CW00690827

U CALL
I HAUL
GREEN OR WHITE
DAY OR NIGHT
SMUGGLER ROGER REAVES .COM

Printed in the United States of America

First Printing 2016

ISBN - 13 978 0 692 63053-2

Marrie J. Reaves Publishing

www.smugglerrogerreaves.com

For Marrie

My sweetheart

My wife

My forever friend

MAP KEY

1 St. Augustine, Florida

2 Early years, Jacksonville, Georgia

3 Redondo Beach, California (Fireman)

4 Santa Barbara, my home for many years

5 Palm Springs, unloaded first ten loads of pot there

6 Mazatlan, Mexico. Marijuana – tortured in prison

7 Shor down, toe shot off

8 Los Mochis, plane on fire

9 Mulege, searching for pot on mule

10 Juan's goat ranch

11 Police shot me, I shot them

12 Cedros Isle, sailing with family, escaped from jail

13 Dry lake bed near Twenty Nine {alms – where I unloaded at least fifty loads

14 Lake Ozete, unloaded 7 loads of hashish with floatplane

15 Cabo San Lucas, kept yacht and airplanes

16 Birth of Medellin Cartel, one angry Pablo Escobar

17 Crash of DC-3 deep in Amazon jungle

18 Carter Ranch- Belize

19 Nicaraguan Military Base- where Barry photographed Escobar unloading cocaine with Sandinista officials

20 St. Tamathy Airport

21 "Mena" Clinton's domain, cocaine offloads, gun-running, Iran Contra

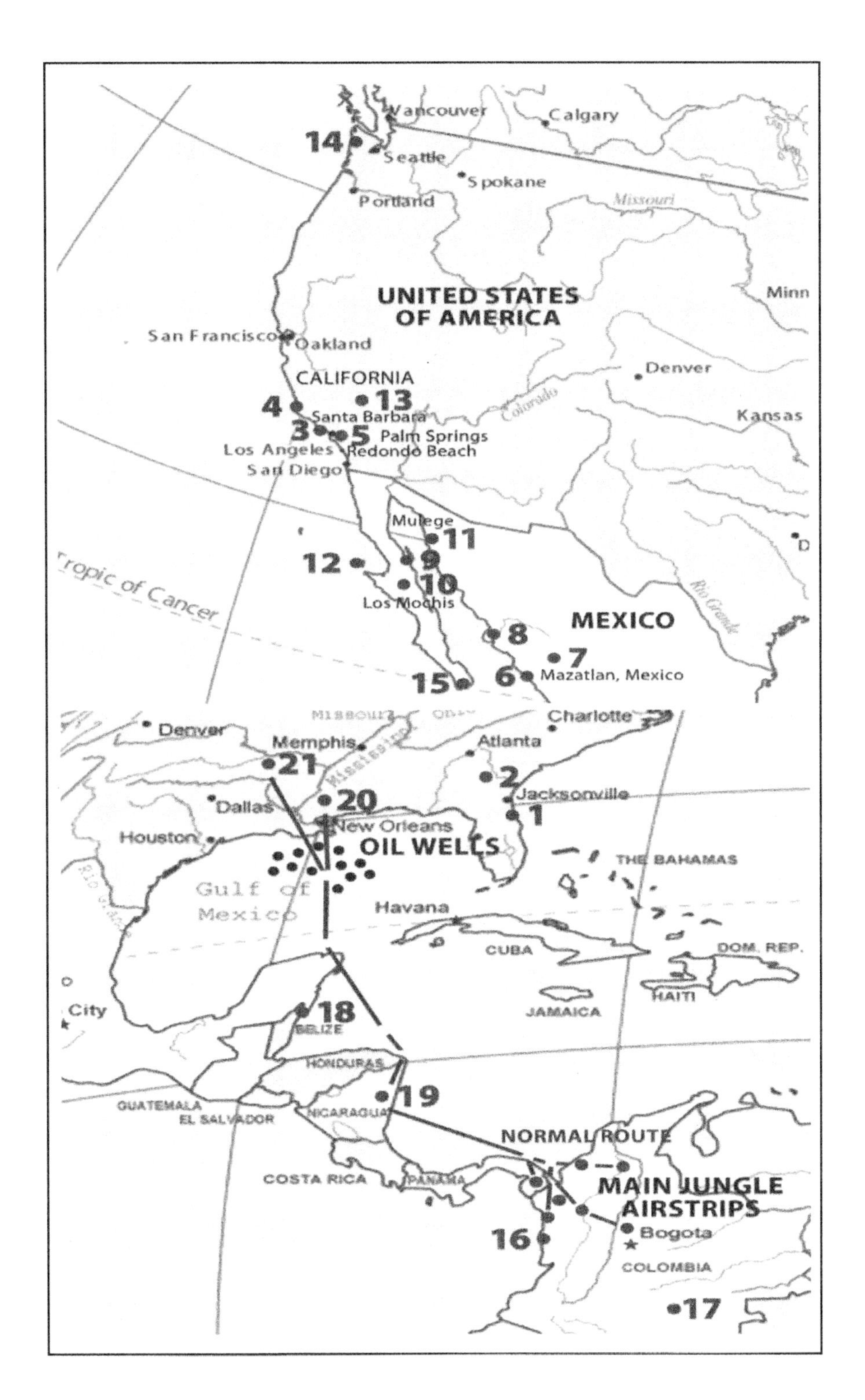
Vancouver
Calgary
14
Seattle
Spokane
Portland
Missouri
UNITED STATES OF AMERICA
Minn
San Francisco
Oakland
CALIFORNIA
Denver
4
13
Santa Barbara
Colorado
Kansas
3
5
Palm Springs
Los Angeles
Redondo Beach
San Diego
Mulege
11
12
9
10
Tropic of Cancer
Los Mochis
Rio Grande
MEXICO
8
7
6
Mazatlan, Mexico
15
Charlotte
Denver
Memphis
Atlanta
21
Mississippi
2
Jacksonville
20
Dallas
1
New Orleans
Houston
OIL WELLS
THE BAHAMAS
Gulf of Mexico
Havana
CUBA
DOM. REP.
HAITI
City
18
BELIZE
JAMAICA
HONDURAS
19
GUATEMALA
EL SALVADOR
NICARAGUA
NORMAL ROUTE
COSTA RICA
PANAMA
MAIN JUNGLE AIRSTRIPS
16
Bogota
COLOMBIA
17

TABLE OF CONTENTS

1. INTRODUCTION

Today is January 26, 2016, my birthday. I am seventy-three years old. I am serving a life sentence in Australia for importing cocaine. I read a lovely card from my wife, seems everyone else forgot. I also received a warrant for my arrest in the United States, stating that U.S. marshals are to arrest me and take me to the Metropolitan Detention Center in Los Angeles for a parole violation. I owe them seven-thousand nine hundred and thirty-five days, or twenty-one years, nine months, for the possession of two hundred kilos of marijuana in 1976, thirty-seven years ago. I have served fifteen years of a non-parole period of eighteen years. In three years, I go up for parole, I have never seen a lifer get parole on the first application; they always say 'come back in three years.

I was probably the most prolific smuggler of the last century, flying in well over a hundred loads of marijuana, hashish, and cocaine into the United States, plus sailing twenty-ton shiploads from Pakistan to Thailand. I made untold millions and lived a life few can believe; and I have paid dearly, with interest, for the privilege. This begins the twenty-eighth year, out of the last thirty-four, that I have been in prison for non-violent drug offences. I do not consider myself much of a criminal. I do not lie, cheat, or steal and I always take up for the underdog. Violence makes me sick. Yet I know I am an outlaw and those that break the law must be punished. We cannot live in a lawless society, but why change the laws so drastically? Before Ronald Reagan, the maximum sentence for marijuana was five years in prison. My crimes pale next to those of presidents in office.

Real crime? The Clintons were up to their eyeballs in cocaine. I paid millions for protection to offload my cocaine laden planes at 'Mena'. Roger Clinton, Bill Clinton's brother was convicted on cocaine charges. You can search the internet for "Mena Arkansas" the full story. George W. and his brother Jeb, who was governor of Florida, stole the election from Al Gore by not allowing the citizens of Broward County, Florida's votes to be counted. Then he and Dick Cheney went after the oil in Iraq using "Weapons of Mass Destruction", a blatant lie, to bomb everything in Baghdad except the oil ministry, and museums from which five-thousand-year-old artifacts were crated and sent to the big boys in the New York art scene. Two-hundred thousand were killed and countless maimed. Ruthless politicians, bought by big business, voted to ship millions of American jobs to China. Congressmen are bribed to vote against clean energy. Cheap land mines are manufactured in the United States and sold to impoverished countries in the third world where children are killed, mutilated, and blinded every day. Yes, my crimes pale next to these scoundrels.

When I received the life sentence in Australia, I was in a special housing unit, a maximum-security jail within a maximum-security prison, a bad place, reserved for the worst of the worst. I knew that I would never go home, never again dance with my lovely wife or sit with my family around the dining table and bounce my grandchildren on my knee. I had already been in prison so long that my children hardly knew me, and my grandchildren never would. I thought of my own grandfather who had served time a hundred years ago in Reedsville, a maximum-security prison in Georgia. I thought how wonderful it would be if I could read about his life, of where he grew up, who he loved and why he killed a man in the courtroom. With that, I decided to tell my story.

At night I would lie on my bunk and as I thought something was interesting, I would write it on a scrap of paper. The next morning, I would take it to the computer room, a small glassed in room directly in front of the control box. Guards would keep watch through a one-way mirror. I knew how to type, but how do I turn the computer on? There was not a program on it, so I typed a continuous line that must have gone on for miles. Sometimes tears streamed down my face as I remembered events from my life and got them down. Often, another prisoner would turn off the electricity at the breaker box and I would lose what I had written for the last ten minutes. It was difficult, but after three months the stories were told.

Two years later I was able to enter it into a Word format and was surprised to learn there were over a thousand pages. I bound all that and sent ten copies to my family and began cutting. I cut out the stories where I was not directly involved, or anything I was not sure of. I wrote the truth as best I remembered. I left nothing out though I've changed a few names to protect the guilty. Statute of limitations means the law will not be bothering friends and associates though the law of karma may.

You may ask, 'What did you learn?' I have learned that it wasn't worth all these years in prison, that you cannot trust your fellow man when he is facing a long prison term and the prosecutors tell him he will go free if he tells on his friend. I learned to read men like you read a book. Give me one minute with someone and allow me to hear the sound of his voice and I know volumes. But most of all I learned that love is the essence of happiness in this life; that the love of just one person can lift you from the deepest despair and make life worth living.

Regrets? Of course, there are many. I regret that I did not apply myself when I was in school. I would have liked to have been a medical doctor helping the poor and sick. I regret all the nights I have been away from my dear wife. We were married fifty-two years ago and I have been in prison for half of that time. She has waited all these years for me to return and it breaks my heart that I cannot go to her. I regret that my children never really got to know me, the true Daddy that I am in my heart, and the happy farm boy that lives within.

By reading the first part of this book you will get to know me and realize how easy it is for a good man to go astray and end up in places, maybe he just should not be. With that in mind, some say a man's destiny is 'written' and free choice is an illusion. Some say life is all about choice, in which case, I wish I had made different ones.

The second part of my book tells of high adventure, of numerous escapes from serious injury and death and comedic routines out of a Laurel and Hardy episode. Of time spent in fantastic isolation in the most beautiful landscapes imaginable and of time spent with family, sailing the high seas and landing at exotic island ports; to flying my personal aircraft over the Arctic Circle and the South American jungle. I have lived a life.

You can see me on YouTube on National Geographic's documentary "Australia's Hardest Prison." I still run five miles a day.

I hope you enjoy my story.

2. CRASHED IN COLOMBIA

Three Tons of Pot -- Fighter Jets and Thunderstorms -- Tangled DC-3 -- The Roadblock -- On My Own -- Missionary Aviation -- So Much Trouble for a Simple Stamp

Douglas Dakota DC-3, "workhorse of the sky." She carried three tons for a thousand miles, and could land on a short rough dirt strip. I owned two of these haulers.
Image courtesy of user "Townpilot" - Douglas DC-3, SE-CFP - Operated by "Flygande Veteraner," Sweden. Wikipedia

I bought November Nine Eight Hotel, an immaculate DC-3- from Union Oil Company. There was not a ding on her anywhere. Blue and white leather seats, white leather ceiling and plush blue carpet gave the interior a stately appearance. The luxurious seats had pull-down tables with inlaid wooden maps. Each country was carved in a different colored exotic wood. Marrie and I proudly flew friends all around California in this nostalgic aircraft. Everywhere we landed people wanted to look it over, inside, and out.

I hired Al Shines from Tyler, Texas as a full-time co-pilot and gave him a monthly salary with a promise of a big bonus on each marijuana run we made. He visited our home in Santa Barbara, met my wife Marrie and the girls and was impressed. This was the lifestyle he was after.

Dan came with a sample of some sticky buds worth 400 dollars a pound. He had three tons secured in Colombia and was anxious to get it out. However, he had two obstacles; one, he had no money, and two, he had no airplane. He showed me exactly where the strip was located in Colombia and said it was five thousand feet long and all was ready to go. We soon struck a deal. For a certain percentage I put up sixty-thousand dollars and flew the pot to the United States. I refused to give Dan the money. I would give it to the Colombian owner directly as I had done business with Dan previously the turbulence

Dan left for Colombia to tell his people that transportation was on the way. Al and I flew from Santa Barbara to San Antonio, Texas where we filled twenty 55-gallon drums inside the cabin with aviation fuel. The wing tanks held another thousand gallons. The old workhorse felt rather loaded as she took off and climbed out on a flight plan for San Jose, Costa Rica.

Stretching across our path from Cuba to Guatemala was a line of severe thunderstorms. As we approached, all we could see was lightning and black towering, boiling weather, stretching from horizon to horizon. There was no way to go through on the Caribbean side, so I turned right and followed the squall line west across Central America and on out over the Pacific and then turned south. It wasn't long before my mistake almost jarred my eyeteeth out and the wings off the aircraft. The turbulence was horrendous. We turned back as best we could and headed for Tapaculos, on the very southern tip of Mexico and landed.

No one bothered us that night after we landed, however, the next morning there were inquiries. A customs inspector got in the plane and looked over the shiny new green drums. He asked what was in them and I replied that it was medicine for bees and went on to explain that a virus had infected the honeybees in Central America and was heading north. This medicine was to help stop the plague. He seemed satisfied and did not ask to have one opened. Phew!

We filed a flight plan to San Jose, Costa Rica, and departed. Fifty miles out I turned east and went to the isolated strip near Tikal, Guatemala. It was deep in the jungle, built back in the 1930s by Shell Oil Company for oil exploration in the area. The runway was smooth but badly grown over in weeds and scrubs and I could never find a trail leading to it. Some weeks earlier I flew down a planeload of Mexicans and cleared it in a day with chain saws, machetes, and mowers. We landed, unloaded the drums, rolled them in the bushes, laid cut foliage over them, and departed for San Jose to wait for Dan. After waiting a couple of days, he showed up and told me that the Colombians had to have eighty-thousand dollars or no deal. He had a stash of fresh marijuana buds to wet my greed. I knew the extra twenty was probably for Dan. He had me committed and now he was squeezing. OK asshole, it was no more than expected. Marrie flew down with the twenty thousand.

Early next morning Dan was anxious to get started. In fact, he got rather ugly about getting an early start, getting there on time, and checking out the load.

I said, "Listen, I don't know what your problem is, but it is nothing you can't work out in the twelve hours we will be on the ground. From here to your airstrip is nine hundred miles. The DC-3 flies at 150 mph which means it will take us six hours to get there, give or take a few minutes, depending on the winds. We will touch down thirty minutes before dark. Is there anything about that you can't understand?"

We departed at noon the following day and flew directly to his five-thousand-foot strip that had shrunk to half that length. I circled in light rain and I knew there was no way to get off that strip with three tons. It was dusk and I had two hours of fuel remaining in the tanks. I had to land.

I taxied up to a red-tiled house near the end of the strip where we were met by a charming Colombian gentleman of around sixty years of age with white hair and a stately appearance. He could have played the part in a Colombian coffee advertisement without any prep. My anger subsided somewhat. Perhaps not all was lost.

Dan said this was a staging stop. The real airstrip was four hundred miles further south and that was the reason he had wanted to get here earlier. I exploded, "You are a lying, sniveling piece of shit. I should have known better than to ever have anything to do with you. You're shiftier than a shit-house rat!"

He took the 'cussin' with stoical grace. He knew it was coming and was just waiting for it to be over. He had been planning the deception for a month. He showed me new hoses with clamps to attach them to the wing. He had a drill to make a hole in the fuselage for the hose to go through and he had two DC-3 fuel tank caps with holes drilled in them and a nipple to connect to the hose. There was also an ample supply of gasoline for the extra eight hundred miles. His plan was to lighten the load by a ton and bring out two tons, the other ton being the extra fuel in drums. He would stand in the cabin and pump into the wing tanks as they burned off.

"You thoroughbred, asshole! Why didn't you tell me all this in Santa Barbara?" Even though Dan was almost seven feet tall and a bodybuilder, I could have whipped him at that time.

"I knew that if I told you it was fourteen hundred miles from your strip in Guatemala you would never have come. We can still bring out two million dollars' worth of good pot if you will just listen to me." He whined.

What the heck, I was already down here; there was good pot and plenty of gasoline. Why not? It began raining hard, so we made a tent out of a tarpaulin to cover the refueling and began pumping. There was sufficient to fill the tanks and another five-hundred gallons loaded in the cargo area. We drilled holes in each side of the fuselage, ran the hoses through, and attached them to the wings with numerous clamps.

The grey-headed gentleman was the owner or broker of the pot and I gave him the eighty thousand dollars. He introduced a young man as a local crop duster who was to fly with us as a guide to the next landing spot. He did not strike me as a crop duster, but perhaps he had ridden in an airplane. Dan wanted to leave right away, said his people were waiting with fires along their strip. However, there was no way I was going to take off in rain and fly through the night over unknown jungle without a radio beacon or any navigation aids. Dan accepted the logic.

We took off at four a.m. and headed south. The grey-haired gentleman had marked roughly where the strip was located on a chart. The crop duster stood between Al and me and soon it became clear he was as 'lost as a loon'. Everything looked the same and I could only dead-reckon my position. When I figured we were in the vicinity I flew a twenty-mile grid trying to get our location.

Around eight o'clock I found the convergence of two rivers that matched the description and from there the 'crop duster' directed us on to what one might call a strip, if you used a lot of imagination. Termite nests stood blood red like twenty-foot sentinels along both sides of the track. There were light impressions of tracks in the wiregrass where other planes had landed but they were barely visible and not recent...

A dozen irate white Colombians met us. Some had red hair and beards. Some were blonde with no beards. However, they all had one thing in common; they were armed to the teeth with AK-47's, pistols, and shotguns with banana clips and they were yelling most emphatically for us to get the hell out of there. Seemed the marijuana had been there the evening before, and they had waited all night for us then at daybreak moved it out. This was a guerilla group fighting government soldiers and the area was frequently flown over by military aircraft. We were to come back just before dark.

Dan knew all this. How easy it would have been had I known.

We took off in a hurry and returned to the ranch we departed from early that morning. When we landed the grey-haired gentleman seemed quite disturbed. However, he had a woman prepare lunch, if you could call it such. I got enough down to kill hunger, walked under a big mango tree, and crawled into a hammock and went to sleep. I was dreaming peacefully when an awful noise, like an explosion blasted me awake. I rolled out of the hammock, hit the ground, stumbled out from under the tree, and looked up into the ass end of two military jets climbing straight up with their afterburners aglow.

All the Colombians ran for a flatbed truck, piled on, and took off with the gentleman driving away with my eighty thousand dollars. I didn't think of that at the time as I was running for the plane, followed closely by Al, Dan and the silent Mexican American who had flown with us earlier that morning.

I fired her up and took off without warming the engines for even a second. As soon as we were airborne the two military jets swarmed on us, shooting a string of tracers across the windshield. I stayed low, probably around three hundred feet above the jungle and headed north. The jets dropped their gear and flaps and flew right on my wingtips, one on the left and one on the right. I could see the pilot's faces clearly. They kept pointing for me to turn toward their airbase at Villavicencio. "No thank you gentlemen." I waved and gave the hippy peace signal and began to slow down. The jet's nose rose higher and higher, black smoke poured from their jet. I knew they were sucking up fuel fast at this low altitude in a stall position. When they couldn't fly any slower, they began circling, shooting tracers all the way down the left wing until it looked as if they would hit the propeller. On another pass one filled the tail section with fifty caliber holes. My throat ran dry. I didn't think they would really shoot us. If they shot the fuselage or wing tanks with tracers the aviation fuel would explode, and we would go down in a ball of flames. We flew on. Tracers began coming from beneath and skimming up from just under my feet. They looked like they were curving upward from our perspective. Twenty-millimeter cannons jarred the aircraft with their explosions so near.

To keep them from getting underneath me, I pushed the nose over and flew at treetop level. I heard later they thought I was trying to crash into them as one almost hit the jungle trying to get out of the way. Finally, one jet left, I presumed for fuel.

Stout metal pins with a red plastic flag attached are stuck through the struts each time one lands to prevent the gear collapsing in case of hydraulic failure. In the frantic rush to get airborne, I had forgotten to pull the pins in the struts, and with the gear hanging down the performance of the aircraft was greatly diminished. I couldn't retract the gear. I needed to land for a few seconds and take them out. I saw a pasture ahead and put her down. It was rougher than it looked, and fuel caps popped off as we pitched and bucked to a stop. I ran out and collected the pins, got back in, and took off.

Meanwhile, back in the U.S., the World Series baseball game was in full swing. The announcer said, "We interrupt this broadcast with a special news bulletin. Colombian jets have just shot down an American DC-3 believed to be on a drug-smuggling run. This is the first aircraft shot down in the new war on drugs."

With the wheels retracted I climbed to get over the approaching mountains. The jet stayed with us firing a string of tracers sporadically. Black clouds reaching to the heavens were boiling straight ahead. I thought, 'we can get away in there, and I flew straight in. A wall of water met me, and the updraft had my ears popping as I watched the altimeter spin. I had no way of knowing how near the mountains were and I knew these tropical thunderstorms hang close to them. I was afraid to continue further in, so I spiraled up to twenty-thousand feet; too high to be safe without oxygen. However, it would have to do for now. I stuck the nose out and there was the jet. Boom, boom, boom, the cannons thundered. Right back into another crash of thunder and lightning I dove.

At that altitude she was icing up. There were inches of ice on the windshield and leading edges and she began to respond sluggishly. I was starting to feel the effects of oxygen deprivation and realized I had to think fast. Deducing he had us on his radar screen and we were not going to get rid of him without more drastic measures, I pulled it up into a stall, kicked the right rudder and went into a tight spin, spiraling down eighteen thousand feet in a very short time. At five thousand feet the clouds began to break up. At two thousand a layer of puffy white clouds stretched to infinity.

I pushed the nose over and dove under this fluffy blanket. What a glorious peaceful world underneath as we flew over the lush green jungle spotted with sunlight. Dan was begging me to go to Costa Rica, but the adrenalin had made me bulletproof and there was no way I was going to toss in the towel now. What we needed was a quiet place to set her down and rest for a couple of hours and go visit the guerillas.

As we flew along the south bank of the Rio Guaviare, I saw a level area of tall grass on a bluff above the river. It looked perfectly smooth and I figured it should be as I could see that it was formed by the river during flood stage but was now ten or fifteen feet above the level of the river. I circled low, had a good look and touched the wheels down, skimmed along for a half-mile, pulled up, and repeated the process several times, putting more and more pressure on the tires each time. After several passes it resembled a landing strip.

"OK Al, this is it, we're stopping this time. Hey Al, take your foot off the brakes!" I shouted.

"I'm not touching the brakes!" He screamed back.

Instinctively I knew we were in trouble as I slammed the throttles forward. The engines roared to life and the whole aircraft shuddered with the sudden burst of power, but it was too late. The tires had broken through the six-inch crust and we were in the soupy mud underneath. Thirty thousand pounds of weight was on less than a square foot of tires and digging in. The forward thrust dug a deeper and deeper ditch for a hundred yards as the aircraft started doing a headstand. I saw what was happening, undid my seatbelt, and yelled for Al to get out of his seat. I fell on the floor between the seats and pulled Al down with me. As the tail rose, we changed from the horizontal to the vertical position. I watched as the nose caved in and crushed the instrument panel toward us. The radial engines held the weight as they plowed through the mud. It came to a stop in a perfectly vertical position with the fuselage ninety degrees to the ground. Gasoline was pouring out of the wing tanks, sizzling, and fuming as it hit the hot engines. What had once been overhead was now a wall in front of me and there was the emergency hatch! I quickly undid the wing nuts, it swung open, and I jumped out into the grass, Al followed.

I yelled to the men in the cargo area and watched as the door opened and Dan's face appeared, looking a little dazed. He was forty feet above the ground. They threw out a length of fuel hose and shimmed down, bruised and shaken, but in good health. The risk of an explosion was still great as fuel continued to spill from the ruptured tanks, but we ventured back in regardless and collected our suitcases and an aerial map of the area. The fuel continued to sizzle as we beat a hasty retreat to the edge of the jungle. All I could think of was Marrie waiting back home, worried sick. As we walked along, I kept repeating to myself, "Marrie I'm OK."

There was a village ten or twelve miles to the north. We could get there before dark if we hurried. I picked up my suitcase and started off. Dan just stood there; I saw that he was crying. He said he couldn't carry his suitcase. Such a huge strong man completely undone by fEar was pathetic. I picked up his case and the three of us took turns carrying it.

The grass along the trail was as high as our heads. It was hot and muggy, and our clothes were soon soaked through. Biting insects covered us so thick that we inhaled them. We were in serious danger; over and above the usual. We were deep in guerilla territory with a war raging between leftist rebels and the Colombian army. The guerillas were kidnapping foreigners at will. If the soldiers saw us, they would most likely shoot us down rather than arrest us. Warplanes were circling just above the clouds. As we hurried along the trail the thought came to me with crystal clear clarity, *'We're 500 miles from the coast and I'm 5000 miles from home, deep in the southern Colombian jungle. If I don't think very clearly and plan very carefully, I am not going to get home to Marrie and the children.'*

A boy and girl of about twelve years of age came down the trail riding on a horse and a spotted ox. After some greetings I asked, "How far is it to the village?"

"Twenty kilometers," was the response.

"Are there any policemen in the village?" I asked.

They smiled and said, "No Señor, there are no policemen."

This was what I wanted to hear. I said, "We will pay you U.S dollars if you will carry these suitcases on your animals to the village."

"Si Señor, with much pleasure." The boy answered.

We tied the suitcases to the saddles and the six of us started down a path through chest-high grass. Insects swarmed around us by the millions. I was soaked with sweat; there was not a dry thread in my clothes. The children had seen the airplane's nose sticking down in the mud, but neither mentioned it. We learned they lived in the opposite direction. When we came near the village, I paid them and insisted they return home. They waved to us as they disappeared down the trail and we walked on to the village.

It was a large place on the south bank of the river. The first building we came to was a small store with a stand-up bar. We walked in and ordered cold drinks. I was having my second coke and telling big lies to the proprietor when armed soldiers surrounded us. They demanded passports. They scrutinized them carefully, failing to notice that three did not have entrance stamps.

I told them that Al and I were botanists, searching for plants in the Amazon to cure diseases. Dan was an assistant and the Mexican was the boatman. Our boat had broken down fifteen kilometers down the river and we had walked here looking for a mechanic. This pacified the sergeant somewhat, but they were still skeptical. Something was said about the radio being off until six the following morning and I knew we were quickly running out of time.

We had a good meal by lantern light and the soldiers escorted us to a vacant house where we were to sleep on the floor. All the doors and windows were locked, and a soldier placed on guard. I sat on Dan's shoulders and slowly and quietly removed the tiles from an area of the roof. We waited until the roosters began crowing and crawled out and eased to the ground. The previous evening, we had passed a house with a long outboard leaning against the wall and a dugout in the river below. We made our way there as quietly as possible and knocked on the door. The man was just getting up and we explained our situation of being broken down fifteen kilometers downstream. I offered him a handsome price in dollars to help us, showing him the money. As soon as he agreed I picked up the outboard and hurried to the dugout. With his help we attached the motor and within five minutes we were on our way.

It was a big dugout, perhaps thirty feet long and with the outboard we were moving along at a good twenty miles per hour. After some time, the man became concerned and asked how much further? We assured him just a little way to go. He stopped for gasoline at an Indian hut on the bank and from the Indian we bought a block of unprocessed brown sugar. We continued down the river. I could see he was getting nervous. In the middle of the morning he ran the boat up on a sandbar and stopped. He explained that his boat was the official transport and mail carrier for the village, and he was not going any further. We explained as kindly as possible that he had to. There wasn't another boat and we were desperate for a ride to San Jose Del Guaviare. I offered him a thousand dollars for the rent of his boat for two days and handed him the money. He was none too happy to be going. Perhaps he was afraid, but a thousand dollars was more than a year's salary.

We were making good time, the rhythm of the motor and the passing of the water beneath the dugout soothed my apprehension. The dense jungle scenery created an almost surreal real-life picture book. My thoughts drifted back in time to my childhood and the news report of a massacre of five missionaries led by Nate Saint on the Curray River in Ecuador, by a band of Native Indians. I also read 'Jungle Pilot,' the biography of Nate Saint, the founder of Missionary Aviation Fellowship. In my youth, my heart burned within me to follow in his steps. I knew I was not a preacher, but flying missionaries, their children, and native people in and out of the jungle were within my scope. As soon as I began taking flying lessons, I had this career in mind. Shortly after arriving in California, I went to Pomona and to the headquarters for Missionary Aviation Fellowship for an interview. They informed me that I would have to get my airframe and engine mechanics rating before they considered having me join their organization. I understood the need, so I went away disappointed. Three years in an aircraft school was too much at that time in my life. That career evaporated quickly and somewhat disappointingly. However, my brush with Missionary Aviation Fellowship was not over. I was now in South America as I had wanted to be in earlier years, but I wasn't carrying missionaries in my aircraft. Despite this radical change in transportation career, Missionary Aviation Fellowship and Roger Reaves continued to be linked by synchronicity over time.

I was jolted from my daydreaming late in the afternoon as we came to some rapids. The dugout owner was scared. A couple of substantial houses were nearby, and we walked up to them and met a young man who said he could run the dugout through the rapids safely. We took everything out and the young man shot the rapids with yours truly riding in the bow. People pay a lot of money for experiences such as this. We bought a 55-gallon drum of gasoline and continued down river.

Feeble lamplights and several small canoes tied to a tree-like fish on a string suggested we had reached a village on the north shore. Our chart showed an unimproved trail leading out. We came ashore and squished up the muddy embankment. The place was poverty-stricken and filthy. Everyone came to the small store to look us over. We inquired if there was a vehicle we could hire to take us to Villavicencio and the headman said there was a jeep ten kilometers up the road. The Mexican American and a lad from the village mounted two horses and set out to fetch the jeep. A woman killed a chicken and boiled it not long enough. She then forked it out of the water and chopped it into four pieces with a machete. It was hot, stringy, and without any salt, but I ate every morsel and licked my hands.

Around midnight the boy returned with two horses and said the Mexican American had left for the city. Dan cursed. It was then I learned he had given him all his money to rent the jeep.

A request went out for hammocks and soon several hung under the open thatched roof. The man and woman lifted their two children into a wooden box several feet off the ground, climbed in after them, and closed the door. The box was like a big coffin and I could not see how any air could get in. After a few minutes in the hammock I wanted to break in with them as the mosquitoes were murderous. It was impossible to sleep. I opened my bag and put on extra clothes to survive the night.

Daybreak was a gift from heaven. The family emerged from the box; hair matted with sweat. The woman cooked a stack of tortillas. I ate and drank three Coca Colas. The drinking water had fermented fruit added to it giving it a slight alcoholic rotten fruit taste. Everyone in the area drank this water because the alcohol killed the amoebas and other harmful intestinal bugs. The young man knew three words in English. He looked around at the chickens scratching and the pig rooting in the dirt floor of his hut and said, "I want more."

After breakfast, a slim man set out to look for a jeep, with me following. He thrust his hips forward and struck a gait so fast that I had to jog to keep up. We carried a bottle of this strange water and walked hard for hours, at least fifty miles through jungle trails. Eventually we came to a sawmill around nine o'clock that night. A jeep was there and the young man working there said he could not take us until his father returned from a trip with a lumber truck. Eventually the young man took us in the jeep, and we drove for some miles until we came to a house built in a clearing enclosed with barbed wire. He and the 'walking man' entered and left me waiting in the jeep. I could see them sitting at a table eating supper and I still do not understand the rudeness. Finally, a couple of young men came out. One was the sawmill owner's son and the other was a guard with a shotgun. The owner's son said he would take us to Villavicencio for four hundred dollars. I gladly accepted.

It was after midnight when we arrived back in the village. Dan fooled around for half an hour politicking and shaking every hand in the village. Once he got in we started out at a good speed as the road was built up ten or twelve feet above the jungle. Everything was fine until we came to the first stream and saw the remains of a washed-out bridge. The road wound down through deep ruts and soon the jeep was stuck. The driver refused to budge, and the guard was completely indifferent. Guess who got out, attached the cable to the winch, and found a tree? We winched across and soon we were on the road again doing fifty miles an hour until the next stream. This process went on all night.

As a pale light shone through the jungle the driver told us to get our passports and papers ready because there was a roadblock ahead. I shouted, "Stop! Stop the jeep! Let me get this straight. Are you telling me there is a roadblock ahead?"

"Yes, there is a permanent roadblock where the two roads meet. Soldiers are always there searching everyone, as this is a dangerous area for drugs and the guerillas."

In English I said, "Boys we can't go through a roadblock, we'll have to walk around."

Dan said, "We have eight hundred dollars, we can pay them off."

I replied, "Dan, you can do whatever you damn well please, but Al and I are going to get out now."

"There you go, always overreacting. Those poor soldiers make fifty dollars a month and they will gladly let us through for a few hundred dollars, I'm going through."

I was livid, "Get out Al, you work for me. Do not listen to this idiot. Just because they speak Spanish does not mean they are stupid. News of the DC-3 sticking straight up in the jungle and the riverboat man kidnapped is enough to have a large search party already in motion," I said emphatically.

"I'm tired, Roger, and I believe Dan is right. I'm going with him," Al said.

"Listen Al, I will crawl through this jungle on my belly and eat snakes for as long as it takes before I put my head in such a noose."

Dan interjected. "We will get through easily. If you get to Bogotá, call me at the Hotel Simon Bolivar. We have eight hundred dollars and I know you have credit cards. You take two hundred dollars and we'll take six hundred."

"That suits me. If you do get through call Marrie as soon as you get to a telephone and tell her I'm safe."

We divided the money. I took my old leather suitcase out of the jeep and stood in the road watching the red taillights fade into the distance. I turned and began walking back the way we had come.

A well-worn footpath crossed the road and I took the route north. My suitcase got heavy, so I put it on top of my head. I was exhausted from four days of high drama and hard work. Alongside the path appeared a little white house with a red tile roof and a vegetable garden. There was also an acre or more of fruit trees, all enclosed with a stout fence. An old woman sat on the porch peeling oranges. In the yard was a well with a round red brick casing. I must have been a sight, encrusted in dirt. Perhaps the whites of my eyes showed through. I stopped at the gate and said as politely as I could, "Good morning Señora, May I use your well to wash this dirt off myself?"

"The water is a gift from God, help yourself" she replied.

I thanked her, opened the gate, walked in, and poured bucketful after bucketful over my head. I took my shaving kit out of the suitcase then lathered my face all over with soap. I shaved, rinsed and shampooed my hair, then poured more water over my head. Oh God did it feel good! Next I got out a bottle of Zuzini after-shave and poured it over the insect bites. It stung but smelled wonderful. I rinsed out the clothes and hung them on a bush for whoever wanted them. Then I put on clean fresh clothes. I was a new man.

Down the trail a way, I found a nice shady area covered in soft grass, and I laid down and slept most of the day. I woke up refreshed and hungry, picked up my suitcase, and continued down the trail. A man on a tractor came along pulling a feed grinder. He stopped and was surprised to see such a sight as me walking through the jungle carrying my suitcase on top of my head. He offered me a ride to his ranch and invited me to spend the night. His wife prepared fresh river fish for supper. He hung a hammock on the porch and this time there was a mosquito net. While we were chatting, I asked if there was an airplane in the area and he replied, "In Loma Linda there are many airplanes." I asked for general directions and learned that it was far, and in the direction I was headed.

I slept like a log and the next morning I drank two cups of strong sweet coffee and ate homemade sausages and eggs. I said goodbye to this wonderful couple then picked up my suitcase and walked on down the trail.

After some time, I came to a bigger road and a school bus. The driver was returning home after delivering the children to school and he gave me a ride to a small town. I explained to him I was going to Loma Linda and he gave me further directions. I had to wait a long time before a flatbed truck gave me a ride to the next village. This mode of transportation continued throughout the day. Late in the afternoon I arrived in another town and noticed a policeman which immediately made me nervous. There was a rather large grocery store where I exchanged a few dollars for pesos. While I was making the transaction, I asked the clerk for directions to Loma Linda. She pointed to a primitive-looking indigenous man and said he was from Loma Linda. I thanked her, walked over to the man who was picking out a hundred or so coconuts, and said in Spanish, "Good afternoon I understand you are from Loma Linda."

"Yes, I am from Loma Linda and do you speak English?" He asked.

"Yes, I speak English. I am from the United States. Are there any Americans in Loma Linda?"

"Yes, there are many Americans."

"Are there any English there?" I wondered if this man was quite with it.

"Yes, there are English there."

"And what about Canadians. Are there any Canadians there?

"Oh yes, there are many Canadians."

I thought, 'this guy is touched', and I asked about Germans, Dutch and French. They were all accounted for at Loma Linda.

"May I ride to Loma Linda with you?"

"Yes, you may ride with me," He replied somewhat like a robot.

When he had finished buying a truckload of food we loaded up and drove through the jungle on a good graded road for perhaps twenty miles, and then the land began rising and falling as we came to higher ground.

On the left appeared cleared land, fenced with strong properly braced posts. Simmental cattle grazed on lush pastures. Here was something out of place, or time. The driver turned off the road, went through a large metal stock-gap and skirted around rolling hills. Ahead I saw a long clay airstrip, a large hangar, several airplanes, and a radio tower reaching hundreds of feet into the sky. What could this be, here in the middle of the Amazon jungle? He stopped in front of a low white wooden building with green louvered windows and a lovely veranda. It gave the impression of Hawaii in the 1940s.

With suitcase in hand, I walked into an informal office or reception like room. A lady behind a desk looked up somewhat surprised and I said, "Good afternoon."

"And a good afternoon to you sir. Who are you and what brings you to Loma Linda?"

Just from the sound of her voice, I knew she was a wonderful person. I answered, "My name is Roger Reaves and I am touring Colombia."

"Welcome to Loma Linda Mr. Roger Reaves. My name is Kati Sue. We do not get many tourists here."

"May I stay for a few days?"

"You are most welcome. The cost is ten dollars a day and that includes three meals."

"What is this place?"

"Oh, you don't know. This is Loma Linda. Headquarters for Missionary Aviation Fellowship for the Amazon."

I shook my head and laughed quietly. The Lord works in strange and mysterious ways, '*His wonders to perform*'.

A radiotelephone operator patched a call through to Marrie via a man in Houston, Texas. She was ecstatic to hear from me and said, "Darling, we are all worried, everyone thought you were dead. But I knew differently! As I was taking a shower a few days ago I clearly heard your voice say, 'Marrie I'm OK.'"

She had not heard from Al or Dan.

Friendly gentle folks filled the dining room. I sat at a table with a redheaded electrician from Torrance, California. He had formerly worked for the same electrical company as I had. He said he spent his vacations working at mission stations anywhere in the world he was needed. He was a good witness for the Lord, and I felt like an imposter.

A Missionary Aviation Pilot flew a retired Canadian missionary out to Villavicencio the next morning and I was allowed to accompany him. The pilot reported every ten or fifteen minutes as we crossed rivers and other landmarks. Of course, you can guess where my thoughts were.

At the airport in Villavicencio, a military policeman lifted my suitcase out of the plane and placed it in the boot of a taxi. The old missionary and I had a pleasant ride up the mountain to Bogotá.

From a telephone house, I first called the Hotel Simon Bolivar. They had no record of Al or Dan ever registering and I knew they were in prison. I called Marrie and had a good long talk. I told her I would be home just as soon as I could get an entrance stamp in my passport. I hung up and took a taxi to the airport.

From a seat in a coffee shop I carefully observed immigration officers as they drank coffee or walked by. I focused on one and invited him for a cup. We chatted for some time and I noticed a film over his eyes that I call 'the killer eyes' and backed off. When the crowd thinned out I took a taxi to a nearby hotel.

Next day I was back at my post. I went from coffee shop to restaurant, to bar, so as not to draw attention to myself. Late in the afternoon I strolled past the British Caledonia Airways counter and a young man in uniform said rather cheerfully, "Good afternoon." He was slim, white and his aura was bright.

"And a good afternoon to you too sir," I replied.

We exchanged the proper courtesies and I invited him for a cup of coffee.

Without moving from behind his counter he said, "I perceive that you are in trouble. Perhaps I can help?"

"Yes, you are correct. I need an entrance stamp in my passport. Can you help?"

"That should not be an insurmountable problem."

"I have two hundred dollars and credit cards. Would two-hundred be sufficient?"

"That is not necessary but would be appreciated. Here is a visa application. Fill it out and come back at seven o'clock. An Avianca flight is scheduled to arrive from Miami at that time."

Somehow I had complete trust in this young man. I went away, filled out the visa application, and returned at the appointed time. He ushered me behind his counter, and we went through an employee door and down a hall. Then through more doors and down a set of stairs that led to an underground walkway. We followed this tunnel for some way and then stopped at a ladder leading to a manhole. We climbed up, pushed the cover open, and climbed out onto the airport apron where the Avianca flight was deplaning. He ushered me into the middle of the line of passengers walking toward immigration.

A female immigration officer asked, "How long is your intended stay in Colombia?"

"Two weeks."

Stamp, stamp, stamp. She tore the visa in two, handed me one-half, and said, "Have a pleasant stay sir. Next!"

I walked directly to the Avianca counter and bought a ticket to Miami on the same plane on which I had supposedly just arrived. I paid with a credit card as I had been doing for everything. I discovered there was a ten-dollar departure tax which had to be paid in dollars. I explained I did not have dollars. Too bad, there are no exceptions. I went to British Caledonia and found my friend who gave me the ten dollars. I paid the tax, received the stamp on my ticket, and walked onto the 707 bound for Miami.

Al and Dan spent three years in a Bogotá prison for kidnapping the riverboat captain and violation of airspace.

Al's wife Gaye came to visit me and explained she had visited Al and that they were getting a divorce. She had two little children to support on her own. Her plan was to go back to school and finish her certified public accountants' degree. She asked if I would help her financially and I agreed. From time to time she would call and say she was behind on house or car payments and I would send her five thousand dollars each time. She graduated as a CPA and sent Marrie and I an invitation to her graduation.

I never heard from Al himself, but Gaye told me he married a Colombian woman he met in prison. I wondered again at his judgment. In 1982 I sent my brother Larry to Colombia with one hundred thousand dollars to buy Al a nice house. Larry flew down to Bogotá, telephoned Al, and told him he was Larry Reaves, Roger's brother. Al said he never wanted to hear from Roger Reaves again and hung up. Larry returned with the money. Seems Al was still making bad judgments.

Safe in my home, reflecting, I thought that would be the first and last great escape story of my life. Once was enough. Crashing aircraft, running through the jungle far from home, avoiding roadblocks, apprehensive and anxious, thinking about my wife and children back home, worried I may not see them again. It is not something you expect to be putting into your resume when you start out in life. However, it would not be the last time events would spiral out of my control and I would have to think fast to get back to Marrie and the children.

3. EARLY YEARS

Hog killing weather -- Mules, Grandpa, and Poor Aunt Sadie -- From the Mouths of Babes -- Huntin' and the 'Lectric Chair -- Field Hand to Watermelon Stand -- Robbed in Chattanooga -- Dynamite Tractor -- An Angel Moved Me -- The Mexican Pinto -- The Wreck Of Daddy & the Doctor

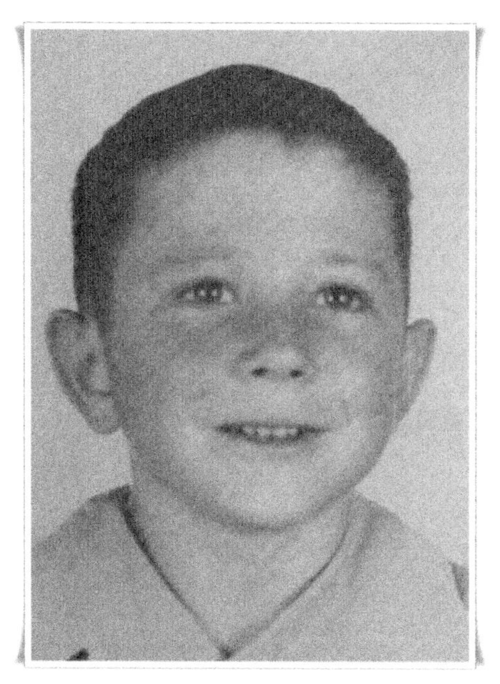

Roger Reaves age six.
Copyright - Marrie Reaves

Show me the prisoner
Show me the jail
Show me the prisoner whose life has gone stale
And I will show you a young man
With so many reasons why
There but for fortune
Go you or I
Joan Baez

World War II was raging. I was born during the siege of Stalingrad where thousands died every day. I see myself in a khaki uniform, a river of warplanes flying overhead; streets are paved with bricks in the herringbone pattern. These vivid dreams and memories continue to this day.

My mother, Hortense Rosa Garrison, was a strikingly beautiful woman and still is, at age ninety-six. While carrying me under her heart, she worked in a veneer plant during the day and stood in a watchtower at night looking for enemy planes. My father, William Joseph Reaves, was a gentle, kind man, foreman of the veneer mill where he and Mother worked.

When I made my debut, Daddy drove Mother from Espanola to St. Augustine, Florida where she entered the Flagler East Coast Railroad Hospital. I was born at six a.m. on January 26, 1943. I was late, ugly, red and crying. They said my Dad took one look at his long-awaited firstborn son and cried. He never told why.

On day four I turned blue and 'Old Dr. Rose', as Mother called him, diagnosed me as having asthma, a malady that has stayed with me ever since. Mother got sick and was feverish and delirious. Her breasts swelled until they were bursting. There were no breast pumps in those days so Daddy went under the house where his bird dog had seven speckled puppies, brought them out, put little socks on their feet so they wouldn't scratch Mother and they went happily to work. A colored woman was hired to nurse me.

During the night I would wake up suffocating and I believe my earliest memory is of someone holding me and walking up and down a platform and stopping before giant furnaces of burning wood. I vividly recollect the flames and red coals; sometimes this person put me down and I would stand there mesmerized.

I was three years old and I can remember this clearly: it was a dark rainy winter night. I was standing on the narrow back seat, leaning over between Mother and Daddy. The heater was blowing warm air and the few instrument lights barely lit the interior of the Ford coupe. Feeble headlights made an effort to illuminate the dark road ahead and I could tell my father was concentrating. I was looking at the road ahead with him when suddenly a Brahma Bull appeared, and we hit him before Daddy could touch the brakes. I shot over the seat, my head hit the floorboard beside the gear shaft and I almost bit my tongue off. The bull attacked the car and hooked out its headlights. I was bleeding like a stuck pig as Daddy turned around and took me to the hospital. A jagged scar across my tongue attests to that incident.

Late one afternoon Daddy lifted me into his 1940 Ford coupe and just as we started to drive away, Mother ran out and pulled me through the passenger window. He left with tires spinning in the gravel. She said he was, "three sheets to the wind." I knew this meant he had been drinking whiskey.

She said that if William stepped over a rotten grape he would get drunk. He went speeding down that country road lined with palmettos and palm trees, came to a ninety-degree turn, skidded sideways through a fence, flipped upside down, landing in a canal, surfed to the far side, flipped right-side-up and not one drop of water got in the car. The next day a wrecker winched the car back through the canal.

Uncle Grover and Uncle Walter, Mother's brothers, came home from the war in the South Pacific in military uniforms, I thought they were the most beautiful people I had ever seen. Uncle Grover took out his knife and peeled me a large orange, round and round he peeled until he had one long peeling that reached the floor in one hand and the peeled fruit in the other.

Uncle Walter had been fighting at such famous places as Iwo Jima and Guadalcanal. He laughed as he told of jumping in a shell hole during heavy shelling. A Jap was already crouched down in the hole, and when the shelling was over, they both ran in different directions.

One Sunday morning we were all dressed to the nines, going on a long trip to visit friends in Uncle Walter's 1937 touring car. The rear tire burst, so we got out and had a look. Uncle Walter said, "William, I don't have a jack, but I'll pick her up and you change the tire." He took off his coat and tie, next his shirt and then his trousers and carefully draped them over the front seat; he was down to polka dot shorts, shoes and long socks. The women screamed with laughter at the sight. He backed up to that big car, picked it up and held it while Daddy changed the tire.

Grandma, Daddy's mother, lived in the house with us and I slept in the bed with her from before I can remember. One day she received a telegram from Georgia with news that her father was sick and dying. This was Mr. Murdoch Odom, my Great Grandpa, and he was rich!

Grandma took me with her on the trip to Georgia. I was three years old and I vividly remember scenes from the journey. Both she and I were dressed in our finest clothes as we boarded the passenger train. A cheerful Negro porter with several gold teeth helped me up the stairs and made a big to-do, bragging on me and saying what a fine little man I was.

Great Grandpa's house was old and made of unpainted pine lumber with a steep roof covered with cypress shingles. The inside was dark except for the places where the sun peeked through holes in the roof. When it rained, the women scurried about placing buckets, tubs, and pans under leaks. Clothes hung on racks in the front room covered with cowhides to keep them dry. Little bags of sulfur, garlic and mixtures of medicines hung from nails on the wall, because my great-grandmother Johanna believed this killed germ and warded off disease.

The weather turned cold and Daddy said this was hog-killing weather. The next morning Bud Graham, a wonderful black man, and several others came to help. They built a big fire under a cauldron that was usually used to make syrup, filled it with water, and when it began getting hot a tar cup full of pine tar was added to the water. This was to make the hairs stick together. Bud kept testing the temperature with his finger and said they had to be careful not to get the water too hot or it 'set' the hair and then it might never come off.

Daddy shot a hog between the eyes with a .22 rifle. His legs just folded, and he fell to the ground without as much as a grunt or wiggle. Everyone got hold of an ear or a leg and carried the hog to the pot. They laid him down and Bud pushed a corncob right up into his anus. I was impressed and asked, 'Why'd you do that?" Bud smiled and told me quietly, "That keeps him from soilin' the water."

They lifted the hog into the water, turned him this way and that, and then scraped the hair off with butcher knives. If a patch of hair was stubborn, Bud dipped the tar cup full of hot water and poured it on the spot and then the hair came off. Soon all the hair was gone. His skin was white, and his feet were pink. Daddy sliced the skin on both hind legs, pulled out the hamstring and pushed a tapered stick between the leg and this white cord, tied a rope to the middle of the stick and ran it through a block anchored to the eve of the barn. Several people pulled on the rope, hoisting the hog high in the air. It swung back and forth with his nose almost touching the ground and his feet near the roof of the barn. Daddy held the pig by the ear and stuck a long butcher knife in his throat. Hot blood gushed out. Mother put a washtub on the ground in front of his belly and Daddy stood on a chair and started cutting between the hog's hind legs. Steam came out and formed a white fog in the cold air.

Then I could see pink guts, lots of them. They bulged out and stayed together like a tangle of ropes. Then they started hanging down toward the head, more and more steam, and more and more guts. One last cut far back and the whole mess fell in the tub overfilling it. Then Daddy cut the liver away from the backbone and handed it to someone. It was cranberry-colored, clean, and shiny. I liked the looks of the liver. Mother told me she was going to make liver pudding out of it.

Next to come out were the 'lights', as the lungs were called. Mother threw them to the dogs. Then off came the head, WOW! then the hams and shoulders. A sharp hatchet cleaved the ribs from the backbone, which was later chopped up. Belly and fat went into one pile and lean in another. The women turned the intestines inside out and cleaned them for sausage casings. Some people eat the intestines, called chitterlings, but Mother will not eat a chitterling, or allow one to be cooked in her house.

The women were busy grinding meat, making sausage, souse meat, liver pudding, and boiling the fat into lard and cracklings. Then it was time to shoot the second hog. Daddy killed four hogs that day. For lunch, we ate milk toast, because nobody wanted to eat meat just then. Late in the afternoon, everyone went to their homes with backbone, a hog head and liver pudding, happy with the rewards of a hard day's work.

My father had three mules, Mike, Cora, and Slow Kate. You could only come up to Mike on his right side. No one could ride Cora and anyone could ride Slow Kate. Our house was a half-mile from the field, and I cried if Daddy didn't let me go to the field and help him. He built a small seat across the plow for me to sit on. Sometimes he would say, "Roger, the ground is getting hard so sit heavy." I would pull on the plow shears and push down with my butt as hard as I could.

In the wintertime he picked up lighter'd knots and threw them in a wagon. This is the best wood to burn in the fireplace as it burns hot and long. He would say, "Roger, you drive the mule while I pick up knots." I felt ten feet tall as I took the reins. Perhaps I did drive, but my guess is the mule obeyed his commands.

Johnny Pace, a colored man, and his beautiful wife, Ida Lee, moved to the Old place. They had no children and they loved me. Ida Lee made delicious cakes and would stuff me until I couldn't eat anymore. Johnny would say, "Oh, you can eat it, Roger. Pick up your right foot and stand on the left so the cake can go down in that one." Then he would have me stand on the other until I ate it all, then he would laugh a wonderful deep chuckle and brag on me.

Johnny was a strong, hardworking man and he needed a pair of strong young mules. I sat between Daddy and Johnny on the trip to an auction at Fitzgerald. Two big black mules trotted into the arena. The auctioneer said, "A fine matched pair of three-year-old, seventeen hands, fresh from Texas and ready for work. Who'll bid three-hundred dollars?" Daddy nodded his head. The bidding was swift and soon the auctioneer said, "Sold to Mr. Reaves for five-hundred dollars." That was a lot of money in the 1940s. That afternoon a truck backed up to our lot and the mules came prancing down the loading chute. Oh, they were beautiful creatures with the sun glistening off their shiny coats. The next morning Daddy went to harness them---not a chance. They turned their tails to him and kicked something fierce, scaring the other mules.

Daddy lifted me into the truck and we drove to the convict camp and went in to see "Little Dave," the warden. Daddy told him the trouble and the warden said, "Yeah, William I got a couple of men that can handle that problem." He sent a guard who returned with two tough-looking sun-burnt men dressed in prison stripes. They jumped up on the flatbed and we drove home. One shook out his lariat and tossed it over a mule's head and wrapped the other end around a corner post. The mule reared and bucked but with each antic he was pulled in closer and closer to the post until he was hard up against it, and it looked like he was choking.

The other convict grabbed the mule by his lower lip, pulled it out, and placed a loop fastened to a stick around it. He began to twist. The mule began to piss, spread his feet wide, and rolled his eyes back into his head until only the whites were showing. In this condition the bridle and harness were fastened on and he was released and led out. Then mule number two received the same treatment.

They were hooked to a nineteen-inch Oliver turning plow and worked all day breaking ground. The next morning, they were still difficult, so off to the convict camp we went. After three mornings they gave no more trouble and Daddy said they were broke and gentle as a couple of kittens. I wanted to ride one. I went into the barn, climbed the ladder up into the hayloft, and looked down through the hole where one threw hay into the manger. Standing directly below and not three feet away was "Boaz," one of the new mules. I didn't hesitate for a moment. I jumped down onto his back. He bucked so hard that my head hit the ceiling and split open. Mother found me lying unconscious under a bunch of mules munching hay.

The following episode is something that was in no way mentioned in our house and I would have never had known what had happened to Grandpa Lee Reaves had I not picked a lock on an old trunk. Oh, what a treasure chest! A fetus in a jar of formaldehyde, a jar of old coins taken from dead people's eyes, a wad of confederate money, and fifty pages of court transcripts; handwritten in beautiful flowing script telling the following tale.

Grandpa, Lee Reaves, had trouble with a young man at school named Woods. In those days, it was common to have young men twenty years old in school, as they went to school only part of the year because they had to work on the farm during the farming seasons. I don't know what happened, but bad blood boiled, and Woods senior took Grandpa to court. Woods got up, told his side of the story, and sat down. Grandpa stood up and just as soon as he started telling his side, Woods jumped up and yelled,

"You're a god-damned liar!"

Grandpa pulled out a 38-caliber pistol and shot Woods twice in the chest. At that very moment, Grandma opened the door to the courtroom and the bullets went through Woods and into the heavy oak door by her head. The judge said, "Reaves, I do believe you have killed him!"

Grandpa laid the smoking pistol on the judge's desk and said, "I hope to hell he's dead."

Papa was tried and convicted of murder. The transcripts, in a beautiful flowing script, are still available. The judge sentenced him to fifteen years hard labor at the notorious Reedsville State Penitentiary where he became the bookkeeper. The light was poor and within a few years he went blind due to cataracts. Doctors were looking for human guinea pigs for experimental eye surgery and Grandpa volunteered. They removed the cataracts and he could see, however, a few days later they came and did further surgery, splitting the irises and he was permanently blinded.

Because of this mutilation, the Governor of the State of Georgia pardoned him.

Daddy often took Grandma to visit Aunt Sadie, who was in her nineties. Her house was dark and cool. A deep porch covered with wisteria ran across the front. At one end of the porch was a well with a hinged cover. On one of our visits, I watched a quack doctor bleed her. She sat in a rocking chair with wide armrests and this man cut a vein in her arm and she slowly bled a dishpan half-full of dark blackish blood that spattered up the sides of the white enamel pan.

Just a little way further down the road lived Cousin Annie Parrish and her simple-minded brother Charlie. Annie had hair dyed bright red and favored colorful clothes. Charlie followed me around, showed me the stubs of his teeth and the inflamed gums, saying over and over, "Charlie's toof urt, Charlie's toof urt." Even as a little boy, I felt so sorry for him and I knew that if I was big I would take him to the dentist or a doctor.

Annie died while sitting in a rocking chair and Charlie didn't understand. The neighbor drove up and asked for Annie, and Charlie said, "Annie sleep, Annie sleep." The weather was hot and after a couple of weeks vultures were sitting on the roof. The stench was terrible! When they tried to get her remains into a plastic body bag, she came apart.

Mother was busy cleaning house, shelling peas and cooking supper and somehow I got crossways with her and a great injustice occurred. I stood there so mad I didn't know how to let it out and then a big loud "damn" just busted out. Every hand stopped in midair as they all turned and looked at me. I can still remember the shock in Grandma's blue eyes. I fled.

It wasn't long before it started getting dark and I realized what a big mistake I had made. I knew they were all sitting around the big table eating fried chicken and peach pies and I wondered if they were missing me. However, I was too scared to go home and face the awful whipping I knew I had coming. Mother would make me go and cut my own switch and it had better be a good one or she would go and cut one herself.

I just couldn't get up the courage to face the crowd. About that time, I heard the jingling of trace chains and I knew it was Rosier Williams on his way home. He was sharecropping down on the Belemy place and he passed the house every morning at daybreak standing on his little sled pulled by a mule and he returned every evening just after dark. I stepped out of my hiding place in the bushes and called, "Rosier, can I ride to the house with you?"

"Whoa mule! What you doing way out here in the dark Roger? Stand here behind me and hol'on. Get-up Kit."

Everybody was sitting around the table eating supper and my place was set. Not a word was said as I slinked up to my chair and sat down; however, after supper it was the old "go- and- find- a- switch" routine.

Daddy went hunting and I was waiting in the front yard for his return. Leather-winged bats filled the air as it started getting dark. To pass the time I threw a big butcher knife spinning high into the air and watched in amazement as the leather-wings dove at it, turning away at the last moment. Whippoorwills began their lovely clarion calls. Fireflies came out by the thousands and went through the woods blinking their little lights. I saw Daddy coming down the lane and ran to meet him. He was wearing a brown leather jacket, a felt fedora and carrying a double-barrel 12-gauge shotgun in his left hand and two big cottontail rabbits in his right. This was my Daddy, the hero, home from the hunt. My little heart was filled with awe and love. I ran up to him and asked to help carry the rabbits and he gave me one. I held it up by the hind legs and it was almost as long as I was tall.

Electrical power came to towns and some parts of the country, but as yet we still cooked on a wood stove, lighted the house by a kerosene lamp and mother ironed the clothes with a series of flat irons. She built a fire in the fireplace, placed the irons near the flames until they heated up. When she had used one for a couple of minutes it lost its heat and she traded it for another. This was all right in winter, but in the summer, the work was brutal. One summer day I was lying on my back with my feet propped up on the wall watching Mother iron. The sweat was dripping off the end of her nose. She was beautiful.

I said, "Mother, when I get big I'm going to buy you a 'lectric iron."

"Oh Roger, that will be wonderful, then I won't have to build a fire in the summertime."

"And when I get big I'm going to buy you a 'lectric stove."

"Oh boy, that's great. Then I won't have to build a fire three times a day in that old hot wood stove."

"And I'm going to buy you a 'lectric Frigidaire."

"Why that's even better. We can make ice cream every day if we want to."

I looked around the room for something else to buy my mother and said, "And when I get big I'm going to buy you a 'lectric chair."

"Oh no, not an electric chair, for that will be the end of me," she laughed.

I went to the Old Place with Daddy most every day. I could drive a mule and was allowed to run the stalk cutter, a round wooden drum with sharp iron blades attached horizontally at six-inch intervals. Over the drum is a little platform with an iron seat with holes in it where one sits while driving. It's a bumpy ride as the cutters chop up the cotton or corn stalks, but I was so proud of myself. I was really working, and everyone could see where I had been. I could only use Kate because she was the gentlest mule. Daddy was busy with two mules throwing up beds to plant watermelons. As soon as the beds were ready we went to town in Daddy's big red International two-ton truck and bought a load of 200-pound burlap sacks of guano. When we got to the field Daddy said, "Roger, I want you to drive down this row slow and when we get to the other end I'll help you turn around."

Oh my god, I was driving all by myself! I thought I would bust with joy. Daddy pushed in the clutch and I moved the gear stick all the way to the left and then down. This was "Grandma," or double low, and away we went down that long row. He would tell me to slow down or speed up a little as he rolled a bag off every so often. It was getting dark when we finished unloading. I looked through the spokes of the steering wheel and saw those big bags scattered across the field and thought they looked like giant turtles crawling across the black earth.

From the age of five or six, I had a watermelon stand beside the highway every summer. I would sell quite a few melons for a quarter or fifty cents apiece, but the wait between customers could be hours and it was very boring for a little boy and I got excited when a car stopped.

One clear, hot, sunny afternoon a shiny new car stopped, but didn't pull off the highway as one normally did, but only partway off. I ran up to the car and said, "Hi, do you want to buy a watermelon, Mister?" The man jumped; He had not even seen me. He said, "No son, my car is overheating, and I've just stopped here to put some water in the radiator."

He was wearing a white shirt and tie. A suit jacket was draped over the back of the passenger seat. From the trunk of the car he took a five-gallon can of water, went to the front, raised the hood, and opened the radiator cap. Steam billowed out for several minutes and when it somewhat subsided he poured water in. The car was running the whole time. He replaced the can and got in the car to drive off. I had both hands on the passenger door and the nice man was saying goodbye to me when a tractor-trailer truck loaded with bricks hit him square in the rear. The car went flying out of my hands and went perhaps twenty feet up into the air. The tractor-trailer truck jack-knifed and went sliding down the highway sideways.

After that, I couldn't see because a cloud of yellow-grey dust engulfed the scene. After a few moments, the dust drifted away, and thousands of sheets of paper came drifting down onto the road and ditches. I ran toward Uncle LG's house and nestled into the hollow of an ancient pine in their yard. I was terrified. I saw Aunt Lucille coming and I started back toward the wreck with her. Then we met Daddy who was running toward the wreck with an ax and crowbar. He told me to go to the house and I knew he meant it. The truck driver recovered, but the nice man spent the next thirty years in an iron lung.

Black Diamond watermelons were five feet deep from the front of the semi-trailer to the rear, each packed in a handful of yellow straw. What a beautiful painting and the combination of smells was a bouquet. As soon as the truck was loaded, Daddy and I pulled out on a long journey to sell the watermelons. I was excited because this was my very first such trip.

We went to the Farmers Market in Macon and nothing was happening there, so we pulled out for Atlanta. The Farmers market there was as big as a city. Daddy rented a space and we unloaded some watermelons underneath the shed and sliced a few open to show how beautifully ripe they were, and then we waited, and we waited. We sold very few that day, so Daddy loaded up, closed the tailgate and we went into a big restaurant there in the market and ate supper. The food was delicious.

After supper, we pulled out for Chattanooga, Tennessee and that was far away. Late that night as we were driving along a narrow, dark highway in North Georgia, Daddy said, "Roger I'm getting sleepy, sing me a song."

I let rip with "Uncle Ned" which went like this, "There was an old darkie and his name was Uncle Ned and he died long ago, long ago, He had no teeth for to eat the hoecake so he had to let the hoecake go. His fingers were as long as the cane in the break and he had no eyes for to see, he had no hair on the top of his head in the place where the hair ought to be. Now you lay down the shovel and the ho-o-o-e, for there is no more work for poor old Ned, he's gone where all good darkies go."

Daddy said, "Hush that and sing a happy one." I didn't realize it at the time, but Daddy was anti-racist, and he didn't approve of such songs, then common in all white schools. "OK, I'll sing another one,"

I tear off at the top of my lungs because Daddy needs me to keep him awake, "I'm coming, I'm coming, for my head is bending low, I hear the gentle voices calling, Old Black Joe."

He said, "Don't sing such songs son."

"All right Daddy, tell me about cannibals."

He told me about the cannibals in New Guinea.

"OK, now tell me about an animal that I have never heard of."

This went on into the wee hours of the night. We started getting higher and higher into the mountains, the weather started to get cooler and we pulled the front windshields shut. Then we came to a tunnel in the side of a mountain and drove straight in. There was a row of dim light bulbs spaced at long intervals hanging from the roof rocks. The tunnel made a turn to the left and it took a long time to go through. As we came out, there below us lay the city of Chattanooga, Tennessee as if it was in a big bowl with city lights twinkling as dawn was breaking. I had never seen a sight so beautiful and then it dawned on me and I said, "Daddy, I stayed awake all night for the first time in my life, didn't I?" And I wondered how many nights in my life I would stay awake.

Daddy said, "You sure did son."

We rented a space at the Farmers Market and started selling the watermelons at a good price. Storekeepers, housewives, and pin hookers were all buying our watermelons because they were fresh and beautiful. By the second night we were almost sold out. We talked about getting on the road home but decided to stay until they were all gone. That night Daddy started drinking whiskey with two men. I got into the cab, wrapped up in burlap bags because it was cold, and went to sleep.

Someone shook me awake. He was a nice farmer from a truck nearby who had befriended us during the day. He told me to go and look after my daddy because those men were going to rob him. I went to the rear of the truck and tried to get Daddy to come with me, but he was already too drunk, and I was too little. Soon the men were gone with all our money. The next morning Daddy was sick in both his stomach and his soul. He just hung his head in shame. I counted the watermelons. We had forty-seven left. If we were real careful these would bring enough money to buy gasoline to get home. It was a long sad trip to home and Mother.

Just as I was turning seven years old Daddy bought an M.T. John Deere, two-row tractor and all the equipment that went with it. That thing was beautiful! It was green with big bright yellow hubs for the tires. The rear tires were taller than the top of my head and the two front tires were close together and sloped into a skinny v. It had only two cylinders and made quite a racket when fired up, going pop, pop, pop so loud it could be heard for a mile and everybody knew if you stopped plowing. There were very few tractors in the country at that time and I was proud of ours.

Daddy sold Mike and Cora but kept Slow Kate to plow the short rows and garden; in reality, Kate was retired.

It was hard to get me away from the tractor; I would have slept with it if I could have. I scurried around helping Daddy hook up the plows, which was a difficult job back then because it took several hours or a day to hook up the turning plow as the rear tires had to be let out to make room.

Covering the rear tires were wide fenders where Daddy allowed me to ride on from the field to the house if there were no implements behind. On the way we had to go through a boggy branch, and beside the road lived a giant coachwhip snake that was over ten feet long. She had a nest of babies and the popping of the tractor really angered her. Every time we passed by she came out and attacked the hubs. Her head was at least four feet off the ground as she glided along beside us and I slid over closer to Daddy who laughed and said that she couldn't hurt me. Never mind, she was angry and fearful looking, and I was afraid of her.

Lighter'd stumps presented a real problem while farming with a tractor and our field was thick with them. These stumps were almost fossilized hearts of long-dead yellow pines. Sparks flew if you tried to chop them with an ax; however, if they were split into small pieces or splinters they burned vigorously. Hercules Powder Co. makes gunpowder out of them. My great grandparents had been burning them off for many years. With mules, they were no problem to work around, but plows got broken and twisted using the tractor.

I went with Daddy to Lamar Brown's dynamite store. We backed up to the door, loaded cases of these dangerous sticks on the old red two-ton truck, and drove home. Both Daddy and Mother worked hard-punching holes ten feet deep under the stumps with an iron buggy axel. Daddy would press a dynamite cap onto a roll of fuse, make a slice in a stick of dynamite with his pocketknife and stick the cap into the slice. Then he poked it all down the hole, adding several more sticks on top. He then cut the fuse and packed the earth around the hole, lit the fuse, and got a long way off. The explosion shook the ground as a two-ton stump catapulted high into the air. We would wait a little while for the smoke to clear, or else we got bad headaches from breathing the nitro-glycerin fumes. Daddy dragged the stump away with the tractor while Mother filled in the big hole with a shovel. We kept finding stumps for years and each time a plow tripped or broke, we flagged it for the aforementioned treatment.

We all worked hard in the field hoeing. Mother could hoe a row faster than anyone I ever met. She hoed her row and helped the stragglers on theirs and she always kept some joke or story going. Everyone worked like the dickens to stay up so they could hear. Every once in awhile the colored women burst into peals of beautiful laughter. We did a lot of hoeing in a hurry.

There was a good fish hole under the bridge where Highway 441 crossed Alligator creek, about a half-mile south of our house.

One hot sunny afternoon, I hurried to the creek, dug some worms, and had just started fishing when this really strange feeling came over me. I thought that perhaps a cottonmouth moccasin was about to bite me. I was sitting near the bridge on grass that had been recently mowed by the highway department. I looked all around and there was nothing. The longer I sat there, the more afraid I became. In a few minutes, I could stand it no longer.

I grabbed up my pole and can of worms, ran across the foot log, up the embankment, across the bridge, and headed for the house. I had not gone far when I saw an old flatbed truck come speeding down the hill. It didn't have a cab and on the back was a big sawmills motor that must have weighed a ton. Three men were riding in front, and in back, five muscular black men with their shirts off were laughing and jumping up and down on the rear of the truck, causing the front tires to jump off the pavement.

The three men in the front were laughing too and I can still remember the big smile on the driver's face. The road had settled and there was a lip of several inches where the road met the bridge. When the front tires hit this lip, they bounced four feet into the air. The driver touched the brakes and the left rear wheel caught first, spinning the truck to the left, throwing the sawmill motor and men over the banister. I saw the men sliding down the highway and the truck running over them. Blood and limbs covered the white cement bridge. The big motor dug into the ground where I had been sitting only a minute earlier.

Is the same guardian angel still with me? I believe he is.

It was August 1952, "Mother, Grandma is going to buy me a pony real soon."

"Roger, just hush about that pony, you know she's not going to buy you one."

"Grandma, Mother said to just hush about that pony because you are never really going to buy him for me."

"Go and get your Daddy and tell him to come here and we'll see about that."

We went to *Boney's Mule and Horse Barn* in Fitzgerald, which was right next to the courthouse where Mother and Daddy got married. Inside the big barn was a wide passageway covered with fresh pine shaving. Big stalls made of heavy timber-lined both sides. Mules were in the front stalls, a hundred or more, with fifteen or twenty to each pen. In the rear and on the left was a stall with a few horses. There he was! A Mexican Pinto. His coat was glistening white, with big dark brown spots. His mane and tail were thick and long. Yellow hooves with a black streak down the center caught my eye. His neck arched and I could tell he was spirited by the look in his eyes. The other horses were dull and drab in comparison. I knew this was the one for me, but the salesman tried to discourage me and warned that he was a handful for a boy. That was even better! He recommended a gentle dappled grey filly that he saddled and had me ride.

And as he said, it was liked sitting in a rocking chair, but this was not what I wanted. The price for either was one hundred and forty-five dollars, including a bridle. The money exchanged hands with a guarantee to deliver him the next day. I was one excited boy! All I wanted to talk to or think about was my horse.

The truck finally showed up the next day after lunch and there were two horses. The man first saddled the grey mare and I went for a ride galloping up and down the road. Everyone bragged on me and said what a fine horse she was. Nothing doing, don't you know I can read all of you like a book? You all think that pinto is too much for me, but there is no choice. The pinto didn't have a saddle and the man said the saddle belonged to the mare. Later I found out why he lied. I climbed onto the bare back of the pinto while the man held the bridle. We walked a ways up the road, the man turned the bridle loose and the horse trotted back to the truck. Not too bad. The truck left with the understanding that if I couldn't handle him he would come back and trade.

As soon as the truck left, I tried to ride him, but he whirled around and bit at me and I couldn't get on. I got help, climbed on and then he acted like a fool, dogtrotting sideways, and jarring my guts out, then whirled around and ran for the barn gate and come sliding to a stop. Pretty soon I was crying. Daddy came, made a stout rope halter, tied a short rope to a heavy corner post and told me to ride to my heart's content. This took some time, but we got to know one another. I found he knew what a switch was and acted like a new horse when I had one. I named him Silver and after a few days I rode him to the Old Place and had him prance up and down the rows as the field hands picked cotton.

He knew very well what he was doing. He would walk gently along and then suddenly throw his head back and hit me in the face, busting my nose. Or he would run by a tree trying to scrape me off or lie down in water and wallow; this was why he didn't have a saddle. He bit me on the butt when I was trying to get on. I jumped down, grabbed him by the ear, and bit down. He threw his head back and nearly jerked my head off my shoulders. I came in every evening with a bloody nose or scraped up and finally the folks had had enough. I must trade horses. They called the man to come and make the exchange. I rode Silver into a thick woods and hid him until the man left.

I got a club and waited for him to throw his head back and try to bust my nose and then I hit him between the ears. It wasn't long before we came to an understanding. Little by little, we worked everything out and by and by I had a horse no one could ride but me.

On a beautiful spring morning in early June, when the yards are a bouquet of flowers and the bumblebees are drilling holes in the porch beams, Uncle Walter, Aunt Martha, and their three children, Jack, Gary, and Dianne drove up in a magnificent automobile. It was a powder blue Ford Victoria loaded with all the extras. Uncle Walter brought a quart of Crown Royal bourbon whiskey and he and Daddy eased on off and had a snort or two, as Daddy would say. I struck up a fire under the wash cauldron to heat water to scald chickens. When it got hot enough, Mother rung the necks of several pullets, and we children watched as they jumped and flopped around the yard. I never did like that part. The garden was full of ripe corn, tomatoes, peas, beans, okra, potatoes, squash, onions, cucumbers, and soon delicious aromas were permeating throughout the house. We ate a big dinner and afterwards the children cranked out a churn of fresh peach ice-cream, ladled out over a thick slice of warm pound cake. Mama bragged on Uncle Walter's car so, he took her and showed it to her. She said, "Walter, it's beautiful, if I could drive I would go to town tomorrow and buy me one just like it". He said, "Miss Mary, driving a car is the easiest thing in the world, now that they have automatic transmissions. All you have to do is turn the steering wheel and it will carry you wherever you want it to go. Sit down here in the driver's seat and I'll explain everything to you. "Mama got in but kept one foot on the ground.

"Miss Mary, get on in and close the door, it's not going to bite you".

Mama closed the door and adjusted herself and her tight corset. Uncle Walter lit up a cigar and began explaining. I was standing by the door. I knew how easy it was to drive, and boy I was hoping Mama would buy a new car and I knew she had the money. "Miss Mary just turn that key there and it'll start up all on its own." This she did and that new Ford purred like a kitten. "Now all you have to do is pull the gear shift to the 'D'. Mamma did this and nothing happened. Uncle Walter said, "That's fine, now Miss Mary, just push gently down on the accelerator and we will drive forward a few feet, nothing could be easier." Mamma stepped down on the accelerator with her fat foot, it went to the floor and stayed there! That car shot forward like a rocket, went through a tall wire fence covered in rose vines in full bloom, knocked down a twenty-foot pear tree, and tore through the vegetable garden, through the far fence and on into the potato patch. This started it to bucking hard. I could see their heads snapping back and forth. Uncle Walter got it stopped just before they got across ten acres of field and into the woods.

P.S. – We did not get a new car.

Uncle L.G said, "Bo, you've got a job at Popes, starting Saturday morning at eight o'clock. Be on time." Uncle L.G had always called me Bo as long as I could remember, his nickname for me. This was his way of telling me something important, short, and to the point.

Saturday morning Mother made me a sack lunch of biscuit sandwiches. One with pork and the other with homemade bullis jelly. I walked to the highway; stuck my thumb out and one of the first cars passing gave me a ride to Pope's front door. Mr. Pope smiled, shook my hand, and told someone to get me an apron. He put it around my neck and the bottom dragged on the floor. Then he showed me how to shorten and tie it properly. Pete Fulford, the butcher, walked around studying me in a most serious manner.

He said, "Why, he's too short to reach the counter. Reckon what he can do, open the paper bags, or what?" I had just turned fourteen, and really and truly I wasn't tall enough to stand on the floor and reach into the bags on the counter. They all picked at me good-naturedly and I enjoyed it.

Mr. Pope taught me to sweep without raising too much dust, to bag potatoes in five-and ten-pound bags, to go to the wholesale warehouse and fetch bales of sugar and flour on a hand truck. I learned to clean heads of cabbage and lettuce and to keep the produce display fresh, to pack groceries with the heavy tins on bottom and bread on top; I did the latter while standing on a wooden box.

At lunch, Mrs. Pope asked what I had in my sack. I showed her and she asked if I would like to trade. Of course, I did, and she just raved over Mother's biscuit and jelly sandwiches. We traded many lunches over the next five years.

Wade Harbin had a hotdog and hamburger place down on Railroad Street, the dividing line between white and black McRae. This was an invisible wall, but as real as the Berlin wall. Next-door was Wades Barbershop where old Mr. Wade had cut my family's hair for five generations. Restaurateur Wade sold hamburgers for ten cents each. They were small, but delicious. I ordered five.

Someone yelled out, "Hey Wade, wattcha use to cut out these patties, a Coca Cola cap?" This kind of happy jesting was always going on.

I was standing at the counter wearing a Pope's apron and smiling at the foolishness when the deputy sheriff drove up in front of the barbershop. He got out, swaggered his fat ass around the car, opened the passenger's door, and out crawled a most decrepit old tramp in handcuffs. Dirt had grown into his skin and filthy tangled hair stood out a foot long all over his face and head. He looked like he had spent the last ten years in a dungeon. He was one ugly creature!

Everyone in the place craned their necks trying to get a better view. Wade said he was the dirtiest, ugliest man he had ever seen. Someone wondered what he had done. Another said he hoped Wade boiled his clippers and fumigated the place once he finished with the beast. At a short break in the talk, I laid my fifty cents on the counter and with a clear voice, said, "That's my Daddy."

You could have heard a mouse fart as I eased out, leaving the crowd with their mouths open. I walked back into Pope's just as he was hanging up the telephone and his belly was shaking with laughter. Wade had called immediately after I left to see who the new boy wearing the Pope's apron was. The story was told all over town and for weeks, men came up to me, shook my hand, and laughed.

I worked from eight in the morning, until ten at night, with a few minutes off for lunch. I packed and lugged groceries all over town. In those days, the sidewalks were packed with people and many parked a half-mile away. Mr. Pope kept us there at night until he had counted his money three times. He was probably afraid of being robbed and felt safer with all of us around. At around ten o'clock, he paid off and I received three dollars. With this, I paid for school lunches. Each year I got a dollar raise and the county raised the price of lunches or another child started to school. There was never anything left over.

One late spring Saturday morning, I walked out to the highway and put my thumb out. The first car that came along started slowing down before it reached me and came to a gentle stop where I stood. All I had to do was open the rear door and get in, so I did. The car was a light grey four-door sedan from back in the '30s. The interior was in immaculate condition, looking as though it had just come out of the showroom. The driver was a nice-looking clean-cut man of about forty years, wearing a grey suit and tie. He greeted me with a 'good morning' in a most polite manner and started off ever so smoothly. A short plump shaped woman was slumped in the right seat holding a white towel over her face. She did not look up or acknowledge me. I felt the tension. Something was wrong here. I could not see what it was, but it was thick, and I could definitely feel it. The man asked me where I was going, and I told him I was going to work in McRae at a grocery store. He then asked if I wanted to buy the suit hanging in the back seat. I laughed and said that I didn't need a suit. He said that it was new, and I could have it for five dollars. I told him I didn't have five dollars

The woman took the towel from her face and turned to me. Oh, God! She was just a bloody piece of meat. The towel was covered and dripping with blood.

She said, "The only reason he picked you up was to try to sell you that suit he stole. I told him you wouldn't buy it, but the imbecile wouldn't listen. He got out of the insane asylum in Florida yesterday, but he's still crazy, they didn't cure him one bit." The man continued driving calmly along without responding, acting as though she had not spoken. I wondered which one was crazy and figured it was both. We drove by a little roadside rest area and saw a family cooking breakfast. There was a momma, a papa, and two teenage daughters wearing shorts. The man turned his head as I did and looked. The woman screamed, "Look, you lecherous son-of-a-bitch, look, look, take a good look, that's all you're good for! Yes, lust, lust, and lust."

Blam! He hit her with the back of his fist, her head hit the window with a pop that told just how hard he had hit her. She put her face in the towel and was quiet. So was I. We rode on in silence for approximately ten miles. As we were getting closer to McRae, just before Nubby's service station, so named because the owner was missing both legs from the thigh down due to a railroad accident. Nubby had raped his eighty-year-old mother and the state had sent him off for a spell. It was at this bad luck place that the woman lifted her bloody face and started cussing the man with the most insulting words imaginable, accusing him of the same acts as in Nubby's case. The man slowed the car down, drove gently to the front of the abandoned filling station, and stopped. He switched off the motor, pulled on the hand brake, turned slowly toward the woman, and began beating her in the face with his fists. Her head was bouncing off the window, blood was flying in every direction and she never lifted a hand to ward off the blows. I truly thought he was going to kill her and probably would, had I not intervened.

I was only seventeen years old and clearly no match for that man, but something deep down inside me rose up and I had all the strength needed for the job. I reached over the seat, grabbed him by the hair, jerked his head back, reached around his neck with my right arm, and jerked backwards with all my might. He started clawing my arm trying to get loose. I supported it with my left hand, I could feel it choking his windpipe. He clawed the skin off my arm and then grabbed the steering wheel twisting it all out of shape while kicking the dials off the radio. I felt him go limp and still I held on until I was sure he was unconscious. I got out, went around and opened the woman's door, but she wouldn't get out. I urged her to come with me, explaining that he was only unconscious and would be coming to any minute. He must have heard, because he stumbled out choking, gagging, and staggered off into the pines. I caught a ride into town and told Mr. Pope who called the sheriff to whom I related the whole story. The car stayed at Nubby's for a month or more and then one day it was gone. I never heard what happened to them.

Daddy began drinking more and more. If he went to town, he was drunk when he came home. I remember once he had been sober for months and there was peace in our home. Then one afternoon we all went to Fitzgerald, we were waiting in the car, a 1949 Studebaker. When I saw him come staggering down the street I was sick to my stomach. Mother got so angry that she let into him and they went to cussing one another. Mother never said a swear word and Daddy wouldn't say 'damn' if he was sober. Mother would take the fire poker and break his bottle. He would go into a rage, get in the truck and go buy a gallon of moonshine on credit and she would break this if she could find it. Over the years, this got worse and worse. We were ashamed to ask anyone to come to our house, even the preacher. Because just as sure as someone came, he was drunk. I think it was partly just bad luck, but he made a pure fool of himself.

Old Doctor Frank Mann was driving out to his hobby farm near Jacksonville one rainy night. Just as he was passing Larkey's Store, Daddy and I were crossing the highway in a barely lit old two-ton truck. Dr. Mann hit the left rear tire and spun us around in the road, doing little damage to our truck, but demolishing his new Cadillac. Not surprisingly, Daddy was about drunk, but sober enough to hand me his quart bottle of moonshine and tell me to get rid of it. He staggered out of the truck and told the doctor that he should watch where the hell he was going. It was getting so a workingman couldn't cross the damned road without some damned blind fool running over him.

I didn't feel very sorry for the old doctor because I knew something of his history. Years before, my Grandpa Garrison, Mother's daddy, was critically ill. Mother walked to a country store that had a telephone and called Dr. Mann. She told him she thought her Poppa was dying and asked him to come quickly. He said, "Do you have the money?" They didn't have the money and Grandpa died without the aid of the doctor.

4. TEENAGE YEARS, GROWIN' TOBACCO

Bobby Jack -- Grandma's Piano -- Bad Fight -- Run Away -- April Fools --The Saddest Day

Many of the clearest memories of my childhood are of working in tobacco. This always included the entire family and young people from neighboring farms. For all of you that weren't fortunate enough to be raised on 'Tobacco Road,' I will explain the growing of the weed, the hard work that goes into the production, and some of the camaraderie and laughter that accompanies the work.

First, you cut the stalks of cotton or corn from the previous year. Then 'burn off' the field to get rid of as much stubble as possible. One must then 'break the ground'. This is done with two big mules pulling a 19-inch Oliver, a turning plow that turned the earth to a depth of eight inches or more. In later years, the job was done by a tractor pulling a tiller or bottom plows. The land is then harrowed smooth, beds are 'thrown up' and fertilizer applied during the process.

Setting out tobacco was a major production. First, we had to go to Coffee County and buy the plants because their season was a couple of weeks ahead of ours. We all loaded up on the back of a two-ton truck before daybreak, went shivering in the wind, and then pulled plants all morning. In the afternoon, we set the plants out. This was done with a hand planter; a V-shaped tin contraption that held a bucket of water and had a funnel attached to the front. The bottom was shaped like the beak of a bird. Mother pushed the beak into the loose soil and someone else dropped a plant in the long narrow funnel. Then Mother pulled a trigger and the plant dropped along with a cup of water. A little boy, named Roger, crawled along behind doodling the plants. That is, packing the wet soil around the roots.

Scattered across the field were tar barrels full of water and two children were busy totin' water to the transplanting team. I preferred this to doodling, as one was freer, and we cut up and had lots of fun. Mother was worried we might fall in a barrel and drown and kept warning us not to dip them dry, because we had to jump up and lean far over into the barrels when they were low. Once I tipped the barrel and dipped all the water out and then stood on my head in the bottom and yelled," HELP! HELP! HELP!" Mother came running from far across the field leading the pack. She was hot, pregnant, and peeing on herself. I was swinging my legs back and forth and smiling to myself as I was jerked from the empty barrel and got the worse whipping I ever had, right there on the spot. There was no "Go cut a good switch, Roger." No sir!

In 1953, Daddy bought a one-row transplanter that carried 100 gallons of water. He set the spacing of the plants at thirty inches. This meant that every thirty inches a pint of water sprayed into the groove where a hand was waiting to release a tender young plant. Each spew was accompanied with a loud clink.

The little *Super A-Farmall* was purring along in low gear, Daddy was smoking a Lucky Strike cigarette and driving. Marijo and Clayton were sitting on metal seats that almost dragged the ground. They were dropping plants while laughing and carrying on. I was walking along behind with a handful of plants, uncovering any that were covered and planting any they missed. To be mean, they would skip half a dozen and laugh when I got angry. Marijo said something to Clayton and he answered, "Ah, go buck a fuzzard!" Daddy jumped off the tractor in a huff and I thought he was going to hit Clayton. Daddy didn't care if he did say 'buck' but it was no way to talk in front of women folks and he wasn't going to put up with it.

When the plants were about six inches high we hoed them and Daddy plowed behind us, using narrow 'snakehead' points that went deep into the soil beside the plants and he tried to move the young plants just a little forward as he slowly plowed down each row.

Budworms were a constant problem and we poisoned them by shaking a flour sack with poison dust over each plant. This was done very early in the morning while the plants were wet with dew. Before this job was finished, we looked like a family of aliens. Our hair, clothes, and skin were covered in white poison and it was caked on our face and arms where we had sweat. This job was repeated weekly, undoubtedly poisoning us as well as the worms.

Plowing took place every two or three weeks and when the stalks got about knee-high, we hoed it again. Once the plants reached four feet and had 32 leaves, we broke out the top of the plant to stop the vertical growth, forcing the plant to put its energy and weight into the leaves. After the plant was topped, suckers grew by each leaf and it was a never-ending job keeping them off.

When school let out for summer we went to the barn and cleaned tobacco sticks of all old thread, worked on the long tobacco bench under the big black walnut tree at the Old Place, then got the tobacco sleds in order by lining them with new burlap. Next, it was to the tobacco barn to burn wasp nests, blow out the burners and fuel lines, and make sure all was ready for the big day.

When the bottom two or three leaves, called sand lugs, turned a lemon yellow it was time to "crop tobacco." The ripe leaves were picked off and flung under the opposite arm by the cropper until leaves were hanging to his knees. Then he dumped his load into a sled pulled by a mule. At the end of each row, the sled was exchanged for an empty one. When I was little, I drove the mule. Years later, we skipped every fourth row and used a tractor to pull the sled.

At about age nine or ten, I was driving the mule and the croppers held me down and 'sanded' my dick in a very rough manner. Oh, how they laughed! I was humiliated and terribly angry, particularly with Bill, as he was the leader of the pack. He was probably seventeen years old and weighed 250 pounds. I took out my Barlow knife, found the longest tobacco stalk in the field, cut it down, and stripped off the leaves. With this weapon, I slipped up behind Bill who had his head down cropping with his back parallel to the ground. His back was as broad as the row and his faded denim shirt was stretched tight and streaked down the center with sweat. I brought my weapon up over my head and behind me until the tip touched the ground, then swung with all my might and yelled, "You son-of-a-bitch!" Bill's shirt split from the collar to his belt and that was all I waited to see. We took off through that tobacco field tearing down everything in our path. He would have done me serious bodily harm had he caught me, but I got to sanctuary under the old walnut tree where Mother was 'stringing' and Daddy was unloading a sled. Bill said I called his mother a bitch and I told on him for sanding my dick. Bill quit and I was happy to see his split shirt going down the road.

Tobacco hornworms can get as big around as your finger and up to five inches long. They are ugly, blackish green creatures, with whitish markings, five pairs of bright yellow spots on the sides, a horn on their tail and numerous pairs of feet. They are the larva of the big grey hawk moth and they can strip a tobacco leaf overnight and a field within a few days. One afternoon we were all taking a break under the tree along with the stringing crew when one of the girls found an especially big worm.

Clayton picked it up and said, "Don't he look yummy?"

The chorus went up, "Eat him Clayton, eat him, I dare you!"

"Whatchu'bet I won't eat him?"

"I'll betchu' a dollar."

We all took it up, bets were taken, heads counted and then Clayton held that worm up real slow, looked at him like he was a piece of candy and then took a bite right out of the middle and said, "yummy, yummy." Then he ate the two ends very slowly and licked his fingers. Daddy took a dollar out of each of the betters' pay and gave it to Clayton. We received two dollars for our days' work and Clayton got fourteen.

One scorching hot day we were short one cropper and Mother filled the place. This was no job for a lady. She was wearing a wide straw hat, loose blue trousers, and what had once been a white shirt. She was bent over double cropping on the row to my right when she yelled, dropped her armload of leaves, and ran over me. One look at her red sweating terrified face and I knew something was dreadfully wrong. She squeezed my arm hard with one hand and pointed with the other. There coiled under the plant she had just cropped was a tub full of a deadly diamondback rattlesnake.

He was coiled with his head reared back, poised to strike and shaking a long pod of rattlers. We couldn't hear this warning because of the noise of the tractor motor. There was nothing to kill him with and they can disappear in nothing flat. I unhitched the sled, drove the tractor over several rows tearing up the tobacco, and stopped almost on top of him. I took the heavy hand crank, stood on the front axle, and threw the crank down with all my might. That serpent struck and his head came up as high as the front tire. I saw that his back was broke, got a tobacco stalk, stripped it, and finished the job. He was six feet long, as big around as my ankle, and had seventeen rattlers in his pod. Mother had just had a close encounter with death.

Once the leaves were cropped and the sled was full, it was taken to the tobacco bench underneath shade trees where it was unloaded onto the long table. Wayne Jones, a retarded neighbor, always had this job. Then two 'handers' handed three leaves at a time to the 'stringer' who tied them on a stick with a series of half hitches. A fast stringer could keep four handers busy. When the stick was full, and this was every minute, the stringer called 'stick-off' and Wayne would say, "Yes Ma'am."

Mother said, "Wayne, don't say 'yes Ma'am' every time I say, "Stick off.'"

Wayne replied, "Yes Ma'am."

He took the stick full of tobacco and stacked it onto a pile, into what looked like the pleats in a woman's skirt. At lunchtime, and again late in the afternoon we loaded this tobacco onto a truck or wagon and took it to the tobacco barn, where it was passed from one to another like a bucket brigade at a fire until they reached me, where I hung them on tear poles, the top ones being twenty-five feet above the ground.

When most of the tobacco was harvested, the market opened, and we loaded the sheets onto a two-ton truck and hauled it to a tobacco warehouse in either Douglas or Fitzgerald. Sometimes twenty or thirty trucks stood in line ahead of us and it was a slow stop and go until it was our turn to get unloaded and have our sheets weighed, tagged, placed on low wicker baskets and put in a long row on the floor. The warehouseman told us what day ours would sell, and on that day, we got all dressed up and went to town. On the big day, we children had a real outing, eating 10-cent hot dogs and drinking 5-cent Coca Colas.

Sometimes we waited for hours on the government inspector to come down the row with his entourage, tearing our beautiful work to shreds. His assistant 'tagged it' with a grade and minimum support price. Once this government geek finished his work for the whole warehouse, the buyers showed up. Pretty farmer's wives and daughters sat or stood by their tobacco, hoping the auctioneer and buyers would be a little more attentive. The auctioneer, followed by a dozen or so buyers from different cigarette companies, came down the aisle raising a finger, nodding or winking and in that wink our years' work belonged to someone else.

Daddy took his government tickets to The Farmers Bank, where he owed money. He cashed his check, paid off the loan and we loaded up for the long ride home. He stopped off at Russell Clark's service station and paid Mrs. Doris Clark for the gasoline used over the past year. Next stop was the Simms Store in Jacksonville, where we bought only the very necessary groceries and Mother kept the bill under ten dollars a week. The only item she splurged on was when once a month she bought a side of smoked bacon, and it was delicious. After Daddy paid this bill, we departed on the four-mile ride to the house, arriving home at dusk. Without fail J.C Anderson, the fertilizer dealer was waiting in his car. J.C was a good friend of Daddy's and they sat on the porch and talked for a long time. When he left, Daddy was broke.

Hopefully we will have a better crop next year and maybe prices will rise.

No account of my youth would be complete without telling of the times and adventures with Bobby Jack. This colorful character showed up one day in our fifth-grade class with his longish hair combed back in a D.A., wearing clothes too big for him, as later became the style of gang members. He took a seat on the back row where he stayed. He was three years older than the rest of the class and he didn't talk to any of us underlings. That afternoon he got on the bus and I sat beside him, but he didn't say anything, just looked out the window as we rode along over bumpy washboard roads. When we came to the Lawson Jones farm, Bobby Jack got off and went onto the porch and directly into the house without once looking back. It was as if we didn't exist.

Gossip spread quickly, and the word was that Lawson had advertised for a bride, and Rea, a pretty redhead with a nice figure, had shown up on his doorstep with a fourteen-year-old son. Lawson put her in his old beat-up pickup and took off looking for a preacher. His farm joined ours on the north side and between school the school bus, and working across the fence from one another, I got to know Bobby Jack better than anyone else knew him, even his mother. He didn't say much, was extremely stubborn, opinionated, and didn't try at all in school. He could repair cars, trucks and tractors and build whatever he chose. His legs were almost dwarfish as they were short compared to his long upper body, but he could run faster than anyone I have ever seen, even to this day. He could run twice as fast as I could and I'm no slowpoke. Also, he was exceptionally strong; perhaps he was some Neanderthal throwback.

I never had any trouble with Bobby Jack, but sometimes he was as mean as a rattlesnake. We were cropping tobacco one stifling hot afternoon when I got the cold shivers, a sure sign that I was about to get 'bear caught' (colloquial for heatstroke). Daddy told us to take a break until we cooled down, so we went down to the new waterhole, a little pond of about a half-acre in area and fifteen feet deep.

Us, white boys stripped off naked, but the colored boys kept their trousers on. Most of them couldn't swim and were wading and splashing one another near the bank when Bobby Jack gave Orace a tremendous shove right out into deep water. Orace went under a couple of times and it was obvious that if someone didn't help soon he was going to drown. I yelled, "Bobby Jack, pull him out. He's drowning!"

He said, "Let the black son-of-a-bitch drown. I don't care."

I knew Orace was drowning and I knew that if he got a hold of me we would both drown, so I dove deep and pushed his legs up and toward the bank. After a couple of lunges, his brother Press grabbed hold and pulled him out. Orace never forgot this. I visited him many years later in Miami and he recollected this story with much embellishment.

Bobby Jack could save money and he saved up enough to order a bicycle from the Sears and Roebuck catalog. It was bright red with big fat white sidewall tires so he could ride on the sandy roads. He rode far and wide and on Saturdays, we went long distances together, he on his bicycle and me on my horse. Silver liked to gallop and could keep it up for hours. I believe he would have run himself to death if I had let him. I carried along plow line and on hills and deep sandy areas, I threw one end to Bobby Jack who looped it over the handlebars, and I held on to the other end and away we rode.

He saved up fourteen dollars and ordered an eleven-foot prefab boat. When it arrived, he worked on it non-stop, gluing, planning, sanding and varnishing.

When he finished, it looked like it came out of a show-room. We carefully placed it on a wagon and took it to Horse Creek where we launched it, just as proud as if it was a big yacht. It was cold and the creek was full. We set trotlines all up and down the creek, built a big fire and dragged up lots of wood. For several days, we hunted, fished, cooked and ate.

Paul Hester, a colored boy who lived nearby, was about the age of Bobby Jack. His sister had recently competed as a sprinter in the Olympics, yet Bobby Jack bragged he could 'smoke her' in a race. I asked him why he didn't try out for the Olympics and get famous. He said he didn't give a tinkers damn about that sort of thing. Early one morning Paul went to the creek with us. There was ice in the puddles and in the boat. The trotlines were full of catfish and we were having a good time, but the weather kept getting colder, so we rowed hard against the current until we were back at camp. I was looking forward to the fire and frying up some fish.

Paul had probably never been in a boat before and when we reached the landing he stood up in the bow. I was sitting in the middle and Bobby Jack was in the rear. When the boat nosed up to the bank, Paul jumped out, kicking the boat backward. Bobby Jack was pitched on his head into the creek. I was bent over laughing when Bobby Jack came up. He was waist-deep in ice water, holding on to the boat. He reached over in the boat, picked up the .22-calibre rifle and shot Paul. I think I went into shock worse than Paul did. Bobby Jack took off down the road all in a huff, carrying his rifle. I helped Paul hobble along for a couple of miles until we came to a road where we flagged down a car that took Paul to the hospital. The Hudson's moved away and I never heard from Paul.

Grandma got sick and went to the hospital. I didn't think much of it because she looked the same to me and the ailment wasn't serious. Also, Grandma went to the hospital often. I was in our big feather bed when Daddy came into the room and turned on the light. I asked how Grandma was doing and he came over to the bed, put his hand on my shoulder, and said, "Son, Grandma died tonight."

I could not digest it. I didn't cry. I must have been in shock or denial. I lay there thinking about her and wondering what my life would be like without her. I wondered where she was right then. I drifted off to sleep and woke myself by jerking the bed with silent sobbing.

The following day I went to the funeral home and it almost killed me to see her lying in the casket. Oh, how I would have gladly exchanged places if only I could. The tears just streamed down my face, splattering on her jacket. We buried her at Sand Hill on Thanksgiving Day, 1957. She was sixty-seven and I was fourteen. On the way to the cemetery, we passed the creek just before reaching Virgil Cameron's farm. Some children were fishing by the bridge. One little boy had on a new straw hat and I thought, those people shouldn't be fishing on Sunday.' It wasn't Sunday, it was Thursday.

Now comes some facts that are difficult to tell. Nevertheless, they are the truth, but they involve one I love dearly, and he is no longer here to tell his side of the story, as he lays buried beside Grandma.

Grandma was dead. The whole family went to Harris and Smith Funeral parlor in McRae, where we stayed all afternoon. We drove home in a quiet, reflective mood, got out, and went in. What had happened? The house looked bare. The beautiful piano that Grandma and the girls played on every day was gone. So were the dining room table and all the nice cherry wood chairs and the lovely dish cabinet and all the china and silverware. The closets had been rifled. Blankets and quilts were strewn on the beds. Gone were all the old family photographs and ancient hand-woven blankets made from wool grown on the farm in times of yore.

Uncle L.G. came from a back room and no one said anything. It was deathly quiet while all of us children held our breath. Then Uncle L.G. very deliberately took a picture off the wall and reached for another. Daddy walked over to him and said, "Put it back G!" He did and left.

Monday evening Uncle L.G. came by and called Daddy out on the porch, handed him some papers, and said, "Brother, I was in town today and there was no key to Momma's lockbox, so I got the sheriff and had it drilled open. There was nothing in it except these old deeds."

We never did learn what was in the box, but I do know it happened exactly as described and Daddy never allowed anything to be said about it for as long as he lived.

After Grandma died, Daddy took to drinking more and more. Had he expected an inheritance? I'm sure he did. Did he believe his mother had gone through every dime? Did he believe his only brother had robbed him? Whatever he thought, we never knew. Grandma had *always* had money; now there was not a dime on the hill. For whatever reason Daddy became a hopeless alcoholic and our family suffered terribly.

Even so Uncle L.G. and Aunt Lucille loved me, and I loved them. Many evenings I ate supper at their house. They took me to the Ringling Brothers and Barnum Bailey circus. I called them Uncle Snaps and Miss Lucy. He was my fishing buddy and he often took me with him. However, I was the only one of seven children so honored. Perhaps it was because I inserted myself when I wasn't particularly wanted. I know that was sometimes the case, but both the fishing and the food were great, and I truly loved my aunt and uncle.

Uncle was at odds with Thoreau when he said many men fish all the days of their lives and never realized it isn't the fish they're after. Uncle went after fish! He worked hard at it and he usually got them. He fished seven lines at a time, and it was a serious business.

The piano, now over at Uncle L.G.'s, had been bought for Marijo when she was a little girl. We all played it and practiced for little recitals at school. Every evening our house was a happy place with the girls practicing or Larry playing 'by ear.' Grandma was a pianist of some renown and she played the old hymns and a circus waltz, where she'd crossed her hands on the keyboard. Jimmy Jones would come by, flop down on the stool with a cigarette dangling from the corner of his mouth, and beat out a ragtime tune.

Mother was beautiful and kept her good figure for many years. She would take her apron off and do 'The Charleston' on the living room floor and would she ever cut the rug. The piano was moved to Uncle's house and put in a dimly lit room with Venetian blinds only partially opened. An embroidered doily lay on top and an empty vase placed on the doily. I never again saw the lid open or heard a chord vibrate with sweet music. 'The Touch of the Master's Hand' was missing.

Carol Clements was a pretty girl, kinda' shy and sweet. Her long glossy hair and large gentle brown eyes glowed with youth and vigor. Her skin had a touch of color and there was a dewy freshness about her. Her parents were poor farm laborers, but she always dressed nice. She was just a year older than I was and when she turned fifteen, heads started turning. Carol and Bobby Jack started courting and Bobby Jack fell in love. Thereafter, his hair was combed, his clothes ironed, and his shoes shined. But unbeknown to either of us he was not the only one in love with Carol.

The weather was warm for a Saturday morning so early in the spring. The sun was shining bright, bees were buzzing and me and Bobby Jack were lying on his front porch reading comic books when Jarvis Hullett and Gigger Hatten walked up in the yard.

I sat up and said, "Hey there, what are you'll doing way over here," and was shocked when Jarvis cussed Bobby Jack. Rea came running out of the house armed with a dishrag and told the intruders to get on down the road, that nobody wanted any trouble. They walked off a little way and called for us to come. I figured Jarvis and Bobby Jack were going to fight and they may as well get it over with now rather than later. I wasn't worried one bit, for I knew how strong Bobby Jack was. Jarvis was already a man, but so was Bobby Jack and my money was on my friend. They said they didn't want to fight in front of Rea and dared us to go over the hill. I told Bobby Jack for us to go and for him to whip his ass and that would be the end of it.

We followed them over the hill and there waiting at the bottom by the branch was the whole male population of the Hatten and Hewlett clan. There was George Hatten, already married with a houseful of children, and Fred Hewlett, who was six foot six, weighed 250 pounds and home on leave from the army. A dozen or so other rough-looking customers were standing around, all ready for a fight. Jarvis and Bobby Jack squared off. Jarvis gave Bobby Jack a quick punch to the head and Bobby Jack fell face down in the road with his arms and legs all askew, and never moved a muscle. We all stood there a moment looking at him. I couldn't believe my eyes.

Gigger ran up to me and took a swing. I ducked and ran backwards. I didn't want to fight him. He was two years older, bigger, and meaner. Plus, my daddy rented his daddy's land to grow cotton. I had never thought of fighting Gigger. We squared off and he hit me a couple of good sharp jabs in my right eye and I saw that I was no match for him, so I ran into the woods and came back with a broken tree limb, meaning to do some damage. Now it was Gigger's turn to run backwards but the limb was partially rotten and didn't do much damage before it broke. It was tooth-'n-nail from then on. He started working on my right eye with his left hook, so I changed tactics and tackled him. We rolled in the ditch with snot and blood flowing from my nose and me cursing him for every kind of son-of-a-bitch imaginable.

This fight went on for a long time. I got my legs wrapped around his neck and commenced to pulverize his face. Big Fred jumped down in the ditch, undid my legs, slapped my face, and yelled for me to fight fair. Next round Gigger got on my back and repeatedly shoved my face down in the shallow water in the sandy bottom. When the fight was over the skin was sanded off a portion of my face and my right eye swelled shut.

As soon as the pack left, Bobby Jack miraculously recovered, staggered around for a bit, and asked, "What happened?"

We went back to the house and I took Lawson's .22-calibre rifle off the wall, checked to see if it was loaded, and found seventeen long-rifle cartridges in the magazine. I slung the rifle over my shoulder and set off for down the road, high on adrenalin. When I passed Cap Jones' store, Cap saw me, took a look at my mutilated face, and tried to get me to come in and talk with him. I looked neither to the right nor left but continued up the red clay road with a determined step.

A little farther on a big wharf rat ran out of a field and I shot him in the head. The gun was working. At George's house I found Mabel in the yard repairing an old electric stove. I always did like Mabel. She took one look at my face and then the gun, and she knew it was serious. She tried to get me to stay awhile with her and let her attend to my face. She told me the whole gang had come by earlier and had gone on down to the wash hole over on Horse Creek, and that I should just wait there, and George would take me home. I wanted none of that and headed out hot for the wash hole.

I imagined walking up to the bank, finding all of them down in the water, white and naked, and me shooting 'em all dead. Would they float or sink? Nah, I wouldn't shoot George, he was Mabel's husband and daddy to all those little children, plus I liked him, and he really hadn't done me any harm. And Gilbert? He was Ellis's boy and I liked Ellis and usually Gilbert.

So it went as the adrenalin high wore off and I kept exonerating. Letting every one of them off the hook, everyone except Gigger and Fred. I would only shoot those two. I wished I'd never got so far into this mess, but now I couldn't turn back. Perhaps they would all run for their lives when they saw me coming with the gun. This was a comforting thought. I heard a car coming up behind me and I stepped to the side as Daddy drove up.

He stopped his Studebaker, got out, looked me over slowly, then took the rifle out of my hand, and told me to get in. He even opened the door for me.

A handsome young stranger driving a new Chevrolet began visiting the Clements's home with a guitar under his arm. One evening, while on my way home from the Old Place I stopped by, met this stranger, then went on in and sat by the fire with Mr. Clements while he tried to teach me to roll a cigarette with one hand. The guitar picker and Carol were sitting in the swing on the porch and after a while, we heard a lovely soft tune as the man began to sing. I still remember the chorus to his song. "You're the only star in my blue heaven, and you're shining just for me. You're the guiding light that brightens up my night…" It worked, because soon Carol was married and moved out of our lives.

My black wool cheerleader sweater with the golden trumpet embroidered across the front was getting dirty so I washed it by hand in cold water and hung it on the clothesline to dry. When I got back from school I went out back and lowered the forked pole holding the clothesline up high out of the weeds and retrieved my sweater. Low and behold, it had two tits sticking straight up on each shoulder. Disaster lurks in the darndest' places.

Mother wasn't home to help because she hadn't got home from the corset factory. My sister Charlotte and Nell were laughing and wetting the tits, trying to get them to shrink down when Daddy staggered in. He said, "Get outta' those damned ball game clothes and get on some work clothes, hogs got out and we have to fix the fence." The bus would be there in less than an hour and I protested strongly. Nothing doing, we had to fix the fence! I hurriedly put on some work clothes, ran and got a bucket of shelled corn and tolled the hogs into a pen, nailed the gate shut, and told Daddy it would hold them until tomorrow. He was just drunk enough to be mean and sober enough to be dangerous. I tried to reason with him, telling him it was getting too dark to drive a nail, but he said, "Hell no, we are going to fix the damn fence once and for all!"

I angrily slung the hammer down and it landed in a warm juicy hog turd, spattering all over Daddy. I stood there in shock, unable to believe my bad luck. He just came undone and hit me a few sharp blows, something he never did. The bus stopped and blew the horn, a few times before driving away. That was it, I wasn't going to put up with this kind of life any longer. I'd run away and never come back nor let him ever hear from me again and then he would be sorry!

Three pairs of jeans, five shirts, and a jacket were my complete wardrobe. I climbed into each item, one over the other, gathered up all my money (which consisted of a fifty-cent piece) hugged my brother and sisters goodbye, and headed for the highway. As was usually the case, the first car stopped and gave me a ride.

I thumbed my way through McRae, Alamo, and on to Glenwood. By this time, most businesses had closed, and it was getting cold. I started walking out of town and came to a fork in the road with a little country store still open. I went in, bought a penny box of matches, and watched as the clerk dropped each coin of my forty-nine cents change into my hand.

The stars were shining bright as I walked with my hands deep in my pockets along the shoulder of the highway. My ears were cold, and I wished I had remembered my cap with earflaps. The highway was going downhill and after a considerable walk I came to a high bridge over the Oconee River. I stopped, peered over the edge and gazed at the reflection of the stars in the water silently flowing by on its way to the sea. The Oconee was only a hundred yards wide at that time of year, but the bridge was over a mile long, built on creosote poles forty feet high to accommodate the water when the river flooded. Up ahead I could see the glow of a fire from under the bridge. I walked up, leaned over the banister, and saw two men and two boys about my age. I called out, "Hello down there, this is Roger Reaves up here, can I come down?"

They were somewhat startled by this voice out of the darkness and talked amongst themselves for a minute and then told me to come on down. It took a while to walk to the end of the bridge, down the embankment, and then back over to the camp. They were very hospitable and offered me channel catfish and hushpuppies hot out of the grease, mmm, delicious. They asked where I was headed.

I lied and said I was going to New York City to visit my Grandma. Two of my new friends got in the boat and went to check the trotlines and one of the boys invited me to lay down on the canvas near the fire with the others. When I woke up it was getting light. I helped load up the boat, fish, and gear on an old pickup and we headed north. After a few miles, we turned off onto a dirt road, and a little farther on pulled up in the yard of an old house. They invited me into the kitchen where a woman served a scrumptious breakfast of hot biscuits and fresh cream. I thought this was just wonderful. I'd never sopped' fresh cream with biscuits. At our house we sopped' syrup and churned cream into butter. I ate until I was ashamed of myself, but they kept eating and pushing it on me, so I kept eating 'till I was full. After breakfast they drove me back to the highway and wished me well on my journey.

They were poor folks and throughout my life I have found that poor people will give you a ride and invite you into their homes for a meal, but never the rich.

Late in the afternoon I came to the sign. *Welcome to Orangeburg, South Carolina, home of Edisto Gardens.*

Somehow, I found my way to 15 Church Street, situated in the heart of town. I walked up the steps of a colossal old three-story house and rang the bell. A kind lady answered the door, and I said, "I'm Roger, William Reaves' son." Come in, come on in, why you look so like your Daddy. How is Hortense? Tell me about everyone, you don't have a suitcase? Why are you wearing all those clothes? Oh! I can't believe you are here. I look at you and see William again after all these years. We always did love him so. She hugged me a couple more times and then showed me to a room as big as a house. Aunt Leila's daughter Dorothy came over with my cousins, Tommy, Nancy, and Woody, I was impressed with all of them. It was a good warm feeling to get to know such wonderful kinfolk. Sometime after my arrival I was sitting in the parlor with Aunt Leila, when the telephone rang. I didn't pay it much attention, until I heard her say, "Why yes Hortense, he is sitting right here with me." She handed me the phone and it was good to hear Mother's voice even though she was crying. She asked if I didn't think it was time for me to come on home, and I answered in a rather sheepish voice "Yes Ma'am." Aunt Leila scolded me for not telling her the truth. Early the next day I was on a Trailway bus headed south. Late that afternoon with airbrakes hissing the bus came to a stop at the end of our lane. Everyone was sitting on the front porch and that walk from the highway to our front gate was a long one. I was scared. No one got up or said a word. Finally, Daddy said, "Did you get enough to eat, or did you go hungry?" The spell was broken, and I was a hero, home from the wars. I had to tell everything from start to end and the good parts several times.

Sunday morning, June 7, 1961 Daddy's hand was on my shoulder gently shaking me as he said, "Wake up Son, I need some help. That old sow tore into the chicken house again." He sat down on the bed beside me and let out a low groan. I jumped up realizing something was bad wrong. My brother Larry was in bed with me and he got up. Daddy lay back in the spot where I had been lying and told me to take his shoes off. I took them off and his toes were turning blue. He held his lower left side with his hands, sweat popped out on his forehead and his face was contorted with pain. He whispered, "Son, something's awfully wrong, I think this is the end. Go quick and get your Uncle G." I ran down the sandy road to Uncle LG's as fast as my bare feet could carry me. In a couple of minutes, we were back at the house in his new Buick 88. I ran in and picked Daddy up in my arms and slid him in the back seat, got in with him and cradled his head in my lap as I watched the roll type speedometer change colors and roll out to 120 miles per hour. The seventeen miles went by in a blur and within minutes, we were in front of the hospital in McRae. I picked Daddy up and carried him in. A nurse came running with a gurney, I laid Daddy on it and she rolled him to the emergency room. Doctor Mann examined Daddy and looked very grave. He said he thought he had an aneurism but wanted a second opinion. Soon Doctor Smith arrived and confirmed the diagnosis. Both doctors were most kind and sympathetic. Doctor Mann said that Daddy would die within a few hours. He explained that there was a blockage where the main artery forked with one going to each leg. The main artery had swollen up like a balloon and no blood was getting through. "Can't we put him in an ambulance or an airplane and take him to Macon or Atlanta. We have a farm and we will pay anything it takes." I begged. Both doctors just sadly shook their heads. Doctor Mann Jr. said, "There is nothing anyone can do, even if it were my own father I would not move him. The pain will get unbearable and we can stop it with morphine, but that will knock him out. We will wait on that until the family has all come and said goodbye." Even though I knew it was bad, these words almost killed me. Uncle LG went to get Mother and the other children, and I stayed by Daddy, holding his hand. He had heard the doctors and he knew he was dying. I could hardly talk for the great lump in my throat choking me, but somehow I got out, "Daddy, are you going to heaven? Have you been saved? Do you believe in Jesus?" He said in somewhat of a whisper, "Yes, Son." However, he didn't seem very interested. He was just pleasing me. After a bit he summoned some strength, looked me in the eye, and said, "Son, I don't mind dying so much, knowing you are there to look after your mother and your little sisters and brother." Mother and the children arrived, and I slipped on out. It was just too terribly sad to watch each little child kiss Daddy and say goodbye forever. Larry and I walked around the block and up and down the oak-shaded street. We agreed that this was the longest day of our lives. Each member of the family has their own memories of that day. I remember Mother being in denial, thinking it was all a big mistake, and saying that he was going to get well and come home. Daddy died at seven o'clock that evening and the undertaker came for his body. We put his worn khaki clothes in a brown paper bag along with his watch, an old wallet, belt, shoes, and pocketknife. It made such a sad, pitiful little pile.

Somewhere, it felt like another lifetime. I remembered him being young and handsome and Mother, young, beautiful, and dressed in the latest fashion. They took me to the Uncle Remus movie, "Songs of the South." The theme song was 'Mister Bluebird on My Shoulder.' A cartoon bluebird landed on a little boy's head and Uncle Remus sang, 'zippity doo da, zippity aye, hi ho hi what a wonderful day, plenty of sunshine coming my way…' Someone was selling a likeness of the little bluebirds in the lobby and Daddy bought me one. The bird was attached to a stick by a string and as I swung it, the brilliant blue wings flapped up and down as the bird flew around. Could I ever know happiness like that again? Would sunshine ever come my way?

April 1, 1962. I remember stories of long ago about when my Great Grandpa rafted timber down the Ocmulgee River. The lookout would call to the men on the sweeps, "Indian" or "White." Indian meaning the Coffee County side, because for many years this had been Indian Territory and the law stopped at the river. Over the years outlaws running from the law settled there and lived a more backward way of life than their northern neighbors. The men wore overalls and chewed tobacco and the women wore long dresses and bonnets, when these were no longer seen north of the river. The soil on the Indian side was fertile and the season three weeks ahead, causing those farmers to lead a prosperous life. Yet, tales of darkness came out of those woods. One Grantham cut a Negro's head off, stuck it on a fence post, and traded hats with the corpse. He said he did it because the Negro had a newer Stetson. The bloodline was still there.

Gordon Beacham asked my sister Charlotte for a date and Cecil Dumile asked Barbara Garrison, our cousin. These sixteen-year-old girls were all a-flutter, this being their first date. Both boys were in my class and I thought it was fine. The next Saturday, Gordon, and Cecil came in and acted like gentlemen. Charlotte left with them and they picked Barbara up and went to the movies.

When Charlotte came home that night she woke me up. She was crying and shaking all over. Her dress was torn in the front and her chest looked like she had been in a catfight. Between sobs, she told me how they had taken Barbara home, and then Gordon drove into the woods and attacked her. She begged Cecil for help, but he sat on her head. She fought like a wildcat and fortunately, she wasn't raped. Nevertheless, she had been thoroughly traumatized and I meant to put *paid* beside that debt.

The next morning, I went to Sunday school and talked with my friends, Bill and Pete Cameron. I explained that Gordon was bigger than I was, but that I meant to put one on him and Cecil. They told me to get something for an equalizer and beat the tar out of them, but to be careful and make sure not to kill them. They were emphatic that I leave my pistol at home, saying they wanted to see me in church next Sunday.

After lunch, I went to Jacksonville and met Stanley Wells, who was five or six years older than I was. He and his daddy, Mr. Walter, ran a store in Jacksonville, Georgia, the local gathering place. Stanley asked if I wanted to ride across the river with him, which, of course I did. He drove slowly over to the roller rink at Red Bluff. The place was crowded. Cars and pickups were parked for a half-mile on both sides of the road. We went in, slipped through the crowd, stood by the rail and watched the skaters go whirling by. Well, I'll be damned, if it ain't Mr. Gordon himself, dance skating around the rink with a gal in a long white dress blowing in the breeze.

I didn't say a word to anyone, went over to the Coca Cola box, reached down in the ice water and got me a Coca Cola, paid the dime, and dried the bottle with the towel there for that purpose. I walked out onto the rink. No one paid me any attention. Everyone just skated around me. Gordon came by with his skates screeching on the corners and put the girl on the outside just before he got to me. He didn't realize I was there. Next round he was on my side. I hit him in the head with the bottom of the bottle and he went down like a pole-axed ox and slid forty feet. I ran along beside him as he slid along. When he stopped I gave him several more licks. Bill Newman the owner of the rink ran over and grabbed my arm, fell down, and broke his glasses. The oak floor was covered in blood and so was I. Someone took out a big pocketknife and I gripped my bottle, but he cut the laces on Gordon's skates. Everyone was frozen in place. No one made a sound. The song, "It's a Cotton Candy World," continued to play.

As I walked out someone asked, "Why'd you do that, Roger?"

I answered, "April fool" and walked on out.

Stanley was waiting and visibly upset. He asked, "Why didn't you tell me what you were planning to do?"

I said, "I didn't *plan* to do anything, it just happened."

"There will be bad trouble over this. Why on earth did you do such a thing?"

"Stanley, Gordon and Cecil took Charlotte out to the woods last night and tried to rape her. She came in all clawed up and crying; her clothes were torn from where those two brutes traumatized her. I can give them both as much trouble as they can handle."

"Gordon has some tough kinfolks."

"Yeah, I know something about the Grantham's." Gordon's mother was a Grantham.

Stanley drove me home and I'm sure he was glad to get rid of me.

When I walked in the house Charlotte saw my clothes covered in blood, all the color drained from her face and with a hand covering her mouth she looked me straight in the eyes and said, "You killed him, didn't you?"

"No, I just gave him a taste of his own medicine."

That evening I went to a Methodist Youth Fellowship meeting at China Hill with Emily. On the way home we saw Uncle L.G. parked at the crossroads in Jacksonville. Roy Cowart, Beverly Ann's husband, was with him. I got out and went over to his car, he said, "Roger, a carload of Gordon Beacham's folks have been to your house with guns 'n ropes and are threatening to come back 'n kill you., Your mother and the children are terribly upset. Go get Johnny--the two of you take turns staying up. If that crowd comes back, make sure that not one of them gets out of the car."

Johnny stayed at our house every night for a week and we were ready with five twelve-gauge shotguns loaded with double-aught buckshot. Fortunately, that mob did not return.

Still I knew there was going to be trouble. Someone was fixing to die, and I didn't count on it being me. Let's get it over with! The waiting was the worst part. I kept the old .38 caliber pistol Grandpa killed the man in the courthouse tucked in the back of my trousers and a razor-sharp knife in my pocket. I waited for something to happen. I was nervous. This was no way to live.

Three weeks later he sent word. "If you have the guts to fight fair and put your gun up, then I will fight you anytime, anywhere and we will get this over with for good."

The time was fixed for late Friday afternoon at the cemetery on the edge of town. Friday came and the whole town and regions beyond turned out. I should have sold tickets, as there were two or three hundred people there. I had Johnny close by holding my pistol under his shirt with instructions to hand it to me if I needed it.

Gordon came up walking fast and stopped near me. I stepped out and started to take off my jacket. When my arms were half out of the sleeves he ran up and took a mighty swing. I ducked and as I freed one arm I hit him over the eye, splitting it open with the first punch. He went crazy, swinging hard and wild, missing me in every round of flurries. He got knocked down a few times and his buddies stepped in, grabbed him, and told him to stop making a fool of himself. His face was in bad shape and bloody.

The only lick I got was self-inflicted. I blocked an overhand haymaker and the back of my fist hit my mouth, knocking my lower front teeth loose. Pharmacist Denton gave me some alum that tightened them right up.

Cecil Dumile got away with his part of the act and I never saw him after graduation. His father shot and killed my friend Tom Kennett over nothing.

My sisters couldn't get a date.

5. YOUNG MAN - SOJOURN TO CANADA

Bear Wrestling -- Meeting Marrie -- Movin' On -- Strange Bedfellows -- Riding the Rails -- Out of Body -- Finding Marrie – Lost in the Swamp

Someone told me they were paying twenty dollars a day in Canada for tobacco croppers. That was four times as much as I was making, and I was anxious to go. I didn't have a dollar and knew I would need enough to survive until I could get there and start working. With discomfort I told Mr. Pope the owner of the grocery store, I was quitting. Why I was so embarrassed I can't imagine because I should have quit years before and gone to work at the Piggly Wiggly where I could have made double what he was paying me but for some mysterious reason, I wouldn't leave Mr. Pope, who probably didn't even care.

Mr. Allen, Johnny's father, hired me at one dollar an hour to hook cables to logs behind an old bulldozer. I was tough but this work was tougher. Some days my clothes were torn off, and I had to pin them until I got home. Oh, how that crew laughed at me, but I didn't care because I was making a dollar an hour.

Friday afternoon I received four ten-dollar bills, a fortune to me.

Early Saturday morning, I said goodbye to Mother, walked to the highway and waited under the shade of the old oak tree. It was some time before I got a ride. Five hours later I stood melting under a South Carolina sun, until a car finally materialized in the distance through heat waves shimmying off the deserted highway. I stuck out my thumb and was happy to see an old Dodge with a sun visor over the windshield coming to a stop. I opened the door, threw my battered suitcase on the back seat, and got in. The driver was a sporty looking black man wearing a plaid hat perched at a rakish angle, and he welcomed me aboard. He started off with a jerk, missing second gear and I grew suspicious. Sure enough, he was drunk all right, really plastered! He weaved down the highway. A tractor-trailer truck was barreling fast onto a head-on collision when its driver swerved, passing on the wrong side of the road, his air horn blaring.

Casually I suggested, "Hey buddy, how about letting me drive?" He didn't say anything, his head dropped lower on his chest and he looked asleep.

"Hey buddy, there's a store just ahead. Stop and let me out. I haven't eaten for a long time!"

He pulled off on the gravel driveway, I jumped out, took a deep breath and thanked my maker. The driver took off, tires spinning in the gravel. But before he reached the pavement, I realized I had left my suitcase on the back seat containing all I owned in the world, my clothes and half the money I had earned by working hard all summer. I ran over to three men sitting on nail kegs, whittling, and playing checkers in the shade. I quickly explained the situation and asked them to give me a ride to catch him. They looked up and one of them drawled, "He's going mighty fast, I don't reckon we can catch 'em."

Damn! I stood by the side of the highway under the sweltering July sun waiting. Not a single car came by. I felt like a complete idiot, my guts were on fire with anxiety. Suddenly I heard tires crunching on the gravel behind me and I turned to see a most unexpected, but welcome phantom who slurred, "Hey buddy, you forgot your suitcase."

That first night I spent with Aunt Leila in Orangeburg, South Carolina, and was on the road early the next morning. By nightfall, I was in Washington, D.C. The following day I went to the Washington Monument where I met a girl from Holland, whose father was a newspaper correspondent for a Dutch newspaper. We met each morning for three days, went to the Library of Congress where I threw my straw hat from the top floor and watched it circle all the way to the ground floor and land on a table. I had my first mixed drink with her and didn't like it at all, but otherwise, we had a good time together and I was sorry to have to leave.

As I crossed the George Washington Bridge, the lights of New York City were really something for a country boy to behold. I rented a room right downtown at the YMCA for six dollars a night. The next morning, I climbed the Empire State Building, then caught the ferry over to the Statue of Liberty and climbed out to the torch in the lady's hand; something not allowed these days.

Day six out of Georgia I was in Niagara Falls, New York with my thumb out when a kind old gentleman and his wife stopped and gave me a ride. He drove slowly along in a lovely old antique car while asking me where I was from and where I was going, questions I answered gladly. We drove by the falls and they invited me to return in the winter when it was frozen and lit with colored lights. Then they kindly asked me to dinner in their home. It was a cozy California bungalow, with a wide porch across the front. The gentleman was a retired railroad engineer and they had not been blessed with children. That night I slept in a wonderful room with a big fluffy bed, clean white sheets, and lace curtains. The next morning after a hearty breakfast, we studied his maps, and then he drove me out to the highway where it was easy to catch a ride. I was sad to leave my lovely friends and I knew I was welcome to stay longer with them.

Before nightfall I arrived in Delhi, the heart of the tobacco-growing area of Canada, rented a three-dollar room at the only hotel in town, and went downstairs to the bar. I was impressed that the bar had a partition dividing the men and women. No mixing of the sexes was allowed on the premises.

Bryan Smith, a bearded young man, befriended me over a pint of ale and told me of a farm out on the Brantford Highway that was looking for a cropper. Bryan drove me out in his 1950 Ford and introduced me to a big Belgian with enormous hands and a kind smiling face. His wife was a sweet Yugoslavian lady who spoke with a strong accent. The couple lived in a two-storied white farmhouse flanked on one side by a greenhouse, and the other by a kitchen orchard with bountiful fruit hanging from the trees. For a backdrop, there was a mammoth red barn to store forty acres of tobacco once it was cured. Beyond the main barn were six big tobacco barns for curing the tobacco. The setting would have made a lovely postcard and I'm sorry I don't have a photograph.

I moved into the bunkhouse with an old Greek named Tony, who had been returning to this farm every year for over twenty years. The next morning two French Canadians from Quebec City showed up in an old car and unloaded their gear. Then two Italians came in with duffle bags overflowing with dirty clothes. The bunkhouse was no longer appealing. Those men stank!

We all sat around a big table in the basement with the owner at the head. His wife served up big bowls and platters of food, which I didn't care for. Either the lady was a bad cook or the food was strange, probably a combination of the two. Fried bologna and eggs for breakfast was a regular with an occasional repeat for supper. One thing I did like was the big bowl of boiled potatoes and gravy, but most everything else had a strange taste, for instance they poured vinegar on french-fries and fish. It was peculiar, but I got accustomed to it.

Two Belgium brothers came from a neighboring farm every day and cropped with us. Their father owned a big tobacco farm that was *hailed out* the week before harvest started. They were very friendly to me and I enjoyed their company. The table crew was from several European countries. When we all came together at the worktable I was reminded of the "Tower of Babel."

We cropped sand lugs for a solid week and though I was toughened up to hard work, I'd never bent double like that for so long and we were all mighty sore in the legs. The early mornings were cold, and the tobacco was wet with dew so we wore rain gear until the sun warmed the world. Then we'd begin to steam under the plastic. It was too wet 'n cold to take the gear off, but it was like being in a sauna to keep it on. One by one we made the chilly removal.

Tilsonburg, Canada put on a big fair every fall. One Saturday afternoon my friend Bryan came out to the farm in his car with a load of his friends and invited me to go to the fair with them. I was already clean because I always took a hot shower in the greenhouse every evening when I came in. All I had to do was put on a pair of nice black trousers, a white shirt and I was ready. Ours was a jolly crew and we were in a festive mood even before we arrived. The fair was truly spectacular and risqué, very different, and something definitely not allowed in Georgia.

Of course, we all had to go to the hoochie-coochie show, and what a show it was. The sideshow was even better. One of the strippers asked an old gentleman with a snow-white beard and mustache for his beautiful gold-headed cane. She took it in hand, admired it, then rubbed it back and forth in her crotch, kissed it, and handed it back to the old gentleman. He took it very deliberately, looked it up and down, and then suddenly came alive, beating the woman hard on the head and back with the cane. Several men jumped in to stop him, her friends jumped in and it was a free for all. When it all died down, he broke the cane over a chair and threw down the pieces.

I thought to myself, "*This fair has promise.*"

A little ways further down the lane a gigantic man with long black hair and a flowing beard draped over his chest paced a platform in front of a circus wagon bellowing into a microphone,

"FIVE BRAND NEW ONE HUNDRED DOLLAR BILLS TO ANYBODY WHO'LL WRASSLE MY BEAR AND GET ALL FOUR FEET OFF THE GROUND, OR THROW HIM!"

"TEN DOLLARS TO ANYONE WITH GUTS ENOUGH TO GET IN THAT CAGE AND GIVE IT A TRY!"

"What's your name, young man?"

"Roger Reaves"

"Where you from Roger?"

"I'm from Georgia."

"I mighta' known. These yellow-bellied Canadians ain't got guts enough to wrassle my bear."

"How much you weigh?"

"145 pounds."

"Show'em your muscles boy."

"ONE-HUNDRED-FORTY-FIVE-POUND-MAN-AGAINST-SIX-HUNDRED-POUND-BEAST-MAN-EAT-BEAST!"

With those words, he opened the door to the circus wagon and threw me in with a 600-pound muzzled black bear. As soon as I stepped onto the platform people started flocking in. This should have told me something, but I figured a mule stumbled sometimes and five hundred dollars was a lot of money. The old bear hadn't looked so big while lying down, about the size of a big old sow, but once he started getting up, he was. A monster! I decided to take my chance before he got ready, I slammed into him with all my 145 pounds, knocked him off balance and we slammed into the side of the cage. I grabbed him around his neck, but it was all loose skin, kinda' like the neck of a bloodhound. He drew back his neck like a turtle and I was holding an armful of nothing. He caught me just above the ankles with a lightning swipe of his padded paw, laying me out horizontally, chest high, and headed for a wreck. The floorboards were purposely loose, and I did make a racket when I hit. The crowd cheered. Someone whistled and yelled to me, "*Sic-em.*" I was barely on my feet before the same thing happened again and I hit the floor hard. There were several rapid repeats. My head was hurting, and I was weakening. A new strategy was desperately needed.

I lay on the floor catching my breath and clearing my head, jumped up, grabbed the bars in the top of the wagon and swung my puny 145 pounds into the bear, hitting him in the face with the heels of both shoes. This drew blood. The bear went insane! He lunged at me and with a fearsome growl threw me to the floor as though I were a rag doll, knocking the breath right out of me for the longest time, to where I thought it was never coming back. He was pawing frantically at me with his heavy padded paws, growling and trying to bite my head off at the neck. I was covered in bear blood and foaming slobber. The big bearded Alaskan rushed into the cage, snapped a chain on the bear's collar and pulled him off. The bear then turned on its owner, knocking him backwards and ran outa the cage and through the crowd.

You should have seen those yellow bellies stomping all over one another as they struggled to getaway. Yeah, "Sic-em!" The chain got tangled on one of the stakes supporting the tent and pulled it out. That side of the tent collapsed, but this held the bear.

My clothes were literally torn off. I asked the Alaskan for my ten dollars and he told me to go to hell. When Bryan dropped me off at the farm, I collapsed as I stepped out of the car and had to be carried into the bunkhouse. I lost two days of work and a set of clothes in that debacle.

Toward the end of July, it rained for several days and the weather turned cooler; nevertheless, we continued slopping up and down the rows cropping the big brittle leaves. Everyone was miserable, even the Belgian draft horses hung their heads low. That evening at the supper table the boss said, "Men, the tobacco is too green to continue gathering. Take two days off and that should give it time enough to ripen. Go where you like but, be back here by daylight Tuesday morning."

The next morning was bright and sunny as I hitched a ride into Delhi. Bryan was home and he invited me to go to Lake Erie for the day, so off we went, arriving at Turkey Point an hour later. It was just a village on the lake with vacation cottages and a few snack shacks. Somehow, we got separated and I went strolling down the packed beach.

A long wooden pier stretched out over the water for a good hundred yards. Near the beach end, boys were wrestling and throwing one another in the icy water fifteen feet below. They looked me over as a prime target, being I had on black slacks, a white short-sleeved shirt, a tie, and a new straw dress hat. A couple ran at me. I fought rather seriously, and they went laughing into the drink. I ran down the pier to discourage further confrontation. I most definitely did not want to get thrown into that ice water. The pier was T-shaped and sitting on towels were three bathing beauties. I was shy and walked on by and turned around at the end. As I sauntered back past a second time I said, "Hello."

They all smiled and acknowledged me, and the heart-stopper said, "Is that a university ring?"

I laughed and said, "No, it's a high school ring."

"Oh, we don't get high school rings in Canada, may I have a look?"

"Surely." I gave her my hand, not wanting to take the ring off over the water with all the cracks in the old pier.

"It is lovely, is that a real sapphire?"

"No, it's just glass. You are from Holland are you not?"

"Yes, how did you know?"

"I heard a little of the Dutch accent slip through."

She looked at me and said, "Please sit down and tell me how you know about Dutch accents." She moved over and made room on her towel and I sat down.

I teased and said, "Oh, international accents are one of my hobbies." All the girls got a laugh out of that one. Then I told her about meeting the Dutch girl in Washington.

"My name is Marrie." She rolled the r's rather strong and I couldn't say her name properly, so I improvised with a soft *Moddie*, which she assured me was wonderful. We talked and time stood still. The other two girls disappeared, and we continued talking. I remember one of her first questions being, "of what faith are you?" I told her I was a Christian of the Methodist denomination. She was of the Dutch Reform Church, one of a similar belief. She told me she was a Dutch immigrant, one of the millions who left Europe after the Second World War. She had celebrated her nineteenth birthday only three days before. I told her of my family on the farm and about my father dying the year before. After a while, we went to the beach, sat on her towel and continued to talk. I had never opened up to anyone like that before. She was good, honest, and compassionate through and through.

"Would you like to go out with me tonight?"

"I'm sorry, but I must refuse."

She was so sweet I dared not question her, but I wondered if perhaps she was engaged.

A man with a kind face and ruddy complexion came up and said, "Marrie, it's time to go." She jumped up and introduced me to her father, Henk Rink. We shook hands and said a few niceties and he told Marrie they were already late. She scurried around trying to find a pen to write her address. Someone had a new yellow unsharpened pencil, so I took out my knife and quickly sharpened it. Marrie wrote her address on a scrap of paper and with a firm handshake, she left with her father.

Empty cannot describe my feelings after she left. I walked around, but nothing interested me. Then I realized the place wasn't so big that I couldn't find her if I kept walking up and down every street. Therefore, I set out on my quest. Then, down a side street, I caught sight of her in a back yard with a lot of people having a barbecue. She recognized me, waved, and called my name. I walked over and was invited in. She introduced me to everyone; Jake Folks and his family, Jerry Den Otter and his family are two that I remember. Jerry, Jake, and Hank were the stars of the show. Laughing, pulling pranks, having a ball! About sunset, I thought I had better leave before outstaying my welcome. Again, I asked Marrie to go down to the local gathering place where the young people danced to an open-air jukebox, drank beer and Coca Colas, and again she mysteriously refused me.

Later that evening I was sitting on the hood of Brian's car when a tough-looking girl wearing white lipstick over chapped and sunburned lips walked over and was chatting me up when Marrie and several girls walked by. She looked over with a quick glance and I read her thoughts. I didn't know what to do. I had the strongest urge to run after her and try to explain but wound up doing nothing as I was too ashamed.

I woke early. The bunkhouse was cold and stank of stale sweat. Someone was snoring loud. I pulled on a pair of jeans, a work shirt, slipped on my tall rubber boots and stepped outside. Burr! The weather had turned icy. I walked across the yard and down the steps into the cellar. It was warm inside; coffee was perking, and breakfast was about ready. The boss was sitting at the head of the table and he looked worried. He told me it was freezing, and the tobacco was destroyed. I felt real sorry for him. There was a foot of leaves left on each stalk and that spread over forty acres was a lot of tobacco, a loss of tens of thousands of dollars. After breakfast, he gave me a check for six hundred and eighty dollars. That was what was left after my weekly draws and deduction for my rain gear. I had been there for six weeks and worked every day except four, two when the bear mauled me and two when the tobacco was green.

I went back to the bunkhouse, put my belongings in the big cardboard suitcase without a handle, and said goodbye to everyone except the boss, who was in the field. I was sorry I didn't have a chance to say goodbye to him. I started walking down the road and looked across the rolling hills at the sea of tobacco stretching to the horizon. The sun came out bright and I felt the warmth on my back. The frost on the leaves sparkled like glass. As I watched, a most unusual transformation occurred. The tobacco leaves turned from a yellow-green to a wine red, starting on the top of the hills on the west side and slowly spreading down to the valleys. Within a half-hour, the country was painted a deep burgundy. I walked out into a field and saw that as the leaf thawed it changed color. The scene was like something from another world.

That afternoon I was traveling down the Queen's Highway, paralleling Lake Erie, passing through inviting little farms of fruit orchards. I made good time, probably couldn't have driven any quicker myself.

The next day I was somewhere down in Kentucky in front of a whorehouse with my thumb stuck out. A man came out and got in his car and I noticed he had another one hitched behind. He offered me a ride and I got in. He was a handsome man about thirty-five years old with jet-black hair and a three-day beard. As we rode along through the beautiful scenery, he started talking. He said he had been to an automobile auction in Detroit and bought the two cars and then got drunk, a state in which he stayed for several days. Then he went to the whorehouse and spent his last night and money. He said he had no idea why he acted so, as he had a lovely wife and several little children waiting at home. He just hung his head and shook it back and forth. He was truly repentant and ashamed of himself and probably afraid to go home.

He offered me the 1956 Buick he was towing for a hundred and thirty-five dollars, the price he paid for it. He had the bill of sale from the auction. At the next intersection he unhitched the car and we parted ways with me driving my very first automobile.

College was fun, but I wasn't ready to buckle down and study, so right after Christmas 1962, I traveled to New York to buy a car to bring back to Georgia and sell. Being that I'd bought one the year before and sold it for over three times what I paid for it, I thought perhaps there could be something to this business. Newer model cars that were rusting out were cheap in snow country, but that was not a problem in our area.

In Rocky Mountain, North Carolina, the snow was knee-deep and falling. It was bitter cold, and my clothes were not made for those temperatures. I went to the train station and slipped aboard a fast passenger train headed north and kept dodging the conductor. In the lounge car, I met two girls from the south who had a drawing-room. I told them what I was doing, and they were all too happy to hide me. I rode to New York City in style with those two pretty girls while looking out the big picture window as the snow-covered landscape sped by.

After detraining in Grand Central Station, I walked outside and looked up through the falling snow at the colored fluorescent lights, a sight so romantic that I felt cheated at not having someone to share it with. I asked for directions to the YMCA (Young Men's Christian Association-- they had inexpensive rooms in every city in the United States in those days). I rented a room for a few dollars and found a steam room, sauna, pool, and games room. That evening I met Scotty, a nice young man of perhaps thirty years of age from Madrid, Spain. We had supper together and became friendly. He said he had lived his whole life in the cities of Madrid, Paris and New York and had never been on a farm or in the country. As we often did in the south, I invited him to go home with me and to my surprise, he accepted.

Early the next morning I caught the underground train to Long Island and walked all day, going from one automobile shyster to another. Late in the afternoon, I decided on a 1954 Ford Victoria that cost me two hundred and seventy-five dollars. I drove back to the '*Y' and* collected my things; Scotty was packed and waiting. We loaded up and headed south down the frozen highway.

Somewhere in Virginia, the water pump went out and I parked beside the road, caught a ride into town, found a junkyard, bought the part and hitched a ride back. It was dark by the time I crawled under the hood. I didn't have a flashlight and the wrenches were so cold they stuck to my hands. I gathered some straw and a few sticks, built a little fire right beside the fender and in that way I had some light and warm wrenches. I remember it being a long miserable job lying on my back in the snow while changing that pump and how warm the heater felt when I was again driving south. We had no further problems and the next afternoon we arrived at home.

Scotty made a big hit with everyone. My sisters asked him about his love life, "Do you have a girlfriend?" Oh yes, he had a beautiful girlfriend in Paris named Sandy and they planned to be married next year. He was a nice-looking fellow and ever so kind and considerate, wanting to help in any way he could.

We were growing chickens under contract with Purina Feed Co. and they paid starvation wages. Many growers supplemented their income by feeding a few hogs on company feed and dead chickens. Mother had a boar and six or eight big spotted Poland China sows, and they all had large litters of pigs. At weaning age, they brought the most per pound and that was when Mother sent them to the auction. We fed the hogs a good way off from the chicken house so that when the inspector came by, which he did once a week, he wouldn't see the hogs eating chicken feed. Late every afternoon, when there was no danger of the inspector coming around, Mother rolled a heaping wheelbarrow of chickenfeed to these hogs and poured it in a trough. Naturally, the hogs were like Pavlov's dog. When the chain on the gate rattled they all jumped up and came running.

One afternoon Mother started across the pasture straining against the heavy load. Scotty ran up and insisted he roll the wheelbarrow for her and she gladly put it down. He picked up on the handles and went weaving across the pasture like a drunk. As soon as he went through the gate, the hogs jumped up and ran toward him squealing. He threw the wheelbarrow over and took off running and yelling for dear life. He ran through the fence cutting his stomach and legs on the barbed wire. He was terribly upset and kept repeating, "Those animals were going to eat me, those animals were going to eat me!"

This was falling down funny to all of us, but it triggered something in Mother's brain, and she went in and riffled his suitcase. There she found a 10X12 framed photograph of *Sandy* and a stack of love letters. Sandy, of course, had a mustache. Now, I was sleeping in the same bed with him and I felt most uncomfortable. We were never rude to anyone, but Mother had no qualms about this; she politely told him it was time for him to move on. He packed his bag and we took him to the bus station where we all shook hands and parted.

Thanksgiving holidays came and Johnny and I went hunting wild hogs in a big dismal swamp, known as 'The Devil's Smoke House'. Mr. Stewart, Johnny's father, logged the area some years prior and built a seven-mile land bridge from the hill to the river. Bulldozers cleared the trees, logs were laid horizontally and massive oak timbers, called runners, were nailed to the logs with heavy spikes. The logging project was abandoned; briars and brambles grew thick in the open area, yet we could still walk fairly well on the half rotten runners.

The day was cold and overcast with a light mist falling as we eased along, listening intently for any sound of razorbacks. After several miles we decided to separate, agreeing that if either of us got lost we would shoot occasionally and go toward one another. Johnny went south and I went north, easing through the swamp treading ever so softly, trying not to make any noise and keeping into the slight breeze. Billows of white fog occasionally engulfed my world and then it cleared for a short while. I sat on a log to eat my lunch when a doe came almost to me, stopped, and looked me over. I didn't move an eyelash and it was some time before she bounded away. Telltale fresh rootings from the razorbacks were everywhere, and I just knew I was going to find hogs any minute.

I kept easing along through the dense swamp, light was diminishing, and I decided it was time to turn back. From overhead came the swoosh of wings as a flock of mallard ducks dove through the trees and landed not far from me. I took the double ought buckshot out of the old single barrel and put in a number six birdshot and crept forward. The ground became soggy and wet as I tiptoed from one dry place to the next. Beaver dams had flooded the area and I had to go a long way out of my way to reach the ducks. I squatted behind a log and waited patiently until two drakes passed one another. Then I shot. The flock flew before I could reload, but I had killed two. I thought. Off came my clothes that I draped over a cypress knee and then I propped my gun against the tree and waded into the cold water. I was in waist-deep when I picked up the first duck. As I reached for the second, he seemed to come to and fluttered out of reach. I picked up 97 speed and tried for all I was worth to catch him, but he was getting stronger by the minute. Oh well, as bad as I hated to I would have to shoot him again. I turned around and headed back for my gun. Soon I was swimming in black ice water with no land in sight. Ever way I looked was cypress trees with thick bulbous trunks covered in slimy algae and grey Spanish moss hanging like long beards from each limb. I felt I was in a prehistoric world as I swam through lily pads, the natural home of alligators and cottonmouth moccasins. Light was fading fast.

Was I swimming in circles? Would I die from hyperthermia in this cold water? How long could I last? Surely not all night. I held onto a tree and rested, trying to get my wits together. Sticking high above everything else was a huge cypress about a half-mile away. I headed for it, knowing that I was swimming in a straight line. It was dark where I was, but the tall cypress was silhouetted against the lighter sky. After a while I came to this giant and still no land. I took a bearing and continued in a straight line. Finally, I came to a beaver dam. I crawled out of the water onto dry land and sat there shivering for a few minutes, I got up and tried to follow the shoreline around to find my clothes. There was no shoreline, just a maze of beaver dams and fingers of water. I came across a well-used game trail and followed it up a slough onto higher ground. I stumbled along as fast as I could, trying to warm up, but the briars and brambles stuck in my feet and palmettos slashed my body. I thought that if I stayed in this game trail it would go somewhere and I didn't care as long as it was on dry land. I also knew that as long as I hurried along I could keep from freezing. The trail was bad, and I often had to crawl. In the better areas, I ran until I fell over logs and other obstacles, skinning myself up and getting completely covered in red clay mud.

For hours, I groped along like this yelling for Johnny until my throat was raw and my mouth awfully dry. Sometime around midnight I heard dogs barking in the distance. Someone was hunting and not too far away. The barking became louder and louder. They were coming my way. The baying of a dozen hounds got so close it scared me. I thought, 'I must be right in the trail of whatever they're after.' There was a logjam beside a cypress tree, and I climbed up. The dogs came to the base and went crazy, barking and trying to climb up. I shimmied on up the cypress and got covered with more moss and mud. About twenty feet up was the first limb and when I got to it, I squatted on it and held to the tree. I yelled at the dogs and thought they might go on after whatever they were pursuing, but they were satisfied with me and kept baying up at me like I was a panther or bear. I was treed! In a while, I heard men yelling, "Whoa! Hold him Pit, Whoa, sic him Blue!" Now I knew two of their names.

I got to wondering what the men would think and wondering what they would do. Here I was, buck naked, blue from cold, covered in moss and mud and sitting on a limb twenty feet up in a tree in the middle of a swamp at midnight, wearing nothing but a beard, my Daddy's old felt hat and a shiny sapphire class ring with the engraving, Diligence, Integrity and Citizenship. Three men rode up on horses with their guns at the ready. I yelled, "Don't shoot; it's me, Roger Reaves, up here!" They kept the lights and guns on me, called off the dogs and I slid down the tree. Eddie Morris Vaughn said, "Boy, do you live in here?" They thought they had found the wild man of Borneo.

I explained as best I could, and Mr. Vaughn handed me his long coat. I swung up behind his saddle and they took me to the land bridge where we found Mr. Stewart and Johnny riding in a Willis Jeep, shooting guns trying to locate me.

As college wasn't for me and I didn't make any money on the car deal I had to find a job. The railroads had changed from steam to diesel-electric in the late forties, early fifties, they hadn't hired firemen for fifteen years, because they weren't needed to shovel coal. However, all engineers were promoted firemen and they were running out of men to drive trains. A big hiring spree took place across the country.

A new fireman made one dollar a day less than an engineer who had been there for forty years. I applied, took the written test, and passed, had a thorough physical exam with several x-rays. The railroad demanded a perfect spine because so many men were suing for back injuries and winning large settlements, including full retirement. I was hired and told to start riding the rails in the district as a "cub." This was an unpaid initiation, where one had to familiarize himself with all the lines and equipment. Once this was accomplished, you were paid to ride. I rode from Albany to Thomasville on a ten-mile-per-hour track and from Waycross to Albany on The City of Miami, doing ninety miles an hour. I rode fast through-freights, slow pulpwood shufflers and switch engines.

Some of those old engineers were cranky old coots and insisted I keep my head out the window looking backwards for *hot boxes*. They never tired of telling me how easy we featherbedders had it and pulled up their britches leg to show the knot of muscles on the calves, acquired by years of shoveling coal. I thought, yeah and I bet you had to walk five miles to school through knee-deep snow and it was uphill both ways. But some were real sweethearts and I became a pet of several. Here I will tell of my friend Wendell Davis and a woman named Mabel.

As the old country song goes, "I had a girl down in Waycross Georgia, but she had unfaithful ways." When the train pulled in, she'd be waiting at the station in her new Cadillac. She was several years older and was showing me the town. On Saturday nights, she wore a slinky sequined or fish-scale dress to the dance.

She caused quite a stir amongst the railroad men. Wendell Davis, the senior engineer on *The City of Miami* would get on the radio as he was barreling through at ninety miles an hour and call. "Hey, fire boy! Are you out there?"

I would be working a switch engine and get on the radio and say, "Yes sir, Mr. Davis, I'm here."

"Who was that gal I saw you out with Tuesday night. Boy, she was as pretty as a bed of speckled puppies under a little red wagon. You be careful now. You hear?"

The railroad transferred me to Brunswick for a couple of months and when I got back to Waycross, she was married. Damn, that smarted.

Some years later, I looked her up. She had three chins, five young'uns, and it'd take two ax handles to measure her backside.

Uncle L.G. asked me to take a car out to Oklahoma to my cousin Emily. It was a two-day drive and then I'd hitchhike back. Having been awake for five days with only an hour or two of sleep, I went to bed and fell into a deep sleep. In a couple of hours, Mother woke me for supper. I ate in a stupor and when I got up from the table, I walked straight into the wall. Mother said I was in no shape to go to work that night, but I felt I had to go. I headed out on the two-hour drive to Brunswick and just past Lumber City the water pump went out. I hired someone to drive me the remaining seventy miles and that cost me more than I was going to make.

I arrived at the train yard just before midnight, serviced the engines with sand and water, and made a big thermos of coffee. My friend Wendell Davis was the engineer. It was raining hard as we pulled out on our way to Brunswick with three big locomotives pulling over a hundred loaded flatcars and gondolas. The windshield wipers were beating a rhythm in time to the big headlamp punching figure eights into the blackness, causing the raindrops to sparkle like a million diamonds falling, slantways. I was sitting on a high stool with my feet propped on the empty brakeman's stool when it happened.

I came out of my body. My spiritual body had the same shape as my fleshly body. I know because I could see the shadowed outlines. The 'I am' was entirely in the spiritual body, sitting up on the radio looking down at my breast rising and falling as I breathed in my fleshly body. I observed the cabin carefully looking at Wendell's face in detail. I stayed in this state for some time. I got to wondering *how* I was going to get back into my body and became anxious with this thought, and instantaneously I was back in my body.

Wendell laid his raincoat on the floor and said, "Go to sleep, Fire Boy."

Every day I wore a clean shirt. I could afford to do this since I had received fifty-two as graduation presents. I put my dirty clothes in the trunk of the car, often forgetting to take everything out of the pockets. When I got home Mother washed, ironed, and folded them ever so nicely. Any money she found was hers!

She always got up before daylight and started breakfast while I made a fire in the fireplace. I sat in the windowsill and talked while she made biscuits. Mother asked me about girlfriends, and I told her about the girl I met in Canada and said that if I ever married I wanted to find someone like her. She asked what happened to her and I said that I lost her address and had no idea how to find her.

One dark, rainy night on my way to Brunswick I had a flat tire. When I pulled the spare out of the wheel-well in the trunk, the dim glow from my flashlight fell on a rusty piece of paper, worn partially through and sticking to the bottom of the tire. As soon as I glimpsed at it, I knew what it was. My heart soared. Here was the *pearl of great price*, the address of the lovely girl I met the summer before in Canada.

As soon as I walked in the front door to the YMCA in Brunswick I picked up a piece of their stationery, sat down at a desk in the parlor, and with a pencil I scribbled out a short note and put it in the mail. The following week I received a beautiful three-page work of art on expensive stationery, monogrammed with flowers in the corner. As I read the lovely words and saw the flowing script written with pen and ink, my face turned bright red. To think that I had written her in pencil and with such crooked lines!

We exchanged several letters, then she wrote that she was going to Florida on Spring break and would like to visit me; I was stoked! She was really coming to see me. I waited. The day came and went. I waited some more. Then I received a postcard from Hollywood Florida, informing me that she was unable to stop in Waycross because she was riding with others and had taken another route. I was very disappointed and when she'd returned home, I telephoned. Her mother answered the phone in a strong Dutch accent and I could not understand her, nor could she understand me, but she understood that a man was asking for Marrie and I heard her call, "Marrie, it is for you!" Marrie was excited that I called and explained the situation about not being able to visit me in Waycross. We talked for a while and she told me that on the first of August she and her family were going to Turkey Point for a three-week vacation and asked if I would like to come up. You bet I would!

Early the next day I was in the train master's office asking for three weeks off in August. He was a kind and considerate man and explained that August was the busiest month for the railroad, and nobody took a vacation at that time. I asked for a leave of absence and he said it would be seen as another way to say vacation and he just could not grant it. With this, I told him I regretfully had to quit. He was concerned in a fatherly like fashion and asked me to take some time to think it over before I made such a major decision.

I went home and talked to Mother and she was dead set against me quitting. She said it was the best job a young man could hope for in our part of the country and that I was making more than many men with a college education.

That weekend a devastating earthquake struck Alaska, destroying Anchorage and surrounding cities. Newspapers and televisions were full of the story. They told of the thousands of workers needed to rebuild and the fabulous wages construction workers were earning. That was music to my ears. I would quit the railroad and go to Alaska, stopping in Canada to see the radiant lady with the lovely voice.

The trainmaster reluctantly accepted my resignation and I worked two more weeks. Mother washed and ironed all my clothes and packed them in a couple of new suitcases. I closed out my bank account and headed north.

The second evening I drove through the tunnel between Detroit and Windsor, Ontario, and stopped for the night. The little hotel had a restaurant. I ordered the meal of the day and soon I was vomiting my guts out. I was so sick that I telephoned Mother and told her where I was, in case I died. She told me that Chester Jones died that afternoon, and I thought I might soon join him.

The next morning, I was weak and ghostly white, but forced myself to push on. I didn't get far before I was trembling. I stopped and rented a nice room in a small town where I slept through the day and that evening I was feeling better. I got up and walked around for a bit. I could not see Marrie in my condition.

The following day I got up late, drove on to Turkey Point and parked. The beach and pier were crowded with young people in bathing suits and it seemed that every girl had long brown hair. As I walked along the beach I got nervous. What did she look like? Would I recognize her? What should I say? Several times I thought I found her and walked around the group, but it wasn't her; thank God! She knew I was coming but didn't know when. I came to the pier and started walking out. There she was, waving her arms. My heart skipped several beats! She ran a few steps toward me, then walked, and then hurried and I had no idea how to act. I was nervous! How could I have ever entertained the thought that I had forgotten what she looked like? I remembered every molecule. I didn't know how to greet her. We were shy and excited but reserved. We shook hands.

She invited me to their cabin and introduced me to her mom and dad, who invited me to stay at their place and share a room with her brother Matt. I got my suitcases out of the boot of the car and moved in. Marrie and I went for a walk and met my old friend Bryan Smile, which was a happy coincidence. We talked a bit and decided to take a ride over to Fort Williams. I invited Bryan to drive and Marrie sat in the middle. The road was crooked and on the curves, Marrie had to brace herself to keep from sliding over on me. She had on a white tank top and occasionally our skin touched. Zap! "We touched!'

When we returned Mr. Rink was cooking supper. He had caught a large sheep head that afternoon and was cookin' it up. He was as jolly as Mr. Santa Clause, and his eyes sparkled as he cremated the fish. Of all the men I have ever known, he is one of the best. A more sincere Christian would be hard to find, a worse cook, impossible. He ruined that fish and he knew it. We tried to be nice and eat a little, while he made lots of noise crunching brittle bones, smacking his lips and bragging on how good the fish was. It really got funny. After he had eaten as much as he dared, he served dessert and coffee. As soon as supper was finished, he read a chapter from the Bible, said a prayer, dismissed us, put on an apron and started cleaning up. No help allowed.

Marrie and I took an after-dinner stroll down to the far end of the beach. There we found *dead cars*, as Marrie called them, placed in a long row out into the lake to prevent erosion. Only the tops were above water and we jumped from one to another until we could go no further, and then backtracked to the beach. Marrie was wearing a white skirt with a small slit on the side and white flats. She walked on my left; I was nearer the sea. The sun was setting, there was not another person on the beach or in our world. Like magnets, our hands found one another, they just slid together, and the sparks flew; real sparks, not imaginative ones. I could not speak.

We sauntered along in silence until we came to the end of the beach where we took a trail to a golf course on a hill. We continued along the edge of the course, trying to find a route back down to the beach. I saw a dim path going down through thick trees and I thought we could descend there. Halfway down Marrie's white shoes sank in mud and we turned back. I was above, holding on to a limb with one hand, with Marrie's hand in the other. I pulled her back up and when she was even with me, our faces met, and we kissed. I thought I had been kissed before, but I was wrong. At that moment I knew it was the once in a lifetime. This is what men fight duels to death for! We walked back along the edge of the manicured golf course and found an inviting place by the trunk of an oak and there we sat and kissed and held one another until long after the sun had sank below the horizon. Time stood still. A full moon rose in the east casting a silvery glow on the trees and golf course.

I told Marrie I was on my way to Alaska and she said, "I will wait for you." No need, I am not going anywhere. We would kiss and all I could say was, "Gosh." I was in love.

For the next couple of days, we were inseparable. I understood we would be married, but we had not talked about it in so many words. I drove up to the golf course, parked and asked Marrie if she really wanted to marry me and she said that she did. We told Jerry and his wife, who were guests at the cabin. I believe they told Marrie's parents, but they did not let on that they knew.

On the third day, we decided to tell her parents. I was to take Dad for a walk and tell him while she told Mom as they were doing the dinner dishes. I invited Mr. Rink to take a walk. He accepted, perhaps a little too quickly, and we walked down to the beach.

I stopped and with a fluttering heart I said, "Mr. Rink, Marrie and I are planning to get married."

He put his palm out toward me and said, "Let us go back to the house." He took his sweet time, stopping and playing with a little boy and any other distractions he could find. It seemed he had forgotten what I said. We entered the cabin, Marrie was drying a plate and Mrs. Rink was wiping the stove.

Mr. Rink said, "Mom, I have found this Georgia boy guilty of stealing!"

Mrs. Rink's hand flew to her mouth and she gasped, "What?"

He answered, "Yes, he is guilty of trying to steal our daughter!"

A big smile broke over Mom's face and Dad turned to me, shook my hand and said, "We are happy to accept you as our son." There was much rejoicing, hugging and kissing. Oh what a wonderful day!

That evening Marrie and I went to a payphone and I called Mother and told her I was getting married. She said, "Have you been drinking Son?"

Mr. Rink said that as they knew nothing about me, Marrie was to go and visit my family for one month and then if she still felt the same way we had his blessings. I was shocked at the prospect of Marrie going to Georgia with me for a month! What happened? She always had to be in by ten-thirty if she had a date.

We played at Turkey Point until their vacation was over and I followed them to their home on Lowell Street in Galt, Ontario. I stayed with them for another week and then we packed up and headed for Georgia. I was in a cocoon of pure happiness. The glass-pack mufflers purred. The radio quit. I smacked the dash with my shoe. It came on again and Marrie laughed. The tires were singing and so were we. Marrie sat close beside me and smiled when I looked in her direction. We lunched on a balcony overlooking Niagara Falls on the Canadian side, crossed over Peace Bridge into the US, and drove south through the hills of Pennsylvania.

Late in the afternoon, we stopped in a little town and found a darling guesthouse on a shady street. I was wondering: should I get two rooms or one? What had Mr. Rink thought by sending us on a one-month trip together? I asked the nice woman for a room and Marrie quickly corrected me and said we required two rooms and explained that we were only engaged. The kind lady gave us big rooms with iron and brass beds and deep fluffy feather mattresses, directly across the hall from one another.

I remember that night so vividly. We lay on the bed and held one another. Marrie was radiant and her eyes overflowed with love and happiness. She wanted me to stay, but her conscience just wouldn't allow it. I went to my room, but there was no chance of sleep, so I knocked on her door again. Finally, she packed me off and we got some sleep.

Marrie had not driven much and I insisted she drive. The Chevrolet had 'four in the floor' and no reverse. She drove through Pennsylvania, West Virginia and into Kentucky. We were hungry so she pulled up in front of a restaurant and before I could say 'don't do it', she parked head-on. We ate and then I had to jack the car up and manipulate the gear linkage to get it into reverse. She backed out and then I did a repeat of the former to get out of reverse. Back on the road again, she drove through Dixie with her long brown hair blowin' in the wind.

Marrie was curious as to what our house looked like and as we rode through Georgia I pointed out shacks and said it was somewhat like that one, but she didn't believe me so I told the truth, kinda. I told her it was a big white house with nine rooms and a porch stretching across the front with white pillars resting on red brick buttresses.

Home! There it was. I don't know what Marrie thought, but I was happy to get there. Everyone was expecting us. Mother was forty-three years old, beautiful, and a little shy. Sharon was standing in a cane bottom chair and when she saw me, she was so excited she peed. It ran through her diaper, through the rattan chair bottom, hit the sloping wood floor, and headed south. I picked the baby up, hugged and kissed her. It felt like I had been gone for a long time.

Mother did her best to make Marrie feel at home. She fried chicken, okra, corn, squash and baked biscuits. However, she had a hard time with fried food, particularly in the heat, but she didn't want Mother to know. Each morning, she ate biscuit and jelly and would have eaten it three times a day if it was available and it usually was. Grandma's old living room was now a large bedroom, and this became her private domain.

Marrie loved the Rubin Hole, a swimming hole on Horse Creek. The water was crystal clear, and the sand beach was as white as fresh snow. Large oaks and poplar trees grew all around and one had the option of the shade or the sunny beach, all within a few steps. We spent most of our month at the swimming hole.

We invited Johnny to go to Fitzgerald one Saturday night and as we came into the edge of town, we saw a 1949 Ford upside down in a ditch and a lot of people standing around. I asked a man what had happened, and he said there had been an accident and a little boy was trapped inside the vehicle.

I said "Well, wattcha' fools waiting for?"

I crawled down in the ditch and stuck my head in the crushed car and sure enough, there was a little boy about four or five years old trapped underneath the dash with part of the windshield across his neck and bleeding to death. I squeezed in, lay on my back, and using both feet pushed the debris and windshield off his neck and pulled him out. I ran up out of the ditch holding the little fellow in my arms and saw the boy's drunken father arguing with a highway patrolman. The patrolman took one look at the little boy and hit the father a blow that knocked him cold. He took the boy from me, put him in the front seat of the patrol car, and sped away to the hospital. My white shirt and shorts were soaked in blood. We got into our car and returned home.

Johnny was logging with his parents who were batchin' in a cabin in Jacksonville. He was usually alone on weekends and Marrie offered to cook us a feast since it was for Saturday night. We went shopping and bought steaks and all the trimmings. She was peeling and chopping away when it dawned on her that we needed wine to go with the spread. We laughed and explained that Georgia was a dry state and you had to drive to Florida for a bottle of wine. Johnny asked, "Would moonshine do?" She thought so, turned the stove off and we headed out to Graham Town.

The night was pitch black as we drove into Hardy Fowler's rutted clay yard and blew the horn. His bulldogs were barking and lunging at their chains; hounds were yapping and running frantically up and down inside the fence. We sat there for what seemed a long time and then two white eyes and a big mouth full of white teeth appeared at the car window. Hardy was just as black as the night, soft-spoken and ever so gentle. I introduced him to Marrie and then told him we wanted a pint. He smiled and faded into the night. In a little while, he returned with a pint of moonshine in a used whiskey bottle with a corncob stopper. We turned on the interior light, he shook the bottle and watched as the little bubbles formed and slowly rose to the top, indicating the strength of his "liquor." This was no low wine. We paid him two dollars and left.

Back at the cabin, Johnny divided the shine equally into three parts, mixed it with Coca Cola, and we all had a fine time. Wasn't long before we decided we needed a wee bit more, so off to Hardy's we went and repeated the whole process. I do believe we ate, but my recollection is rather fuzzy. I do remember Marrie being most happy. I was trying to sneak her back into the house, but everyone was up and waiting for us. Nell was sitting at the dining room table, Marrie hugged her and told her how much she loved her and that she understood if they didn't approve of her as a sister-in-law, and so on and on like this, all the while slurring her words. They all thought she was putting it on and had the biggest laugh, but I knew the moonshine had gotten to her. This was one of her favorite stories for a long time.

One morning I looked in my wallet and found it bare--too much fun for too long. What to do? Marrie had to fly home, I had to buy the ticket. Pinecone season was just beginning so we went to work, gathering the cones with the whole family pitching in. Wasn't long before we had the hundred and thirty-five dollars, and a good time earning it...

We set a tentative wedding date of December 21, 1963 giving Mr. Rink a good laugh. When I asked him what was so funny, he said we chose the longest night of the year. Mother couldn't leave home during Christmas, so we changed the date to February 15, 1964.

On day thirty of Marrie's allotted time, I drove her to Atlanta where she caught a flight to Toronto. This was the first time I had ever been to an airport. In those days, visitors were allowed to accompany passengers right up to the boarding gate, so I walked with Marrie down the long corridor and waited for an hour looking through the glass at the four-engine Constellations and DC-8's taking off and landing. My heart burned with excitement just thinking about flying one of those machines. A new passion was born that day and still is with me today.

What should I do for work? I had to get a job and I didn't want just any old menial job. I wanted to make the most money possible for my labors. One Sunday we were sitting in a swing in the back yard visiting with Jimmy Jones and he said that Standard Oil was hiring equipment operators to work in Saudi Arabia and they were paying over twenty thousand dollars a year plus housing and many other benefits. This was five times what I could make in Georgia.

6. CHICAGO

Broke -- The Big Red Boil -- A Country Boy Needs the Soil Underfoot -- Wedding Plans and President Kennedy -- The Wedding

I loaned my car to Charlotte and Nell and set out hitchhiking to Chicago to see about the job with Standard Oil. Folks stopped and gave me a ride as soon as I stuck my thumb out. Traveling in this fashion, I met all kinds of nice people. For the last several hundred miles, I rode with a young man from Chicago who said I could stay at his place for a few days. I was pleased with the offer because I had very little money. He drove into the very bowels of that giant city, going deeper and deeper into the slums. We came to a whole section of town filled with shabby, wooden four-story tenement buildings. He found a parking space among stripped and abandoned cars. He parked the car and walked down an alley and up several flights of stairs. His brother opened the door, and I could tell we were not welcome, only marginally tolerated. This was not his place but his brother's and his brother's skinny wife and a bunch of pale young'uns that looked as though they had just stepped out of a Charles Dickens novel. For supper we ate cabbage and horsemeat. I was squeamish about eating horseflesh, but I was hungry, so I chowed down. That night I slept on a linoleum floor and left early the next morning before anyone woke up.

Madison Street was the cheapest, seediest street in Chicago. Every building had heavy roll-up bars across the front and strong wire mesh in front of the windows. It was on this street that I found a hotel room for a dollar a night. What a dingy little hovel it was. The room had a sagging cot and one rickety clothes bureau. Fortunately, I had a raincoat that I spread over the bed and slept in my clothes.

Each day I walked the streets, going from one high-rise office building to the next. I filled out an application with Standard Oil and was told to wait. Then they gave me a test. Since I was only twenty years old, they offered me a job in Oklahoma for one year; if that worked out, perhaps they would send me overseas. Crapola! They can kiss my shiny.

That night I spent my last dollar on food. I was *totally* broke and there was no family or friends for support. A fellow inmate of the hotel told me of a place called *Rent-A Man*, located just down the street. He said I could find work there and get paid the same day. I was there early the next day. A fat man behind a narrow desk took my name and social security number. He said that if I got work I would be paid one dollar and twenty-five cents per hour and the house took the twenty-five cents. This was fine with me, so I took a seat. The place was only about five feet wide and a hundred feet deep with a long bench on one side and a mirror on the other. By eight o'clock there were over fifty men waiting on the bench. However, they didn't look like much competition as workers; most were winos on their last leg.

A fat man with a shiny bald head, wearing a cheap suit and tie sauntered down the aisle puffing on a cigar. He would stop in front of a man, look him over, point his finger straight at him and say, "*You*", and then jerk his thumb towards the door. I received the "*you*" and the thumb jerk and got in line at the desk where each *you* received a dollar for lunch money as we filed past.

Twelve of us loaded into a utility van without seats. The big man got in and his chauffeur drove us across Chicago until we came to the wharves. We unloaded and went into a new unvented warehouse made of concrete blocks. The place was airless with a strong smell of fresh cement. There before us was a mountain of small tools, tiny Allen wrenches, miniature sockets, open-end wrenches and screwdrivers by the millions. Mingled in this mess were the boxes in which they once belonged. Had there been a shipwreck? I had no idea. Our job was to fit the correct tool in the correct spot in the correct box. Looking this mess over I knew I had work until retirement. We suffered through orientation with the fat man swaggering back and forth showing us just how it had to be done. Then we settled down to the most boring work imaginable.

Did you ever have a boil? A big red one, filled with puss and right between your cheeks, the ones you don't smile with? If you haven't, you are most fortunate and if you have, well then, you will sympathize with me, 'cuz I had a hum-dinger and it was killing me. In fact, I was sick and feverish from it. After working an hour, I went into the toilet to have a look.

On the wall above the sink was a mirror that must have been placed there for a seven-foot-tall man as I could barely see the top of my head. I folded toilet paper and held it under the hot tap and then applied it to the boil, held it there for a minute, and tried to squeeze. The only thing that came out was tears. Oh boy, did I ever want to eyeball that thing! I took out my pocketknife and tried to chip a piece off the mirror, but it was anchored to the wall with thick black goo that wouldn't budge or chip.

With my britches down around my ankles, I climbed onto the commode and then stepped ever so gently onto the sink, putting my weight on it a few pounds at a time. It held. Whew! I opened the hot water faucet and got more paper, wet it, and bent over, all the while applying the hot poultices looking upside down between my legs. When I thought it was soft enough I gritted my teeth and gave it a hard squeeze. A bloody glob shot against the mirror as I yelled with pain. I must have shifted my weight because the porcelain washbasin tore loose from the wall and broke into a thousand pieces as it hit the concrete floor. I landed boil first in the glass. Both hot and cold-water pipes broke off. My butt and arms were cut and bleeding. All this made a terrible racket and the boss man came running and opened the door. I was still trying to get out of the wreck with my trousers 'round my ankles with both hot and cold water spraying on me. The fat man didn't wait for any explanation, he just went to cussing and yelling, flung away his cigar and fired the whole crew.

It was a long walk back. The winos were so angry at me they wouldn't let me walk with them. Back at *Rent-A-Man* I was paid for four hours, the minimum allowed and received another three dollars. I wound up with four dollars and a lanced boil for my troubles.

I walked to a diner, ordered two eggs and a bowl of soup, the bill was fifty-eight cents. After the meal I walked to Grand Central Station, went up to the Illinois Central Railroad counter, laid my money down, and asked, "how far will three dollars and forty-two cents take me, mister?"

The agent asked, "In what direction do you wish to go?"

I answered, "I don't care one whit. I just want to get out of this city and off concrete."

The agent took my three dollars and forty-two cents and handed me a ticket to Woodstock, Illinois. I went to platform nine stepped into a train pulling out. Oh! What a relief to be leaving that metropolis. I know Chicago has its good parts, but I didn't see any when I was there, nor any as the train glided through mile after mile of slums. It must have been Monday because clothes were hanging on lines stretched from one tenement building to another and over every fence and shrub.

About sundown, the train pulled into Woodstock. I detrained, walked to the road, and stuck my thumb out. A quiet young man of about thirty, driving a new car stopped and I got in. He asked me where I was headed, and I told him I was going to Lake Geneva, Wisconsin. We rode along and talked for a while. It started getting dark and he said he would drive me to Lake Geneva.

Johnny's sister Sara and her husband Dave Hackett lived there. The driver stopped and asked directions several times and after some maneuvering, we arrived at their door. I told them who I was. We were invited in and soon the young man left. I was burning up with fever and Sara put me to bed where I stayed for a couple of days. She washed my clothes and I was ashamed of how dirty they were. What lovely people! They treated me like family, and I stayed with them for several weeks.

When I got better, Sara and Dave invited me to go bow hunting for deer in the Wisconsin Dells. It was during the fall of the year and the woods were magnificent, glistening in every color of the rainbow. We camped beside the banks of cranberry marshes and I was amazed at the way the berries were grown and harvested. Dams enclosing a few acres of paddocks, constructed at intervals along the course of a stream and the berries are grown in those paddocks. When the berries get ripe, the farmer closes the sluice gates and the marsh floods. Ripe berries pop off the vines and float to the surface and on downstream to the overflow where they are scooped onto waiting trucks. Red berries were thick floating on top of the water. It looked as if you could walk across them.

Case Tractor Company in Racine, Wisconsin was hiring. I applied and got the job. It paid four dollars and thirty-five cents an hour and I was to work the shift from three until eleven p.m. Dave loaned me some money and I rented a room near the factory at the Hotel Racine, which catered to the workers. We were paid on a piecework basis and I often exceeded the minimum, plus we were paid time-and-a-half for Saturdays and double for Sundays. I worked every chance I got and saved my money.

Eight hours' work in the afternoon wasn't enough, so I got a job selling Watkins Products door-to-door. The man who trained me was very assertive and made money, but when I was by myself I didn't do so well. I just couldn't be pushy, plus I didn't like trying to sell people things they didn't want or need so I quit that job.

The following morning I walked down the street, stopping at different businesses asking for part-time work. The owner of the Lincoln-Mercury dealership had trucked in houses that had been in the path of a new highway and the houses were sitting on beams next to the basement that was waiting to be finished. The man wanted a ditch dug the length and breadth of the basement with a two-foot deep hole for the sump pump. The pay was ten dollars for each basement. He gave me a shovel and left.

The basements were in heavy red clay and covered with several inches of water. I stuck the shovel in and there was a strong sucking sound as I tried to pull it out. When I did get a shovel-full out, it stuck like glue and the clay wouldn't come off. I had been conned.

All right, there is more than one way to skin this cat. I found a big heavy hoe and went back down by sloshing the wide hoe back and forth, I had a ditch washed out much deeper and wider than required in just a few minutes. Within a couple of hours I had completed seven basements and was headed for the eighth when the owner drove up in his new Lincoln and asked why I was way down here. I said I had finished the others. He didn't believe me, so he got out of his car and had a look. My ditches were so deep all the water had run off the floor and into them. I told him how I did it and he promptly fired me. We went back to his office and he wrote out a check for twenty dollars and said that was all I was going to get for the two hours I worked. I said, "Mr. Big Shot, did you see how easy I dug those ditches. Well, if you don't pay me, I'll beat your ass right here and right now, just as easy as I dug those ditches."

He took a good look at the muddy young man standing before him and without another word, he wrote out a check for seventy dollars.

For the Christmas holidays, I planned to visit Marrie, but just before I was to leave, my car broke down, and my mechanic said it would take some days to repair. I grabbed my suitcase, left the car in the shop, and stuck out my thumb. Late that night someone dropped me off at the turnoff to O'Hara Field outside Chicago. A big neon sign was flashing, *temperature -20 Time 3:45 a.m.* The wind was blowing a gale, my trousers were thin, and I was freezing. It wasn't long before I got a ride and made good time on to Canada.

Marrie was glad to see me, but something was wrong. Next evening as we were doing the dishes, she stopped, turned to me and said that she didn't think she wanted to get married. Ouch! I had been thinking the same thing and told her so. It was all right with me; I was scared, and this was somewhat of a relief. How does someone know if this is the one for life? When one is twenty years old, beautiful women are everywhere. Is there only one predestined for each of us? Perhaps it was best this way. Should I get my suitcase and leave? First, I had to tell her how I felt.

We went into the living room and sat on the sofa. I took her hands in mine and told her I also had reservations about getting married so young, but I was in love with her beyond a shadow of a doubt. I had never loved anyone before and felt that I could never love anyone else. If we broke the engagement, it would break my heart, but if both of us were doubtful then we should definitely wait. With these words, Marrie fell into my arms and with tears in her eyes said that she had been crazy and didn't know what came over her, but she wanted to marry me more than anything in the world. At that moment, I had no more doubts; I would love and cherish this woman all the days of my life.

It was bitter cold, and Marrie insisted I fly back to Wisconsin. To be honest, I wasn't exactly relishing the hitchhiking trip back. Marrie went to a travel agency and purchased a ticket and I gave her a check for the amount. When I returned I paid for the repairs on the car, which cost more than I expected and unbeknown to me my check to Marrie bounced. My first bad check was to my sweetheart. She didn't understand what the stamp *insufficient funds* meant.

It was November 22, 1963. I was in the bank checking on this mess when the lady behind the counter told me that President Kennedy had just been shot. I was sick at heart and I believe every American who is old enough to remember can tell you where they were when they heard this tragic news.

An old movie theatre in the center of Racine had recently been renovated and converted into apartments. I rented a furnished studio for thirty-five dollars a week and cleaned it up spick and span. Oh how excited I was as I prepared everything, imagining carrying Marrie across the threshold of our first little home. I tried to picture what she would say and what she would think of it. I couldn't wait! One wasn't made to be this happy.

Wedding day February 15th, 1964. A fresh snow had fallen and the sun had come out. The world sparkled in all it's splendour.
Copyright Marrie J. Reaves

Case Tractor Company gave me a week off and I headed for Canada. Marrie had lost a lot of weight running hither and thither, getting ready for the wedding. Mother, Nell, and Johnny drove up from Georgia, and Mother took me to the best men's store in Galt where she bought me a dark blue suit. I had to take my shoes off to try on the trousers and when I walked out, I thought, darn this sidewalk is cold! Then I realized I had walked out into the snow in my socks. Was I nervous?

February 15 was a fabulous day. Long icicles were hanging from trees and houses, a fresh snow had fallen, the sun came out and the world sparkled in all its splendor for our wedding. I went to the church a little early and found it full of flowers and a few older ladies already waiting. Pastor Baird took me to his office in the rear of the church and entertained me as best he could. I didn't see Marrie arrive in the Chrysler New Yorker covered in flowers, but I heard the organ start playing 'Here Comes the Bride' and I knew it was happening. The doors opened and there was Marrie on Mr. Rink's arm, walking towards wearing a gorgeous white wedding gown and a lovely smile. Mrs. Latimer sang *I Love You Truly*. Marrie had three pretty bridesmaids and Johnny stood with me as best man. We exchanged vows without a hitch and became man and wife.

Everyone was invited to the basement for refreshments where so many people shook our hands and congratulated us and we smiled for so long our faces were sore for a week.

Marrie had invited a hundred people to Fern Lodge on the Galt River for dinner. Gary Pluim was MC, he told jokes and kept everyone laughing. There was food, whiskey, wine, cigars, and good music. Mother had always said she would dance at my wedding if I would do this or do that and she really did dance. I handed her a glass full of whiskey and the men twirled her around the floor. She was truly beautiful. Nell was decked out in a lovely dress and she won everyone's heart. I have no idea what I ate for dinner, but I do know that it came in many courses. At the end when desserts came, I was too full to sample them and have always regretted it. Mr. Rink had driven to Niagara Falls early that morning and bought them from a Dutchman he knew, who was famous for his pastries. The party broke up late. The family went to Marrie's house where we had coffee, she changed into a black and white traveling dress. It was after one o'clock in the morning before we departed.

A honeymoon suite was awaiting us in London, Ontario, but when we got to the 401 expressway it started to snow. By the time we got to London a blizzard was blowing. Cars were stalled in the middle of the expressway, but I kept *easing* along. 'Just married' was written all over our car that was stuffed high with gifts. A Royal Canadian Mounted Policeman drove up and approached us. I told him where we were trying to go and he said for us to follow him. He put on his bright fog lights and his emergency flashers and guided us up to the door of the Holiday Inn, London, Ontario. By the time we got to the room, it was almost three in the morning and we were exhausted.

Marrie was extremely nervous. She went into the bathroom and took a long time and then came out dressed in her white nightgown and robe. She sat on the side of the bed trying to hold back the tears. I took her in my arms and soothed her, telling her not to worry, that we were too tired to think about making love and we had a lifetime to work all that out and for her to relax and we would sleep in one another's arms. She cried and thanked me profusely. We went to bed and tried to sleep face-to-face holding one another. This didn't work out, so she turned her back to my stomach. We fit like two spoons in a drawer.

Next morning we drove on up to the border. Customs agents were hostile and antagonistic. They made us unload each and every gift and told Marrie she was not allowed into the US. After pleading and explaining a higher up agent said we could enter the U.S. if we paid duty on each item. What could we do? Add it up and we'll pay.

God does look after his children. Each present opened had 'Made in the USA' printed on it. When the agent saw this he said, "You two get out of here." We repacked and headed west on Interstate 94, arriving at the apartment after dark.

I couldn't find the key to the door and I knew I had put it in a safe place, but for the life of me, I couldn't remember where. We stood at the door while I searched through my pockets and then I left Marrie standing there, went outside, shimmied up the frozen drainpipe onto the wrought-iron balcony, and jimmied the door. I opened the front door and carried my bride across the threshold in my arms. Marrie was delighted with our small apartment and said that she did not expect so much. Next afternoon I went to work and Marrie went to cleaning. She said the place was filthy. What? I had just cleaned it!

One morning I went out to get in the car and found a bare spot in the snow where the car had been parked. We reported it stolen and was informed that it had been wrecked. A man had escaped from prison and stole it. A gas station attendant was filling it up with gas when the thief sped off, tearing the hose out of the pump. A police officer saw the hose sticking out of the side of the car and gave chase. The escapee slid around a curve, lost control, and went through a fence. Damage to the fence was two hundred and sixty-five dollars and I was responsible. No way! Have you all gone crazy?

I sold the damaged Chevrolet, still covered in '*Just Married*' graffiti, and bought a 1959 Pontiac. That thing was big!

We didn't think about distances. On Friday night, we headed out on the 600-mile trip to Canada, spent a day or two, and drove back in time for me to go to work on Monday afternoon.

One morning as we ate breakfast, the tranquility was shattered by loud banging on the door. I jumped up, opened the door, and there stood a huge policeman with a paper in his hand. He handed it to me and said most rudely that he had come for the license plates on my car. This was because of a lien of two hundred and sixty-five dollars by the state of Wisconsin for the damage to the fence, which I did not intend to pay. I followed the rude giant out and watched as he took the tags off my car, I felt violated.

He said I would be arrested if I even *moved* the car. I thought, "Don't hold your breath, buster! To hell with Wisconsin!" I quit my job and we packed up, putting as many of our belongings as we could pack inside the car with the rest on a roof rack and headed south. We were happy and singing as we drove through the cornfields of Illinois. We came around a curve going a little too fast and the loaded car leaned with the weight on top and two boxes slid off. I stopped as quickly as I could and turned around, but before we could get back a Cadillac loaded down with Negroes stopped, picked up one of the boxes, and took off. I waved and tried to get them to stop, but they had no intention of stopping.

We came to the first box, Marrie jumped out, got it and I took off after the Cadillac. Soon I had her pegged at 120mph and she was floating over the hills. The Cadillac came in view, he saw me, floor-boarded it, and away we went. Directly I was on his bumper and rammed him every chance I got. Young black faces with big white eyes filled the rear window. The driver slowed down, stuck his arm out the window, and waved it up and down. The brake lights came on and at twenty mph the back door opened, and my box slid down the highway. I picked it up and headed back for Marrie. Mile after mile I kept expecting to see her. How could I have missed her? Did she run afoul of bad people? Where was she? It couldn't have been this far. Should I turn around? Then I saw the most beautiful woman in the world walking along the berm of the highway in Bermuda shorts, swinging an electric frying pan by the handle. The truck drivers were blowing their air horns and whistling. Eat your heart out boys, she's mine!

We stopped early at a motel with a pool, swam and lay on chaise lounges while I smoked a big Cuban cigar. The world was our oyster and we were shucking it. We were headed to the farm to build our home and our future. We drew floor plans for our dream home with a big swimming pool. My plans were to have enough chicken houses for 100,000 chickens and at that time each chicken earned a dollar per year. I planned to plant the farm in Bermuda grass and fertilize with chicken manure and with irrigation, I could cut 15 tons of hay per acre during the summer months. We would have children and grandchildren and live in our dream farmhouse under big shade trees with an orchard on the north side that'd produce all kinds of fruit. We would make wine from a few acres of vines outback; a long grape arbor would shade the path to the kitchen garden and barn. A palomino mare with a colt trotting beside would pull our buggy down sandy country roads as we went fishing or swimming in the creeks. Our barn would have an oak floor and once a month we'd invite friends to a barbecue or fish-fry and square dance 'til midnight. Such were my dreams.

We moved into the house with Mother, Larry, Kay, Sharon, and Tara. Grandma had built an addition of three rooms on the south side of the house that could be called a separate apartment, and this is where we set up housekeeping, but really, it was just one

7. MOONSHINE

Flying Lessons -- First Born -- Moonshine -- Largest 'Still' in the County -- Pass the Sugar and the Ammunition

One morning I had business in Douglas and afterwards I drove out to the airport where a crop duster was giving flying lessons. I told the man that I wanted to learn to fly. We walked across the apron and strapped in an old Ironic Scout with *Death Trap* written on the side. It was a clear spring morning as we taxied out and I took off for the first time. The fool didn't want any return business, because he rolled it as soon as it was off the ground, kept it low, and ran directly at trees, at the last moment pulling up hard. His specialty was finding two tall pines on a fence row that were too close together for the tiny craft to fit. When he got so close that I was sure we were going to lose both wings, he'd roll it on its side with wings vertical to the ground and slice between the trees. I didn't think he was going to kill himself, so it was a thrill. I yelled that I wanted to go to Jacksonville and fly over my house. When we got to the river I took over the controls and with his help we circled low. Marrie came running out, he idled the engine and I yelled down, "Hi Sweetheart!" I had not told her of my intentions of flying.

Marrie glowed with health and beauty throughout her pregnancy. We spent the morning cutting brush and burning the area where we planned to build our house. That afternoon Marrie went to the doctor and learned she had dilated so many centimeters. We went home, packed a bag and leisurely returned to town. Late in the afternoon of September 14, 1966, Marya Jacoba arrived. My heart expanded when I held her. She was beautiful. Where did all this new love come from?

Our house was full of people all weekend. Marrie tried to nurse the baby, but it wasn't working. The infant gave up and cried. Marrie pumped her breast, put the milk in a bottle and by then she was crying. Mrs. Stewart came in, saw the young mother in distress and ran us all off in no uncertain terms. Marrie still loves her for this kindness. Mrs. Stewart was wise and calming, a truly lovely lady. She spent the afternoon with Marrie and came back several times thereafter.

We loved our baby and took her everywhere. When Marrie hung clothes on the line, Marya was in the clothes hamper, when we picked up eggs, Marya was in an egg box riding along on the trolley. When she was big enough to sit up, she reached for the eggs and one was all right, but two were a disaster, as she would smash them together, and then there were none.

Early one spring I was working the tractor near the old over-grown water hole, trying to clear up some new ground to plant watermelons. Each time I passed, I noticed a big ripple near the edge and figured an alligator was living in the pond. Later, as I was breaking ground I saw whatever it was made a big swirl as I passed by and it looked like the swirl of a very large fish. Then I remembered putting all those little Channel Cats in years before.

Saturday afternoon, Marrie and I took the baby and laid down a big patchwork quilt for a pallet in the grass. We baited our hooks with fresh chicken livers and cast out to the center. Marrie hooked him as soon as the bait hit the water and what a fight it was. He just kept peeling off the line as she reeled it in, eventually wrecking her gear. Wasn't long before I had him on my line, and it was a repeat of the show. He must have regurgitated the hook and thereafter wouldn't bite if he could see us. We kept going back, hiding in the weeds and throwing in baited hooks from a distance, and each time he spat them out without even a good fight.

The following Saturday afternoon I borrowed a salt-water reel from Ewell and sharpened the treble hooks on a whet-rock until they were needle-sharp. We laid Marya on the bright plaid quilt, threw in our lines, and waited on him to bite. I figured he had eaten all his brothers and sisters and was the only one remaining.

I had killed several big diamondback rattlers in this area, and we were afraid to walk in the knee-deep weeds. Suddenly a loud *buzzzzzzzz* went off under our feet. We both jerked Marya up off the palette and jumped in the middle of the quilt. Then we laughed, realizing it was the drag on the salt-water reel making the noise as the line peeled off. This time he stayed hooked and when we landed him he was over four feet long and weighed thirty pounds. Later on I told that he was nine inches. Folks would look puzzled and say, "Only nine inches?"

"Yeah, I measure em' between the eyes."

With only four acres of tobacco and three houses full of chickens, I could not make ends meet. I paid Mother 50% for the rent of her chicken house and Wylene, our neighbor nearby, the same, plus I paid for all the shavings and electricity.

I bought a ten-wheeler International L170 and started hauling shavings for other growers. Loading and unloading tons of shavings with a seed fork is backbreaking work and sometimes I worked all night. I remember the movie

Doctor Zhivago was playing in the theatre in Douglas. We didn't have the money for admission, so we broke Marya's piggy bank and went, taking my sisters and brother. The movie was so sad that we all had tears in our eyes as we walked out. When we got to the edge of town I stopped the car so we could all have a good cry and laugh.

My income was just not cutting it. Some months we could not pay the electric bill and the Rural Electric Association sent men out to disconnect our power. I climbed the pole, put shims in the break and we were back in business. Marrie thought this was great.

Forrest Grey, an old schoolmate, worked for the REA and they sent him out with orders to climb the pole and disconnect the transformer so that Roger Reaves couldn't bypass their block. Forest arrived late one Friday afternoon and told Marrie that he was sorry, but he had orders to turn it off for good. Marrie begged him to wait until I came home and then we would pay. She explained that we had a freezer full of food and a little baby and the trailer was as hot as Hades without the air conditioner. She invited Forest in for a cup of coffee and a piece of pecan pie, but he refused and said he had to go to work. He got out his tools and climbing gear and started up the pole. Marrie came out with a rifle in her hands and said, "Mr.Grey, it's Friday, and if you disconnect the power it will be Monday afternoon before it can possibly be restored and by that time all our food will be ruined. I have worked all summer putting it up and I am not going to allow you to climb that pole and cut the power over a ten-dollar bill that is a few days late."

Forest climbed down off the pole and said, "Miss Marrie, a piece of that pecan pie sure does sound good."

I came in a short time afterward; we had a good laugh and I paid the bill.

Looking back in time I can see that the following choice was a major turning point in my life. Had I not made this choice; my life would have been very different.

Homer Boone was a most likable man who lived near China Hill with his wife and seven young'uns. He was a big farmer and could have run for any public office and won, except for the fact that he was a notorious bootlegger. His encounters with the law were legendary. The old cars he drove were ragged-lookin', but souped-up to run fast and it was said he could burn a new set of tires off the rear end between traffic lights.

Once he drove up in his circular drive and the Federal Revenuers were waiting on him. He rolled down his window and asked what he could do for them and they replied that they had a warrant to search his house. He asked to see the warrant and as soon as it was in his hand, his foot came off the clutch and away he went. By the time they drove the twenty-five miles to town for a new warrant there was no evidence left in his house. Homer had never been caught, but he was as hot as a firecracker.

I guess Homer heard I was in financial difficulty, as it was no secret. In any case, he drove up late one Saturday evening. I went out to meet him and he invited me to sit in his car while we talked. He offered me one hundred dollars a week if I allowed him to put a "likker" still by the stream behind our trailer. He said I would never see him and that he would leave the hundred dollars under a brick by the doorsteps every Saturday night. His men would enter before day and leave after dark and they would go in and out by the chicken house, so I was not involved. This sounded all right with me. A little excitement and some money were both welcome. I agreed.

Marrie was ironing when I came in. I told her what I was going to do, and she was hard set against the idea, but I prevailed with the argument that we needed the money and we were not involved. I remember her tears falling on the little dress and her ironing them dry.

Homer asked me to take my truck to Ocilla and pick up the new still at a metal fabricator. I couldn't believe the size. It was twelve feet long, six feet wide and four feet deep, with a 20-inch truck rim welded in the top center and a two-inch gate valve in one end at the bottom. That monster almost filled the bed of my ten-wheeler. I hauled it back in the middle of the night. Early the next morning Homer drove up with Jim, his oldest boy, and two colored men, Roosevelt and Elijah. Our job was to unload that thing and set it up on concrete blocks.

They brought a nifty little gasoline operated water pump and hooked up a series of mufflers, then stuck the exhaust pipe underwater in the branch. When they cranked it up you would only hear the bubbling of the exhaust. The vat was filled three quarters with water, a ton of sugar, four hundred pounds of wheat shorts, and twenty pounds of yeast were added, and all stirred together. Next they put a three-inch steel pipe with holes drilled along the sides under the still and attached large butane bottles to a manifold. They lit the fire and heated the water just enough to dissolve the sugar and Homer said that one had to be careful not to let it get it too warm and kill the yeast. A burlap bag stretched over the opening kept out bees, wasps, and other insects. Every day or two I slipped through the woods to check on the progress. The brew was working, turning and foaming, with a head of foam almost a foot thick, then one day the foam disappeared, and the brew was ready for distillation.

Roosevelt showed me how to tell if all the sugar had *worked off.* You put your arm down deep into the mash, bring it out and grip it with your dry hand. If the wet hair on your arm sticks to your hand, the sugar has not worked off, but if it comes away clean, it is ready to run. It took about five days in the summer and seven to ten in the winter for the brew to work off.

Jim, Roosevelt, and Elijah (known as Lish) arrived before daybreak and put the fire under the still. After breakfast, I walked down and had a look. Roosevelt was busy changing gas bottles, as one iced up he put it in the edge of the flames and added another in its place. Lish was standing on the periphery looking this way and that, his head swiveling around like a wild turkey's gobbler sticking up over the palmettos. He was looking for revenuers. It took several hours for the mash to heat and while they waited, they attached a twelve-foot long *shotgun distiller* to the top of the tank, sealed the cracks with a glue made of cornmeal, flour and water. On the end of the condenser hung a large funnel filled with layers of cotton baton. This was to strain the whiskey in case the still puked.

This sometimes happened when a sudden change of temperature caused the sides to flex, spewing mash through the condenser, contaminating the clear alcohol. The whiskey ran through the cotton and into a fifty-five-gallon stainless steel drum where Roosevelt kept checking the purity by shaking a sample in a bottle and noting the size of the bubbles and how long it took them to dissipate. The bigger the bubbles and the longer they lasted the higher the percentage of alcohol. As the alcohol evaporated, the heat had to go higher and higher until in the end, you only got 'low wine' that was used to cut the pure alcohol.

After about six hours, they had 250 gallons of moonshine whiskey in stainless steel drums. They mixed it together to get a uniform proof and then poured it into clear, five-gallon, collapsible, plastic containers. They told me a man named Sugar Boy would come from Atlanta, sometimes in the night and pick up the liquor and leave a load of sugar. I was in no way to meet him or to let him see me. He must have been a valuable contact.

Within a couple of weeks Homer added two more stills of the same size and shortly thereafter he brought in another. I told him he owed me four hundred dollars a week, but he wouldn't agree and said he didn't say how big a liquor still he was going to put there. I knew I was being taken advantage of, but at that time in my life I was too immature and trusting. They were now making 1000 gallons of whiskey a week and selling it for three dollars and fifty cents a gallon. It cost less than a dollar a gallon to produce, so my hundred dollars was less than a pittance.

Roosevelt and Lish were delightful company and I spent many days sitting around the still while they cooked off the liquor. Several times I stuck bushes in my hat and belt and crawled on my belly right up to one of their feet, jumped up and shouted, "Gotcha." They jumped up 'n started to run before they realized it was me. After a couple of good laughs, they turned serious and asked me not to do it again.

Lish was about thirty-five years old, and already had fourteen head of young'uns. One morning he came in drunk, smelling of strange perfume and went to sleep on the sofa. His wife boiled a pot of water, added a can of Red Devil lye, and poured it in his face, blinding him in one eye and leaving one side of his face snow white. He must have thought he had it coming because they stayed together.

The still had been in production for eleven months and the path coming through our yard began to look like a well-used logging road. I was getting nervous. I plowed up the whole field and road, then harrowed it smooth. I went to Homer and told him it was time for him to move that thing off my land. He asked me to wait until he could find another location and I showed him two other good sites. They began using the gate by the chicken house and that looked better me, but I still wanted it out of there.

On a cold, foggy February morning, I was sitting at the table drinking a cup of coffee and Marrie was frying eggs when we heard and felt an explosion from the direction of the still. I jumped up and looked out the rear window just in time to hear, feel, and see another giant explosion, immediately followed by two more. "That's it, the Feds have blown all four stills."

Six or eight more explosions close together shook the house and then it tapered off to one every now and then. After a while, all was quiet. I knew something bad had happened down there. Though I was afraid, I eased out the door, ran for the woods, circled through the branch and came up on the backside, all the time hearing a high pitch whistle. The scene looked like the aftermath of a battlefield. Ten or twelve two-hundred-pound butane tanks had exploded in the middle of a batch of a hundred or more. Several had the necks cracked and the gas was spewing 30-foot flames. It looked like a tangled mess of flame throwers from World War II.

I grabbed a hoe, dragged the flaming bottles into the creek, and even under water, they continued to screech. After a bit, I managed to get all the fires out and the bottles in some sort of order. Lish showed up and explained how they were placing the partially empty iced-up bottles in the flames, when the sides of the still flexed, knocking the bottles over onto the others. These exploded, knocking others over. Both he and Roosevelt ran and I can't say as I blamed them because it's a wonder they weren't killed. We started hooking up bottles and had the fire going when Roosevelt came back. The weather was foggy with a fine drizzle falling and I left it to them and went on back to the house.

Marrie was cooking me a second breakfast when we heard gunshots. She looked out the rear kitchen window and said, "Oh my goodness, here comes Lish with Waymond (the deputy sheriff) right behind him! Waymond is shooting at Lish! Waymond fell down in the Bahara grass. Lish is outrunning Waymond! Waymond lost his hat and has stopped, oh-oh, he's found his hat."

I took off up the highway to see my old friend Jimmy Jones to get a little advice. We talked for a while and then saw the truck from the convict camp come flying by with bloodhounds and 'dog boys' to run 'em. We stood there and watched as carload after carload of lawmen came speeding by. I went on back to the chicken house to tend to some pullets who had scratched underneath the house and were out. There were over twenty law enforcement cars and trucks in the pasture with lights flashing. Waymond came up to the chicken house, "Waymond," I said, "what did yawl find back there, a rattlesnake or what?"

"You know what we found and if you go back there I'll put the cuffs on you."

"Why, Waymond, I haven't lost a thing back there and I have no intentions of going near that circus."

A GBI (Georgia Bureau of Investigation) agent came up and tried to get me to sign a confession before the Feds got to me, but I graciously thanked him and declined. What I didn't know was that the sheriff arrested me, and Mother signed a ten-thousand-dollar property bond. Perhaps he did this so the Feds or the GBI wouldn't arrest me. Anyway, he was paid protection money, and surely, he did not want to arrest me.

A.J. Giddings, our closest neighbor, had called the sheriff and showed them where the explosions came from. He said he was milking, and his cows tore out of the pens thinking a plane had crashed.

Roosevelt had made it through the creeks to his home late that afternoon, but when Lish didn't show up, we began to worry that he had been hit and lay hurt or was dead. There was no way we could ever find him, even the bloodhounds couldn't track in that weather. Thankfully, he showed up the next day unhurt.

Headlines of the *Telfair Enterprise* read:

'Largest moonshine still in county history found near Jacksonville, Georgia. Four vats containing over 40,000 gallons of mash, 500 gallons pure moonshine, 200 butane bottles, 12-foot condenser. One man arrested and sheriff says there will be more to follow.'

Similar articles appeared in the *Macon Telegraph* and *The Atlanta Journal*; the news covered Dixie like the dew.

When this hit the news, General Motors Finance Corp. came and repossessed the pickup. The International Tractor Co. repossessed the tractor and ten-wheeler. People came to the house and demanded their money. I was paralyzed broke with zero credit. I bought an old 1952 Dodge car for two- hundred and forty-five dollars and a Black Diamond International pickup with a five-gallon can and a rubber hose running to the carburetor for a gas tank, all for a hundred dollars.

Quarter annually, the circuit judge came to town and the grand jury met. This was 24 men and women from our county and when they met, I made sure to be around and shake a few hands. Billy Walker, an attorney friend of mine came by, took me by the arm and led me around the corner where he explained that a charge of interfering with the Grand Jury was worse than the one for making whiskey. I eased on out of the courthouse and went on down to the drug store for a milkshake.

After a while some of the jurors came in and one old man eased up beside me and said, "we ain't a gonna get no bill agin' you, but don't you let Homer put nara' another still on yore place." He was correct, they voted 12 to 12 and the case was dismissed.

After a few months things had cooled down and I went to Ocilla and had a still made just like the others. I stayed up all night helping the fabricator solder fifty brass rods into a twelve-inch pipe, loaded all this up, and took it to the Wiregrass Hole on Alligator Creek, which was about two miles east of our house.

Getting sugar was a problem. I had to go to Ambrose one week and Douglas the next. One Saturday I was loading bales of sugar on the back of the pickup while keeping a sharp eye out for the law. I looked up and saw three young women walking abreast holding hands. One was on the highway and two were on the shoulder. I told the grocery man handing the bales out to hold up, because three women were coming.

While we were waiting for them to pass, I saw a car coming from behind them at an insane speed. At the last moment, the driver saw the girls and swerved to miss, but the rear side of his car hit the one on the highway throwing her into the air; she fell near the front of my pickup. I was sick as I walked over because I knew from the sound of the impact that she was dead. The other young women got hysterical and I learned later they were all sisters. Police cars began arriving and I eased on back to the truck and put a cover over the sugar. About an hour later the coroner took the body away, yet the police stayed around taking notes, sometimes leaning on the hood of my pickup (half loaded with sugar) to write their reports.

Each week I made 250 gallons of high-grade moonshine and Charles Purvis, an old friend from school, helped me sell it. We got four dollars a gallon and I paid Charles fifty cents. After subtracting all expenses, I was making seven hundred dollars a week. Not bad. If I could keep this up I could get out of debt and start farming again.

I bought a 1956 Buick, without reverse, for five hundred dollars, outfitted it with air shocks that leveled out the frame, no matter how much you loaded. I often put 200 gallons (over 1200 pounds) in the trunk and seats and she still set level.

Every three runs the vat needed cleaning with strong soap and steel wool to keep unwanted bacteria from accumulating. The first time I did it by myself it took three hours. The whole time I was afraid the revenuers would slip up and catch me in the vat and there would be no chance to run. The next time I needed to do this job, I talked my brother Larry into standing lookout. It was in the early spring and as we walked along the trail, the huckleberry bushes were in full bloom with bees buzzing in the flowers. In clear or burned off places little blue violets and white daisies gladdened the woods. It was a most beautiful and peaceful day. Larry and I arrived at the still and I found him a good hiding spot a little way up the road behind some gallberry bushes. I told him to wait there and if anyone came to shoot the shotgun three times and take off running.

The inside of the vat smelled of old sour mash it took three hours of scouring to clean it out. Once it was clean, I began running water in the vat, then went to look after Larry. I found him easy enough. He was lying in the road on his stomach, holding the shotgun in his hands above his head, sound asleep. I took out my pocketknife, cut a gallberry switch and cut him across his butt. He woke up looking lost and bewildered. That sting across his ass didn't jive with his dream.

That fall, the woods caught fire from the still and burned several acres before I could extinguish it. The pine trees burned all the way to the tops, and I was sure this brown spot stuck out to anyone flying overhead while patrolling for stills. I needed to move it and I needed help. I asked my old friend Jimmy Jones and we moved it one night from the Wiregrass Hole to a spring behind where Elmo Pace used to live. Jimmy was holding a gun in one hand and a flashlight in the other. Later he said that was the most insane thing he ever did. The new site for the still was one of the places I had shown Homer, and I decided it was best to tell him, so if he heard anything from the sheriff he could let me know. How stupid can a young man be?

On a foggy Monday morning, just before day, I loaded up the sugar, condenser, and several stainless steel barrels and headed for the still. Shortly after passing the Belemy place, I saw a car backed up in the bushes and figured it was the Feds waiting on me. I turned left and drove by the turn-off to the still. At the corner, I saw another light blue four-door car stick its nose out from the old abandoned Annie Parrish home site, there was no question, Homer had turned me in! My old pickup had a big strong motor and it was fast. I put the pedal to the metal and went flying around the corner by Carrabelle's, slinging off the condenser. I tore down the rutty hill toward Buddy Studstill's place.

By now, both cars were right behind me with sirens blaring. I'm sure that part of the woods had never heard a siren before. The Studstill place was at the end of the road, but I knew of an old pulpwood trail that went on through the woods where I had ridden my horse years before. I busted through Buddy's wooden gate slinging off more evidence and tore out through the woods. I ran over a log and the truck bounced high in the air causing my head to hit the roof -- hard. A steel drum flew off and I thought this would slow down my pursuers. I looked in the review mirror to see what happened. The first car crashed into the drum almost wrecking, but both stayed right behind me. This wasn't working, I came to a sliding stop and jumped out and ran through the woods. As I ran, I realized what a foolish place I'd chosen, because it was open pinewoods. The Fed's cars pulled up and eight doors flew open and eight men jumped out and began shooting. They were definitely trying to kill me because the bullets were hitting limbs and trees by my head. I believe that each one shot at least six times and that adds up to 48 hunks of lead that zipped by my ears; it sounded like more. As soon as I got in thick brambles, I crawled back up to the edge and lay flat on my belly looking out.

Several men ran on in the branch and two stopped near me and talked. I thought they might be able to feel my heart pounding against the earth.

After they all loaded up and left, I struck out and walked through hog pens and a herd of cows that had bedded down in the bad weather, hoping to throw the dogs off my trail. When I came to Horse Creek I jumped in and swam a mile or more in some mighty cold water. When I could stand it no longer I got out and walked to Mother's house. I borrowed her car, drove to McRae and went to see Nicky Rawlins, a young attorney. He told me I didn't have anything to worry about since they didn't catch me.

The Fed's dynamited the still, the new pump and the pickup. A few days later, they came to the Old Place, told me they knew the still was mine and that Homer had turned me in. They tried to get me to work with them against Homer, but I wanted no part of that.

The newspapers and television were full of the story. Everybody knew the still was mine.

Marrie and I were ashamed to go to church.

8. FAMILY MAN, CALIFORNIA

Family Reunion -- The Right to Workbook -- Fire Fighter -- Pop Goes the Robber -- Dog Food -- Taking To the Air -- Private Island -- The Firefighting Bee Keeper

It was August 1968, Saturday afternoon. We dressed up, left Marya with Mother, and started to Fitzgerald to buy groceries because we didn't want to face people we knew in McRae. We had only gone a couple of miles when the old $245 car swerved sharply to the left. I turned the wheel all the way to the right and slammed on the brakes, but it just kept on angling across the highway, over the berm, and into a ten-foot deep ditch. As we went over Marrie screamed and grabbed my leg, pinching blood where each finger grabbed. The back seat flew over in the front seat. A huge cloud of dust and debris covered us, and we were badly shaken up, but the old car was undamaged. The car behind stopped and gave us a ride on to Jacksonville where we told Mrs. Clark what happened, and she sent her wrecker and towed the car in. The tie rod end had come off the left side. Had a car or truck been coming our way we would have been killed.

My sister Marijo was visiting from California and she told me they were really building the place up, paying top dollar for construction workers. She thought they were making about seven dollars an hour and invited me to return with her and have a look. I had no intention of leaving home and going so far, but for that amount of money I would go and work the fall and winter, save my money and return in the spring to farm. The chicken houses were empty, all the equipment was gone, and I was paralyzed broke. Marijo wasn't going back for two weeks and I was anxious to go and have a look. If things were as good as she thought, then Marrie and Marya could ride out with her.

I borrowed a hundred dollars from Ewell, gave Marrie fifty and I kept fifty to make the trip. Marrie washed and ironed my faded clothes, packed them neatly in a suitcase and kissed me goodbye. Ewell came over to give me a ride to McRae. As we drove away, I felt my heart would break. My spirit must have known I would never get back. In my innermost being, I felt I would lose Marrie in California and perhaps lose myself. I rode away from the farm, my home of twenty-six years, with tears flowing down my face.

That old Sun was bearing down as I rode my thumb to California. Several short rides took me to Macon and Highway 82 where I headed west. I had to thumb both day and night because I didn't have enough money for a hotel room, there was barely enough to eat on. It seemed so slow, but it wasn't, it was just a very long way. The journey across Georgia, Alabama, Mississippi, and Louisiana were a multitude of short rides, always with poor people who liked to talk, ask a hundred questions, and always wished me good luck. I could have gone home with most all of them if I had asked.

In East Texas, a hot pink Cadillac with a six-foot set of cow horns mounted on the hood stopped and I stepped into a plush air-conditioned world, smelling of leather and money. The man was jovial and told me I could ride as long as I talked and if I could keep him awake, we would be in west Texas by daylight. I was tired and sleepy, but I talked and told him the biggest yarns I could think of just to keep myself awake. He kept the speedometer pegged at 120 mph and we just floated over the hills as that Cadillac ate up the miles. Sometime during the night, he asked if I was hungry and I said I was.

We came sliding to a halt at the gas pumps of a truck stop he said, "Fill-er up please sir! Let's go get some grub."

We sat down at the counter and a waitress came over to take our order.

"Bring us a couple of the biggest T-bones ye got." the man said.

"How'd y'all like those cooked?" She drawled.

I answered, "I'd like mine medium."

"Oh man, we ain't got time for that, just knock his horns off, wipe his ass and bring him on out here!"

"Bring me a hamburger kinda medium please."

Within fifteen minutes we were again speeding across Texas at 120 miles an hour.

About daylight, he let me out at a little truck stop west of Midlands. I hung around there all morning, but only local cattle haulers stopped. They told me there was a town three miles down the road with a crossroad and heavy traffic, so I started walking. As I walked along, I nodded to a man on a tractor mowing grass on the shoulder of the road. Shortly after, I came to a bridge where Highway 82 crossed over another highway. I stopped to wait for a semi-truck I saw coming my way, and of course stuck out my thumb.

As the man mowing grass went to turn around, he swerved out into the highway. The semi hit his rear left wheel and it flew up twenty feet. The tractor driver was thrown down the embankment on my left and the truck jack-knifed to the right and started sliding toward me. I dropped my suitcase and jumped over the guardrail. I looked up and saw the terror on the driver's face as he came sliding past. The loaded trailer pushed the truck into the heavy cement banister of the bridge and the truck went through and over, nose-diving straight down into the other highway. The trailer was loaded with paint. It landed on the cab, squashing it flat and burst into flames. I had to put my arms in front of my face because the fire was so hot.

Outside of El Paso, a worn-out old Pontiac stopped, and I got in. The driver was a thin middle-aged man who looked kinda down on his luck. He told me he was headed for California if his old car would make it, but he didn't have enough money for gas. We had about 700 miles to go, I figured we needed fifteen dollars for two more fill-ups. I agreed to pay, and we had a most enjoyable ride through New Mexico, Arizona, and California with the windows rolled down listening to country music. I bought cheese, crackers, and Coca Colas as we picnicked at a rest area. This man was from Arkansas and had worked in California off and on for years, so he knew his way around and kept pointing things out.

The sun was coming up as we came into San Bernardino, but I could barely see it through the thick smog. I was thoroughly disappointed in sunny California. The nice Arkansas man was headed to Bellflower but went out of his way and drove me to Torrance. After finding Marijo's apartment, he continued on his way and we parted company.

What a lovely surprise! Marijo had a posh apartment, with two big bedrooms upstairs, and a kitchen, dining room, and living room downstairs. The dining room looked onto Anza Avenue, a wide new street with young trees and red bottlebrush bushes. A pool just out the front door was surrounded by women in bikinis. I met the manager and explained who I was and went to bed.

After a few hours, I got up and went outside. As I was walking around I came to a group of people being entertained by two men arguing. They were standing by a big hole under the front of the apartment building and I could see that new plumbing had been installed. The owner, Mr. Waterman, was arguing with the plumber over the price of six hundred dollars he was demanding to fill and pack the earth back in the hole. The plumber was inflexible on the price and complaining about the cost of labor. I listened a bit, then stepped up and said I'd like to do the job for three hundred dollars. The plumber angrily asked just who the hell I thought I was. I walked right up to him and told him just who I was and if he ever had any more holes like this to fill up, I hoped he would call me. Mr. Waterman gave me the job and I went to work.

It was all sand, and a group of children was around, and they all wanted to help. I had them shovel the sand into the hole while I packed it underneath the concrete slab and before night it was all filled and raked smooth. Mr. Waterman paid me and I was in the chips.

Kitty-corner across the street was a big apartment building just beginning construction. I walked across, found the contractor, a Mr. Picar, and told him I was looking for work. He said I could start immediately toting lumber to the carpenters and being a general handyman. The pay was four dollars an hour and I could work as many hours as I liked. I went back to the apartment that evening and called Marrie and told her to come on out, that this was the land of opportunity.

Seven o'clock sharp we started work. I carried six, eight-foot lengths of 2 by 4's on my shoulder to carpenters on the third floor, dropped them, and hurried back for another load. We had a half-hour for lunch, so the day's work was over at 3:30 and I wasn't tired. The boss was paying 75 cents to have each sheet of 4X8 plywood nailed and I asked for the job. This was before pneumatic nail guns, so I bought a little creeper that was only a couple inches off the floor, and I scooted around on my butt driving nails. I made more from 3:30 to 7:30 than I did carrying lumber all day.

The family arrived from Georgia utterly exhausted and sunburned. Marijo drove a new convertible and kept the top down all the way. Marrie was the most worn-out I have ever seen her. She told me that on the way across the country, whenever Marya saw a man on a tractor, no matter what color, she would point and said, "Daddy, Daddy!"

The next day after a good long rest, she hopped on the back of the motorcycle I had borrowed from my brother Larry, and we rode down an avenue lined with tall palm trees, flowers and lovely old early Californian homes. We came over a rise and Marrie gasped as she saw the blue Pacific Ocean laced with whitecaps and sailboats. All this on a motorcycle with the wind blowing in our faces and her arms tight around me is about as close as one can get to heaven on earth. It was a moment to remember and cherish-such beauty, such happiness. Marrie was ecstatic and I do believe she fell in love with California at that moment.

We were happy living with Marijo and had a comfortable unspoken agreement. She paid the rent and I bought the groceries. Marrie cooked, cleaned and kept the children. Marijo worked nights, slept in the daytime we didn't see much of one another. I walked back across the road for lunch and Marrie and Marya brought me sandwiches in the afternoon to keep me going until dark.

January came and I went to work framing. This paid by piecework and I was making a hundred dollars a day, but it was killing me. The other men were toughened to the work and it was wicked. We had to drive a 16-penny nail with only two licks and we were nailing joist on 16-inch centers with short-handled heavy hammers. We wore canvas shorts and nail aprons and you didn't dare stop to pick up a dropped nail. The boss came around every once in a while and his favorite words were, "Ass holes and elbows boys, that's all I wanna see!" I got off at 3:30, went to the house and cleaned up, fell across a bed and slept till' supper, ate, and then went to bed. After a few weeks, I developed bloody dysentery and quit. I'm glad I did, because those men looked much older than they were. That job will wear a man out.

Next, I got a job with Ralph Bless, a cement contractor. For a month, we built forms for a huge subterranean garage. I liked this work and was learning daily. Finally, the big day came when we were to pour over 200 cubic yards of concrete. Early in the morning, a cement pumper with a long boom showed up and then what looked like a convoy of cement trucks started pumping their innards. I worked shoveling cement until I was totally exhausted. My boots were full of the soup, it was burning my legs, and someone was always cussing and waving their arms. Late in the afternoon, the boss's brother cussed me. I threw my shovel in the soup and quit. That is the only job I ever just walked off, and I wish I had done it early in the morning because I got cement poisoning on my legs.

One evening I came home late from working in the cement and my Levi's virtually stood in the corner where I retrieved them at daybreak the next morning. No need to wash what would be in the same shape after ten minutes. Sometime in the wee hours of the night, Marrie woke me, nudging my ribs and whispered that someone was downstairs. She said he had just gone out the door. I jumped up and looked out the window, sure enough, there was a man wearing a black raincoat walking by the pool. I pulled on the cement jeans and ran downstairs and out the front door. Rain was gently falling, and it was cool to my naked torso and feet. As I came around the corner, I saw a shovel handle the children had been playing with and I grabbed it. What a weapon.

The man was walking nonchalantly through the apartment garage and I ran silently up behind him on my bare feet and said, "What were you doing in that apartment?" I expected him to stop and explain, but he took one terrified look at me and took off running as fast as he could. It took a second for this to register and then I was hot on his heels. We ran through rough ground, I cut my foot on something and it was hurting, but I kept gaining on him.

When I got close enough, I swung the shovel handle back and came down on the top of his head hard. He fell down so suddenly that I tripped over him and came to a stop in the dirt twenty feet beyond, skinning my chest. By the time I got up, he had a good lead going in the other direction. I ran hard. My lungs felt like they were on fire and his must have been about done in because he ran into an apartment complex garage and by then I was close behind with the shovel handle. As I went to catch him he slid under one car and then under another. This went on for a while with me poking him with the sharp end of the stick. He stood up on the far side of a car and went to crying and begging. My intention had been to knock him out and drag him to the police, but his begging got to my soft spot, so I admonished him strongly and let him go.

Tw's back to framing. It paid good money, but it was killing me. Every day I ate lunch with a soft-spoken gentleman who wore an old fedora of a style from back in the forties. He was the electrical supervisor for the job, and he told me I should get a job as an electrician. I said I didn't know much about it, but anything was better than framing. He started teaching me for a few minutes every day. He taught me the names of all the tools, boxes, how to drill holes for the flex and particularly how to drill the corners. He taught me how to hold and cut the flex with a hacksaw and told me not to worry about what wire went where, because it always took two men to pull wire and everyone was happy to attach the wire while the other did the heavy work of pulling it through the flex. As to the union, he said that obstacle could be overcome by stating that I was an electrician from out of state and I should ask to sign the Right to 'Workbook.' He laid out his tools and drilled me on all the names: dikes, side cutters, strippers, etc., he advised me to try to find used tools so as not to look like a novice.

There were no used tools to be found, so I went to Sears and bought everything new. Early one morning, I strapped on the new yellow leather pouch, hung all the tools thereon, mounted Larry's motorcycle and headed down the freeway to Wilmington. After finding the IBEW (International Brotherhood of Electrical Workers) union hall, I parked and was in a dilemma as to what to do with all those new tools. If I left them hanging on the motorcycle they would be stolen, if I walked in everyone would laugh and wonder where this new guy came from. There was no choice, so I carried the tools inside. I looked around and found a vacant bench, slid them underneath and walked boldly up to the counter. The big-bellied union official had the personality of a junkyard dog and growled as he asked me what he could do for me. I told him I was an electrician from Georgia and wanted a job. He asked for my ticket and papers, which of course I didn't have. He looked up and said, "Next."

I said, "Mister, I demand to sign the right to the workbook."

Oh, was he pissed as he fumbled through the ledgers and found the hated book.

He slammed it down on the counter. Dust flew. He said, "You'll have a long white beard before you're ever called out of that book."

Next morning I was back early and the growly man wasn't on the counter. I waited as fifteen or twenty men were called and given jobs and when the man was about to close the window I walked up and asked about work. This man said he had not seen my name and I told him it was registered in the right to work book. He pulled it out and sure enough, there it was. He took a card and wrote, Webb Electric and an address in Inglewood. I saddled up, drove back up the freeway and found the address, just a couple blocks from downtown in the Chinese district. The job was thirty-two apartment units. Several men were working, and I met the contractor, Jim Webb, who took me around and showed me what he wanted to be done. Naturally, I didn't understand half of what he said, but I grunted like an old pro. This job paid seven dollars and fifty cents an hour an' if it required a little acting, I was game. One apartment had been completely wired and half the others were exact replicas. The other half was mirror images, which was confusing for a while. I worked for two years as an electrician, going out on all kinds of jobs and no one ever knew

The Redondo Beach Fire Department was reducing their working hours and they needed twelve new men. I answered the ad and was informed that they already had over four hundred applications, with more coming in daily. The big day came for the exam and so many men showed up that they sent us to a school auditorium where we took a test lasting several hours. That thing was hard, and I couldn't remember how to solve some simple fraction questions and got angry with myself.

After waiting a few weeks, I received a letter telling me to come for the physical agility test. First we had to do twenty-five pushups and 10 chin-ups. This eliminated over half the applicants. Then we had to run and climb over an eight-foot solid board fence, climb a one-hundred-ten foot ladder on the back of a hook-and-ladder truck, ring the bell attached to the top, come down and run around a field as fast as possible. There was no pass-fail. The twelve winners became firefighters.

I sat back and timed each man as he climbed the ladder and ran around the field. A good many couldn't get over the obstacle and I saw that if a man was just a little overweight he didn't make it. I also noticed the timing started when one began to climb the ladder and ended after the run around the field. The big difference in time was going up and down the ladder, with very little difference in the time it took to run around the field. I waited until late in the afternoon when everyone else had done his best and then I stepped up.

Up, up, up I ran without looking down and after jingling the bell I let the railing slide through my hands as I almost free-fell backdown, with my feet only hitting one rung in every five or six. My overall time was easily the fastest and I thought I would get an interview. Sure enough, I received an invitation for an interview by Chief Black. It went fine and I was hired. Later I learned I came out third on the written and first on the physical. The man who came out first on the written didn't pass the interview and only my friend John Crookston came in .01 percent ahead of me overall.

Twenty young men showed up at the Inglewood Academy for Firefighters, twelve for Redondo Beach and the others were from surrounding cities. We rappelled off the tower, folded fire hoses until we were sick, sprayed water on aluminum fires while the instructors laughed at us running from the explosions; we tied knots, practiced CPR on life-size dolls, did calisthenics, and had a good time.

April 12, 1970. Graduation night and stag party: Everyone was three sheets to the wind when we received a call from Captain Sanders at the Fire Department demanding that we all show up at the fire station forthwith or suffer his wrath. "What the hell, boys. Let's load up and go on down." We did and had a great time. What a way to meet the crew!

I was assigned to B shift, with Capt. Sanders as my boss. The first day I showed up for work the captain assigned me to pumper 2. After hanging my coat on the back of the truck, I sat down to a cup of coffee. Bells clanged and over the speaker came the announcement of a child not breathing. We arrived at the location within a minute. The place was dirty and greasy. The table and floor were covered in empty liquor bottles, beer cans and other trash that told of a bash. On the dining table was a big cake decorated with a penis and the caption, 'happy birthday cocksucker'. The woman of the house was young and a rather attractive redhead who directed us into a children's bedroom where a medicated humidifier was blowing. In a crib was a baby with a bluish-grey color. Cliff Bertrand took the child and began resuscitation and heart massage and color returned to the face, but every time he paused, the blue returned. He worked on that little blue corpse for a long time, but the baby was dead. A few months later, we were back to the same house and the woman was bleeding to death from a miscarriage.

The summer was a scorcher and I went with a pumper crew to help protect homes in the path of a huge forest fire in the mountains north of Los Angeles.

We fought fires for ten days and my eyes were as red as coals from all the smoke and ash, but the paycheck was the biggest I had ever received.

We were called out several times a shift, sometimes on big fires, but on another, a child might have a pin stuck in his foot; we got all kinds. Most of our runs were to the poorer, dirtier places. Seldom did a nice clean house catch fire.

Captain Sanders was getting a divorce and he offered to sell me his twenty-acre avocado ranch in Fallbrook, Orange County. Marrie and I drove down and looked it over. There was no house. It was in the dry season and everything was brown. The payments were reasonable, and he would finance the whole thing. I seriously considered buying, but finally decided against it. In hindsight, it was like telling Bill Gates you didn't want to buy his Microsoft stock before the initial offering.

A robber went into an antique store near the fire station, stuck a pistol in an old lady's face, and robbed her till of twenty dollars. As he was leaving, she threw a two-hundred-dollar vase that hit him in the back of the head, breaking both. He staggered to his feet and ran. She called the police. Soon cop cars were sliding in from all directions. Tow truck drivers heard the report and at least a dozen got in the melee. Two police helicopters circled low overhead. This was all in our front yard and the big doors were open. We were anxious to know what was happening, so several of the firemen packed into the cab of the hook and ladder truck, the only vehicle we had with the police frequency. Larry Denhart saw this, ran to his locker, returned with a cherry bomb, and threw it under the truck. The explosion shook the big empty building. I was looking at a policeman across the street as he started to go under a house with his pistol drawn. He banged his head so hard that he fell and lost his hat. He lay on his back, jerked out his radio, and yelled, "Shots fired at Pearl and Broadway, shots fired at Pearl and Broadway, officer needs assistance!" I almost busted my sides laughing. When I could catch my breath, I picked up the radio and explained that it was a firecracker at the fire station.

The communication center was in the rear of the station where a female operator took the calls. This was the private harem of Battalion Chief Louver and off limits to us common mortals. Anyway, when the firecracker went off Chief Loover was on duty at his usual station and he locked and barred the door. After my radio call, the police dispatcher called the fire dispatcher and Chief Loover confirmed that shots had been fired in or near the fire station. Soon it looked like World War II with so many guns pointed at us. I walked out on the apron waving my hands and explained to the police captain that it had indeed been a firecracker and he started yelling at me. Captain Sanders came running out, slung his hat in the street and said to me, "You loudmouth piece-a-shit. If you have anything to say, say it to me and I will kick your ass right here, right now!"

Thank you, Captain Sanders!

Next day the headlines read "POP GOES THE ROBBER."

Captain John McBride transferred to our shift and we became friends. Work was a real pleasure with him on board. There were three shifts and I became the cook for ours. The men chipped in a couple of dollars each. I always took a portable radio whenever I went to the supermarket to buy groceries and we did eat well. I was always calling Marrie and asking questions about cooking and sometimes she would come to the station, take my hand and show me how it was done.

However, C-shift had a bunch of porkers who were always trying to lose weight, therefore they didn't have a food fund. We'd put our leftovers in the refrigerator and attach signs, but they'd get hungry and would eat every morsel. OK, now, what to do? John came up with an excellent idea; we made special beef enchiladas. We bought half a dozen cans of Heinz dog food, pulled out the biggest veins and made a tray full of enchiladas. After they were golden brown, we took them out of the oven, sprinkled grated cheese on top and melted this. The enchiladas were beautiful, a work of art. We cut out one quarter, threw it in the trash, the remainder we covered ever so pretty with tin foil and taped the sign *DO NOT EAT- LUNCH FOR B SHIFT*, in big bold letters.

We were off the next day and when we came in the following morning, the tray was empty, unwashed and covered with crumbs. Captain McBride acted angry and demanded to know just who ate our lunch. The men started confessing, one ate three, another four and Gary Edmonds ate seven! A quarter each was duly collected. Then out came the empty dog food cans with the veins and bones. Some of them tried to vomit, others got angry and we laughed to our heart's content. The following day there was a big announcement on the bulletin board stating: "Gary Edmonds killed. Yes, he was lying in the road licking his balls, when a car ran over him."

Working a 56-hour week and doing 24 hours at a time meant we worked nine days a month, with the other twenty-one free. Marrie was managing the apartments and I began contract painting. We put an ad in the newspaper. She answered the phone, screening the calls and soon I had more work than I could possibly do. I raised my price, hired several painters, and started making money.

One-third ownership of a Cessna 150 was for sale for eleven-hundred dollars and I became the proud owner of a third of an airplane. I never met one of the partners, as he never flew, so it was between just two. I hired a flight instructor to give me a few lessons and as soon as I had soloed and been signed off, I was at the airport every chance I got. Cessna Aircraft Company sold a kit course that had 600 questions of which the Federal Aviation Administration would ask 60 on the Private Pilots examination. I took the test and made 100 percent.

Marrie and I traveled throughout southern California. We made Marya a pallet in the luggage space behind the seats and flew to Catalina Island for a lunch of buffalo burgers. This was our favorite spot. The airport was on a mountain top with a rustic lodge and a big patio. Hummingbird feeders hung from the eves and I'd never seen the likes of so many beautiful little creatures. Sometimes we took a van down into Avalon, spent the day strolling about the little town, went to the wharf and watched the seaplanes landing and taking off.

When it was time to leave I pushed the nose over at the end of the runway and skimmed down the side of the mountain until we found a herd of bison grazing, then circle for a bit. On the far side of the island, the water was an unusual turquoise color where we often saw sharks lying in the shallow water. During certain times of the year, we could see pods of whales frolicking between the island and mainland, we would circle, turn into the wind and get right above them. From that distance and at such a slow speed they were clearly visible.

Another favorite spot was Meadow Lark Airport in Orange County; they made delicious hamburgers. On day excursions, we'd sometimes go to Jim's Air in San Diego or up to Santa Ynez, rent an old 1958 Chevy Impala, go for a ride in the oaks, and look for deer. We flew over Montecito, Santa Barbara and Hope Ranch and were in awe of the beauty and amazing wealth of those places, never dreaming we would soon live there.

Westward, forty miles beyond Catalina, lies the tiny island of Santa Barbara, the farthest island out and approximately seventy miles from the mainland. This was my private get-a-way for several years. The Island is less than two miles long, one mile across, and reaches a height of 600 feet on the west end. The NW side is steep, but the SE side is more gradual, and I'd land uphill and come to a stop within a hundred feet.

Many years before, wheat had been grown on the island. During W.W.II, the Navy had a runway with two Quonset huts and a landing pier on the SE quarter. There was no sign of the old dirt runway, but the two Quonset huts were still standing. There were several canyons with steep rocky sides full of red rabbit dens. The government had released foxes to eat the rabbits and I would sometimes see a beautiful red fox. I brought diving equipment and dove among exquisite coral, and bright red garibaldi perch, the state fish. The Island was literally covered in rare and unusual plants. There is one palm-like plant that was completely covered in bright yellow flowers at a certain season and this is the only place on earth it grows. Whales seemed to be attracted to the island and I often watched them playing directly below the cliffs.

On the NW section of the island and at the highest point, the island stops as though a huge knife sliced one part off leaving a perpendicular wall straight down for over six hundred feet. At the top is an acre or so of smooth looking pasture and I wanted to land and take off over the cliff. Ann, a pretty blond nurse from Georgia, was visiting my sister Marijo. I told her about the island and she and I flew over one afternoon. We circled, and on a whim I decided to land on that green pasture. I turned into the stiff breeze, brought the plane in at just above stall speed and touched down, going no more than 15mph. The tail flew up, it slid forward on the nose wheel, came to a sudden stop, and fell on all three tires. That smooth looking ground cover was a knee-deep ice plant. We got out and found large stones scattered all through the plants. What a predicament! Should I radio an SOS? I felt like a pure idiot! I tried clearing a space and found the job impossible. I removed the tangle of vines off the nose wheel and struts, then stomped out somewhat of a path. To heck with seeing the Island, we were in a dangerous situation.

There was nothing to do but try to take off. I showed Ann how the throttle worked. Next I held the tail down and yelled for her to give it full power and pull back on the yoke. The propeller blades bit into the juicy ice plant and both the plane and I were instantly covered in green goo. Once the plane was rolling as fast as I could run, and Ann was screaming for me to get in, I managed to climb aboard just before going over the cliff. The door was still open, and my feet were not yet on the rudder pedals as I pushed the yoke full forward praying the belly or tail wouldn't snag on the cliff. We headed straight down with full throttle the stall-warning horn blaring. Almost immediately we were flying. I pulled back on the yoke and headed for the mainland with shaking knees. It was impossible to see through the goo-covered windshield. I had to stick my head out the open window to see how to land at Torrance airport.

Back at the fire station, I related my adventure with the pretty nurse, my passenger to Santa Barbara Island. Captain McBride wanted to meet her and check out this tale. I invited him over, both passed inspection and it wasn't long before they were engaged.

At the fire station we told tales and John started writing some of mine down. He declared that *no one* my age could have possibly done all those things. He'd say, "Now *who* was the man you made moonshine with?"

Or, "*Who* was it that you almost shot his damned legs off at the knees?"

This went on and on until he had something written down. John went to Georgia to visit Ann, and while there, he looked up some of the people in my tall tales. First he went to Homer's and got a gallon of moonshine. From there he went to see Terrell Clements and told him that Roger Reaves had an airplane and was going to land on the highway right in front of his store and give him a ride. Terrell said, "You tell that silly son-of-a-bitch that I wouldn't ride with him if he was pushing a wheelbarrow!"

John returned with a good report on my versions of the tales. He and Ann were married in Georgia. They had one daughter and lived happily ever after.

—Herald-Examiner Photo

FIREMEN ENJOY TASTE OF VICTORY AFTER DEFEATING A 'HONEY OF A BLAZE'

Munching honey combs taken from fire — Roger Reaves

Post fire, munching on honeycomb. I'm on the right. This event led to a life long fascination with bees. Eventually I had 500 hives.
Image courtesy Herald Examiner 1070

Flames were gushing out the windows and licking up the side of an apartment building when we arrived with the first pumper. We put the fire out, but the apartment was charred. We began to tear into the hot spots, to make sure there'd be no rekindle. Suddenly the guys started throwing down their tools and running out, yelling that bees were stinging them. I looked around and saw the floor was covered with bees, but they weren't bothering me. I saw a stream of hot honey oozing through a crack in the ceiling and began tearing plaster away with my pike pole. Running across the entire ceiling was a heating and air-conditioning duct and on top of this was a beehive that extended from the outside wall all the way across the living room and bedroom. At the rear, the honeycomb was old and black, but near the outside wall, it was bright and golden. I ran to the ladder truck, grabbed two washtubs, and put one on a stepladder and started filling it with honeycomb. A newspaperman came in and told me to take a bite. Sure enough, as soon as I did, he snapped a photo. The next morning there I was on the front page, taking a big bite of honeycomb with the caption 'BEES IN FIREMAN'S BONNET'. Naturally, my new nickname became "Bee Man."

The next day after work, John McBride and John Crookston came home with me. (Thank goodness, Marrie wasn't there.) We carried the tubs of honey into the house. I commandeered a pair of pantyhose and we started heating and straining smoked honey. I don't remember how many pints we ended up with, but it was delicious! We gave it as gifts and had honey for a long time. We left the kitchen spotless, and to my surprise, never got in trouble.

Roger Keeney, a jewel of a man with a twinkle in his blue eyes and a gold mine in the mountains, owned an FBO (fixed base operation) at the Torrance Airport. I bought gas from him and he kept the airplane in excellent mechanical condition. One day he took me behind his hangar and showed me an old derelict building where bees were busy coming and going through a knothole. I had an idea. I went home and brought back a fireman's helmet and some veil material. Wearing this armor, I cut into the building, took the honey, and placed the bees into a proper hive behind Roger's hangar. Thus began my bee-keeping days.

Whenever a fire department in the area reported a swarm of bees landing, they called me, and I would go and collect them. It wasn't long before I had over thirty hives. However, later the City of Torrance made me move all the hives from the airport property.

Bees interested me, I studied and read all I could about them. Sometimes I would remove a swarm with my bare hands and have photographs of them hanging from my chin and reaching to my knees. Jim Roberts, a friend from church, had a dear old friend who lived in the desert a couple of hours drive north of Los Angeles. Both our families decided to visit the man and his wife.

The couple invited us to spend the night. The next morning the old man was flipping pancakes for breakfast and said, "Let us thank the Lord for our new friends and this bountiful breakfast." We all bowed our heads and he began to pray, however, I noticed he was still flipping pancakes and putting them on our plates while he prayed. It was wonderful. I told him of my problem finding a place for the beehives and he invited me to bring the hives on his property. It was a perfect location situated on a bluff over a dry riverbed covered in sage and wildflowers. I kept collecting bees until by 1974, I had 500 hives.

9. NORTH TO ALASKA

Moose Hunt-Commercial Fisherman- Together Again- Chichagof Island Flag

Mark Howard, a young man from Alaska, lived in our apartment complex and he loved to tell tall tales of the frozen north. Being that I had always wanted to go to Alaska, it didn't take long for us to get up a trip. A few shift trades at the Fire Department gave me thirteen days off. We loaded up the 150 Cessna with sleeping bags, tarp, frying pan and a few groceries and headed north, following the coast of California, Oregon and Washington. The scenery was stunning.

We spent the first night in a hangar on Vancouver Island, Canada. The next morning I purchased charts for the Canadian portion of the journey and was advised to take the inland route, however, I wanted to see the famous old mining towns and glaciers along the coast. We got a late start and after a few hundred miles, I ran out of charts. The salesclerk had skipped one. What should I do? I had been following the Inland Passage and every now and then we could see fishing boats, or tugs pushing barges loaded with logs traveling on a northerly direction, however, there were many channels, all looking alike and running in every reading of the compass. I continued on a northerly heading. Just when I was about to turn back, I saw a passenger liner coming our way and I knew I was on track. Late in the afternoon we crossed the border into Alaska, landed on Annette Island, where we parked in a humungous hangar, rolled out our sleeping bags under the wing, and spent a good night.

The next morning we headed out for Juneau. After a hundred miles we encountered low lying clouds and had to climb over them. Juneau weather was reported as being good, so I kept heading north.

The clouds below became thicker and higher. We continued at 9,500 feet with a dark layer of clouds above. I was nervous. We had to continue because we were beyond the point of no return. I didn't have an instrument rating nor was our small Cessna equipped for instrument flying.

All at once the layers merged and we were in the soup. I turned around, but the clouds closed in thick and dark. We were past the half waypoint, the point of no return. I kept heading north and climbing, trying to get a signal from the VOR at one of the stations along the coast. What I didn't know was that we had an 80 mph wind blowing from the west and we were being blown inland over the Rockies.

I could not get a signal from anywhere. I turned the radio to 121.7, the emergency channel, and called out a mayday. No answer. I gave the mike to Mark and told him to keep calling and I decided the best thing to do was to head west, figuring that when we had to descend we would be over water and not the mountains.

We ran into ice! The windshield was soon covered two or three inches thick and I could see it building on the leading edges of the wings and struts. Next, the wind instruments went out and I knew the Pitot tube had iced over. I applied pitot heat but to no avail. I wasn't strong at flying in instrument conditions, making it more difficult with the few instruments I did have; without the airspeed indicator and altimeter, our tiny airship was going up and down like a roller coaster. The only way I could determine the airspeed was by the sound of the wind on the airframe. The weather became worse, it seemed we had flown into a dark night. Ice pellets pounded the small aircraft with a deafening noise.

Mark started screaming, "We are going to die! We are going to die!" I yelled at him to shut up. I was also of the same opinion but determined to fight to the end. After an hour of this, I figured we must be over water and I pushed the nose over and headed down.

After a bit I saw granite out my side window, pulled up, and turned hard to the right. I tried climbing on a westerly heading, but she wouldn't climb as she was just mushing through the air loaded down with all that ice. I heard the radio pick up a station ever so faintly. SIT in Morse code beeped in my ears. Sitka VOR was coming in intermittently and the radio-heading needle swung intermittingly to the southwest. The fuel gauge indicators were dead on empty, I had to descend. I did not want to end up over the islands all iced up, out of fuel with a dead stick, so I took the chance and headed down, every fiber of my body tensed.

I prayed, 'Oh Lord, don't let it be now.' We came out the bottom of the clouds at what I guessed to be three thousand feet. There below was the sea whipped into a white fury embracing scattered islands covered with boulders and huge green trees. Sitka radio was coming in clear and I headed for the signal. All the ice came off, but still the pitot remained frozen. I held my breath, willing it to make Sitka, meanwhile rolling the wings back and forth to slosh the remaining gasoline into the pickup tube.

I declared an emergency, and Sitka radio kept encouraging me. There was an 80 mph wind from the west, so the controller advised me to come over the hangars and land on the apron, crossways to the runway, as they did not have an east-west runway. When I flew over the hangars and reduced power and started flying backward, I had to apply power to reach the apron. Once down I had to apply power to *stay* on the apron. A fish truck drove in front of me. Men jumped out, secured ropes to the plane and I shut her down.

We were given a warm welcome and large whiskeys. The man and woman who had spoken on the radio were especially nice. The firemen invited us to sleep in the station, the lady from the weather service invited me to dinner. She prepared a dish of halibut, smothered in tomato sauce. Mmmm—it was delicious! The fire department engineer, Don Reaver, invited me to his home where I met his wife Donna and their children. He took me fishing the next day. I caught a 20-pound king salmon, but I was the one hooked. Don laughed at my enthusiasm and invited me to come to Sitka and work for the fire department.

After a couple of days, we said goodbye to our new friends and headed north. I had learned a valuable lesson about getting on top and being suckered in between clouds, so now I stayed in sight of the ground. I thought of my old friend, Bud Graham, who I had invited to go flying. He just answered, "No sirs, Roger, the good Lord don't want me to fly in nary air-o-plane."

"Why d'ya say that Bud?"

"Cause the Lord said, 'Low. I will be with you always, even to the end of the world.'"

Just south of Yakutat, we started seeing moose and I wanted to go hunting. We landed in the village and I bought a hunting license and rented a 30.06 rifle from a bush pilot. We spent a miserable wet night under a tarp stretched over the wing of the Cessna. Next morning we ate breakfast in a local restaurant that was so expensive I ordered two eggs and toast, and left off the two strips of bacon, saving four dollars. As we flew back south, I saw several moose in the bend of the river. One was an old granddad with a big set of antlers. A half-mile on, I noticed a rough bush strip. I landed and taxied up to a small hut where we found four wooden bunks, a wood stove, and a few emergency rations.

We sloshed out on the tundra and after wading around an hour in ice water I found my prey. Moose have such poor eyesight that I was able to walk within a hundred yards. I shot. He started to run, and I shot again. He froze, picked up his rear leg, stood like that for the longest time, and then toppled over. I eased over to him and poked him with my rifle. He blinked those big soft brown eyes at me, and I was sorry, truly sorry. I took out my pistol, delivered the coup de grace behind his ear, and watched as the life left his eyes and they slowly clouded over. I repented that I had killed such a magnificent creature. Right then and there I knew I would never kill another beast like that again unless I was hungry.

The work began. He most likely weighed a thousand pounds and his antlers were six feet across. I skinned him. The hide was a good inch thick. After quartering up the carcass, I had to carry it back to the hut and by now grizzlies were closing in on the smell of blood. There were six or seven that I could see and they were not afraid but kept their distance in the bushes. I left Mark with the carcass and rifle while I stumbled the half-mile back to camp through the ice water with a 100-pound chunk of moose on my back. The job was exhausting. On the last trip, I carried the antlers with Mark walking behind. I turned around and saw he had the pistol cocked and pointing at my back. He was terrified of the bears. So much for all his brave stories!

In Yakutat, I packed the meat for shipping to Anchorage on Alaskan Air Lines. That day a Boeing 727 crashed on approach to Juneau killing all one hundred and sixty people on board. For the next week, the flights were full of bodies. The law prohibits fresh meat and human bodies on the same flight, a law that I most definitely agree with. I left the meat with the agent and flew on to Anchorage. A week later, the meat arrived, and I took it to an abattoir where it was sliced and packaged. We took one quarter to Mr. Holland and had a big cookout. The meat was delicious, but that which went through the abattoir and reached California was rank and inedible. The abattoir had swapped the meat for some old bull in rut.

On the return trip we flew north to Fairbanks and from there turned south, following the Trans-Alaska Highway. The country was barren with reddish-brown tundra blending into the horizon. Off in the distance I saw a pack of wolves loping across the desolate landscape. I turned and dropped altitude to get a better look. There were fifteen or twenty in the pack with a black male as the leader. As I came closer, he looked up and bared his teeth. The hair stood up all around his neck. He quickly changed directions and the pack followed. I took out my camera and started clicking, continuing to tighten the circle. The circle got too small, the lower wing stalled and in the twinkling of an eye, it rolled on its left side and dove for the ground. Miraculously I recovered only inches from the tundra. I continued south with my knees shaking, having used up another of the numerous lives allotted.

The fire department no longer held any charm. I couldn't get Alaska out of my mind. I dreamed of buying a salmon trawler and fishing in the summer for the two or three month season and fly as a bush pilot the remainder of the year. My friend Don, from the Sitka fire department, found a converted 38-foot Bristol Bay gill-netter for three thousand dollars. So, on April 1, 1972 I took a leave of absence from the fire department and caught a commercial flight to Sitka. Don was happy to see me, and we went directly to look the vessel over. Her lines were graceful, and she looked so inviting sitting amongst all the colorful fishing boats with their outriggers reaching for the clouds, which were not much above them. Yes, I wanted to buy her, and the transaction was soon completed.

The fire chief invited me to stay at the fire station free of charge, so long as I made runs when I was there. What a deal.

Sitka has extreme tides, making it an easy matter to clean and paint the bottom of a boat. You find a piling or tree, tie alongside and when the tide goes out, she sits high and dry for several hours. I tied her to a tree and went to work cleaning and painting the bottom with anti-fouling paint. Then I began above the waterline. Within a week, she was all painted with happy colors. The inside was Spartan. There were two wooden slabs to sleep on, a fuel oil stove and a chemical toilet. That was it, nothing else. I built a few cabinets and painted the whole inside a glossy white, trimmed in sunflower yellow, and she looked cheerful. The stove worked *most* of the time, I kept it going around the clock because of the cold and damp, often leaving the grate open so I could see the flames.

Don taught me all he could about fishing for the Kings, as these particular salmon are called. However, no one can learn from instructions alone. You gotta get wet, cold, seasick, and slimy with fish guts. You gotta run aground, get lost in the fog, have the native fishermen curse you for some stupid mistake, and make a couple thousand more blunders before you are a real fisherman. I literally hated baiting hooks on a rolling deck. I gagged, vomited, got dizzy, cursed, and wondered why anyone would choose a profession such as this.

Most days I trolled for sixteen hours without catching anything except big red bass, which only brought ten cents a pound and weren't worth keeping. If I was in sight of land, a Bald Eagle would recognize the free feed and soar out. The bass came up from the depth so quickly that its air sack inflated and popped out of his mouth. When I took him off the hook and threw him back, he couldn't get down under the surface of the water, an eagle would swoop down, snatch him up, and fly back to his perch onshore and eat him. Sometimes the fish was too big for the eagle and it was a struggle for the eagle to get his claws unhooked. I once saw a bird get pulled down and only his wings beating the surface kept him up. If that bass had not had his swimmer hanging out, it would have been the fish that caught the bird! There were so many eagles—an Instamatic snapshot we took had sixty-five eagles in one photo!

The whole game was feast or famine. Sometimes I got into a school of 20 to 40-pound Kings, and within a few minutes, the deck would be literally covered in fish. During those rare times I couldn't do anything but bring in fish and snap-on hooks; and a lot of hooks are needed for these special occasions.

Once I lost the school, I started gutting and packing them in ice. Salmon are soft and delicate. You can't just gaff him and throw him on the deck and watch him flip- flop around until he dies, this knocks off scales and bruises the skin, and people won't buy such a fish. You take the leader and guide him to the back of the boat, lift his head out of the water, and hit him at a special place on the back of the head that kills him instantly. Then you gaff him in the gills, lift him into the boat and lay him on burlap. When you get the time, you place him belly up in a trough without ends and gut him. Then he goes into the ice hole. Pack him full of shaved ice and ice all around him, and then he is worth a dollar or more per pound.

That little vessel was named the Capella II. She was built of wood in 1890 as a sailing vessel, but someone had converted her to power with a four-cylinder gasoline engine, capable of five knots in good weather. Her claim to fame was that she had caught the world's largest salmon and there was a brass plaque by the entranceway with the date and weight of the fish. As I remember, it was a King, over six feet long, and weighed one- hundred twenty-two pounds.

Now the following is the truth and not just another fisherman's tale. One grey morning, I was twenty or thirty miles out beyond the last island, putt-putting along at about two knots. I hadn't gotten a bite all day. Suddenly there was a hard jerk on the rear starboard outrigger, the cable started coming up and swinging out in a long arc at a terrific rate. I flipped the lever to the gurney that wound in the cable and soon there appeared the biggest salmon. He was so big my hands trembled just looking at him. I took the gaff in my right hand and with my left, I pulled his head out of the water and gave him a sharp rap on the back of the head. This tore the hook out of his mouth, and he rolled over belly up. He seemed to follow the boat for a few feet and then began sinking. I tried to gaff him, but the handle was too short. I had the strongest urge to jump in and grab him, but it dawned on me as to where I was, and this only caused me to shake worse. I don't know how big he was. I'm sure he weighed a hundred pounds or more. In any case, he was huge, and I was sick that it was now just another fish story and not a world record.

Every week I came in with the catch and sold it to Sitka Cold Storage, where I purchased fuel, ice, groceries, bait, and fishing tackle. This purchase usually included a number of lead cannonballs. It was hard work staying even. The fish weren't running that summer and I learned that 10% of the fishermen catch 90% of the fish; a fact that can be applied to all businesses.

An old cannery building on the waterfront was a happy watering hole for a rowdy boisterous crowd and I liked to go there on Saturday nights. The song '*Put Your Hands in the Hands of the Man from Galilee*' was popular and I was offended at it being sung in such a place. However, there were other new ones out in 1972, such as *Jeremiah Was a Bull Frog*. I wondered if the whole world was going to hell. A lady bartender began giving me beers on the house and asked a lot of questions about my coming to Alaska and fishing all alone.

One night she leaned across the counter, looked me deep in the eyes, and said, "If there is ever anything I can do for you, just let me know." I thanked her, but it excited me.

The following Saturday as I was shoveling out the old ice in the fish hole, there was a knock on the hull. To my surprise, there stood the woman from the bar. I invited her aboard and made her a cup of coffee and it looked like she was going to spend the day. As I was at the commercial wharf I had to move the boat. I untied and started up the engine to move to my regular slip, but when I put the gear in reverse the shaft broke and water began rushing in. I quickly crammed clothes and bedding in the hole, partially stemming the flood and got someone to tow me to a boatyard. This shed me of the woman problem, but now I had one I couldn't fix.

I took the broken shaft out and my friend Don told me of a machinist who could repair it, if I had enough money to keep him in whiskey. We met and he was a caustic old cuss, but I soon found it was all bluster and that he was really a pussycat in disguise. He drank and welded, told stories, drank some more and then put the shaft on a lathe. This went on all night long and by breakfast, I had a virtually new shaft.

The next day as I was getting ready to depart, Don came down with his daughter and told me I needed help on the boat and his daughter would work for 10% of the catch, which was a normal percentage. I couldn't believe it. To be cooped up all summer in a space not much bigger than a closet with a good looking eighteen-year-old gal with flaming red hair, and no telling what *other* flames. It sounded like more trouble than I could afford. I declined the offer, and he looked at me like I was the crazy one. He told me of an incident the previous summer; a young man and his girlfriend ran on the rocks and sank the boat. She was the stronger swimmer and got to land, He drowned. It was three weeks before the rescuers found her on a small island in a near-death condition. Don and his daughter left disappointed and I steamed into the sunset wishing Marrie was here.

The next Saturday at about noon, I entered the harbor and as I was nearing the cold storage, I saw Marrie and Marya standing on the dock. They were dressed in identical white sailor suits with a deep blue anchor embroidered on the collars. My heart almost exploded. I couldn't get the boat tied up fast enough. They had found a room with some nice people and we stayed there for the night, sleeping double in a single bed. The next day they moved aboard. There was plenty of space; Marrie and I each had a narrow bunk and Marya slept on the floor between us. With Marrie steering, life was now easy.

After a couple of days, we pulled into Saint John the Baptist Bay, a virtual paradise. It was after eleven o'clock in the evening, but the sun was still shining on the placid water. The scenery was indescribably glorious. I tied a line around a large limb hanging out over the water. We cooked dinner and then placed paper and jackets over the hatches to block out the light and soon fell asleep. I woke up dreaming that my neck was breaking and realized my head was pressing into the bulkhead at a forty-five-degree angle. The tide had gone out and left us hanging from that limb. The deck was so steep I had to climb to the bow. Once there, I found the line pulled as tight as a banjo string. It would never have come untied. I cut it and the bow of the boat fell straight down ten feet. We were learning fast.

The way a king salmon catches his dinner is to run through a school of small fish and whip his tail back and forth, stunning or even killing some. He then turns around and gobbles them up. Naturally, when other fish see the tail slapping and the belly flashing, they rush in for a free meal.

We lost a fish or two most every day to sharks or seals. When these big salmon get on the line, it takes several minutes to bring them up from the deep. On the way they fight for their life, thrashing, their white bellies flashing, a sure signal to the shark that dinner is ready. It's just sickening when the shark cuts the salmon in two, sometimes one after another. I do believe a shark will purposely follow a vessel knowing he will have easy pickings. Usually they strike four or five inches behind the gills and cut the salmon in two as clean as any razor-sharp knife. Oftentimes I had the twenty-foot leader in my hand when I saw a shadow coming up from the deep, and felt the line go limp. Then, for supper, we dined on one-inch thick steaks. This was the only time we ate salmon steaks, as we never thought of butchering one of those big fish for ourselves; they were too expensive.

Goddard Hot Springs is located on one of the outer island's southwest of Sitka and this became our favorite anchorage. Fishermen have their favorite spots, and some become jealous of what they call their area and are secretive about it. I preferred to fish in the open ocean, yet not too far from land and preferably along the shelf before the bottom dropped off to infinity. Goddard wasn't too far to come in when we got tired of blue water and wanted a rest and a change of scenery.

Every few days we pulled into Goddard, dropped anchor, put three big Idaho potatoes in the oven, lowered the dinghy and rowed ashore. The island looked as it must have a thousand or a million years ago, I felt as though no one had ever walked on it. Massive trees with *bear bread* growing as big as a hat was attached to most of the trunks and giant ferns grew anywhere they could get a bit of light. Big granite boulders were scattered haphazardly. Everything was covered in a bed of soft needles from the tall conifers overhead. Drizzle fell continuously. We pulled our dingy up on the shore and secured it firmly. Then we were off through the woods. The three of us tramped until we found the hot spring. Years before someone had carved a small pool out of stone and a two-inch plastic pipe lay nearby with boiling water gushing out. On the other side was a similar hose with cold water flowing. I put a four-inch log stopper in the drain and started filling the pool. When half full, we climbed in and regulated the temperature, making it hotter and hotter. This was a lot of fun and sometimes the three of us bound out at once because it got too hot and sprayed each other with the cold water to cool down. We usually stayed the better part of an hour soaking in the hot water, then walked back through the woods, steam rising from our pink bodies. We had to be careful with our young daughter Marya, whenever she got too hot she would vomit, and I realized her little body became too hot much quicker than ours. The heat drained our energy, sometimes we could barely get back to the dinghy.

Once back on our cozy boat, we made hot buttered rum drinks. Yum, yum, were those things delicious! Marrie put a pat of butter in a large iron frying pan and cooked the salmon steaks. Nothing ever tasted better! After dinner, Marya curled up on her soft pallet on the floor and Marrie and I would have the sweetest sleep imaginable. The next morning, while they were still sleeping, I pulled up anchor and headed back out.

We passed that summer lost in love and happiness. Life was wonderful. We were young and beautiful, and the world was ours.

We met a couple in town who had a little girl Marya's age and they invited Marrie and Marya to stay in their home. I was lonely out there all by myself, so on the next trip I asked Marrie to come with me. The couple insisted Marya stay with them and that was all right with us.

Thirty and forty pound Kings were hitting the deck left and right. We were having the best day of the season. Suddenly over the radio we heard a little boy crying and begging for help. He said their boat had an explosion and his father was lying on the floor, blood coming out of his ears, his legs were broken and twisted, the boat was on fire, please, please, please, somebody help me. The child was crying in hysterics and the plea made my blood run cold. I knew he was nearby because of the reception. I got on the radio and asked if he knew where he was, and he said he didn't. That was his last broadcast.

The Coast Guard came on the air asking if anyone could see a vessel drifting or on fire. I gave my position and so did several other boats. We were told to be on the lookout for a partially sunk or burning boat. Soon the Coast Guard helicopter was overhead.

The cries of the boy lingered in my mind and laid heavy on my spirits that day; I was always on the lookout for any sign of the boy and his boat. While standing in the fish well at the stern, facing to the rear, I was gutting a big thirty-five pound King, and as I turned to lay him on the deck I noticed the bow of a vessel upside down. The bow was covered with barnacles and sticking ten or twelve feet up out of the water. I could see the shadow of the overturned hull just beneath the surface and I was concerned my propeller was going to hit the keel. I jumped out of the fish well, ran forward and disengaged the gear lever. By the time I could look again, I saw my mistake. It was not an overturned boat. It was a giant blue whale surfacing under my boat.

What I thought was an upside bow was his dorsal fin covered with barnacles. He surfaced only a few feet from the stern and blew his warm stinking breath all over me. Hooks began biting into his blubber; he felt the pain, rolled and sounded. My rigging folded like it was made of haywire as the four six-thousand pound cables brought it all crashing down around me. I grabbed a little instamatic and started snapping pictures because I could never expect anyone to believe *this* fish story. The brakes were set on the hydraulic gurneys and they were smoking as the cables peeled off. Capella II was going backward faster than she had ever gone forward with the transom nearly underwater. We looked like a giant cork on a big fishing line. When it was all over, everything to fish with was gone. We were out of business.

The cries of the little boy were a hoax.

As my brother Larry says, "When life gives you lemons, make lemonade," and that is just what we did. We went into town, had all the twisted iron cut off the deck, and made a cradle to hold the skiff. Marya stayed with friends and Marrie and I set sail into the wild blue Pacific. I suppose this became the most memorable vacation of my life. We went to Chichagof Island, an area larger than Rhode Island that few have ever heard of. We explored old gold mines, abandoned at the turn of the previous century. Rain gear and rubber boots still hung in the bunkhouse. An ax stuck in a block of wood by the fireplace looked as though it had not been touched for a hundred years. The table was set with dinner plates, broken after they filled with water and later froze. The overseer's house was askew from the movement of the earth over the past century, although the roses in the wallpaper were still a lovely dusty-rose color. We followed the rails into what was the richest strikes on earth. We read receipts for groceries bought a hundred years before and a few old love letters that had been left behind. We read one stained but elegant letter on personalized stationery and wondered if the recipient ever returned to Kentucky and the lady with the beautiful handwriting.

There's gold and it's haunting and haunting.
It's luring me on as of old.
Yet it isn't the gold that I'm wanting
So much as just finding the gold.
It's a great, big broad land way up yonder,
It's the forest where silence has lease.
It's the beauty that thrills me with wonder,
It's the stillness that fills me with peace.
--- Robert W. Service, *Spell of the Yukon*

The normally graceful Canadian geese were feeding in the area and some get so fat they can't fly. I took my 30.06 rifle out and tried to shoot one in the head so as not to spoil the meat. Sometimes I nicked feathers, however with the boat rocking and his bobbing in the waves I couldn't hit my target. I decided to run him down and kill him with a paddle. What a chase! Each time I got within striking distance, he would dive underwater, and I would paddle like mad with Marrie laughing and yelling that I would never catch him. I was determined to prove her wrong and have goose for supper, and he was determined that I shouldn't. I wanted to get the rifle and shoot him, but by some unspoken honor, I couldn't cheat. Round and round and up and down we went. He must have lost weight, because he finally got up and walked, his wings beating the water into a white spray. In the end, he wore me out. What a wonderful afternoon!

For thousands of years, Asians employed glass blowers on their fishing vessels. The artisans blew glass balls of all sizes for floaters to hold up the nets. These glass balls come in all colors and often have the stamp of the particular artisan or vessel. Naturally, many were lost during storms and it is estimated that some will float on the endless currents of the vast 70 million square miles of Pacific Ocean for the next million years. Each spring after the fierce winter storms they can be found in the log jams on the beaches of Alaska. Once we were out of the fishing business, hunting for glass balls became our favorite pastime. We would anchor behind an island, Marrie would walk one way and I the other. We scrambled over and searched amongst the tangle of bone-white logs washed up in huge piles along the shoreline. We found several glass balls and were really getting into this hobby.

The woods were filled with both Black and Grizzly Bears, Marrie always carried a .44 caliber pistol and I took the 30.06 rifle. One afternoon as I was coming to the end of the beach a doe ran out and right behind her was a big grizzly. She saw that she was hemmed in by a rocky bluff, turned, and ran back through the surf, but the bear was faster and headed her off. As she dodged back toward the pile of logs, he struck her down in the surf. I was perhaps a hundred yards away and this angered me to see what I knew went on daily. I fired my rifle over the head of the bear he turned and looked at me, then loped off into the forest, abandoning his kill. I walked up to the deer and saw why the bear chose this target. She was in the process of giving birth. I could see the little nose sticking out. I carried a razor-sharp knife in my pocket and with a couple of swipes I laid her open and took the little fawn out, still wrapped in the placenta. He was alive and frisky right off. I took off my T-shirt, dried him off, put him down my coat sleeve, and hurried toward Marrie.

I tried to act nonchalant as I walked back to where I had left her on the beach. She eagerly asked what I had shot. I told her it was a big grizzly; she threw her head back and laughed. I told her I found something pretty and she was to close her eyes and put her hand down my coat sleeve.

She replied, "Roger Reaves, I would never put my hand in your pocket. There is no telling what kind of varmint you found!" I promised she would be happy and finally persuaded her to touch. When she felt the whiskered nose, her eyes opened wide with sparkle and wonder. You should have seen the radiance on her face as she pulled the fawn out and held him to her breast.

We carried him back to the boat, made him a nice bed in a box and tried to get him to drink milk from our fingers and made a milk and sugar tit. Nothing we did encouraged him to even try to eat and by the following afternoon, we decided he would die. We took off for Sitka and arrived the third day. When

Marya saw the little fawn she squealed, picked him up and hugged him to her. He grabbed her ear lobe and started sucking for all he was worth. Marrie hurried for a doll bottle that wasn't much bigger than my thumb and filled it with milk. As the fawn sucked on Marya's ear, Marrie stuck the tiny nipple in his mouth and he drained it immediately. Soon he had the hang of the bottle. Marya came on board, and the three of us took off with the deer. He couldn't walk on the linoleum floor, his tiny hoofs slipped, and his legs went in all directions, so we tacked burlap sacks on the floors which made him right at home. We named him Flag for his little white flag of a tail.

Fall came all too soon, and we decided to return to California and the fire department. We sold the boat and packed up. What to do with Flag? It was illegal to take wildlife out of Alaska and it was particularly difficult on a commercial aircraft. I went to town and bought the biggest shopping bag I could find with a zipper across the top. Flag fit perfectly! We boarded without a hitch and soon were soaring toward Seattle. Flag began crying for his bottle, we tried to quiet him, but to no avail. The stewardess came by and Marrie gave her two baby bottles filled with milk and asked her to heat them. She looked surprised, looked all around, and asked, "Where's the baby?"

She seemed like a nice lady, so I unzipped the bag, and Flag's head popped up. He looked around with those big brown eyes, his ears alert and his fawn speckled coat glistening.

The stewardess's mouth dropped open, she stooped and asked in a whisper, "Can I tell the captain, he would love to see this?"

The captain, the co-pilot, and all the stewardesses took turns to see Flag. The captain said, "Sir, I have had most everything smuggled on my aircraft over the years, but never a deer. Would you be so kind as to wait a couple of minutes when we reach Seattle, so my wife can see him? "

Mark and Lois Arwine, their two daughters, Carol and Ann, were in Texas on vacation and we were house-sitting for them. They had a large enclosed backyard that was perfect for Flag.

After a few weeks, he got diarrhea. We took him to a veterinarian in Beverly Hills who specialized in exotic animals. Marrie and I were on time for our appointment and the receptionist told us the doctor was running a little late. We took a seat beside a former belly dancer dressed in colorful gypsy clothes and around her neck was draped a twelve-foot boa constrictor.

As we sat down the reptile saw Flag and came alive, sticking out his four-inch forked tongue in rapid succession. The owner had a job on her hands restraining him. Marrie quickly exchanged seats with me and sat down beside a 'man' in a hot pink outfit, holding a South American ocelot in his lap. The cat jumped down, licking his lips and staring our way with his big yellow eyes. I pushed Flag down in his bag and zipped it shut. The vet was a friendly man who explained that the molecules of cow's milk are ten times larger than the molecules of humans or goats and if we switched to goat's milk, the problem would clear up.

Flag grew quickly and began to knock Marya over and we realized we could not keep him any longer, so we gave him to neighbors who owned a horse farm in Apple Valley. We visited several times and watched as he grew into a big stag with impressive antlers. One day we received a call from the neighbors who told us that a pack of dogs had scared Flag and he had jumped an eight-foot chain-link fence and ran off. Later we read in the news that a deer had gone up to campers in the Angeles National Forrest, nuzzling and following them around. They called a ranger who took Flag to Santa Claus Lane California, where he spent his remaining years in a petting zoo.

10. CALIFORNIA ANTIQUE DEALER

A New Addition -- The Ghost -- Miriam

On one of our trips across country, we stopped overnight in Natchez, Mississippi, where I found a Cessna 182 for sale for seven-thousand five-hundred dollars. The price was too rich for my pocketbook; however, I was tempted to sell the 172 Cessna I owned and buy it. Back at home, I told Mark Arwine about it and he offered to go halves. Mark had been a jet fighter pilot in Korea and was then the principal of a high school. I called Mississippi and made an agreement with the owner, flew back commercially and flew the airplane to California. It was a big step up from the 172. Mark and I both thoroughly enjoyed the 182 and had a good friendship and partnership for a long time.

All the fuel gauges in airplanes of similar vintage were erratic and the only way to really know how much fuel one had left was to keep close tabs on how long you had flown. Because of the unreliability of the gauges, Mark and I agreed to always fill her up upon landing.

Early one Saturday morning Marrie and I flew to San Francisco for the day, then on to Palm Springs, where we met friends and had dinner. It was after two in the morning when all of a sudden it became very quiet. I quickly checked the cockpit instruments to see if anything was amiss, all seemed normal. I rocked the wings back and forth, she started up, ran a little, and quit again. I realized we were out of gas. Thankfully, we were flying at four thousand feet. I could see the white sand of the long beach from which the city took its name and headed for it while putting out a mayday and switching the transponder to the emergency frequency.

The controller informed me I was directly over Long Beach Airport. I tilted the plane on its side, looked down at the brilliant lights flashing in sequence, indicating the direction to land. I never imagined an airport could be so bright. It took a few minutes to circle and land. As soon as I touched down the nose rose, the engine started, and I taxied to a hangar. We took a cab home. The next morning I had the mechanic check the plane over and sure enough, it was out of gas. Mark had flown it, came in late and didn't fuel up. I bought Mark's share. He was disappointed and our friendship was never the same afterward.

Antique hunting had been a hobby of ours for some years. One Christmas we were visiting Mom and Dad in Canada. An old, retired minister who lived next door was selling-out and moving to a retirement home. Marrie found a washstand in what must have been a chicken coop because it was encrusted in crud. However, she wanted it. I scrubbed it clean enough for the airlines to accept, and we checked it in as an oversized piece of luggage. The piece arrived on the baggage carousel to the smiles and wonderment of the other passengers. We put it in the trunk of the car, secured it, and hauled it home with the trunk lid open.

I went to a local paint store in Redondo Beach and met Sam, a happy and informative man, who explained in detail how I should strip and stain our new treasure. I had my doubts, but Marrie never wavered. That old thing came out magnificent and I was hooked. We started frequenting antique shops, which were numerous in the beach cities those days. By talking with the proprietors we learned quite a bit. After refinishing a few more pieces, we put a two-word ad, *Antiques Wanted,* along with our phone number in the Los Angeles Times.

We already had an existing ad in The South Bay Daily Breeze stating, *Expert Painting*. Marrie screened the calls. We didn't want to bid on painting jobs for apartments; we wanted houses in Beverly Hills or Rolling Hills Estates. Whenever there was a call from a rich area for a bid on a house she made an appointment. I put on my white overalls, grabbed my clipboard, and headed out. I had enough work for three painters, and I stayed busy bidding and doing pick-up work after the painters.

We got some real winners on the antique ad. Shortly after we had placed the ad, an attorney called from Los Angeles. He said he had a client who died recently and there were two old cars in the garage that he wanted to liquidate. Marrie called me at the fire station and told me about it. I asked the men if they knew what a LaSalle was. No one did, but Cliff Bertrand said he would like to go with me to have a look. The next day we headed out. I expected some old house, however when we arrived at the address, it was a new and luxurious condominium complex. The attorney met us and opened the garage.

On an immaculately green painted floor, jacked up on stands were two cars in museum condition. One was a yellow 1951 Cadillac that looked like it had never left the showroom. Beside it was a 1934 LaSalle, light grey, with running boards, sun visor, original horsehair seat covers, and only 700 original miles. My heart was beating fast as I wondered if I could afford either. I asked the price and he replied that he would take one hundred and thirty-five for the Cadillac and seven hundred for the LaSalle. Cliff said he wanted the Cadillac and I didn't blame him. Nobody argued with the price. We each wrote checks and the treasures were ours. Both vehicles cranked at the touch of the starter and we drove them home, leaving my old pick up.

A wife can be a real pain sometimes and that was exactly what Marrie was that day. She thought the car was nice, but we couldn't afford a second car and how much did it cost. When I told her seven hundred dollars, she thought I had lost my mind and said this left us virtually broke which wasn't so. In any case her nose was bent and insisted I sell the car. We took some pictures and went for a ride, but even so she still couldn't see the treasure. The very first person I told that I was going to sell the car, asked me how much I wanted. I said two-thousand dollars, and he bought it.

One evening the phone rang, Marrie answered and talked for a few minutes. Then she put her hand over the mouthpiece and told me she thought I should take this one. A sweet lady's voice began telling me of an old couple in their nineties, who lived in a large house near UCLA. She went on to explain that the couple hadn't been able to climb the stairs to the second and third floors for years and they needed a thousand dollars to pay their taxes and wanted to sell everything on those two floors; she was wondering if I might have a look. I thought, would tomorrow morning be too late?

Marrie and I met the lady at the address, and we were invited into what had once been a stately home and introduced us to Mr. And Mrs. Conger. We fell in love with this old couple. He was 93 and she 95 and they got around quite well. She was cooking lunch, and the food bubbling on the stove smelled delicious. Everything was clean and orderly. We sat down and they were happy to talk. We asked how long they had been married, he said forty-five years. They went on to tell that both had been married previously. They bought adjoining poultry farms back in the 1930s and the two had fallen in love and had a clandestine romance for some years. Her husband found out and hit him beside the head with a fence post, leaving him for dead. He proudly showed us the scar that marked the day his life changed.

After a long visit and coffee, they invited us to go to the upper two floors and informed us that everything there was for sale for the thousand dollars and they were happy for us to have it all. To this day I can't believe the treasure-house we walked into. There were over a thousand hardcover books, many complete sets, each signed Conger Library # 976, etc. Mr. Conger's father had owned Los Angeles Brick Co. and this old man had inherited all this from his father. Amongst the treasures was a marble bust of a young woman, it looked as if it had come out of a museum in Rome. Carved fern stands, bow-front carved stair chest, a 10-gauge Parker Brothers engraved shotgun with high brass shells, and all the cleaning apparatuses were just a few of the hundreds of pieces. The list of treasures is long, and I regret we ever sold one piece.

We paid the couple the thousand dollars and rented a twenty-four foot U-Haul truck. I found two men to help load and we took it all back to the apartment complex where we had two vacant apartments. We sorted and priced each piece.

Once this was done, we placed an ad in the paper advertising an estate sale. On Saturday morning, we were swamped. People were almost fighting over the books. To this day I have no idea how much we lost due to our ignorance. We saved several choice pieces of furniture and the shotgun. When we counted the money, we had cleared over five thousand dollars for our efforts. That was a lot of money in the early 1970s, however, I was not happy. It made me sick to part with the treasures. We visited the Congers several times during the following years.

With the windfall from the Congers, I surmised there were other similar finds in the neighborhood. The area was changing color, housing prices were dropping, and the older white homeowners were moving out. I parked my pickup and began knocking on every door on both sides of the street. I never got far before I was invited in to look at something. I believed I had a nose for this work. Once I was invited in, I asked to look in the attic and basement, oftentimes finding things the owners had no idea they had. Whenever my truck was loaded to the very top, I drove to antique row. I had my favorite customers and soon I was sold out and on my way home to tell Marrie I had earned our bread for the day.

Late one afternoon I was talking to a Chinese man who took me behind his house to what had once been the stables for horses. The ground floor had been converted into a large room and it had the biggest carved ornamental table I have ever seen. I tried several times to get him to sell, but he wouldn't budge. I bought the Queen Anne chairs that went with the table.

Upstairs in what had once been the hayloft I noticed the room looked shorter inside than it did from the outside. I stepped off the distances and found it was indeed shorter. Upon closer inspection, I saw where a door had been plastered over. The owner got excited. He had his sons run for a crowbar and we broke the wall from the hayloft into what had been the tack room. Once we entered, it was obvious this place had been sealed up for many years. Hanging from the ceiling was a canoe about six feet long, inlaid with mother-of-pearl. Inside the boat we found a pair of paddles, we couldn't imagine what it was. Over in a corner was a hand wine-press that could have been a thousand years old from the look of the wood and the type of bronze screw. Several saddles and all the tack from the past century were hanging on the walls.

I bought everything for next to nothing and took the canoe to the museum of natural history where I found a curator who knew what it was. He identified it as a two-hundred-year-old Solomon Island ceremonial canoe.

Marrie came to me, said, "Sweetheart, I have something to tell you. We are going to have a baby." I was overjoyed! Marrie told me she felt good this time and knew there would be no problems. This baby was special.

We began looking at houses and one afternoon she called me at the fire station and told me she had found a house and that we should put a deposit on it immediately. Houses were selling the same day they came on the market. I asked her to wait until I got off from my shift. I hurried home, changed clothes, and drove to Danaha Street in Walteria, an older suburb of Torrance, a few blocks from the airport. The house was a darling three-bedroom bungalow, a detached garage, and a split-level back yard, with a charming lemon tree hanging full of yellow fruit. Over the back patio was an arbor of cane poles covered in ivy, leaving the kitchen shaded and cool. We bought it for thirty-two thousand dollars and were to move in within a couple of weeks. As soon as the previous owners vacated, we went over to clean and noticed the lemon tree had been stripped of all its fruit, even the unripe green fruit. It made me sick to see such sacrilege, the tree died from the shock. On top of that, they had taken every light bulb from both inside the house and out. Did you ever want to kick someone's rear end? I sure did.

I built a bookcase across one wall in the living room and put down a new carpet. Marrie painted the kitchen cabinets a pale lime green and wallpapered one wall to complement the paint. I thought it would be awful, but true to form, it turned out splendid. By then she was beginning to show and looked stunning.

Del Conte's restaurant and bar were just a few blocks walk from our house. Sometimes we strolled down, ordered prime rib and baked potato. Afterward we'd dance in the lounge to the music of a combo that played Tom Jones and Rod Stewart Songs.

Tony lived a few blocks from the fire station, and we worked the same shift. One afternoon after a particularly heavy rain, his three-year-old daughter was playing in a ditch with her little girlfriend. A grating had been removed from a drain and the friend fell in. His daughter held on to her friend's hand for a long time but finally had to let go. The child drowned. Shortly afterward, wherever Tony's daughter went into the house there was a knocking in the wall. He invited the firemen to come over and give our opinion. The only thing I can say is, it was real... and spooky.

Ghostbusters came with their equipment and removed the plaster from the walls, yet the knocking followed the little girl. Tony resigned from the fire department and moved to Lake Ellsinore, where he bought a bar.

While I was visiting Tony, I noticed a vacant house in poor shape. The yard was full of holes and dog shit. I found the owner who was losing it for lack of payments. We came to an arrangement, with me catching up the back payments and giving him a few hundred dollars. I became the new owner.

We hauled off the manure-encrusted carpets, sprayed disinfectant and let it air out for a week. Then with the aid of my new airless sprayer, I gave it two coats of paint, installed new carpet throughout, and laid new linoleum in the kitchen and bathroom. The inside was like new. We spent one day in the yards with a rented rotary tiller. Marrie and I raked it level, scattered grass seed, and bingo! We had a new yard. Now, to keep it and rent it, or sell it was the big question. We decided to rent it and see if we could make a similar deal once or twice a year.

This was my cup of tea and I thoroughly enjoyed all aspects. We figured we could do this twice a year and work on the fire department. After twenty years, we would be in Fat City when I retired. However, farming was still pulling my heartstrings like a magnet. I thought if I could just save up three hundred thousand dollars, I would move to the farm and live happily ever after. Marrie saw the real-estate deal, and wouldn't even take a peek at farming, saying I must not remember as well as she did.

Marrie went to natural childbirth classes, stretched and breathed for months. One night after supper, she experienced a sharp pain and told me she thought the baby was coming. Her bag was packed, and it was a five-minute drive to the hospital. Shortly before midnight the contractions were coming regularly and more frequently. We slowly got in the car, laid Marya our seven-year-old daughter in the back seat with a pillow and blankets, and drove to the hospital. The hospital charged two hundred dollars a day for a room and the rates began at midnight. To save the two hundred dollars we sat in the car, listened to classical music until 12:01 on August 14, 1973, and leisurely walked in with bag in hand. Marrie had an easy delivery (her words) and soon the nurses were showing me my beautiful daughter through the glass. There is something heartwarming to look at your own little baby for the first time. I fell in love. No matter how much you love one, there is always plenty more for the new one.

Next evening Marrie was feeling good. She said the food was awful and asked me to bring her a hamburger and French-fries from McDonald's. It was past nine-thirty and visiting was over at ten. I hurried downstairs, peeled out of the parking lot, racing to McDonald's, had the attendant rush the order. Before you knew it I was back in the car speeding and pulling into my own driveway. Oh, shoot! Put the car in reverse, tires spinning I made it to the hospital just as the doors were closing and I slipped in.

Marya wanted to see her baby sister and her mother. This was a no-no in those days, so we devised a plan. Bringing down the largest suitcase from the attic, Marya stepped inside in the hospital parking lot, and as I walked in under my breath I said, "Marya we are about to pass the nurses' station so pull your elbows in."

The bulge disappeared. When we got to the room, I unzipped the suitcase and Marrie beamed with joy. We hid Marya under the bed and asked the nurse to bring Miriam, so she could nurse. We spent over an hour together and Marya got to hold her baby sister. Then repeated the suitcase trick in reverse.

END PART 1

THE SMUGLLER - 1973 TO 2003

11. SMUGGLER BILL

Fashion Guru -- First Trip -- Second Time Lucky -- Goodbye Smuggler Bill

My old truck was loaded down with antiques when I pulled up in front of an antique store in Hermosa Beach. I went in to make a sale; and the proprietor bought a few pieces. When I walked out a man followed me. He introduced himself as Mike, a wholesale dealer. We got into a long conversation--something I later found to be Mike's trademark. He seemed to know a lot about the business, and I invited him to come over to the house. He was a good talker and unusually handsome. He told us he originally came from Missouri where the early settlers, traveling from the east, came with all kinds of furniture on trains. Once they crossed the Mississippi into Missouri, they had to leave everything that wouldn't fit in the covered wagon, leaving Missouri rich in old treasures.

Mike invited us to go to an antique auction on Pacific Coast Highway in Redondo Beach that night. I accepted, but Marrie declined because Miriam was only three weeks old and she wasn't ready to leave her even for a couple of hours. When Mike and I arrived, the auction was in full swing and I was surprised by the speed at which things sold. Two pretty women were serving cake and coffee from a side room. One of them was the most beautiful woman I had ever seen, and I made a comment to that effect to Mike. Well, this was just his cup of tea. Soon he was chatting up these ladies and one of them, in particular, was eager to get to know him.

After the sale and while the men were loading and settling accounts, Mike invited the ladies to go for a drink. Both ladies had auburn red hair, deep blue eyes, rosy complexion, and full figures; Susan was the one who liked Mike and was giggling. Christy, the goddess, was timid and held back. Mike took Susan by both arms and soon they were in the back seat of Mike's car and off we went to a bar. Christy had both hands over her face laughing at how crazy the world was. She said she would never have done such a thing and Susan was crazy, because her husband Ed was insanely jealous and would kill her. To tell the truth I was nervous about it myself and knew it was insane, but fun. We didn't stay long and when we returned no one had missed us.

Mike and I made plans to go to Missouri and buy a load of antiques. I made three-shift swaps, giving me thirteen days off. Then I scraped up all the money I had or could borrow. Mike did the same and we flew back to Joplin, Missouri where we rented the biggest U-Haul made and then drove to his parents' home near Diamond, Missouri. They had a lovely old stone house, a big barn, and white sheep grazing in an apple orchard. Mike's parents were very nice and made me feel at home. I could see they idolized their son.

Every morning Mike and I went to antique auctions and shops all over that part of Missouri and parts of Kansas. We heard of a firefighter in Kenosha who sold antiques and we went to see him. He had a barn full and we almost filled our truck there. After several farm auctions, thc truck was packed to the max and we had to rent a two-axle twelve-foot trailer to get everything loaded.

We said goodbye to the parents and started the long drive back to California. The ride was most uncomfortable as we bounced along at forty-five mph pulling the overloaded trailer. The trailer was far too heavily loaded with oak tables and over a hundred beautiful four foot by ten-inch oak leaves, for which we had paid zilch.

National Geographic had recently run an article on the element Mercury and explained how it was found in Mexico and the difference in price there and the USA. Just for conversation, I told Mike I would like to have a contact in Mexico to buy the stuff and fly it to California. He then asked if I was interested in transporting marijuana. I told him about Jim Kalk, a young man who worked for me, who had talked of shipping it back to Johns Hopkins University in Maryland.

Mike said the problem was *finding* it in California because the stuff went like hotcakes- he'd never seen anything like it. I asked him what the penalty was if one was caught; he thought one would probably get probation for the first offense. We talked about this for miles and before we reached California, I knew as much about that business as he did. He said he had a friend who knew someone in the business and that he would introduce us.

We unloaded the antiques in our garage, house, and yard, and advertised for a big sale on Saturday. We sold out and made a nice profit, but I had been gone too long and worked too hard to want to go back to the Midwest anytime soon.

Shortly after our return Mike introduced me to Allen Niger, I was impressed. He lived in downtown Hermosa Beach, right at the center of the hippie culture. He was a handsome man of about forty years, with thick black hair, white complexion and spoke with a beautiful baritone voice. His wife, Judy, doted on his every wish while taking care of their little boy and new baby. It was some time before I realized Allen was paralyzed in his legs. He had been a famous racecar driver and a cold had settled in his spinal cord, causing bleeding around the nerves. Allen overcame this with his winning smile and personality. He spoke flawless Spanish and seemed to know about everything. He knew the price of marijuana in Mexico and the price in California and yes, he had someone who would just love to meet a pilot with his own plane.

In a few days, Allen introduced 'Smuggler Bill,' a tall thin blond man who played the part. It was nearing Christmas when Bill came over to the house with a dozen new shirts and just threw them on the sofa, saying he'd come across them and wanted me to have them as a gift. He continued to tell me that he had a friend in Jalapa, Vera Cruz, Mexico, who had a couple of loads of marijuana and would pay ten-thousand dollars a trip.

Dick Irvine hired me to build a real estate office in an old store on Pacific Coast Highway in Manhattan Beach. It was a big job. First, it was a big building and second was all the work they wanted to be done. They wanted five separate offices with windows and doors, all kinds of electrical and telephone hook-ups, a hundred feet of paneling, and a bathroom. The job got rather involved and I was on it for a couple of months.

Next door to the site was a boutique named "Charlie's Girl," owned and operated by Donna Davis. I loved the smell of that shop. It smelled like potpourri, laced with French perfume. Several attractive attendants worked there and we would visit during breaks. Across the street was a superb sandwich shop that piled sprouts on avocado sandwiches. We ate there frequently and after some months, we all became old friends. One Saturday night someone threw a Molotov cocktail through the window of the Italian restaurant next door to "Charlie's Girl" and the flames went through the partition and smoked up Donna's' Shop.

She was devastated, cursing the low life, cowardly, Italian mafia. All her clothes had to be cleaned and then they wouldn't be new. She was in a mess. The insurance adjuster estimated a 30% loss. Donna was livid! She didn't want the damaged merchandise and she was crying.

I came over and told her I could fix it, to just hang on until everyone went home. Once the area was empty, I took a five-gallon metal paint can with just a little paint in the bottom, poured a speck of acetone, and struck a match. Black smoke boiled out and flakes of smut settled. We kept an eye on it and when she thought there was enough I put a lid on the can and the job was finished. The next day Donna called for another estimate and he recommended a 100% loss.

Donna wanted to take the clothes to Mexico to sell so there wouldn't be a record in the US. She hired me to fly them down to Guadalajara. Smuggler Bill was ready, so I decided to smuggle both ways. Donna packed over a thousand articles of clothing in suitcases. Luckily, it was the era of miniskirts and flimsy fabric, so a couple of hundred pieces fit in one bag. We departed early one morning and reached Guadalajara in the late afternoon. We had never fixed a price, but a percentage had been discussed. When Donna left, she gave me a chrome Seiko watch and a peck on the cheek. This was all I received for my efforts on her behalf.

Cressna 182. In 1973 I flew my first load of marijuana across the Mexican border and made $180,000. This was more than I made in a year as a fireman.
Image courtesy Adrian Pingstone - Cessna 182 Skylane - N2231F - Cotsworld Airport England - Wikipedia

From Guadalajara I flew on to Jalapa, the capital of the state of Vera Cruz, located high in the mountains and a long way from the famous city of Vera Cruz. Women were washing clothes in stone basins carved into the rock on a stream flowing through town. Donkeys laden with goods were clip-clopping about on cobblestone streets. A policeman wearing white gloves stood in the main intersection directing what little traffic there was. The setting was so quaint and romantic it felt like a glimpse of life a thousand years past.

Three o'clock the next morning all was ready and I went to the airport. A guard questioned me, asked for my papers (which he couldn't read). I showed him my fireman's badge and then he was all smiles, wanting to help load my suitcase. I taxied to the end of the runway and stopped. Bill and his friend drove up in a pickup with the load. We quickly stuffed the bales in the luggage compartment and back seat of the plane, placing sleeping bags and other camping equipment on top.

We took off into a clear star-studded night and headed NW, following the Sierra Nevada Mountain range. The mountains rose at about a thirty-degree angle to my left with the Milky Way strung across the sky glittering brightly. Somewhere in my mind was a strong desire for the earth to be horizontal with the stars, and no matter how hard I fought the sensation, I got vertigo. It was so very strange. I knew what was happening; yet my mind wanted the plane to bank to the right and each time I saw the artificial horizon instrument show a roll to the right, and the compass began to swing. I became dizzy and nauseous trying to shake this illusion. My training had warned me of the phenomenon, but that was the only time I ever experienced it. I stopped looking outside and relied on the instruments until the dawn's rosy fingers reached across the heavens and put my mind level.

I planned to cross Mexico and reach a large dry lake near Hermosillo, Mexico, unload, fuel-up, and clear customs for Los Angeles. But there was a steady wind out of the NW right on the nose and we were not going to make it. I spotted what looked like an abandoned airstrip in the dry country filled with cacti, scrub, and rocks. I circled, saw a little boy tending a herd of goats, and landed. At the end of the strip was the remains of an old stone house and we put the marijuana behind the walls. I left Smuggler Bill with the goat herder and I went to Ciudad Torreon for fuel. It didn't take long and was back with cold drinks and sandwiches. We had a picnic with Lazarus, the young goat herder joining us, before heading out.

We reached the Sea of Cortés and followed the eastern shore northward until we reached Isla Tiburon, famous for cannibals. Nathan Pritikin wrote about the descendants of these people, noting their ability to walk a hundred miles through the desert, loaded with children and gifts with what seemed to be the greatest of ease. By studying their diet, he discovered cholesterol and wrote several books on the subject. Mexican soldiers killed the last of the cannibals, in1950's.

Directly opposite *Isla Tiburon* and perhaps ten miles inland is a good-sized dry lake. A barbed-wire fence stretches across the center giving it a surreal look of another world. I landed near the edge and taxied amongst some shrubs and unloaded. Bill was hesitant to be left alone in the desert and wanted to fly with me. I could tell he was afraid, so I left a .22 caliber automatic pistol with him and this seemed to calm him.

By the time I reached Hermosillo, filled out the paperwork, fueled-up, and returned, it was dark. After landing and taxiing up, I saw Bill running from behind the bales shooting. This scared me. I assumed I was being followed. When a slug hit the plane's windshield I realized that the idiot was shooting directly at me. When the pistol ran out of cartridges he took off running through the shrubs. I jumped out and yelled at him, but he kept on running. I loaded up with the fullest intention of leaving him there.

Yet, as I was getting ready to take off, he came sneaking back, hiding behind the shrubs. I called out, asking what the hell his problem was, but he didn't say a word, just scurried in. Then I grasped that he was stoned out of his mind, and he admitted he had taken some pills, not the marijuana.

The headwinds continued and grew stronger as we flew north. By the time we crossed the border they had reached gale force. We had planned to unload in Banning, California, but fighting this headwind I knew we wouldn't make it.

When we came to Brawley, I landed at Tri-County Airport. It was a full moon and blowing sand obscured the desert. The runway was made of white cement and the desert sand was the same color. When I came to a fork on the taxiway, I continued straight ahead and ran off the runway into soft powdery sand. The tires sank past the axles. What a fiasco. We stepped out, scouted out a depression in the sand dunes fifty yards away, and stashed the marijuana, partially covering it with sand.

I told Bill to stay out of sight, that I would get a wrecker and a fuel truck. I walked to the terminal, entered, and explained the situation to the two weathermen working in the office. The men were surprised, as they hadn't seen or heard me land and I didn't tell them that I had coasted in with the lights off. They were exceptionally nice and asked if I was alone and I told them I was. They telephoned the fuel truck driver and he said he would be out in a few minutes. Bill burst through the doors saying he was dying of thirst and headed to the water fountain. We had water in the plane. The men asked if this guy was with me and I replied he was, but I wasn't claiming him.

The fuel truck came and pulled the plane out of the sand and onto the taxiway. I started the engine and followed him to the ramp where he topped it off with fuel. I gave him a good tip and we were off.

We couldn't take the chance of stopping and loading as we had to keep the running lights on and the men in the terminal were talking to me on the radio. We had no choice but to take off and fly to Palm Springs. There I hailed a taxi and went to town. I saw a young Mexican man driving an old Chevrolet with a miniature steering wheel. I stopped this young fellow and offered him five hundred dollars to rent his car for a few hours. To seal the deal I had to leave him my driver's license, credit cards, and fireman's badge.

We hustled back to Brawley. I removed the fuse for the brake lights, turned off the headlights and eased up to the airport, opened the gate, and drove down the runway to the spot where we had hidden the stash. We filled the trunk and stacked bales of marijuana to the roof of the back seat, even put a bale under Bill's feet, then headed north with Bill bitchin' the whole way. I was either going too fast or too slow. We stopped at the edge of Palm Springs where I rented a room in an old motel and backed up to the door. We unloaded just as it was getting daylight.

Bill called his friends, who were waiting less than an hour's drive away. He began complaining and I had had it with him. I shoved him in the corner and gave him a couple of kicks right in the butt. Nothing ever felt so-o-o good!

His friend showed up and passed me a brown paper grocery bag filled with ten-dollar bills. I counted the stacks at random and recounted and was satisfied that it was close to correct. I left the room.

Next I contacted the owner of the car and we met at a restaurant downtown where I had a big steak and egg breakfast. Then he drove me to the airport, and I flew home. I arrived about nine in the morning, took Marrie into the bedroom and shook the bag of money out on the king-size bed. That afternoon I took her shopping. Her eyes sparkled as she tried on clothes, and I know mine did too, just watching her. When we ate out I told her not to look on the right-hand side of the menu, to order whatever her heart desired. She said it was like having Christmas every day.

Ten-thousand dollars was a lot of money in 1973. It was more than a year's pay for a fireman, and we didn't owe anyone a dime. Once we bought some new clothes and ate out a few times, we didn't want anything else, so we rented a safety deposit box and stashed away the money.

Smuggler Bill returned, apologized, and wanted me to go back for another load. That was alright with me, but we had to come to an understanding on several important issues such as he was *not* to take any kind of drugs, his partner was to meet us at Banning airport and take the load, and I was to be paid ten-thousand dollars upon landing.

Bill readily agreed to all the conditions and then flew down to Mexico commercially to arrange things. I flew to Finn Air in San Diego and had special tanks installed. This allowed me three extra hours of flying time. My trip south was a repeat of the first but without Donna. Upon landing at Jalapa, I met the watchman from the earlier trip, and he smiled and was happy to see me. A smile is the same in all languages.

The following day I walked through the old city, taking in the sights for the second time. I went into an old church and was impressed by the twelve Stations of the Cross, beautifully carved in niches along both sides. Later I learned that this was a common practice in the Latin culture. Whenever I entered a Catholic Church, I would look for the stations.

We loaded up and took off identically as the first trip. This time I had plenty of fuel to reach the dry lake near Hermosillo. We unloaded and I left Bill with the load, went into town and fueled up. By then it was around lunchtime, so I went into a restaurant and ordered a big lunch and ate leisurely. After lunch, I strolled through the streets of the old city. A group of uniformed school kids talked to me and escorted me around for a leisurely hour.

At the airport I filed a flight plan for Los Angeles International Airport and took my sweet time before going back for Bill. He was beside himself when I returned, and I just laughed.

We flew north to the upper reaches of the Sea of Cortez and followed the Colorado River north. It was ebb tide and mudflats stretched for miles on both sides. The silhouettes where the water drained into the river, looked to me like giant naked trees lying on their sides their roots in the river, and trunks in the mud, branching smaller and smaller until they were just twigs. The late afternoon sunlight cast shadows across ravines of sparkling wet silver-grey mud.

Just after dark, I flew the pattern for Mexicali, skimmed down the runway, hung a sharp right and crossed the border. I hoped that if customs were watching us on the radar, it would look like I was taking off from Mexicali. We flew north to the Salton Sea where I pushed the nose down and watched the altimeter unwind until it read 200 ft. below sea level. We flew low over the golf courses of Palm Desert and on past Palm Springs before turning west into Banning Pass where we ran into sixty-mile-an-hour headwinds. We landed on the apron on the east end of Banning airport and were pushed backward upon touchdown. I had to apply power to taxi over to where we were supposed to meet our un-loader.

There was no one waiting, so we unloaded the pot and stacked it in the bushes. Still no one showed up. We put several bales in a sleeping bag, dragged them fifty or sixty yards into the thorny scrub and hid it all in a ditch. We repeated this until we had it all hidden and covered with the sleeping bags, limbs and bushes. I left Bill with the load and he started walking to the other end of the strip where there was a payphone to call his friend. Since I had a flight plan to Los Angeles, I had to get going.

Landing at LAX between the jetliners was exciting. I had to be mindful of the wingtip vortices that can easily flip a small plane. Ground control had me taxi for a mile or more, turning many times in different directions. Suddenly I ran into something solid and hard. One propeller blade went through the right wing, rupturing the fuel tank and spilling all the fuel, and the other cut the front tire off the rim. It became deathly quiet. I got on the radio and told ground control I had an accident. They sent a car around to check and found that someone working for Flying Tiger Airlines had left the tail end of a train dolly strung almost to the center of the taxiway. Officials from the airline came and promised to rebuild the engine and repair the plane. We shook hands, they towed the plane away and drove me to customs. I had no problems clearing and soon I was in a taxi on my way home.

When I opened the door, Marrie fell into my arms and held me so tight that I can still feel her heart beating against my chest. After assuring her I was all right, she calmed down enough to tell me what had happened. Bill had called her from Palm Springs and told her that I had been arrested and he had only narrowly escaped. I couldn't imagine what he was talking about, but knowing Bill it could be anything.

Around 2 a.m. I headed for Banning in our 1968 Mercury Park Lane. It was 1974 and the rationing of gasoline was in effect, a scam imposed by the oil companies on the American people. Automobiles with license plates ending in even numbers could only buy gas on even days and odd numbers on odd days. This was strictly enforced and soon gasoline prices doubled and never came down, yet there was no shortage at all... This fraud was also pulled in turn with lemons, silver, and beef to name just a few of the more blatant ones. I stopped at a truck stop on Interstate 10 just east of San Bernardino and it being the wrong day for me, I bribed the attendant with a fifty-dollar bill to fill my tank, and paid for the fuel.

Shortly after Banning, I turned right and drove down side roads until I found a dirt trail paralleling the airport. The runway lights were barely visible through the scrub. I could make out the Vasey lights on the east ends; parked as near as I could and crawled through thorns and cacti until I came to the ravine where we had left the marijuana. Everything was exactly as we left it. I walked a way down the runway and saw nothing, I began dragging the sleeping bag with four bales at a time. Polyester fabric had just come out and the thorns were playing havoc with my clothes. It was daylight by the time I dragged it all to the car and loaded. The trunk was full, the seats were stacked to the roof with burlap-covered bales. I got on the freeway and drove for about an hour before reaching the house on Ripley and Ridge in Redondo Beach, pulled in the garage and shut the door. With great effort, I hefted the bales into the attic, drove home, and crashed.

For several days I wondered what to do and then decided to heck with those fools. They ran off, left it, and said the police had it, I figured it was mine.

Allen and I talked it over and Allen agreed with me, but Howard, a marijuana dealer, warned to never burn *anyone* in this business. Against my better judgment, he talked me into calling Bill and telling him I had the pot. They came over with big smiles and zero money, said they had to sell the product before they could pay. I took their truck, loaded it up, and returned it to them. Oh my, they were so happy. They kept shaking my hand, one guy kissed me on the cheek as they got in the truck and drove away waving. After several days without a word, I called. Ring, ring, ring, ring, no answer. A couple of days later: ring, ring, "This number has been disconnected and there is no forwarding number." The blood drained from my face. All that work and then betrayed with a Judas kiss. I was livid!

Mike was a most thorough man and I hired him to see if he could find them. He was happy to oblige and left immediately for Bill's last address, which was a cabin in the giant redwoods near Walnut Creek, California. He arrived after an eight-hour drive and found the cabin stripped clean. In the fireplace, Mike found the ashes of a quarantine document for a dog shipped to Vancouver, Canada. Luckily, the ash was intact, and Mike got all the numbers before touching it, causing it to disintegrate. With a few telephone calls, he confirmed that the dog did go to Canada, but was then shipped to an address in Queens, New York. Mike flew there directly.

The next day I was on duty at the fire station when Mike called and said Bill was walking the dog past him as we were talking. I traded shifts with a co-worker and flew to New York. Mike met me at the airport, and we drove to Queens. In less than an hour, Bill came strolling down the sidewalk with his dog. I opened the door, stepped out, stuck a pistol in his ribs, and told him to get in. You should have seen the petrified look on his face. He grabbed the dog up in his arms and said he must take Leslie. He stumbled into the back seat and I slid in beside him. All was silent, not one word was spoken as Mike drove down to a rundown area amongst old wharves and warehouses.

Bill tried to light a cigarette, but his hand shook so hard he couldn't connect the match and the cigarette. He finally threw it on the floor.

He said he had spent all the money and his wife was expecting a baby any day. With all the shaking, tears, and snot, I began to feel sorry for him. He had eight-hundred dollars at the apartment and promised to raise the balance within thirty days. We drove him back to the apartment where he got out and went in. A few minutes later he came out with the eight-hundred. Then I told him I was keeping the dog as collateral, if he didn't pay within thirty days he would receive the dog's head in the mail. He was terribly upset to learn I was *dog-napping* his pet and said he wished I would take his wife instead.

We bought a kennel and shipped the dog to California. When I brought her home, the children loved her, combed her long red hair, and covered her in ribbons and bows. I fed her the special dog chow he recommended, and she was happy in our yard. After a couple of weeks Howard came by and asked me to *please* give the dammed dog back, because the fool was calling everyone and making more waves than any of us could afford. I called Bill and asked him how much money he had raised, and he said he had two-thousand five-hundred dollars, so I told him to bring it and get his dog. He flew from New York that night, came to the house early in the morning with the money, and took Leslie with him. That was the last I ever saw or heard of Smuggler Bill. What a relief!

12. POT RUNS AND MEXICO

Tricks of the Trade -- Bohemian Folk Hero --

Howard called and asked me to come over. He lived in a nice house in Manhattan Beach, California, a block from the strand. I walked in and found him naked in his Jacuzzi wearing dark John Lennon sunglasses. He got out of the Jacuzzi, put on some jeans and a shirt, and came to the reason for my invitation. He knew a man with a Mexican connection who would meet me in Palm Springs in the lobby of a plush hotel. I would recognize the man by the *News Week Magazine* held in his left hand as he walked through the lobby at *exactly* ten p.m. I was to bring a gift of marijuana so he would know I wasn't a Fed. Feds are not allowed to give or sell drugs. I find that hard to believe.

The following evening I drove to Palm Springs, took a seat in the lobby, and waited. At *exactly* ten o'clock, there he was, a short man walking briskly with a News Week in his left hand. I couldn't believe my eyes. He was wearing new Levi's and a bright red-checkered cowboy shirt with a bandana tied around his neck. His boots were made of ostrich skin with at least four-inch lifters. His Stetson would've turned the head of any Texan and I thought I'd come to the circus and he was the first of the clowns. I followed him to the parking lot, but he kept on walking until he came to a second lot further down the street. He opened the passenger door of a utility van, told me to get in the back, and show him the weed. He didn't like the quality or the amount.

He gave me a black hood and told me to put it on and pull it all the way down to my neck, and to lie down and stay down. I thought, who is this fool? By now it was getting funny, so I decided to play his little game. He took off swerving around corners, going first to the right and then to the left, obviously trying hard to disorient me. If he only knew I didn't care. After a bit more screeching around corners he got on the freeway for a distance, got off, and back on again. Next we came to a rough dirt road, bounced along for a while, and then stopped and he got out. I took the hood off, looked around, and began to laugh.

"I suppose you think you lost me with your little act. I know exactly where we are. Over there are the tracks of the Southern Pacific Railroad, off to our right is Interstate 10, and at two-hundred-fifty degrees and three thousand feet up is the light at the top of the tram."

He was peeved but invited me into a house trailer. Draped over chairs in the living room were short-barreled pistols in quick-draw holsters. The walls were decorated with wanted posters for Jessie James and other famous outlaws. I went to the bathroom and there was a big hardback book on *The Ma Baker Gang*. He introduced himself as Terry Thornton, which I later found to be his true name. When he quit putting on his act, he was all right.

He said he had a contact near Mazatlán, Mexico and he would introduce me if I paid him five thousand dollars for each load I hauled. I could also use his airstrip and hangar for another five thousand per landing.

Terry's only redeeming factor was his girlfriend, Elizabeth. She was at least six foot four, a rodeo trick rider, and pretty. When Terry stood beside her, minus his four-inch lifter cowboy boots, she put her hand down on the top of his head and messed his hair. I chuckled, picturing the two in bed. Something about a toy poodle fresh from the groomers, wearing a rhinestone collar, mounting a sleek greyhound.

In front of the house trailer was a runway that ran under two clusters of overhead wires. There was a major group of high power lines near the east end and a short way down the runway was a hundred or more sagging telephone wires adding to the obstacles. Off the center of the strip was a new hangar with a Cessna 207 with one wing missing. The strip was not worth the five- thousand dollars per landing, but Terry thought it was ideal because no one could follow you in at night due to all the wires overhead.

I rented his hangar in the name of Leslie Baumgartner, for Baumgartner Funeral Services; to coincide with the false ID he gave me. I studied the papers until I had memorized each detail, I even learned the star sign. I heard of someone being caught entering Israel with false papers.

The female immigration officer asked ever so sweetly, "What is your star sign sir?" He had no idea.

The following week Terry and I flew to Mexico and stopped on the Mexican side to clear customs. We walked up to the desk and I presented the false papers to an immigration officer. He turned them around so he could read them and asked me my name. My mind went blank.

I stood there for a second and said, "That's always been a hard one," reached and turned the papers so I could see the name and then everything came back. The General laughed and Terry almost swallowed his chew of tobacco.

We flew on to Guaymas where we spent the night and had a good time. *Catch 22*, had recently been filmed there and left a long smooth runway. The following day we flew south until we were about fifty miles north of Mazatlán, where we turned east until we reached a pueblo with a blue cathedral and twin bell towers, the exact landmark he was looking for. We continued east through semi-desert landscape until we came to a shallow river running through a sharp narrow cut in a rock cliff. To the west of the cut was a very short landing strip. One would have to be imaginative to call it that.

We circled once and then landed. Several men met us and shook hands with Terry. To my surprise, he couldn't speak one word of Spanish. We started walking up the deeply rutted trail to the village and met Joaquin, the head honcho, an ugly hair-lipped little mouse of a man riding a starving donkey. We got right down to business; I understood he had all the marijuana I wanted at seventeen dollars per kilo. I also made him understand I'd return the following evening shortly before dark.

We took off in the hot afternoon sun, using every inch of the runway and barely skimming the rim of the rocky mesa straight ahead. Half an hour later we landed at the international airport south of Mazatlán and closed the flight plan. Terry caught a commercial flight back to California and I took a taxi into town. I loved the place right away. It was an old city right on the shore of the Pacific Ocean with a picturesque harbor. Hundreds of shrimp boats in a multitude of brilliant colors, including rust, were tied three deep for over a mile. Sailboats, sport fishers, and pleasure boats filled the rest of the marina. All along the quay were open-air restaurants with white tablecloths and smiling waiters scurrying in and out with platters of fresh seafood, a charcoal burner beneath to keep it hot while one ate.

I chose Señor Frogs, a noisy, happy restaurant. A waiter would tie a bib around your neck and squirt a stream of red wine from a goatskin into your mouth for as long as you could keep your mouth open. Hanging on the wall were famous photographs and interesting posters. I remember one of Poncho Villa with his handlebar mustache and the bandolier of cartridges crossed over his chest with the caption:

RIDE TO GOLD AND GLORY WITH PONCHO VILLA.

WANTED, RAILROADERS, MACHINE GUNNERS &

DYNAMITERS. PAID IN GOLD MONTHLY.

Had I lived in that era I would have signed up. The California in-crowd was having a ball and I wanted to bring Marrie and laugh and dance in the cantinas; something we did do our share of later.

The next afternoon I fueled up and filed a flight plan to Mulege, Baja where I knew there wasn't a control tower. I found the village of Pechilingue without a problem and lined up with the strip, which faced due west. The sun just touching the horizon blinded me as I tried to land. The aviator sunglasses were useless--I needed welding goggles! In order to take my bearings I looked out the side window. I was greeted by a group of people on the strip which was about a half-mile from the village and they insisted on carrying my satchel.

We walked along by fields of corn, fenced entirely with spiny cactus so tightly planted that even a baby goat couldn't squeeze through. Other patches had wire fences with living posts. Since it was the end of the dry season, it was hot, and the animals were starving. Some of the donkeys looked as if they were going to die that day and Joaquin was still working them and had several harnessed in front of his house.

Joaquin introduced me to his wife, and I saw right off that she was the brains of the village. They took me into a big empty room with a hammock and she told me with sign language that this was where I would sleep. Darkness came quickly, a generator cranked up and men brought benches and placed them in rows in the square. Someone started up an old reel projector and people began arriving. I learned that every Saturday night this man played a Mexican western and most of the village would come to watch. When all were seated, a man went down each row collecting money and making change. After the movie, the generator shut down and the village was dark.

We returned to Joaquin's house, where his wife prepared dinner for me, and me alone. A red and white-checkered tablecloth was laid on the table. A kerosene lamp was placed in the middle beside a place setting for one. I sat in the hot bright light while a dozen or more stood back in the shadows looking me over.

The supper was bony fish in onions and tomatoes, piping hot, even the lamp was hot.

The sweat was dripped off my nose. I ate while everyone stared at every bite I took. When I finished eating the woman brought me a glass of milk. I didn't expect it to be cold because there wasn't electricity and I don't like to drink milk with fish. Some old wives tale said the two together would make one sick. I turned the glass up, took a drink, and immediately spewed it out all over the table. Was it spoiled-I'd seen the cows? Then it dawned on me--*condensed* milk from a can. I apologized profusely, but no one seemed to mind, they were only interested in the fifteen-thousand greenbacks in my pocket.

I remember wearing khaki trousers and brown wing-tip shoes. I placed the shoes under the hammock and lay down, swinging one foot on the rough concrete floor in the hot windowless storeroom. Donkeys brayed all night with the most infernal sounds imaginable--like they were having orgasms with their vocal cords.

It didn't seem long before a chorus of roosters joined in. Then there was a knock on the door. A dozen men walked me down to the river where I brushed my teeth in the stream and waited for daylight. At the first hint of light, Pedro got on the plane with me. He looked to be about seventeen years old and seemed to catch on to what I was saying faster than the others. We took off with Pedro directing me. In about ten minutes we came to a new major highway and followed it east until we saw the truck from the village pull out onto the highway, blocking traffic. About a mile down the road, I could see another truck stopped crossways on the highway. All traffic ceased. I landed and taxied up to the first truck, loaded with men armored with rifles. They passed bales of marijuana from one to the other like a bucket brigade. I got out, shook hands all around, and then took off, passing over the other truck. Perhaps fifty vehicles were stopped, and I noticed a highway patrol car with the lights on top (not flashing) in the queue.

I flew close to the border where I landed by a dry salty lagoon called *Salido Seco*. Earlier, I had hidden several jerry cans of gasoline; plenty to reach Palm Springs. I poured the fuel through a chamois, ate the lunch Marrie had packed, and found a love note. The temperature was well over 120 degrees Fahrenheit and I baked in that oven all afternoon. As soon as the light began to fade, I took off and crossed the border east of the San Diego mountain range. When I landed at Terry's, most of the fuel had burned out of the wings causing the center of gravity to be in the rear. The wind was blowing a gale and as the plane came to a stop, it fell on its tail from the heavy load in the rear. I jumped out and ran like a scared rabbit. I got about a hundred yards away and waited in some bushes to see what would happen. Terry came out with a small tractor and pulled the plane into the hangar, then I eased-on back.

Howard sold the load and paid me sixty dollars a pound. Much later I learned the correct price was one hundred a pound. That year I hauled so much that it brought the price down throughout California. I'd had fun and soon was ready to go again. So I did, again and again, until I had lockboxes bursting with money all over Los Angeles. I'd empty shopping bags full of the green stuff on the king-sized bed and Marrie and I counted it. Miriam was a crawling little rascal and she knew this was important, so she grabbed a couple of fists full of hundred dollar bills and scrammed. She always was partial to the hundreds.

One day, Clark Bennet, the realtor who sold us the house, came over and we got into a friendly wrestling match. I had him up in the air and he was headed for a wreck on the grass, so I squatted to shift his weight on my upper leg. When I did that a small bone broke in my foot. With a cast up to my knee, I had to use crutches for months. I'd go down to the fire department, drink coffee with the men, and joke about them having to work.

However Howard was out of pot and a load was waiting in Mexico, but I couldn't fly with the cast on my foot (which I use to brake). So, I took out a handsaw, cut off the cast, and flew the trip. Of course the foot hurt like the dickens without the cast, but the forty-thousand earned eased the pain. The doctor cussed like a sailor when he saw what I'd done, but two weeks later the saw came out again, and I did another trip. This time the old doc cussed like a *drunken* sailor and swore he would *not* put on another cast.

Mother, Sharon, and Mother's husband George flew out for a visit. We showed them the sights of southern California. Mother took me aside and asked, "What are you doing to make all this money?"

I said, "I'll be truthful with you. I'm flying marijuana up from Mexico."

"How much do you make a trip?"

"Forty thousand dollars."

I could see this worried her and she asked, "What would they do if they caught you?"

"Mother, I talked with a lawyer who handles such cases and he told me I would probably get probation since it would be my first offense, but at the worse I would serve one year in one of those posh farm facilities. What do you think?"

She said, "Do you need a co-pilot, Son?"

I resigned from the fire department in April 1974, four years to the day from when I started.

Howard introduced me to a pilot from Milwaukee and this man wanted to know how I crossed the border without getting picked up on radar and I was happy to oblige him. We loaded up several jerry cans with aviation fuel and headed out. We stopped at the Palm Springs airport for a leisurely lunch and then flew on down to the Seco Salido where I stashed the fuel. The Mexican government had recently dug a canal to drain the lake when it rained, and dozers graded the banks of the canal rather smooth for miles. I found a cluster of Manzanillo trees near the canal, with a small entrance to a perfect circle, just enough space for a plane to park. No one could see me except from directly overhead. This was my private lair, yet for some reason I shared it with this particular man.

We flew back across the border, both on the lookout for new landing sites, remote yet easy to find. We continued north until we were east of Paso Robles, California. As we flew over an Omni radio beacon, I noticed two dry lakes. They were covered in stark white powder with a dark dirt road running through the center--a perfect landing site for a dark night. I eased her down on the dirt road dividing the two lakes, stopped and got out to take a leak. I looked behind and there was the cavalry.

Leading the pack was an Air Force AWAC plane, one of those big jets with a huge radar dome on top and all around this mother were the little sharks that started landing one after the other and came bouncing up the road toward us. Men hung out the windows with machine guns pointed at us, I raised my hands just like they do in the cowboy movies. One young customs agent ran up and stuck his pistol right in my face. He was ghostly white; his lips were caved in and he was shakin like a bird dog shittin' peach seed. I thought, 'this idiot is either going to shoot me or pass out.' I asked the older agent to have the scared man remove the quivering gun from my face.

They were obviously disappointed at finding nothing in the plane, but they handcuffed us and put us on the floor of a twin-engine aircraft without seats in the passenger section, most likely a plane confiscated with a load of pot. Two agents took off in my Cessna and then we took off behind them. They landed in Bakersfield and put us out on the runway. I told them we lived in Santa Barbara and since they were flying directly by, we'd appreciate a ride. No way, absolutely not, we could walk for all they cared! We hired a taxi for the hundred-mile ride home.

A few days later I called U.S. Customs in San Diego and found that the bond for the airplane was ten-thousand dollars. I needed the plane right away because Marrie and I had planned a trip to Brazil with her Dutch cousins. I dug up the money buried in the back yard. The bills were damp and stuck together. This was our spending money as I didn't put five and ten dollar bills in the lockboxes because they took up too much room. Friday afternoon I drove to San Diego, showed up at customs at four-thirty, flopped the wad of wet bills on the boss's desk, and told him I wanted my airplane. The entire office stopped and went to counting. Five o'clock came and they were angry and still counting. Around six they were through, and the boss said I was twenty dollars short. I said, "No way José, I counted it just before I left and there was exactly ten thousand."

He cussed a blue streak, reached in his wallet, and threw a crisp, dry, twenty on the pile. I smiled and flew away in my plane.

A year later, I received a check from Washington for twenty dollars and I smiled again.

alled and invited me over to his house. To my surprise, I had thing of a folk hero in the bohemian circle of Manhattan Beach unding area. I was welcomed with honor and people wanted to meet me. t season was beginning in Mexico and Howard boasted that if *anybody* could smuggle it across, Roger could.

Howard told me that Terry had repaired his Cessna 207 and wanted to sell it for thirty-five thousand dollars. I flew to Palm Springs and looked it over. This was the biggest single-engine plane Cessna built, carrying three times as much as the 182. I gave it a test flight in the stifling heat, doing short-field landings and takeoffs. I was impressed with its performance and before nightfall I was the happy owner.

Everyone was anxious for me to get going. Howard wanted the product to sell, Terry wanted the ten-thousand per load for his part and the hippies wanted something to smoke, as did about half of the population of California according to a referendum in which 49% of the Californians voted in favor of legalizing cannabis.

Clearing customs and obtaining all the paperwork in Tijuana or Mexicali was old hat. Nevertheless, this is a must if one is to penetrate very far south of the border, and failure to do so has had many an airplane confiscated, and the crew thrown into prison. Once one has all the paperwork and filed flight plans, he is welcome anywhere as a tourist. I flew south to Mazatlán and rented a VW dune buggy. With this tin contraption, I bounced along rough washed out roads until I reached Pechilingue. The whole village was happy to see me, and Joaquin had fresh marijuana. He showed me a sample; however I had no idea what good pot was or even what it was supposed to look like. I bought 1,100 pounds for seventeen thousand dollars, drove back to town and at dusk returned with the plane.

At the crack of dawn, Pedro hopped in with me to show me where to pick up the load. As I was barreling down the short strip, an old sow trotted out in front of us. I locked the brakes and applied full right rudder. The plane slid sideways and in doing so, the tires kicked up rocks that cut the brake fluid line to the right wheel. We got out, examined the damage and clamped the brake line. We taxied back and gave it a second run. All was fine until I had to land on the highway between the trucks and couldn't stop. I kept the left brake locked until it burned all the rubber off one side of the tire. When I finally let up, we went bump, bump, bumping down the highway. I realized the idling propeller was pulling us along, so I killed the engine and she stopped.

The airplane was quickly loaded, and I took off over the truck with the mounted machine gun. Flying north, I worried that the tire would blow out upon landing.

I touched down ever so gently on the right tire, let it settle onto the left and bumped down the hard dry lakebed, taxied over to the side, and unloaded in tumbleweeds and cacti. The town of Caborca, Sonora had an airstrip with several duster planes. I filled up with gasoline and was fortunate enough to find a new tire. This sounds simple enough, however in Mexico, this could have taken a week, so I was lucky. It was almost dark when I got back to the lakebed. The load was safe, and I reloaded and headed north. Terry was busy trying to look important and justify his ten thousand dollar cut. He had parked his pickup on top of a small mountain that I had to pass over in order to land on his strip and he pretended to talk me down, as one directs a pilot in thick fog from the radar room. What an idiot!

Joaquin had an unlimited supply of marijuana and I had an unlimited market, so I made weekly runs. Each week we opened another bank account and filled another lockbox with greenbacks. The pot cost fifteen dollars a pound and sold for sixty. My expenses were the ten-thousand to Terry and a couple of tanks of gasoline for less than two-hundred dollars. Loads averaged just a little over 1,100 pounds, I was making forty-five thousand dollars each week. My original plan had been to make three hundred thousand dollars, quit, and move back to the farm, but I just rocketed past that goal so fast I couldn't believe it.

I looked at the bundles of pot that just looked like bales of hay to me and I couldn't fathom why anyone would pay thousands of dollars for it. During a trip north I figured how much I was making per hour--it averaged around six thousand dollars. As I graduated to bigger and faster planes that figure increased exponentially.

Marrie and I went to the grocery store and bought apple boxes full of candy and goodies for the children in the Mexican village. They loved the big red apples as they had never seen such fruit from the colder climate, so I always took a box or two. We shopped at Toys "R" Us and bought toys. For a few hundred dollars, we could fill the plane. When I landed on the strip I would pass the goodies to the children and to some of the adults present. Joaquin was a dog in the way he attempted to grab the boxes and pass them to his men. Even though I couldn't understand the language, I knew he was telling them to hide the boxes. He was getting seventeen thousand dollars a week and couldn't stand to see those children even get an apple. Pox on him wherever he is! However, this may have been my undoing, because every week even more children showed up until it became dangerous to land. There was no way all those children came from that one small village. News of the American Santa Claus was spreading.

13. A STRIP OF FLESH

The Thirteenth Trip -- Lemonade from Lemons – Yugoslavia, Europe, Home – Senor, You Come with Us -- Day Fourteen -- A Firm Mistress -- A Ghostly Passenger -- Good Weed in the South

Mike and I flew over Baja, looking for suitable landing strips that were far from roads and people. We spotted a short strip marked off with white stones on a tiny island north of La Paz. It looked perfect. I put her down and as she slowed, the nose wheel sunk into the soft sand, causing the propeller blades to bend out of shape. What a mess! We looked the situation over, and I never dreamed she would fly, but we soldiered on. In the luggage compartment were two ten-ton hydraulic jacks for Joaquin to press marijuana blocks. Mike held one behind the blade and I beat with the other. They straightened out fairly well, although both had bad kinks in them. I started the engine with my hand on the kill switch, fully expecting it to vibrate the engine mounts loose. Not so, she purred like a kitten and no vibration. I revved her up and to my amazement the blades were perfectly balanced.

We noticed the land was of a strange formation. There was a foot of sand and then a strip of hard earth running diagonally across the island. If we went directly across these hard strips the plane would taxi, but to turn parallel with them, the front tire sank. We loaded everything in the rear baggage compartment and Mike sat on the tail. This caused the tail to drag on the ground and lifted the nose wheel off the ground. In this attitude, we taxied to the end of the strip and angled her diagonally across the lay of the land. Mike continued to hold the tail down while I held the brakes and gave her full power. When we got going, Mike crawled into the baggage compartment with his legs hanging out.

The plane veered off the strip and was quickly approaching the water at a 45-degree angle. I saw she wasn't going to fly before she hit, but there was no choice I could only hold to what I had. Just as the tires were about to touch the water I pulled the nose up hard, jerked on full flaps and the main tires skied across the water, causing rooster tails to fly high into the air and soak poor Mike who was hanging half out of the plane. Just as soon as she was airborne, I rolled her over on the right side and kicked the left rudder, and Mike tumbled into the cabin. He crawled upfront and climbed over in his seat grinning from ear to ear. We were two proud boys.

We flew directly to California where I purchased a new propeller. The next day we were back in Mexico, looking for the perfect spot. We found a narrow dry lake about a mile off the beach in the upper Sea of Cortez near Cabo Tepoca.

It looked good! On one side was a bluff with a mesa on top and the other was endless reaches of desert with cacti and scattered thorny scrubs. We dug a long trench, covered it with plywood, brought in five-gallon jerry cans full of fuel, and stashed them in the hole. Mike drove me crazy with his meticulous ways, spending hours sweeping the area with a branch and then throwing sticks and leaves back over it. He wouldn't leave when it was obvious to me the job was finished.

We started unloading there every week. I flew to Caborca or Hermosillo, fueled up, bought hot lunches, and brought them back. An hour before dark we headed for the border.

Easter Sunday morning 1974. We were heading north with a load of kilos packaged in red cellophane. The beaches were packed. Surely everybody in Mexico had gone to the beach that day. We flew low over the bathers until we were approaching our dry lake, then turned right across the chaparral, landed on the dry lakebed, and unloaded in the scrub. I taxied a hundred yards away and began sweeping out the plane. Mike was busy hiding the load when an old maroon Pontiac came barreling down the lake, kicking up a plume of dust. Hanging out the right window was a man with a rifle pointed at me. The car slid sideways to a stop and three very determined young men jumped out with guns all over me. They were policemen from the town of Caborca.

In their search one of them found two marijuana seeds either on the ground or in the plane and then the barrel of one pistol was in my mouth and another in my ribs. The leader laid the .45-caliber pistol beside my temple and pulled the trigger. A strip of flesh was shot or burned off the side of my head and I was deaf in my left ear.

After a few minutes of haggling, a small plane came into sight circling a thousand feet above us. I have no idea what he was doing, but these men assumed he was meeting me with a load. When the plane continued on, they figured whatever deal I was doing was off and they changed their tune. I had two-thousand dollars in my wallet in one hundred dollar bills, and they got into a hot argument as to how they were going to split the loot. I told them I had to have two- hundred for fuel and that the next week I would visit them in Caborca. When they saw they weren't going to get anything better, they gave me the two-hundred dollars, an address, phone number, and were emphatic about my meeting them the next week.

I flew into town and fueled. When I returned I was expecting an ambush, so I landed fast and downwind. When I turned around, the Pontiac came peeling out of the bushes just as I had envisioned. I feinted as to go left. They slid to their right to head me off and then I turned back to my right where I had more room. As I passed them, they put three slugs in the airplane; one hit the window about a foot behind my head. They were shooting to kill. I headed north, and at five-thousand feet I turned to see if they had left the lake. The car was just a dot as it left the dirt road and turned on the highway heading east across the desert.

Hidden underneath the dash was a Browning High Power 9mm automatic pistol with thirteen cartridges. After making ninety-degree turn to the right I slid over in the right seat and took the pistol out. Within minutes I was on top of them at two thousand feet. They were traveling at eighty mph. I adjusted the throttle and attitude until they were directly below and then I began reducing power.

The highway was perhaps six feet above the desert. No shoulders, only a cement berm along both sides, and perfectly straight for as far as I could see. The windows on a Cessna open horizontally and have a hinged brace to keep them open. I slid over in the co-pilot's seat, pushed the right window fully open and locked it in position and kept easing the plane down until it was no more than twenty feet above the top of the car. My ears were ringing, blood was oozing down the side of my head, and the powder burn was still smarting as I lined up on my prey…

I kept her just above the chaparral on the way back to the dry lake. We loaded quickly and took off, crossing the border just after dark.

Mike was getting on my nerves. I had been shot, police tried to kill me, and I didn't have a good place to leave the marijuana while I went to town and fueled up. Changes had to be made. Terry wanted me to come across the border in the middle of the day, but I would not consider doing that. He was not afraid to cross during the day; in fact, he preferred it. With that, we came to a new partnership, whereby he would meet me on a dry lake near Hermosillo with fuel and I would fly the southern portion of the trip. We became fifty-fifty partners, and this worked out better for me because I didn't have to cross the US Mexican border or pay the five-thousand-dollar landing fee, nor the five thousand to Mike.

Everyone was happy. Joaquin had plenty of pot and we were in demand in California. I spent each night in the village of Pechilingue and departed at first light with Pedro riding shotgun, directing me to a new spot most every morning. They loaded 1,100 pounds of marijuana and I headed north to the dry lake. I'd meet Terry in his old Cessna 336, the stiff-legged version of the Cessna push-pull (The plane with one propeller on the nose and the other on the tail). He brought fuel, sandwiches, and ice-cold beer. We transferred the load to his plane quickly, making it ready for take-off in case anyone came our way, and then topped off my plane with fuel. Afterward we would sit under the wing and enjoy a good lunch. There was no hurry because we could see for ten miles in all directions across the stark white dry lake.

On one trip, Terry brought his father, Allen Butts, who wanted to get in on the action. Allen was a likable, jovial man, probably twenty years older than I was. He was a heavy equipment operator who also flew single-engine planes. He hopped in and we flew south.

Allen was a riot! That evening Joaquin told me there were two Americans in the jungle who wanted to meet me. After supper, several of the men led us through the scrub. The path was bad. Rocks, thorny bushes and cactus were everywhere. Allen knew one word in Spanish, 'caballo', meaning horse, and he kept putting two fingers from his right hand over one finger on the left and yelling, "caballo, caballo!" He kept the men laughing as we struggled over the stones trying to follow a dim lantern. Howard in California had been complaining about the pot being green and I was saying, "My people want the brown stuff."

After three or four miles, we came to a camp lit up with bright lanterns. The place was a hive of activity with fifteen or twenty men pressing marijuana into kilo bricks. Two Americans introduced themselves as Allen Whitsitt and Mark Reich. Allen was a big bruiser who looked like a bouncer in a nightclub and Mark was a wiry redhead, with a red beard and piggish blue eyes. They were both happy to see us and very friendly, in fact, too friendly. I should have guessed they wanted something. Mark was learning Spanish and teased me about saying, "My people want the brown stuff." Both were from Southern California and we exchanged telephone numbers. They said they'd watched me land every evening and were impressed with how slow and short I brought her in.

We made twelve successful trips in twelve consecutive days and I was done, ready to go home and take a break. On trip thirteen, I had a bad gut feeling. That night I talked with Joaquin about my daily landings and asked if he thought this was bringing attention. He laughed at the idea and said the Federalés were paid off and there was nothing to worry about. Still, I didn't feel right, that warning bell was going off in the pit of my stomach. The following morning I walked down to the river. I washed my face, brushed my teeth, and at the crack of dawn Pedro and I got into the plane. I cranked her up and when I did I heard a loud bang. I thought a tire had blown out and as I looked down at the left tire I realized Pedro was yelling, "Policia! Policia!" It registered! I slammed the throttle to the firewall and went tearing down the 600 feet of strip left in front of us.

As I checked the air-speed indicator I heard another loud crash and then there was no more windshield. Gasoline was gushing in like it was being poured out of a bucket and blowing into my face. A slug slammed into the wing support beside my head. The impact was as loud as if someone hit it with a ten-pound sledgehammer. Bullets splattered against metal, sending slivers of lead in my eyes and all over my face. Then came the moment I was hit in my right foot and it felt like I was on fire. Bullets were hitting the plane hard and fast. Like hailstones in a storm.

All this happened just as I rotated at the very end of the strip. I went up probably a hundred feet into the air and then realized there was no resistance, backward or forward to the yoke, and at that split second I thought the elevator cables had been shot out. Five hundred feet ahead was a cliff of solid rock and directly in front were big, smooth, round boulders that looked like wet turtles all packed together. Something strange happened in my mind. Everything turned yellow and moved in slow motion.

I vividly remember pulling out the mixture-control to stop the engine, turning off the fuel, the oil shut-off valves and all electrical switches, as if I had all day. I watched as we plummeted toward the rocks and I knew if it didn't explode into flames we would live. I found out later my mother woke up in Georgia having a nightmare that I was burning to death. As we hit I saw the nose and motor come off, we bounced once, and on the second impact the wings folded, and we stopped. The engine and nose assembly were underneath the plane.

I was knocked unconscious and as I came to, I heard Pedro yelling, "Come on Roger, come on!" Our doors were jammed so we jumped out front where the engine used to be. I look back and saw four men with rifles running our way and shooting. There was no doubt they meant to kill us. I reached in, pulled out the 9mm pistol, crouched on one knee, and fired five or six shots in their direction. They ran for cover in the rocks.

We started down a dry sandy streambed, but he steered me up the mountain. As he led the way I saw he was running on a jagged bloody mess. His foot was almost shot off from where an AK-47 slug had ripped through his ankle bone. I stopped him, took off my T-shirt, and wrapped it around in his ankle, tying it as tight as I possibly could. This staunched the flow somewhat. We hobbled on up the path with Pedro in the lead. I suggested we head downhill but Pedro said that was the way the Federalés would go so we continued up the mountain.

After a short distance we came upon an old white donkey ambling along in front of us. Pedro managed to get astride, and I mounted behind him. Without bridle or saddle, we rode for the next seven miles until we came to the house of a friend or distant relation of Pedro's.

Pedro stopped the donkey beside a rail fence where a man was plowing with a speckled ox and told him what had happened. The man took us to his house where his wife and daughter were; and insisted we go in. The daughter was so very shy she wouldn't look at us.

The toe of my boot was blown away and a bullet hole gaped at the center of my foot. I cut the boot off. The bone and nail were shot right off my right big toe and there was a deep gash across the top of my head where a slug had grazed my skull. Most of Pedro's ankle was gone. Flies crawled all over our wounds. The woman brought diesel fuel and poured it over the raw flesh and draped the wounds with a cloth. The man left for help. I sat all day in a hard, straight chair.

I must have drifted into delirium because there was a heavy hunting rifle hanging on the wall and I insisted I needed to take it, slip back over the boulders and shoot those cowards like fish in a barrel. Pedro and the woman looked at me as if I was crazy.

As it was getting dark, a band of men rode up on horses and mules. Amongst them was Dr. Benjamin Sosa, a Red Cross doctor from a town twenty miles away. The first thing he did was give us both a shot of morphine, and a tetanus shot. Then he began cleaning the filthy fly-encrusted wounds. He was tender and meticulous, but it was an ugly job. He dug for a long time trying to find the slug in my foot; later x-rays found it lodged between the anklebones. He advised us both to get to a hospital as soon as we were able but further asserted that it was too dangerous for me to go to one in Mexico as they were looking for an American who had been shot. He gave us big white pain pills, along with penicillin tablets.

We mounted mules and rode toward the nearest road. Sometime after dark, a ten-wheeler truck loaded with corn on the ear arrived with a dozen or more men. They dug holes in the corn, and buried Pedro and me, leaving a tiny space for our noses. Each time we hit a bump, which was often, we were covered entirely. We went through three roadblocks and searches while in route to Mazatlán, and learned that an army division was looking for an American pilot shot down - believed dead. Joaquin's brother had been killed in the shooting and another man seriously injured. These were the men that had walked me to the river that morning, laughing, and joking as I brushed my teeth. I had heard what murderers the Policia Federalés of Mexico were. Now I knew.

The truck stopped in a small village just north of Mazatlan where Pedro and I were invited into a house. We each bathed in washbasins of cold water. The man of the house kept changing the water as it soiled with the dirt and blood. After considerable effort, we were clean. They gave us decent clothes. Pedro went to a hospital, and I had to get out of the area, so we parted company. I figured there were roadblocks on the highway going north, so I decided to head south to Guadalajara. The men took me downtown where someone found a rather new taxi willing to go the distance. The driver was a dwarfish man who loved to talk and did so all night.

"I was living at home with my widowed mother and had a taxi that was paid for and I had money in the bank, but I was little and ugly and couldn't get a woman to go out with me. I had my eye on Dora, a girl in the neighborhood, but she was shy and wouldn't talk to me, even if she had liked me. One holiday there was a parade in front of our house and Dora was playing the flute in the band. I hid behind the gate and when she passed by I pulled her into the yard, and with the help of my mother, we got her into the house where we kept her until the next morning.

We treated her good, and I told her I had loved her for a long time and my mother told her she wanted her for her daughter. Still Dora was so shy she wouldn't even talk to me, so the next morning we sadly sent her home. When she got there, her parents wouldn't let her in the house, thinking she had spent the night with a man. She cried and begged them to let her in, but they wouldn't change their hard hearts. I watched Dora walk away with her head hung low. It was then that I ran up to her and told her how much I loved her and asked that she and I go to the priest right now. And sir, that is how I got my beautiful wife."

"After two years, our first son was born. At that time, I owned a Ford taxi, so I named him Ford. A year thereafter, we had another son, and this time I was driving a Dodge taxi, so I named him Dodge. Wasn't long before the third son arrived and at that time I owned a Chevrolet taxi, but the priest wouldn't name him Chevrolet, so I had to bribe the priest by teaching him how to drive and then he christened him Chevrolet. And that sir, is how I got my three boys, Ford, Dodge, and Chevrolet."

As day began to break, we were high in the Sierra Madre Mountains, on a steep upgrade with trees overhanging the highway. Clouds were boiling and mingling with one another as we approached the crest. Some were dark blue, others swirls of pink with lacey white borders, and then suddenly the sun shone through, giving a celestial view. It looked as though we could drive straight into heaven. I had the driver stop the car as the sight was so breath-taking that tears sprang to my eyes. It was the most beautiful scene these eyes ever looked upon. I imagined that the Prophet Elijah was about to appear in his flaming chariot.

The driver took me to the International Airport in Guadalajara where I boarded a flight directly to Los Angeles. Marrie met me at the airport and immediately we went looking for a doctor who wouldn't report the gunshot wounds. I remembered a Chinese couple, both doctors, who owned a hospital in Wilmington. I had painted their house and hospital some years before, so we went to them. He was none too happy to oblige, but I told him I had been shot in Mexico and he finally agreed to work on me.

He removed twenty or thirty slivers of lead in my face and chest where the AK-47 bullets had hit metal and splintered. My big toe looked like hamburger meat, but the most searing pain came from the slug embedded in my foot. The doctor had to operate for a long time, cleaning, and sewing.

My foot continued to throb and ache with every heartbeat. Pills simply would not dull the pain. Inspired, I cut the toe off the right boot of my pair of army combat boots, I slipped my bandaged foot inside, laced it up tight and got some relief. Then I discovered that if my foot was higher than my head it didn't ache nearly as much. So for the next month I went around with my foot high in the air. It sounds ridiculous, but if something hurts badly enough, you find a way to get relief.

For the first time, I realized this job could kill me,

I couldn't walk therefore I couldn't work, so why not take a real vacation? I mentioned Hawaii and Marrie jumped at the idea. Before nightfall, she had reservations and tickets. The very next morning we took our two little girls and flew to Honolulu for three memorable weeks. Our five-star hotel was on Waikiki Beach. Between the hotel and beach was an acre-sized swimming pool with deluxe white lounge chairs. The most sought after places were next to the beach and bar. Early each morning I hobbled out and draped towels over four of the choicest chairs, and each morning I saw the same nice-looking young man doing the same. We introduced ourselves and became friends during the vacation. "Concerning your shot foot," he said, "I don't care if the story is true or not, just make it interesting." Gary was a clever man and we remained friends for many years.

In the years when sailing ships cruised the oceans of the world hunting whales to render into oil the sailors would while away their idle time carving on whale-bone. Many of these carvings are exquisitely detailed, depicting life at sea. This art is called Scrimshaw, and it was a hot item when we were in Hawaii. The shop attendant told us that it was being outlawed. When I heard this I bought the shop out with twenty-dollar bills. Gary liked the action, however, he laughed hard the next day when the shop window was again full of the same.

We visited sugar and pineapple plantations with Marrie driving and my right foot elevated out the window in the cut off combat boot. Marya learned to sign for room service that trip and the things those two little girls ordered made us smile.

Each night the hotel put on different entertainment. We enjoyed our first luau. I was impressed with the way they heated rocks, threw them in a pit, then wrapped the hogs in banana leaves and placed them on top of the hot rocks, then threw in more hot rocks and covered all this with earth. Several hours later they took the meat out and it was succulent, cooked to perfection. We danced by torchlight, I would leave my cane beside the chair and Marrie and I would sway gently to the romantic Hawaiian love songs played by the band. One night a tall thin man dressed in rags danced to the song "Mr. Bo Jangles" behind a curtain so all we saw was his shadow. It was fantastic.

Puka shell jewelry was in vogue and we sifted through the sand, digging for shells on the beach. Marrie and the girls made necklaces and bracelets with them. I relaxed in the lounge by the pool, drank piña coladas, and read books. Whenever I got hot the girls poured cool water over me. What a delicious vacation it was! The only time in my life I can remember going anywhere with just vacation on my mind.

Mike told us that Stan-the-Man had arranged a gambling junket. If we put up five-thousand dollars we got a free trip to Dubrovnik, Yugoslavia. Once we arrived at the casino, we would receive our money and gamble as we chose. I swallowed hook, line and sinker and put up the money. We were to leave on a B.O.A.C charter flight departing at 9 pm. from LAX. After a *very* long wait we finally boarded. Between me and the window sat a very fat man with a long cheap cigar which he puffed on all the way to London. We had a four-hour layover in N.Y, then a six-hour stopover in London. It took forty *miserable* hours to reach Dubrovnik. Once we arrived, we were booked into a dingy little hotel that couldn't have cost ten dollars a night and were informed by Stan that the Yugoslavian government would not allow the funds to be transferred, thus we were free to return anytime we wished. The junket was over. Stan hadn't done too badly if you multiply five thousand times one hundred and then subtract the cost of a cheap charter flight. What a crock! I determined I would get my money back.

Marrie and I rented a little red V.W. Beetle and headed south to the Albanian border. I had my right foot stuck out the window and my left arm around my sweetheart. We laughed as she sped around sharp curves, sometimes almost going over onto two wheels.

Once, as she came tearing around a bend, we saw soldiers in the middle of the highway with a big *HALT* banner stretched between them. Through gestures, they made us understand that they had comrades positioned ten kilometers back on the highway and we had driven the distance too quickly, thus we were speeding, and the fine was 500 Dinars. Marrie was laughing and trying to take their photo, but they kept covering their faces. I told them we didn't have 500 Dinars and they would have to take her to jail. She stopped laughing and asked me how much that was in dollars and I told her it was several thousand and then she got real serious. After a little fun, I paid the fine, which amounted to about five dollars.

The southern coast of Yugoslavia had a most unusual pink rocky landscape along the Aegean Sea. Of particular interest were castles built on tiny islands connected to the mainland by a narrow causeway and drawbridge. It was all stark and strange to me and I was ready to leave after a few days.

Next we flew to Rome and spent two wonderful days visiting Vatican City, with St. Peters Basilica and the Papal Palace housing the Sistine Chapel and the paintings and sculptures by Michelangelo. They were so wonderfully carved it looked as if they could step forward out of the marble. We loved Rome. At the airport, we got to talking with a priest from Rhodesia and became so engrossed in the conversation that when they called our flight to Holland we didn't hear the announcement. No one stood up to board the plane, so we just waited.

After a few minutes, the flight to Carthage was announced and the entire waiting room stood up. We ran over to the counter and asked about the flight to Amsterdam and were told the plane had already left the concourse and was taxiing out. We didn't mind and soon had reservations on another flight to Holland, arriving within an hour or two after the original.

We were received most graciously in Holland. They loved Marrie and told wonderful stories about her childhood during the Second World War. One of their favorites was of the very hard times when the cities were being bombed and Marrie's mother took her to the country where they stayed in a barn. Her father was working for the Dutch Underground and was a fugitive from the Germans. Somehow Marrie went missing, it was dark and everyone there went searching for her. Suddenly she appeared, crawling out from under the hay, smiling and calling for Mamma.

From Holland, we flew directly to California where two little girls were overjoyed as we came through the door. Their little faces were radiant sunbeams. Holding these two precious daughters to my chest was without a doubt the best part of the vacation.

"It takes a heap o' livin' in a house t' make it home,
A heap o' sun and shadow and you sometimes have t' roam,
A' fore you really 'preciate the things you left behind
And hunger for 'em somehow, with 'em always on your mind."
--Edgar A. Guest

Terry proved to be a coward, as I had always suspected. He did a lot of swaggering around with his pistols. Perhaps he might have enough guts to shoot an unarmed man in the back, but that was doubtful. When I didn't show up on the dry lake, he put his tail between his legs and ran under the house. He knew I was in trouble when I didn't show up and he also knew where I was taking off from and the route I was taking. It would have been so easy for him to have flown down and take a look, but he didn't, and he never told anyone I was missing. Over half a million dollars was floating around for the twelve previous trips and he was hoping I was dead.

When I did show up, he was cocky and hard to pin down on anything. Thanks to Howard, I collected what was owed me and went to take the pickup and camper rig I had paid for. Terry had hidden it and it took several trips before I came across Allen Butts who told me where it was. Terry never did give me the title, so I drove the truck until it was ready for the junkyard.

I asked Allen one day how he came up with a son like Terry and he replied, "I don't know, he just got caught in my trap."

Allen was eager to work, but I had lost my enthusiasm. Joaquin owed me seventeen thousand dollars and I knew I would never get the cash. The only chance was to get up a load. Allen was anxious and Terry was hiding from me, so Allen and I struck up a partnership whereby he would fly down and get the load and we would split the profit down the middle.

I meticulously explained everything he had to do. I told him to stop in Mexicali and clear customs. Then fly on down to Mazatlán where I would be waiting in the Hotel El Camino Real, under the name of Roger Ardell. I would have the load secured on a safe strip and on the way home he could stop for fuel at a specific cattle feedlot, five miles south of Hermosillo where he would pay the gasman five thousand dollars to top him off. I gave him the money and explained exactly where this place was located. You couldn't possibly miss it as it had thousands of cattle and a mile-long dirt airstrip.

I flew down and arranged everything and called Allen to come on down.

The Camino Real was a lovely hotel right on the Pacific with hanging flowers cascading from the balcony of every room. A large pool meandered around huge boulders with a submerged bar at one end with stools just below the surface. I was laughing and having a good time when a gentleman came over and asked if I was Mr. Ardell, I answered in the affirmative. He nodded to his assistants who came over and handcuffed me. They escorted me to my room and told me to change and pack. No one would tell me what it was about. I hadn't done anything, so I wasn't very worried. Gogan shirts were popular at the time and one was hanging over a chair. I chose it and a pair of jeans and sandals.

Two carloads of Federalés escorted me through town and deposited me in the prison. A more horrible, loathsome, filthy place would be hard to find if one searched the world over. The Federalés took my clothes and suitcase which I never saw again. I had over three hundred dollars in my wallet and the receptionist took that. When I protested he took a blackjack and slapped it in his palm in a most threatening manner, all the while glaring at me with black, glassy killer eyes.

I was taken to a courtyard with one large cell, perhaps ten by fifteen feet. The iron grill slammed behind me and I looked on a pitiful sight. A dozen men were sitting and laying around on the filthy floor. Over in one corner was a five-gallon bucket half-full of piss and shit. In another corner was an old pillow so slick and dirty the stripes from the ticking were barely visible. I shuddered just to look at it. I learned that this was just a holding cell for men passing through or men who had just been arrested. The afternoon grew hotter and hotter and I grew tired of standing and for the longest time I refused to sit down, thinking something must happen and I would be taken out.

All the men were stripped down to their undershorts. A boy came to the grill and took orders for sandwiches and cold drinks. I would have loved a big, cold Coca Cola, but I had no money. The boy brought someone a Pepsi bottle full of water and I eased up to the grill and asked him to get me a drink. He took the bottle, went to a faucet nearby, filled it, and brought it to me. I took a swallow and spewed it out; it was the temperature of horse piss.

That night was endless and stifling hot. I tried to sit as near the grill as I could, it seemed a little cooler there. Every so often the door opened, and another thief or drug addict was thrown in. Before the night was over, there were eighteen of us in that cell with standing room only. The following morning around ten o'clock the cell started to empty, and that filthy, greasy pillow started looking mighty good. When the man sitting on its left, I grabbed it and didn't dare let go.

In the afternoon, a rather well dressed young man was being released and wanted to buy my brightly painted Gauguin shirt. The shirts cost a hundred dollars at the time, however, under the circumstances I agreed to sell it for ten dollars in pesos. He stood on the other side of the door and asked for the shirt, but I demanded the money first, for I knew if I handed him the shirt he would walk out laughing. I took it off and kept several wraps around my hand while he did the same with the money. He would gain a wrap on the shirt as I gained a wrap on the bills. Once I had the major portion of the bills in my hand, we completed the swap. The boy came around with hard roll sandwiches and I bought one and a cold drink but had difficulty swallowing.

Day three found me exhausted, probably from not eating and getting little sleep. Around noon a busload of tough-looking prisoners came in. They were being transported to Tres Maria's; a large prison colony located on three islands some distance out in the Pacific. One convict was a hard-looking, yet handsome man, with several days' growth of rough black beard. He nodded and sat down beside me, his presence had a calming effect upon me, and I believe others in the cell felt it also. We had been sitting there for several hours when an old woman dressed in a long black dress with a scarf over her head, brought him an open basket filled with tortillas rolled tightly around the succulent spicy chicken. When the woman left, he sat down again and took the cloth off the basket and I saw him slowly bow his head and pray.

When he looked up he passed the basket to me and I gladly took one and said, "Muchas Gracias, Señor!"

He looked me straight in the eyes, held up his right hand, negatively shook the index finger and then pointed up. I have heard many wonderful sermons in my life, but never an equal to the one that was but a demonstrative gesture.

During the fourth night, I was taken from the community cell deep into the bowels of the prison and thrown into a small cell with nothing but bloodstains. There was no window, no peephole, no bunk or slab to sit or sleep on, nothing but greasy black concrete with a small light bulb behind an iron grill in the high ceiling. How long I stayed in that cell, I have no idea. The only sound I heard was the sound of torture, the muffled sounds of a struggle, and then the sounds of a beating and begging, moaning, or screaming. Every so often, the door opened, and I was allowed to empty my pot. Then I received a plate of rice and beans and a jug of water.

The jailer would say, "You next, son-of-a-bitch!" He wasn't lying. They came and got me, and handcuffed me to a wall. Then they started beating me with rubber hoses and leather blackjacks. When they figured they had me softened up, a man who spoke English came and told me this would all be over if I just signed the confession. I said I didn't know what he was talking about. He then explained that Allen Butts was in prison in Hermosillo and had confessed everything. It seemed Allen had landed at the international airport where he was arrested. Still, I couldn't imagine what the problem was. Of course I refused to sign.

The next treatment was affixation in a tank of what looked like water. Three men held my head under until I had to inhale and then found it was some type of gaseous water that burned my eyes, nose, and throat. After the first snort, the three couldn't hold me down. I figured I must struggle in the same way just before I had to take a breath, and this worked somewhat. Each time there was a beating and then something new. The third night they applied cattle prods to my testicles and stubbed out cigarettes and cigars on any tender spot they chose. I knew I would never sign the confession, even if they killed me. In the community cell, I learned that once you signed it was all over. They then took you before a judge and you were sentenced. If one didn't sign the confession, the paperwork took two years and all kinds of bribes could be arranged during that time.

After two weeks, they brought in a frozen corpse wrapped in inch wide strips of newspaper and hung him from a meat hook stuck between his ribs with the other end attached to the wall. First, his eyes started thawing and as the water trickled down his face it looked as though he was crying. As he thawed out, the hole where the meat hook was inserted pulled his ribs apart and I could see his liver, heart, and lungs. The longer he hung there the more the newspaper unraveled until parts of him were naked. This was a bad sight and worse smell, but it had no adverse effect upon me at all. I had butchered too many large animals for this to bother me. The formaldehyde smell was nauseating, so I kept my face to the floor and breathed the air through the little quarter-inch slit underneath the door. I learned to sleep with my face plastered to the filthy floor with my lips puckered, trying to suck in fresh air. I dreamed in living color and woke to a black and white nightmare.

After the corpse, they got heavy-handed in their beatings. They knew just how hard to hit so as to jar one's very bones, yet not knock you out. They stripped me naked and stretched me over a barrel. They greased my rectum and started packing something up inside me. I caught on fire! There was no doubt it was a very hot pepper treatment. The pain was excruciating. I screamed, yelled, and cussed until my voice went. After a while, they came with a water hose, shoved it up and washed me out. The pepper burned the lining off my colon, and it was painful for several weeks thereafter. This was my lowest moment, still, I never considered signing the confession.

Some days after the pepper treatment, they moved me to a small section of the prison in the general population. When I learned the date, I found I had been in the torture chamber for two weeks.

My new home was an open courtyard with a corrugated iron lean-to extending from the wall. Underneath the lean-to were stalls made of cardboard, or whatever one could find. These condominiums were sold or rented by the month. Usually two men shared one and the others had to sleep on the concrete floor underneath the roof. There were two Americans there, named Mel and John and they lent me a blanket. I felt like I had died and gone to heaven to be out in the open, breathing fresh air.

The first morning I was sleeping soundly on my back when something hit me in the face, hard. As soon as I could see, I saw a mean looking Mexican standing over me holding a bag of clothes and I saw this was what he had struck me with. He told me I was late for muster, so I got up and stood in line with everyone else while the guards walked by and counted. Mel and John were very nice and invited me to eat with them; otherwise, I would have had to find an empty tin can and scoop from the tub of rice and beans brought in once a day. That was it, period. There was nothing else whatsoever for the men to eat. However, they were all local and there was always someone at the grill bringing in food. Also, a boy ran across the street and bought anything you could afford.

A tall, blond, pencil-necked, piece of functionary from the American consul showed up and questioned me. I asked him to telephone Marrie. The only thing he did was send a report to the DEA.

Two men were being released and I gave them Marrie's telephone number and begged them to call her. One man knew Alberto and Rafael Pardo, two big marijuana dealers whom I had met, and I asked him to contact them. One of the men did call Marrie and let her know where I was. I learned later that he also contacted Rafael Pardo and things began to happen.

Marrie went to our friend, Allen Niger, and explained what had happened. He introduced her to his landlord, a Mexican-American named Gus. They flew to Mazatlan and met an attorney whom Gus knew. On the ride from the airport, Marrie's dress was torn on the springs from the car seat and the lawyer apologized for the sad shape of the car, explaining that his Mercedes was in the shop for a few days.

Marrie and the lawyer met me in the lawyer visiting area which was the best-looking part of the prison. This lawyer was an obese, pig-eyed man, with greasy black hair combed straight back. He was wearing a striped seersucker suit with a loud yellow tie. With one glance, I knew there was no way he was going to be my representative before the court. I asked Marrie to find another lawyer. She gave me forty dollars and left.

The next morning John, Mel and I made up a shopping list that included two bottles of whiskey. We were planning a celebration. The boy returned with all the foodstuff, but only one bottle of whiskey. I asked the prisoner in charge of the transaction about the other bottle of whiskey.

He pulled out a big knife, stuck it under my chin, looked me right in the eye, and said, "You only paid for one bottle."

Mel ran over, pulled me back, and said it wasn't worth a bottle of whiskey, even if I killed him. He was the same man that hit me in the face the first morning. This ruined the party for me and that afternoon I bought a razor-sharp shank. There was no doubt that if I stayed in that area one of us would die and I did not plan on it being me. My guess is he heard I had an equalizer because he left me alone from then on.

Wednesday was visiting day. Visitors were allowed a twelve-hour visit and they could bring in food. The section I was in was back toward the rear of the prison. Leading to our patio was a low, dark, dome-shaped corridor eight feet wide, lined with cells on both sides. I was waiting at the grill on our end of the corridor and I saw her hurrying through, walking as near the middle as possible, holding the picnic basket close to her chest. The cells had iron bars across the front and as Marrie walked down the dark corridor wearing a crisp white sundress, brown hands and arms reached at her from both sides.

Tw's another scene from *Dante's Inferno*. I rented one of the little huts for the day and after a quick introduction to my new 'friends' we hurried inside and sat down on the worn brindled cowhide stretched between two poles that sufficed for a bed. This seemed strange and we didn't have very much to say to one another. After a while, we went outside and joined the crowd.

Lupe, the resident gay and washer person, was parading around in a negligee, holding a puppy in his arms. Mexican music was blaring from a dozen busted speakers, all from different stations. Dancer was waltzing on his one leg with the aid of crutches, having lost his leg up to the hip since arriving. It all began when he stubbed his toe. The toe turned black and shriveled up before he saw a doctor. The doctor amputated the toe as gangrene had set in. Then his foot became infected, which they cut off. That didn't stop it. The next slice was at the knee. Still not enough, so they took the leg off at the hip. Dancer was still a big happy man, twirling around on crutches.

The day following visits was always depressing and the men were quiet. One morning, a young man climbed on the roof and got onto the wall before the guards shot him off. He hit the corrugated iron roof and made a clatter before rolling to the edge and falling hard onto the concrete patio. Several men ran to him. Shots rang out and bullets ricocheted off the cement. A voice came over the speaker, ordering everyone to stay away from him. The man was shot in the upper leg and it was obviously broken. He lay there all day under the blistering sun while his blood ran out in a little stream across the cement floor and into the gutter. That was one tough hombre. He never cried out or made a sound except to ask for a drink of water several times, however, the guard on the catwalk above acted as if he didn't hear him.

One young American, about twenty years old with a shaved head and wearing a bright yellow and white striped T-shirt went over to him, caught flies off the wounded man, snapped their wings off, and popped them in his mouth. He said he did this to keep them from tickling his stomach when they buzzed. If someone threw a banana peeling in the trash this man jumped up, grabbed it, and ate it. He was a rather nice-looking young man and seemed strong and healthy, but insane. Late in the afternoon guards came with a stretcher and took the wounded man away.

One morning a guard came in and told me I had been released and for me to get my things and follow him. I didn't have any things, so I shook hands with John, Mel, and a couple of others and hurried away. I thought it was some kind of trick and they would just put me in another part of the prison or transfer me to Hermosillo, something they had been threatening to do. However, I was escorted to the front door and released.

There waiting for me was Rafael Pardo in a new Ford pickup with a palomino horse's head painted on the door. We shook hands and he drove me directly to a bank where we met the president, who spoke English. This man explained that Joaquin had given Rafael the 500 kilos of marijuana that I had paid for and Rafael had paid this money as a bribe to have me released. Rafael said there was an Aero-Mexico flight to Los Angeles leaving at 12 o'clock. It was already after ten. He sped through the narrow side streets and dropped me off in front of the hotel where Marrie was staying.

I ran upstairs to her room and knocked on the door. Thinking it was the maid she called, 'Come in.' I opened the door and you should have seen the surprise on her face. The first words after her gasp were, "You escaped didn't you?" She hurriedly packed her clothes while I paid the bill and we just barely made the flight. It was only after the Boeing 727 accelerated down the runway, lifted off and I heard the clunk of the wheels as they retracted, that I really believed I was free. It was Independence Day, July 4, 1974.

Allen Butts spent the next year in the big prison in Hermosillo, with his family spending over a hundred thousand dollars to get him released. For some unknown reason he landed at the International airport in Hermosillo without papers. A Federale saw the money, tried to take it and Allen refused.

Seven years later, I met him in Miami, bought a Terex bulldozer from him and *loaned* him two-hundred-thousand dollars to buy a Mammoth dragline to dig lakes where golf courses were being built. He was married to a nice German woman and they had a little girl. I learned that I had been on their daily prayer list for all those years. He died a few years later and I felt the loss.

Terry Thornton thought I might use his airstrip some night without his knowledge, so he set a deadly trap by scattering boulders on the strip, painting them green, and letting the grass grow. The following year, he was coming in with a ton of pot to a strip in the desert, the weather was socked in and he didn't have anywhere else to land, he attempted to land amongst the boulders on his old strip. This he managed to do, however not before the Twin Beech aircraft disintegrated, scattering bales of marijuana over a quarter mile and breaking Terry's neck. Some call it karma.

Terry was killed in an ultra-light accident in May 2003.

The crash in the 207 left me shell-shocked. If I ran over a rock in the road that made a loud bang the hair on my neck stood on end. I decided this was a good time to find a new profession and began looking diligently at other options. My compass needle was always pointed toward the farm in Georgia, but no matter how hard I tried, I couldn't persuade Marrie to join me.

I bought a couple of lots in San Diego, had contractors build on them and we split the profit down the middle. This was profitable but slow and boring. Something was seducing me back to my old ways.

Mark Reich, one of the men I met in the jungle, called and wanted to meet. With strong misgivings I agreed to have lunch with him at Del Conte's Restaurant.

He said he had someone who would buy a plane if I would fly it. His deal was that he loaded and sold the merchandise and we split everything three ways. I refused and said I would fly it for half. He argued hard for thirds, but I held my ground saying that my part was what changed the price from fifteen dollars a pound to seventy the minute it crossed that invisible line called the US border.

I did need someone in Mexico who spoke Spanish, smoked pot, and knew good weed from bad. Everyone was begging for the good stuff and I didn't have a clue. I also figured that if I didn't have to tramp around the jungle of Mexico looking for weed and didn't have to sell it in California, then my chances of getting caught were greatly reduced. Reluctantly he agreed to fifty percent.

Mark introduced me to Jerry Wills, a tall handsome blond man with blue eyes and gentle manners. I saw Jerry was several cuts above anyone I had met in the business and liked him right off. I also learned that Jerry was the man for whom Mark and Allen were loading the campers. They were flunkies pressing bricks in the jungle. Jerry knew of a Twin Beech aircraft in Wisconsin with long-range tanks that would haul a ton for a thousand miles. We agreed to meet in Milwaukee in a few days.

Jerry picked me up at the airport and drove to an older, wealthy section of town with houses shaded by hundred-year-old elms. We drove up the drive to one of the mansions and went in. The place was exquisite, with Persian carpets throughout. Tasteful antique furniture decorated the lower floor and the walls were adorned with paintings by old masters. Classical music was playing, and several attractive young women were going about their business in long flowing dresses. Jerry introduced me to Tom Stanton and his girlfriend Carol, and Jerry's fiancée Mary. The whole scene could have stepped off the screen from *The Great Gatsby.*

After a few drinks, we went to a fancy restaurant in an antique Duisenberg. I sat between Mary and Jeff Brine, a spry young man who told tales of helping Tom steal stained glass windows just for sport. They would drive up to a house while the owner was eating dinner, run up with crowbars and pry the window out, ran back to the truck, and drive off leaving the family sitting at the dining table in dismay. They also stole two half-ton bronze eagles off the flagpoles of the governor's mansion.

After dinner, I asked Mary to dance and we had a good time even though she was expecting a baby soon. She was radiant with sparkling blue eyes and very much in love with Jerry.

Twin Beech, a hauler and a pleasure to fly. She carried one ton for a thousand miles. I owned twelve, all five models.
Image courtesy United States Airfore - Wikipedia

The following morning, Jerry and I drove out to a charming farm with a gently sloping grass airstrip. We could see the D18 Twin Beech in the hangar and was she a classy machine. The owner was expecting Jerry and since I had just talked to the man over the phone with my strong southern accent, we agreed I would be Jerry. I walked up, held my hand out, and said, "Hello, my name is Jerry Wills."

Then Jerry walks up, holds out his hand out, and says, "Hello, my name is Jerry Wills."

The Beach Boys previously owned the plane and the interior was luxurious. The seats were a soft turquoise and white leather, the ceiling covered in white pigskin and a thick red carpet adorned the floor. And wow, was that thing big!

I had limited time in a twin-engine and that had been in a Piper Seneca for my multi-engine training. I was nervous as those big radials fired up. The seller flew with me for a few minutes and then we landed. Jerry paid forty-five thousand dollars and I headed south for Atlanta where Marrie was to meet me the following morning at Hangar 1 on the international airport.

About dark, I ran into turbulence and bad weather over Illinois. Ice began building on the leading edges of the wing and windshield and I switched on the de-icing device and watched as the rubber expanded and the ice popped off the wings. In a couple of minutes, a little hole appeared in the ice on the windshield. I made an approach for Lexington, Kentucky, and broke out at four thousand feet. Far ahead, I could see the lights of the runway through the tiny hole. The runway looked mighty short for such a big airplane. My hands were sweating as I approached. Would I get it down where I wanted? Could I get it stopped? She touched down on the numbers ever so gently. I turned off the runway at the first intersection and had to taxi a half-mile to get to the apron.

The following morning: I heard, "Atlanta approach, November seven nine seven Juliet foxtrot, twenty miles north for landing."

"Roger, seven Juliet, foxtrot, number four for landing, zero eight left, maintain 180 knots, switch to tower frequency 129 point 5."

"Roger Atlanta approach, 129 point 5."

Hot dog, I was flying with the big boys! In years to come, I would graduate to much larger planes, but the jump to the Twin Beech was the one that made my heart soar.

I was wary of landing on the strips in Mexico. I envisioned Federalés or soldiers riddling the plane with bullets as I landed or took off after the crash in the 207. I felt a little better after installing steel plates under and around the pilot's seat. Then I purchased a world war two German military helmet and had the lining redone and padded. Next I bought a set of full-body armor that was over an inch thick. To try it out I had Mark shoot the back piece with a .306 rifle while I held it. The shock almost tore it from my hand, but the slug only penetrated a few layers. It wasn't the best way to conduct the experiment, but it gave me some confidence even if in real life it was unlikely to stop an AK 47 round at close range.

After hauling three loads, I learned that Mark had cut Jerry and Tom out of the deal. The plane was in Tom's name and I felt bad about flying where there was dissension, so I said I would pay for the plane myself. Jeff was unloading me in the desert, and he was a friend of Tom's, so I gave him forty-five thousand dollars to give Tom. I was in Canada with Marrie's parents for Christmas when Jeff called and said Tom wouldn't give him the title to the plane after he received the money. I called Tom and he said I would have to pay him his share in the first three loads. I explained that that was between him and Mark, as I had only received my share. He cursed badly and said I would never get the title.

This sent me spewing! "Ok stupid, I will fly it without the title and if I get caught, guess who owns the plane?"

I did fly it repeatedly, bringing in ton after ton of pot into Southern California. I bought in so many loads that I bought the price of pot down from a hundred dollars a pound to sixty.

Thunderheads towered to the heavens as I wove a path through on my journey south. The past winter had been good, and I must have hauled thirty loads without incident, but for the past six months no pot was available. It was early September, somewhat early in the season for a load, but Mark had scored one and was waiting in Mazatlán. November seven nine seven Juliet Foxtrot had been one lucky plane and those big radials were purring like contented kittens.

Curious to know how things were on the ranch where I unloaded, I made a long, slow descent and landed on the most isolated strip in Mexico. From this ranch to the nearest rough track where someone could get a truck was a long hard twenty miles. Lush green grass covered the ground. As I landed, doves flew from the mesquite trees by the thousands. Juan rode up on a mule walking as fast as most horses trot. He looked awfully grave as he dismounted, and I knew something was wrong.

I gave him a big smile and said in a happy jovial voice, "Buenos Dias, Juan. Como estas?"

"Not very good Señor. There have been many problems on the ranch since you were here," he said with a serious countenance.

"What happened?" I asked with a heavy heart, thinking this perfect strip was finished.

"Well Señor, after your last trip the soldiers came and camped all around the airstrip. They hid their tents under the trees and waited for you to come back." he replied.

"How long did they stay?" I asked.

"They were here for three months and ate over a hundred of my goats. I saved the bones to show you. Come with me, they are just over there."

We walked a little way and came to the cache, and what a pile of bones it was! I said, "Damn, they were a bunch of hungry sons-of-bitches. I'm sorry about this Juan. I'll pay you for them and your troubles. How much were they worth?"

Weight fell from his face with those words. He thought a bit and said, "Well Señor, they were females in their prime, and most had little kids. The soldiers didn't care; they just shot the one nearest the pot. They ate half my milking nannies and my cheese production is way down."

Now the weight fell from *my* shoulders as I realized the problem could be fixed with dollars. "How much damage did they do you, Juan?"

"Well, every one of those nannies was worth at least twenty dollars." He said not very convincingly while looking at his toes.

"Would three thousand dollars cover everything Juan?"

From the look on his face, I knew it was more than he expected.

"Si Señor. That will be good."

I paid him and we worked out a warning signal. He leaned a sheet of tin on a milking shed and as long as it was there, it would be safe for me to land.

"Would you care for a bite of lunch with me before you go?" he invited.

I declined, remembering the last time we had dined together.

Juan's ranch covered twenty-five thousand acres, mostly unusable rocky outcrops where little vegetation grew. I asked him if there was anywhere to plant a crop of marijuana and he said there wasn't a suitable spot on his place, but he knew of a likely spot only five hours ride by mule. We set out just after dawn on a pair of young mules. The desert was carpeted in wildflowers. As we rode along the mesa, Juan pointed out a spot and said that he had shot two mountain lions there. He explained how he rolled boulders off the rim and as they bounced through the scrub below it frightened out the deer. However, two weeks ago, two big mountain lions came bounding out in the open and he shot them. I asked him what he did with them and he said he ate them and that they were very good eating.

We stopped for lunch, he built a small fire from the stalks of dried cacti, and quickly it burned down to white embers. He placed corn tortillas on the coals and soon they were hot. We took them out as needed, blew the white ash off, added a bit of dried meat, and ate it. A delicious feast, until I picked up a tortilla and saw a big fly pressed in it. Juan laughed, pinched it out and continued. I asked what kind of meat we were eating, and he said, "Lion."

Before noon, we arrived at an absolute paradise. As we rode through a pass in the mountains, we stopped and looked down on a stone house beside a clear pool with water cascading over a dam on the lower end. A cluster of the biggest orange trees I ever saw grew nearby. After leaving that area, the stream went underground. We rode on down to the house and met the owner who said he would like to grow some marijuana, but the neighbors had tongues that unrolled onto the ground. We arrived back at Juan's ranch before nightfall and I could hardly walk, my ass was that raw and sore.

Departing Rancho Providencia, I had to climb over three miles above the desert to clear the thunderheads and at that altitude it was freezing in the cockpit. I put on an old military jacket that I kept on the plane. Both pockets contained a 'fuzee', a phosphorus torch that will light under any circumstances; it will even burn in water. Beside me under the co-pilot's seat was a gallon of high-test aviation fuel in a plastic jug. Those two articles were part of my insurance policy. In case the feds followed me in, I intended to pour the gasoline on the load and throw in a lighted 'fuzee', and hopefully there would be no evidence after the aluminum fuselage burned white-hot.

After La Paz the clouds cleared, and I started a long descent for Hotel Cabo San Lucas down on the very tip of Baja California. I came in from over the sea and landed uphill, stopped at the far end, and stepped out into an oven. My arms felt cold and hard as I stood there in the sun, breathing in one hundred and twenty-degree air while waiting for the car from the hotel.

While registering, a pretty señorita dressed in Mexican folk tradition came in with a silver tray full of margaritas. I took one. It was delicious and immediately she was there with another. Damn, service like this was rare and the drinks were free. I was the only customer in sight, and I wondered, what's going on? A private jet landed and soon a lively group arrived in the lobby and the margaritas began to vanish. It was Andy Williams and his entourage. A couple of his minions befriended me, and we had several more of those special margaritas in glasses that held what was normally three drinks. I thought there must not be much alcohol in them because it was not affecting me in the least. A porter took my bag to the room while I accompanied my new friends to a beautiful open-air bar and ordered another round.

A band struck up and folks started dancing. Sitting with a group at a nearby table was a gorgeous woman with short black hair, a golden tan, and wearing a striped black and white zebra dress. I was dressed in jeans and a denim shirt, not exactly the proper attire for the occasion, but I sauntered over and introduced myself. Her group was most sociable and soon our parties merged. It was apparent that she was only interested in Andy Williams and I insisted on introducing them as I had already noticed the looks they were giving one another. I got up, went over to Mr. Williams and told him I would like to introduce him to a lady. He thought it best to send a note and since he didn't have anything to write on I pulled out a hundred-dollar bill and handed it to him. He wrote something on it, I walked back to my table and found miss gorgeous had vanished. Oh well, it saved me a hundred dollars.

We all went in to dinner and ordered another round or two. It began to come on as the waiter served the main course. Suddenly I was very drunk and found it challenging to keep my face out of my plate. I excused myself and staggered to my room, falling on the bed fully clothed, keeping one foot on the floor to slow down the spinning world.

At 4 a.m. the alarm jarred me awake. God I was in awful shape! If I was flying for anybody else, I would have quit. A shower washed out a few cobwebs, but not near enough. It was cold in the desert as I walked to the airstrip. I fired her up and took off over the hotel shaking everyone awake an hour before daybreak.

Constant sheet lightning caused the propellers to look like they were under strobe lights as I crossed the Sea of Cortés. Static electricity streamed from the ground wires on the wings. As day broke, I could see the lights of Mazatlán to the south and I headed for a narrow asphalt highway leading to a village near the coast. This road was too narrow for the plane to land safely as there wasn't six inches of asphalt to spare on the outside of both tires and the wings barely clearing embankments on either side. The road was blocked with a two-ton truck at the further end and I could see Mark standing beside it. Everything looked fine, the same as last year. I wished Mark would find a better strip. I approached straight in at one hundred and twenty miles an hour and slowed her down as I came over a bridge before touching down. Even before the wheels connected with the ground, the wings were cutting bush. The noise was awful. I thought the beating they were taking was inflicting real damage. In the tropics, vegetation will grow three or four feet during the wet season. This is exactly what happened, and Mark hadn't considered having it cut and cleared.

After getting out and checking it over, I found the leading edges were battered up, but there was no serious damage. They quickly loaded a ton of forty pounds pressed bales on board and I departed northbound.

The tin signal indicated all was clear at Juan's, I landed and unloaded, then flew on to Mulege where someone washed her and filled the tanks. I rented a room and slept for a few hours. At around four in the afternoon, I flew back to the ranch, which was twenty minutes away, and loaded up. Upon takeoff, it was so hot she used every foot of the runway, barely clearing the canyon rim. The stall horn was blaring, and the yoke was shaking like she had palsy. The yoke shaking is the second warning device indicating an imminent stall.

Over Los Mochas, at eleven thousand feet, I felt a slight thump in the bottom of my feet. Not a good sign. I started looking for trouble. Around the right cowling, I saw black oil running out and while I was looking on intently and wondering what to do, she caught fire. Flames engulfed the left engine and streamed back past the tail. I quickly shut that engine down and closed the oil and fuel shut-off valves. There was no change in the fire. I looked on, horrified of burning to death two miles above a sea of water that I couldn't get to. Only one thing to do and that was to try to blow the fire out before the wing came off. I opened the cowl flap, pushed the nose over hard, and watched the airspeed indicator go into the red and stop against the peg. The altimeter was unwinding so fast the hands were a blur. I knew the tail might come off at that speed, but that was secondary to losing the wing before I could get to the water. Down, down, down I dove, swallowing hard and fast to equalize the changing pressure in my head.

Like magic, the fire went out and I started pulling out of the dive. I was probably doing twice the 'never exceed' speed and I was afraid to pull too hard because the wings would come off. Ever so slowly the nose started to come up, but she was still headed for the water at an alarming rate. At fifteen hundred feet, she finally leveled out.

California was still five hundred miles away and every mile I could ride would be one less to worry about. I pushed the right throttle to the full position to slow the descent, passed Guaymas at five hundred feet, and flew over the strip where *Catch 22* was filmed. She was still far over the weight to fly on one engine, so I kept the beach close on my right wing, slowly descending at a rate of about one hundred feet per minute. The water was relatively smooth, and I wasn't worried about getting hurt, as I knew I could land and get out safely before it sank. I was all prepared to ditch when I felt it hit the cushion of air compressed between the wing and the water. This phenomenon comes into effect at one wing length from touchdown. She continued to sink, and I thought I would touch down within a few seconds. Five feet above the water, she leveled out and started riding on this cushion. Warning lights were flashing, the stall horn was blaring, the yoke was trembling in my hand and the oil temperature needle for the right engine was well in the red. Thinking I was going swimming any second, I stayed as close as possible to the coast.

Trim tabs are not designed for such conditions and it took a lot of pressure on the right rudder and the yoke. After an hour, I got to thinking she might just make it. To relieve the pressure on the yoke I ran off the left wing tanks and transferred all the fuel to the right side. This helped somewhat, but the situation was so delicate I couldn't move a hair. My head ached something awful and I was dying for a drink of water… just out of reach. My bladder was bursting and there was nothing to do but make a puddle in the seat. The tension was dreadful. Never in my life had I concentrated for so long without moving. I had both feet on the right rudder, both hands on the yoke and all four were in dire need of movement. However, there was a strong incentive to remain at this strenuous post.

Arriving at the northern-most end of the Sea of Cortez was imminent. Would she crash on the mudflats? Perhaps I could find the mouth to the Colorado River. My ground speed was less than half of what it should be, and it was getting dark. A half-moon was up. Saturn was shining brightly from due west. (On the first few crossings, it scared me as I thought it was an airplane keeping the same distance and watching me). She burned off enough fuel to fly on one engine, but I kept it just skimming the water and the speed continued to increase.

I found the Colorado and it was difficult to follow. I was doubling back, headed south, and then every point on the compass as she wound her way through the Sonora Desert.

At Yuma Arizona, I crossed the US border. By then she was flying a little better and I pulled her up to two hundred feet. The hills to the north were unfamiliar so I headed west right down interstate eight. A highway patrolman was giving someone a ticket and I laughed as I skimmed across his head, knowing I blew his hat off. An unlit overpass crossed the interstate and I saw it only a split second before feeling the concussion of the compressed air from a near miss. I went spastic! Three feet lower and I would have been a pancake on the side of that dingy bridge.

At Mexicali, I turned right and flew across the Salton Sea at 280 feet below sea level, the lowest place in the United States. At Palm Springs, I turned east, following Interstate 10. Not far out of Palm Spring, and unbeknown to me, the highway began to rise, rising faster than I could. A front was moving in from the east and I ran into a wall of water. The windshield wiper was flapping as fast as it could go, making little difference. The lights from an oncoming semi blinded me. It was crash or start up the bad engine. There was no choice. I quickly turned a few valves, pushed the propeller control from feather to start. She wind-milled a few times and caught.

It felt like a thousand horsepower rocket kicked her in the ass as she reached for the sky. My pucker factor was mighty high as I watched that left engine, just waiting on it to catch fire. The weather was rough, and I was bouncing all over the sky, but I was afraid to keep it running any longer, so I shut it down at six thousand feet. Immediately she started losing altitude.

Jeff was waiting on a dry lakebed east of Twenty-Nine Palms, California. This strip of white sand is situated in a narrow canyon between two jagged ridges known by locals as 'The Devil's Backbone.' I broke out of the soup at two thousand feet and radioed Jeff on channel 123.45. I said, "I'm ten miles south with an engine out and I can't go around. It's rough as hell, so give me all the room you can."

All was silent for a moment, then Jeff answered very calmly, "Understand... there has been a lot of rain, I am bogged down about a third of the way down and I am almost ninety degrees to the strip."

I thanked God he had waited.

"OK. How far are you from the east side and which way is the truck headed?" I asked quickly.

"Headed west and fifty yards, stay as close to the east edge as you can, there's no standing water there," he answered.

"OK, give me some lights, I'm right overhead and trying to get down." The updrafts from the ridges were tossing me around like a rag doll.

The truck lights reflected off a lake of water. I was six hours late and exhausted. She would probably flip over on her back if the water was very deep. I turned on the landing lights (something I had never done as they can be seen for miles in the desert) and got as close to the bush as possible and saw there was no water there. I held her off and kept pulling the nose up until she stalled just as she touched and plowed through the mud, coming to a quick stop.

Jeff had the truck free and came up all covered in mud. We transferred the load and Jeff departed for Long Beach with instructions to send Jerry back with some tools and oil as quickly as possible.

The trip to Long Beach took two and a half hours so it would be six or seven hours before Jerry got up, found everything, and drove back. I cleaned all the evidence from the cabin, a chore made easier by the professionally installed linoleum-lined interior.

I was so tired, thirsty and hung-over, that I was trembling. A gallon of water was sitting by the air-stair door, I sat down and took a big long drink. Gag! Puke! Spew! Death and Destruction! My eyeballs almost popped out! It wasn't water, it was 130-octane aviation gasoline and I had swallowed a big slug. I tried to puke, but my brain simply refused to endure the torture of that poison flowing both ways. Soon I was shitting my guts out, with nothing to wipe with. The night got freezing cold and I had nothing to wrap up in, so I lay on the cold linoleum floor shaking like a bird dog shittin' peach seeds. It was one long miserable night!

Jerry arrived at dawn and we took the engine cowling off. The top cylinder was split wide open and the two spark plugs were hanging in the open, spraying gasoline and igniting it. Jerry cut the fuel lines to the plugs and crimped them shut. Then we poured in several gallons of oil, put the cowling back on and she fired right up, popping and backfiring something awful. I took off without incident and climbed through weather to fourteen thousand feet. Over Mt. Palomar, I started my descent to John Wayne Airport, the busiest in the United States.

Taxiing down the runway to Orange County Aviation, she made a spectacle of herself by backfiring like a cannon every time the busted cylinder fired, leaving puffs of black smoke spaced at perfect intervals down the runway. And if that wasn't enough to get everyone looking and pointing, the paint was burned from the left engine and the left side of the fuselage was scorched black.

I was thankful there were no bullet holes this time.

Good weed in Mexico is elusive and every winter I searched diligently for a sufficient quantity to fill my airplane. In the fall of the year, it was relatively easy to find, but later in winter and spring, it became scarce. A small amount was grown during the summer and this brought a high price if one could score a load. All of my competitors quit and went to Hawaii or Europe for the summer, but I was tenacious and kept searching.

Over the years, I must have ridden a mule from one end of the Sierra Madre Mountain Range to the other. I rode mules through deserts, rugged mountains, and enchanting valleys and saw many marvelous waterfalls.

One particular trip stands out in my memory. We parked the truck in the clouds on the crest of a mountain and headed out with a caravan of about twenty mules, riding along a trail cut into the side of a mountain. As I looked down under my right stirrup into a void a mile deep, I recalled the words to the old hymn:

"When I tread the verge of Jordan, bid my anxious fears subside.
Death of death and hell's destruction, land me safe on Canaan's side."

We descended down to a river and came to a ranch that must have been at least fifty miles from the nearest road. The children and women were very reserved and sneaked sideways glances as they silently went about their work of grinding corn, making tortillas and killing chickens. The men took me to the stash and showed me what they had to offer. A certain amount of haggling was required before a deal was struck and then out came the Tequila and guitars. A young man with a beautiful voice sang Mexican country songs. We ate a scrumptious supper by lamplight and later slept in hammocks hanging on the veranda.

One bright sunny summer morning I was driving east through a dry scrub and cactus area in the state of Sinaloa en route to the mountains. It must have rained here occasionally because the highway was built up six or eight feet above the surrounding desert. The road had a tiny cement berm on either edge about the height and span of a hand and no shoulders. In some places, gaps were missing from one side or the other with little stones marking the death traps. Big semi-transports, doubly overloaded, passed at high speeds without a whisper of space between. Dead cows and burros in all stages of decomposition lined the sides of the road.

In the distance, I saw several cars and trucks parked in the road and as I drove up, I saw a pickup truck down in the scrubs with all four tires in the air. Twenty or more men, women and children were picking it up. I jumped out and ran down to see if I could help. The vehicle didn't seem damaged in any way as it had a heavy chrome roll bar behind the cab. I got down on my knees and saw two young boys trapped underneath and this bunch was just picking the truck up and putting it back down in the same place. I jerked the tailgate, opened and crawled under. Gasoline was all over the ground and men were smoking. One little boy about five years old was trapped between the cab and the roll bar. His right arm was broken and dangling. I dragged him out and passed him to his mother. The other boy was about ten or twelve and the roll bar was across his chest. A small stream of blood was running out the corner of his mouth. I yelled, "Arriba, Arriba," (up, up) and as they lifted the truck, I pulled the boy out. There was a deep indention across his chest. I tried to find any sign of life, but he was dead. I lifted him out and gave him to his grieving parents.

As I continued on my journey, I had the strangest feeling that the boy was sitting beside me. His presence was so strong I could almost see him. I don't *believe* in such things and had never even thought of it but I can only say the feeling was *very* real and it persisted for several hours. When I stopped at a gasoline station I realized the left sleeve of my shirt was caked with dried blood from the wrist to the elbow. I took off the shirt, draped it over a flowering shrub, and washed my arm in a water trough used to check truck tires for leaks. I told the boy to go on to where ever he was supposed to go, got in the car, and continued on my way. I never felt his presence again.

Cessna 210 - She could carry half a ton for 1,500 miles.
Image courtesy Adrian Pingston - Cessna 210 Centurion - D-EBWS - Wikipedia

High-quality marijuana was coming out of southern Mexico. This was out of range for the Twin Beech, so I bought a new 1974 Cessna 210 for fifty-seven thousand dollars. Then I flew directly to Finn Air in San Diego and had fuel tanks installed on the wingtips, giving it a range of 1500 miles. The 210 had retractable landing gear and was supposed to fly 210 miles per hour with the capability to take-off fully loaded on short strips. The factory test pilot must have worked as a jockey on his days off testing the plane before paint and the interior was added. I won't say Cessna lied. All I can say is, I couldn't extract such stellar performance from it.

With Marrie sitting beside me and the girls in the back seat, we took off from the Torrance Airport one March morning before daybreak. Suddenly the right door popped open on takeoff scaring the livin' crap out of us. I immediately landed and closed the door. On the trip across country, we flew at 27,000 feet to take advantage of the 200 mph. jet stream. All I had were visual flight charts and with our ground speed exceeding 400 mph I was turning the maps like pages in a book. We made it across the USA before dark and deducting the three-hour loss due to time change, it must have been a record.

Once Marrie and I flew the new plane deep down into Mexico to Zihuatanejo, in the state of Guerrero. It was a real paradise. There was no coastal highway then and the only way to the secluded villages was by boat or small aircraft.

One morning as we were flying along the coast I saw a long narrow pasture parallel to the beach that somewhat resembled a landing strip. I circled and as I did children ran out of the jungle waving towels, chasing off the horses, goats, and cows. It was obvious, this pasture was sometimes used as an airstrip and they thought I was landing, so I did.

Bronzed Indian men and boys rode up with saddled burros and invited us to mount. We climbed on, set out at a brisk walk, and soon came to a stream cutting through the beach. The donkeys waded right through the water that reaches up to the saddle. We laughed, put our feet on their necks until we came to the far side dry. The donkeys walked into a yard beneath thick coconut palms and stopped in front of a shack.

A middle-aged white man appeared who seemed surprised to see us.

"Welcome, welcome strangers, I was expecting someone else, but this is a pleasant surprise. Get down and make yourself at home. My name is Pepe and you are most welcome." He invited us into his sand floored home and had us sit while a woman prepared coffee over an open fire. He truly did make us feel comfortable.

An ugly hairless pig came in and Pepe said, "Buenos Dias Gordita, do you want a tortilla this morning?" The pig grunted 'un hu' and Pepe petted her on the head and reached for a tortilla, "Take it gently now, roll over and go outside to eat." The pig did exactly as directed.

Later we watched the local boys casting nets into the surf and marveled at the beauty of the nets whirling and opening like the skirt of a dancer. I asked to have a go and was given a net. I waded out thigh deep and noticed a shadow, cast, and caught a nine-pound snook. I said, "That's how it's done where I come from. The gringo can teach you something about fishing."

What sheer luck!

We lounged all afternoon under the palms, swinging in hammocks, sipping coconut milk mixed with rum, taking photographs of the locals with our new Polaroid. We gave the photos to the owners who screamed with delight as their image slowly emerged on the white paper. Most had never had a photograph taken, and they brought people dressed in bright colors.

We learned that Pepe was a famous television star in Mexico, and this was his retreat.

We left on the burros late in the afternoon and returned to Zihuatanejo. The evening was enchanting, a full moon shining through tall gently swaying palms. Marrie and I danced to soft music on the patio of the hotel overlooking the Pacific, a lovely ending to one of the most enjoyable days of my life with Marrie, Pepe, the Indians, and the talkin' pig.

14. NEW ORLEANS, HASHISH SMUGGLER

Motley Crew -- Million Dollar Gift

Russian grain ships were rusting at anchor all up and down the Mississippi River with no one to clean them. The World Court in The Hague had fined the United States seven billion dollars for selling contaminated grain to the eastern bloc. There wasn't anything wrong with the grain, it had just been loaded in ships previously transporting oil or chemicals and had not been cleaned properly. Nine hundred-foot supertankers worth a hundred million dollars, with crews of fifty or more were lying idle for months. Captains were offering as much as a million dollars to have their ships cleaned.

All the grain silos were jammed full and barges loaded with grain were rafted together for miles along the banks of the Mississippi. The Mississippi and its tributaries are one of the largest and longest river systems in the world, draining two-thirds of the United States. A few barges had come from as far away as the Rocky Mountains or the northern Appalachian.

A crew would clean a ship and call for inspection. A functionary from the U.S Department of Agriculture would crawl around, inspect with white gloves on. If he found even the tiniest bit of oil he would refuse to certify the vessel for loading grain. This was political. Grain is a very important export for the US economy and this situation was threatening the grass-root voters of America. Senators and congressional representatives from the wheat-growing states were screaming for ships to be loaded.

So, Roger throws his hat into the fray.

While working at the Redondo Beach Fire Department I studied hydraulics at Long Beach City College, and I thought that cleaning these ships was a rather simple matter. As it turned out, I was right. I just hadn't considered the floor.

We packed up and moved to a two-story house in New Orleans on the banks of Lake Pontchartrain, enrolled Marya in an elite private school and rented an office in Shell Square, a tall skyscraper overlooking the Mississippi River. Mr. Tom Wheeler, a distinguished elderly attorney in New Orleans guided me through the legal labyrinth. Marrie and I frequented the better restaurants of New Orleans and Fat City. Brennan's for breakfast and Chris Ruth Steak House for dinner were favorites. Then there was the restaurant with no name in a private house on an obscure side street where some of the best dishes imaginable were served.

Marya wanted a horse and we bought her a young grey and white appaloosa named 'Jubles Rebels'. He was a handsome steed but proved too much for a little girl. We rode him bareback one night in the Christmas parade with little Miriam sitting in front and Marya behind. He began bucking as if he was in a rodeo. We managed to stay on but he scared me, and the next day he was gone. After some searching we found a gentle red mare, approximately thirteen and a half hands high, not much bigger than a pony, named Ginger Snap. She was so gentle she would let the children swing from her tail, four could ride at one time. If one fell off, she stopped and waited for 'em to scramble back on. I have never known a horse so gentle and we cherished her for many years.

I bought a used Wheatley pump, a gigantic contraption previously used to hydrostatically test pipelines before they were buried. It could pump water up to a pressure of twenty thousand pounds per square inch and hold it there. This was the ticket. I mounted it on a lowboy trailer and took it to the wharf.

After acquiring steel-jacketed hoses that could withstand the extreme pressure and finding spray guns and nozzles marginally suitable, I was ready to try it out. The thing was deafening and the backward pressure frightening. No way could a man hold it at twenty thousand pounds, and I found that a pressure below five thousand pounds was ample. Even at the lower pressure, the tiny stream of water could cut a crosstie in two like it was butter. It required yoking two men, one behind the other, to the same gun to operate it.

A Greek shipping magnate had been wining and dining me and was anxious for me to get started on one of his ships. He chose a nine-hundred-foot mammoth with sixteen holds a hundred and five feet deep. The offer was one million dollars for it to pass inspection within thirty days with a guarantee of all costs in case of failure.

The inside looked like a rust bucket with thick slabs of built-up crud. Holes were cut in the deck and two men on hydraulic scaffolding were lowered in. The blasting began. An additive was added to the water to prevent the metal from rusting for a time. It was dangerous work. Water got behind slabs of rust weighing hundreds of pounds breaking away and falling. Once water started pouring in from a hole around a fitting where only rust had been holding it together. Working three crews around the clock transformed the rust bucket into a bright new ship in three days. That was... to within two feet of the floor.

Barges were secured alongside, and the sludge pumped out of the ship. Most of the liquid was pumped, but hundreds of tons of soupy slop filled with rusty debris remained on the floor. An absolute mess!

The Maritime union sent men out by the hundreds. They were lowest-life guttersnipes from the sewers of New Orleans with no intention of working. The foremen would ask their names as they climbed the gangplank and they'd mumble something. Some shimmied down the anchor chain or ropes thrown off the riverside and there wouldn't be half the number leaving a shift as got on. I found them sleeping on the giant beams, not even pretending to work. I was inspecting the work when a five-pound scraper dug into the timber at my feet missing me by inches. I looked up and saw several hostile smirking faces. It was a dangerous situation. On payday, we had to have twenty or more police officers on hand and the paymaster protected by a glassed-in cage.

Next door to my office on the seventeenth floor was a colorful character named Rene Martin, who knew everyone in southern Louisiana. He was connected with the Japanese in a fishing deal, owned the power station on the island of Utila in Honduras and had a brand new eighty-five-foot shrimp trawler, but couldn't afford lunch. He was forever borrowing 200 dollars. He would come and say, "Roger, I ought to be wearing an asbestos suit this morning, fire is licking my ass. Will you loan me two-hundred dollars to put it out?" The total I loaned him I'll never know because I liked him and enjoyed his company. He told funny jokes, drank the same brand of whiskey, and loved to fish.

Rene knew of my labor problems and introduced me to Carlos Marcello, the Dixie Mafia boss. Marcello hooked me up with another labor union resulting in a war between the two of them. Shots were fired. Television crews arrived along with congressional representatives. What a fiasco!

The ship was cleaned before the thirty-day limit and the Department of Agriculture was notified. They sent out an inspector who refused to certify the vessel. I asked him what he had found offensive. He replied that there was a workman's cloth cap in hold number six. I removed the cap and called and scheduled another inspection for the following day. This time the ship was cleared, and I received a check for one million dollars. It looked great for a short time, however, after paying all the expenses, labor, tugs, barges, and palm greasing there wasn't much leftover.

Labor became more difficult to find as competitors moved in. I cleaned two more vessels and put the business up for sale. The first day it sold, making two men very happy.

Rene drove me to Mobile, Alabama to take a look at his new six-hundred thousand dollar eighty-five foot shrimper. She was a beauty. There was one problem, the Bank of Mobile had her chained to the dock for lack of six payments each of six-thousand dollars. I told Rene I could find work for the boat. Since he was anxious to save her, he was very interested.

My friend Jerry and Mark flew down to have a look. They were as impressed as I was. She had a ship class cabin with a brass wheel and the latest Loran, radars, and sonar. Two General Motors twelve-cylinder diesel-powered her with two four-cylinder generators supplying the electrical power and hydraulic systems. Fuel tanks with the capacity of over forty-thousand gallons gave her a range of halfway around the world. With the shrimp holds filled she could make it all the way around. Everything was brand new, ready to go, and we had work for her.

Jeff Brine, Reich, and Dennis Boxer and I boarded a flight in Los Angeles bound for Karachi, Pakistan, with stop-overs in New York, London, and Istanbul. Between L.A. and New York we got drunk and slept all the way to London. Over Europe the drinks began flowing again and Mark was making a complete ass of himself. He pretended to stumble and splashed drinks on our heads. From eating boiled eggs and drinking bourbon my farts were deadly. It was time for revenge. I took a seat behind Mark and folded a blanket into a tent and waited. I gathered the gas, enveloped Marks's head, and held on for dear life as Mark kicked and clawed. Boxer laughed for the next 500 miles. To top off the adolescent behavior Mark sat on the head of a woman sleeping on the front row. A mighty row ensued. Officials threw him off the plane in Istanbul. He paid a bribe and got back on.

I was impressed as I looked down on the high, jagged, snow-covered mountains as we crossed Turkey, Iraq, and Iran. Upon landing in Karachi we taxied by an airliner smoldering on the apron of the runway, victim of one of the first airline hijackings in the world. We deplaned through a corridor of machine-gun-toting soldiers. Cameras were not allowed. Whiskey was contraband. The heat was suffocating. We suffered through officialdom and walked into hell. A throng of beggars attacked us, thrusting babies with hideous deformities into our faces. Mark, who was familiar with the place, told us not to pay attention that the parents of these children had maliciously deformed them to inspire pity. It was sickening to see such suffering.

We were met by Mark's hashish contact 'Diesel', a lowly taxi driver who was aptly named. What a disappointment! He drove us to a marginal hotel which was probably the best in Karachi. The new KLM Hotel was under construction. Camels pulling enormous loads intermingled with the traffic. We drove through an affluent area and saw men laying or sitting in front of garage doors, waiting to open it when the owner returned. To throw him a coin was cheaper than installing an electric door opener. The first night I accompanied Mark and Diesel to the depths of hell; they popped pills and drank moonshine in clandestine bars with dirt floors. Little boys dug holes under the tables and curled up to sleep like stray dogs. We were returning to our hotel soon after daybreak when I saw a ragged tramp in a big pile of rubbish. He was bent over with his trousers around his ankles, a stream spewing from his behind in full public view.

We were prevented from going into the interior until we had acquired the proper documents and that was to take some days. While waiting, I met the crew from a KLM passenger airliner, and they invited me to go sailing on an Arab dhow. The day coincided with the time we were to pick up our passes and I asked Mark to get mine. I can't remember what I had to promise, but knowing him, it wasn't anything small.

The KLM crew consisted of twenty persons including the pilots and flight attendants. We boarded the vessel and several Arabs sailed the heavy craft with lateen sails, only running aground twice. A bed of sand covering the planks served as a fireplace. A fire was built, and a rather good lunch of crabs and fish served. I returned to the hotel late in the afternoon sunburned and happy for the first time in days.

"Hey Mark, did you get my papers?" I asked.

"Yeah, I got em. Wanna see?" He threw a rolled scroll on my bed. I untied the ribbon, unrolled it, and read in beautiful calligraphy:

Name of person: WILLIAM ROGER REAVES

Place of birth: BUMFUCK GEORGIA

Occupation: NIGGER STICKER

"Very funny, asshole!" However, I made the mistake of keeping it and storing it along with other mementoes.

The following day we raced camels across the desert and that was it for me. This crew didn't need me to find hashish. I was going home, and I caught the next smoker west.

Jerry Wills and I flew the Cessna 210 north to Canada, cleared customs and immigration in Victoria, British Columbia, and checked into the Empress Hotel. I truly loved the place. It's a marvelous old historical monument with gracious service.

The tops of tall pines slipped underneath the cockpit window at dizzying speed as we headed north along the west coast of Vancouver Island. We were looking for the perfect place to unload the hashish. We saw several promising spots but continued on to Port Hardy near the northern tip where we stopped for fuel and lunch. Then the minor irritations began. To begin with, the lineman refused to pump the fuel and told us if we wanted fuel to pump it ourselves. We bought a quart of oil and didn't have an opener; the attendant would not lend me one. We went to an outside bar for a drink and a sandwich. I propped my foot on an empty wooden chair, the waitress chewed me out. Time to leave Port Hardy.

On the way south, we passed a waterfall cascading over rocks into the ocean. Hidden behind an outcrop of rocks was the entrance to a perfectly enclosed deep-water lagoon, a hundred yards wide, and a mile long and shaped like a banana. Beyond this was a short sandy beach. This was just north of the Peninsula, the oldest landmass in North America. We landed on the beach, looked it over, and decided we need search no further. My hands were sweating as I taxied to the end of the beach. I looked down our short runway and applied full power. It took every foot to get off and then we flew on to historic Nanaimo where we rented rooms above the harbor observing the colorful floatplanes flying in and out.

Thirty-six thousand dollars unchained the shrimper and brought her to Houma, Louisiana. Rene's son-in law was a welder and with his help we removed the insulation off the rear of the freezer compartment and built another complete wall three feet from the rear of the vessel. This made a "stash" to hide the hashish on the long trip home. Then a trap door was built in the floor over one of the drive shafts. We sprayed the whole freezer area with new foam and painted it throughout. It looked brand new.

Rene and I took the boat up and down the canals and bayous in order for me to get accustomed to operating it. She was big, over three hundred tons gross in weight. I enrolled in a celestial navigation course for merchant marines. It turned out to be one of the most educational subjects I have ever studied, and I took to it like a hog to slop. Soon I was competent with the vessel and my new pride and joy, an 800-dollar sextant.

Marrie and I began buying groceries. We had fun pushing cart after cart to the register. Eventually the manager told us we should just push them to the backroom, give the butcher our meat order and he would cut and wrap to our specifications. Grocery stores in South Louisiana were used to such orders. We planned three meals a day for four men for six months and that takes a lot of groceries… and beer.

I bought charts, specific charts, harbor charts and weather charts. I wanted charts for the great distances of water without any land and the clerk laughed and explained that there were no such charts.

Jerry didn't trust my skills with the sextant, so he bought a thirty-five thousand dollar 'Onan' contraption. At each landfall he bet me his position was closer than mine. It never was and I heard later that he learned to use the sextant.

August 3, 1974, Don Whalen, Pete Counsel, Jerry Wills, and Captain Roger Reaves departed Houma, Louisiana on a trip around the world. A greener crew had never before set forth. The things we didn't know and needed to know were encyclopedic.

The first fiasco was in the middle of the Gulf of Mexico. It was a bright Sunday afternoon. The vessel was on autopilot holding her course within a degree or two. I grabbed some fishing gear and began trolling a lure off the fantail when a Barracuda over six feet long struck. We immediately stopped the vessel and began reeling him in. His head was the size of a bulldog's and his teeth were ferocious. After a lot of excitement and sweat we had him on deck. We placed him in the freezer then proceeded on our course. Later in the afternoon I noticed the sun going down in the east. This was confusing. Oh Shit! We were going the wrong way. When we resumed our course after catching the fish, the autopilot engaged on the 180 degrees heading. I felt like an idiot. Moreover, it was not to be the last time I was to have that particular feeling'. A motley crew indeed.

The freezer units went out, so we diverted to Tampa, Florida for repairs. 'Tw's a mighty long way from open water to the shrimp docks, perhaps twenty miles. We tied up and a mechanic checked it over and said it would take several days to repair.

This was good news to me because it gave me a chance to go home and visit with Marrie and the girls. Marrie and I were having marital problems and I was sad to be away from her.

On the return trip I sat beside a rather attractive woman who asked, "Where are you going?"

"To Tampa," I replied.

"I'm going to Tampa also," she answered in a rather sexy, teasing voice.

"And may I ask where it is in Tampa that you are going?" she continued.

"I'm going to the shrimp boat docks," I said, thinking this would stump her.

She cracked a Cheshire cat smile and said, "I'm going to the shrimp boat docks too."

I thought 'damn, is she trying to pick me up?' I said, "I'm getting on a large shrimper."

She said, "I'm going to get on a big shrimper too."

Who was she, FBI or DEA? Surely such a pretty woman wasn't blatantly trying to pick me up even though she was pretending pretty well.

After more joking she told me her boyfriend was a shrimper from Texas who owned a fleet of boats. He had been working the Florida coast and she was flying down for a few days. What a coincidence! We got off the plane together and she introduced me to her partner. He was a rather charming rascal and offered me a ride to the boat. When I told him I was going to the Howie he burst out laughing.

"No shit, you're one of that crew?"

"Yep, I'm the captain of that motley crew," I admitted.

"Well, you better sell me the winches and freezer units. Tell you what I'll do. I'll give you fifty grand for all the equipment you don't need for your trip. I'll even throw in some old nets so you can hang 'em up. Might make it look better from a distance," he said rather seriously.

"What are you talking about?" I replied.

"You sure ain't goin' shrimping with that crew. Now you take that tall blond fellow wearing those linen shorts and matching shirt. Are you telling me he's your deckhand? You're going to have him dump nets and sort shrimp? Who do y'all think you're foolin'?"

"Is it that bad?" I asked.

"Tell you what. I'd just love to be a little bird in the cabin watching. I'll venture to guess that in two weeks y'all be off La Guajira, Colombia, loading thirty tons."

"Nope, you got it all wrong, we're delivering the boat to Singapore," I lied.

He knew better and being a southern gentleman he let it go.

I did wish we were going to Colombia though, but early next morning we set out for points east, stopping off in Miami for a week.

Marrie flew down and we treated ourselves to a suite at the Coral Gables Hotel. It was like a honeymoon before I set out across the Atlantic. It was great to see her. We were missing each other terribly.

We rode the Gulf Stream north making good time until we were clear of the Bahamas then bore east for Bermuda, a thousand miles away. We saw a few ships on the radar until we were a day out of Bermuda when a fleet of grey navy ships overtook us. They had an ethereal, lethal appearance as they glided by only a few hundred yards off our port side.

The Island of Bermuda rose gradually from the ocean as we approached. Surrounding the island is a deadly reef. The chart showed it to be about three miles off the coast on our approach from the southwest. I decided to head directly for the island and have a look as we sailed on to the far end, twenty miles on. I kept watching the radar, planning to turn when we were five miles out. The houses were coming into view and it dawned on me that it couldn't be over five miles. I looked up at the fathometer painting a solid black picture. We were on the reef! I jerked the throttles into reverse and gave her full power. She stopped on a dime and I dashed to the side, looked over, and went weak in the knees. The water was crystal clear and looked about three feet deep. We needed eight. Every way I looked it was shallow with a goodly crop of dark coral heads showing rather thickly. The six-hundred thousand dollar sucker was about to lose her bottom and go to the bottom.

A large cabin cruiser throwing a gigantic bow wave headed our way. I thought, 'Oh boy, here comes the cavalry. How much trouble are we in? Fifty-ton fuel spill. Environmental impact. Destruction of the reef. These were the first offenses that came to mind. A black man at the wheel was waving frantically for me to stop. I was stopped! He came alongside; told us we had crossed the reef and were in the lagoon. He instructed us to follow close and he would lead us to safe water. Onboard his boat were a dozen or more rather attractive passengers and I thought he was a dive charter boat? I stayed close on his stern as he slowly maneuvered through the coral heads. To show my appreciation I brought out a case of Rothschild's Bordeaux, 1964, rigged a rope to a boom and swung over onto the cruiser and met the entire crew filming the Hollywood movie, 'The Deep". Author Peter Benchley was present; however he continued with his paperwork and never once spoke. I'm sure he was upset at having a half-day filming ruined.

It was dark by the time we reached St. George and we were afraid to enter the harbor. It was most confusing with the runway lights, television, radio towers, and harbor entrance lights, so we decided to drop anchor and wait. The next morning we eased in and tied to a lovely stone wharf built by slaves centuries ago. Sharply dressed customs and immigration officers welcomed us most cordially and I was soon through the formalities. These officials had been at this for hundreds of years.

Motor scooters were the rage. Everyone was riding one, so we rented four. I went off by myself, rounded a bend on sand blown asphalt and came straight off, skinning my hands and elbows. Being the lucky guy that I am, a convoy of women rounded the bend on mopeds and picked me up and dusted me off. They were concerned over my abrasions and followed me to the docks where I invited them all aboard. After applying iodine liberally to my wounds, I opened a few bottles of wine. In appreciation for my hospitality they invited me for dinner at their hotel for which United Air Lines paid as they were a flight crew. Strange how one remembers things; one of the ladies was Muriel Stevens, a cute petite blond. We got to talking and I discovered that I knew her boyfriend! A rather elderly captain for United. Marrie and I had an unpleasant experience with him and his wife over an antique deal some years before. It's a small small world.

My crew was dizzy drunk when I returned. Jerry had Don on the handlebars of the moped and was going in circles on the wharf. As the speed increased so did the circumference of the circles. Both weighed well over two hundred pounds. It resembled elephants riding a bicycle. Finally, they couldn't make the turn and ran into a stonewall folding the front wheel to a perfect ninety degrees. This was knee-slappin' funny to 'em and their audience, so they mounted another steed and resumed the fun. When the speed exceeded the moped's ability to make the circle off into the drink they went! The moped gurgled as it sank in forty feet of saltwater while the 'clown act' scrambled back onto the wharf, well pleased with their circus performance. Everyone was crying with laughter.

After a week of fun we were ready to leave. I went to the harbor master's office to pay for the berth and was presented with a bill for eleven hundred dollars. This was outlandish and I protested vehemently, all to no avail. They had registered us as a foreign commercial fishing vessel, and we must pay and pay we did.

Next port 'Horta' in the Azores Islands. All day we watched the phallic-looking six-thousand-foot rock slowly rise above a white mist. It didn't appear to get any nearer; it just grew taller.

We sailed into the harbor late in the afternoon and I was awed by the town's peaceful beauty. I strolled along cobblestone streets covered with stones brought from Europe over the centuries as ballast in countless sailing ships. I stopped by an open window and listened to a young lady playing classical music on a grand piano. She was dressed in a red gown, performing as if she were on Broadway. A pony appeared pulling a two-wheeled cart with a man dipping milk from cans and pouring it into bottles left on doorsteps. I entered a local café and had a delicious meal of octopus, beans, and rice. The Port wine was superb.

The following day Jerry and I took a taxi around the island, stopping off at a windmill grinding wheat. A couple of cheerful red-faced men waved for us to climb the ladder and look around. The gigantic blades were turning slowly, and the wooden gears of the mill turned the heavy millstone while the men leisurely shoveled in the wheat. A longhaired sheepdog lay in a box along with a bed of young sucking puppies. The view looking down on the south side of the green island was breathtaking. I could have moved in and been content.

A woman from Boston was on a small sailboat in the harbor, and when she heard we were headed for Ibiza she invited herself along. After the journey, Don married her. They lived in Amsterdam and had a son. Elizabeth turned out not to be the best choice for a wife, however. After both she and Don divorced, I guess she was bitter. Years later she testified before a grand jury in Los Angeles and said that we shot machine guns off the fantail of the ship and told numerous other outlandish lies. So much for giving her a ride. I'm sure the jury found it interesting.

We left Horta in a gale. It was rough, much rougher than I had expected. The ship bucked and pitched for a good twenty-four hours. Once the seas calmed a following breeze of about ten knots blew. Exhaust drifted to the rear and the breeze kept us enveloped in a cloud of diesel fumes giving us headaches and making us nauseous.

We entered the Straits of Gibraltar after dark with fifteen or twenty ships on the radar screen. I nervously crossed the stream of traffic and pulled up under the Rock of Gibraltar and called, "Gibraltar control, this is the vessel Howie, we are a half-mile off for customs and immigration."

"Roger Howie, I can't see you."

"I'm an 85-foot shrimper lit up on a heading of 20 degrees."

"Roger that Howie, I still can't see you, I'll shine a light."

"Thank you Gibraltar, I have your light."

"I have not shined it yet, Howie."

The radio was full of captains laughing for the next ten minutes.

"Gibraltar to the vessel Howie, I presume you are at Algeciras?" So much for my navigation.

Two hours later, at one o'clock in the morning, we tied up to the docks in Gibraltar. I wanted to go ashore just to get off the boat and stretch my legs. One of the crew chose to join me. I won't name names. The other two said they were tired and sick. My sidekick and I caught a taxi to the only place open, which happened to be a rather seedy bar on the waterfront. We had a couple drinks and as we were getting ready to return to the vessel in walked two whores. They were wearing miniskirts with pantyhose tops showing below the hemline. Best I remember, there were some warts with long bristly hairs protruding. The price was twenty dollars for the pair. I didn't haggle. We had the taxi wait while we took them aboard. I explained in my best sign language that they were not for us but for two other gentlemen. I pulled the lever on the electrical breaker and the interior blackened. We began banging on the walls and yelling, "We've got women, let's have a party!"

"Send mine on in here," came a sleepy response.

"Mine too," came an echo from an adjoining cabin.

In a few minutes, I turned on the electricity. You could hear choice words flying as one crewmember ran on deck naked and douched himself in gasoline from the outboard motor tank. The other washed with a bottle of brute aftershave. Later they were known as 'Eighty Octane' and the other as 'Foo Foo'.

The next morning as I was putting on my boots shit squirted from the boot to my knee. Touché!

We began our Mediterranean cruise early in the morning heading for Ibiza, Spain. We had brought along two- hundred eight-track tapes and the deal was that whoever was doing the cooking for the day had control of the music. I liked country music and the other three were hard rockers. I can't remember who began pitching tapes first. When I missed one of mine, two of theirs went overboard. By the time we reached Ibiza I had one 'Hank Snow' tape left. Somehow, they appreciated his singing.

In 1976 Ibiza was an unknown, laid-back, Spanish island visited by a few hip celebrities. I rented a room in a small hotel to place a call home and was informed to expect a wait of twenty-one hours. The next day the phone rang. An operator in Madrid placed the call; I could barely hear Marrie's voice. We yelled for three or four minutes. I told her I was coming home. I was sick at heart from being gone from her and the girls for so long.

Originally I had planned to ride as far as Alexandria, Egypt, then fly home and prepare for the offload. However, I had had enough. I returned to the boat and told Jerry I was leaving. Pete had learned to use the sextant on the way and was competent. All was in good hands. It was time for me to leave.

Jerry and the crew would arrive in Canada with the load in January 1977. It was my job to fly the hashish from Vancouver Island to Washington State and I needed a plane. A Cessna 206 on floats was advertised in Trade-A-Plane. I called the number and Ketch Ketchum in Anchorage, Alaska, answered the phone. I asked a few questions and it sounded like the plane I was looking for.

Cessna 206 on floats. I moved part of a 20 ton load of hash, from Canada to the U.S. with this aircraft.
Image courtesy of user "Pauljoffe" - Cessna 206 ampbibious - Wikipedia

Anchorage was knee-deep in ice and snow. I stayed at the famous 'Captain Cook Hotel' overlooking Cook Inlet which was frozen over for as far as the eye could see. The plane was located on Lake Hood a few miles out of Anchorage and I caught a taxi out the following morning. Mr. Ketchum was a cordial gentleman and soon the airplane changed hands. The floats were frozen in the ice and blowtorches were needed to thaw it out. A line was secured to the left wingtip and a man in the back of a pickup truck held the other end as I taxied over the ice. There was a lot of loud jarring and banging and it sounded like the aluminum floats were coming apart. The pickup stayed right under the left wingtip with the man in the back holding the line to ensure I didn't get blown sideways on the ice. Eventually I was airborne, and Mr. Ketchum flew a Cessna 185 along beside me to the lower finger of Cooks Inlet and on through the pass leading to Prince Williams Sound. We slid underneath with only fifty feet of clearance between the top of the pass and the bottom of the icy clouds. After clearing the pass, Mr. Ketchum waved a hardy goodbye and departed.

Prince William Sound was breathtakingly beautiful, indescribably so. Words cannot portray the exquisite beauty of the white-capped sea, emerald green islands, and picturesque little villages. As I flew on a stiff breeze began blowing from the south as I approached Valdez. I called on the radio and the lady who answered advised against landing and suggested I go further south as there was a three to four-foot chop in Valdez. It was going to be risky bringing my new floatplane down.

Daylight only lasted four hours at that latitude in January and it was getting toward dusk. I had to put it down, so I circled the town a few times and saw several men come down to the dock to watch the show. Due to the strong headwind I was probably not doing over twenty miles per hour over the water. I stalled her directly into the wind and waves. There was a horrific jar and saltwater covered the plane as it hit and came to a sudden stop. Luckily no damage was done and we bucked and pitched on to the fuel dock.

The hose from the pump to the plane was a couple of hundred feet long and since it had not been used for some time it had to be stretched and drained to ensure no condensation polluted the fuel. The salty spray had frozen on the wings and they were slippery as a slick of oil as I crawled out on the far wing. After filling the tank I passed the nozzle down ever so carefully and closed the filler cap. The ice caused the lock lever to be stubborn about closing so I gave it a sharp rap with the heel of my hand. It closed all right, but my hand kept on going, pulling me with it. I slid off that eight-foot-high wing in slow motion and hit bone-chilling ice water. The cold took my breath away. I was wearing a heavy sheepskin jacket and it soaked up gallons as I swam for the dock. I climbed up the ladder and darted across the way until I reached a little store where a fire and several women were sitting around. I said, "Ladies if you don't want to see a naked man you had better turn your heads!"

They laughed good-naturedly and someone got my suitcase out of the plane. I put on dry clothes and gladly accepted the offered cognac.

The following day I flew down to Canada and visited several hunting and fishing lodges within an hour flight of the unload site. Fuel was going to be somewhat of a problem in that I didn't want to frequent the same place. Several of these lodges were ideal and they served bear, elk, moose, venison, or salmon steaks. Gasoline was sold in five-gallon jerry cans at thirty dollars a jug.

Sleeping bags, air mattresses, tent, ax, ropes, fishing tackle, freeze-dried food, and a hundred other items were purchased in Vancouver. I flew them to within ten miles of the spot and stashed them on an interior lake with no way in except by air.

David Gunn flew up to help me and Peter Davis flew up to look after his, Mark's, and Allen's interest. We flew to the spot a couple of days ahead of schedule and set up camp at the far end of the lagoon. From experience gained while fishing in Alaska I knew of the tremendous tides, so I selected a spot above the high water mark in an area with plenty of grass and we set up the large tent. I tethered the plane to a long overhanging limb, leaving plenty of slack. After a good supper and ample drinks around the campfire we blew up our air mattresses and turned in.

Sometime later in the night I was jarred awake by Peter's high-pitched screaming, "I'm freezing to death! I'm freezing to death!"

I bolted upright and as I was getting up to check on him I stuck my hand in freezing water, only the salt kept it from turning into an ocean of ice. By the time we got up and lit a lantern the water was over our ankles. We made a makeshift bench with gasoline jerry cans and piled all the perishables on top. Still the water rose and the jerry cans, filled with gasoline, began to float off. The lantern fell in, flashlights shorted out and we were in pitch darkness. Peter grabbed his sleeping bag and ran for the hills still yelling, "I'm freezing to death!"

David and I began tying gasoline cans together and collecting the flotsam. There was a ditch between the tent and dry land and the water came up to my chest. David kept collecting everything he could find and I made numerous trips carrying it to the hill. It wasn't long before I was overcome with hypothermia and David had to help me get into my wet sleeping bag. The hill was very steep so he propped me up in the branches of a shrub. It was a terrible cold and miserable night. I thought daylight would never come. When it did the water was gone and most of our belongings too. We built a fire and spent the next day thawing out and moving camp. I remember the freeze-dried eggs and sausages that sizzled in the fire tasting scrumptious.

The boat was overdue and every day I flew out fifty or more miles looking for them. On the fifth day I went to one of the fishing camps that had a radio-telephone and called my sister Nell. I said very deliberately, "Hello Nell, I am calling from a radio-telephone and lots of people can hear what you say, so don't talk ugly now, you hear?"

There was silence for a space of a few seconds as Nell thought. She always had a cool head and she answered, "Now you know I don't talk ugly. How are you all doing?"

"We are all fine and you?" I asked as casually as possible.

"Jerry is in Seattle at the Hyatt and he wants you to give him a call. Do you want the number?"

"Sure, give it to me." She did and we signed off.

I flew directly to Nanaimo and used a landline to call Jerry. He told me they had come in a week early and he had been sitting in the room by the phone ever since. He described in exact detail where the hashish was stashed.

I returned to the camp late in the afternoon, loaded up seven hundred pounds and headed south. It was well after dark when I crossed the Strait of San Juan de Fuca and entered the United States. I headed for Lake Ozette, approximately seventy miles south of the border. It's a round lake with several little islands covered in tall trees. The islands are spaced random enough to make it interesting on a homemade instrument approach. The night was crisp and clear, and the moon was full and bright as I arrived at the north end of the lake. For a fleeting moment I mused over the fact that I was a little early and shrugged it off as probably having a tailwind. I saw the black water and the islands as clear as you please. Surrounding the lake was a narrow white beach. I didn't remember that. I pulled the power and prepared to land. I was gliding down without any doubt what-so-ever about landing. When I got to within twenty feet of touchdown I saw black stumps and trees lying in a tangled mess. I gave it full power and pulled back hard on the yoke climbing out of the jaws of certain death. There would have been no lucky escape from that sea of tangled wood.

I circled to see what had misled my eyes and all my other senses of reason. It was an area of approximately the same size and shape of the lake that had been clear-cut and burned. The white beach was a sandy logging road surrounding the area.

Several miles further south I found the lake and landed without incident. Allen and Greg Riley were there in a boat to receive the load. I didn't bother telling them about the near-miss.

As I flew toward Puget Sound a bright moon reflected off the snow-covered peaks of the Olympic Mountains sticking just above thick clouds that blanketed the northwest. I continued steadily on toward Seattle and saw a break in the clouds. Reflecting off the water was a Pabst Blue Ribbon sign. I didn't know where I was, but this would do. I spiraled down, landed, walked into the bar that was filled with lumberjacks and wild women, laid two hundred dollars on the counter, and yelled for drinks on the house.

The five following loads were hauled in snotty weather with rain and fog coming right down to the water. On the north shore of Lake Ozette stood a commercial radio station. I came over it at 500 feet and made a completely blind approach, usually seeing nothing until I hit the water. It was hairy! Several nights the unloading crew could not find me for hours, even with the rotating beacon on.

The hashish was of good quality and it was selling fast at 1,100 dollars a pound. I decided to hold mine and rightly figured that when the others sold theirs they would create a demand. When it was all gone, I could raise the price. I ended up selling my share of a little more than four hundred pounds for fourteen-hundred a pound, clearing a little over half a million dollars.The return should have been double that and would have been had we not been ripped off by Mark and Allen. The deal was for six of us to put up sixty thousand dollars each, which would pay the expenses of the boat and purchase three tons. Mark

Reich and Allen were to go to Pakistan and load. I was to rent the vessel, put the lease in my name, captain the vessel to the Med, and fly the product down from Canada. Jerry was to get the vessel on around the world. Greg O'Riley and Peter Davis didn't have a job.

Jerry had arrived off the coast of Pakistan and ran into the beach with a big Boston Whaler where he met Mark and Allen who loaded him with a ton-and-a-half and told him to hurry back. He returned in a few minutes and as he approached the beach machine guns began firing over his head with plenty of tracers. Flares lit up the night sky and he got out of there. This was just a show by Mark and Allen. They never put up a dime, so we were short half the load.

Peter Davis and Allen made a big fuss about getting back their share of the floatplane. I said, "No way! I've risked my life making seven trips across the border in treacherous weather. None of you could have found another pilot for any price, so I'm keeping the plane as a souvenir." There was a lot of bitchin' but I wouldn't budge.

There was so much anger and hatred after the load was finished that I never wanted to work with most of them again. Rene Martin got a full share even though he should have received a swift kick in the behind. Every month I gave him six-thousand dollars to make the payments for the boat which he pocketed like petty cash. The bank was looking all over for its vessel and Rene was flying here and there trying to find it. Every time he could catch me he whined about the bank demanding a new survey on the boat for insurance purposes.

Despite this, Jerry and I made plans to make up for our losses and go to Thailand for a load of Thai sticks. We had a meeting with Rene in the living room of my house and Rene showed his true face by becoming irate over a freezer unit that had gone out on 'his vessel' and demanded Jerry pay him ten-thousand dollars. That killed any future deal with him. He had just received four-hundred thousand dollars plus the six-thousand dollar payments all for nothing but hindrance on his part. It just shows it's hard to find good quality help sometimes. All you end up with more often than not is a motley crew of greedy assholes.

Flush with money and plenty of time on my hands I was ready for a long slow trip around the world. Trans World Airlines was offering enticing deals on round-the-world tickets. I purchased four with stopovers scheduled in Tahiti, New Zealand, Australia, Hong Kong, Bangkok, Singapore, Rangoon, Colombo, Bombay, Kabul, Tehran, Istanbul, Rome, Paris, Amsterdam, and Montreal. I pictured us in each exotic place and secretly hoped we would find that special place to call home. Somewhere we would be safe with all that money. I knew I could not continue to live in the US without paying taxes and to do so opened a bigger can of worms than leaving it alone.

We flew to Guadalajara, Mexico and looked at houses. Marrie was somewhat interested in one. I especially remember it because of its brick-lined domed ceilings which I thought was dangerous in case of an earthquake. It was a handsome place set tastefully in a garden of boulders as only a Mexican architect dared.

We then visited Costa Rica and looked at Cervantes on the west coast. It reminded me of California a hundred years ago and I liked it. However, it had not been developed sufficiently to have proper roads. We stayed in a hotel with white sand floors for two dollars a night. The girls loved it. We then toured the east coast. This was a hot tropical area that did not interest me at all.

We went to a 'fish camp' on the border with Nicaragua where Tarpon fish were caught. If one got off the hook another struck before you could reel the lure in. We passed several days there in a grass hut and in the next hut was a retired couple from the US Midwest. They were amateur lapidaries and the girls loved them, calling them grandma and grandpa.

Our family in Hope Ranch, Santa Barbara, California. 1979.

As our departure date drew near we went up to Santa Barbara for some reason, I don't remember why. Marrie was particularly fond of this area. I remember her being enchanted with it when we flew over Montecito and Hope Ranch in a small Cessna some years earlier. While I was out tending to whatever, Marrie visited a realtor and when I returned to the hotel Marrie said, "Sweetheart, I found a house and you will just love it!"

"Where is it located?" I asked as gently as possible, having no desire to live in a city, or California, ever again.

"Hope Ranch, and Roger it is wonderful, it's all I have ever dreamed of and then more."

"How much do they want for it?" Perhaps it was out of reach.

"Two-hundred and twenty thousand dollars and Marylyn, the realtor, says they will take less. Come with me to look at it now please."

Marrie never asked for anything for herself and it was an exception for her to like a house so I said, "OK, sweetheart. Call the realtor and we'll have a look."

The house was lovely with the look and feel of home. I told the realtor we would think it over and we went back to the hotel. I said to Marrie, "Sweetheart, the house is wonderful, and I know it is a good investment, but with the income tax problem I don't see how I could ever justify buying it."

She answered rather sharply, "You seem to find a way to buy ships and airplanes at your whim. I like this house. I want a home to raise our children and you can well afford it."

"But honey, you don't understand. Nobody knows who owns the ships and airplanes but I don't see any way to hide a house?"

With that she turned her back to me and I got a chilly response to any words of endearment. It's not very pleasant sleeping with the Ice Queen.

The next morning I said, "Call the realtor and make an offer of one-hundred and seventy-five thousand."

"Oh Roger, you don't really mean it, do you?" she said with her beautiful blue eyes sparkling.

"Yes, I mean it. I'll find a way."

A deal was struck at one hundred and seventy-nine thousand dollars. I called my friend Roger McKenzie, a realtor in Newport Beach and he agreed to put the house in his name. Marrie was ecstatic.

The movers arrived from New Orleans only a couple of days before our scheduled departure. Marrie stayed busy arranging furniture and covering everything. I could tell she was in her element and did not really want to go on a trip around the world.

We flew directly to French Polynesia landing in Papeete. Roger McKenzie had given us the names of several people to look up, the first being the owner of the Bali Hai Hotel. He was a handsome California surfer type, about forty years old and received us graciously.

Introductions were made all around. He had his twelve daughters line up and introduced each one. They were from eighteen all the way down to two years, all clad in bikini bottoms and sarongs. Twenty-four firm brown breasts of all sizes were pointing at me. I was terribly embarrassed and he could see it. He said something in French and the girls all ran off and soon returned with tops. He explained that each of the children had a different mother and he was raising them himself.

Next stop was a visit to a local Tahitian village to look up the family of Naomi, a UTA flight attendant McKenzie knew. We were most welcomed and invited to a picnic the following day.

We arrived around noon, waded out to a motorboat anchored near the house and climbed aboard. He sped through an exquisite coral lagoon and came to a small island with tall leaning palms and a brilliant white beach. I climbed a giant breadfruit tree and picked the big green fruit. The children gathered wood from the beach and we built a fire laying the breadfruit on the coals. Our new friend punctured holes in a large tin of New Zealand corned beef to allow steam to escape and placed it near the fire. A jug of rum punch had been prepared for the occasion and we all drank freely. We water-skied, swam and snorkeled at our leisure. After a few hours when the fruit was cooked, we sliced the breadfruit and placed generous portions of corned beef on top making a delicious and memorable meal. We all got sunburned, a painful reminder of a wonderful day at the lagoon.

The *Kei Ora* was a new five-star hotel that had opened on the Island of Moorea. We made reservations and flew over. It was a paradise! We asked for a cabin for four and we were allotted number 26. There were no safety deposit boxes and the clerk gave me a stout manila bag in which to put our valuables. We had around forty thousand dollars, passports, and Marrie's four-carat diamond ring. I was reluctant to put all this in a community safe, however, the concierge assured me all was secure. The clerk marked our envelope #26 in big bold black letters and put it in the safe.

After spending one night in #26, we found there was not enough privacy and asked for something larger. We were given the Captain Cook suite, a large detached grass-thatched bungalow. No thought was given to the valuables in the safe.

We played for a week in the enchanting wonderland. A glass-bottom boat took us to an outer reef where we snorkeled amongst angelfish and a myriad of other colorful sea life. We were warned not to step on the giant clams that could latch onto one's leg and not let go. I was standing next to the reef in neck-deep water and looked down. Not more than three feet away was a moray eel as big around as my thigh slowly opening and closing his dog-like mouth. The water was a strange yellow color as I swam away. We climbed Mount Orohena, the highest point in Tahiti while Marrie talked about what color curtains to hang in our new house in Santa Barbara.

One morning we decided to rent two mopeds. We placed a picnic lunch in the moped basket and started on a trip around the island. Marya was riding behind Marrie and Miriam was behind me. It was a glorious day. I was thinking this was about as close to heaven as one got in this old world. Marrie was riding in front taking in the beauty of the island when she came to a curve she continued straight ahead and ran off the road and down the twenty-foot drop over the coral embankment. Marya saw the danger and jumped off at the last moment. Coral outcrops and shrubs stopped the wreck from falling all the way to the bottom. I climbed down and lifted the moped off Marrie.

She seemed all right other than her leg was burned where the exhaust lay on it. I helped her back up to the road, she stood there a minute and then fell backward without bending her knees. Her head made a sickening pop as it hit the pavement. She looked dead. I thought perhaps she had burst her spleen in the accident or was bleeding to death from internal injuries. She was cold and clammy, a sign of shock. She lay there in the bright sunshine and the girls began crying and calling Momma, Momma. I didn't know what to do. I was sick with dread. After about five minutes she sat up and looked around as if lost. She said that she was in an indescribable place, and had a most beautiful vision of little children running in a field of flowers and tall grass coming towards her and saying how glad they were she had come. Marrie had a near-death experience and was caught up into heaven.

This experience shook me to the depth of my being. I thought she was dead or was going to die. Now nothing else mattered. She needed to get into her own house and do her own thing. If Tahiti didn't impress her she would be miserable in the outback of Australia or riding a camel across the deserts of Afghanistan. We went back to the hotel and I arranged to fly back to California the next day.

Checking out took forever. The twin-engine plane that was to fly us back to Papeete was revving up its engines. The clerk was shamelessly ripping customers off and there was a din of arguments going on in French. My turn came and I paid the extra four hundred dollars without arguing, as I had seen the results of the previous customers. I asked for bag #26 from the safe and the clerk shoved a big parcel over the counter. I saw it was larger than mine should have been but, it was marked just as I left it. I took it over to the side and opened it and there were one million dollars banded in stacks of ten thousand dollars to each stack. A receipt for the transaction from a bank in Milan, Italy was lying on top of the money. I immediately realized the mistake.

Never in my life had I stolen anything but now was the perfect time if I was ever going to do it. My heartbeat fast. My face burned at the thought. I figured it was money for some big deal that was about to go down. Perhaps I should just take it to cabin #26 and say, "Let's make a deal."

"Marrie, I need your help. That fool just handed me a million dollars. Go up to one of the other clerks and ask for the packet from the Captain Cook suite."

"Are you out of your mind? Give it back!" She demanded.

Rather sheepishly I returned to the counter with the loot and told the arrogant attendant that he had given me the wrong package. He was indignant, cursed in French and jabbed his finger at #26.

I said, "Ok stupid man, I tried."

"Marrie darling, I tried, now ask for the Captain Cook suite bag. Just look at all this beautiful free money."

I opened the bag and showed it to her, and Marya looked in. At eleven years old she was savvier than her Mother, she held her dress open. "Put some in here, Dad."

I returned to the counter with a sick heart. The French clerk glared at me as if to say, 'Not you again.' I headed him off with, "Look, I have told you three times that this is not my package; there is a sweet million dollars in this bag that does not belong to me. Had you rather I pour it on the counter or talk to your boss?" I opened the bag. The color drained from his face. All the haughtiness disappeared. He replied in a low voice, "Pardon Monsieur, excusez- moi, pardon me indeed, my mistake entirely."

The swap was made and I wondered "what if "all the way across the Pacific.

15. SANTA BARBARA

Re-incarnation -- The Clenet -- Race Horse

Santa Barbara is, in my opinion, one of the finest places in the world to live. It was home to our family for many years and I suppose it will be home to our children all their lives. Our house was an old classic two-story early Spanish-Californian style with hand-plastered walls, a red tile roof, and situated on an acre and a half of land. A formal rose garden edged by a manicured boxwood hedge held a variety of roses. Apricot, lemon, orange, pomegranate, and kumquat trees were scattered throughout. A stable was built for Gingersnap, our pet mare. Adjacent to the stable we built a tack room and a chicken house with stones the children and I gathered from the riverbed nearby. We had a variety of chickens, each laying different colored eggs, blue, dark brown, white, red, and speckled. Each morning the hen nest looked like an Easter basket and the children loved to gather the eggs.

I tended a large garden in which I grew an abundance of vegetables. We installed a Grecian style pool with a Jacuzzi in one end. Marrie kept pots overflowing with flowers around the pool. Huge ferns and fuchsias hung from porch beams. Miriam loved to pop the fuchsias between her fingers. Several beehives behind the garage kept the fruit trees pollinated and honey on the tables of the neighborhood.

I was serious about the large real estate deals I was financing in Orange County. I often got up early, flew down, and left the plane at Orange County aviation. Bill J. met me at the hangar and we spent the day looking over prospects. Marrie is a fabulous cook and I tried to be home for supper, so around five o'clock I would head back to Santa Barbara. The house was five miles south of the airport and on my way in, I circled at about 700 feet and pushed the throttles in and out. Marrie would call out, "Daddy's home" and she and the girls ran out and waved. The image of those precious ones standing amongst the flowers waving is stamped indelibly on my memory.

As I was browsing through a pet store in Montecito, a lovely voice said "Hello." I looked around and there was no one about. Again, "Hello" and then I saw it came from a brilliant green Amazon parrot with a bright red head, a rare specimen indeed. I wondered if the proprietor knew what he had. I asked about the bird and the owner told me that he was a good talker and the price was one thousand dollars. The lady took him out of the cage and as he sat on my arm he spread his wings, rolled his eyes back until they filmed over and made the most wonderful gurgling sound. He loved me! There was no doubt. I looked him over.

He had blue, yellow and red feathers peeking out here and there through the green and I thought, 'He is more beautiful than any Picasso, and with that, the name stuck. I paid and walked out with Picasso on my arm. Marrie was visiting with Pam when I called and I told her I had bought a Picasso. They screamed with delight and asked me to describe it, and that I did. I told of the vibrant green with a touch of red and a dab of yellow showing here and there. They were excited and told me to hurry home. The girls were somewhat disappointed as they had expected something to hang on the wall, not something to feed and clean up after. To top it all off, Picasso was a one-man bird. He was in love with me. He would not allow anyone else to come near as he spread his gorgeous wings and looked menacing. Whenever we put him down he hopped immediately on my shoe and rode.

We purchased a large ornate wrought iron cage and placed it in the dining room. It is our custom to hold hands around the table, bow our heads and say, "Pardon us of all our sins oh Lord, and make us thankful for these and all other blessings, we ask in Jesus name, amen. "Wasn't long before Picasso had that down pat and as we held hands he bowed his head, looked at us sideways and out came the sound of my voice mumbling the blessing and ending with a clear 'amen'. We laughed so hard that I couldn't say the blessing in his presence so we moved Picasso to the den.

We were standing at the counter of the Airport Inn across the street from the John Wayne Airport when I noticed her eyes. They were a pretty light blue filled with light and her blond hair was cut in a pixie fashion. This and the look of her skin made me think that perhaps she was really from Venus.

I was surprised when she said, "Excuse me sir, I believe I know you?"

"Hello, you must be mistaken, because I'm sure I would remember you," I said with a smile.

She took a step backward, looked me directly in the face, her eyes filled with tears and she said, "Sir, I know you."

I was uncomfortable and didn't know what to say, so I said, "Perhaps, but I don't remember. My name is Roger Reaves," and I held out my hand.

She took my hand in hers and said, "Will you please come with me."

The lobby was virtually empty as we walked across to a sofa beside a fireplace. We sat down on the sofa and she took both my hands in hers and said, "I know that I know you, but I can't remember. Please close your eyes and tell me what you see."

As soon as I closed my eyes a vision appeared. I was a military officer in World War11, dressed in a long trench coat with wide lapels without insignias, high boots, and a cap with a solid visor that prevented me from seeing my face. I was in a passageway lined on both sides with large burlap sandbags. A shelter of some type was built over these walls and a section had just been shelled. In front of me was a ten-foot gap in the left wall. Smoke and cordite filled the air. I picked a young soldier up in my arms and walked through the hole in the wall. I was taking long steps as though I was floating and calling 'Medic---Medic---Medic.' The soldier was perhaps eighteen or nineteen years old and I could see that he was dead. As I looked at his face I realized it was the face of the woman whose hands I was holding.

I have no memory of what happened after. I did not get her name or address... was I entertaining an angel, unaware?

Marrie and I in our Clenet parked next to the DC-3 which pater crashed in the Columbian jungle.
Image courtesy user "Arden - flikr

A sleek roadster drove past and I thought it was the prettiest car I had ever seen. I followed it until the driver stopped and I inquired as to what make of automobile it was. He said it was a Clenet, hand-built by a small outfit in one of the hangers at the Santa Barbara airport. I found the place and met Alan Clenet, the owner, who showed me around. He had one completed that he was using as a demonstrator and asked me if I would like to take it for a spin. I was sold within a block. He said this was a limited production as he was only making 250. He was then beginning production on a four-door sedan model. The price was thirty-two thousand dollars. I bought two positions; numbers 28 and number 200, for a deposit of five thousand each.

After a few months mine was ready. It was painted a soft cream with brown fenders. The interior had pale calf leather seats with lamb's wool carpeting. The dash and steering wheel were made from African tigerwood. Marrie's initials were etched deep into the glass side window on the right and mine were cut on the left. A crystal bud vase was mounted in a silver holder beside the passenger's seat.

One Sunday we went for brunch at the Biltmore by the sea. When we came out, a group of people were milling around the car looking it over. A priest wearing a rather worn cassock said, "Sir, May I ask what you do for a living to be able to afford an automobile like this?"

"Why certainly, Father. I'm the Baptist preacher over on the south side." The crowd got a chuckle and Marrie laughed so hard her mascara ran down her face in tears.

As we would drove slowly through Santa Barbara and Montecito, people would point and say, "Movie stars."

Ron Sage, from somewhere in Kentucky, owed me five thousand dollars after we settled up on a load. He said, "I am a little light on money right now but I'll make you a deal in which you can't lose. I have a racehorse that I'll let you have for the balance."

"Ron, the last thing in the world I want is a racehorse."

"Now just hold on a minute and let me explain. This ain't no regular racehorse. This horse is fast! And I mean really fast! A neighbor had him and the same trainer who was training mine was training his. This two-year-old was tearing up the track during workout when his shinbone split. They were talking about putting him down and I offered to take him to my place and give him a chance. The vet pinned the bones back together and they've held for the past two years. He will be ready to run next season and since he has never been on a track no one knows just how fast he is. We'll put him in the five-thousand-dollar claimer race with mostly two-year-olds. A four-year-old will intimidate the younger horses. Come up to the farm and look him over."

We rode across the rolling hills of Kentucky and came to a farm way out in the country with a small house and a big barn. As we walked by I noticed it was a commercial chicken operation, but one like I had never seen before and most likely the only one in the world. Ron was raising fighting cocks in a most unusual way. The barn was built on a steep hill with a vertical drop of 20 feet from the foundation of the barn to the flat ground below. On the side of this hill and under the eaves of the barn was a long row of cages 4 by 4 feet and 30 feet high. Young roosters were placed in wire cages, straw, a foot deep covered the floor, and grain was thrown on top of the straw. The roosters developed powerful muscles in their legs scratching to eat. Every week the water trough, with a perch attached was raised a few inches higher forcing them to fly straight up to drink the water. Once the water reached 20 feet, they were on the same level as the hens in the barn where they liked to perch, flying down only to scratch for grain. Ron had a standing order from someone in the Philippines to buy every rooster he produced for two hundred dollars.

Horses on this farm were not pampered with such luxuries as quilted covers or warm stables. Ron threw the hay and feed on the ground and they had to spread their front legs and bend their necks down to eat. Ron said this was how horses in the wild ate and they were never sick with the sniffles. His horses were all smooth and healthy and I liked the looks of Twist-a-Song, my new steed.

Six months later, I was visiting my sister Marijo in New York when I received a telegram from Ron, *Twist a Song will run at River Downs Ohio on July 4th, be there and bring your money.* Ron met the plane at Huntington, West Virginia. We drove through the scenic countryside to River Downs Racetrack. The odds were 16 to 1 on old Twister and Ron told me to put every dime I had on him. I only had two thousand dollars and I put it all on a 'to win' ticket. At the sound of the gun twelve horses busted out the gates and were away in a pack. About a quarter of the way around Twister broke away on the outside, left the pack and it was a one-horse race from there on to the finish line with Twister coming in a hundred yards or more ahead of second place. I was escorted to the winner's circle where a pretty woman hung a lei of roses around my neck and a bigger one around Twister's while we had a photo session.

'Twas a fine feeling to be standing at the winner's window while the clerk counted thirty-two thousand dollars into my palm. Later, Ron gave me the five thousand from the claimer so I came out thirty-five thousand dollars to the good and thoroughly enjoyed myself. It's strange how the money will just fall on you when you have more than you need and how hard it is to come by when you need it.

16. FEBRUARY 1978 - DON'T TAKE YOUR GUNS TO TOWN

Dan the Jinx and the Vampire Bat -- Crash and Burn -- Orange County Land Developer – DC-3

Queen Air 80-B. I owned three. Bought my first one from World Aerobatic Champion, Bob Hoover.
Image courtesy aeroprints.com - flikr

Mark and Peter bought a Beechcraft Queen Air 80, one of the bigger models. They had scored a load of lime green sinsemilla buds with long purple hairs that would easily bring six-hundred dollars a pound. Their only problem was they didn't have a pilot to fly it across the border. They called me and I flew down, had a look, and offered to haul it on halves. There was a lot of shouting from Peter's side. I didn't care one bit and was about to leave when they offered 40% if I used their plane. I agreed since the loss of ten percent was compensated by not risking a plane.

Peter said, "All right, I'll agree to the deal, but you stick to the flying, I'll do the thinking."

I went back to California, checked out the plane, flew down to Mexicali, cleared in and flew on to Mazatlán, a thousand miles south of the border. That night we all went to dinner and agreed to meet on the tidal flats north of town shortly after six in the morning. I arrived at the airport early and filed a flight plan for Mulege, a fishing village across the Sea of Cortés. Ten minutes north of town I came to the strip and found it half covered in water. I circled a few times, didn't see anyone, and landed. With water covering one end, and sand the other, there was barely enough runway.

I did a short field takeoff, called Mazatlán tower, and said I had engine problems and was returning to land. Permission was granted and I returned. Back at the hotel I found Mark and Peter both asleep. After some harsh words Peter said he would be on the strip with the load in two hours. I strongly emphasized that the last hundred yards had to be packed down with a tractor before I could taxi onto it.

I departed Mazatlán and landed on the strip finding it exactly as I had left it three hours earlier. I sat in the cockpit a few minutes with the engines idling and while I was sitting there Peter drove up in a one-ton pickup. He jumped out in a thither and began waving me forward. I motioned back with a slice of my hand across my throat to emphasize it was a bad idea to try to put three small tires on soft sand with six tons of plane pushing down on them. Peter was adamant and angrily waved me forward. I shook my head and pushed the throttles forward. The nose wheel bogged before the mains even reached the sand and I shut her down. Peter tied a short rope from the tail of the plane to the truck loaded with a ton of marijuana and started backing up and running forward. The truck came to the end of its rope like a bulldog on a chain, jerking the back wheels of the pickup off the ground without so much as shaking the plane. I got out and Peter ordered everyone to push while he jerked with the truck.

I said, "OK asshole, you think fast while I push hard!"

Off in the distance we could hear the chop, chop, chop of a helicopter, we saw it, but just as it got 90 degrees to us he turned a sharp right and came directly to where we were. We untied the truck quickly and sent it on its way, and took off running through the jungle, with me yelling for Peter to think fast, but run faster.

Mark Reich was arrogant, devious, and dangerous. In fact, he was bad to the bone. One night I had a vivid dream. Mark came up to me in his most winning smile with white teeth sparkling. He was dressed in the robe and turban of an East Indian. He put his arms around me as though he was going to give me a hug and I felt a curved dagger enter my back, pierce my heart, then felt the life flowing out of me.

Mark was supposed to load a maximum of 2,200 pounds on the Twin Beech, but the loads kept getting heavier and heavier to fly and lighter and lighter on payday. One morning after he loaded me I took off down the highway, and as I rotated, the plane started to porpoise. Despite pulling back on the stick with the nose off the horizon, she drifted down on full power. I was going to crash. She barely cleared the low hills a half-mile ahead and only climbed at one hundred feet per minute. I was afraid to touch the gear or the flaps until I reached a thousand feet and even then I held my breath as I retracted them.

When I unloaded in Baja, Juan found a pair of scales and we weighed the bales. The total weight was over 3,000 pounds and I knew then that Mark didn't care if he killed me. That afternoon when we reloaded I gave Juan 600 pounds and headed north.

Mark was finishing building The Elephant Bar & Grill next door to Señor Frogs on the beach in Mazatlán. He had spent well over a million dollars and was always holding up my half of the money, and I was sure he was getting more than he was telling me. When I drove down to collect my money he would say, "Fuck off, I just gave you a hundred thousand dollars!"

"No, you didn't give me shit. That was my half, the half that I worked for, and don't you forget it."

I hired Ron Jameson to fly a few loads for me with one of the Queen Airs, and Mark loaded him a couple of times. When I bought the second DC-3, I hired Jameson as co-pilot.

One evening I went by a payphone in Santa Barbara and called the Elephant Bar and asked to talk with Mark. He owed me a couple hundred thousand. Peter Davis answered the phone and spewed some foul name-calling, "Don't be calling here no more! You're out of the deal. You've sat on your powder puff ass in your mansion long enough. We have your plane and pilot so there ain't room for your sorry ass."

"Put Mark on the phone."

"Fuck you asshole! Mark ain't going to talk to you. If you have anything to say you go through me."

"All I can tell you is to sit tight; I will be there on the next flight."

"If you come down here we'll dust your ass for a nickel. If you know what's good for you, stay out of Mexico!" He slammed the phone down.

I threw some clothes in my old leather bag along with my two pistols, a 9mm Browning High Power and a Smith and Wesson 38. A couple boxes of cartridges went along with it and I headed for the airport in Los Angeles. All flights to Mazatlán were full. The only possibility of getting there that day was through Houston, Texas. I bought my ticket, checked the bag with the guns, and headed for Houston. It was storming when we landed and the bag didn't show. I got a room in the hotel at the airport and waited. Every couple of hours I walked over and checked with the lost luggage counter.

The next morning it still hadn't shown up and I called Peter and Mark in Mexico. Peter answered the phone crying. "Oh Roger, they shot Mark. He's in the hospital and they don't expect him to live. We sent for a private jet to fly him back to L.A." All the bravado was gone from him and he sounded like a little boy. His courage came from Mark.

The ambulance plane arrived and Mark died on the way from the hospital to the aircraft. He was cremated and Jerry Wills, along with a Mexican girl Mark was living with, took his ashes out to sea. They smoked a joint and threw the roach overboard. Not a tear was shed. A fitting end to the life of Mark Reich.

Mark's tragic end was uncalled for. He was spending every dime he could scrape together to complete his restaurant and was withholding the money he owed Roberto for the loads

Roberto and Mark had been good friends for years and Roberto had given Mark a lot of credit. However, this time Mark had been too slow-paying and Roberto sent word to Mark asking him to come out to the ranch. Mark kept avoiding him. One night Roberto was drinking and sent three ranch hands to town with orders to bring Mark out to the ranch. The cowboys waited until Mark closed the Bar around one in the morning, and as he walked across the street to his car they confronted him. He told them to "Fuck" off and a scuffle ensued. One of the buckaroos pulled out a pistol. Mark took it from him and shot one of the men, then Mark was shot with a bullet piercing his spine. Mark brought his tragic end on himself because Roberto is a kind and gentle man who liked Mark.

A month later the airline returned my bag of wet mildewed clothes and rusty pistols. Would I have killed Mark or would he have killed me? Did my guardian angel cause the bag to get lost?

How or where I met Dan the jinx I cannot, nor do I want to remember. He appeared in my life for a short time on four occasions, bringing tragedy and disaster each time.

He was a seven-foot-tall, bald, ugly, weight lifter covered in stretch marks, with a whiney voice that gave one the creeps. He said he was a medical student in Guadalajara, Mexico, and had an endless supply of good marijuana down in the state of Guerrero. He described his runway as a deserted mining strip two-thousand feet long and running uphill into a sheer mountainside with no possibility of a go-around.

Glenn Tiller, the owner of Orange County Aviation, had been doing mechanical work on my planes for a couple of years and was keen to get into the business.

I told him about Dan and the claims he was making and Glen wanted to work but he didn't want to go so far down into Mexico. I told him I didn't mind shuffling it around inside Mexico, it was the border that scared me. He was bulletproof regarding the border. He had a Cessna 337, the new push-pull type with a surprisingly large cabin. We decided to go partners in the transportation with me hauling it from Guerrero to Baja and him flying it on into California.

I knew of several strips in central Baja where we could meet and transfer the load so we arranged to meet at the Serenaded Hotel in Mulege and go from there to look them over. Dan flew down with Glen. Marrie and baby Miriam came down with me a few days earlier, and I got in some fishing while Marrie lay around in a hammock, read, walked on the beach, and potty-trained Miriam.

For some unknown reason we decided to take two planes out to the desert strips. Glen got in the 337, did his run-up, taxied just a little way down the mile-long runway, and turned around. I was still sitting on the apron waiting for my engine temperature to climb into the green when I saw the dust fly as he gave it full power. I thought to myself, 'Glen must think he's flying a rocket. I believe I'll time his take off' and punched my stopwatch. He came roaring by me and beyond was the end of the strip and the Mulege River. He ran off the end of the runway and I could not believe my eyes as the nose of the plane came up, up, up until he was nearly vertical. She fell from fifty feet elevation tail-first into the river. I was in shock for a second or two and then jumped out of my plane and ran towards the crash crying and yelling, "Glen, Glen, Glen!" I was sure he was dead.

All was quiet. Part of the plane was above water. No one was around. Several skiffs were chained to the wharf and I couldn't get one loose. A post was lying nearby and I grabbed it and knocked the front plank out of the bow. The chain and lock went flying. A paddle was lying on the floor. I took it and started paddling frantically. It only took a couple of minutes to reach the crash but it seemed an eternity. The cabin had peeled off the plane. Glen and Dan were sitting, strapped in their seats. Both were conscious, but in shock. Glen's legs were broken with bones sticking out and Dan had a deep cut in his head, blood running down into his lap.

Somehow I got those two big men into the skiff and paddled to the far bank. An old fisherman was there in a dilapidated pickup and he helped me load them into the back. He eased off down a one-lane road at about ten miles an hour. I kept yelling for him to hurry to the doctor. About halfway down he met a man in a nice car. The old man stopped and began backing up. It was a good half-mile back to where they could pass. I banged on the roof and ordered him to stop. When he did, I yelled for the other car to reverse telling him we had two casualties for the hospital. I shoved the old man aside, got in, and drove quickly to the first aid station where a young female doctor was in charge.

As the Doctor was looking at Glen's legs, Dan was raising hell about how stupid she was to even look at broken bones while he, a bleeding man, was lying there unattended. She sewed Dan up, but Glen was in critical condition and could not receive the required medical treatment there. A Baja Airlines DC-3 arrived. We loaded Glen in on a stretcher and both were in a San Diego hospital within hours.

Glen was out of commission and out of the deal. I had to do it alone, which I should have done from the beginning.

A month or two later 'Dan the jinx' called to let me know all was ready. The mountain strip was too short for the Beech 18 so I decided to initiate the new Cessna 210. I flew down with enough food and drink to last a week. The weather turned bad causing me to stay low and a mile or two out over the ocean to make any progress at all. Just north of Acapulco the weather was right down on the deck and there was no way to go into the mountains. I flew up and down the coast hoping for a break, however, the weather stayed foul. With night coming fast in the tropics and the light fading rapidly, I had to land. Some miles north I had noted a long dirt strip near a village on the coast and I put her down with some relief.

The interior of the plane was filled with jerry cans of gasoline. I got them out, placed them on the high wings, and climbed up. I used a raincoat sheltering the funnel as I poured the gasoline through the chamois strainer. As I was going about my work a truckload of armed soldiers came screeching to a halt with rifles drawn. The sergeant ordered me to get down. I slipped on the damp wing and fell on the jerry cans below, breaking three ribs. I couldn't breathe. The fools were jabbing rifles, demanding papers. I showed them my papers and everything was in order. The soldiers were fighting a guerilla band in the nearby mountains and they thought that I might be connected in some way because I had landed on this strip in the dark and rain. They promptly arrested me, threw me in the back of the truck, and drove to a nearby army post where they locked me in a new metal barrack with perhaps fifty cots. Water ran in between each two-foot-wide piece of metal roofing. The cots were spaced to miss as much water as possible. I sat on one gasping with pain at each breath. No one came. All was still except for the dripping of the water. After some time I switched off the lights and lay down and dozed off. I woke with in a fright as I felt something on my neck and reached to brush it away and promptly realized a giant vampire bat had attached itself to my neck. I slung the wretched thing off, switched on the lights and there were two of them in the building. A mop was standing in the corner. I grabbed it and flailed at them. They found their hole and flew out. Blood streamed from my neck and wouldn't stop. They inject an anti-coagulating agent in their bite. I spent a long miserable night lying awake on that narrow cot with water running in on both sides and extreme pain with every breath due to my ribs.

The next morning I stood before the Company Commander who was apologetic. He returned my papers and invited me to breakfast. With that sorted and the weather clearing I flew on to the mining strip and landed without incident. The 'jinx' was happy to see me. I unloaded the delicacies and we set off for the village where we stayed in a house with a family.

Early the next morning we loaded 500 kilograms of marijuana in the 210 and I told Dan I expected to be back in one week for the next load. His only instruction was that I not sell for less than eighty dollars a pound.

I lined up in the center of the runway and gave her full throttle, released the brakes, and headed down the strip. At forty miles an hour I was over halfway, at fifty, two thirds. The bushes at the end were approaching fast. It was too late to stop and there was not enough speed for takeoff. "Oh God, Oh!" BLAM! BLAM!, I watched as the propeller cut a path through the shrubs and the world fell away. I was falling into a deep canyon. I pushed the nose over and she started flying. I retracted the gear and continued to fly down the canyon. 'The Jinx' didn't know whether I crashed or not.

The trip back to the US went without incident though my ribs continued to cause me a great deal of discomfort. I unloaded on a dry lake bed in California, hid the pot under Joshua trees, and returned before daybreak in a truck to collect it.

I gave the pot to Tom Stanton, who tried to sell it, but it was old and dry and he returned it after a week demanding I pay him ten dollars a pound as a handling fee. What idiots walk this earth! Against the Jinx orders I lowered the price to seventy dollars and it sold in a day.

Marrie and I shopped at the Deli for a load of ham, turkey, pickles, and beer for another week-long picnic for the Jinx in the mountains. I flew down and circled while I radioed for a response in the code we had agreed. An unfamiliar voice came on the frequency, gave me the code and said Dan left several days previously. He spoke with a soft southern drawl and I didn't think he was a Federale, however, I was dubious. I landed, turned it around, and was ready to take off when a tall handsome blond man about thirty years old stepped out. All seemed to be all right, so. I shut her off and stepped out to meet Dixon Johnson, formerly of Texas.

I liked this man. He took me to his tent a half-mile into the brush and said the Federalés always hung around the women in the cafés and never ventured out into the jungle. We unloaded the goodies and took them to his camp where he built a fire. We drank a good portion of wine and got acquainted.

His story was an interesting one. Several years earlier a Texas syndicate sent him to Mexico to grow cucumbers and tomatoes. They bought a five hundred acre avocado orchard that wasn't producing properly, cut the trees down, and didn't bother with the stumps. Dixon farmed around the stumps and sent the fruits of his labor to Texas where his associates cheated him out of his share. After two years, all Dixon could collect was the stumpy land which wasn't worth very much. He married a local girl in Uruapan, Michoacán, and put the land up for sale.

While he was trying to sell the property large shoots sprouted from the stumps and began producing avocados. Dixon began pruning and caring for the new trees and was getting a reasonable harvest which was doubling each year.

He said he could get me a load if I was prepared to stay for a day. Next morning we got in his pickup and set out. During the summer there is very little available, however, we found a ton of rather dry pot stored in a fire tower on top of a mountain. Dixon and I came to an agreement and I paid for five hundred kilos and a deposit on another load.

We had men cut the bushes at the end of the strip and I got off without incident. That is if one can call running off the end of a runway overloaded and diving into a canyon in order to become airborne, 'without incident'.

This load sold for eighty dollars a pound the first day.

Dan the Jinx came to the house and I paid him his half for the load and told him I had returned and met Dixon and did a load with him. He became angry and said the pot was his and that I owed him for his half. I explained that I was going to give Dixon half and if he had any arguments to deal with Dixon. He was adamant and said I used half of his money to purchase the load. I said I did not need any of his money to buy as I had money of my own and that argument didn't hold. I told him he abandoned his post and it could have got me killed or thrown in prison. He towered over me with teeth clenched and fist balled. I walked into the bedroom and returned with a .22 rifle, pointed it at his balls, and marched him backward out of the house. We are not finished with the Jinx!

Glen was doing an annual inspection on the 210 and I needed it to go to British Colombia where business was calling. I told him to wrap up the job as quickly as possible so I could be off. He said he had it all taken apart and offered me a new Beech Baron to use free of charge. I was delighted and wondered how Glen was managing that swap? Marrie and I flew the new Barron through breathtaking views of the snow-covered Olympic Mountains and on to Vancouver Island where we stayed in picturesque Victoria for a week.

Glen looked rather downcast when I returned the Baron. He invited me into his office and poured me a drink and while looking everywhere but at me, he said, "Roger, I'm really sorry to have to tell you this, but I used your 210 while you were gone. Scott and Jeff were flying and they made an approach to a strip in Mexico. They tried to make a go-around, hit a tree head-on and the 210 burned. Only the front tire was found."

Shit! The sneaky thief, I should have known that when the deal is too good to be true there is always something wrong. Now it was all coming out.

The insurance company paid the original price but I lost because the 210 had gone up in price by at least twenty percent a year. This soured my relationship with Glen. I apparently didn't learn and continued to have him service and repair my planes.

One dark stormy night out over the Pacific I reached up and adjusted the rudder trim. Nothing happened. I cranked the handle a few more turns and suddenly the loose cable grabbed and I was flying in circles. It took a half-hour of working with that thing before it would fly straight.

The next day I took the plane to Volar Aviation in Hollywood-Burbank Airport and had them do an annual inspection. They saw she was a trafficker and gouged me on the price, charging seventeen thousand dollars for the inspection and the small amount of work that was needed. However, they discovered the rudder cable had come out of the roller. It was frayed and almost worn through. Only ten of the sixty strands of cable were intact. Glen lost a customer.

The next I heard, Glen was in prison in Culiacan, Mexico. He had flown down without stopping and clearing at the border. For some reason he had to go into an airport and was arrested for entering Mexican airspace illegally; an amateurs mistake. Glen was in prison for a year. I later saw him at the Airporter Inn, across from the John Wayne airport. He had lost weight and looked sad. It was Christmas, he had no money to buy his wife and the children gifts, and so I went out to my car, came back and gave him five thousand dollars as a Christmas present.

The following winter Glen was returning from Mexico with a load of marijuana in a Cessna 210. The airport was socked in so he landed crossways to the airport at a ski resort. For some reason he landed gear up and slid a mile across the frozen snow and flipped upside down in a snowbank. Glen was trapped and hung there for several hours by his seat belt. His back was broken and he was paralyzed from the waist down. Marrie and I visited him in the Orange County Hospital, and he seemed to be in good spirits.

One day I asked my friend Roger McKenzie if he had seen Glen and asked how he was doing. He said, "I hate to tell you this, but your name came up while I was talking to Glen and he said he never wanted to see you or hear your name again as long as he lived." What in the world? I thought Glen liked me? Was I mistaken for all those years? Was he jealous of my success and downcast at his failures? Did he start hauling marijuana to imitate me? All these thoughts rushed through my mind as I sat there with a red face.

Later I learned that Glen had been called before a Federal Grand Jury in Los Angeles. I read the transcript, it was awful. He told everything he imagined I might have done, embellishing every point. He said he often found marijuana debris in the planes and white powder in the window ledges which was a lie. He told of patching numerous bullet holes and seeing machine guns in the planes. He never saw a gun. I have a homemade truism, 'each low life piece of shit that rats on another, finds a reason to hate his victim.'

Roger McKenzie was a charming rascal and one of the most successful realtors in Orange County. Wednesday afternoon was race time and I was invited to crew on his sleek 50-foot sailboat. Wives were not invited although there were always a few single secretaries on board. One evening Roger said he wanted to introduce me to his friend Bill, who was looking for an investor in a real estate deal. He said Bill was a little dodgy, however, he could come up with some real winners. Bill had one eye, was bald, and a sport. His business was planning and zoning properties and he needed two hundred and fifty thousand dollars as a down payment on a two and a half-million-dollar dairy farm that had shut down. Once the land was rezoned, the value increased tenfold. I put up the cash and Roger raked twenty-five thousand off the top.

For the next ten years I supported all kinds of deals, investing millions, and never got a dime in return. Looking back, I wonder how I could have been so stupid, but at the time, it seemed the thing to do. One deal would make money and then there was always another larger one on the drawing board. We did several land projects cumulating in Sunny Mead, a 6000-acre project later renamed Moreno Valley and according to National Geographic Magazine, it was the fastest-growing city in the United States during the 1990s. Bill and his partner Bill Dyer hooked up with a Toronto based consortium named 'Markborough'. They put in lakes, schools, police and fire stations and thousands of lots on which contractors built houses with prices starting at four hundred thousand dollars. We zoned and built a hydroelectric plant in northern California. Owned 16 oil wells in Petaluma, California, and drilled two successful ones in Taft, California. We owned a company plane and each drove a new 300SD Mercedes.

Bill saved the farm in Plains Georgia when Jimmy Smith, the crooked preacher I bought it from, foreclosed. I purchased it from him and his son-in-law, Ronny Miner. They were happy to sell it and accepted my fifty-thousand dollar down payment knowing it was drug money without flinching and financed the balance at 8%. Interest soared to 16% within a year or two and they wanted their money now, not twenty years from now.

The land was covered with thousands of stumps and litter left by the pulpwood crew. One hot day I called the forestry department and they helped me burn it off. The pine straw was a foot deep and the smoke from the fire could be seen for fifty miles. It burned so hot that 90% of the stumps burned out. The land had a 60-acre peanut allotment and rent for peanuts soared. The value of the farm tripled.

Smith and Miner were filled with resentment.

Mother was taking care of my business in Georgia and she was renting the peanut allotment for sixteen thousand dollars a year. In January she gave Smith a sixteen thousand dollar check and he said he wanted to buy a silage chopper I had for sale and he would take it for the remainder of the payment that was due in June. We thought all was well until the eleventh of June when he foreclosed. Georgia law is hard on such points and lawyers advised me to pay it off before it went to auction. I called Bill and he got it refinanced over the phone.

I've always wanted to go to Smith's Church and walk down the aisle telling his congregation what a sleazy crook he really was.

I also financed an interesting project where we got approval to put a small hydroelectric plant on a stream. The paperwork was legendary with the environmental impact studies on the Indian artifacts and a specific pollywog that existed in the stream. We didn't disturb anything. The water went in one end of a pipe, ran through the generator, and came out the other end and back into the stream. Once the project was approved, it sold for two million dollars. With Bill, it was one interesting idea after another and they all needed a transfusion from me.

For years I worked at what was most likely the most dangerous profession in the world in order to support both my investments and Bill's. Had Bill been honest we most likely would have been billionaires. We got in on the ground floor of one of the hottest real estate booms in history. We drilled oil wells, built hundreds of condominiums, and rezoned over a thousand acres of prime Orange County real estate and I had to keep working to support the deals.

17. UP THE STAKES, DC-3

Pot Plantation -- Flee!!! -- Primo Asshole -- Balmy Days and the Jolly Swagman

QANTAS gleamed like polished silver against the oxidized aluminum fuselage of the old DC-3. The paint over the letters had been stripped away, leaving the virgin metal to tell the tale of years of service under the harsh Australian sun. Etched in the manufacturer's plaque was the date, January 26, 1943. We had the same birthday. The logbooks showed that she was sold to Air America, a CIA front, where she served for seven years in South East Asia. Forty-two jump seats bolted along the sides and the steel platform on the floor by the cargo door told of a mounted Gatling gun. At the close of the Vietnam fiasco she was sold in Singapore and I picked her up for sixty-five thousand dollars. A bargain in anybody's book.

She could easily carry three tons for a thousand miles if one had a two-thousand-foot strip of any kind, but most Mexicans couldn't fathom the wheels being twenty feet apart and the wingspan over a hundred feet.

Fat Ortega, a seedy Mexican I had contracted to install a sprinkler system, swore he could get good pot out of Oaxaca, a state whose name was synonymous with marijuana. I didn't believe him, but it was in the middle of summer, and America was out of smoke. Out of curiosity I agreed to have a look. Fat Ortega was beaming as he left the house with enough money for his trip. After a couple of weeks, he phoned and told me everything was fantastic and to come down and take a look.

My arrival at the airport in Oaxaca was fit for a diplomat. Police cars escorted me to a five-star hotel. I had drinks with them and then their bosses. After a while I saw that these people knew nothing about what I was after, it was Fat Ortega showing off with my money. It took some persuasion to get him away from them.

We stopped by a ranch of someone he knew. It was pitch dark when they brought out the armory and fired hundreds of shots at imaginary enemies. The following day we walked a ways up a river and saw a couple hundred kilos of leafy, seedy pot. It was fresh and they assured me they had three tons. Reluctantly, I agreed to buy it.

There was no landing strip in the area so I stepped off two thousand feet on a bend in the river. Both ends had an approach with a twenty or thirty-foot cliff at either end, something I had found to be a great advantage. An arroyo cut across the middle and they assured me they would fill in a thirty-foot section. I stayed for a few days and waited until a major portion of the work was completed then I returned for the plane.

A DC-3 is required by law to have two certified pilots. In the first place, I didn't know of a pilot who would fly with me, and secondly I didn't want one. That is how my sister Kay began riding right seat on those trips. She put her long hair under a cap, dressed in a jumpsuit, flew down with me and caught an airliner home. She loved the job of pretend pilot.

Kay was an alcoholic and you couldn't keep her from the sauce. You would think she was drinking a glass of water when it was a glass of gin. On our way down we stopped at Houston International for fuel. The gas truck driver was taking forever to pump the tanks full through the small hose. What he didn't know was that I was pumping fuel from the mains into two 500-gallon tanks inside the cabin. While this was going on Kay walked across to a hotel with the excuse that she was going for a bag of sandwiches for the trip. When she didn't return I knew where to find her. After paying for the fuel I walked over to the lounge and there was Kay, true to form, entertaining a group of Texans. I pried her loose, loaded up, and took off shortly after midnight.

At eleven thousand feet I leveled off in thick soup. Kay went to shaking and moaning something about freezing to death. I told her I had some warm clothes in my satchel and for her to go back and put some on. It was somewhat rough and when she didn't return I shined a flashlight back into the cabin and saw her curled up with my clothes twisted around her and the suitcase still open. I smiled and continued flying south.

Suddenly, both engines quit. Silence filled my dark universe. Oh, shit! What could be wrong? We were over the middle of the Gulf of Mexico with the nearest land three hundred miles away. At night and in weather, our chances of surviving

a ditching at sea was zilch. Nothing seemed to be wrong as far as the instruments indicated. I sat there in shock watching the nose dip and the altimeter unwind as we glided to our death. Then it came to me in a blinding flash! The 'drunk' had kicked the lever of the interior tanks to the off position! I unbuckled, jumped out of my seat, and ran for the cabin. As soon as I got up I felt the left-wing dip as we started a diving turn to the left. I struggled on to the rear of the forward compartment and just as I thought, Kay's foot was still on the lever and it was in the off position. I whipped it to the 'on' position and both engines exploded to life as a rush of cold fuel hit the hot cylinders with the throttles still in the 'full' position. The burst of power dipped the left-wing even more and I stumbled back to the pilot's seat, strapped in and leveled off; breathing a little harder than usual. Kay remained fast asleep.

We arrived over our new airfield around nine o'clock in the morning. Nothing much had been done since I left. There was a bridge across the arroyo about ten feet wide, enough for one tire. The trees were still standing across one end. I circled several times and decided to land to have a better look. Man, was it rough, and I know what rough is. But this one took the cake!

Fat Ortega drove up in a fancy pickup smiling from ear to ear. My guess was that he was happy because he had bet someone that I could land it on the strip without getting killed. The strip was seventeen hundred feet long, with three-foot undulations in the earth. The arroyo was three hundred feet from the far end and I thought the wing might hold one tire up long enough to get it across, but it was dicey. Trucks arrived with the pot and twenty or thirty farmers made short work of loading three tons. I stationed a dozen men at the far end armed with axes and crowbars in case I crashed.

It felt like a roller coaster ride as she bounced from one rise to the next. I held my breath as I came to the arroyo. The right side dropped as the earth disappeared from underneath the tire. In a blink she was across and I felt a hard thud as the tire hit the rim of the far side. At the bitter end I pushed the nose down as she sailed over the cliff. The tail was up and she was flying. Within seconds I was in the soup and the world was whirling in a white mist, an undeviating ingredient for the next nine hours.

Nine-thousand five-hundred feet above the sea, four-hundred miles south of the Louisiana coast, with rain beating against the windshield - the lights shorted out. My small world turned black, as dark as the inside of a cow. I couldn't tell north from south, nor up from down. I had to have light! There was a flashlight in my bag in the radio room. I groped my way back and fumble around in the bag. I felt money! In the fiasco on the ground everyone had forgotten the money! Oh God, they would hold Kay for ransom! There was no time to think of that now; I would be upside down soon if I didn't get back to the cockpit. I found the flashlight, switched it on and hurried back. I shaded it with some paper and shined it on a map on the floor. This worked out.

With over three hours to go I was worried. How long would the batteries last? The light progressively got dimmer and dimmer. It turned from a blinding white to yellow, then to a feeble yellow. I put the map in my lap and laid the light on top. The instrument panel was barely visible. Perhaps there would be lights from the oil wells. I descended to five hundred feet. It was still dark and raining. Going any lower was suicide. That area of the gulf was thick with drilling platforms. How high were they? The feeble light faded. My pupils must have dilated to the max. I was seeing in virtual darkness.

Following the red taillights of cars going west across a thirty-mile causeway led me to flashing red lights at the end of the freeway. At that point traffic had to turn right onto a small highway; a detour around a section of interstate10 where several contractors had gone broke trying to build a bridge across the Mississippi River. Beyond the flashing lights were two miles of stark, white concrete, six lanes wide running through miles of black swamp. Three clicks of the radio and a million candle powered beam lit up the stark white highway. I was down and alive. I could have kissed the ground and both Johnny Allen and David Gunn. We used this perfect landing site for over a year and each morning after a landing someone would return and scrub the black tire marks off the interstate

For some time the men had told me of a light that came up beside the power lines that traversed this swamp and I had scoffed at their tale. We were unloading and sweating as we tried to wrestle the oversize bales through the trap door underneath the truck when David stuck his head in the plane and said, "Come and have a look at this."

There, just beyond the power lines, was a ball of smoky yellow light as big as a car. The power poles and wires were clearly visible, being between the light and us. It floated directly in parallel with the power lines. I pulled out my pistol intending to shoot through it but Johnny restrained me.

After unloading I flew to St. Tamothy aviation on the north shore of Lake Pontchartrain where my friend Harvey and his two daughters gave me a welcome. Some days later Kay showed up. Her eyes sparkled as she laughed and told of her adventure in the jungle. I gave the money for the load to fat Ortega who just pocketed it. He had no intention of ever going back.

The Oaxaca load was dry and filled with big black seeds. We shook out over a hundred pounds of seed and during the process I got high from breathing the dust. I filled a suitcase to busting with seeds, put it in the boot of a car, and sent it across country to Johnny in Georgia.

George Doran, Gene Conner, Johnny Allen, and I went into a joint venture to grow marijuana on a grand scale. If ships could bring a hundred tons at a time into America, we could shortcut all that by producing it at home.

Gene had a farm way out in the country near Ambrose, a village notorious for outlaws and moonshiners. He had a 245-acre field surrounded in tall pines with a two rut road going to it. A pivot system irrigated it in one turn. An old house stood empty under ancient oaks, an ideal setting to grow marijuana.

We hauled in four hundred tons of chicken manure, spread it on the land and harrowed it in. Next we planted corn, but not as thick as usual because in every other row we ran a planter with the marijuana seeds. Every seed must have sprouted, because there was a plant every three feet. We needed help!

Fat Ortega said he could get some Mexican Indians who had never been to town. I told him to bring me seven of the most savage of the bunch, which he did. They rode a bus for three days to reach the US Border, then, with the aid of Coyotes, came across into the US. They were all in their early twenties, bronze, slim with long black hair. We took them straight to the barbershop and to a men's store. The transformation was amazing to say the least. They almost walked into the mirrors looking at themselves. We went to Los Angeles International Airport where I bought eight one-way tickets to Atlanta on the Red Eye. I smiled as these men shied, then jumped on the escalators. As we walked through the airport and onto the plane they looked like little children walking in on Christmas morning and seeing the treasures Santa had left.

The flight attendant ushered the handsome young men to their seats in the center aisle and I sat across the aisle next to an attractive black woman with glitter in her hair, an ostrich feather boa around her neck and plenty of cleavage. I had to show the Indians how to fasten their seat belts, interpret the flight attendant's instructions, and show them how to open the toilet door.

My seatmate was enthralled with these young men. I told her some big story about them being wild men I had dressed up so they could ride an airplane across country without being arrested by immigration. I told her I was taking them to my plantation in Georgia. We laughed and had another drink.

My new friend was a nightclub singer who had just finished a show. After a few more drinks she was singing about a wheel within a wheel and apples spinning in space and I understood the deeper meaning of all that. Before arriving in Atlanta, we were buddies. I told her that two prejudice, tobacco-chewing farmers from South Georgia were meeting us and I wanted to give them a shock. We walked out of the airport hugged up and saw Gene and George waiting. The voluptuous singer and I walked over. I introduced each Indian and then introduced her as the cook for the crew. The fellows almost swallowed their chaw! I walked her back inside where she caught a flight to Baltimore and a new engagement. I didn't get her address; something I have regretted.

We took the Indians to the farm and got them settled into their new home. Gene and George had it furnished adequately, with nice beds and linen, a gas stove, refrigerator, freezer, and TV. We went to town and brought back a truckload of groceries. The next night I checked on them and noticed a mound of spaghetti they had cooked. I had bought twenty pounds of hamburger meat and they had cooked it all in the spaghetti sauce. I knew this crew had a lot to learn. I pulled out plastic freezer bags and showed them how to freeze what was left. The young men were excellent workers who never once walked off the farm. They hoed and pulled male plants from daylight until dark. As the plants grew and needed more room they chopped out the corn until there was little left. By August the 245-acres was ten-foot deep in marijuana.

I bought two hay bailers to bail the tops and arranged with a trucker to move twenty tons per trip to California or New York. We began harvesting, just the main colas at first and leaving them in the shade to dry.

Gene noticed motorcycle tracks that had gone around the locked chain stretched across the road. He followed the trail and saw where it stopped. A bale of marijuana had been taken. A woman had walked alongside leaving a long slim footprint in a muddy place in the road.

Gene wanted to mow the crop down immediately. I was hesitant to destroy a billion-dollar crop. Before night, I found out who the culprits were. It was my new brother-in-law Pete and his ex-wife. I told Gene we could let them in on the deal and make workers of them, or I could take them on a vacation to Mexico until it was all over. He was scared and wouldn't listen to reason. He wanted four hundred thousand dollars for his farm and he would leave and go to Mexico. He began walking around with his pistol and was extremely nervous. We had a falling out and I took my Mexicans and left.

Fat Ortega met us in San Antonio, Texas to drive the young men to Mexico and I flew on to California. He told them they would be searched at the border and their money confiscated. He took their money on the pretense of wiring it to them then abandoned them in Texas, broke. May he burn in Hell!

After I bowed out the farmers regrouped and commenced harvesting using a crew of young men from Albany, Georgia. This crew returned home each night.

"Two Hundred and Forty-Five Ton Drug Bust: Biggest in US History"

These were the headlines of The Atlanta Journal, The Macon Telegraph and local newspapers across Georgia. Channel 10 television station in Albany kept it on for days. Paul Harvey even got in on the action with, "The Rest of the Story,"

Johnny Allen, George Doran, and Gene Conner were arrested in Coffee County, Georgia, with bail set at a quarter-million dollars each. There were also indictments in three other counties. The papers said they were looking for 'The Big Rooster' in California.

"It's time to move...Marrie!"

"Jolly Swagman," a stately, 51 foot Ketch.
It was our second home for 10 years.
Copyright - Marrie J. Reaves

We had a brand new 'Force Fifty' sailboat being outfitted in Long Beach. She was a gorgeous machine with carved teak interior, teak decks, and two spruce masts. Within a week the ladders were filled with fine wine, Chivas Regal, and enough food for a two-year cruise. We set sail with Roger McKenzie who sailed with us as far as San Diego. Because of a late start we stopped overnight in San Juan Capistrano, continuing on the following morning. It was one of those glorious days with a gentle breeze at our back, smooth seas and bright sunshine. I was standing in the bow sprint when I saw a fin ahead. I called for Marrie to turn a few degrees to the right and we headed directly toward it. We were almost on top of him before he saw us and gave a twist and disappeared. It was a swordfish so big that if I told the truth nobody would ever believe me. Do they grow to fifteen feet and weigh over a thousand pounds? That night we dined at The Yacht Club in San Diego where we were treated like royalty, our last treat before departing on our adventure.

Ensenada, Mexico was our first stop. We spent several days getting all the permits and insurance, knowing that any infraction could cause endless delays and la mordita (the bite). Once everything was in order and double-checked, we sailed into the Pacific intending to pass Isla Guadalupe well to port.

We were sailing along at a good clip when the autopilot went out. I looked for the problem and found the amp meter was discharging fully, indicating a dead short somewhere. I looked everywhere and could find nothing wrong. The D8 batteries weighed well over a hundred and fifty pounds each and they were a difficult job to get out and heft onto the deck where I recharged them with a Honda generator. After charging them for a couple of hours I replaced them and started her up. She charged until they were all up and I shut her down. Next day when I started up it registered a full discharge. What the devil? After disconnecting the battery lead and looking for the problem I reconnected it and everything was fine again. OK, I didn't know where, but there was a bad diode somewhere. I found the culprit to be an oil pressure switch sticking out the side of the engine. Naturally, it was in the most difficult area to get to. I finally managed to take it out, shook it, blew into it and could hear a click. I examined it carefully and decided it might unscrew so I put the wrenches to it and it turned but it would not come apart. Oh shit! Had I broken the seal? I replaced it, started the engine up and got on the floor with a flashlight looking for any oil leak. There was not a drop. Phew, that was lucky!

I went up on deck, kicked back with a Corona while Marrie served lunch. Marya came up and said, "Daddy, the engine is making a funny noise."

I jumped up and ran below. There was nothing funny about that sound. It was the grinding, popping sound of a new diesel engine eating its bearings. As I shut it down I knew it was for the last time. Where would I find another 120 horsepower diesel this side of San Diego? I could not go back.

Marya was eleven and Miriam turned five that month. Marya was tall enough to see the compass and could take a watch at the wheel so it was two hours on and four hours off.

Isla Guadalupe grew out of the sea as we approached in a strong westerly. There was one small indention on the leeward side but not a suitable anchorage due to the steep drop off. Since we had no current for the electric anchor winch I had the stern anchor with twenty-foot of chain and several hundred feet of rope ready to drop. Marrie stood in the bow with instructions to push it over when I yelled. The fathometer read 600 feet until we were almost on the shore. The bow was close on the rocks before it was shallow enough to anchor. I yelled. Marrie dropped the anchor. I dropped the mainsail and a forty-mile per hour wind blew us back. The anchor held. Phew!

Wind blew through the rigging with a menacing whistle. On our starboard side was a three-hundred-foot cliff with numerous holes in the rocks. As the sea surged in, air rushed out with an awful hissing, blowing sound. Doors slammed on flimsy abandoned fishermen's shacks. Sea lions barked on the rocks to the south. An ill-omened spirit shrouded the place.

Later we learned that the previous yacht to anchor there had been ill-fated. The family was diving near the rocks when a giant shark came up out of the deep and took the father completely out of the water and then spit him out. His femoral artery was severed and he bled to death before they could get him on board.

Now I know to move when I get such a clear warning of danger. At that time, I had not learned to listen to that inner voice.

I strapped a 30.06 Winchester across my back took a camera and a few supplies and prepared to go exploring. We lowered the dinghy and the four of us got in. As we reached the rocky shore a wave swamped the Zodiac. We got drenched and the camera was ruined. Disappointed, but now landed, we pressed on. A short distance up a trail and heard coyotes barking. A strong haunting feeling was present making me want to hold the rifle in my hands. We all agreed, this was enough and returned to the yacht.

Marrie prepared fresh fish for supper. When night fell we lit the hanging lanterns and all was cozy below deck, although the wind continued to whistle through the rigging. Marrie and the girls went to bed and I sat on the stairs with a glass of Grand Marnier. Someone had to stand anchor watch to assure the wind didn't change directions and blow us on the rocks.

Around midnight the boat surged ten or twenty feet straight up and fell on its port side with a tremendous crash. I was thrown down the companionway along with dirt and rocks. Marrie and the girls were banged up and crying. I thought for a minute that I had DT's.

By the light of the half-moon, we saw that the three-hundred-foot cliff with the blowholes had collapsed into the sea.

I grabbed a fire ax, cut the anchor rope letting the wind blow us out to sea. We hoisted a small jib and assessed the damage. The inside of the cabin was a disaster! Doors were torn off cupboards, food items were broken and scattered and we had no idea what had happened. Later we learned there was a massive earthquake and we were directly over the epicenter. The place had us spooked from the beginning. We were all relieved to be getting out of there.

Adjusting my new camera on one of my trips.
Copyright - Marie J. Reaves.

Isla de Cedros, being interpreted, 'Island of Cedars', sounded beautiful and green. What a disappointment! Sailing in at a good clip and excited to be among civilization, we found a hot, dusty, dirty low island, without a single tree. Near the anchorage was a drab village of concrete blockhouses, a few stores, a jetty, a jail, and not much else.

We dropped anchor in front of the jetty around seven o'clock in the morning and rowed ashore. The place was deserted. We walked down a wide dirt street until we came to an open-air café with a concrete floor, a tin roof, and a few flimsy aluminum card tables with an assortment of rickety chairs. We sat down and ordered coffee and breakfast from a most pleasant waiter. While we were eating, a couple of men came in. One young man had a pair of shoes wrapped in newspaper tucked under his arm and *he* kept gawking at Marrie in a most disrespectful manner. I looked him straight in the eyes and said, "Buenos Dias!" He sauntered over, stood beside Marrie and asked how we got here. Marrie was friendly, probably sensing trouble, and said we had just arrived by yacht.

"Yacht! Me," as he pointed to his chest, "Jefe de immigration! Papers!" He demanded in a brusque manner.

I felt there was going to be trouble and replied, "No problem, I'll get the papers as soon as we finish eating, so please, excuse us."

He stepped back one-step, crossed his arms across his chest, and said, "Veinte minutes" (twenty minutes) and continued to drool over Marrie. I stood up, ushered him out into the street, and said something about his mother as my right hook connected with his jaw, knocking him down in the dusty street. He was stunned for a few moments, got up and staggered off.

We finished our breakfast and as I was paying the bill he returned with an old fat policeman. The policeman talked to the proprietor of the restaurant and then shook his head and said there was nothing he could do about it since the immigration officer was federal and he was municipal. I could see he was pleased. The twerp got what was probably long overdue.

We took a walk around the place and when it started warming up we returned to the boat. Around noon, a boy rowed out and said the port captain wanted to see me. I got dressed, rowed the dinghy to the jetty, and waiting for me was the Jefe and two soldiers armed with rifles and bayonets. They promptly marched me off to the jail located on the hill and locked me in the only cell. The cell was in the back of the building that was stuck into the side of a hill. Red dirt and rocks reached almost to the window.

Marrie came and she was angry, angry with me for being such an idiot, idiot being one of her kinder accusations. However, she brought me sandwiches,

Coca Colas and candy, then took the only taxi in town to look for the only lawyer in town, who resided on the next island.

After Marrie left, a little boy and girl around ten years of age with dirty faces and tattered clothes came up to the window. I offered them Coca Colas and candy and in exchange they passed different size stones through the bars.

The lock to the iron door was lower than halfway and I could pull the top corner out of the jam. By placing a small flat stone in the crack and pounding on it with a bigger stone I forced the gap wider. I did this with larger and larger stones until I could crawl through the opening. When I came to the front door I kicked it off its hinges and walked out.

Down at the harbor I found Marya and Miriam safe with a baby sitter from another yacht that had arrived. The owner of the vessel had met Marrie earlier, knew about the situation, and suggested that I depart for Turtle Bay immediately. He told me to take his daughter and he would bring Marrie when she returned. The girls and I hoisted the anchor by hand and sailed away.

It was after midnight as I stood at the helm sipping Grand Marnier. A light chop on the ocean caused the phosphorescence wake to teem like a billion blue fireflies. I turned around to marvel at the twinkling blue lights and saw that we were being followed by a golden canoe. It was big and perhaps just beneath the water, however, it was glowing and gaining on me. I looked a bit, I thought a bit, I shook my head and pinched myself to see if I was o.k. It was still there, dead astern and gaining. I dashed below, shook Marya awake, and said, "Hurry honey, wake up, there's a golden canoe following us!" She came on deck rubbing her sleepy eyes and there following us was a golden crescent moon, now just above the horizon. "Is that a golden canoe?" is still a joke between us. She refers to it when I get outlandish.

Early next morning we sailed into Turtle Bay and dropped anchor. Marrie was there on the other yacht and we were happy to see one another safe. Turtle bay was an improvement over Cedros Island. There was sheltered anchorage, a processing plant for abalone which employed a hundred women, and an excellent restaurant.

Six soldiers spoiled the day when they arrested me and placed me in a proper jail. A telegram and radio message had gone out all across Mexico with the message:

Arrest the bandito Capitan
On the yacht *Jolly Swagman*
For assault, insult and jailbreak

The policemen were kind and thought my 'crime' was wonderful. The story was that the immigration officer was the spoiled son of a politician in Mexico City and had caused trouble at every post he was placed. Cedros Island was the last and most remote location. It seemed no one liked him, but they all loved my family and me. In the evenings I invited the policemen and the mayor to dinner in the restaurant along with Marrie and the girls. We ate and drank abundantly. It is seldom one comes across such a hospitable group. The party is where you find it.

One evening Marrie and the girls came to visit. I was sitting on the bunk and the grill was locked. Miriam was dressed in a pretty little calico dress with a full skirt and a sash that tied in a bow in back. She turned sideways and squeezed between the bars and out of the folds of her dress she pulled out my 38 Smith & Wesson, handed it to me, and whispered, "Shoot them Daddy." I had never been so surprised in my life, but my heart swelled with pride as I hugged her and told her they were all nice men and my friends and shouldn't be shot.

We had to wait five days until the DC-3 stopped on its way north to Santa Rosalita, the capital of Baja, Sud. I had to pay the round trip tickets for the immigration officer and two policemen.

We all boarded and flew north to court. The chief stared at me the entire trip, however, I noticed he kept a good distance. We arrived in Santa Rosalita before noon. They locked me in a dirty cell until after siesta and then escorted me to court. The verdict stated that I must apologize in court and pay six hundred dollars for damage to the jail. Marrie paid the money and I made my speech in English which was accepted as an apology.

Getting the anchor out of the mud was more than I and the girls could manage by hand, however, as they say, 'necessity is the mother of invention.' We attached a line to the anchor chain by placing a screwdriver through a chain link. Next I tied on a line that was wrapped around a headsail winch and ever so slowly we winched it up and into its cradle.

Three days later, in a strong wind from the north, we rounded the cape at Cabo San Lucas. Once we got behind land the wind was contrary and we couldn't make the last half mile to the anchorage. We lowered the fourteen-foot Zodiac and the 35 horsepower engine and tried to tow the twenty-six ton Jolly Swagman. No go. The Zodiac zigzagged back and forth. Then we tied it fast alongside and off we went with Marrie steering the yacht while I stayed down in the Zodiac running the outboard. This worked out to be a perfect tug and we used it whenever we needed to move. As we were the first yacht of the season, the choice of anchorages was ours. We anchored in crystal clear water and drifted back until the stern was only a few feet from the beach. We all agreed we had arrived in paradise.

In those days, Cabo San Lucas was still a small Mexican village with a sandy road, three or four hotels, a bakery, and a place where you could eat a great pizza. There was also a disco without a roof situated on the beach and several open-air restaurants. We ate in restaurants cheaper than we could from our larder. The seafood was fresh and the Mexican beer superb. Is it any wonder we stayed for a year? Now I question why we ever left.

Yachts arrived daily. Perhaps fifty anchored up and down the beach. We made friends quickly and almost every evening fifteen or twenty of us would meet for the happy hour at each of the hotels. Everyone's children came along. We ate pizza or whatever struck our fancy afterward. They were glorious days.

Marrie is good to the bone and the goodness seeps out. She ironed our clothes despite the heat. We looked like we had come out of the bandbox whenever we went out. She was very beautiful. I often wondered how I ever got her. Her figure was sculptured and her weight never varied five pounds. She was the queen of the ball. As the old Marty Robbins ballad goes, 'Everyone stopped to stare, at this one young and rare, even the women remarked of the charm she possessed.'

Marya and I were pals. I taught her seventh grade and to water ski. The Zodiac could go twenty miles per hour and I would tow her near the tuna cannery. I told her sharks were lurking just below the surface and she had better not fall. I probably was correct to warn her.

Miriam turned five on August 14, 1978 and we enrolled her in the village school. The teachers were proud to have this little blue-eyed angel. They touched her hair and would say "Aye, que linda" (how beautiful). Marrie plaited her hair in a French braid, dressed her ever so nicely, and walked her across the street and up a sandy path to the school. We left her with the intention of coming back in the afternoon to fetch her. Around noon we were on our way to a restaurant for lunch when we heard Miriam's voice. She was standing in front of the police station, a policeman with a handlebar mustache was holding her by the hand and she was kicking his shins, yelling and pointing towards the boat. We ran up, rescued the poor policeman, and then realized what all the fuss was about. The school closed for lunch and the children went home. Since we didn't show up, the teacher handed Miriam over to the policeman at his station next door. Miriam was trying to explain that her home was the yacht just across the way and if he would just turn her hand loose she would go home.

The first time I went to the grocery store in Cabo I returned with excitement and said, "I found out the word for peanut butter."

Before I could say it, Miriam rolled out "*Crema de cacahuate*, Daddy."

Steve, Connie and their thirteen-year-old daughter Justine arrived in Cabo on their Chinese Junk. Steve did some varnish work. He was a hard worker and honest and didn't drink my beer or proposition Marrie. I knew I had found my man. We became good friends.

We were still without an engine since the episode at Guadalupe Island. I had a local mechanic take a look and assess the problem. The engine had to come out.

Marrie and I took the 1,200-pound engine up the companionway with not a quarter inch to spare on each side. We used the boom, winches and tackle with good effect. Next we lowered the engine into the Zodiac which was a feat. Then I sent it to Los Angeles where it was rebuilt to the highest standards.

I flew from La Paz to Tijuana taking a chance going back to the US. I went home, got my pickup and Spunky our pet cat who Miriam was missing. I then drove to LA and collected the engine and headed south.

Spunky had gone somewhat feral and drove me crazy! He wasn't still one minute and kept trying to get out whenever I cracked a window or door. I drove the thousand-mile Baja trek stopping only for fuel. Never again!

I had my airplane brought down and I did a load every couple of weeks throughout the winter without mishap.

Stephen and Alexis, friends from Manhattan Beach, came down to Cabo for a visit. One day we went whale watching in the Queen Air. We must have seen a hundred or more of these amazing giants of the sea. It was mating season and Baja was their dancehall. One morning we saw an unbelievable sight. Four large whales, two of which were mating. They were lying on their sides and we could clearly see the white penis connecting them. Underneath the two mating whales were two more of equal size holding the top two up. It looked as if they were pushing upwards so that the blowholes of the mating pair were above the water. A rare and remarkable sight for anyone.

Another day we went fishing in the Zodiac and I hooked a six-foot hammerhead shark. There wasn't a chance of landing him with my light rig He swam up to the boat and I grabbed him by the tail and dragged him aboard. Marrie, the girls, Stephen, and Alexis screamed while running to the bow, which is not very far in a 14-foot rubber boat. They yelled for me to throw him overboard, however that proved to be a much harder job than getting him aboard. He was most docile for a few minutes, squirming back and forth and looking around.

Suddenly he went wild. The hammerhead grabbed my plastic tackle box, shook it like a bulldog shaking a cat, and splintered several rods I had tied together. His little pig eyes, stuck out on extinctions to his head were looking me over. My passengers also had the same look in their eyes and I must admit I had overdone it big time. As he flopped and slid toward the bow the outboard came out of the water as everyone tried to stand on the small forepeak. I thought I was going to lose my crew if I didn't do something quick. I grabbed a butcher knife and as I went to stick him in the head he jerked to one side and I stabbed the floorboards instead. I finally connected, he quivered and died. I put a line around his tail and dragged him back to the Jolly Swagman where I hung him from the boom as a trophy.

We replaced the engine and did some sailing in the Sea of Cortés. After living in paradise for almost a year we reluctantly headed south down the west coast of Central America, traversing the Panama Canal tied to the biggest tug in the world. Steve and Connie took the vessel on to the Leeward Islands. We flew down several times sailing and playing in the Caribbean.

The Jolly Swagman was also a very photogenic boat. She was photographed a thousand times when the famous train robber Ronald Biggs was led across her deck handcuffed to a bounty hunter. These characters kidnapped Biggs in Brazil and sailed into Barbados. Since the harbor was crowded they rafted up to the Jolly Swagman. Later, the courts returned Biggs to his family in Brazil. Another claim to fame for the Jolly Swagman is she was used in the movie, "Beggar-Man Thief," based on the famous novels by Irwin Shaw. She was beautiful and we have many happy memories of the years we spent owning her.

18. THAI STICKS AND THE MOTLEY CREW

Lost and Found –Cutter Abandoned–Storing Pot Next Door to the President -- The Chain Gang

The Taurus was a 125-foot World War 1 coast guard cutter. She was long, narrow, fast and the worst roller I have ever been on. She rolled to one side so far that you braced yourself with one foot on the wall and waited for the long slow roll in the opposite direction. The bridge was twenty feet above the water and you felt you were in an upside-down pendulum. She was fabricated early in the last century from riveted pig iron plates and trimmed in lovely brass rails, portholes, and fittings. A big brass and teak wheel adorned the cockpit. Twenty-five aluminum skiffs were stacked on deck and fifty beds were stacked three deep in the forepeak to accommodate the fifty fishermen who manned the skiffs. Rene scammed the Japanese out of a million dollars to convert her into a mother ship for the fishing skiffs, plus another half million for the license to fish her in Honduran waters. He fished almost a year and should have made a fortune, but that was not Rene's destiny.

After the round the world trip on the Howie I wanted to go to Thailand for a load of Thai sticks which were bringing a thousand dollars a pound. The other investors were flush with money but were not ready to risk any. A few told me that if I got a boat over there they would be interested in investing. This meant I was alone in the venture until it was half done.

I leased the vessel from Rene and he hired Charles Whitfield to get a crew together to ferry the vessel to Manila, Philippines. Charles hired Paul Garret, not the smartest shrimper on the Gulf of Mexico to skipper her. He got to Grand Cayman Island, less than a thousand miles from home before he called and said he broke down. We invited Roger and Dianne to fly down with Marrie and I and make it a vacation.

Charles met us at the airport. He was a giant of a man who said he had smoked marijuana, but it didn't have an effect on him. I laughed, went out, and bought a lid. Back in the bungalow on the beach I rolled a joint and passed it around. Charles inhaled deeply, still denying it could get him stoned. All at once it hit him and he went to laughing and crawling on the floor, following the joint and asking for more. We laughed 'til we cried and I know that was the happiest joint I ever smoked. We took a stroll through town and enjoyed watching the Americans with their satchels taking their money to the eighty banks on Main Street.

We got the problem repaired on the Taurus and Paul Garret headed out for the Panama Canal where he reversed and damaged the propeller shaft. I flew down to help. It only took a come-a-long and four bolts and we were underway. I decided to ride for a couple of days and give the crew some moral support before they set out across the Pacific for Manila.

Puntarenas, Costa Rica was somewhat of a disappointment as we sailed up the dirty river and tied to a dilapidated wharf. Across the street was a row of seedy open front bars with working girls. I walked in with my motley crew and sat down at a table. A pretty woman with beautiful green eyes, curly black hair, and wearing a green dress with matching high heels walked over, pinched me in the ribs, and asked, "Ver' you from, sailor?"

"I'm from Santa Barbara, California," I answered.

She got excited and said, "My boyfriend es from Santa Barbara."

"Really? And who is your boyfriend?"

"Jerald Vills. I got picture in vallet." She quickly dug in her purse and brought out a small picture of Jerry.

This was just too much to believe. Puntarenas is three thousand miles from Santa Barbara and I had never heard of the place.

"When did you meet Jerry?"

"Oh, he here one month. He left two months ago. He took me San Jose and buy me new clothes. He bery nice man. I go Santa Barbara to vesit him."

This was too good to keep and the first thing I did when I returned home was to contact Jerry. He was in a restaurant with a group of people and I said, "Jerry, I was in a whore house in Puntarenas and there were posters with your picture on every wall. He laughed and said," Wasn't she pretty? I felt like some company and she was a perfect guide for Costa Rica. So you liked that dress, huh?" A United Air Line pilot later married her and they moved to a hundred-acre site on the Pacific, a few miles north of Santa Barbara, thanks in part to the pretty new clothes.

"Mystery Ship Abandoned in Keawaiki Harbor" filled the front pages of newspapers across Hawaii.

Paul Ray Garret almost made it to Midway Island in the Pacific before he turned back to Hawaii. He called from Hilo and said he was broken down again. I asked what the problem was this time and he said the autopilot had gone out. I asked if it would not have been easier to go on to Manila and he said they were a tad nearer to Hawaii. For some time I had suspected Paul was afraid to do the load and was doing everything in his power to make it look like it was mechanical problems rather than his fear that was stopping the vessel. I flew over and spent a week in Hilo Harbor fixing things.

Once the autopilot was repaired the crew sailed for Manila and I returned to Santa Barbara. Two weeks later Rene called and said the ship had been abandoned in Keawaiki Harbor, on the Kona Coast of the Island of Hawaii. I flew over and found an absolute mess. Paul had stripped her of all the brass portholes, the wheel and navigational equipment and had abandoned her. She dragged anchor one night in a storm and a group of hippies boarded her and were claiming salvage.

Marrie and I flew over with the girls. We rented a condominium for two months and went to work.

I loved the Kona coast. Marya was about thirteen and wanted to drive so I had her chauffeur me around. One day she was doing seventy miles per hour through a virtual desert of black lava and asked, "Daddy let me go a hundred."

I slid over by her and said, "Go for it." She kept easing the pedal down and the speedometer kept rising. I could see for miles along the deserted highway. When she reached a hundred I said, "Marya, there's a highway patrolman behind you."

She didn't look in the rearview mirror. Instead she jerked her head around with the steering wheel going in the same direction, I grabbed it. We had to stop and just laugh for a while.

The volcano Mauna Kea erupted and we had a ringside seat. We stood by a river of red-hot lava as it flowed by our feet and slid into the ocean. Tourists poured in from all over the world to see the majestic sight.

Asthma is a malady that has been with me all my life and I have never felt better than when I was there.

After fifty thousand dollars in repairs and lawyer costs, I hired a new crew to return the vessel to Louisiana. Rene didn't want it and sunk it while it was tied to the dock and collected the insurance.

While I was in Mexico, Johnny Allen, George Doran and Gene Conner were indicted in three different counties. Johnny was held in the city jail in Albany,

Georgia. His bail was a quarter of a million dollars and my sister Charlotte, bless her heart, went his bail.

They stored several tractor-trailer loads of pot on my 700-acre farm near Plains, Georgia in Sumter County, home of former President Jimmy Carter. All this added hype to the media. The trial lasted for weeks. Miraculously they won!

The next trial was in Albany and the prosecutor kept referring to 'The Big Rooster' in California. My photograph was held up to every witness and thankfully none had ever seen me. They spent a small fortune on lawyers and as the old prison saying goes, *they received as much justice as they could afford* and walked away from that trial.

The third trial was held in Coffee County, home of George Doran and Gene Conner, who didn't think the prosecutor could find a jury to convict them.

Uncle Grover had gone to school with the judge and upon Mother's request he put in a good word for Johnny. The Judge excused himself from the trial, saying that he was too good of a friend of Grover Garrison not to be influenced by his statement. This was a tactical error as that judge was fair.

Their peers found them guilty. Johnny received a seven-year prison term while George and Gene got five years. Johnny was sent to a penitentiary in north Georgia for a couple of years and then transferred to a chain gang in southwest Georgia.

I visited Johnny and I found it strange to see him in black and white stripes, but he looked great. He had filled out with muscles. His skin was bronze and his hands had layers of calluses from swinging bush axes.

The warden came through the visiting room, stopped, and spoke to us for a minute. He seemed a nice enough old farmer type who I thought might have had to take a state job out of necessity. Johnny said he was all right but tough.

Without mentioning a thing to Johnny, I bought a quart of Chivas Regal and called on the Warden that evening at his home. I figured if he took the whiskey, he might take more. He was friendly and invited me in. I presented my gift which he accepted and we went on through to the kitchen and sat down at the table. He took down two glasses, added ice, and poured a couple of stiff ones. After some getting acquainted and a few more drinks I got down to business.

"Warden, is there anything that can be done to make life for Johnny a little easier?"

He thought a bit and then said, "Well, let's see. I suppose I could make some changes and put him outside as a dog boy."

"What in the world is a dog boy?" I asked.

"Oh, he's the man who looks after the bloodhounds. Whenever a convict runs he goes after him. There are two dog boys. Most every day one runs and tries to get away. After two hours, the other one takes the dogs and runs him down. They have a lot of fun doing it and it keeps them in shape and practice. They take bets on how quickly they can catch one another. It's the best job here. The only bad thing is the other convicts hate them and they have to be careful not to ever get near them"

"That sounds great. I'd like to try that myself, just for fun mind you."

"Hell, it is a lot of fun. They run down creeks, down the center of highways and back and forth over fences. That slows the chaser down because he has to lift both those heavy sons-a-bitches over the fence and they weigh eighty pounds apiece. Now they agree beforehand as to how many fence crossings they can make."

"Will you give Johnny the job?"

"Yeah, I'll put him out there tomorrow morning first thing."

"Is there anything I could do for you?"

"Well now, my wife has been wanting to open a blue jeans store in town."

"How much would it cost to open a nice store?"

"We've been figuring and it comes to about ten thousand dollars."

I reached in my inside jacket pocket, pulled out a ten-thousand-dollar bundle of hundred dollar bills and laid it on the table and said, "And in continuing appreciation for your looking out for my friend, I will see that you receive a thousand dollars on the first of every month,"

"It will be most appreciated and you can be assured that I will do the best I can."

He walked me out to the car and gave my hand a strong, heartfelt shake and I drove away with a good feeling.

Johnny was moved outside the prison walls into a mobile home that he shared with another convict. Naturally, I kept him furnished with the best food, a TV, and a new device called a 'video recorder'. Johnny and the other prisoner drove the dog truck all over the county and were allowed to stop at the video store and shop for groceries.

On one visit, I was at the trailer when the warden came in, and soon thereafter Johnny's girlfriend from Albany drove up. The other prisoner grilled steaks, cooked supper and cleaned up. Nobody noticed him. He went quietly about his work like a subservient slave. After dinner the warden went home and Johnny and his girlfriend retired to his bedroom. The prisoner and I stayed up late into the night, drank whiskey, and talked. He told me of the murders he had committed. I remember he had killed his stepfather with a frying pan and several others for different reasons. He said he would rather kill a man than a dog. He also said that Johnny and the warden treated him like a dog. I gave him a hundred-dollar bill and he was delighted.

Next day I talked with Johnny about the man. He said he didn't like him, was afraid of him, and didn't have any more to do with him than he had to.

Towards the end of Johnny's sentence he began getting furloughs, first for a day and later on several days at a time. During Easter, Johnny invited the warden and his wife to accompany him and his girlfriend to the Gulf of Mexico in Florida where he had a cabin and an offshore fishing boat. The warden accepted. While they were out fishing it began to rain. They were coming in from the weather wet, cold and shivering and there waiting on the dock was an FBI team who arrested them for escape with a firearm. They were taken to the Federal holding facility in Atlanta, Georgia and held incommunicado for some days. The women were released, but the warden and Johnny were held without bail. They were charged with escape and because the warden had his pistol they were charged with escape while using a firearm. The Feds handed them over to the State where they were quickly tried and convicted. Judge Kato gave them ten years each and at sentencing he said, "I want to see you busting rocks in the freezing cold and burning heat. Nothing is good enough for scum like you." They were sent to Reedsville State Penitentiary, the worst joint in the state, a hell hole where prisoners see lights dim as one of their mates is fried in the electric chair.

The whole debacle started when the disgruntled dog-man went up for parole after twenty years and was denied. He had been making threats about what he was going to do in case they turned him down. The parole board, knowing his history, had no choice but to deny him release. This malcontent piece of human garbage wrote the FBI a ten-page letter, in pencil, telling of all the sins Johnny and the warden were committing. I read the letter. It was a piece of art in snitching. He had even recorded conversations and body language, telling on me for giving him the hundred dollars.

This was unjust, something had to be done!

I drove to Thomasville from Key Biscayne, Florida, stopped at a gas station and asked a man changing a tire, "Excuse me, do you know where Judge Kato lives?"

"Yeah, I know where the son-of-a-bitch lives. Are you sure you wanna know?"

"Yeah, I wanna know. Is he all that bad?"

"He's worse than bad, pardner'. He'll put you on the chain gang for spitting on the sidewalk."

"I've heard something about him. He put my partner and the warden in for ten years for taking a legal furlough."

"That's him, that's him all right, I heard about that. So, they are your buddies. It was in the news around here while the trial was going on."

"What kind of a man is he really?"

"He's an arrogant, tobacco chewing son-of-a-bitch, not over forty-five. He's so bad his wife couldn't stay with him. He's living with his daughter now, and there's a whole lot of gossip about that."

I thanked him and got directions out to the house. A long driveway winding through pines led to a brick house on a lake. It was ten o'clock on a warm spring Sunday morning when I knocked on the unused front door. The judge answered. I told him who I was. He stepped out and we walked out under the pines. His daughter came and stood on the porch, looking kinda worried. He told her to go on back inside, which she did.

I told him how Johnny was an innocent man caught up in the marijuana business and that it was all my fault. I told him I knew the warden and as far as I could see neither had done anything wrong.

He said, "So you admit being in the marijuana business?"

"Yes, I have been in that business and I am the one who talked Johnny into quitting his job and joining me. He was happily married with a beautiful little girl and if it hadn't been for me he would still be with them."

We talked for a half-hour or so with me taking all the blame for Johnny. Monday morning first thing, he commuted the two sentences from ten years to time served. Both were released and placed on probation for ten years with the stipulation that if either met with or talked to Roger Reaves, they would serve the sentence in full.

That conversation was probably my Waterloo because I believe he called the Feds as soon as I left.

Mr. Allen, at age ninety-five, still lived in his home on Highland Avenue. I knocked on his door about ten at night and he was very happy to see me. I had him call Johnny and ask him to come over on an urgent matter. Johnny walked in five minutes later looking rather anxious and I stepped out and gave him a big hug. We had a short get together. I could see that he was afraid of being caught with me and going back in for ten years. I handed him a brown paper bag with twenty-five thousand dollars in it for which he was most appreciative.

19. MAY THE FORCE BE WITH YOU

Close Encounters with the Federalés the DC-7 and NTV13

Prospects for marijuana in Colombia were promising. The only problem I had was that my airplanes could not fly from Colombia to the US without refueling. To solve the problem I went to Central America to scout out potential landing strips. They are more difficult to find than one would imagine.

I flew a Queen Air to Guatemala City planning to use it as a base. At the hotel I met two Pan Am Stewardesses who wanted to go to the Mayan ruins at Tikal to see the actors in a movie being filmed. As this fitted in with my plans I invited them to fly over with me. When we landed there was barely room to park for all the other aircraft. Futuristic model aircraft buzzed about as we climbed the pyramid. From the summit we watched the people filming. Some were shouting, waving their arms, while others scurried about. We had to come down off the pyramid so that the small flying machines could zip by for filming. The name of the production was "Star Wars." Little did we know that we were watching the filming of one of the most popular movies ever made. The opening scene consisted of space ships flying out past the peaks of Tikal.

After leaving Tikal I flew the short distance to the potential landing strip in the jungle and found it had slender reeds about twelve feet tall growing all over it. I landed and taxied to the far end. Upon turning around I saw the propellers had made two big bites down the center of the strip. That looked interesting, so I decided to mow the grass. Back and forth I taxied, shredding the flimsy reeds with the propellers and after a few swipes the strip had a new look.

We took off and flew to Guatemala City International where I was cleared for a straight-in approach through heavy rain. On final I lowered the landing gear and got two green lights and one red on the left main gear. I called the tower, explained my situation, and asked them to have a look at the gear on a close fly-by. They reported all three wheels down. I was not satisfied. I retracted the gear and climbed. At altitude I went into a steep dive and lowered the gear, pulling up hard. I hoped the high G's would ensure the landing gear was fully deployed and locked in place. After several tries I still only had two green lights so I decided to bring her in regardless. I shut down the engines and feathered the propellers on the final. There are three blades on each propeller and I kept bumping the starter until only one blade was hanging down. I held her off just inches above the runway and touched down on the right main so gently I didn't feel it. I held it on that gear until she slowed down and gently settled on both, then she collapsed onto her belly.

When retracted, the tires on a Queen Air protrude a few inches below the fuselage in line with the runway. The propellers made a terrible scraping sound but there was little damage as the few inches of tires hanging down saved the belly. Not even the rotating beacon underneath was broken.

Fire trucks arrived with sirens blaring. They helped the girls and I push it to one side of the big runway. A KLM Boeing 747 on a flight from Amsterdam had to go around twice. When he did land his wing tip vortex almost knocked us over. A Beechcraft dealer sent a truck and towed the Queen Air to his hangar.

Back at the hotel we were at the bar celebrating our health when in walks Marrie. It was all innocent, but I was terribly embarrassed.

Marrie and I took a commercial flight back to Santa Barbara and since I did not have time to work with the wrecked Queen Air I began asking around for a pilot-mechanic. Someone who would go down and fix it or fly it home straight-legged, (gear down).

David Mann came to the house one morning and said he was a pilot-mechanic. He was about thirty years old, blond with longish hair and serious. He sat straight up on a soft chair with a clipboard on his knee like a pilot flying instruments and took quick notes of all I said. In a very short time he had all he needed to know and was on his way to Guatemala City.

While we were talking, he mentioned his wife Pam and that she was touring Europe with her grandmother. I pictured a special woman. She did eventually become a very special person in the life of our family.

David returned within a week with the Queen Air and finished the repairs at his hangar. When I received the bill it was nowhere as much as I expected. From then on David was my mechanic and friend. The friend part was often challenged because he was a fanatical perfectionist and I take life much less seriously. We came to an agreement whereby he kept the planes in perfect running order and delivered them to me south of the border. This arrangement worked well for some years.

All my contacts were out of commission. Roberto had been shot while running away from the landing strip moments after I had taken off and was now in prison in Culiacan. Asiento, his older brother, was being hunted like a wild animal by every agency in Mexico with orders to shoot to kill. Their sister Dora, who ran a beauty salon on a rough dirt back street in Mazatlán, told me that

Ramon, her fourteen-year-old brother, could find me a load since he had been working with his brothers for years and knew everyone.

Ramon was a bright-eyed happy kid. A little small for his age, but wiry and street-wise. We loaded up in an old car and headed into the Sierra Madre Mountains looking for 'the kind.'

Ramon brought a couple of other youngsters along to help. One was a pinched faced weasel looking character that I wouldn't have trusted as far as I could throw a bull by the tail. He was the one who was supposed to have the load. We first went to have a look at what he had to offer and it wasn't up to the mark and I turned it down. He had a temper tantrum, stalked off and I thought, 'good riddance.'

An American had been living for some years in this area growing excellent 'sinsemilla' (without seed) during the wet season and I had seen a sample. It was beautiful lime green with purple hairs and would bring five-hundred dollars a pound instead of the sixty we were getting for the commercial grade. We walked and rode mules for several days before I agreed on a ton of good stuff and then returned to Mazatlán. I gave Dora sixty thousand dollars for the load and she promised delivery to a Nayarit beach at daybreak, two days hence.

After a much-needed scrub at the Camino Real Hotel I went down to the open-air bar overlooking the Pacific and ordered a Bombay gin and tonic. It was getting on happy hour and the place was filling up. A full moon was rising, a mariachi band was playing and pretty ladies were swaying solo to the music. To do my part I walked over to a cute brunette with freckles across her nose, bowed slightly, and gave my old line, "Pardon me, Ma'am. Do you happen to know a gentleman by the name of Roger Reaves?"

She thought for a minute and said, "I don't believe that I do."

"Well let me introduce myself." This got a laugh and a dance. Her name was Molly, a travel agent from San Francisco. She was there with her identical twin sister and twenty-five co-workers. We had a few drinks, danced for a while and she insisted on spending the night with me.

We passed an enjoyable night and early the next morning I called room service and ordered coffee, orange juice, and huevos rancheros for breakfast. Soon there was a knock. I slipped on a pair of trousers and opened the door. Standing there was a big red-faced waiter with a tray balanced on his left hand and a pot of steaming coffee in his right.

He said, "Buenos Dias Señor," in a good loud voice, and set the coffee pot on the table. With his right hand he lifted the tray and in his left was a pearl-handled .45. He stuck it in my face and said, "Federal Policia de Mexico, you make one move I keel you, comprende?"

"Si, comprendo."

In broken English he ordered us to get dressed. While we were getting our clothes on he looked through my wallet and passport. I took a glass bottle of Coca Cola out of the minibar and thought very seriously of knocking him in the head. I considered we were on the sixth floor, there were no balconies and I didn't know how many were waiting in the hall or lobby.

With that in mind I decided to back off and with a trembling hand I opened the coke, took a swallow, and reluctantly passed on the idea. He took a firm grip on my shirt collar, stuck the pistol hard in my ribs, and marched us to the elevator.

Five more black-eyed killers were waiting in the lobby. Three cars were at the entrance. They loaded us into the back seat of a new LTD Ford. The first thing I noticed was that there were no door handles in the back. The lead car zigzagged through the empty early morning streets with us close on its tail. The other car hard on our rear. I thought we were headed to the prison where I had been tortured a couple of years previously, but we passed on by and headed out into the country. They played a tape of me talking to Dora, but I didn't say anything incriminating.

I leaned over and whispered to Molly, telling her I planned to escape and for her not to worry because they were not interested in her.

They turned off the highway and followed the railroad tracks along a rough dirt road. After a mile or so they stopped in a clearing of red clay, about an acre in size. Scattered everywhere were carcasses of mules, cows, burros, and all kinds of roadkill in various stages of decomposition.

At the back of the clearing were banks of clay pushed up by a bulldozer the previous year. Sticking out of these mounds were bones of all descriptions. Gourd vines grew rank in this fertilizer.

The big red-faced waiter opened the door and said, "Get out ".

We walked perhaps fifty steps from the car and stopped right in the middle of all that carrion, stench and blowflies. Then old red face said, "Donde esta su avión?" (Where is your airplane?)

I said, "Sorry, I don't speak Spanish."

He hit me hard with an open palm on my right ear, knocking me down and yelled, "Speak Spanish, son-of-a-bitch!"

Five Federalés worked me over while one stayed by the car with Molly. They made me kneel and tied my hands tightly behind my back with my leather belt. Then they grabbed my white dress shirt in the back, pulled it over my head, and commenced to kick and knock me about. When they seemed to tire of this they started on my privates with a cattle prod. This went on for several hours with them occasionally grabbing me by the hair, jerking my head up, shoving a bunch of papers under my nose and shouting for me to sign and this would all be over. They told me I gave Dora sixty-thousand dollars the day before and that I owned three airplanes and a large yacht. It didn't take long to see 'the weasel' all over the questions. I hoped Dora and Ramon were safe. I knew that if I signed the confession I would be in a Mexican prison for years and they had nothing on me.

They said they were members of a joint task force between the American DEA and Mexican Federalés. That I had been operating out of the state of Sinaloa for a decade and they had come from Mexico City with orders to stop me.

After three hours the fabric, skin, and some meat was gone from my knees. My shirt was torn and I was covered with blood. Ol' red face ground out his cigar on my neck. I looked up into a clear china blue sky and was completely at ease. I somehow knew I was going to get away. The temperature was rising. Ol' red face was wet with sweat and I could see he was tired. They tried the cattle prod again. Fortunately, the batteries had weakened. They radioed back to the city for someone to bring new ones. Everything stopped while we waited.

After half an hour a car drove up and stopped behind the others and the boss got out. Four of the killers left to go back to the cars to kiss the ass of their boss and gawk at Molly and her rather large cleavage. They hung around her laughing and talking, leaving me alone with Ol' red face. I strained for all it was worth at the belt tied around my hands and managed to get them free, pulling the skin off the top of my right hand. Red rocks, about the size of baseballs were scattered everywhere. I squirmed around, got one in my bloody right hand, and in a trembling, crying, sniveling voice, I whimpered to Ol' red face, "Señor, I will sign." He couldn't believe his ears! He bent over and I remember his big gold chain with swordfish pendant dangling as my hand came overloaded with five pounds of stone. It hit him in the forehead and he fell to the ground like a bull in a slaughterhouse hit with a sledgehammer.

A waist-high bank of red dirt with bones sticking out was fifty steps away. I ran out of my Bally shoes trying to get there before I was shot down. At about the halfway mark six Federalés started shooting. As I leaped over the embankment bullets were hitting the dry dirt all around me, kicking up tufts of dust and twanging off trees and limbs. A machine gun opened up and was tearing up the jungle when a vine caught me across the bridge of my nose. This stopped my forward motion and slammed me down on my back. I hit the ground so hard it made a thud. I lay there for a second as bullets shredded the foliage overhead, and then I started screaming like a wounded dog, "Ahh! Ahh! Ahh! Ahh!"

Silence. All shooting stopped. I quickly crawled through the jungle and got behind a large tree and yelled, "Molly, I'm fine. I'll see you in San Francisco!"

Molly's clear thin voice came back, "Oh, thank God. Be careful Roger!"

An animal trail led into the jungle. I ran down it stooped over. I saw a flock of wild turkeys ahead and I knew if they flew it would give my position away. I backtracked and went around them. My bloody white shirt was like a neon sign in the jungle. I took it off and crammed it under a rotten log.

Back on the trail I came upon an exquisite blue parrot feather lying in a little patch of sunshine. This was my talisman. At the hotel I had been reading Richard Bach's 'Illusions' and on the front cover of the book was a painting of this feather. I picked it up most reverently and tucked it in a pocket. Before long I found that I was rather in a small area of perhaps a half-mile square, the railroad on one side, a road on the other, and fields on the other two sides. I came to the edge and lay there for a few minutes. I heard a two-way radio crackle only a few yards to my right. I thought of going back and covering myself in leaves and waiting for dark but decided against it as soldiers might come in and search. A car came tearing up and stopped. My heart pounded against my ribcage. My throat was bone dry. The radioman got in the car and they sped off. I stuck my head out looking both ways. It looked clear. I scurried across the two-rutted road and slithered under a sagging barbed wire fence into a long narrow pasture with tussocks of grass and weeds growing here and there. An old swaybacked white mare picked up her ears and trotted over to welcome me. Damn! Any other time a horse ran from you, but she pranced around as I half ran, half crawled across the pasture. Beyond this area was a thousand acres of young mango trees. The red earth had recently been harrowed and there wasn't a sprig of grass in sight. One could see for a mile under the trees. My only hope was to climb up in one and wait it out. I had just squatted on my perch when a military Huey landed in the pasture. Seventeen soldiers jumped out and swarmed into the jungle with AK-47's at the ready. The Federalés' cars kept circling the area. After a couple of hours the soldiers came out, loaded up, and flew away. Then I saw the four cars with Molly and the Federalés drive away.

Never in my life have I been so cramped and thirsty. When I climbed down off my perch I could barely walk. My throat was so dry I couldn't swallow. It was several miles across the mango orchard before I came to a dirt road. By an empty chicken house I found a spigot sticking out of the ground about four inches high. I turned it on and let it run for a few minutes. The water stayed warm and tasted like plastic, I didn't care. I drank my fill and then washed the blood off.

A school bus came by, stopped, and unloaded some children. The back window was covered in several inches of red dust. I ran up and grabbed onto a ladder that led to the roof. The children couldn't see me. I rode like that for five miles until we came to a village on the main highway. Fortunately I kept my folding money in a money-clip in my front pocket and it was still there. I knew I looked a bloody sight as I walked down the dirt street without a shirt and my trousers torn off at my bloody knees. The first store I came to I bought a bright yellow and blue Mexican cowboy shirt, a pair of jeans, a straw sombrero, a pair of huaraches, and walked out feeling like a new man.

A deluxe bus was leaving for Mazatlán so I boarded and eased on to the rear. We had only gone a few miles when we came to a roadblock. A trooper entered and looked around. I sunk over in my seat making myself as small and Mexican looking as I could while trying to hide my battered face. He walked about halfway down the aisle, then turned around and left, leaving me weak in the knees.

Nicholas, a taxi driver, knew Dora and I asked him to find her. He went to her house and found it boarded up. The neighbors knew nothing, or if they did, they weren't talking. After some searching he found her and we had a scary reunion. Everything was good as far as the marijuana was concerned. We decided to go ahead as planned. I called David Mann who was waiting with the Twin Beech two hundred miles away at the Hotel Cabo San Lucas on the tip of Baja California. David arrived just at daybreak. When he saw my face and hands he decided to ride out with me. Usually he delivered the plane, got out, and caught an airliner home. This time he rode to Mulegé after we unloaded at Juan's goat ranch. I rented a room, took a shower, and had lunch while someone washed and polished my airplane. Around four o'clock in the afternoon I flew back to the ranch and loaded up. I paid Juan the rancher five hundred dollars and headed north for the border where the value of the load increased by a multiple of five.

I made a low approach to a dry lake near Twenty-Nine Palms, California, and clicked the radio button three times. Truck lights barely lit up a short distance of sand. Just enough for me to get the position and heading. I descended at 200 feet per minute and watched for the shadow of the wing to get near the plane and then I flared. Once down and stopped, I turned on a flashlight because Jeff Brine, the driver, had a hard time finding me as the plane was the same color as the lakebed.

Jeff left with the load and I stayed put until he was well clear of the area then I fired her up and departed for San Diego. I landed at Love Field and taxied to Jim's Air where a line boy took over tying her down. I breathed a sigh of relief. This little saga was over. Or so I thought.

Stashed in a lockbox in Banamex, downtown Tijuana, was forty thousand dollars, a passport, and titles to property. But the key to the box was in Santa Barbara. The Federalés in Mazatlán had my wallet and in it was a business card from this bank.

Tijuana, or TJ, as Californians call it, is thirty miles south of San Diego. I took a taxi to the border, walked across, and caught another ragged old taxi to the bank, arriving shortly before noon.

Banamex is a large one-story building taking up most of the block. I walked up to a receptionist and explained my problem. She listened attentively and then excused herself and walked over to the manager. He was a young man, not more than thirty-five years old, sitting on a raised, glassed-in platform overlooking everyone. She talked a minute and I saw his head jerk up. He looked directly at me and his hand reached for the phone. I read him loud and clear and got up to ease out. The receptionist returned and said, "Señor Reaves, the manager is calling a locksmith and one should be here shortly. Would you like a cup of coffee?"

This confused me. Perhaps I was paranoid? He wouldn't be so blatant about calling the Federalés. I sat down on a large soft leather sofa and drank my coffee and watched nervously as a bank guard prevented any new customers from coming in and allowed everyone to leave. This was normal because the bank was closing for lunch. The receptionist came by and told me to wait and that the locksmith should be here any minute. I waited, but I was extremely nervous.

Seven of them came through the door. They were wearing dark sunglasses, dark green fatigues with trousers tucked into spit-shined combat boots. They had .45's on the hip and one was holding a MAC-10 machine gun pistol. My guts froze. What could I do?

I heard the clicking of high heel shoes on the marble floor behind me as someone ran up. I turned, it was a teller with whom I sometimes did business. She whispered, "Señor Reaves, Federal Police are here for you, come with me."

She trotted down an aisle while slightly bent over. We came to a large men's restroom and she whispered, "Hide in there."

"No," I said, "that's no good."

She then took me by the arm and hurried on, coming to a pile of construction blocks in front of a large tinted one-piece window. I thought it might be made of the unbreakable kind, but who knew? I picked up a forty-pound block and was about to heave it at the glass when a policeman with a .38 hanging to his knees sauntered up and stopped right in front of the window. Oh, shit! If I break the window and run he'll shoot me in the back, thinking I have robbed the bank. Again, she took me by the hand and ran into a warehouse area. She showed me a stainless steel door in the wall and told me to squeeze through when she pushed a hidden button some distance away. She quickly wrote her phone number on a scrap of paper, gave it to me and said, "My name is Alicia. Call me after three o'clock."

The small hole was for armored trucks to back up solid against the bank and pass money through. It definitely was not made for a man. Somehow I squeezed through and fell on top of my head onto the sidewalk, four feet below. In a flash, I was up and running. At the corner I jumped on a bus and rode for a few blocks. I was too nervous to sit down or stay on. I got off, caught a taxi, and felt somewhat better. After a few miles I got out and walked a ways then caught another taxi to a restaurant where I had several stiff ones.

To telephone Alicia or not to telephone Alicia? What if they arrested her and she talked? What if she was sitting by the phone waiting for me to call? She had probably saved my life. For sure, she had saved me from being tortured and thrown in prison for years. I called. Half an hour later she drove up in a big old Oldsmobile. I noticed the University of San Diego parking sticker and a frequent border-crossing permit on the windshield. We would have no problems.

When we came to 'La Linea,' as the Mexicans call the border there were twenty-five lanes of traffic backed up for a mile. It would take an hour to cross. Mexican police were watching from the sidewalks which made me more nervous than I already was. Alicia suggested I lie down and put my head in her lap. I did as instructed and she smoothed my hair down ever so softly. After about an hour, with no further trouble, I was back across the border and safe. To say I "owed" Alicia is putting it mildly. I never did see her again.

My friend Jerry Wills heard the story of my escape and good-naturedly presented me with a large antique etching of a rabbit diving into a hole with vicious hounds snapping the air only inches away from his tail. It wasn't far wrong in its presentation of events.

"Hollywood-Burbank tower; Twin Beech, November, seven nine seven Juliet Foxtrot, five miles south, landing runway three zero with information bravo."

"Roger Juliet Foxtrot. Follow the seven twenty-seven, two miles ahead landing on the left, keep visual separation. You are cleared to land on three zero right."

"Roger, three-zero right."

"Turn right on taxiway Delta, contact ground one-two-seven point nine"

Thus ended the flight from Orange County John Wayne Airport to Hollywood-Burbank. I taxied to Burbank Aviation where several large planes were for sale and parked underneath the wing of a McDonald-Douglas DC-7. Wow! That thing was gigantic!

DC-7. This monster could haul 30 tons of pot, 6,000 miles.
Image courtesy Peter Ehrbar - DC-7 of Swiss Air-July 1961 - Wikipedia

A big, red-haired, red-bearded, red-faced, rough-looking South African strolled out. He enfolded my hand in his and told me to come in and take a seat. The chairs were a row of seats from some airplane scrapped long ago. His desk was salvaged from the galley of perhaps the same plane as the seats. A wicked-looking razor-sharp dagger with brass knuckles for a handle served as a paperweight. On the wall behind this giant was a blasphemous sign printed in fancy Old English script and framed as though it was a museum painting. It read, "Yeah though I walk through the valley of the shadow of death I will fear no evil, for I am the meanest Son-of-a-Bitch in the valley."

He asked what he could do for me and I told him I had come to look at his DC-7. He slapped the desk with both hands, jumped up, and said, "Well, let's go have a look at that sweetheart. I just flew her in last week from the wars in Africa. As you can see she only has three engines and we haven't had time to patch up some of the bullet holes she acquired upon leaving Mozambique. They had removed the left inboard engine thinking it would stop somebody, but me and a couple of the boys went back and convinced them of the error of their thoughts. She flies like a dream! I flew her from Mozambique to Brazil by myself."

It was Mammoth, weighing one hundred and forty-four thousand pounds, one hundred nine feet long, with a wingspan of one hundred seventeen feet. A man could easily walk around in the wings where they attached to the fuselage. The engines had 54 cylinders attached to a round engine that produced 3250 horsepower. This monstrosity had four of them. One engine was missing and the belly was covered with oil and grease. We climbed up a twenty-foot aluminum ladder leaning against the cockpit. The inside looked like a big dark tunnel a hundred feet long, twelve feet tall and fifteen feet wide. The cockpit was familiar except for the four throttles. The flight engineers station was alien. There was a glass bubble in the ceiling for taking star sights and I looked forward to trying out my sextant at 400 mph. This machine could operate out of a dirt strip and carry thirty tons of marijuana five thousand six hundred and thirty-five miles. What a machine!

We agreed on a price of three hundred thousand dollars and I gave him a deposit of twenty-five thousand cash to hold it for a few days. The South African said he would have a new engine installed within a week and have me 'comfortable' flying his sweetheart within a few days.

I called Johnny Allen and asked him to hire a construction crew to grade a 6,000-foot runway on the farm at Plains, Georgia. I telephoned Roberto Davila in Santa Marta, Colombia, and told him I had bought the plane and he could expect me in three or four weeks and I needed thirty tons of good fresh weed. I asked if the terms were still the same as I did not want any surprises, particularly since I had partners. "Yes," the deal was still the same. They got the first fifty dollars a pound and we got the rest which was approximately two hundred and fifty dollars. With no losses, we would walk away with over fifteen million dollars a load and I would be dirty for less than a day. This kind of deal was hard to beat.

Saturday morning I started down the stairs and there curled up on the landing in her nightclothes was my twelve-year-old daughter, Marya, sobbing inconsolably. I picked her up in my arms and said, "What's the matter baby? It can't be that bad, tell Daddy all about it and I'll make it better."

She said, "Daddy you were driving your train and the bad people took one rail out of the track and the train turned over and over and caught on fire. I was there with Aunt Kay and she was drunk. We tried to get you out of the fire but we couldn't." With this, she started crying even harder.

I said, "Sweetheart, Daddy hasn't driven a train in years so don't worry about some old dream."

"But Daddy, it wasn't like a dream, it was like it was real and I was there. Oh yeah, before it was a train it was an airplane and it had a happy face just like your DC-3's. But it was bigger and one engine was off and it was all greasy and had a long ladder going up to the cockpit."

Did you ever see a man covered in goosebumps?

Early Monday morning I was at the home of one of my partners. I told him of Marya's vision and said I wanted out, in fact, I was out. He was more understanding than I had expected and gave my deposit back.

One month later the plane landed at Rio Frio, near Santa Marta, Colombia on a tide flat that was a shade too short. The propellers could be reversed after landing, but they had to be in the forward position before the ship slowed to fifty knots. Obviously the pilot came in too hot and held them in reverse too long while trying to stop. They loaded thirty tons on board and then couldn't start the right outboard engine because the prop was locked in the reverse position. They had to take the propeller off, order another one from Miami and have it flown into the clandestine airstrip. I wonder what the bite was to keep everything cool for that long.

The mechanics changed the prop and all was ready. The engines started, # 1, # 2, # 3, difficulties with #4. It kept grinding down. Then it was on fire. The pilot turned the fire extinguisher valve to #4 and pulled the discharge handle by his seat. The hoses were rotten as they had not been changed for years. They blew out and the cockpit filled with fire extinguishing chemicals. The pilot, co-pilot, and flight engineer barely escaped with their lives. The pilot broke his ankles in the jump. The aluminum plane and 10,000 gallons of high-grade aviation fuel was a crematorium for the thirty tons of marijuana.

Landing in Belize to refuel was a danger that could be eliminated with the right equipment. David and I began searching for aircraft that could fly non-stop from Colombia to Louisiana, a distance of two thousand miles. The Merlin 3 was at the top of the list with several other twin turboprops that were able to make the journey if they were tanked. David found an Aero Commander 690 B for the price of a half-million dollars. She was a sweetheart of an aircraft, designed by the same man who designed the F model fighters for the military. It was a jet-prop version of the plane in which Bob Hoover performed his amazing aerobatics at air shows all over the world. She belonged to TV channel 13 in

Los Angeles and that's how she came by her numbers, NTV13. The pilot was giving me instructions and on the first takeoff he asked how high I wanted to fly before turning downwind. I looked at the altimeter and saw I was approaching three thousand feet and spooling upward at over five thousand feet per minute. Damn that thing was hot! I had to go ten miles downwind to get her down, but it didn't take me long to get the hang of it. She flew like a dream.

Aero Commander 690 N13TV. This photo was taken a month after the D.E.A confiscated her in September 1982. The right engine caught fire when they attempted to fly her away. I admit to chuckling.
Image courtesy of Zane Adams

Shortly after I was checked out I loaded up the family and we set out for the Canadian arctic, arriving in Victoria, British Colombia within three hours with an average ground speed of over three hundred miles per hour. We spent that night in the lovely old Princess Hotel. The next morning we went shopping in an elaborate toyshop where we bought the girls stuffed animals that looked and felt real. We departed and started across the snow-covered Rockies. The girls walked around pretending to be stewardesses and the plane pitched up or down as they walked. This caused the autopilot to keep adjusting and the sound of the engines to change. I was unfamiliar with the aircraft and flying over thousands of miles of sharp, jagged ice-covered peaks was making me a little nervous so I made the girls sit down and buckle up. After a three-hour flight we descended over Lake Labarge, where Robert Service wrote 'The Cremation of Sam McGee,' and landed in Whitehorse, Yukon Territory.

Marrie's brother Matt worked for an oil company out of Inuvik, Northwest Territory on the Arctic Ocean. We flew to the site where the team of blasters was doing seismic mapping, landed on a dirt strip in the endless tundra, and asked where we could find him. Someone pointed out the camp where he bunked and we found him sitting around a table with ten other men playing poker. Hands froze in the air and silence fell over the group. Matt looked up as if he was seeing a ghost and then got a huge smile on his face and shouted, "I can't believe it!"

We had a wonderful reunion.

Matt had to go to work that evening and invited us to go to his cabin on the Great Bear Lake. We flew down and landed. Mounties came out to the airstrip inquiring about our business. I told them we were there to visit Matthew Rink. They asked if we had anything to declare and I said, "Only the ten cases of bourbon we brought for him." They jumped to attention and were quite peeved to learn I was only joking. I knew about the prohibition of alcohol in the Northwest Territory.

Elsie, Matt's Indian wife, made us welcome in their one-room cabin with an oil drum for a heater. People from the village came and stared at us through the windows for hours as we went about our business. They slipped silently through the door and lined up against the wall with serious faces and it was difficult to get one of them to smile. Most of them had rotten teeth from drinking Coca Colas and smoking constantly. Some had knife cut scars on their faces. Huskies and Malamutes were chained to stakes throughout the village. We enjoyed a visit from the missionary who had been there for twenty years. He had not had a single convert.

The following day we hired a guide to go fishing. It was late July and cold. Whenever we lined the boat up with the church steeple and a certain tree, a couple of three-foot-long Northern Pike would strike. It was great fishing, however, little Miriam cried and begged us not to kill the fish. She became so distraught we quit and went back to the cabin where we cleaned and cooked one of the bigger ones. The fish grow an inch per year in that cold water and the meat is firm, pink, and delicious.

Two days in the village was enough for us, so we flew south to Yellow Knife and spent the afternoon sightseeing. That night we stayed in a log cabin hotel with just the basics. The next day we flew to Spokane, Washington where we were met by a nasty custom agent. She insisted that we take everything out of the plane and then spent six hours tearing it apart.

20. RHETT, AN OIL RIG AND A MERCEDES WITH A PINK BOW

Marrie flew to Orange County where I met her at the airport. We drove to the Marriot Hotel where I was staying for a few days and that evening we went to The Chanticleer, one of the best restaurants in Orange County. While we were having cocktails a colorful elderly lady, who reminded me of Mrs. Santa Claus, passed our table with her large entourage. She was blind and as she passed my table she told her guide she would like to meet the man on her right. Once she was seated at the head of her table her guide came over and told me the lady would like to meet me. I was delighted and accepted. When I came up she held my hand in hers and they were hot. I was strongly attracted to her. She said some nice things and then said she saw rooms full of money surrounding me.

Marrie and I had a delicious dinner along with a couple of bottles of Rothschild's Bordeaux 1964. A few weeks later she came to me and said, "Sweetheart, we are going to have another baby."

"What? We are thirty-eight years old. Who do you think we are, Sara and Abraham?"

"It was the wine at the Chanticleer," she teased.

I was secretly happy and she knew it.

Somehow or another Rene got possession of 500 acres of fertile Louisiana bottomland. The only problem was, it was three feet below water. That didn't bother Rene in the least. He acquired a worn-out dragline, loaded it on a barge, and started dredging up 'lots' and selling them to duck hunters. His dredging was going faster than sales when a dapper young man drove up and gave him a good spiel on why he should buy a Bible. Rene converted this shyster on the spot with tales of the millions he could make selling 'lots' and they did do exceptionally well. That was until the Feds shut them down on environmental impact charges for destroying the nation's wetlands.

Rene landed on his feet when an oil company drilled on a neighbor's property and got a flow of twenty million dollars a month in natural gas. Dry wells on both sides proved that the gas dome was under Rene's property. Texas Drilling Company dug a canal to the location and floated in a big rig and began sinking the well.

Being that I had the inside skinny I just had to have a piece of the action. Governor Edwin Rose had brokered the deal and received the override; the difference between 7/8 and 3/4 percent of the deal. This amounted to twelve-and-a-half percent in the way royalties are divided. I organized an appointment with him and on the day we were to meet I was running late. I was driving my grey Cadillac when Rene said, "Put the pedal to the metal, son. I know the Governor!"

I eased it on up to 120 mph and heard the siren coming up behind. Rene didn't bother the trooper with his tale about knowing the Governor.

The Governor's Mansion in Baton Rouge is a big ostentatious copy of antebellum plantation home and Governor Rose was a slick dandy to complete the façade. Rose invited us for cognac and cigars. I accepted the former and told the tale about Rene knowing the governor. We all had a big laugh and Rose asked for the ticket and that was the end of it. I gave him a hundred thousand dollars in small bills and he signed over the title without counting the money. How millions of people can vote for such an obvious crook belies the imagination.

I held little Rhett close as we climbed the ten flights of stairs on the Mammoth offshore rig. The first rig had been replaced because more pressure was needed and this one was capable of putting 400,000 pounds of pressure on the bit, two miles below. We had a fabulous dinner at the chief engineer's table as he explained that we were over 11,000 feet deep and right over the granite dome covering the apex of the gas field. The pressure of the gas on the granite formed billions of years ago, made it extremely hard. Every day they pulled over two miles of pipe out of the hole and installed a new bit. The granite was so hard they were only making 25-feet a day and at tremendous expense.

We were enjoying an after-dinner cognac when a floatplane landed. A man climbed up and handed the engineer a letter. He read it, shook his head, and said, "That's it, we are to shut down immediately and dismantle; funds have run out."

The well was cased in a thick steel pipe to over 6,000 feet and as they attempted to pull the casing out it twisted off. They poured several truckloads of cement in the hole, 'capping it off'. Two tugs came and towed the rig away.

July 27, 1977. Marrie loves chocolate. I once took a photo of her lying on the beach reading a diet book while eating a big chocolate bar. For her birthday present, I wanted to give her something chocolaty.

On the corner of Pacific Coast Highway and State Street in Santa Barbara was a Mercedes dealership. As I drove by with Marya and Miriam we saw dark chocolate, 450SL, convertible, Mercedes sports car in the showroom. It caught my eye and I knew I had found the present. We circled the block, parked, went in, and looked her over.

"Do you girls think Mommy would like it for her birthday present?"

"Oh yeah!" they cried in unison with eyes sparkling and smiles that lit up their little faces.

The price was thirty-two thousand dollars. I paid cash on condition that it was ready by the following afternoon.

The three of us hid in Marya's room and made up a super big pink bow then conspired to send Marrie on a mission while we hurried downtown. I can still feel the excitement as we drove home and parked our present in the detached garage and attached the big pink bow on the dark chocolate lid of the boot. We agreed not to give the secret away in any way and to act normal.

It was getting dark and Marrie was not home. The girls were playing in the den and I was having a glass of wine when she drove up. She got out and I heard the car door shut and then I heard this delightful scream. I looked out the window and saw her standing in front of the garage looking at the chocolate car with the big pink birthday bow. We ran out and joined in her excitement. She was ecstatic!

I asked why she went out to the garage and opened the door since this was completely out of character. She said the light was on and she wanted to switch it off. In our excitement we had forgotten to turn it off, but the gift coming a day early and so unexpected was better than what we planned.

21. RETURN TO WORK

Marrie, Where's My Pot? -- The Ranch and Mr. Carter -- Sonya, the Bitch From Hell -- Paranoia is a Terrible Thing -- The Switch -- Fatal Crash

The Queen Air was packed to the gunnels with bales of good pot as I dive-bombed friends on a deserted strip in southern Baja. Flapping against the fuselage outside the pilot's window was a fabric bag containing five kilos held by a string clamped between my teeth. As I neared the spot I opened my mouth, released the string and smiled as they received their Christmas present.

The border was getting hot with Reagan's new 'war on drugs.' Operation 'star track' had recently netted three pilots and a dozen airplanes. My new route was just north of Isla Guadeloupe, situated two hundred miles out in the Pacific off central Baja. From there I turned north until I was a hundred miles west of San Clemente and the Santa Barbara Islands. At that point I turned right and entered the US by flying just above the waves until I was west behind Santa Rosa Island. I would then pull up near an airstrip on the island, hoping that on radar it looked like a departure. Whatever the reason, it worked for a long time during some of the hottest surveillance in US history.

Wild Bill, Ed's friend, was to meet me with his pickup and camper at Santa Inez Airport at eight p.m. I landed at eight-thirty, the place was deserted. I taxied to the tie-down area and parked. Next to the office was a payphone which required a dime, but all I had was twenty-one, one hundred dollar bills. The village of Solvang was a good five miles away and I marched off at a lively clip, cursing Bill with every step.

In one of the restaurants I obtained a dime and called Marrie. I asked her to come in any kind of truck as fast as she could. I ordered dinner and somehow managed to eat. Marrie walked in looking worried. She sat at the bar while I took the truck to the airport. When I opened the door to the plane it was empty. Oh, shit! Wild Bill must have waited until I left so he could steal the load. Somehow I couldn't believe that. I went back to Solvang, picked up Marrie, and drove through the pass to Santa Barbara and home.

It was two a.m. when the phone rang, "Hey Rog, old buddy, where you been?"

"Where the hell were you?" I almost shouted.

"Well, we waited till about eight-thirty and then went to get something to eat. When we got back we found a Christmas present. Everything's fine old buddy."

"I got there at exactly eight-thirty." I said with as much restraint as I could muster.

"Yeah, I figured that out when we got back. We saw your landing lights on approach but thought it was an airliner landing and decided we couldn't do anything until they left, so we went to McDonald's. See you around noon."

Marrie drove me back early the next morning. I asked her to stand by to see that I got off ok. I took a broom and began sweeping out the plane as there was enough evidence on the floor and in the windows to send me to prison. Behind the cockpit was a coffee-making compartment, the door was wide open. Sitting under the table was a burlap sack stuffed with seventy pounds of good sticky buds.

"Oh shit! What a fucking idiot!"

"Marrie, pull up to the door quick!" I called, as I dragged the sack out.

It wouldn't fit through the truck door.so I had no choice but to lay it in the truck bed where it stuck up above the sides several inches.

"Sweetheart, in the past, I have never allowed you to get near this stuff, but this is an emergency. I have to get the plane out of there quickly. Go and get rid of this as soon as you can."

She said, "I can't lift it Roger."

"You don't have to lift it. Just go into the woods somewhere, open the tailgate, back up and slam on the brakes and it'll slide out. I'll pick it up later."

We both got out of there in a hurry. Twenty minutes later I was at the hangar in Santa Barbara and Marrie arrived shortly thereafter.

"Did you get rid of it all right?" I asked.

She looked a little sheepish and said, "You're not going to like this. I think it got wet."

"Got wet! You must be joking. There's nothing between here and Santa Inez but a mountain of rocks. How did you manage to get it wet in a desert?"

"Well Roger, I did what you told me to do. I found a spot, opened the tailgate, backed up and jammed on the brakes and the marijuana went flying over the cliff and I heard water splash down at the bottom."

"Honey, just how far down did it fall?" I asked as gently and sarcastically as I could manage.

"Maybe three or four hundred feet; it fell for a long time. I heard it crashing through vines and limbs and then I heard a splash."

"OK Sweetheart, let's see which way it went."

She drove me up into the Santa Barbara Mountains, took a side road and stopped on a precipice overlooking the Santa Ynez valley. The sides of the cliff were steep and covered with poison oak and scrub. I needed ropes and some help.

"Damn Marrie, couldn't you have found somewhere a little gentler?" I asked. Really? I found her first and only experience with smuggling quite humorous.

Dennis Boxer had borrowed my one-ton pickup and camper and I needed it for this job. I called Dennis's house, and his sidekick Delbert answered. Dennis was gone for a few days, but the truck was there. I went over to pick it up and asked Delbert to help with the mountain climbing task. He was all for a little adventure, so we headed out. The terrain was as rough as one could imagine. We worked our way down to the bottom and found the sack of marijuana in good condition. It had hit the stream and bounced out. With blood, sweat, and swearing, we wrestled it up the side of the mountain and loaded it in the pick-up.

Delbert begged, "Let me sell it. This is some good shit and I know who will buy it."

I said, "No man, Dennis would be pissed if I crossed the line and do business with his man."

"Oh, come on man, I won't tell Dennis. He'll never know. Plus, he don't pay me shit and I need the bread bad for Christmas. Come on, I've helped you get it up the side the mountain and you're gonna need someone to sell it for you. I know you don't touch the shit."

Dennis was a real jerk. I had tolerated him all the way to Pakistan. He and I had been in several deals and I always got the smutty end of the stick; plus, he was a big bully. He thought of himself as a boxer and walked around bridging. In any dispute he thrust out his chest and got in your face in a threatening manner. No one I knew liked him, but as my friend, Jerry said, "If you don't work with assholes in this business, you're going to be lonely."

"OK Delbert, you can sell it, but just don't tell Dennis." I reluctantly agreed.

It was Christmas Eve. Mother and my baby sister Sharon had flown out from Georgia for the holidays. The stockings were stuffed. Santa had come and gone. The family was sleeping snugly when the phone jarred me awake. I looked at the clock and saw that it was two in the morning.

Wondering who it could be, I picked it up and heard Boxer inebriated voice. "You double-dealing sons- of- a- bitches, I'll teach you to use my help. I'll be at your door in ten minutes and I'm going to beat the hell out of you!"

I got up, dressed, and slipped a long-barreled, .38 Smith & Wesson in my belt. I grabbed my leather jacket and waited for Mr. Tough Guy. He drove up, I opened the door before he got to it and invited him and Delbert in. I said, "Calm down Boxer, let's talk this out reasonably."

"Fuck you and talk! I'm going to kick your ass all over your house!" With that he came for me. I whipped out the .38 and aimed it at his chest. The click was loud and clear as it cocked. I said, "You take one more step and I'm going to jerk this trigger five times and save the last one for your lapdog

The color drained out of his face as if his throat was cut. His shoulders and chest sagged, his hands opened slowly as he held them up and backed off the porch stumbling over flowerpots.

Thankfully that was the last time I ever saw Dennis Boxer. He told Jerry that it was the scariest experience of his life.

With Marrie in Belize, Central America, Exploring. 1970
Copyright Marrie J. Reaves

The strip near Tikal in Guatemala was marginal for an overloaded plane in the heat of the day. To compound the danger the place was surrounded by tall gnarled trees, laden with bromeliads and Spanish moss. The area exuded a strange, prehistoric, haunting spirit that gave me the creeps. I felt death surrounding the area. While flying low overhead, the trees radiated a shimmering disturbing aura. Could it be from the spirits of countless souls sacrificed on the gruesome altars over the millenniums?

I found the perfect spot on a twenty-mile by twenty-mile sand ridge in the center of Belize. A two-rutted trail used occasionally by hunters and plant gatherers traversed the area. The vegetation was sparse, with stunted palms no bigger around than your arm scattered here and there. Rene Martin, his girlfriend Rose, Marrie and I went down with axes, machetes, and shovels and cleared a seven-thousand-foot runway in three days. While working on the runway we stayed at the Paradise hotel on Ambergris Cay. This is the northernmost landmass of the second-longest coral reef in the world. The diving and fishing are superb.

A Texan, flying a Lockheed Lodestar, was staying permanently at the hotel and he was a grass hauler, but a lazy, vulgar one. We had a few drinks and after a couple of days I asked him if he knew of a safe strip where I could refuel. He cursed a mouthful about how easy that problem was to solve and invited me to take a short flight. We flew to a 30,000-acre ranch south of Orange Walk, landed, and walked up to the house. A maid said she expected Mr. Cotter back soon, so we walked around to the front of the house and sat on the steps to wait.

A community of Mennonites living on small farms nearby bought fresh beef from Mr. Cotter. A young man was sitting in a buggy hitched to a cream-colored mare with a young colt romping about. The vulgar man began cussing, complaining that Cotter was not coming. The young man whipped the horse several sharp licks and put both hands over his ears as the rig tore out down the road. A witness in pantomime!

The following day I drove out to the ranch and met Mr. Cotter. He was a fine old Texas rancher, working as a foreman on this big ranch. For ten thousand dollars I could land anytime I wanted and fuel up. It was none of his business to snoop around inside other people's airplanes. This arrangement worked to both our benefit for several years. I would hazard to guess that he made from three to four hundred thousand dollars from the agreement that day.

Sonya de Attila had artificial tits as hard and cold as billiard balls, with a heart to match. I will tell how I came to know this vicious piranha.

Cameron was a distinguished-looking old airplane trader from the era of the barnstormers. Over the years he had sold me several DC-3's and Twin Beeches while working out of Hollywood-Burbank and I knew this old reprobate had his fingers in a bunch of pies. One afternoon he drove up to my door with a tall blond Colombian gentleman and introduced me to Roberto Davila, an attorney from Bogotá. I invited them in and they presented us with a bottle of superb wine.

We went into the den and they laid out their objective. Roberto Davila was related to the famous marijuana Davila's of Santa Marta, Colombia. He had someone with a ship who wanted to bring thirty-five tons of pot to the west coast of the United States and asked if I was interested in unloading and storing it for twenty-five percent. I did some quick figuring. Thirty-five tons was over seventy-five thousand pounds and at three hundred dollars a pound that was over twenty-two million. One-fourth of that would be mine, approximately five and a half million dollars. We quickly got down to particulars.

Davila was brokering the deal and he had to guarantee the shipowner that someone would be there to unload. The shipper required a thirty-five-thousand-dollar deposit to cover his cost of fuel in case the un-loader didn't show. This all sounded rather fishy to me. However, I liked Cameron and Davila was an impressive looking man. The two had the looks and presence of Clark Gable and Robert Redford. How could I miss it? Furthermore, every time I did a deal I was risking considerably more money for a much smaller expected return. Regardless, I accepted the deal, gave them thirty-five thousand dollars in the smallest bills I could find and they left.

Several months passed with one excuse after another, so I flew down to Bogotá and went to the home of Mr. Davila. I was received like an old friend, introduced to his lovely wife who prepared a delicious meal while we drank good wine and listened to his classical record collection. He said he gave the money to the ship captain and couldn't get it back. He mentioned several other problems.

To make up for the loss of the money he promised to hook me up with the very best contacts in Colombia. His cousins in Santa Marta were the biggest marijuana dealers in the world, doing twenty or thirty-ton loads daily. They would load my planes completely on credit and I paid fifty dollars a pound once it sold. However, he had a better deal for me in Medellin. His very own compadre, Fernando Correro, was the number one cocaine trafficker in the world and that was where the real money was.

We flew to Medellin for free on Avianca as Mr. Davila's wife had connections in that department. The jet maneuvered between mountain peaks before lining up on the runway for its final approach. The descent was steep and we came to a stop on what is renowned as the most dangerous airport in the world.

A taxi took us to a tall apartment building overlooking the city and emerald green mountains. The elevator stopped on the top floor and we stepped off into lavish luxury.

Fernando Correro was an ugly man, fat, his skin was pallid, his head was too big for his body, and he was drunk. However he was a likable rascal. After talking with him for some time it was obvious that he was a genius. He reminded me of a Latin Winston Churchill.

Roberto told him I was a pilot who had all kinds of planes and experience smuggling loads into the United States and asked if he might need my expertise anytime in the near future. Fernando assured him there was more than enough to keep me busy. He was looking for transportation and paid five thousand dollars for each kilo delivered to Miami.

While we were talking, in sashayed a woman with high Indian cheekbones. She was dressed in a snow-white ski outfit with matching white calf-length boots trimmed in white rabbit fur and wearing a white beret. She kissed Fernando on his cheeks several times and after their greeting, she was introduced. Her name was Sonia de Attila from Santa Cruz, Bolivia. Following in her wake was Anita Tomaya, a gentle lady from Cartagena, Colombia.

We were sitting around the window on white sofas having a drink looking out on the panoramic view of Medellin. Sonia told Fernando she was on her way to Miami to buy an airplane. Roberto asked what kind she was after, but she had no idea. She wanted one with two motors. Roberto turned to me, winked and said, "Roger you have several planes for sale, don't you?"

"Yes, I have a Queen Air I want to sell."

Sonya finally looked at me and asked, "How many people will it carry."

"It has seats for eight, but it will carry much more than that."

"How far will it fly without stopping for gasoline?"

"Right now I have two large fuel tanks strapped in the interior and it will fly four thousand kilometers without stopping."

"How much do you want for this Queen Air?"

I noticed she had tripped to the name, 'Queen Air.' Roberto turned to me and kept jabbing his thumb up in short little jerks. "It has new motors and is tanked for a very long range and I will take one hundred and fifty thousand dollars for it."

That had been the normal price a year earlier. However, the news about several wings burning off in mid-air and killing all on board had caused the price of these aircraft to plummet. I bought three for sixty-five thousand each and with a minimum of work they were as safe as they ever were.

"When can you have the plane here?"

"Señora, I have no idea whether you will like the plane or not. If you want it brought down I can have it at Panama City International tomorrow. I will require a deposit of five thousand dollars to be applied to the purchase price if you decide to buy."

"Money is not the problem. Miguel, give the man five thousand American dollars." Miguel was one of her two muscled up bodyguards.

I called David Mann and told him I had a big fish on the line and asked him to fly the Queen Air to Panama as soon as possible. He assured me he would be there the next evening.

Sonya, her sister in law, the two bodyguards and I flew to Panama the next day. I followed her around the expensive shops as she bought everything that caught her fancy. She just threw it in a bag and had Miguel pay. When the bag got full, she sent the other slave to the hotel to dump it and return.

David called and left a message with the hotel saying he was leaving Honduras and expected to land in Panama at nine o'clock that evening. We all went to the airport and sat on the veranda, drank cocktails, and waited. I saw the landing lights on approach and knew it was him. The Queen Air looked great as she taxied in.

After David cleared customs we went out, and had a look. The interior with the two big aluminum tanks strapped to either side of the cabin looked bad to me, but Sonya didn't seem to notice as she climbed into the pilot's seat and played captain for a bit. We laughed, not because it was funny, but because it was so childish and she had the purse.

"I want to go to Isla San Jose tomorrow morning. If I like it, I buy it. OK?" This Island off the Pacific coast of Panama was famous because the Shah of Iran had been living there recently as a guest of the CIA. He died most conveniently. For the CIA that is.

Ten o'clock the next morning I went to the airport, filed a flight plan, and prepared for the flight. The tanks were low and I didn't fill them as the strip on the island was short. Sonya showed up with at least fourteen people; many were carrying suitcases. I thought, 'Oh boy, can they all pack in and if they do, can I stop it on that short coral strip. No way can it get off this afternoon in the heat. Perhaps some are staying or they wouldn't have brought their suitcases.'

Sonya jumped in the co-pilot's seat and the others somehow jammed in like sardines. Someone closed the door and we took off. She landed like a dream with plenty of strip to spare. Sonya was beaming with her new toy. We had lunch at the hotel and soon she was ready to return to the action at the casinos of Panama City.

Sonya said, "I like it and I buy it. The money is in Santa Cruz. You fly me there tomorrow and I pay you, OK?"

That night we went to the casino and had dinner. While we were eating Sonya asked, "Do you have other bigger planes?"

"Yes, I do."

"I need a pilot to fly cocaine base from Bolivia to Colombia. I can send a ton or two every week. Are you interested?"

"How much do you pay per kilo for transportation?"

"I pay one hundred dollars for every kilo."

"I will think about it," I said.

This amounted to one or two hundred thousand dollars a week with little or no risk from the authorities which was a big relief. The danger was the thousand miles across the Amazon without navigation aids, fuel in rusty drums, and short muddy strips recently hacked out of the jungle. Also, there was jealousy between these people and whole groups were wiped out regularly.

The following day we left early and flew directly to Santa Cruz, Bolivia. Customs and immigration bowed to her as she strutted through. Two limos were waiting. The chauffeur drove us to the outskirts of town to a monstrous square white house situated below a water tower with Santa Cruz written across it. An armed guard opened the gate and we drove in. Sonya invited me into a marble-floored mausoleum. Everyone was silent, red-eyed, and crying.

Sonya yelled, "What is wrong with you idiots!"

Everyone was afraid and cowed away. Finally, it came out that the lion had eaten the maid's baby that morning.

"You stupid fools, why did you leave the baby on the floor in front of a lion? It is not the lion's fault. You are all stupid and I want everyone gone in ten minutes and I never want to see one of your stupid faces again!"

The servants disappeared, Sonya walked over to the male mountain lion, cuddled and kissed him on his mouth. That was too much for me. I collected my money and left as quickly as I could.

Sonia had many people murdered over the next five years. She was arrested in the United States by the DEA and became a star witness against many of her former employees. For her assistance the DEA gave her a new American passport and placed her in a witness protection program.

Some of her stories, along with photographs and a paragraph or two about me can be found in the book, "The Big White Lie - The CIA and The Cocaine Epidemic". It says the DEA told her I was on their ten most wanted list and I had flown for almost every cartel in South America and they would give her anything if she could lead them to me.

Anita Tomaya, the nice woman I met with Sonya, lived in Cartagena, Colombia where I visited her. She lived in a big house on Sixth Avenue and Sixth Street in the old prestigious Boca Grande section. I was graciously welcomed and she insisted I check out of my hotel immediately and stay in her home. The household was a hive of activity with five daughters, all with boyfriends and a husband with as many girlfriends. Anita was a good person, born and raised in Cartagena, and knew everyone. Twice weekly, the socialite ladies gathered at her house to play cards and gossip. Her nights were passed in the casinos gambling; Anita knew what was what in the area.

Anita kept introducing me to big marijuana dealers hoping I got loaded and she received her cut. She introduced me to two Cuban brothers, Rene and Raul Benitez, two of the funniest men I have ever met. I flew to Cali and stayed a week with Rene at his house. Things were going along just fine until they took two American DEA Agents out to a garbage dump, shot them in the ass, and let them go. The Americans made a big deal in the press about how they had escaped an assassination attempt. That was not the case at all. If the Benitez brothers had wanted them dead, they would have been very dead indeed.

Anita found another group and we reached an agreement where we went halves on each load. I would fly it to the states and give Anita and her partners their half and I would sell my half. This was price gouging on a grand scale, but it was the best I could arrange at the time.

David arrived a few minutes before dark on a strip on the Magdalena River near El Banco. We passed a pleasant evening by a campfire and the next morning he said he wanted to ride back with me. By noon we were unloading on the sand ridge in Belize. David flew to Belize City for fuel while I stayed with the load. A fire had recently swept across the area burning the grass and everything else in its path. The ground was an inch deep in powdered ash and with every step a puff of smut flew from under my feet. Soon I was covered in black soot.

A couple of hours passed, and I began to worry. Then I heard the airplane and could see David flying low, searching for me on a ridge some miles to the north. He was lost and kept getting farther and farther away. I ran all over, picking up partially burned limbs, and kicking splinters off stumps until I had enough fuel to get a fire going. It burned hot and smokeless until I smothered it with green brush and leaves. David saw the signal and came directly to me. While loading he also got covered in smut. We climbed into the cockpit looking like two grinning chimney sweeps.

At midnight we landed at Saint Tamothy Parrish Airport and taxied off the end of the runway and down the overrun area that was covered in young pine trees about three feet tall. We threw the pot in the trees, taxied back to the apron, and parked in a vacant space. We walked over to a faucet at the corner of the hangar and washed our face and hands, pulled off our shoes, and began washing our feet.

Screech, screech, screech came the alarming sound of someone burning rubber. I panicked and ran into the canal climbing the farther bank before looking back. I could see men walking around the plane shining a flashlight all over it.

Oh, shit! My greatest fear was before my eyes. The Feds had followed us in. I took off running with David close on my heels. We ran through a sagging barbed wire fence getting scratched and cut as we cartwheeled through the pines. We scrambled up and ran through a couple more ditches filled waist-deep with cum-covered water before we came to a blacktop highway with a white line down the center. We took off running down this road and soon my bare feet were bleeding. I decided to run on the white painted line which was smooth and easier on my feet. We slowed down somewhat, then I heard the bloodhounds barking. We sped up.

After a while David called out for me to hold up because he had a nosebleed. My chest was on fire and about to burst from running so fast for so far. As I was standing there bent over with my hands on my knees, I saw a police car driving slowly down the highway. We ran into the canal and squatted in the slime-coated water until only our heads were showing. The car was a 1950 Ford with a red bubble on top. The sheriff was driving with the window down and his arm resting in the window. He was wearing a stiff brimmed hat and looking straight ahead. It was about midnight and pitch dark; however, he was lit up in an eerie grey glow. For some reason, David couldn't see him and never did see him, but he was there.

It's strange what fear and exhaustion can do to one's mind. As far as I know it is the only time I ever hallucinated, and I did, big time. Or was I seeing back in time?

Ten miles farther on, we came to a house with a pack of barking dogs. I yelled until the people woke up. I told them we had bogged down back in the swamp and needed a ride to town and offered to pay a handsome price for a ride. The man obliged and took us to Picayune, Mississippi where we rented a room, fell on the beds, and slept soundly until noon.

From downtown New Orleans, I called Saint Tamothy Aviation and Hal's wife Pat answered. I asked about Hal, thinking he might be in jail, she laughed and asked, "Where did you run off to?"

Not daring to commit myself I asked, "Where's Hal?"

"He's sitting right here eating dinner. Do you want to talk to him?"

"Yeah, put him on." I just knew it was a trick and the DEA was standing there listening and trying to trap me.

"Hey there old buddy, where'd you run off to so fast last night? I took care of everything after everyone cleared out."

"What are you talking about Hal?"

"Last night after you landed Doctor LaSalle and his wife flew in from Biloxi and you were parked in their space."

"Who was shining the flashlight?"

"That was Doctor LaSalle."

"OK Hal, I'll be there in an hour."

I left David at New Orleans International so he could catch a commercial flight to California as there was no need for both of us to go to prison if Hal was lying. My courage was barely up to the task as I drove across Lake Pontchartrain, the longest causeway in the United States. Fortunately all was well. Hal had stored the pot, that is, except for a couple hundred pounds he took for himself. I didn't mention it.

September 1981, I remember the date because I left my plane on the tarmac at Belize International and flew commercially to Colombia. While I was gone, Belize celebrated her independence from Great Britain. Dignitaries flew in and they needed the tie-down space. My plane was dragged to the woods and they declared me persona non-gratia.

Roberto Davila met me at the airport in Medellin and we went directly to Fernando's apartment. He was still drunk, but we went directly in and had a drink, hoping to get some sense out of him. However, this was impossible, he could drink a fifth of scotch as I drank a glass of water. Several toadies were there to supply his every need. He called in a boy and girl about fifteen years old and asked if we wanted either. He said they came every evening after school to listen to records and take care of any desires his guests might have. A bowl of cocaine on the coffee table seemed as normal as peanuts on mine.

Roberto asked him when he expected to have work and he slurred that there was plenty of work and for us and to go see Marta his wife.

We arrived at a nice house where I met Marta. She said Fernando would sober up one day and there was a lot of work for pilots who would risk running the US border. She said they paid five thousand dollars per kilo for delivery to Miami. As we were about to leave she seriously invited us to Fernando's birthday party in a couple of weeks. They were planning a big festival on their Pacific property with Avianca Air Line shuttling guests from Medellin to the coast.

We gave up on Fernando for the moment and headed for Santa Marta. On the flight over Roberto told me that Fernando owned sixteen miles of oceanfront property on the Pacific and from this property ships and planes were loaded.

Jacob Davila, one of Roberto's poorer cousins, met us at the airport. He was not the Davila who shipped the big loads, but he assured us he could find me a ton of choice 'Santa Marta Gold.' Early the next morning we loaded our gear in a truck and headed into the mountains of La Guajira, zigzagging our way up the narrow road toward the towering snow-covered peak of Cristobal Colon. Six thousand feet above Santa Marta we stopped for breakfast in the little town of Minka. The view was breathtaking as we looked down on coffee farms nearby and beyond them the red-tiled roofs of Santa Marta and the dazzling white beaches and fishing boats on the Caribbean.

At the end of the road was a big corral with at least a hundred mules. Hundreds of bridles and saddles hung in what must have been the biggest tack room in the world. These people were in business. A 'muleteer' lassoed and saddled two mules and we set forth up the trail climbing steadily toward the snow. Occasionally we met a string of twenty or thirty mules laden with a big bale of marijuana strapped on each side. A man rode in front of the caravan while a boy trotted along behind with a switch in his hand bringing up the rear.

We stopped at several houses and looked at tons of marijuana, but it was all the regular run of the mill commercial grade loaded daily on shrimp boats and ships in lots of up to a hundred tons. Since I could only carry one ton, I wanted a better grade. We followed a stream up the side of a mountain and came to a small farm in a deep narrow canyon. The slim young farmer opened the door to his shed and there it was, the elusive 'Santa Marta Gold'. Bales upon bales and all packed with gleaming yellow buds the buyers would fight over in California. We need to search no further. I gave the farmer a deposit on a thousand kilos, marked the bales, and said I would return soon.

We set off down the mountain to have a look at a nearby 'landing strip.' It was on the crest of a ridge on a steep grade. At one end was a house and shed with ample aviation fuel. These people were set up for business.

Back at the hotel I made a deal with Roberto and Jacob to pay them twenty percent of whatever the load brought, minus the thirty-five thousand Roberto owed me.

I called David Mann and asked him to bring the plane; a Beechcraft H18, one of the last models made. David was an excellent mechanic and kept the planes in perfect running order. He had just finished installing an oak floor and he was proud of, it and it did look good.

The next day the marijuana was brought down to the strip and I waited until dark, but he didn't show. This was most unusual for David and I began to worry. The next day I waited all day and that night I went to town and called. David answered the phone and I asked what happened. He said the Feds were following him and he abandoned the plane.

"You abandoned the plane? Where?"

"In Fort Stockton, Texas; they were all over me, following with three planes."

"Well if that ain't a hell of a how-do- you -do! They follow me all the time. If you're empty, there ain't shit they can do. Are you going to bring it or not?"

"No, I'm not going near it. The key is in the rear wheel well boot, pinned to the canvas with a safety pin."

"If you are scared to bring me an empty plane I suggest you find work elsewhere."

"That's fine with me, adios," thus ending several years of teamwork.

The fixed-base operator in Fort Stockton told me the Feds' had climbed all over the plane and photographed her from one end to the other. I searched for bugs but found none. It took some feeling around up in the canvas-lined wheel well before I located the key and departed for Colombia.

The first stop was San Pedro Sula, Honduras. I cleared in and filed a flight plan to Roatan Island, forty miles off the coast. Instead of going to Roatan, I went on to Puerto Lempara where I was to look up a woman named Elizabeth Eden. I remember because I thought the name was so beautiful.

A devastating hurricane had all but destroyed the Mosquito Coast, and I had to walk a series of planks above the water to reach her house. She was seventy years old, black, and the matriarch of that part of the world. I introduced myself and told her who sent me. She received me graciously and we had supper by lamplight in her house. I told her I was looking for a refueling site nearer to Colombia so I could load deeper into the interior. There was a long clay airport a few miles away and also a sizable army outpost as it was on the border with Nicaragua. Her response to the idea was not very promising.

At midnight I left Mrs. Eden's house and walked through the rain to the runway. It was pitch black and there were no airport lights. I walked to the far end of the strip, switched on my flashlight, and left it lying in the middle of the strip.

With mud weighing me down every step, I plodded back to the plane and fired her up. While I was waiting for the engines to warm up I saw the lights from what must have been army jeeps bouncing fast in my direction. I took off and disappeared into rain and clouds.

North of San Andres Island I noticed the right engine started running rough and backfiring something awful. It would completely quit for a second or two and then start up with a bang that jarred the whole aircraft. I had to shut it down and turn back. Turn back to where? North for the time being. Flying in the soup over water at night on one motor is not something I relish.

The clouds were broken as I passed over Roatan Island and I could see the outline of the coral strip. I decided it would be very difficult getting a mechanic and parts out there, so I continued on. The concrete runway at San Pedro Sula was shining white against the dark jungle background. There were no lights anywhere near the airport and there was no answer to my radio calls. I turned on my landing lights and made a half dozen low passes trying to get someone's attention. I thought it most unusual that no one responded, but nevertheless I landed and taxied to the apron. As I was shutting down and preparing to get out of the seat two army trucks came racing up and screeched to a halt. Twenty soldiers jumped out and surrounded the plane with rifles at the ready. I opened the airstair door and slowly stepped out with my hands raised. A lieutenant walked up with a pistol held in both hands. The soldiers were in a perfect circle with twenty rifles pointed at me. I thought it humorous in a cartoon way. If I had jumped, all twenty would have fired, killing everyone.

Off I went in handcuffs to the army barracks where they kept me under heavy guard for the remainder of the night and the following day. After dark, they transported me to a prison with an open courtyard and a few trees. Surrounding the small yard were a half-dozen cages with thick iron bars. The jailer stopped in front of the first, which was packed with brown naked humanity. He acted as though he was going to open the door and throw me in, then shook his head in the negative and we walked on to the next cage. This one was more interesting as they were all women. It was sultry hot and not many clothes were visible. The jailer stopped, scratched his head while looking me over and again shook his head in the negative fashion, and walked on.

The enclosure had two trees. Tethered to one was a spotted goat, to the other a very fat bulldog. The jailer looked me over and tried to figure out where he should chain me and decided on the bulldog. He fastened a chain around my ankle, locked it, and did the same to the tree with the other end, leaving me about ten feet of slack. The dog was young and frisky and tried to lick me to death while drooling slobber.

The jailer brought me a blanket and left me chained under the stars. The days were very hot, long and boring. The only entertainment was the women teasing me from their cell. Some of them were completely naked and quite brazen.

The authorities were softening me up for 'the bite' and I knew it. I had done nothing wrong. I had cleared out of San Pedro Sula in the afternoon with all the papers in order and returned the same night after the airport had closed. Their complaint was that during the day the airport was civilian and at night it converted to military. Therefore I had landed on a military airfield without permission; never mind the emergency.

No one would take the bribe even though I asked several times to settle the matter locally; this was too big a deal for the lower echelon. After three days, thinking they had softened me enough to pay, they released me and told me to go to the transportation minister in Tegucigalpa, the capital of Honduras. I caught a bus that wound and climbed through scenic mountains for a half-day before reaching its destination. I checked into a hotel and went to the transportation ministers' office. Naturally, he was not in and it was Friday. There was absolutely no way General Castro could be disturbed on his days off.

Teguc, as the locals call it, is a city of over a million inhabitants. However, ninety-five percent are poor, leaving only five percent of the population living in areas of affluence. Finding the residence of General Castro was as easy as asking the taxi driver to take me there.

A maid came to the front gate and I asked to see the General. She went away and in a few minutes a man of about forty-five years of age came to the gate wearing a singlet and looking as though I might have disturbed his morning coffee. Of course he knew who I was and with very little foreplay I came directly to the point. "How many American dollars will it take to get you to release my airplane?"

He looked me over, looked at his slippers while trying to divine just how much I would pay. After a bit he said, "Twelve thousand dollars."

"The plane is hardly worth that much and it is low on fuel. I will pay you twelve thousand dollars if you will throw in 400 gallons of aviation fuel."

He agreed. I gave him the money and he guaranteed the plane would be released that day and 400 gallons of aviation gasoline delivered the following morning. Seeing as the plane was worth sixty thousand and aviation fuel was almost impossible to find, I didn't come out so bad.

Back in San Pedro Sula I taxied over to Bill Karl's fixed base operation and had his mechanic install a new magneto. She ran as smooth as cream and I was ready to go. The gas truck came and the lineman instructed him to pump it into the underground tank. I explained that the fuel was for me and should be pumped directly into the plane. After the truck left the lineman refused to pump the fuel.

I had been chained for three days and nights with a goat and a bulldog, paid twelve thousand dollars for a landing fee and a tank of fuel. I was ready to go. A million-dollar load was waiting and this jerk wouldn't let me have my fuel. I went to the mechanic who held his hands out open and said, "'There is nothing I can do."

Well there was something I could do and I had been itching to do it for some time. I commenced to punch him. When he couldn't get up I picked up a wrench and walked toward the mechanic who all of a sudden got religion. He was only too happy to pump the gasoline and apologized profusely for my troubles with the stupid lineman.

I arrived at dusk and Jacob was waiting on the strip. I noticed two gateposts as big around as a man's waist at the far end and asked Jacob to have them removed before morning. With a ton of pot and a ton-and-a-half of gasoline she was far over gross and I was going to need all the room I could get for take-off. An Indian woman prepared a meal, while Jacob and I sat around a fire on the hearth and talked. When it was time for bed Jacob left and said the plane would be loaded before daybreak.

It was still dark when the woman served me a cup of coffee, tortillas, and eggs. After breakfast I walked out to the plane and gave it a thorough pre-flight examination. I opened the door and found the cabin filled with dry, black, marijuana. It was old stuff from the previous year, packaged in paper bags, many already coming apart and this black crap was everywhere. Oh, the sorry, low-life, scum-sucking, thieving, sons of bitches!

My first impulse was to throw it all out and sweep the plane clean. However, after I cooled down and giving it some thought I decided it was better to take a chance of making 'something' than to return empty. What a difference between the merchandise I bought and what I received!

Over the 'shit' and into the cockpit I crawled, busting bags as I went. I fired up the engines and while waiting for the motors to warm up I looked down the strip and saw the two posts on the far end still standing. I considered shutting off, walking down, and removing them. This would take an hour if I could find tools. In that time, military jets could very well find me on the clandestine strip and all would be lost. Being that the strip was on a steep downhill grade I figured I could get over them. I pushed the throttles to the firewall. A hundred yards before the post I pulled her off hard and hauled back on the yoke, but with the load she just couldn't climb fast enough. Somehow the post went through the gap in the propeller without touching, but the right tire caught it dead on. I felt a horrendous jar as the tire slammed into the post and I thought the gear was knocked off and perhaps hanging in pieces underneath. The mountain dropped away sharply, and soon I was at a thousand feet. I reached for the gear lever and pulled it into the retracted position, half expecting all hell to break loose. I could feel the tires coming up and the doors closing and then three little green lights popped on in the panel and I marveled at the toughness of the Beech 18.

As I flew north the engines began to run slower and slower. Quarter throttle, half throttle or full throttle was all the same. By the time I arrived at the refueling strip in Belize she was barely staying airborne. When I landed she went bump, bump, bump, down the runway. The tire was still pumped up, but the aluminum rim was flat for twelve inches on one side. I took the cowlings off and found the fuel strainers packed with crud. I cleaned them out and she ran fine. The insides of the fuel bladders were old and somewhat brittle and from the hard jolt the old hard dry rubber came loose and stopped up the strainers.

Over the Gulf of Mexico she began shutting down again. By the time I arrived at my landing site on a dusters strip in a sugar cane field she was struggling to stay airborne. I landed almost silently as she was barely running. As I came to a stop the plane was covered in a mist of oil. I opened the door. Spray filled the air. A loud hissing noise filled my head. I looked around, saw the oil derrick, and knew what happened. The farmer had struck black gold and was probably out celebrating.

Nearby were several trucks and many men. One spark and there would be a lot of work for Red Adair and his fighters. I had to get out of there quick.

The truck backed up to the door and within ten minutes she was unloaded. I fired her up and 'mushed' down the strip. Being light on fuel she came up just enough to clear the new cane and flew reasonably well on over to Saint Tamothy's Aviation where I put her to bed.

The black trashy junk smoked very well indeed. Within three days it had all sold for three hundred dollars a pound fetching a whopping six hundred and sixty thousand dollars. Jacob was ashamed to show up and sent an emissary. We met in a hotel in Atlanta and I explained that I had been cheated. I had paid for the 'Gold' and received the 'Trash.' There was no argument from his side, just a song and dance about how they had been cheated by the farmer. I said I would have a hard time selling it and offered to give him their twenty percent. Of course he didn't want it. I offered him ten thousand dollars and wiped out Roberto's debt. He gladly accepted the money and ran.

After we fell out, David Mann went to work for Jerry Wills. On his first trip they loaded a ton of sinsemilla in a Twin Beech and he headed north following my old trail over the Pacific and coming in behind the Channel Islands. On this first trip David didn't show up. Jerry sent planes to look for him. They didn't find a trace. It was too vast an area to search as he could have gone down anywhere in over a thousand miles of ocean.

David and I were partners in a *Bellanca Scout* which we rented to the operator of Santa Ynez Airport. This woman said that David called her several times from Argentina and asked her to tell me that he was fine. This just didn't fit. The load was worth over two million dollars, and David Mann was not a thief.

Seven months later a Mexican shepherd working on San Clemente Island was selling premium pot in San Diego for thirty dollars a pound. He told his girlfriend he was getting it out of a crashed airplane and that there was a skeleton sitting inside the cockpit. The girlfriend called the navy and they found David's body. The bones were clean and white, his blond hair had continued to grow.

Friends become dearer as tombstones thicken.

22. BIRTH OF THE MEDELLIN CARTEL

D.E.A Mid-Air Stalkers -- Handshakes and Hand Guns

Jorge Ochoa and Pablo Escobar, founders of the Medelin Cartel. I knew them both and considered Jorge my friend, until my 3.5 million dollars went AWOL. Jorge and myself are left.
Image courtesy Drug Enforcement Agency

Fernando's birthday party was coming up, and Marta said he was still drunk, but the party was going ahead as planned. Little did I know that I was about to take part in a little bit of 20th-century history by attending a gathering in the middle of the Colombian jungle.

I decided to fly to Panama and leave the plane there. Before heading south I found a pressure-operated transponder in the tail cone of the Twin Beech. I carefully removed the deluxe model and added it to my collection. The Feds wanted me bad.

I stopped overnight in Louisiana. Early the next morning there was a lot of activity in the small airport. A man was reading a newspaper in his car while parked backward to the norm. Others were looking over a plane in the hangar with too much attention. Upon taking off the tower vectored me first to the right and then to the left. It was obvious they were setting me up for an intercept. A hundred miles out over the Gulf of Mexico and beyond the oil wells I flew by black clouds. As I passed them I hung a left and then did a tight 180. There they were, sitting right in front of me in an old sub chaser.

The pilot pushed the nose over and dove for the deck with engines wide open. I smiled and wondered if they thought I was armed with missiles.

I flew on to Belize, landed on the ranch, and had lunch with Mr. Cotter. All was well. He had installed an underground fuel tank and told me the Mexicans were fording the river regularly with loads of gasoline. This made me wonder just how many other pilots were using what I thought was 'my' refueling site.

Upon takeoff I felt a slight vibration coming through the bottom of my shoes. I quickly scanned the instrument panel and saw the oil temperature gauge for the right engine climbing into the red. I had just taken on four hundred gallons of fuel at the ranch, so she was heavy, plus the weather was hot and humid, giving less lift. I had to shut down that engine and feather the prop. On the one engine she was able to maintain altitude but could not climb.

That motor was finished. The only feasible thing to do was to go to Belize City and land. I was unable to raise anyone on the radio because the tower and approach frequencies had been changed. I did a flyover at ninety degrees to the runway, rocked the wings, and expected a green light from the tower, but one was not forthcoming. On final approach I shut down the good engine and feathered the prop so both sides were equal. By landing hot there was enough momentum to coast to the apron. I pulled in and pivoted around between two other planes and stopped perfectly in the tie-down space.

The cavalry arrived in a jeep with guns drawn. British troops were behind sandbags looking down machine gun barrels. Harrier jets were on the apron nearby and these fellows in camouflage fatigues looked menacing. I explained that I had landed in an emergency and was unable to raise anyone on the radio. They did not believe an engine was out because I had taxied and parked normally. Something that could not be accomplished on one engine.

They called a mechanic to check out my claim. A British soldier-mechanic came out, took off the oil strainer, and found it full of shredded metal; metal never before found in an engine. They were shavings from some unknown metal shop. The engine had been sabotaged, and I knew exactly who the culprit was. Some over-zealous American DEA agent who thought, 'If I can't catch him, I'll kill him.'

Whose was the greater crime? His for attempted murder or mine for hauling pot?

I spent the day arranging and for a new engine to be flown down from Miami and a mechanic to install it while I was gone. That evening I caught a commercial flight to Panama and the next day boarded a flight to Medellin.

I arrived just in time. Avianca Air Lines was shuttling guests from the Medellin airport to the Pacific coast in several twin-engine aircraft. The flight was over verdant, jagged mountains that dropped away sharply on the Pacific side. There was not a road within a hundred miles. The plane approached the sea and landed on a mile-long clay runway at a place in the jungle called Curiche, halfway between Panama and Buenaventura. It was as though we had landed on a remote island.

As we rolled to a stop I saw a fortune in abandoned machinery littering the shoulder of the runway. Two new D8 Caterpillars were rusting in the rain without even a can over the exhaust pipes. One was missing a track and apparently left where it broke. A pristine Cessna 180 on floats was tilted over on its side, a large wasp's nest under the wing, abandoned so a new one could use the papers, avoiding the high tariffs.

As we deplaned, handsome young black men carried the luggage to brightly colored cottages built on high stilts along the beach. However, I didn't rate a cottage, they gave me a room in a large bunkhouse.

A muddy red river coming out of the mountains flowed swiftly into the ocean. The silt turned the sea red and washed onto the beaches coloring them red as well. The weather was hot and muggy. Fifty or more sleek private airplanes and a few helicopters were parked haphazardly. Two or three hundred people were already there and the party was well on its way. People were strolling about with clear plastic bags of cocaine offering samples.

By the bank of the river and facing the ocean was an old log house which was the centerpiece of the place. Cooks were roasting steers, hogs, and goats over an open pit. A long slim pole stuck through an open window. Swinging from the small end inside the house was a baby lying in a basket. His mother was cooking on a wood stove. Whenever the baby made a noise she gave the pole a tug and the baby had quite the ride for several minutes. Sometimes his little sister came up and talked to him, took his scrotum in her fingers, and gave it a good shake and the baby would smile. I was surprised at what was normal in that world.

On the flight over I met Marcus and Esmeralda Cervantes, a handsome young couple from Medellin. Esmeralda was exceptionally beautiful and radiated an aura of light in that crowd, though I'm sure she would have done so in any crowd. Marcus was a tall, blond, blue-eyed Don from old Spanish blood who was quite serious and very aware of what was going on. Esmeralda spoke both English and French fluently and I gravitated towards them.

Late in the afternoon I pulled my shoes off, rolled up my britches legs, and took a walk in the surf. An attractive barefoot young woman wearing an old-fashioned dress joined me. We walked along in the shallow water as sandpipers darted in and out in front of us. She spoke in a sweet soft voice and I realized she did not belong in this crowd. She said she had flown for the first time that day and she was afraid. She came with a man named Pablo Escobar and his friends. I wondered what her relationship was with this man and I asked. She said she hardly knew him and did not really know why he invited her. She followed me wherever I went and I was concerned. Whoever Pablo was, he did not bring this woman to the beach to spend the day with me.

Marcus and Esmeralda were also taking a walk on the red sand. When they came to us Esmeralda said in a very sweet voice, "Roger, do you know that you are walking with the girlfriend of the most vicious killer in Colombia? Marcus suggests you get away from her as quickly as possible." I smiled, thanked her, and walked the young lady back to the crowd and excused myself.

The gala consisted of a motley crew with people from all walks of life. Three bands took turns playing all afternoon and late into the night. Colombia's most celebrated stand-up comedian performed and famous actors and actresses performed skits. Governors and police chiefs of major cities made short speeches. A female Supreme Court judge befriended me and danced the evening away. One never knows when one may need friends in high places.

That night I was standing in the door to my room smiling and talking with people, when a man shoved the girl from the beach roughly into the room and said something angrily. I thought, 'Oh shit, here I go again with a real killer this time.' She started crying and several of his friends gathered close around him, patting him on the back saying, "Calma te senor, calma te senor and the situation was defused. Later I heard she refused to go to his room, so he shoved her in mine. That was the first time I met Pablo Escobar.

That weekend was the birth of the Medellin Cartel. Cocaine producers from all over Colombia got together and made agreements to co-operate and work together. Some were growers, some manufacturers, while others had diverse chemicals. I was the only one there interested in transportation.

Friday night, all day Saturday and on into the wee hours of the morning the party raged. Sunday morning found everyone worn out and quiet. Planes began to depart. By noon they were all gone. Avianca flew in three planes and took out the 'VIPs,' leaving the common clay for the following day.

The barbecued goat was scrumptious. I made up a heaping plate, went behind the house, sat in a hammock, and ate in peace. After I finished eating I lay back in the hammock, picked up M.M. Kay's, "The Far Pavilions" and started reading. I was somewhere between reading and dozing off when, BLAM!!! BLAM!!! I was almost deafened from the report of a big pistol much too close. Blood splattered across the pages. I rolled out of the hammock and kept rolling across the dirt. When I raised my head I saw a white dog with a black ring around his eye flopping around on the ground slinging blood out of the hole between his eyes. A young black man grabbed the pistol out of a middle-aged white Colombian's hand, pointed it at his head, and pulled the trigger. I flinched and closed my eyes every time it went click, click, click. The pistol was obviously out of cartridges.

I saw blood gushing out of the femoral artery of the black man's leg and I knew that in a very short time he would be dead if the bleeding was not stopped.

"I am a doctor. Let me stop the bleeding or you will die." I said in Spanish as I walked towards him. I could see he was going into shock, the color of his skin was turning death grey.

He whirled around, stuck the pistol in my face, and hobbled backward. I wanted to save his life but I did not want that pistol to go click, click, click, in my face. He hobbled on toward their village which was at the far end of the runway. I kept following and calling to him. Marcus came up beside me and tried to talk some sense into him, but he just kept limping on. As we approached the village, which was hidden under trees, an old crone came out and told us to go away if we knew what was good for us. She said her people were angry with these new white people and there was going to be plenty of bloodshed before daylight.

After a bit we heard screams and undulating cries coming from the village, and we knew the young man had died.

Fifty or so women were left: actresses and musicians mostly, and only four men: the shooter, a tall Avianca pilot, Marcus, and myself. As the light faded we all very solemnly gathered around the old log house and stayed near one another for comfort. Suddenly we were plunged into pitch darkness as the generator shut down. Someone fetched a flashlight to check on it. The cap was off and the tank was filled with sand and water.

The screams and shrieks coming from the village sent cold shivers up my spine. This carried on well into the night. The tall Avianca Pilot started crying shamelessly and I was disgusted at his cowardice.

We gathered all the cans we could find and partially filled them with gasoline and oil, twisted a piece of cloth for a makeshift wick and lit pitiful little smoky lights. The insects came out in force. We all drew together in front of the old log house within the circle of little lamps. I found that Esmeralda had a snub-nosed .38 in her purse and I stayed close. We passed a slow, smoky, buggy, miserable night.

Daylight came and we saw that the runway was covered with trees, oil drums, and all manner of debris. About nine o'clock three serious soldiers arrived in a canoe with a big motor and arrested the killer. He asked to have a shower and change clothes before he went with them and the sergeant agreed. While he was taking a shower he escaped out the back by prying two boards loose. The soldiers were irate over losing him and treated us rudely.

Later, Avianca planes arrived and began circling overhead. We were warned not to move the obstacles because the locals had rifles and were good shots. I went down the red sand beach and stomped out a big SOS.

We spent that day and the next night under house arrest. The soldiers had lost face and they were not going to let us go until we produced their man.

Someone in Medellin sorted out the problem. The soldiers cleared the strip and the planes landed.

Marcus and Esmeralda invited me to visit them in their home where I met their two lovely children. Nicholas was nine years old and entertained me by feeding the fish in the aquarium and telling me about them while Esmeralda cooked supper. Amelia was a shy little girl of five.

Supper was delicious! Esmeralda boiled fatback and then fried it, something I'd never had before. She served red beans that melted in my mouth and would have made a fine meal all by themselves. Thick tortillas cooked over an open fire added the finishing touches. She served strange native fruits for desert and afterward coffee and pastries.

Marcus smoked his cigar while I sampled his wine. We talked late into the night with Esmeralda interpreting whatever we could not convey with our limited vocabulary and sign language. A bond was formed that has withstood the trials of the years.

23. MY NAME IS BARRY SEAL

Cocaine Smuggler -- Jorge Ochoa and Pablo Escobar -- Fogged in, Pucker Factor High -- Barry and the Boys -- Roger the Banker -- Gentleman Cuban Smuggler

An hour climbing drive from the east coast of Honduras, nestled amongst mountains hanging with tropical vegetation, lies a lake with some of the biggest Large Mouth Bass in the world. The lake was discovered after a particularly strong earthquake struck, leaving twenty-pound fish floating by the shore. The shock only killed the larger ones. On the shore of this hidden lake was a well-guarded greenhouse containing ferns with mold on the spores that were thought to cure cancer and tumors. A German pharmaceutical firm set up a laboratory and was doing research. A mile on down the road was a 1000-acre farm on the river that fed the lake. The farm was for sale and this is what brought my family and I to this tropical paradise.

The soil was rich volcanic ash, hundreds of feet deep. A seed dropped was all that was needed to grow. Papaya stalks twelve feet tall were loaded with fruit as big as watermelons. Giant mango trees with fruit bending the branches shaded the house. A narrow, fast running river cut through the property with sleek cattle grazing in lush pastures on both sides. I have never seen a more ideal spot to spend one's life.

Unfortunately we couldn't work out a deal and we sadly returned to San Pedro Sula - a city that was to become in later years the murder capital of the world.

Our suitcases were full of dirty clothes. We took the clothes to the laundry and asked the proprietor if they could be ready Tuesday evening because we had to catch the flight to New Orleans Wednesday morning. He assured us they would be ready. Late Tuesday afternoon I went to get the clothes, they were wet and I was told to return at eight o'clock the following morning. This was cutting it too close for comfort, but I had no choice. The next morning I sent Marrie and the children to the airport with instructions for them to go on without me if I didn't make it, as it was easier for one to catch a later flight than five.

I had a taxi waiting at the curb while I paced around the laundry as the clothes were collected. On the way to the airport the taxi driver was puttering along with the flow so I offered him a hundred dollars to make a dash for the airport. He began blowing his horn, but the speed remained about the same. When I got to the gate the 727 was taxiing out. I ran on through the gate and out onto the apron with a big pile of clothes in plastic, draped over my shoulder. I waved to the pilot. He waved back. He had no intention of stopping, and then I saw Marrie's face appear in the cockpit and the plane's nose dipped as he put on the brakes. The ladder was partially extended and then retracted. I saw the pilot smiling as he let the ladder down and the door opened. I ran up the ladder, and received a round of applause from all the passengers.

My seat was by the aisle with Miriam in the middle seat. Sitting by the window was a handsome man that I thought had to be CIA and was most likely working with the Contra's fighting the Communist Sandinistas in the area.

We took off. The wheels retracted with a thud. Shortly thereafter there was another smaller jerk. Miriam asked, "What was that Dad?"

I said, "The pilot just engaged his autopilot and the plane's altitude was different from when he turned it off."

The CIA man leaned over and said, "So you also fly these?"

"Yeah, I've logged a few hours."

"My name is Barry Seal." He reached across Miriam and we shook hands.

On the two-hour trip to New Orleans I learned he had been released from prison that morning, having spent over a year in prison for landing with a hundred kilos of cocaine in his plane. He was now on his way home. He said he was once a Captain for TWA Airlines - the youngest ever. His career was blossoming at the time and he very quickly moved up to instructing other pilots on the Boeing 747. He lost that job after being indicted for flying a DC6 load of arms to anti-Castro forces in Cuba. I thought, 'If this guy is for real, then I have found my man.' We exchanged addresses and phone numbers and I watched a jubilant family meet him as he walked through customs. He introduced us to his wife Debbie, three little children that were hanging all over him, and to an older son. My lingering suspicions about him soon withered as it became obvious he was telling the truth about being released from prison that morning. You couldn't fake the tears, smiles, and hugs.

He checked out to be all he claimed and a lot more. In a few weeks I called and invited him to Santa Barbara. I told him I was a smuggler and needed some help from time to time. We met for a coffee and then headed over to my hanger for a chat and a walk around. We went for a flight in my Aero Commander, with Barry in the left seat. He handled the plane like he had been flying it for years and I saw right off that he was a pro. When we got to 5,000ft he leveled off and said, "Let's check this sweetheart out. Mind if I do a few maneuvers?"

Well, that was a pretty big plane to be doing aerobatics in, but of course I had to say, "Show me what you got."

I immediately began to ever so slightly regret having given the green light for Barry to stress my airframe! He rolled it onto her side and did two 360's and it looked like the altimeter was welded in place. Then he pushed the nose down, picked up airspeed, and performed a smooth loop and a half. At the top of the second he rolled it upright and then pulled it up into a tight spin. At about two thousand feet he stalled it and did what aerobatic pilots call a 'falling leaf' and we stalled from side to side until he was almost on the runway. Within seconds the gear was down and we landed like a feather hits the pavement with the barest 'jolt' as the undercarriage touched the tarmac. We stopped within a few feet. The only other person that I had ever seen do this was Bob Hoover, the aerobatic champion of the world. I wondered, 'who is this guy? He must have been a member of the Blue Angels when he was in the air force?' I had no further doubts about his flying ability. Barry had been flying since he was 16 years old and took to it like a duck to water. Only much later did I find out that Barry had served with Special Forces in Vietnam; and had a thousand parachute jumps under his belt (starting at age 16 in Air force Cadets) including combat jumps; served with Army Intelligence and was a member of the CIA.

Aero Commander 690B. I had just taken Barry up for a test flight where he has shown me his first class piloting skills.
Copyright Marrie J. Reaves

The plane needed modifications to the fuel tanks and Barry said he knew a mechanic in Mena, Arkansas. I gave him ten thousand dollars and off he went with the plane. Some days later I flew to Baton Rouge, went to Barry's house, and spent time with him, his wife Debbie, and his three children where I had a most enjoyable time. In a short time of getting to know Barry, I was pleasantly surprised to discover that he didn't drink, smoke, or swear and his children were polite and well behaved.

We went to the hanger and inspected the new fuel tanks recently installed in the Aero Commander. There were four of them in the fuselage and three in the baggage compartment; all professionally hooked up to transfer pumps. That was enough fuel to fly from Colombia to Canada with plenty to spare. I flew to Montego Bay, Jamaica, where I hid her in a hanger until needed.

The Reaves family rented a suite at the Las Velas Hotel on the water in Cartagena, Colombia. The view was breathtaking and the disco one floor above was nerve-shattering. Miriam befriended 'Wild Bill', a beech combing tramp and his broken jawed old dog. Marya made friends with Anita's five daughters and Marrie took Spanish lessons from the maid. Rhett was breaking out from the Colombian diapers and Marrie insisted we import pampers.

Marcus and Esmeralda came down and stayed a week and I returned to Medellin with them. Marcus drove me to the home of Jaime Cardona, the killer I met on the beach at Fernando's party. After a short introduction we got in his new Seneca and flew to his ranch where I herded cattle on horseback with a machine gun slung over my shoulder. Jaime had been caught with one ton of cocaine, the biggest bust in history at that time. Sixteen judges and prosecutors were murdered before the trial was over. Jaime was nervous and jumpy. To be honest, so was I. We reached a deal whereby I would fly 300 kilos of cocaine to the United States and deliver it to Miami and he would pay me five-thousand dollars a kilo. For insurance he wanted my family to stay in Cartagena with Marcus and Esmeralda and he would put someone in the plane to take care of the product. This didn't bother me as I was going to do the right thing by him and therefore have no problems; I thought.

The strip at El Banco was covered in water and the plane slipped and slid around like it was on ice skates with the wheels up to the hubs in gummy red clay. Men standing on a farm wagon pulled by a tractor rapidly cranked a hand pump filling the tanks with jet fuel. Others came out of a banana field on a horse and wagon piled high with bales of cocaine. This was quickly loaded into the plane along with Reynaldo, a bad-looking fellow holding a Mac 10 machine-gun. He climbed in back, sat on the bales, and didn't speak.

I took off, and so much mud stuck in the wheel wells that the gear wouldn't retract. No matter how much fuel I had it wasn't going to make it two thousand miles with the gear hanging down. There was nothing to do but land on the ranch in Belize and clean the wheel wells out.

Ugly said we were not supposed to land before we reached the United States. I explained that we were going to land one way or the other and it would be better to do so on dry land where we were welcome. Reluctantly he agreed. I landed at the Carver Ranch and fortunately Mr. Cotter was home. He had the plane washed while we joined him for lunch.

We landed in Louisiana after dark. It was then that I learned there were not 300 kilos but 165. My pay went from an expected one and a half million dollars down to eight hundred and twenty-five thousand. Was I ever pissed!

The driver drove to Miami non-stop and I flew down with Ugly and met Bill Barber, the man who was going to sell the cocaine. I liked Bill. We had a bite to eat and he and Ugly left with the cocaine.

Two weeks passed, then three and no word. I heard Bill had been shot several times in the stomach, was in the hospital and not expected to live. A month later Bill was released. I went to see a much slimmer Bill who gave me part of the money. It took another month to collect it all and by then I knew I would never work with those people again.

Back in Cartagena, Marcus told me he had some very nice people to work with and wanted me to go to Medellin and meet them. We drove up a narrow winding mountain road through lush vegetation and turned off at a barricaded drive. Marcus chatted with the armed guards who raised the barricade and we drove through. A half-mile further we came to a lovely old hacienda shaded by giant trees filled with orchids. Men were standing around, obviously waiting for an audience with El Jefe. We were escorted in and a beautiful woman offered us a coffee. In a few minutes we went into another room and met Jorge Ochoa, a soft-spoken, gentle young man of perhaps thirty-five years. On his desk were ten or twelve telephones of different colors. He explained that each one was for a different city in the United States.

After some small talk we got down to business. He said I could fly 300 kilos every day of the week if I wanted to; that he would pay five thousand dollars per kilo, but not until the merchandise sold, which took an average of three weeks. I told him my wife and children were waiting in Cartagena and if I was going to work for him I would appreciate help to find a house for my family near Medellin. He called the pretty secretary in and related my request and said he would have a house within a couple of weeks and invited us to his ranch for the weekend.

A nice-looking young man walked in unannounced and Jorge introduced as Pablo Escobar, his partner. I recognized him, but he did not remember me. We shook hands, he asked a few questions about my skills as a pilot, planes I owned and experience crossing the U.S. border. He seemed pleased with my response and reiterated that they had as much work as I wanted.

Marcus and I returned to Cartagena and took our families to the Ochoa ranch for the weekend. It was wonderful. Jorge's Mother, Father, eight or ten sisters and two brothers were present. Bathing suits, clothes, shoes, sports gear, cosmetics whatever you needed and didn't bring was available. Two motorboats pulled skiers all afternoon on a large lake while an ultralight on floats gave anyone a ride that wanted to go up. We strolled through a giant aviary filled with exotic birds. Elephants, zebras, and giraffes wandered freely around the property. A herd of capybara frolicked in the lake beside a flock of pink flamingos.

In the late evening we went into a playroom where I rode an artificial bull. No alcohol or drugs were present. They didn't even smoke. The next day we witnessed a bullfight with Favio, the younger brother, as the matador.

The three brothers and I sat down and discussed business. I said I would like to work more than once a month and asked what would happen if they owed me for several loads and I was arrested? Juan David, the elder brother, spoke very gently and said they were all honorable men and no matter where I was they would make sure I was paid. Those false words still ring in my memory.

We enjoyed a wonderful weekend and Sunday night three new Toyota Land Cruisers drove our exhausted crew back to the hotel in Cartagena.

Marcus had learned a lot over the weekend. He said the Ochoa brothers and Pablo Escobar had formed a cartel with other cocaine producers. They were providing transportation for ten thousand dollars per kilo and if it was lost they replaced it in Colombia. Up until that time transportation had been a problem for small producers. They would give the product to someone to deliver, but if there was a bust anywhere in the United States that slightly resembled the load, they claimed the cocaine was busted. Thousands of people were killed each year because of such rip-offs. This insurance policy ended all that and made the insurers very rich.

I kept the Aero Commander in Montego Bay, Jamaica. From there it was only a two-hour flight to the coast of South America where I descended over the San Blas Islands, a string of exquisite emerald green islands set in crystal waters. They are famous for the 'hammock' and the colorful intricate designs in their weavings. I made a quick flyover of the strip on the Colombian border that was situated in the center of the village and army base of 'Acande'. As soon as I landed and came to a stop, soldiers loaded 300 kilos in the back of the plane. I took off without shutting down the right engine or taking on any fuel. My stay on the ground was less than five minutes.

My un-loader met me and made three trips to Miami with the cocaine in the trunk of a car. A man in Tampa, Florida purchased three Marques Mercury's and Ford LTD's every week, paying four-thousand dollars for a good used one. Another thousand was spent on new tires, fan belts, water hoses and load leveling air shocks. I flew to Miami and met the driver who pointed to the car in a hotel parking lot and turned over the keys. Lito was waiting nearby and as we drove by, I pointed to the car without speaking and handed him the keys. I had explained beforehand that the title was on a clip over the sun visor and the price was five thousand dollars. For a while they balked at the cost, but then they came to realize the value of not using the same car twice.

Two weeks later I did a repeat. Lito and his helper Ache brought me three boxes of money, each containing five hundred thousand dollars. Collecting money became my main job. I would park at a restaurant and go in and have a drink. They would drive up and park next to me. When I finished my drink we would walk to the parking lot, transfer the boxes from the trunk of their car into mine and in less than a minute and a half the job was done.

Marrie and the children were flying up from Colombia to Miami and for some reason we had not arranged where we were to meet. I flew down from Louisiana and during the flight I asked a stewardess if she could recommend a good hotel on the beach that my wife and children would enjoy. Without hesitating she said, "Try the Royal Sonesta on Key Biscayne." I rented a two-bedroom suite and ordered flowers. A half-hour had passed when there was a gentle knock at the door. I opened it and there stood Marrie holding Rhett in her arms and Marya and Miriam by her side. I was shocked and asked, "How on earth did you find me in this city of over a million people and nobody knew where I was?"

"It was no problem at all sweetheart, I can find you anywhere and you had better remember that!"

"Come on, really, how did you find me?"

After a bit more teasing she fessed up and said, "On the flight up, I asked a stewardess to recommend a hotel, she suggested this place. When I went to register, the clerk said I was already registered."

Of all the hotels in the Miami area what were the chances we chose the same one?

We rented a charming house on Cape Florida Drive in Key Biscayne across the causeway from downtown Miami. There was a deep-water canal behind the house with a 100-foot dock where Steve and Connie tied the Jolly Swagman when they sailed up from Martinique. I bought a 25-foot Magnum Marine runabout, hung it from the electric davits and winched it out of the water after water skiing and fishing. We bought four bicycles with a baby carriage on the back of mine and rode through the level streets and bicycle paths of Key Biscayne stopping for lunch at an Italian pizza parlor or 'Ye Old English Pub'. When the shrimp were running we anchored in the stream, hung bright lights off the sides and scooped up shrimp in dip nets. Life was wonderful.

In a few weeks I collected three million dollars, stacked it in front of a wall mirror and took a photo. I began making a trip each week and money was flowing in. Once a week, Marta Ochoa dressed in a nurse's uniform met me in a restaurant to go over the accounts. One time I forgot that Lito had given me a half-million dollars.

On a trip north the temperature and dew point came together and the world fogged in. As I was coming across the Gulf of Mexico I kept receiving radio broadcasts telling of airports closed from Dallas, Texas to Tampa, Florida, with zero, zero visibility. The Southern States were fogged in and all airports were closed. If there had been a parachute on board I would have bailed out and let the plane go to sea and crash, however, I didn't have one, I had to land.

Louis Armstrong International in New Orleans is two miles long with a glide slope. At eleven at night I intercepted the glideslope five miles out and wondered if they were watching the screen since the airport was closed. I was sick with dread as I flew blind toward the concrete runway at a hundred knots. A heading error of a couple of degrees would put me in the lake or into the airport buildings. I set the radar altimeter for an alarm at 50 feet and continued down the glideslope. All was well at the outer marker. I was sweating profusely at the middle marker and puckered right up at the inner marker. The decision height light and buzzer came on. I flared and held it and held it and held it ---touchdown---bounce ---- another touchdown, this time she stayed down. Runway light went under the left wing and I stopped in gravel on the verge of the runway and shut down. As soon as my knees stopped shaking I walked to the end of the runway which was over a mile. I had plenty of room to take off.

I was in a dilemma, I couldn't obtain a car and drive it out on the international runway at midnight. Nor could I move the cocaine by hand, and I didn't have anywhere to put it if I could move it.. There was nothing to do but wait it out and see what happened. Every hour I turned the radio on to check the weather which remained unchanged all night. It was cold. I walked around the plane worried that a security guard might possibly drive down the runway.

It was a long, cold and anxious night. When daylight finally came the fog enfolded the world like a grey blanket. I had three hours of fuel remaining and couldn't bear to sit there another minute. I started her up, lined up on the centerline and took off. At five hundred feet I broke out into bright sunshine and looked down on a world of white fog. After an hour I began seeing patches of earth and at two hours the fog was breaking up. I headed for Hal's, raised him on the radio and told him I was low on fuel and needed to land. From directly overhead the airport was visible. I knew that as soon as I got in the fog I would be blind. I set up a steep approach with full flaps and no power and dove in. When I glimpsed the runway I pulled back hard and landed short. I taxied to a hangar, got out and walked into the lounge, poured myself a cup of coffee and didn't care if I ever saw another airplane again.

The offloader hauled the cocaine away and I decided that had been my last load. I was fortunate to be alive. I had made over seven million dollars[1] in a very short time and that should be enough to last for as long as I lived. I was hanging up my guns. Or so I thought.

Lito and Ache were devastated when I told them I was quitting and asked if I knew of anyone who would fly? They had all been exceptionally nice to me and it was only fair I should help them. I called Barry and he flew down to Miami and we met in the Omni Hotel. I offered to buy the planes and pay him two-thousand dollars per kilo to fly for me.

Barry agreed to the deal but didn't want to fly without a copilot. I argued that he could load another 100 kilos without a copilot. However, he insisted. He had a friend named Emil Camp who was in prison in Honduras and for $20,000 he could have him released in a couple of days. He also wanted a *Panther* to fly the loads. These were Piper Navajos, converted from the firewall forward with new 450 horsepower motors and four-blade props with Q-tip ends to cut down on noise. One equipped with radar, storm scope and a new gyro navigation system cost between $350,000 and $400,000. I ended up buying seven of these haulers for both Barry and Jerry who also flew for me on the same deal.

Barry flew to Honduras and returned a few days later with Emil, who wasn't

---

near the pilot Barry was. I suspect they had become good friends while in prison and Barry wanted to help him. Most men prefer to have a partner or co-pilot, I don't. Whenever he becomes scared his fear radiates and contaminates me.

My favorite landing strip was a small airport way out in the pines of Southern Louisiana where I paid the owner ten thousand dollars per landing. My other choice was on interstate 10 anywhere in Louisiana or Texas where it was closed for construction. Barry didn't even want to hear of my places. He would only land at Mena, Arkansas where Governor William Jefferson Clinton ruled with wife Hillary. Barry said he was covered one hundred percent, right to the very top; that is was impossible for him to be arrested. I balked at his bravado and wondered how you could guarantee one hundred percent? Even with bribes, which were the norm at this level of operation, you could never guarantee one hundred percent. I was soon to learn that when Barry said he was having, "lunch with *the Gov*," he wasn't joking.

The landing fee there was $50,000. I can guess it was spread around through the Sherriff, on up the chain. I never bothered asking, I knew how things worked. It was no secret Bill and Hillary Clinton were up to their necks in mischief in the state of Arkansas. In any case, I had to cough up the money every time Barry landed at Mena and he must have done that at least thirty times on my watch. I found out much later he was doing far more than that. While I languished in prison, Barry kept flying and began operations in a much larger aircraft that was registered to the DEA and CIA. At times he was carrying over one and a half tons of cocaine in a single trip on a C-126 military transport aircraft dubbed, 'The Fat Lady'. Barry was right in the center of one of the greatest political scandals of the last century - *Iran/Contra*. Illegal arms shipments flew out of Mena, Arkansas and landed in Honduras where the arms were then transported to anti-Communist forces in Nicaragua. Then, the same plane landed in Nicaragua at a military airbase, loaded cocaine, then flew right back into Mena, Arkansas. Tons and tons of cocaine and money. No one said, "Just say no." No one in the White House anyway. Nor Mena, Arkansas. Never in my wildest dreams did I imagine that the name 'Barry Seal' and 'Mena' would soar to such notoriety in the years to come.

But for now, early in his career with the Medellin Cartel, Barry went to work for me and flew just as fast as I paid him. This doubled my risk as I was paying out cash for the cartel before I was paid. Nevertheless, I had to pay him before he would fly. Barry bitched and moaned about this and that. In one box containing a million dollars I placed a package of Stay Free Mini-Pads with a big pink bow. He thought it was so funny that he made a place on his mantelpiece for it.

Barry was a likable fellow. We met one night at the Omni Hotel. Marrie, Miriam and baby Rhett were there and we all went to dinner at the Festival Restaurant in Coral Gables. When we returned all the rooms were sold out, so Barry spent the night with us. There were two double beds in the room and Barry stripped down to his striped shorts and T-shirt and made himself at home. During the night Rhett wanted a bottle. Barry laid him on his big belly and gave him the bottle, smacking and carrying on saying, "It's sooo good, ain't it Rhett?"

Before Barry was fully up and running and I was fully retired, I would have to work with him for a while, flying the southern Colombian end while Barry flew the northern end of operations into Mena. I'd arranged to meet 'halfway' at the Carver ranch in Belize and transfer the quarter-ton of coke on the clay airstrip.

This weekly trip began with me flying my Aero Commander turboprop out of Montego Bay, Jamaica, and meeting a Cessna 180 over the Colombian jungle, just above the El Banco radio tower. I would descend from 30,000ft and slow down to 150mph at treetop level and follow the little 180 right into the jungle airstrip.

Quickly loaded, I would have my windshield wiped, a coffee, then be right out of there.

At a climb rate of 5,000 ft. per minute I was soon up at 30,000 ft. and able to reach Barry via radio, 2,000 miles away, 12,000 ft. over Louisiana. Barry flew in his favorite 'Panther' converted Piper Navajo and we would speak in code to time our arrival at the Carver ranch. "One hundred out," would crackle sharply over the radio. "Seventy-five out, descending," I'd reply. We'd land within minutes of each other and pull up outside the home of Mr. Cotter. We'd greet each other and I'd help refuel and transport the load into Barry's Panther.

At times when I landed the clay strip was wet and not being used to prop pitch and the idiosyncrasies of the Aero Commander, I'd end up sideways down the runway with Barry laughing at me sloshing this way and that in the mud.

With the load transferred, I would fly back to Montego Bay then on to Miami, while Barry would fly to Mena, Arkansas, and on into infamy.

I had made some complaints to Pablo about the jungle airstrips and the dangers for my engines as they were sensitive turboprops - essentially a jet engine driving a propeller. Typical of the Medellin Cartel, no expense was spared and a thousand feet of runway was added and smoothed to perfection with hard clay.

Later I heard that particular place was as busy as JFK airport with some large aircraft landing. Glad I could help the cause. I hope Oliver North was happy.

At times, Pablo himself would fly in on his Jet Ranger helicopter and talk with me about procedures and plans. On one particular trip he landed with his entourage and three hundred kilos of produce looking very happy with himself. Both he and Jorge Ochoa had organized with the Sandinista Communist government of Nicaragua for me to land at a military airbase with a large concrete runway and modern facilities. I was extremely happy with this as both Barry and I were growing increasingly nervous about landing at the Carver ranch in Belize with fifteen million dollars' worth of cocaine every week. It was only a matter of time before local bandits twigged as to what was happening and ambushed us, making us instant dead men. Barry had become so concerned he had taken to buzzing low over the jungle around the ranch landing site looking for suspicious activity. As he was empty at that time, carrying no produce until the exchange took place, he had started landing first and scouting the area out on foot. His Special Forces training, and time in Vietnam came in very useful and with both of us getting increasingly nervous about the transfer, Barry was over the moon when I told him about the new arrangement. "No shit!" he said, beaming. He was impressed and made good use of the arrangement well on into the future.

Pablo arranged for me to meet Ben, an American helicopter pilot by trade, he flew right seat with me and directed me to the large military airfield in the east of Nicaragua. On landing, we were taken to see the Commandante in the officer's mess and served a delicious meal of steak with an egg on top as well as beans and rice. It sounds simple but it was delicious.

The commander was a very dignified and gracious man and assured us we were welcome at any time. His only instruction was that we maintain radio silence on approach to the base. Ben and I exited the officer's mess well pleased with the new arrangement and I noted my Aero-Commander was sparkling, washed, refueled and ready to go. I cannot express how relieved I was with this new landing and transfer deal. I was protected one hundred percent in Colombia and Barry was protected one hundred percent in Mena, Arkansas. It was too good to be true.

Ronald Reagan was to make much of the expose of the Sandinistas Government officials with photographs of Barry unloading in Nicaragua. Commentators claimed that it was a "set up" and the Iran/Contra affair was an almost purely Bush Sr., Oliver North/Contra operation, run by a virtual private intelligence group from within the CIA and State department. Not so, the Sandinistas were playing their own part in the cocaine trade. Who wasn't? The Bush and Clinton clan included.

Sadly, I learned Ben was killed in the Andes a week later after meeting him. It was in bad weather. I was quite disappointed as he was a professional and decent young man. As time goes on, the tombstones thicken.

I called my old friend Jerry Wills and invited him to Miami. He arrived with his wife and stayed at the Key Biscayne Hotel which was near the house. We had dinner every night and I told him of the deal I had with the Colombians and invited him to fly if he wanted to. Jerry asked how much I was getting and I was truthful and told him five-thousand dollars per kilo. I offered to buy the planes and give him half in advance to deliver the cocaine to California. A week or two later I had two airlines flying. In the end Jerry would fly more loads than Barry for me. While Barry had the east coast route covered through Mena, Jerry would land in Louisiana on one of my strips and then the coke would be transferred via truck to the west coast.

Jerry hired my old enemy, Terry Thornton to fly with him. He said Terry didn't know north from south about navigation, but that he was a good pilot in clear weather. On their second trip an engine failed on take-off, causing them to almost roll upside down. They got it level before it crashed and scattered 300 kilos of cocaine over a half-mile. Luckily, the 600-gallon interior bladder tank didn't rupture and they walked away from the crash. I bought another plane and they continued working.

No telephone calls were allowed. Every day at noon I passed by a busy Cuban sandwich shop and looked to see if Lito or Ache were there. I parked a ways off and walked up and stood in line with them. We would chat for only a minute or two and then meet that night at an agreed spot. Most weeks they received six cars with a hundred kilos in each and I collected three million dollars. We met fairly regularly.

Believe it or not money became a real problem. I didn't have time to count it and finally accepted Lito's count which had proved to be close to correct. I buried two million under the palm tree in the vacant lot next door. Marrie and Mother helped dig a trench under an oak tree at the Old Place where we buried three million dollars in hundred dollar bills in sealed five-gallon paint cans after removing the metal bail so they couldn't be discovered with a metal detector. I bought four million dollars of gold Krugerrands, six farms, rare and expensive gold coins, silver coins by the hundredweights, and buried them in four-inch PVC pipes. I wonder how many I lost since I couldn't write down the locations.

I chartered a Lear Jet out of San Antonio, Texas to haul money to Grand Cayman Island. The money took up three times more space than the cocaine. Each U.S. bill weighs exactly one gram, so it's easy to weigh the money and get a good count. A million dollars in one-dollar bills weighs a ton or 2,200 pounds and if it is in hundreds, it weighs ten kilos or 22 pounds. The bulk of the money I hauled was in twenties as the Colombians kept the hundreds and I paid Barry and Jerry in hundreds and fifties. I flew down to the Cayman Islands with each load. Sometimes the plane was so full I had to lie on the money with my back against the ceiling. Steven DeFief met the plane on the apron in his white Cadillac and a van. We unloaded the money into the van and followed in the Cadillac without an immigration and customs check.

From the airport we went directly to one of the larger banks of the eighty that lined the main boulevard and unloaded. Ten or twelve young men and women dressed in stiff white shirts and black ties sat behind a long counter and began counting. If I was to blink twelve bills hit the floor on the other side of the table. They managed to steal an average of twenty thousand on each load.

I would always chuckle on the return trip. All the effort placed into 'drug interdiction' while banks are blatantly set up to launder ill-gotten gains and operate with impunity. Wall Street is the biggest beneficiary. The suits in Washington never wanted this goose to stop laying 'liquid cash' golden eggs. They just throw a few of us into the clink now and then as a ritual sacrifice to keep the public happy and their 'Key Performance Indicator' monthly reports up to date. Everyone is in on it - except the public. When one of us went down, there were always fifty hands raised to replace us.

To limit our exposure the pilot would file a flight plan from the air and on the return trip he would file from Grand Cayman to New Orleans listing only the pilot and co-pilot as the sole occupants. They would land after dark. When the plane turned off the runway onto the taxiway I would get out, make my way across the boundary fence, walk to the parking lot, and retrieve my car or catch a flight to Miami.

Rare gold coins were a favorite and I bought several in the 35,000 dollar range along with a box of old Spanish pieces of eight. Of particular interest was a Brasher Doubloon which happened to be the most expensive coin ever sold at that time. The 'Numismatic' journals had a field day with articles such as '*MYSTERY BUYER BUYS MOST EXPENSIVE COIN IN THE WORLD*' and other such headlines. The Bank of Miami asked Sam, the coin dealer if they could display the coin in their bank. I agreed and they gave me an insurance policy for one million dollars and built a pedestal in the foyer to display it.

Marrie and I shopped at the expensive stores along the Miracle Mile in Coral Gables. We bought one-carat flawless diamond earrings and a matching necklace. We took my Mother shopping and bought her a diamond ring and an aquamarine. My five sisters and brother received a thousand dollars a month as a gift. Marijo went to India and worked as a missionary. Kay took to the road and was gone for a few years on the hippie trail to India, Nepal, Thailand, and beyond. Some went to college and got degrees. Charlotte wanted a lump sum so I gave her $50,000 and said I would do better when the others were caught up.

Back at work, Lito was behind to the tune of six million dollars so I told Jerry and Barry to wait until I had collected before going again. Everyone was ready for a little relaxation; we shut down for two weeks.

Marya finished tenth grade and wanted to go to boarding school in Massachusetts. The whole family flew to New York and stayed at the Plaza Hotel on Central Park. We visited the art galleries and museums by day and had front row seats in the theater at night. We dined in famous restaurants and shopped in designer boutiques.

Schools were full for the following year so I offered to pay for an extra teacher. However, that didn't work out. After searching all over New England, we found a spot at Concord Academy in Concord, Massachusetts. It was July third; we drove to Boston for a few days and stayed on the top floor of the new Meridian Hotel overlooking Boston Harbor.

The night of the Fourth, fireworks started up and continued for an hour or more. I had never seen or heard such an extravagant display, bursts of every color in the rainbow and patterns. The five of us stood on the balcony gazing into the sky with awe. I held Rhett in my arms and he kept reaching for the starbursts with his little hands. Unbeknownst to us, we were standing above the exact location where the Boston Tea Party began, which went on to spark the American Revolution. Thousands of people had come from distant places to witness this sight. We were there by chance.

With hardly enough time to count the millions coming in, it defies reason to think that I would go to Jamaica to sell an airplane, I did, sell a Turbo Prop Aero Commander, November, one-three-tango-victor, which looks better as 13TV, was sitting at Toucan Airfield near Kingston. The entire interior was stored in the fixed base operator's attic. She was tanked from stem to stern with fuel tanks. Somehow, I ran across an aircraft broker from San Antonio who was keen to buy. Around this time my baby sister Sharon called and warned me of a vision she had of me crashing into shallow emerald-green water. She has the gift and I paid attention.

This dapper young broker flew down and we both inspected her. The tires were slack from sitting for months. I had the tanks removed and the plush interior replaced while several men washed her. When they rolled her out on the apron she was an orange and white beauty.

We gave her a good walk around inspection, climbed in and took off. I was flying in the co-pilot's seat, everything seemed sweet until we got off the ground and when she turned a sharp left. The pilot yelled, "What the hell! Help me on the right rudder, the right rudder!" The altimeter needle was whirling as she gained altitude in an uncontrollable circle.

The radio tower on a hill above Kingston was directly in our arc. I yelled for him to let me have it. I rolled her ninety degrees onto her side and pulled back with all my might. The tower with guy wires stretching out for a half-mile went by on my right in a blur. I rolled the wings level, thought a moment, and decided a truck or something must have bent the airframe. I feathered the right engine to compensate for the yaw. This hardly made a difference. With the big stable rudders these planes will take off on one engine. The broker was frantically winding the rudder trim and gradually she straightened out. We were over three thousand feet, and my knees were knocking. The whole episode probably didn't take over a minute, but it will remain imprinted on my mind forever.

As we approached Kingston International I noticed how shallow and emerald-green the water was. We landed and taxied to the apron without further incident. Some idle boy had sat in the pilots' seat and wound the rudder trim tab all the way to the left. We had both missed this usually benign item on the checklist.

We went back to the Pegasus, an old hotel built during British Colonial times with a sprawling balcony overlooking Kingston, the harbor and the sea beyond. We ordered gin and tonics and celebrating victory over our brush with death. People at a nearby table were having difficulty ordering as they spoke only Spanish. I listened for a bit and walked over and offered my assistance. They were visibly relieved as they had despaired of ever having the kind black waiter understand them. I interpreted their order and they invited my associate and I to join them.

On our new table was a stout elderly grandma, a slim father, an attractive mother, both about thirty-five years old and two pretty twin daughters in evening wear. I asked what brought them to Kingston and they were happy to relate the story.

The previous year President Jimmy Carter offered to accept all Cuban refugees. Castro said everybody that wanted to go, could go. A flotilla of small boats left Cuba daily. Their Grandma, brothers, sisters, and even the dog departed for Florida. The father was a professor and for some reason he hesitated and lost out.

Castro did a dirty on the US from which it will never recover. He emptied his prisons and asylums of the insane, criminally insane, murderers, rapists, and thieves. This scourge hit the beaches of Florida, killing, raping, and robbing before they got to the high watermark. President Carter saw the terrible mistake and ordered the flood stopped.

This remnant of the family missed the boat and made it to Jamaica, hoping it was easier to get to the US from there. They had been there six months with the father working as an automobile mechanic earning fifty dollars a month with no hope of ever finding a way to the US. This was the twin's nineteenth birthday and grandma had flown down from Miami with presents.

After a while of translating to the broker their story, I asked him, "Are you ready for a little adventure?"

After seeing the fuel tanks in the plane he had no trouble divining what I had in mind. He smiled and said, "Yeah, I wouldn't mind."

I turned to the family and said, "We will take you to The United States tomorrow."

"You can't mean it. How is it possible?"

"I don't want to tell you now, but believe me, I can get you there!"

"Do you really mean it? Where are you staying?"

"I am staying right upstairs. Meet us in the Air Jamaica hangar, come tomorrow morning at eight o'clock sharp. Do not bring much luggage. You can ship your things with your grandmother, bring one small suitcase each."

They couldn't keep it quiet. The grandma called several times and then around midnight the owner of the mechanic shop called with many questions. I was vague.

The next morning we were at the airport at eight o'clock and filed a flight plan to Merida, Mexico. I radioed for permission to taxi. It was granted. I stopped on the apron and informed the tower that I needed to taxi to Air Jamaica for hydraulic fluid. Permission was granted and I taxied right into the hangar. The family scurried in with only one little suitcase for all four. They had misunderstood me. I reversed the props and backed out.

The taxiway was two miles long and parallel to the runway. As we were taxiing the tower called, "November One Three Tango Victor, hold your position."

Oh, Shit! I applied full power and took off down the taxiway. As we climbed out I picked up the radio and said, "Kingston tower, your transmission is broken and unreadable good day."

The co-pilot said, "Seems our adventure is off to a grand start."

At twenty-seven thousand feet the gear and flaps came down. A hydraulic line had come loose and the plane automatically went into landing configuration. Airspeed dropped to half. There was no way we could reach Mexico. Grand Cayman Island was dead ahead and I radioed for permission to land. This was granted and we landed and taxied up to the ramp.

"Get out quick and go around back to the patio of the restaurant and order food," I said.

They scrambled out and had just gone around the corner when a blue van drove up. Three men jumped out. One was holding a pistol, something out of the ordinary for an English protectorate. They searched the plane while my contraband sat at a table drinking coffee.

Once they tired of searching and left, I hired a mechanic who tightened a fitting, filled the reservoir with hydraulic oil, and we were on our way. Not knowing how Cuban passports would go over in Mexico I chose not to find out. We landed on the strip at Chichen Itza, the Mayan pyramid on the Yucatan Peninsula. Halfway down the runway we ran into a wall of rain. I got out with my charges and the co-pilot flew on to Merida.

Immediately we were soaked through and it was cold that afternoon in the tropics. We walked to the highway and waited, and waited. Few vehicles passed and those that did swerved to the far side of the road because we looked like what we were, wet refugees. I took out a hundred-dollar bill and waved it at cars. They waved back. After several hours an old school bus, built in Fort Valley Georgia stopped and we climbed aboard. One of the twins sat beside me and she was nervous with my proximity. It was a long slow ride on to Merida. We arrived around midnight and found the pilot waiting for us in the lobby. The restaurant was closed. Night clothes were acquired and all our wet clothes were handed to the clerk for washing. The next morning we found them washed, ironed and folded.

The next part of my people smuggling operation was tricky. The pilot had to file a flight plan for one person; otherwise he would be in trouble when he reached New Orleans. I found the fuel truck driver and had him park his tractor-trailer between the plane and the flight planning office. While the pilot was filling out the flight plan and the plane was being fueled, we slipped aboard, drew the curtains and hid. Not soon enough for any of us, we were once again in the air and on our way.

Big fluffy white clouds drifted by as we crossed the Gulf of Mexico. Two hundred miles from the coast I put her on the deck and slowed down, weaving my way through the numerous oil well platforms just like I did on smuggling runs. Not very far inland I landed on a crop duster's strip, deplaned with my charge and the pilot took off. Directly across the canal was a junkyard and it looked like a mile or more walk to get around. I suggested we wade the ditch which happened to be much deeper than expected. We were wet once again.

We dripped up to the junkyard and I offered a man a hundred dollars to take us to Bourbon Street in the French Quarter. He hopped at the offer and within two minutes we were doing eighty miles an hour through the cane fields of South Louisiana in a car half sprayed with red undercoat and missing a fender.

We booked in at the Queen Ann Hotel, a lovely little place off Royal Street, and then we went shopping. I gave each family member money as I didn't want to interfere with their choices. However, they constantly kept asking if I liked something or not.

They were frugal and bought only the basics even though I encouraged them to buy more. When they were finished, the father returned the money that was leftover.

That evening we dined in one of New Orleans' finest restaurants and afterward did the town. I can only wonder what they thought America was going to be like after their first evening in the French Quarter with a millionaire guide.

I think they must have stayed up half the night calling friends and family. We boarded a flight to Miami. Upon arrival, there must have been two hundred people at the gate to meet us. Flowers soon covered the girls and many bottles of Chivas Regal were presented to me.

A street in 'Opa Laka' was roped off and musicians were playing loud Cuban Music while pigs and goats roasted over hot coals. Drinks flowed like water. People were hugging, dancing, and crying. I was a hero. I believe they would have paraded me around on their shoulders had I let them.

Before I left I took the mother and father into a front room alone and gave them some money with which to start their new lives. They just stood there and cried, and with tears in their eyes, we said our goodbyes.

24. ALL GOOD THINGS MUST COME TO AN END

Cash to the Ceiling -- Red Light -- No Bail for Me -- Friends who Write Letters

Jerry had three million waiting for me in California. I flew out on a commercial flight and changed planes in New Orleans. When I boarded the new flight a drunk stood up and yelled, "Well, I'll be damned if it ain't Jerry Lee Lewis!" He came up, shook my hand and hugged my neck. Several other passengers also stood up, shook my hand, and before the plane got to L.A. I had signed a dozen autographs, and the drunk was crying and begging me to come and sing at his mother's funeral.

The money was a mess of small bills with about half in Canadian currency. I called the charter outfit who flew out in a jet and picked me up with a load of money. When we arrived in San Antonio where we spent the night, the pilot tried hard to have me leave the money in the locked plane, in his locked hangar, but I wouldn't agree. He hired a van and we hauled it all to his house and put it in a spare bedroom where I slept with it. I could read his mind. It would definitely have been gone the next morning and who could I call?

Early the next morning his wife prepared breakfast and he asked if she and the two little boys could fly down with us. I said that there was not enough room as I had to lay on top of the money with my back touching the ceiling of the Leer. He said they would change to his Saber liner, which was a larger jet. I didn't like the idea but relented. We loaded up on top of the money as there were no seats in the cabin. Then we took off, headed south bucking a headwind all the way and running low on fuel. Upon arrival a small but violent thunderstorm was sitting right over the runway. We circled until two red warning lights began flashing 'LOW FUEL, LOW FUEL,' we had to land immediately. I suggested coming in low over the water and avoiding most of the unpredictable turbulence. The chief pilot agreed. We came in skimming the waves and landed in a crosswind so strong and gusty that the right wing-tip tank scraped the runway.

Half an hour later the sun was out. We packed the van with dollars and followed it to the bank in the Cadillac. This time DeFief and his thieves managed to steal forty thousand dollars. He eased some of the anger by giving me 14% interest and driving me to Doctors Beach and showing me deals in real estate.

It was Friday afternoon and the pilot asked if I would stay until Monday so his family could visit and play on the beaches. I explained that I couldn't because the next day was my daughter Miriam's birthday and also my twentieth high school class reunion which we had been looking forward to for some time. Normally we flew back and landed after dark and I would get out on the taxiway and make my way across the perimeter fence to avoid customs. To accommodate the family, I reluctantly agreed to catch a commercial flight back to Miami.

After dinner and a few drinks I went to bed but couldn't sleep for the feeling of impending doom. I kept waking up with a start, my guts were on fire and I was nervous.

The next morning I boarded the flight to Miami and sat beside a rough talking local fisherman. In our conversation he asked who I was doing business with on the island and I told him Steven DeFief, in a loud voice he said, "Steven DeFief! Why he is the biggest crook on this island. If you got any money in that shiny new bank of his, all I can say is you better take it out!"

I figured he was telling the truth about DeFief, as it concurred with my gut feeling.

A red light came on as the customs agent typed my name in the computer. Three agents appeared, escorted me into a room, and told me I was under arrest on a federal charge from L.A. I wondered whether they meant, LA as in Louisiana, or L.A. as in Los Angeles. The agent didn't know. I asked to go to the bathroom and a nice young man escorted me. I sat down on the toilet, tore up the receipt for the deposit of the three million dollars and other incriminating information, and flushed. They allowed a telephone call and I rang Marrie and told her I had been arrested at the airport and to cancel our chartered flight to Georgia and to clean house.

Four or five hours later a short, tough-looking, Cuban-American DEA agent came out and took me through several doors into a seedy area that reminded me of the torture chambers in Mexico. He read me the Miranda statement, handcuffed me, grabbed me hard by the forearm and we walked to the parking lot where he opened the door to his car and shoved me into the back seat. As we were driving I offered him a million dollars to let me go.

He slammed on the brakes and yelled. "Shut you fukin' mouf you son a bitch!"

His English was terrible; his disposition worse. He drove me to North Dade County lock-up where I was put in a big cell with ten or twelve other men and there we sat looking at one another for the next week. I tried to be calm, but from going full out to a dead stop was hard to adjust to. My elbows started itching and even though I knew it was nerves I couldn't help but scratch. Within a few days both elbows were bleeding.

A handsome young lawyer showed up, introduced himself as Roy DeFox, and said that Barry had sent him. He read my indictment which contained one of the most dreaded charges the American government can throw at anyone; a Title 21-848 or Continuing Criminal Enterprise which carries a life sentence without parole. Then there was a string of marijuana charges for importation, possession and distribution with about 200 overt acts listed. Six counts of income tax evasion followed. To round it all off I was charged with unlawful use of the telephone that carried an additional three years. All added up it came to life plus 81 years.

Council DeFox arranged a bail hearing. We appeared before an old magistrate that had me telling lies and tripping all over them before I knew what was what. Lawyer DeFox's voice was trembling, and I knew the game was lost. It was like putting a boy in the ring with an old pro wrestler. "Bail is set at five million dollars cash with a 'Nebia' hearing. Next."

A Nebia hearing is a hearing before the judge to prove where the bail money is coming from.

DeFox regrouped and hired Albert Krieger, the smartest and most gifted lawyer I have ever met or heard of. When he appeared, the courtroom was packed with lawyers and law students taking notes. Krieger applied for another bail hearing and this time I was silent. Krieger told of my charges and said this was the first time I had ever been in trouble and that all the accusations were for marijuana. He painted a picture of what a fine and upstanding family man I had been for the past forty years and then told of well-known gangsters and their heinous crimes with bail set at two million, surety bond.

After he went through a half dozen of these horrific crimes with bail set at two million dollars surety, the prosecutor stood up and said, "Your Honor, the U.S. Attorney has no objection to a two-million-dollar surety bail."

Krieger gestured a bow and excused himself. The swinging half door separating the audience from the spectators swung back and forth after he walked briskly off the stage and almost ran from the courtroom.

"Well, if that is the request of both parties I set the bail at two million dollars surety." This meant that no money was necessary as property or a bond from a bail bondsman was sufficient to get me released.

"Excuse me, Your Honor, I made a mistake, I meant two million dollars cash bail," said an alarmed prosecutor.

"Sorry, bail has been set," said the old magistrate.

DeFox and Krieger's assistant attorney, Susan, came to the holding area of the court to talk with me. I had been there for hours while the marshals hauled off load after load of human fodder to stoke the furnace of the Federal Department of Justice. It was after seven pm and dark outside. I was dressed in an eleven hundred dollar blue suit, a thousand dollar pair of Weston black shoes and a conservative red silk tie. A Federal Marshal escorted me from an open wire cage and locked me in a glassed-in room to talk with lawyers. They stayed for an hour and during that time the Marshals changed shift. When we were through talking I banged on the window or pushed a button, I don't remember, but a stout black woman came over and opened the door and asked if we were through. I answered in the affirmative. She opened the door to the corridor, elevator, and freedom, then she walked off. I walked out in the foyer and pushed the button on the elevator and DeFox went ballistic. I said, "Just keep cool and walk me out of here."

"You have to go back." He was shitting himself. Susan wasn't saying anything and I think she was all for it.

"Look Roy, if you will walk me down those stairs I will give you a million dollars tonight."

"Guard, guard, put him back inside." He said with a little laugh.

Twenty prisoners were watching from the cage and I am sure they wouldn't have said anything at the time. Of course, there were plenty of informants in the group, but they were afraid to yell out because of the consequences.

Back at North Dade Detention Center the guard said, "Pack up Reaves, you're moving out."

"Where am I going?"

"I ain't got no idea, but yore travelin'."

The U.S. Attorney figured my lawyers were arranging bail and they were making sure that I was unavailable.

Three U.S Marshals chained me and drove me to the airport where we spent the night before boarding a flight to San Francisco. There we had to walk to another terminal and as we were walking across an overpass a cement truck drove underneath. I almost jumped down on it, but at the last moment, I saw the drum was turning, there was no way I could have stayed on. We caught another flight to L.A. where I was taken to Terminal Island Prison in the Port of Los Angeles.

A heavy black woman took my clothes, fingerprints, and mug shot and gave me a red jumpsuit, flip-flops, comb, soap, and safety razor. Two jailers escorted me to A-block, a dark medieval building with three tiers of cages, and locked me in a dimly lit cell. It was barely five feet wide and eight feet long with two metal bunk beds, a stainless steel toilet without a seat, a stainless washbasin about the size of a hat with a button in the wall that took all my strength to push it in deep enough to get a stream of cold water. The cell was dirty, grey and dingy and had an evil feeling about it. This is one of the reasons many men commit suicide when they first come in and are placed in such degrading places.

The next day Marshals took me downtown where Judge Terry Hatter raised the bail back to five million cash with the Nebia hearing. We had several bail hearings in subsequent weeks, however, the amount remained the same.

The prosecutor gave the lawyers the discovery, which outlined their case, and from that I saw who the accusers were.

Peter Davis and Ron Jamison were number one. They were caught red-handed bringing in a ton of pot and they never served a day by giving me up.

Glenn Tiller lied through his teeth, saying he often found white powder in the windows and floor of my planes when I brought them in for repairs after they had been shot up. I was shocked at his betrayal.

Bob Reynolds from Newport Beach, California was in prison in Tucson, Arizona he testified to a pack of lies just to get transferred to Phoenix. He saw 200 kilos of marijuana in my garage in December of 1977 and again in January 1978. This was convenient, since all the other overt acts were over five years old and the statute of limitations had run out. The prosecution needed something within five years and this was it. He said he saw the pot as he drove by, a lie that could be quickly discredited because the garage door could not be seen from the road.

Ron Sims from Arizona, and Barney Swinehart from Llano, Texas were caught with a load. They were working to stay out. Some years earlier I had contracted with Swinehart to fly several loads and he ripped me off on the deal. I woke him up one night around three in the morning, had a chat. From that he must have gotten his feelings hurt.

Albert Krieger said he could discredit all the witnesses, the only thing I had to worry about was the income taxes. That was until he had the bomb dropped in his lap.

My old friend Johnny Allen rolled and dictated a book to the U.S. Attorney. I can say one thing, Johnny Allen has a fabulous memory. He remembered things

I had long forgotten. I was not angry with Johnny, I just felt a great loss, worse than if he had died. They indicted him on the same charges as me and I heard the U.S Attorney spent a week in his cell before he broke.

With such a witness on the stand against me there was no hope, I had to make a deal. Of course, the attorneys went ahead as though we were going to trial. They hired Shallow and Shallow out of Madison, Wisconsin--reputed to be the best appeal lawyers in the United States. I was flanked by six or seven high-powered lawyers each time I appeared in court.

For the out of state lawyers to practice in California they hired Howard Weitzman as the local council. Each time we went to court, Judge Hatter recognized Weitzman and was stern with the other lawyers. On one occasion at a lull, Howard and the Judge got to talking rather personal. I paid Weitzman ten thousand dollars which was only a pittance compared to what the others were getting and I thought I had the wrong lawyer for L.A.

DeFox said he had found an oil baron in Oklahoma who would put up the bail for a million dollars. Marrie and Mother dug up the three million at the Old Place, gave it to DeFox and I directed him to another three million since I was expecting to be released any day. DeFox came to me in his blue dress shirt wet from his armpits halfway to his belt. I could see he was nervous. He told me Marta Ochoa, the woman dressed in a nurse's uniform whenever we met had been arrested in Miami and Barry had paid her bail and had asked him to get her out of the country. The prosecutor was willing to plea bargain and it should go all right. Jorge Ochoa owed me three million three hundred and eighty-two thousand. Barry was continuing to work. DeFox said he wanted one million dollars to take Marta out of the country, make the plea bargain, liaison between Barry and me, and to put the six million in the bank in Grand Cayman.

He had me in a precarious situation as he had six million. Barry was bringing in one and a half million a week and I needed someone to keep in contact. Besides, the three million-plus what Ochoa owed me needed collecting. I felt the hot rush in my face that tells me I have just been screwed. I also knew he arrived at the million-dollar figure because of the million dollars I offered him at the elevator. At the time his cowardice made him lose it, and now he was trying to win it back.

"OK DeFox, I will give you one million dollars after you deposit the six million dollars in the bank and collect the three million from Ochoa. You take your million out of the money that Barry is making each week. Plus, you must bring me half a dozen strands of Angel Wire, (wire coated with diamond chips used to cut bars) this week."

His sweaty shirt was drying.

Barry was doing all he could to help. He paid Marrie full price for the planes, stacking the money up in a big hidden safe in his house; holding it until she could figure out a place to put it. He sent word and asked if I wanted him to hold a load until the Ochoa's paid up the three million dollars. Like an idiot I said "no". I thought they would pay when I got out and I was swamped with money.

Meanwhile I was moved from A-unit to B-unit which had one level with a dozen cells on each side of the wide corridor. My cellmate was Eli, a red headed bank robber who was as anxious to leave as I was. The paint and supply room was next door and Eli made a key to open it. At the back of this small room was a dirty window with flimsy bars. Pre-sentence prisoners wore red jumpsuits, but the sentenced prisoners wore khakis and we had two pair stashed in the ceiling. From the window it was only a short walk to the fence built on the edge of the water. On the other side were fifteen to twenty ships anchored in the roads waiting for berths. Matt, Marrie's brother, was going to be standing by in a speedboat and pick us up when we climbed the fence. I waited for the cutters and DeFox kept stalling for one reason or another. Marrie wouldn't bring them in as she said she kept seeing the number three concerning my sentence.

John DeLorean, the famous car manufacturer, was arrested on cocaine charges and moved in next door. His wife at the time was the celebrated model, Christine Ferrare, who resembled Marrie. When Marrie drove up in her Mercedes the reporters and cameramen swarmed on her. They left rather disappointed when they discovered they had the wrong beauty.

Every day the guards chained me and John together on a long chain with thirty other prisoners and marched us to the exercise yard. We played volleyball on the same team and became friends. Lawyers were lined up in two-thousand dollar suits trying to represent the case, poor John didn't know which one to choose. I told him about Howard Weitzman, how the Judge acknowledged him each time he entered the courtroom, and how he treated the lawyers from the east coast. John asked if I would arrange a meeting. I called Weitzman who was pleased to come out and said that if I could help him land the case he would be forever grateful. He took the case and won on grounds of entrapment. This became one of the most publicized drug cases in the U.S. John sent me a Christmas card each year as long as he lived.

DeFox showed up with a plea bargain that he and the prosecutors had worked out. The government would drop all the charges except two counts of possession of marijuana, six counts of income tax, and unlawful use of the telephone. The first eight counts carried five years each and the last one carried three years. In exchange they wanted my assets. This included our home in Santa Barbara, the farms in Georgia, two airplanes, the Jolly Swagman, and all bank accounts in both Grand Cayman and the United States - this amounted to tens of millions of dollars. I was to pay a fine of $10,000 and the cost of prosecution. In exchange for all this the prosecutor agreed not to ask for any specific sentence. I didn't have much choice.

Everything was fine with me except for losing the house. I tried to exchange money for that point. DeFox and Krieger advised against the move as it would make it look like I had too much money and may increase the sentence. In any case, the IRS would take the house later. I signed the plea agreement, planning to buy the house back before Marrie had to move out.

Mr. Hudson, from Pre Sentence Planning, interviewed me and said he was going to recommend confinement of one year with a lengthy parole period. Sometime before sentencing, Layn Phillips, the prosecutor, got to him and changed his recommendation to seven years, incarceration.

When I asked him about it he hung his head in shame and said that he had to keep his job.

December 21, 1982. I walked into the courtroom, it looked like homecoming at Sand Hill Church. The room was packed with family and friends dressed in their Sunday best.

Layn Phillips stood behind the podium facing Judge Hatter. He rested the toe of one shoe on the heel of the other presenting a hole in the sole of his shoe. "Your honor, Mr. Reaves is not a drug dealer. Mr. Reaves is not a drug importer. Mr. Reaves is a drug industrialist who has spanned the globe for a decade with his death and destruction! Mr. Reaves started as a marijuana hauler, but changed to a lighter and whiter product which was infinitely more profitable."

Albert Krieger jumped up and said, "Your Honor, I object to such slanderous slurs. I'm from Missouri and I say for Mr. Phillips to either put up or shut up!"

"I agree with Mr. Krieger. Mr. Philips, I advise that in the future you temper your accusations to the charges before us and remember that no third and fourth hand hearsay is allowed in my court."

Philips ranted on for an hour. He kept to the letter of the plea bargain and didn't ask for any specific length of incarceration, he said such words as "The accused should be taken off the streets for many years." And again, "The government asks for a lengthy period of incarceration."

When the prosecutor sat down Judge Hatter said, "Mr. Reaves I delayed court this morning to read all sixty-five letters on your behalf and I was impressed. I see that you were raised on a farm where you plowed mules and slopped the hogs. I believe you came out to California and got caught up in the glamour and glitter of it all and wanted to live high on the hog. I sentence you to five years on the marijuana count with a B1 sentence and recommend that you be paroled after twenty months. I am also going to send a message to society. In addition to the five years' incarceration term, I sentence you to twenty-five years on Special Parole. Should you violate the conditions of your parole you will be returned to prison to serve all or part of the twenty-five years. I further sentence you to five years each on the income evasion charges and three years for the unlawful use of a telephone. However, I am going to run those charges concurrent with one another and place you on probation for five years in which time you must complete five thousand hours of community service work at the discretion of your parole officer. You are to pay a fine of ten thousand dollars and the cost of prosecution, which I set at two-thousand dollars. I recommend to the Bureau of Prisons that you serve your sentence at Boron Prison Camp."

Of course, at the time I didn't know how much time I was getting and was anxious to ask Mr. Krieger. He said, "You have to do twenty months at Boron camp. Roger, I know that a lot of people have been praying for you, this is almost enough to make me change my religion."

Marrie, honey you were close when you saw three years, but I got five and have to do sixteen more months, I thought.

When I returned to Terminal Island, they placed me in the general population with the sentenced prisoners. One of the first men I saw was 'Dan the Jinx'. He walked over and asked how much time I got. When I told him he began ranting and raving about how unfair it was and how much money I owed him from the load he didn't load in Mexico years earlier. I reminded him of the $80,000 and the DC-3 his stupidity cost me. He said that when he was released from prison in Colombia he had to eat out of garbage cans. I told him I thought that was most appropriate for a swine like himself. He went to swinging those long arms and luckily I ducked. I knew his heart was about the size of a peanut and that he was just eaten up with jealousy.

25. CO-ED PRISON

Home and the Spirit -- Back To School -- Have You Seen My Airplane? -- Stanley Black, the Most Mean Tempered Son Of A Bitch I Ever Ran Across -- Roger's Home Fitness Program -- Whoops, I Did It Again

January 8, 1983. Shackled, chained and locked in one of the forty individual cages on a bus with thirty-nine other prisoners, we left Terminal Island early on a foggy morning. In the front was a driver, a co-driver and a guard facing the prisoners wearing a pistol and holding a shotgun loaded with double-ought buckshot in a banana clip. In the rear of the bus was another compartment with another guard facing forward with the same killing machines. After three or four hours we stopped at Lompoc Penitentiary and next at the Federal Correctional Institution, unloading some prisoners and taking on others at both places before continuing north. We reached Pleasanton, California late in the afternoon where I was unloaded along with five other happy convicts.

Colorful flowers lined the walkway to the reception. A pretty blond was raking leaves, she paused and gave me a wave... Reception was a shocking change from Terminal Island. We were treated kindly, given jeans and regular shirts until our clothes arrived. Three chalets held 200 inmates each. Two were for the female prisoners and one for the male. I saw right off that the ratio was in my favor. It was rumored the prison was built especially to house Patty Hearst after she was 'brainwashed' into robbing a bank with a group calling themselves 'The Symbionese Liberation Army'. In any case, the place was posh for a prison.

The rooms were very nice, bunk beds made of yellow oak and a four by eight tinted window looking out onto rolling hills. I noticed the blue carpet on the floor and the white porcelain lavatory and commode with a toilet seat. All rooms faced onto a large carpeted split-level general area where men were playing billiards, cards and backgammon. The accommodations were more than I could have dreamed possible.

I took a walk around the track and met Jo Ann Overland and her friend. They asked me what I thought of the place and I told them. I could sense by the look on their faces that I had committed the unpardonable. The girls had never been in a Mexican prison or Terminal Island; I dried up about how nice it was. Men and women strolled past holding hands and chatting as though they were in a city park. At four o'clock we were called back to our units for count and to get ready for dinner. When the doors opened men and women strolled over to the dining hall and sat in booths or at heavy oak tables which seated six or eight.

There was an outside balcony with tables and benches where we ate in good weather.

The next morning, during orientation, the young female guard stopped talking, excused herself, walked to the room next to mine, and opened the door. Two men stared wide-eyed and frozen in place with their trousers around their ankles. One was in the position of the fuckee' and the other, the fucker'. Our quiet spoken guide said, "Flacko will you please disengage your penis from Ortega's rectum and both of you go to my office." She closed the door and continued with her orientation. That is the only time I ever saw anything like that. I hope to never again.

My clothes and toiletries arrived. I was popular because some of the men were poor and wanted to use my expensive after-shave lotions. I wore a London Fog trench coat, a scarf draped around my neck, and walked the track with the ladies. I walked with one of Charles Manson's accomplices and Sara Jane Moore who shot at President Ford and missed. I took one or two strolls with a woman who had kidnapped a little boy and bitten his penis off. When I heard this information I made myself scarce.

A cute blond from Montana latched onto me and I had to be rude to shake her off. There was a wealth of attractive women as a good many were bank employees who had signed the bank manager's name to loans for their building contractor boyfriend or other such scams.

Each month an examiner from the United States Parole Commission visited the prison. I applied for a hearing the first day I arrived and within two months one was scheduled. I hired William J. Genego, a young professor of law at the University of Southern California who taught post-conviction law. Marrie flew up and the three of us walked into the hearing chamber and met Harry Dwyer, a dwarfish looking man with big pointed hairy ears stuck on a bald head far too big for his body. He sat on several cushions. I noticed his feet were a foot off the floor. I had been warned about this monster who hated the world and everyone in it. We didn't have a chance. Professor Genego had a turn and then Marrie said a few words, however, when I spoke he cut me down with well-rehearsed lines from many years of diabolical practice. He said that he didn't give a fig what the judge ordered, he was going to impose a prison term of 44 months.

This was anticipated and I had a right to return to the judge within 120 days of sentencing and ask him to reconsider; which we did. Judge Hatter was angry with the Parole Commission for disregarding his recommendation of 20 months before parole. He changed the sentence to three years of which I would have to do two thirds or two years.

Marrie's vision of the number '3' was fulfilled.

Once a month we had a dance and local bands came in and played. I liked Jo Ann Overland and when she wasn't taken I danced with her. Someone knew a guard who would bring in a quart of Chivas Regal for 500 dollars and every month I bought a bottle, poured it in a clean Clorox bottle, and saved it for dance night. Those women would put it on you on the dark dance floor with or without a drink.

Dan McKeon was a handsome young man from Santa Barbara and he and I became good pals. He loved to gamble at backgammon or most anything else for that matter. One afternoon we were playing for ten dollars a point and the game kept switching back and forth as whoever thought they were ahead passed the doubling cube. I received it on 64 and held it, eventually winning backgammon or triple game for $1,920. Dan fell over backward in his chair kicking his feet in the air.

My roommate Mike was a big stout fellow who wrote letters to three or four of the girls next door. The letters and the ones he received were smutty beyond imagination. He was having sex with one or the other and had no qualms about slipping in the women's dorm and taking on several women. Late one afternoon someone snitched, perhaps she wanted to be first. The screws locked the building and started a systematic search. Mike kicked the bulletproof window out of one of the cells along with the masonry and bricks holding it in place, jumped out the hole, and ran. He came into our room with eyes flashing and nostrils flaring. Months later a woman guard walked in the kitchen freezer and found Mike and a gal going at it on the table. She told Mike to get down, but he refused. Both he and the woman were laughing. The guard called for backup, it took six of them to pull the stallion off. They laughed for weeks about Mike's 'hot pink dick' smoking in the icy air.

There were as many guards as inmates and it seemed it was the sworn duty of several of the former to catch the latter in the act. Wheat grew right up to the fence and a guard slipped in on his days off, crawled through the wheat watching with binoculars and a camera trying to catch a couple. However, the prisoners were slick. The girls wore full skirts without knickers, sat on the lawn with their legs over the legs of the man who was leaning on his elbow at a ninety-degree angle to the woman. It wasn't obvious unless you were directly looking at them.

However it was easier for the women to dress up as men and sneak into the men's unit which was a rather frequent affair. I met a willowy vixen who invited me to get a job at the drapery factory outside the compound where opportunities for privacy were plentiful and the guard didn't care. I turned down the offer as I was happily married and Marrie and the children flew up every second week, visiting for two days. Besides, if one was caught, a letter was sent to your spouse or next of kin stating that you had been caught having sex with another inmate. No mention made as to the sex of the other inmate. Also, punishment was horrific. They administered 'Diesel Therapy', which consisted of putting you on a bus for six months. You rode 12 to 16 hours a day, stopping over at a prison or jail where you went through the fingerprinting and delousing treatment before eating a cold sandwich and crawling into a bunk, only to be woken a few hours and hitting the road again. Some men were broken in this fashion.

I should have stayed at Pleasanton, but I didn't know it at the time. Men kept talking about how good Lompoc Prison Farm was and I put in to go there as it was only an hour's drive from home. The administration denied my request. Marrie visited Congressman Lago Marsino who wrote a letter to the Bureau of Prisons. I was called in and asked why I had a congressman asking for me to be transferred. Had they known I wanted to go to Lompoc they would have moved me earlier.

In June 1983 I was given a furlough transfer from Pleasanton to Lompoc Camp. They gave me a bus ticket and twelve hours to make the journey. Marrie met me at the bus station and whisked me away to the airport where she had a jet waiting to take us to Santa Barbara where we spent an unforgettable day. The garden was lovely, the pool was perfect. We had a picnic on the terrace and played with the children. It was a day in heaven. Late in the afternoon Marrie drove me to the bus station in Lompoc where I hired a taxi to take me to the camp.

What a terrible let down! The living quarters were a twin pair of three-story World War II barracks with a hundred sagging bunk beds in each wing. There was nothing to separate the men except small lockers, some of the men snored, masturbated unashamedly, farted, and moved around all night.

I landed a job mending fences on the ranch that covered Vandenberg Air Force Base and fifty miles of coastline. The area was thick with silos for nuclear-tipped missiles. We watched numerous sidewinders and other ballistic missiles fired. The area was also thick with Western Rattlesnakes. These rattlers were more docile than our Eastern Diamondback and they liked to lie under the lip of the blacktop where the water had washed holes underneath. Sometimes I caught one, squeezed the back of the head, and made his mouth open showing the long fangs. The guard was deathly afraid of them and I would chase him. Without warning I was on the kitchen roster.

A busybody Austrian convict ran the kitchen and the work roster. He also liked to play backgammon and chess and before long he owed me a thousand dollars. I let him pay it off by covering for me while I went home.

Before daybreak I would go to the kitchen, check-in, and then take off running down a two-mile farm track to a highway where Marrie picked me up. One morning, I ran into a barbed-wire gate stretched across the road and fell over it cutting my finger. It ached all day. That evening Marrie dropped me off near the guard's housing where I hid in a garbage truck and rode back into camp.

Bob, the garbage truck driver, made forty dollars an evening by giving four massages and another hundred dollars selling beer. His wife stashed cases in the bottom of the garbage cans in the area where the guards lived and he would take them out and put them in a secret place on the truck. He also did 'river runs', which is swimming the Santa Ynez River, jogging to the liquor store, and bringing back a dozen or so bottles. One Saturday afternoon I got so drunk on vodka and grapefruit juice that my friend Stretch had to help me in my bunk and hold the pot while I puked. That was by far the most inebriated I have ever been. Some call it blind drunk.

Marrie and the children visited several times a week and brought delicious food in a hollowed-out loaf of bread. The rule was, one could bring in anything in the shape of a sandwich, and we stretched the definition of a sandwich.

October 1st, 1983. Prisoners having served one year or more and with only one year remaining were eligible for a furlough if they had maintained clean conduct. The conditions were that if you had to travel over a thousand miles you received seven days, otherwise you got five. Georgia here we come!

Flying Delta's first class with our whole family together after fourteen months separation was another taste of heaven. Marrie was holding on to my arm, her eyes sparkling. Rhett was sitting on my lap pulling my face around each time he wanted to say something to me. Marya and Miriam were snuggled up and loving on me. The stewardess asked, "What is going on here?"

Marrie whispered, "My husband just got out of prison this morning and we are on a week furlough."

She returned with two bottles of special gift-wrapped wine.

In Atlanta we rented a car and drove the four hours to my sister Charlotte's house in Douglas. When we arrived there were yellow ribbons everywhere, a band was playing, and the camera rolling. Tears, hugs, and kisses were abundant.

On Saturday several of us went fishing. We came in early because we were all going to a dance that night. As I went into one of the back bedrooms, Barbara Garrison was getting fixed up. She is a cousin several times removed and I had known her all my life. She was a stewardess with Delta and as the boys around the hangar would say, 'she had a fine fuselage.' She was parading around Charlotte's bedroom in a slip and bra when I came in. I slapped her on the butt and said, "Barbara, if you ever start selling that stuff or giving it away, I wanna get out.

She replied, "Oh Roger, I'm not like that anymore, I've been saved!"

I had seen many people 'saved' for a while and then return to their old ways and I was skeptical, so I said, "Tell me about it, Barbara."

She replied, "When my daughter, Natalie, was six years old she started tripping and falling. I took her to the doctor and after many tests they found she has a rare, incurable disease. The doctors told me that she will become a vegetable and have a grotesquely twisted body. There is absolutely nothing that can be done. I was devastated. I didn't know which way to turn. Then I heard of a healing service in a church and I took Natalie. They prayed for her, but she wasn't healed. However, she started speaking in an unknown tongue and was happy, always talking about Jesus and wanting to go to church. I continued to take her, anytime I heard of someone with the gift of healing I took her. At one of these services I received the Baptism of the Holy Spirit, and I was changed."

"Barbara that is a truly wonderful story, I have always wanted that experience and have prayed for it and had others pray for me, yet I have never received anything."

She said, "You have got to meet Mildred! This lady has the gift of imparting the gift of tongues; she lives in Atlanta and you must go to see her."

I said, "I would like to if it was possible. We are planning to spend Thursday night in Atlanta."

We arranged a meeting. Thursday was a stormy day, traffic was slow back to Atlanta, and we didn't arrive at the hotel until after nine that night. We were tired and in no mood to go out again in the weather and we decided to cancel.

Marrie said, "I don't want to drive across Atlanta with Barbara to get the Holy Ghost. I'm tired, the children are tired, and I'm not going."

As we pulled under the awning of the hotel, Barbara drove in behind us. I got out and told her we had changed our minds. She insisted, I told her to talk to Marrie. They went up to the room while I registered. I don't know what Barbara said to Marrie, but when I got to the room it was already decided that we were to follow Barbara to the lady's house that was just around the corner. We began following in the rain and just around the corner was a long drive. We arrived at the destination at eleven o'clock, went in, and Mildred greeted us warmly. She was in the kitchen drying dishes, her husband was in the den watching television, although he didn't come out. Mildred made a strong pot of coffee and regrettably I drank a big cup that crossed my eyes. Mildred asked if we believed in the Lord Jesus Christ. We answered, yes; she then read a few verses from the Bible and said a short prayer binding Satan. She told me to kneel by one chair and Marrie across the room by another. She told us to let our tongues be limber and free and to say anything that came to us and not to be ashamed or afraid. As soon as she came towards Marrie with the Bible in her hand praying, Marrie began speaking in the most beautiful language. She lit up! Tears streamed down her beaming face.

She stopped speaking in the language and said to me, "Oh darling, God is wonderful. He has a sense of humor and I will never fear again. Then she continued praising God in her beautiful new language. Unfortunately, nothing happened to me. Mildred said that something was blocking me. I hope it was the strong coffee, as it does affect me adversely. For some time afterward Marrie was filled with the Spirit, she wanted to run up to strangers and tell them of God's wonderful love.

Sony Watchman battery operated color televisions had just come out. Five men asked me to bring them one when I returned from furlough. I went shopping in Santa Barbara, purchased them, and put them in a box along with gambling money.

Marrie drove me to Lompoc. We were on the prison property, yet ten miles away from the compound and I asked her to stop so I could stash the contraband. A car was following, Marrie slowed down to let it pass. As it drove around I noticed a couple who looked to be about seventy years old. Marrie pulled off on the shoulder and I ran across the ditch, jumped the fence and ran out a way, and hid the bag under a tumbleweed bush. Marrie was blowing the horn. I sprinted back in time to see the VW Beetle turn around and come speeding back. Marrie took off, the VW tried to follow. I figured the man must have something to do with the prison. We made several turns and went on to the camp where she dropped me off and I received a breathalyzer test.

The next day while working on the ranch the men said that the guard had been calling me over the loudspeaker all afternoon. I knew the game was up and I thought hard about taking off for Mexico. I decided to see how much trouble I was in before doing anything rash. Sitting in the office was the man who gleefully identified me. They made a big production of the TV's and charged me with bringing contraband into the prison to sell for a profit. Then they handcuffed me, transported me to the main prison and put me 'in the hole.'

One afternoon I heard gunshots and wondered what was going on. Later I learned that three prisoners had taken a garbage truck, rammed the fence, and got through. The truck had governors allowing it to run about 20 mph. A woman guard in a pickup drove in front and shot the men, killing one, and critically injuring the other two.

After a month of 'hole' therapy I was shackled, chained, and transported to Terminal Island Prison where I remained for the next nine months. After Pleasanton and Lompoc camp, this place was the pits. Not much happened of interest during those nine months and I don't care to recall the trivia. I had one fistfight where I had the inside of my mouth busted and my knuckles skinned up. We could purchase ten dollars in coins at the commissary once a week to buy from the vending machines. The one on the main square had delicious ice cream sandwiches. One night I lost my last quarter in a drain while trying to put it in the machine. I pried and levered the cover off, found a horde of coins, and extracted over forty dollars out of the muck. I was as delighted as a miner who struck pay dirt.

Howard 350 - the fastest piston engined passenger plane available. She would throw you back in your seat on take off. She could carry two tons of cocaine for two thousand miles at 400mph. My favorite aircraft.

Image courtesy user "RuthAS" - Howard 350 executive standard - Ft Lauderdale, FL 1978 - Wikipedia

Someone stole my Howard 350 aircraft off the tarmac in Santa Barbara and I was angry. A real flying machine! I suppose it was the ultimate in piston-driven aircraft. She could work out of rough strips, fly at 400 mph and carry two tons over 2,000 miles. The only aircraft that could outperform it was the Howard 500 and there were only seventeen left at the time. I couldn't find one for sale. I hired a detective who found it at the Chino airport and got the name and telephone number of the thief. I called the number, his wife answered. I told her I was being released from prison in a month and it would make everything much easier if her husband returned the plane in the same parking space from where he took it. The thief called the prison and accused me of threatening him. Johnson, my case manager, was eaten up with jealousy because of my financial situation and had me locked in the hole for the remainder of my term.

Somehow I heard a whisper that all might not be right in Grand Cayman Island. I asked my brother Larry to go down, buy gold, and put it in another bank. He bought four million dollars' worth as that was all he could purchase at the time. It arrived at DeFief's bank. Larry said it took him several trips carrying heavy briefcases down the street to the Royal Bank of Canada where he deposited it in lockboxes. It wasn't long before Roy DeFox showed up with a proposition from DeFief. He offered to pay 18% interest if I brought the coins back and put the money on deposit. He had heard that I knew something was up. I asked Mother to go down and take all the money out of that bank and deposit it in another. She and my brother-in-law, David Nettles, chartered a private plane out of Miami. On the way down they ran into severe weather, the pilot got lost and if David had not been a good pilot they would have gone down in the Caribbean.

DeFief refused to carry out my instructions and instead gave Mother a check for the remaining millions made out to her, although requiring my signature. When she brought the checks to me in the visiting room at Terminal Island and told me what had happened I knew it was a stalling tactic. Something bad was going on. I refused to allow my Mother to get involved in a money-laundering scheme so I sent further instructions for transferring the money. Too late, the bank had closed, ripping off hundreds of millions of dollars from me and the other depositors.

July 1984. I was scheduled for release at ten in the morning. Marrie was waiting in the parking lot. Agents from the DEA and IRS were waiting in the boardroom. They questioned me about the Grand Cayman Island accounts, Barry Seal and my California connection. I refused to answer their questions. They called in prison functionaries who said that unless I cooperated they would not release me. I said for them to take me on back if that was the case.

It was four in the afternoon before I walked through the prison doors.

As soon as I stepped into the car I took off the prison clothes and put on the clothes Marrie had brought. Driving over the tall bridge leaving Terminal Island I threw them over the rails.

Stanley Black was my parole officer and without a doubt the most mean-tempered son-of-a-bitch I ever ran across. He had been blown up and shot several times by his charges and I know why. For example, I was talking with his secretary who was asking me if I wanted a kitten for my children. When Black walked in at this particular moment he jabbed his finger in my chest and said, "Don't ever let me catch you talking to that cunt again!" Other times he would tell me to have a seat. He would type a while and read his newspaper without speaking or looking at me. After a couple of hours he would say, "You can go for now, but remember, I can put you in prison at my whim and there isn't a damned thing you can do about it. See you next Monday, at ten o'clock." I hated the piece of shit so bad I would sweat under my arms every time I went through the door. I would have loved to have him alone on an island for a few minutes. Just the memory of the creep makes me want to vomit. How does someone hold such hate for their fellow human beings?

Marrie was living in a rented house in Montecito and I wanted to buy a place. I found an old run-down mansion overlooking the Mission in Santa Barbara. For the past half-century it was used as a convent, and had recently been sold. Part of the property was now Mary Mount School with the main house sold as a residence. It must have been sixteen or eighteen thousand square feet in all, counting the basement. President Franklin D. Roosevelt had visited and considered it for his Western White House. I can't begin to explain the beauty and elegance of the place. I paid seven hundred thousand dollars for it. I added another three-hundred thousand for repairs and refurbishing. We had a place fit for any king.

While we were restoring, my sister Kay came out and stayed with us. She met my friend Dan McKeon and they hit it off. I was trying to help Kay get off the booze as she had turned into an alcoholic. She walked around with what one assumed a glass of water. Instead, it would be full of vodka. She drank so much once that the skin on her hands and feet swelled, bursting from alcohol poisoning. One night she and Dan went out with Marrie and I. After dinner they left together and I warned Dan to keep her away from food and alcohol. He assured me he would. However, about five in the morning he called and told me to come and get my crazy sister. I told him to go to hell, that he was the one who had given her whiskey and for him to pay the fiddler. He called again and told me that he and his Mother had her handcuffed in the back of his pickup and for me to please come and help. I went to his farm and found Kay passed out drunk, handcuffed in the back of his truck. We took her back to my house and chained her to a pipe in the basement and left a gallon of water and a slop jar nearby. It was twenty-four hours before I made an appearance although I peeked in several times to check on her. She wouldn't speak, so I left for another day. By the beginning of the third day she was beginning to come around as she had had enough of sleeping on a blanket on a concrete floor with nothing to eat, only water.

"Kay, you can't live like this and nobody can live with you. If you want help, I'll help. If you don't, I will unchain you and you can hit the road for good. Which will it be?"

"Roger, I need help." She replied.

"Alright, I'll help you. You may think it's tough but it is going to take drastic measures to keep you away from too much food and alcohol. There is an observatory apartment on the top floor with a balcony. I'm going to buy a long chain and secure you there. Do you agree to that?"

"That's fine with me. Do whatever it takes Roger."

I went to the hardware store and bought eighty feet of small link chain, made one end tight around her waist, and locked the other to a heavy pipe. I put a stair master, a stationary bicycle, and a rowing machine on the balcony.

"Alright Kay, each of the machines has a calorie counter, start pedaling. Each time they add up to 400 calories or more ring this bell and we will bring you a meal equal to the calories burned."

Kay went to pedaling to eat. Doug and several other workers at the house sat around and smoked with her during their breaks. After two weeks she wore a bikini and had a fabulous tan. One afternoon Black, the evil parole officer, came sliding to a stop in the driveway and Kay leaned over the balcony to see what was going on. He told her to come down. She said, "I can't, I'm rather tied up at the moment."

He busted in, came running up the stairs, and said, "Did Roger do this?"

She answered, "Yes, he did, but he did it with my consent as I am an alcoholic and it's helping me. I can get out anytime I want, there are bolt cutters in case of fire or an emergency."

Black left rather disappointed.

Several 'fat gals' heard about my fabulous 'fit for summer' technique and asked if I would chain them up? I reluctantly declined.

Steven DeFief showed up at the house with his wife's parents, Vickie and Carl Dodgers, and an attorney. DeFief said, that as the bank was going under the only thing he could do to save some of my money was to buy mining stock. He had deeds to over a billion dollars' worth of proven assets and the core samples to prove it. There was also a new roller mill in El Paso with four million of my money 'invested.' However, at the moment he was broke and needed a little money to kick start the venture. He said he understood if I wanted to kill him and if he wasn't telling the truth he invited me to give him the coup de grace. I didn't believe him but I made the mistake of going and checking out the property, got gold fever, and was sucked into the most foolish investment of my life. They gave me half interest in seven mines and the mill in El Paso, plus titles to bulldozers, motor graders and dump trucks.

I went to the farm in Georgia, dug up a bucket of gold, and gave them $600,000' worth of Krugerrands. They went back to Silver City, New Mexico, and started blasting a shaft under a mountain.

David Nettles called me and told me he had some friends who had a novel idea to make millions by putting a computer in every airport taxi in the United States beginning with Atlanta. The computer would have all the attractions of the city along with advertisements for hotels and stores. The numbers were great. All they needed was $300,000. I flew back to Georgia, dug up another bucket of coins, and took out the required amount. The investors were particular, they wouldn't accept gold, they wanted cash.

Carl and Vicky Dodgers had cashed in the coins in New Mexico without a problem, so I called and asked them to change some more. They assured me it was no trouble. David loaded the coins in the trunk of a car and Kay headed out to Silver City. However, the Dodgers were working with the Feds. Kay met them at a hotel and Carl Dodgers told her to take them on to another town. On route they went through a roadblock and the coins were confiscated.

Marrie, Marya, Miriam, Rhett and I were in Vail Colorado for a couple of weeks skiing when I got the news and I knew I was going back to prison. We returned to Santa Barbara and I continued working. My illusion of living a happy life with my family in a mansion in California was rapidly vanishing.

26. BARRY SEAL – REBEL ADVENTURER

Remain Calm and Continue the Restoration -- Flee South Young Man -- "Barry's Dead" -- A Year in Brazil

President Ronald Reagan's blue eyes stared from the television screen directly into my eyes and said, "We now have absolute proof that the Sandinista Government of Nicaragua is in the drug-running business."

I had heard that Barry had turned and was now working for the DEA and this was proof enough. I was worried as to how much he had said about me. A few days later the phone rang. Barry wanted to meet. He named a small French restaurant in Santa Barbara and said he would be there at nine that night. I walked in and he was sitting at the back table facing the door. All the other tables were taken with men and women in their thirties and forties, many wearing leather jackets. I noticed there were no elderly or young couples.

Barry had gained a lot of weight in the two and a half years since I had last seen him. When I sat down the first thing I asked was, "Are you wired?"

"No."

"Are all the others DEA?"

"Yes they are."

"Barry I am not going to say anything, so just tell me why I am here and what you have been doing."

"Five years ago I gave a DEA agent a handful of pills I picked up on San Andreas Island and told him I could buy millions more. That indictment was held over my head for years, but for one reason or another the Feds kept putting off prosecuting. When it came right down to the five-year statute of limitations they dropped it on me. I was found guilty and sentenced to ten years. There was also a life sentence waiting in Louisiana. I just couldn't do it." Here he stopped, put his fingers over his eyes, and tears slid down between them.

Barry wiped his eyes and continued, "I was released on an appeal bond, went to Washington and knocked on the door of the Attorney General, Edwin Meese. I told him that tons of cocaine were coming into the country every month and if he would make a deal with me I could catch the whole cartel. Meese didn't believe me, so I went back the next day and tried again. Meese gave me an audience with Agent Jake Jacobson from Mississippi who thought I might be telling the truth. I told them everything, your part included, I got immunity for you and your family. You are under the protection of my umbrella if you co-operate."

After scrutinizing my face for some reaction he continued, "Me and Jake took a C-126, flew down and picked up a ton-and-a-half of cocaine and stopped with your old friends on the base near Managua and fueled. On take-off I pulled an engine and pan-caked down the runway. I called Jorge Ochoa and told him I had been in an accident and needed another plane quick. He and Pablo Escobar flew over and landed just as it was getting daylight. We unloaded the cocaine from the crashed plane into the new one with Pablo, Jorge and three Nicaraguan Generals helping. We had cameras outside and one in the cabin. The shutters were clicking the whole time we were making the transfer and my heart was in my throat thinking they would hear. We got over a thousand shots of them carrying the cocaine. Then I flew directly to Homestead Military Base and unloaded it into a motor home. Lito drove away and the DEA had a dump truck ram the motor home on the expressway. Cocaine busted all over the highway. A DEA agent posing as a highway patrolman was following, pulled up and turned on his flashers. Lito said he needed to call his boss and the patrolman told him there was a telephone booth across the freeway at the gas station. Lito started walking across when a Good Samaritan yelled, 'That's cocaine,' and tackled Lito. We wanted him to get away and keep the scam going but that idiot blew it."

"Barry, they are going to kill you."

"No, there's little danger of that. We will all get new IDs and passports and locate somewhere new. Plus the two Ochoa brothers are already in jail and Fabio is just a kid, he won't do anything."

"Barry, they are going to kill you! Bring your head honcho over." He motioned to a table nearby and a tall thin man wearing jeans and cowboy boots ambled over. I stood up and Barry introduced me to agent Jacobson. We ordered Chivas on the rocks and Barry ordered a coke as he didn't drink, smoke or do any drugs. We had several stiff ones and got a little pie-eyed together. I rather liked the man, we would have been friends had we been on the same team.

The whole deal boiled down to the fact that Barry had told everything and if I didn't join their little group I was sure to go to prison for the rest of my life.

Agent Jacobson said they knew everything but the name of my man in California. I had to give him up if there was going to be any deal between us. They knew he was doing a load as often as Barry. How they knew this is only speculation as I had never told Barry about him - I kept my small air force compartmentalized. Most probably Lito or one of the other Colombians told

Barry to inspire competition as they were always trying to get us to go more often. Jacobson said that I could fly first class to Miami the next day and testify before a Grand Jury or he would take me down in chains, the choice was mine. I said I would go first class.

I drove out to the airport with Barry. Then walked him to a sleek private jet and watched as he and the agents streaked off into the night sky.

My stomach felt like it was filled with ice slivers. I leaned against a tree and puked my guts out. I went to see Jerry and unloaded it all on him. We were two serious men drinking beer after midnight. I told Jerry I would never tell on him even if they gave me a life sentence or cut my tongue out. He was not to worry.

The next day Marrie and I flew first class to Miami and rented a cottage at the Coral Gables Hotel. I went to the courthouse and waited.

A number of people were coming and going as I leaned against one of the marble columns watching the show. Then I saw the motorcade bringing Barry. The first car had two men and the second had a driver in front and a man on each side of Barry in the back seat. They stopped by the steps. Barry wasn't six feet away from me and they were all looking the other way. I stepped down and slammed my open palm on the roof of the car above Barry's head. They almost tore the car up ducking and drawing guns. I leaned in and said, "See how easy that would be?" They failed to see the humor, but the point was made.

I just could not go into that building and testify against men who I had been in business with for years. They had never done me any wrong. It was just not in me so I explained to the DEA agents that I wanted to talk with a lawyer before I took the plunge and that was alright with them. Barry gave me the name of his lawyer. I knew what kind of lawyer he had so I began looking for the best in Miami.

Someone recommended Attorney Gould and I went to see him. He was working out in a sweatsuit when I went in. He listened without so much as moving a hair while I talked. When I finished he said, "Cooperating is like being pregnant, you either are, or you are not, there is no halfway. I will be happy to defend you for a deposit of six-hundred thousand but I don't represent snitches." My face felt on fire as I walked out of his office. Damn him, I was not a snitch. Later, I heard his office had been bombed and his partner killed for taking on such clients.

The next lawyer was a bit kinder, but the message was the same, the third was no better. I called Barry and told him I needed some time for the lawyer to study the case. He said there was no hurry and he would have them hold off for a while. Just as long as I was on their side there was nothing to worry about.

That evening, January 26, 1985, on my 42nd birthday, I took Marrie to dinner at La Festival in Coral Gables, our favorite restaurant in the Miami area. When we walked in there sat Barry and his wife Debbie. We were surprised to see one another and after dinner they joined us for dessert. I reiterated my belief that the Colombians would kill him and again he stuck his head in the sand and wouldn't look at the obvious. We parted after dinner and that was the last time I saw them.

We flew back to the house in Santa Barbara, continued restoration and kept up appearances considering what was swirling around us. The workers showed up in half a dozen cars and vans, parking everywhere. My good friend Ed came over, he smoked a joint and drank a strong cup of coffee laced with Kahlua. We got in his blue van, which was similar to the one driven by the man refinishing the oak floors, and drove off. Ten minutes after we left, twenty stormtroopers headed by US Customs Agent Allen Doody swarmed the house waving machine guns and automatic rifles. Marrie was still in her nightclothes dressing little Rhett when they burst into the bedroom. The first thing they did was to take the diamond ring off her finger and then systematically vandalized the house. As they pushed an iron bed across the newly refinished floor Marrie asked them to be careful. The agent said, "Don't worry about it lady, it isn't yours no longer, it's Uncle Sam's." She was held under guard for the next twelve hours.

I called home to ask Marrie about something and a stranger answered. I asked to whom I was speaking and he said Bill Johnson, I knew the game was up. I called our friend Mercedes and asked her to go over and visit Marrie and tell her I would meet her at a certain hotel in town after the siege was over. Mercedes went over and had to be rather assertive to get in. She visited Marrie with the agent in the room listening, so they spoke in Dutch. Mercedes opened a magazine and pointed to an ad with the name of the hotel.

That night Marrie came to the hotel and spent the night. I instructed her to pack up and ship everything to Canada and for her and the children to go to her parents and stay there until I contacted them. I called Mother and asked her to fly out the next day and help Marrie pack and give her moral support.

They worked hard at packing for the next three days. Mother returned home and Marrie called the movers and had everything packed and shipped, but left a $20,000 grand piano sitting in the living room. She said it was too heavy to move and store. Why she didn't give it to Pam I will never know. She also sold my moose antlers and a wood and brass propeller with twelve-foot blades that came off a flying boat. Ouch! Finally, Marrie managed to load everything else and send off to Canada.

I called a friend in Canada to tell her to come to Buffalo, New York and go to a certain hotel. The next day as I was walking down the busy street I saw Marrie and the family drive by. I jogged alongside until they stopped at a light and I jumped in. They almost jumped out of their skins. When the screaming stopped there was plenty of laughing and crying.

That night we were snug in bed asleep when the phone jarred us awake. Mrs. Rink called and said they made it home safely. I jumped up and said for everyone to get dressed and within ten minutes we were out of that hotel, in a taxi, and on our way out of town. In the next town, we caught a train to New York City and from there a flight to St. Thomas in the American Virgin Islands. Since they are a U.S. protectorate, there is no immigration check going into the islands from the U.S.

We walked out into sweltering heat amongst tough black men haggling over who was next in line. One big Rastafarian won the contest. I asked the price to the Holiday Inn and he said twenty dollars, a rather steep price at the time. I accepted, loaded the suitcases into a mini-van and climbed aboard. We came to a lonely spot on the highway and the driver pulled over and told us to get out. I asked what he meant and he replied that this was as far as he was taking us for twenty dollars and began unloading our luggage beside the road. He wanted another twenty to continue to the hotel. He was a big strong fellow and I had nothing as an equalizer. I had to let it go. We sat beside the road until another minivan came along and took us to our destination. Welcome to St. Thomas!

From the hotel balcony I saw a sturdy double-ended ketch flying a German flag. I went down and introduced myself to Manfred and Evo and after a bit I asked if they were interested in a charter to Brazil. They were most happy to oblige and we struck an agreement of $200 per day for the trip.

Marrie had packed our photographs, dishes, silverware, and keepsakes in twenty boxes, and Mother had them in her possession. I called her on a secret number and had her Federal Express the boxes to Philipsburg, St. Martin in the Dutch West Indies.

We crossed the six-mile channel between the U.S. Virgin Islands and St. Johns, in the British Virgin Islands via a ferry. My only document was David Nettles' birth certificate. Immigration accepted it for a temporary tourist visit. We island-hopped south to Saint Martin where we rented a charming condominium for a pittance and stayed there a month waiting on the boxes and the sailboat to arrive. Rhett had his fourth birthday on the Island and I remember him standing on the balcony feeding the yellow honeyeaters out of his hand while we ate breakfast.

Every night a group of eight or ten steel drums played on the beach below our balcony amongst the derelict boats left by the last hurricane. Flaming cups of oil fastened on bamboo poles stuck in the sand gave the area a romantic glow. As the cacophony reached its crescendo there was nothing to do but go down and join the party of rum drinking merrymakers. Marrie loved it. I enjoyed the people, not the noise.

Evo and Manfred sailed in and we loaded the boxes on their boat. They then sailed for Grenada where we were to meet them as we didn't want to ride the old sailboat when we could fly.

We enjoyed Grenada. It was shortly after Reagan's invasion and the buildings were full of bullet holes along with talk about the battle. The people of Grenada were definitely for kicking the commies out. We were befriended by staff from the newly founded St. George's University, which grew into one of America's large schools of medicine, where Miriam later returned and studied for her medical degree.

From Grenada we rode the hot, damp, claustrophobic sailboat to Trinidad where the police made sure I stayed on board, because I didn't have a passport. Trinidad had been a British colony and was more British than the British. After fueling, and taking on fresh vegetables we attempted sailing through the cut between Trinidad and Venezuela. The current was running against us at six knots and we were going backward with the engine wide open. Evo turned and sailed around the top of the island.

Our first stop was Georgetown, Guyana. As we sailed up the river, *FUCK WHITES* was written in bold white letters on the sides of the dilapidated rusty warehouses. Our reception mirrored the spirit of the welcome signs. It took a customs broker and a fee of five hundred dollars to get a permit to buy fifty gallons of diesel. It was Friday. Evo went into town, when he returned he said the agent wouldn't be in until the next week.

At that moment I cottoned on to Evo stalling every chance he got. We rented rooms at a hotel and waited out the bureaucrats. I told Evo that in the future I would pay him two hundred dollars for the days we traveled and one hundred for the days he stalled in port.

Eventually we got out of Georgetown and headed for Surinam, formerly named Dutch Guyana, where we sailed up the river to Paramaribo, the capital. This was a drastic change from Guyana. We rented a room in a good hotel and ate in an excellent restaurant. Miriam exchanged dollars on the street for sixteen to one, the official rate was one to one. We ordered decadently but the bill was still less than two dollars per person, including drinks. We purchased airline tickets for Marrie, Miriam and Rhett from Cayenne, French Guyana to Macapá, Brazil for less than ten dollars each. I bought cases of Chivas Regal at a price less than fifty cents each. Marrie was able to converse in her mother tongue and it was a delight for me to see her light up as she spoke.

From Paramaribo we sailed against a strong current to Cayenne, French Guyana. We began naming Evo, 'Evil Evo' because he skimped on the food and was disagreeable in every small way. Rhett tied the lines in knots which drove him crazy. I encouraged Rhett to keep playing with the ropes. Miriam took a turn at the wheel and read a book while steering. Evo would slip up and observe the compass, if it was off even a little he grabbed the wheel in a pissed off manner. He had no idea how thin the eggshells he was walking on really were. He was within a whisper of an ass whipping.

The French were purposely relaxed on immigration as many small two-man vessels sailed into the harbor daily to sell Brazilian products and buy rice and whiskey. I slipped off the boat as soon as it touched the dock and went to a hotel. Marrie and the girls waited for the authorities - they didn't come. They jumped ship and joined me. Cayenne was quaint and tropical, yet it had a definite French flavor. Stately Imperial Palms lined the streets and squares. We walked into a restaurant with simple red and white checkered tablecloths and ordered. The food was delicious and the wine was the best France had to offer.

A rather new Brazilian style wooden vessel of perhaps ninety or a hundred feet lay at anchor in the harbor. From a distance I instantly knew the owner had to be a smuggler from Guyana to Brazil and I wanted to meet him. I had someone row me out and I discovered the caretaker on board was a Colombian who was happy to converse in Spanish. He said the vessel was owned by Monsieur Chevalier who was off in the jungle on his gold dredge and should be returning any day in his floatplane. I knew I had found my man and wondered if he had a diamond implanted in his front tooth. I gave the Colombian my name and hotel room number and asked him to have Monsieur Chevalier contact me as soon as he returned.

Early evening there was a knock at the door. I answered and a short blond Frenchman introduced himself as Jackie Chevalier. I invited him in and introduced him to my family. I could see from the glint in his eyes when he spoke to the children that he was more than all right. I poured a glass of wine and got acquainted.

After a short time of talking I said straight out, "Monsieur Chevalier, I do not have a passport and I am in the need of one to get into Brazil."

"That should not be any problem at all if you have a thousand dollars with which to buy one."

"I have the thousand dollars; how long will it take?"

"My friend is a fisherman who was in a serious knife fight, he will be out of commission for at least three months and I am sure he will sell his. I'll ask him tonight."

"Very good, take the thousand dollars now to help things along."

"There is no need for it, but my friend is broke and perhaps this will lift his spirits."

Jackie was gone no more than a half-hour and returned with a French passport in the name of Simon Bouvier, born in Strasbourg France with three years remaining until expiration. Jackie asked if I had a passport photo and I pulled one out that I had for just such an occasion. He took an X-Acto knife and cut Bouvier's photo out of the rivets, taped that photo over mine, took a straight pin, cut it off blunt and started tapping it with a small hammer in the old punched holes on the photographs. Within several minutes he had the holes on mine that lined up exactly with the rest of the page when my photo was glued in place.

Over another glass or two of good wine we discussed the possibilities of the caiman hide business. Jackie was interested and looking for work for his boat he built in Belém, Brazil. He said he spoke Portuguese fluently which would be a huge asset. He left giving us an invitation to come to his house the following afternoon for dinner.

The next morning I sent Evo and Manfred sailing to Belém Brazil, a city near the mouth of the Amazon River. Thank God that was over.

Jackie's house was located down a two-rutted trail some distance from town in thick jungle that came right up to the edge of his yard. The house was over two hundred years old and thought by the locals to be haunted. As we entered I saw the strangest sight. Lying in a basket by the door was a Springer Spaniel with a bed of puppies and one baby ginger kitten sucking with them. It was a contrast of expectation.

Jackie introduced us to his wife Catherine, a lovely woman who spoke very little English. We later learned she was a pediatrician. Catherine served chilled Rose wine and Jackie prepared a dish of chicken cooked in coconut milk, lemongrass and chilies. After a delicious meal we visited his friends, Jean and Monique who lived in a lovely cottage on the edge of a lake and both spoke English flawlessly. Jean was a surgeon who had lost his right thumb in an accident leaving him unable to operate. Surgeons removed his big toe and sewed it on his hand to replace the thumb. It worked perfectly and was hardly noticeable. Jean joked and said, "Shake my toe."

We took to one another in a warm special way. He loved the children and they crawled all over him. We visited Devil's Island, the prison made famous by prisoner Henri Charriere. His book, 'Papillion', was made into a great movie, starring Dustin Hoffman and Steve McQueen.

One day we loaded up in his jeep and drove to the border of Surinam to see the giant leatherback turtles. As there were no other facilities we rented a small white cabin half grown over in vines in the abandoned leper colony. For dinner we were given three choices - snake, caiman (the South American crocodile) or 'pac', a giant anteater which grows to eighty pounds. I choose the latter and enjoyed it. French wines accompanied our meal keeping our minds less focused on the meat entrees.

After dinner we walked to the beach and waited for the half-moon to rise. As the moon was rising the giant turtles began arriving. Perhaps they swam in underwater since I didn't notice them until they appeared in the surf as they slowly made their way to higher ground. It was amazing to watch them carving and scooping a smooth hole four feet deep and twelve inches in diameter with their flippers, throwing sand as if using a shovel. When the hole was satisfactory she backed up to it and began laying eggs. We counted over two hundred white pliable wet eggs drop from one turtle. Native men with burlap sacks were robbing most of the eggs, leaving only a few. We were saddened and disgusted. I understand rangers have been placed on the beach now, protecting the somewhere between fifty and one-hundred of the twelve-hundred-pound giants who came in to lay their eggs. As they made their way back to the water I lifted Miriam and Rhett onto their backs for a short ride. These gentle giants would remain at sea for another year eating only jellyfish before returning to the same beach and laying another batch of eggs. We left that beautiful sight a little sad and returned to our bungalow. We hoped there would be enough eggs left to keep Mother Nature's gift coming back each year.

"Oh No! " Marrie shouted as she opened the door to our cabin. I quickly pushed around her to see what she was all about and saw that the room was full of mosquitoes. We had left the light on and a window open. The jungle must have been emptied of mosquitoes that night. I dampened a bath towel and began flapping it against the walls and ceiling. In a half-hour I had them reduced so that Marrie and the children could come in. They were exhausted and went to sleep while I stood watch the remainder of the night killing strays as they landed on their faces.

The next morning at the crack of dawn and after driving a few miles, Jean stopped the jeep while a black Jaguar crossed the road. They look bigger in the wild than in a zoo. An unexpected sight. We stopped for lunch at a waterfall on a jungle river, spread a blanket and had a picnic. As we came by the European Space Agency facility at Kourawe we observed a satellite launch. It was a spectacular sight but the view was cut short by cloud cover. We returned to our hotel late in the afternoon tired, having spent one of the most memorable twenty-four hours of our lives.

While Evo was making his way to Belém we had to push on, so we said goodbye to our new friends. Marrie and the children went to the airport and caught a Surinam Airline flight to Macapá, a small city on the northeast coast of Brazil. I chartered a bush pilot to take me to Saint-George on the border with French Guyana and Brazil. On the way the pilot flew low trying to scare me. Shades of the old crop duster's tricks I experienced on my first flight. I just smiled and kept quiet. We landed and I caught a ride to the river where several launches were waiting for a fare. I got in a dugout, the native fired up the outboard and we skimmed along the black waters of the Ouapock River until we came to the Brazilian border town by the same name.

I was nervous as I climbed the wet clay embankment to the immigration and customs shack, wondering if the agent spoke French. I said, "Good afternoon" in as cheery a voice as I could manage and handed him the dodgy passport with twenty dollars folded between the first and second pages.

He asked, "Have you ever been to Brazil before?"

"No Señor.

"He opened the passport to the page where I had placed the twenty-dollar bill, held it up between two fingers as if it was dirty and handed it to me. Oh shit, it isn't what I expected! He leafed through the passport and stopped on a page over near the back with an entry stamp into Brazil, laid the passport down and said, "Please explain how you have this stamp from Brazil since you have never been here."

"Oh, pardon me, I forgot about that time."

He looked at me hard for a full minute before picking up the stamp and marking the passport.

The next plane was scheduled to arrive in four days. I had to wait because it took a week to get out by road. I checked in at the only hotel. The partitions between the rooms were only partway to the ceiling. That evening a couple checked into the room next door. Around nine the squeaking started and it didn't stop. It was a slow deep grind and I was curious as to how anyone could screw for so long. I stacked my chairs on top of one another, crawled up and looked over the divider. The man was sleeping in a hammock with one foot on the floor rocking forwards and backward.

A poor deaf boy and girl of about twelve and thirteen hung around the hotel, the lady proprietor was exceptionally nice to them. In sign language, I spelled out hello and a few other words I had learned in Portuguese, their little faces lit up. The two of them took me everywhere in their realm. One afternoon we went upriver in a dugout, ran the rapids and stopped off at an Indian village. On the way back I stopped at the store and bought them each a bicycle, I have never seen happier faces.

A plane did come and several military men boarded. I offered to pay any amount to get on, but they brushed me off like I was dirt. Undoubtedly they were making too much money robbing timber and other natural resources to look at my thousand dollars. The DC-3 finally came and I flew to Macapá where I met a miserable, unhappy Marrie. The place was hot, humid and muddy with little to offer.

We boarded a flight to Belém that evening and our dear friend Steve met us at the airport. We took two rooms at the Hilton for eighty dollars a day each. Jackie flew down and rented a room next door above a coffee shop for eight dollars a day and I preferred his room to ours. Jackie introduced us to his friend Claude who had twice been before a firing squad and both times the troops refused to shoot him. It was over problems caused by the Secret Army Organization which took over Algeria and threatened Paris. He eventually escaped and made his way to Brazil where he owned a discothèque.

Caiman hunting was illegal and out of the question for the next six months as the rainy season was beginning. They are only hunted when the water dries up which forces them to congregate in water holes and small streams.

Evo and Manfred had been waiting in Belem for some days. Steve had met them, but had no idea our things were onboard. He laughed and told me that Evo had been paying prostitutes with hundred-dollar bottles of Chivas when he could have paid with three dollars. I unloaded our belongings and there was no Chivas.

"Evo, where is the Chivas?" I asked.

"The Chivas is mine!"

"Did you fall on your head on the trip down?"

"I bought the Chivas."

"Evo, you are lying. I bought twelve cases, and you have been giving it to the whores. Bring it out and we will count every bottle and for everyone missing I am subtracting one hundred dollars."

"A hundred dollars, you paid six dollars in Paramaribo."

"That is correct and you also know that I advised you to buy some at that exchange rate."

"I will not pay a hundred dollars, I will pay six."

"Evo, you have been an asshole ever since I met you, now if you don't get the cases on deck I am going to beat hell out of you and get them myself."

Evo brought the cases out of the hole and I subtracted a hundred dollars for each missing bottle.

Belém definitely was not the home I was looking for so we bought tickets to Rio de Janeiro. The flight departed after midnight in rough weather. A distinguished-looking gentleman sitting in the seat to my right was so frightened that he gripped the armrest with all his might and then he grabbed me! Whenever the turbulence had subsided he apologized profusely and began talking. He told me he had concessions on hundreds of square miles of jungle on which to harvest hearts of palm which he canned and shipped worldwide. I always enjoyed hearing about the lives of others, especially if they were in business.

Dawn was turning the sky a swirling pink as the 727 descended into Rio de Janeiro. The city was lit up like a sparkler with Ipanema and Sugar Loaf Mountain for a backdrop. We did Rio for a month, staying in the famous old Oro Verde Hotel on the Beach

The first words of caution people told us was not to wear jewelry and carry only a small amount of money when going out as it was a matter of when we would be robbed. Policemen in shorts and T-shirts holding a German Shephard on a short leash were posted every hundred yards along the beach. A busload of German tourists were stopped in route from the airport and the passengers were stripped clean of their money, jewelry and luggage.

We met an English couple who invited us out and gave us some tips. The man warned Marrie to take off her earrings which she did and put them in the bib pocket of her jumpsuit. We stopped in a busy English pub where the man bought a round of drinks and then took us to a fine restaurant. After a dinner with wine and cognac, our new friend happened to discover that he didn't have any cash on him, so naturally, I paid. As we were ready to leave Marrie reached into her pockets to put on her earrings, but they were gone. Her pocket had been buttoned the whole time and then it occurred to her that when she used the restroom in the pub she had unfastened the bib and the top folded upside down. We rushed back to the pub and Marrie ran into the busy toilet that had been used by many customers during the past two hours. She searched frantically on the floor; went through the wastebasket, but found nothing. As she was searching she realized she had used another restroom which was less frequently used. She immediately went to the spot and began searching. The woman with her suggested she put her hand down the toilet and up into the trap. Marrie reluctantly did so. She felt around, deep down in the trap and her hand touched one of the earrings. She pulled it out and again the second time she dug deeper she found the other. As she was rejoicing she casually mentioned the value of the diamonds. The man asked to see them and she handed them to him. He took a look and put them in his pocket. I asked him to give them back to Marrie and he said he would just hold them for safekeeping. I stopped him and told him to hand them over. He demanded a three-thousand dollar reward for his woman suggesting to Marrie to put her hand in the toilet. The façade was over and I had no further need to be polite. Needless to say, Marrie got her earrings back quickly and we returned to the hotel having had our first night out in Rio.

Our intention was to rent an apartment on the beach, I discovered they were hard to find. We walked from one end of the beach to the other knocking on every door and asking in my five words of Portuguese if they had an apartment for rent. The answer was invariably the same, "No." We found a woman who knew someone who had an apartment for rent, we got into a taxi and went looking for this person. When we found him, we learned that it was not him, but his cousin who had the apartment. He squeezed into the taxi and set out looking for the cousin. The cousin did not have what we were looking for, it was his friend. Next the cousin's friend squeezed into the taxi and we set out looking for the friend. I was in a happy mood that day and I knew each one would demand a finder's fee of 10% from the owner so I put up with it. We continued until we had to hire a second taxi. Before we found the person who had the apartment both rear bumpers were dragging the pavement.

The apartment was a dusty old place that had not been inhabited for years, however, it was right on Ipanema Beach and the rent was four-thousand dollars a month with a security deposit. This made our suite at the Oro Verde Hotel look like a palace so we remained there for our stay in Rio.

Rio has a reputation for thievery and it kept living up to it. Miriam was eleven years old and often caught the bus in front of the Hotel. One morning three young men stepped onto the bus and positioned themselves around her. One of them pulled out a knife and motioned for her to hand over her money. She was also wearing an engraved gold bracelet she had received as a gift when she was four years old. It no longer slipped over her hand and the cowardly bandits cut it off, bruising her arm in the process. The passengers were frozen as they looked on, afraid to intervene. The bus stopped, the brutes leisurely stepped off and stood on the curb counting the loot. An older woman rushed over and hugged Miriam trying to comfort her in a language she did not understand.

I said, "Sweetheart it's time to move on! I have enjoyed about as much of Rio as I can stand."

We shopped for a vehicle in which to explore Brazil and found a new Ford pickup with four doors, a short bed, a winch and a good air conditioner. We had the back seat taken out and had one that converted into a bed installed in its place. We went to a camper dealership and bought a strong fiberglass shell to cover the cargo area and loaded thirteen suitcases, pillows, blankets, books, games and children, then set out on a serious quest for a home in Brazil.

'Buzios' is the African word for the cowrie shells. A village by that name is located on the coast two or three hours' drive north of Rio. We stopped there with every intention of staying a month, having heard it was the up and coming hot spot for the rich and famous and many opportunities for building luxury homes. The red clay road going in was washed out with knee-deep ditches zigzagging from side to side. Our hotel rooms were adequate and colorful with a balcony overlooking the inlet. Around midnight it started pouring down rain. The roof only directed the flow to certain areas of the rooms. Help came running with buckets, bowls and cans trying to catch the water. They might as well have been trying to catch the wind. Their scurrying about and hard work was all in vain, everything got drenched. There were no other dry rooms available, so the next morning we loaded up and headed north, a decision I later regretted. Buzios bloomed and blossomed, becoming one of the hottest places to live or visit in South America.

Ilheus is Brazil's oldest Portuguese city, renowned as the cocoa capital of the world. In Rio, we met a young man who invited us to his plantation of cocoa and ginger near Ilheus. We celebrated Marrie's 42nd birthday on the farm.

Salvador was a colorful city, mostly inhabited by people of African descent. We enjoyed our stay at the Quadro Rhodas Hotel a few miles north of the town. The food was superb and in the center of the grounds was a natural sinkhole filled with goldfish that ate out of the children's hands. Of particular interest to us were the old churches. As you walked in the first thing you saw were thousands of plaster images of body parts hanging from the ceiling, mostly arms and legs. The Catholic religion had somehow mingled and merged with the African Candomble religion and they believed if you took a plaster impression of the diseased part of the body and the priest blessed it and hung it in the church, you would be healed. For two dollars a priest tied a narrow fabric bracelet around your wrist, blessed it and advised you not to take it off until it fell off on its own accord if you wanted to have good luck. Miriam bought one.

Every two weeks I called Marcus and asked him to help collect the three million Ochoa owed. I sent Jackie to Medellin. Marcus met him at the airport and told him they would put a bullet in his skin if he went around there asking for money. My brother Larry went down and received a similar reception from Marcus. At last, he had good news; he said Ochoa had given him six-hundred thousand dollars as partial payments and for me to call back in ten days. I called back on the scheduled day and he was rejoicing and said our problems were over; Barry Seal had been killed. Even though I had expected this, I was so very sad. I felt a terrible loss. Tears welled up in my eyes for the loss of my old friend. Yet, another part of me was happy that the snitch and star witness against me and others was dead. I would not be tried and receive a life sentence for the ten-ton cocaine indictment in Florida.

A federal judge in Louisiana double-crossed the DEA and ordered Barry to do six months in a halfway house from which he went to work every morning and returned at six in the evening. This was 'sprung' on Barry's lawyers at the last moment and was regarded as completely unnecessary. The judge would not allow him to have any arms, bodyguards, or protection. This was effectively a death sentence. Some say it was a complete 'set up' to facilitate his murder. When Barry drove into the parking lot, the ugly man who flew in the back seat of my plane on the first cocaine trip, along with three other Colombians, emptied 'silenced' Mac 10's into Barry. He put his hands over his ears as if to try to block the sound of the gunfire. I heard he had bullet holes through his hands where rounds had passed before entering his body.

After the long bursts of automatic gunfire ceased, Barry was slumped across the steering wheel with a dozen bullet holes in his body. There were rumors Colonel Oliver North of Iran/Contra fame was in on the hit himself. Barry was notorious for protecting his position with dirt on potential adversaries and it was said he had footage of Jeb and George W. Bush with two kilos of cocaine on a plane. He kept a pile of material in the boot of his car. Police swarmed all over that as well as the private papers in his home.

There was also the inside knowledge Barry had on the whole guns for drugs affair out of Nicaragua. Barry was as hot as hell! His lawyer at the time - Ungglesby - claimed Barry had given him a phone number to call to prove just how deep things got. His lawyer rang it and a secretary answered. A Navy Admiral came to the phone and said, "Barry! Where you been!" Barry's lawyer answered, "This is Barry Seal's lawyer." The phone was hung up. It was the office of Vice President George Bush SNR. No wonder Barry wasn't worried about landing at Mena.

Barry had taunted so many in law enforcement in Louisiana over the years they say there was a lineup of local police at the crime scene who wanted to make sure he was dead. Some were convinced it was just a scam by Barry and the DEA to disappear him into a witness protection program. They found different.

Marta Ochoa, the pretend nurse who kept records, and her son was found garroted and wrapped in plastic at the bottom of a Miami canal. Lito did twenty years in federal prison. Ache returned to Medellin where he became an addict. Marcus and Esmeralda bought a coffee plantation near Cali. Pablo Escobar was instrumental in blowing up the Palace of Justice in Bogotá and was eventually hunted and killed by Colombian authorities. The communist Sandinista government in Nicaragua fell along with Oliver North and his cronies. The president of the Turks and Caicos Islands went to federal prison on money laundering charges. I was indicted on charges of importing ten tons of cocaine into the United States. Barry Seal caused all the above and much, much, more. A complete account of Barry's shenanigans and assassination are documented in the book, "The Kings of Cocaine." I am also mentioned in the book. Dennis Hopper played Barry's part in the film "Double-crossed." Former CBS producer Daniel Hopsicker lived with Barry's wife for a time after his assassination and produced the very interesting book "Barry and the Boys". Hopsicker writes Barry was involved in the deepest levels of the American Intelligence community from a very early age and documents many of his claims.

I returned to the Quadro Rhodas and told Marrie the news about Barry and she and Miriam cried. Despite all that Barry had done he was a kind and gentle man at heart. I never heard him raise his voice and never heard him threaten to hurt a soul. May he rest in peace.

The police caught all four of Barry's assassins within hours and they are now serving life sentences in Louisiana. Some say the police investigating Barry's death knew where to look for them from the get-go.

The six-hundred-thousand-dollar payment evaporated with Barry's death.

We traveled on up the coast looking for a home, stopping off in Recife, Natal and Fortaleza, Brazil. We enjoyed the north coast and spent some time investigating the possibilities of buying a cashew estate. The area was dry, the estates large, the business very profitable and the land owned by just a few families. Every part of the nut was used, even the hull which is used in brake pads so they will cool down faster.

A drought had plagued the northeast for several years and over a million perished. The drought was over when we arrived, but we could still see the signs of it in the extended stomachs and red hair of the children. One day we were eating on the porch of a restaurant in a little country village and noticed five or six children standing barefoot in the dirt road holding dented pots and pans. I asked the waiter about them and he said they were waiting for our scraps when we finished our meal. This broke my heart. I could barely eat my lunch. I walked over to them and gave them money to go to the grocery store although a couple stayed back waiting on our scraps.

Sahara Desert looking sand dunes rose to heights of over five- hundred feet along the beach near Fortaleza where we spent a memorable day sand skiing.

At the Hotel in Fortaleza, we met Alexander and Fernanda Sadi from Sao Paulo. Alexander was a lawyer and they both spoke English. He was playing the stock market and quite excited about Massey Ferguson Tractor stock. This sounded good to me and he invited us to rent his parents' beach home on Guaruja, located on the coast just an hour's drive from Sao Paulo.

It was a very long drive from Fortaleza on the north coast to Guaruja in the south. Miriam lay on the pull out bed and read "Gone with the Wind," and sobbed at the end.

We rented the house for six-hundred dollars a month on the condition that we leave for the month of December. I invested a hundred-thousand dollars in the stock market and it soon doubled. Fernanda's mother had a bikini store in the mall and I invested a hundred thousand dollars in a factory for swimwear. We named the enterprise Nandella. The most interesting part of the work was making the expensive brochure with the Brazilian models strutting around in the swimwear. We sent a hundred thousand suits to the US. They didn't sell. The venture was a flop and we ended up storing thousands of bathing suits until the buckles rusted off.

Miriam turned twelve in August and I wanted her to continue her education. We hired the mayor's daughter as a tutor for the Portuguese language. She spent the morning at the mayor's house and the afternoon under the lifeguard stand. Within a few months she was fluent in Portuguese. I insisted she read the classics, which she did, completing dozens of them.

The rich children were all scooting around on mopeds and Miriam wanted one. We bought her a pretty blue one which she rode everywhere. Each month the police stopped her and took it. She and I would go over in the pick-up, pay twenty dollars, and bail it out.

Rhett was four years old and Lija, the maid, had a little girl, named Juliana, the same age. I bought them each a bicycle with training wheels and she and Rhett spent all day playing. Within a few months he spoke Portuguese just like the black children he played with.

Alexander's wealthy parents lived in Sao Paulo and he invited us to his mother's birthday party. It was a highbrow affair held in the garden. A string quartet followed the lady, playing classical music. Suddenly shrieks and peels of women's laughter could be heard. I went around the corner to see what was happening and there was little blond blue-eyed Rhett with his foot propped on the fountain entertaining the ladies. They were asking him questions and he was answering in Portuguese. They were wiping their eyes from laughing and said it was hilarious to hear this blue eyed blond boy speak like a 'garoto' which meant he was talking like a street child from the slums.

One night we hired a taxi to take us to the airport in Sao Paulo. The expressway was closed in our direction so we had to take a small winding road up the side of the mountain. Only one side of this multi-billion dollar project was completed. They opened it on a Friday and traffic both ways was split with Saturday for Sao Paulo to Guaruja and on Sunday and Monday it was from Guaruja to Sao Paulo. Unfortunately we chose the wrong day to go up the mountain and had to suffer the winding two-lane road in heavy rain. After a 5,000-foot climb we reached the plateau and the rain stopped and a full moon shone through patchy white clouds. Directly ahead of the car and up 500 or 1000 feet was an ancient Greek style colonnade supporting an entablature under a gabled roof. It was bathed in a dim golden light. The driver stopped, and we got out and had a good look. We stayed for five or ten minutes while several other cars stopped and the inhabitants got out and stretched their necks. The next day there was a small article in the newspaper about people reporting a church in the sky near Sao Paulo.

Every month or so I contacted Jerry Wills in California and one day he asked if I was interested in investing in a ten-ton hashish venture. The hash would come out of Pakistan, go to Mexico via ship and from there to the US via a DC-3. The deal sounded good to me so I wired five-hundred thousand dollars to a bank in Bahrain.

I toured Mato Grosso del Sul, checking out cattle ranches and soybean farms. The soybean business particularly interested me. The land was fertile and all one had to do was harrow the soil, drill in the seed and wait four months to harvest. No fertilizer or insecticide was used and this method produced three crops a year with large yields. The biggest job and expense was combining. The combines cost a hundred-thousand dollars and a 10,000-acre farm required several. When I got rather serious about buying an estate Marrie said, "Roger, if I die in this godforsaken place, promise me you won't bury my bones here."

I said, "Sweetheart, if you feel that dismal about the place we will leave. Why didn't you tell me earlier?"

Jackie was trying to obtain Brazilian passports for which we paid twenty-thousand dollars for the four. He flew down from Belém with all the necessary paraphernalia to take our fingerprints which had to be entered into the government computer. Miriam's prints were rejected twice so he had to fly down each time and redo them. On the third trip I gave him the pickup to sell when he got back to Belém, as the local dealers were only offering half the value. He later reported his friend wrecked it and I never received a dime. As Poor Richard said in the almanac, "If you want something done, go, if not, send."

Luxury buses constantly crisscrossed Brazil and we took advantage of this comfortable mode of transportation. We rode buses all over the country. We went to Asuncion, Paraguay, stopping off first in Curitiba and from there taking a steam train down to the coast for a few days. Next a day excursion to Ciudad Viejo, an outcrop of rocks a hundred feet tall and covering several miles. The wind and water had eroded them into the most interesting shapes. One looked exactly like a Coca Cola bottle, another an elephant, and so on.

Our next stop was Iguaçu Falls, the largest waterfall in the world. We stayed in a lovely old hotel right by the falls. It was out of season and there were few tourists. One evening while dining in a large empty dining room we heard a note from a flute, followed by a choir of angelic voices coming from the adjoining room. We peaked around the divider and saw a room full of young boys. It was a choir of a hundred German boys on a world tour.

We went on to Stroessner City, now Ciudad Del Este where I met with the son and nephew of the president. We had several discussions, some concerning smuggling through Paraguay. I felt uneasy and got out of there and well away from those dangerous men.

In Asuncion, Paraguay we stayed at the Hotel Presidente on the plaza. While I was having breakfast I heard a group of Dutchmen laughing and talking at a table nearby. They looked like a group of interesting fellows so I ran upstairs and told Marrie. By the time she came down they were gone. That afternoon we came in, went to the bar and there was the jovial group. I walked over and introduced Marrie and myself. They invited us to sit at their table and soon Henk had his back to me, mesmerized with Marrie, and nothing could divert his attention. They talked until closing time and I had to pry Marrie away.

Puente del Este, Uruguay was teeming with excitement as boats from the Round the World Whitbread Race were arriving. We stayed there for a week and it had the best possibilities for a home of any place I saw in South America. However, they were extremely expensive. We looked at one with a price tag of five million US. A good steak in a restaurant cost two dollars and the short ride there in a taxi cost ten.

Montevideo was dead with half of its citizens living overseas. From the deserted docks we caught a hydroplane for the hundred-mile trip across the estuary of the Rio Plate, arriving in downtown Buenos Aires in the late afternoon.

We checked into a rich old hotel and I went to change dollars for pesos. It was one of the numerous holidays all Latin Americans celebrate and the exchange was closed. As I walked off a distinguished-looking elderly man asked if I was interested in changing dollars. I answered in the affirmative. He said he needed dollars and would like to exchange his pesos. He asked how much I planned to change. I told him five-hundred dollars would be sufficient and he asked me to step into the foyer of an apartment building nearby. I counted my five one hundred dollar bills and held them in my hand while he counted the equivalent in pesos. Just as he was wrapping the pesos in a rubber band a man came down the stairs and rather roughly told us to leave his premises. The gentleman was unflustered and we walked out and I handed him my money and he handed me his. When I arrived at the hotel I discovered I had less than ten dollars.

We flew on a military plane to Mendoza, a city near the Chilean border. The area was dry, with vineyards hanging in juicy red grapes. I went to rent a car and met the proprietor who was blind. He spoke English and we had a long chat with him, telling me of the auto accident in which his wife was killed and he was blinded. I rented the car at five in the afternoon and took it back to the hotel. The next morning we left early to drive up the mountain to the famous southern hemisphere observatory for a look at Haley's Comet. In route we came to a huge dry lake where a sail car race was taking place. I was amazed at how fast they went. Miriam wanted to drive so I stepped out and watched as she took off doing doughnuts and laughing. We returned the car at four p.m. and the nice blind man charged me for two days. I protested, saying it wasn't right, that we had the car less than 24 hours and he said that was how it was done in Argentina. If you rented it one day and brought it back the next, it was two days' rent. Afterward I was ashamed I had argued.

We spent several days there exploring Bariel, a quaint village high in the mountains above Mendoza. Rhett did very well on a gentle mare called Tostada. As we rode past a large field of unfamiliar vegetation I asked the guide what was growing there. He said it was mint, exported to a chewing gum manufacturer. Several months later we took an excursion in a glass-covered boat on the canals of Amsterdam and met a family from Argentina. I told them we had recently arrived from their country and asked where they were from. They replied, "Bariel." I said we had stayed in the village for several days, he said he owned the mint farm. T'is a small, small world.

Perfectly preserved mummified bodies are found in the crumbling slate hillsides of this area. A boy, sacrificed hundreds of years before was exhibited sitting in a glass box. It looked as though he was alive with the exception of his skull being split open.

We went to a zoo in a town along this trek. In one big corral was a juvenile elephant and he was frisky and friendly. I crawled through the log fence and petted him. He was curious and began exploring my body parts with his trunk. I held him off for a bit, however, he was much too powerful, and soon he pushed me up beside the fence, stuck his wet snout in my shirt and explored under my arms with the end of the trunk nibbling like cold wet lips. I have never in my life been tickled so. I fell on the ground and rolled back under the fence to the laughter of my family, particularly Miriam.

Moreno Glacier is the fastest moving glacier in the world, Lake Argentina with an ice face three miles wide and 150 feet high. It travels at 12 inches a day and regularly calves with cannon-like explosions into Lake Argentina. The glacier would dam up the river and we watched as the river rose a hundred feet on one side and dried up on the other, then water would break through underneath and shoot for hundreds of feet into the air. We stayed there several days waiting on a flight to Ushuaia, the southern-most city in the world.

Ushuaia is located right on the tip of South America, near Cape Horn. It was cold! It snowed one summer day and the snow remained on the ground for the week we were there. In that cold climate apples grow to the size of plums.

Remaining particularly strong in my memory were the hundreds of miles of stark white stumps standing sentinel over the land as reminders of the brutal work convicts did under the lash to clear the trees for sheep farming. We visited a sheep farm that had gone out of the sheep business because wool prices had fallen so drastically, that it wasn't profitable anymore to shear a sheep. I felt sorry for the farmer and his wife who had lived on the farm all their lives and were now trying to make a few dollars from tourists by showing them the shearing sheds and long whaleboats in the barn.

On our journey north we stopped off at Bariloche for a week. While registering at a rustic ski lodge we met several interesting couples in the lobby. I invited them for a drink, ordered Chivas for the men and wine for the ladies. We tossed those back and ordered a couple more rounds. When I went to pay the bill it was over four-hundred US dollars. Naturally I protested and then the bartender explained that a bottle of good Scotch whiskey cost several hundred dollars in Argentina. In comparison, the wine was free.

The Falkland War was recently over and as we drove north along the coast we saw the markings on the highway made by the Argentine Air Force where they had used the highway to refuel jets during the war.

Back in Buenos Aires the movie 'Out of Africa' was showing and the theatre was full. The old black chief told Karen Blixen that no child taller than a mark he made on a post with his machete could go to school. Karin argued the value of children going to school and the old chief replied, "The English have been going to school for a very long time and it hasn't made them any smarter."

Everyone in the theatre stood up, yelled and whistled, stomped and applauded, except us. Eventually I nudged Marrie and we stood up and clapped also.

27. FLEEING IN STYLE

Trip to Amsterdam -- The South of France and A Small Yacht -- Safari

Jackie met us in Buenos Aries with four new Brazilian passports which made me very pleased. I was all for going to Chile and looking for a home and business but Marrie was fed up with South America and wanted to go to Europe. All coach tickets were sold out for several weeks and if we were going it had to be first-class. A KLM flight was departing from Montevideo the next day so we caught the hydroplane across and I shelled out eight-thousand dollars for four first-class tickets. Marrie's eyes sparkled as she boarded and spoke to the crew members in her native language. Everything was so fresh and cool that even I was impressed. Marrie was radiating as the wine was poured and the meat carved by our seats.

Telephoning loved ones is difficult when you are on the ten most wanted list. We landed in Rio for a one-hour layover. Before we left Marrie called her Mom and Dad in Canada. She came out of the telephone booth crying and looking so terribly sad that I thought someone had died. No, the Royal Canadian Mounted Police had been to her parent's house and told them I was a wanted drug smuggler with agencies all over the world looking for me. They asked them to have me turn myself in and Marrie's parents wanted the children to come and live with them. A few years back I had bought them a new Buick for Marrie's Dad's seventieth birthday. Now they wanted to give it back. It was tainted with drug money. Marrie was devastated. This news spoiled her joy for days to come.

With the flight being so long and arriving in Amsterdam early in the morning the airline gave us luxurious complimentary rooms in the Krasnapolsky Hotel on Dam Square, downtown Amsterdam. Marrie was happy to be out of the squalor of South America and in the country of her birth.

The young man who serviced the minibars every morning knocked on the door and would immediately walk in. I told him to wait until he was invited in before he opened the door again. Marya and Miriam also complained about him walking in on them. The next morning while I was in the shower I heard Marrie gasp and speak harshly to this man. He caught her partially dressed. I quickly jumped out of the shower, wet and naked and attacked him. He ran backward out the door and down the hall with me in hot pursuit. After a few steps I stopped and ran back to the room where the door had closed of its own accord. I knocked and Marrie asked in a sweet voice, "Who's there?"

"Marrie, open the damn door, I'm standing out here naked!"

"What do you want sir?" She continued to mock. She let me stand there dripping for a couple of minutes before opening the door, giggling hysterically at my naked run down the hall.

The following afternoon I went to the hotel barbershop for a haircut. The lady barber was chatty and asked where I was from. I told her I was from California, she said, "Oh, this gentleman waiting is also from California. May I introduce you to Mr. Floyd McClung, a missionary in Amsterdam. This perked up my interest and we began talking. I waited for him to have his haircut and we went for a coffee. I introduced him to Marrie and invited him to dinner the next evening at the Black Sheep Restaurant on the 'Leidseplein'. It was a lovely evening. He told us about his mission work in the red light district of Amsterdam and his ministry to drug addicts and prostitutes. I had a strong urge to confide in him and confess my predicament as a fugitive searching for a home, but decided against it. He had a daughter the same age as Miriam, the two became friends and Miriam spent the night in their home a couple of times. They lived on the top floor of the old Seaman's Mission where the blue sign on the roof '*GOD LOVES YOU*' can be seen for miles by ships entering the harbor.

Around the corner from the hotel and in the cellar of one of the old houses leaning on one another was a wine bodega. As you walked down the stairs the first thing you saw was a huge bouquet of at least a hundred long-stemmed red roses. Every afternoon it was filled with lusty Dutch folks, laughing and drinking wine. Over in one corner was a fireplace and one could order delicious steak dinners served on plates in wicker holders. You had to eat while holding your plate on your knees or on small coffee tables. Marrie and I went there most every evening and one night in walked Henk from Asuncion, Paraguay. He said, "Hello Roger," took Marrie's hand in both of his and turned his back on me. I laughed, winked at Marrie and went to look for someone to talk to.

We looked at houses all around southern Holland and found one near Den Hague that was suitable. However, it rained constantly that summer discouraging us from buying there.

The South of France was calling us out of the flood so we loaded our thirteen cases onto the train and headed in that direction. One night at the George V in Paris was enough for me and the next morning we boarded a fast train to the coast. It stopped in Toulon and we were told we had to catch a different train to Nice. After some inquiries, we found that the next train departed in three hours from quay 17 and we were on quay 1. A broad well-lit tunnel went underneath the tracks with stairs going up to each quay. I took two suitcases while Miriam and Rhett took one small bag each and Marrie stayed with the remaining bags. We went downstairs and walked quite a ways until we came to the very last track and we walked up the stairs to quay 17. I left the children guarding the baggage while I went back for more. After several trips Miriam said, "Daddy, there is a man that comes after you leave and plays with himself in Rhett's face. Rhett tries to turn his head, but the man holds him by the top of his head and turns his face around and goes psss, psss with his mouth."

My eyes went wide, "Sugar, can you point out this man?"

"Yes, he has olive skin, about thirty years old, tall and wearing a jean jacket with a white wool collar."

"Come on children, we'll go to your Mother."

We went back to Marrie and left Rhett with her. I gave her a brief explanation about what had happened and as we started to leave she grabbed me by the lapels of my coat and said, "Do not kill him Roger!"

As Miriam and I were walking past the ticket office the target appeared walking nonchalantly toward us. Miriam whispered out of the side of her mouth, "That's him Daddy."

"Are you absolutely sure?"

"I'm sure!"

Beside us was a pile of lumber. I pulled out a short 2 by 4 and I heard Marrie whisper in my mind, "Be careful, make sure you don't kill him, remember you are wanted all over the world. You can't afford to go to a police station."

Peasants were sitting on the long wooden benches with their parcels as I ran up behind the pedophile and went psss, psss. As he turned I hit him alongside the ear with the timber, knocking him off the quay and onto the tracks. He stumbled and fell, then staggered up on rubbery legs and ran down the track. I threw the 2 by 4 between his legs bringing him down. He jumped up and ran and I went after him. As he rounded the corner I was a step behind. He slipped in his pointed shoes and curled into a cowardly fetal position. I kicked him in the groin repeatedly until a half-dozen American Navy men in whites pulled me off with, "Woah, woah, take it easy man!" I told them what the perpetrator had done and they let me know they were sorry they had interfered. I returned to the platform and it was buzzing. When Marrie explained to the crowd what had happened there was approval and congratulations.

Cannes film festival was in full swing when we stepped down from the train. We booked rooms at the Carlton Hotel for the price of thirty-thousand dollars a month with 'petit dejeuner' included. Both Rhett and Miriam learned to sign for room service. I could tell they enjoyed themselves by the number of seven-dollar scoops of ice cream and five-dollar cokes they ordered. We rented a car and took day trips to Saint-Tropez, Monaco, and Antibes, stopping for long leisurely lunches.

81ft aluminum ketch "Amazon." I paid $1 million in cash in 1986.
Image courtesy Jean Pierre Bazard - 9 June 2012 France - Wikipedia

Away from the coast I was sick with allergies and asthma, but on the water I was fine. I decided to try and find a sailboat to live on and do the Mediterranean for a year from where we would gradually sail into the Indian Ocean. I was walking along the pier in Antibes harbor when a vessel caught my eye. A woman was working on deck and I mentioned that the boat looked nice and asked if it was for sale. She said that indeed it was and invited me aboard. It was grand, inside and out!

The woman's name was Annie. She said 'Chantiers Navel de Biot' built the yacht and that she and her husband had sailed it to the Miami boat show and recently returned. The vessel was an 81-foot aluminum Ketch and she said they often reached speeds of 20 knots on the crossings. The price was firm at one million US dollars. We got in her car and drove to the village of Biot where the boatyard was located. I met the owner of the yard, a Monsieur Puglaise, his wife, and secretary. Puglaise brushed Annie aside and offered me a drink. Later he took me back to the boat and together we went over it thoroughly. She was named

'Amazon' and owned by Señor Bobo from Milan, Italy. Señor Bobo would not consider an offer of less than one million as he had that much in it. I offered full price on the condition that he take the money in three payments of three hundred and thirty-three thousand dollars each over a two-year period, without interest. The offer was accepted and a sea trial scheduled for the next afternoon.

With 25-knot winds she reached speeds of 20 knots. She was too tender for my liking and I wanted lead added to the keel before I would buy her. Puglaise trucked her back to his yard and added three tons of lead to the bottom of the keel in a torpedo-shaped tube. She handled better. We commissioned her with cases of choice wines from the local caves and bought a small truckload of food, enough to last the family for a year or more.

Señor Bobo required a million-dollar worldwide insurance policy that cost seven thousand dollars a month. However, if I stayed in the Med. with Annie and her husband John on board, I could use the shipyard's insurance. The difference more than paid the wages of the two people who were most familiar with the yacht and I presumed it would be a good idea to have them aboard until I was familiar with all aspects of this particular sailboat. The morning we were to sail to nearby islands, John Paul asked me in broken English if I had insurance? I explained that I was using the shipyard's policy, he told me very emphatically that I should go across the street to the insurance broker and put the insurance in my name. I told him it wasn't necessary as we were going to spend time in the local waters before venturing out.

July 14, 1986. Marrie, Marya, Miriam, Rhett, Jackie, and his wife Kathryn from French Guyana, Annie, and John Paul, along with ten other people were on board for a day sail to the Islands. It was a glorious day and soon we were slicing through the whitecaps at 20 knots. After a good sail we turned about, tacked a few times, brought down the sails and started the engine in order to go back. I smelled smoke and went to investigate. John Paul said it was just the new paint on the engines causing the smell, it would wear off, nothing to worry about. After a while smoke started coming up the companionway and I shut the engines off, went below and began tearing food out of cupboards trying to locate the fire. I made a hole to the exhaust and emptied several fire extinguishers but the fire grew hotter with noxious black smoke boiling out. We were only three minutes from the harbor and I tried to go in but was prevented by the water police.

Kathryn had recently had an appendectomy and was sleeping in the forward cabin. I tied a rope around my waist and had everyone hold onto the other end while I went forward and brought her out. Then I thought of our precious photographs, passports, and a hundred thousand dollars in cash, so back down

I went. These items were in the rear cabin and the smoke wasn't as bad there and I handed up clothes through a hatch. Armful after armful went on deck until I had retrieved all the clothes and shoes. I came on deck and saw everyone handing things to a multitude of boats. I saw my new air compressor and diving equipment, which cost over ten thousand dollars, and then a fortune in fishing reels and gear go into unknown hands. I put a stop to this, had everyone get off, lowered our dinghy in the water, and threw the clothes in the dinghy. The drain plug was out, and it filled with saltwater soaking the clothes and shoes.

Black smoke was billowing. People were frantic and yelling for me to get off. They were afraid the fuel tanks would explode.

I remember Miriam asking very calmly, "Will the fuel tanks blow Daddy?"

I said, "No honey, it's diesel, the tanks are below the water line and they are full. She may burn to the waterline, but the tanks won't blow, so don't you worry about me."

Unfortunately, the date was July 14, and the French were celebrating *Bastille Day, all* of France was on vacation. It took three hours for the fire department to obtain permission from Paris to come to the rescue. The fire was a difficult task for the local fireboat and it was several hours before they had it completely extinguished and towed to the dock. The main salon was gutted with severe smoke damage to the rest of the vessel. I could clearly see that the fire started at the exhaust collector box and melted the plastic pipes which caught fire and spread upwards. Afterward I learned that Puglaise and Bobo promised John Paul and Anne 10% if they sold the boat. They reneged on the deal and John Paul removed the insulation from around the exhaust collector and turned the fans on.

As soon as we got ashore, we put the wet clothes and shoes in plastic bags and took them to be cleaned. The owner assured me they would be ready in three days. Every hotel room in the area was booked. The only available rooms were in a whore house above the harbor and we felt lucky to find them. The ladies of the night were most kind and gave us soap to wash the soot off our bodies as there was nothing in the rooms but a bed and towel. On day three I went for the clothes and the place was closed. White paint covered the inside of the windows. A neighbor said the man had gone out of business. Through a crack I could see our clothes in plastic garbage bags in the exact spot where I left them. I got the door open somehow and found the clothes mildewed and ruined. We were sick at heart at the loss of so many personal items.

Twenty-five thousand dollars purchased a first-class safari on the Serengeti Plains of Kenya. Marya was engaged to Michael Simpson at the time and we invited him to come along. In Nairobi we bought safari clothes for a tenth of the price it cost in France. We all got outfitted and Rhett was darling in his khaki safari clothes and hat. For two weeks we visited camps on the Serengeti and saw a goodly number of the three million beasts that roam the plains. We saw so many that we tired of watching lions kill wildebeest. We saw elephants, zebras, giraffes and even a mother leopard and her two cubs napping in a tree. At one camp they fed crocodiles every evening at dusk. We could see the crocs moving slowly up and down the river, crawl out onto the bank, and up to the feeding area where a knee-high brick barricade separated the spectators from the tooth filled beast. Whole, deboned goat carcasses were thrown over and the biggest crocs got them. A 20-foot monster, 4 feet across the back had first choice. He took the whole carcass in his mouth and the rib bones reached around and poked him in the eyes as he crunched.

Ostrich roamed through the dining room and grounds of Buffalo Camp in East Kenya. One morning at breakfast Rhett was sitting on Michael's shoulders offering an ostrich a sausage. For some reason the bird refused the sausage and grabbed Michael by the right ear and wouldn't let go. Michael was bent over trying to getaway. Rhett was yelling bloody murder and I fell down laughing. I laughed so hard my ribs crossed.

Michael was a real sweetheart, however, a bit lazy. Each morning we were awakened at five o'clock, had coffee, and prepared to see the animals at first light when they were most active. Most mornings, Michael refused to get up, but Rhett would bother him until he dragged himself out and climbed in the van without coffee or washing his face. He and Marya broke off the engagement soon thereafter and Marya says that if we had not invited him on safari she would now be Mrs. Simpson.

A week in Mombasa held little interest for us. People were dying from a rare strain of malaria. We cut our trip short and caught the steam train back to Nairobi.

When we returned to France the Amazon was back in the shipyard and the insurance company had paid the yard two-hundred thousand dollars to begin work. Puglaise's wife was openly hostile and he was little better. I asked where the food and wine was. He said a truck hauled that rubbish to the dump. At that moment I knew I had been had. My only hope of getting back the half million I lost in the fire was biding my time and allow him to repair the vessel.

Jean De'zure, the insurance agent and former champion sailboat racer, was kind and helped us find lodgings. We looked at the residence of Pablo Picasso in Mougin, then owned by his widow, but could not come to terms. We looked at other choice properties and ended up renting *Bastide de L'Ibac,* an old sandstone mansion situated on a cliff overlooking the river and a half-mile down a quaint lane from the village of Biot. Every morning I walked to the village bakery where the friendly Madame taught me to count from one to ten in French as I ordered savory pastries, croissants, and bread. A shepherd and his dog were regular visitors, bringing his herd of sheep to graze on the hillside. The tinkling of the bells tied around the sheep's necks was music coming through the open windows. A steep path descended to the river where a hermit lived. This interesting little man grew vegetables, gathered mushrooms, and made goat cheese and we soon became friends, both talking in our own language. Miriam enrolled in Academy Sophia Antipolis and Rhett went to Linc, a private academy in Gulf Juan.

A fawn-colored Jaguar in a showroom in Nice caught my eye one day and I bought it for thirty-five thousand dollars. I learned the license plates cost more than the car. To circumvent this problem I borrowed temporary plates from the dealer, drove to the Kingdom of Andorra and purchased plates for four hundred dollars. The plates were long and red with a gold crown on both ends. People thought I was some kind of royalty.

I studied and passed the exam for my French private pilots' license, rented planes at Cannes Airport and flew regularly into the Alps, landing in remote villages. We would have lunch in the local restaurants and most of these places served scrumptious meals for a pittance.

One day Marrie and I were in a tiny restaurant high up in the mountains. We exchanged greetings in French with a handsome couple about our age at the next table. However, we struggled to make ourselves understood. Struggling on, we even went so far as to exchange morsels of food from our plates but they could not understand one word of English. Suddenly the man began to choke on a piece of meat and ran to the toilet leaving the door open. He slumped down by the commode, gasping for air. I ran over, grabbed him around the middle and squeezed hard and fast and the meat shot out of his mouth. He staggered and inhaled deeply. I returned to the table and ordered a cognac, as our dinner was spoiled. The man returned and said in perfect English, "Thank you, sir, you saved my life. My name is [*I forgot*] and here is my card. If you are ever in Paris, please look me up." Bizarre.

During the winter we drove an hour to the ski resorts which we thoroughly enjoyed. On the way back there was usually bumper to bumper traffic especially on Sunday afternoon. One of us would get out of the car and walk on ahead to the Pizza shack and place an order. By the time we arrived the pizza was hot and ready to go which we ate on the drive home.

The French Riviera grew on us and after a year we began to love it and felt rather at home. Marya was attending the University of Paris and came down often with friends. Miriam was speaking perfect French, had loads of friends and was enjoying school at the Academy Sophia Antipolis. In the afternoons when I drove to 'Gulf Juan' to pick up Rhett from school he would be in a play fight, diving and yelling, "Attaque!" Marrie was painting and attending French-speaking classes. Most days I took long walks into the hills, or down to the river.

One day I said to Marrie, "Let's have our things shipped from Canada, buy a house and set up housekeeping. I can find something to do here as well as anywhere else." Marrie was all for the idea so we made plans to have our belongings shipped over.

28. TWENTY TON LOADS

"Mr. Nice" De-Frocked -- All Over Europe and Spain -- Not Without My Furniture -- The Philippine Connection -- How 'Nice', I Just Lost Ten Million Dollars

Jerry Wills arrived in a private jet with his entourage. Suites were waiting at Hotel Juan-Les-Pins in the village near Antibes. Jerry was then with his Peruvian 'Princess' Ester. Ron Allen was with his German 'Guru' Gertie. 'Flash' was there with his personal physical therapist. He had gone swimming the day after surgery to replace his artificial hip. Subsequently a big hole had developed in his hip where it had become infected.

While on a tour of my 81-foot burned out sailboat the "Amazon ", Jerry told me about Howard Marks. The timing should have been a warning. He said he met an Englishman who had contacts at the top in Pakistan, Thailand, Philippines, England, and the CIA. Marks could have us loaded by the navy of a dozen countries. It sounded too good to be true.

We enjoyed a week of wineries and famous restaurants in the south of France. Jerry checked out of the hotel and the bill was eight thousand, six hundred dollars. They loaded up in the chartered jet for the flight to Mallorca, Spain to see Howard. My daughter Marya flew with them. On the passenger manifest was the name M. Reaves, which was to haunt me, as Interpol thought it was my wife, Marrie Reaves.

Marrie, Miriam, Rhett and I drove to Barcelona from the south of France and took the eight-hour ferry ride across to Mallorca, arriving two days later. We checked into the Palmyra, a sprawling five-star hotel catering to the rich and famous. Jerry arrived with Howard Marks and I cannot explain the disappointment I felt as we were introduced. He gave me a limp handshake. His blue eyes were set to close and darted shiftily about. His demeanor was stooped and subservient and his voice was as patronizingly sweet as a politician's. Oh well, he had loaded Jerry out of Pakistan with ten tons of poor quality hashish and we were there to settle.

Howard invited us to dine at the restaurant of his friend and afterward we visited his wife Judy and their three children in their home. Strong pot and excellent cognac were offered. I drank little and smoked none, I was ready to get down to numbers. The politicking and massaging of egos had gone far enough for my liking and I did a faux pas by saying I was ready to discuss business. I had invested five-hundred thousand dollars to buy a portion of a ten-ton load of hashish. When it arrived, the shit was so full of yak fat it wouldn't stay lit.

Some customers returned it and the price dropped from sixteen hundred dollars a pound to seven hundred. This drop in price made a tremendous difference in what I would receive as the exuberant expenses remained the same. At sixteen hundred a pound we would have made thirty-five million dollars but at the reduced rate we were lucky to get fifteen million. The fault lay directly with Howard Marks. The hashish he presented to entice us into the deal was much different from what we received.

Marks was all pawning and sniveling, claiming that it was not his fault. Malik in Pakistan had bought the best and there was a war going on and it was lost etc. It worked out that I had two million dollars coming for my investment. I had furnished the crew and their pay came out of general expenses. Two million was about a fifth of what I should have received. Howard said that everything was sweet in Pakistan now. The new crop was coming in and Malik could reserve twenty tons of 'first shake' if we put our order in now. Only two million dollars was needed to secure our place. Besides, any one of us could go and stay there to ensure we got *the kind.*

I didn't need the two million dollars cash and it was in the US anyway so I told Jerry and Ron to let all mine ride on the next load. This gave me thirty percent. They were surprised at this, although they knew I had always been a gambler and a child of chance.

Howard was happy. He called his brother in law, Patrick Stuart, in Karachi and told him to expect a wire of one million dollars and to tell Malik to secure twenty tons of the best.

I bought a 120ft King Crabber like the one above to transport 20 tons of hash with Howard Marks ("Mr Nice") and others.
Image courtesy Michael Thebarge - "Cornelia Marie" - Wikipedia

Our vessel, the Axel D, a 120-foot Alaskan king crabber, was waiting in the Maldives not far from Pakistan and we were ready. It had recently come out of a million-dollar overhaul (rip-off) in Darwin, Australia.

My million dollars was wired to Pakistan.

Kobe and Dopey were two supposedly CIA agents in town to see Howard. A lot of 'I spy' was going on and I surmised it was a lot of I spy 'bullshit'.

Howard met us one evening excited. Dopey had told him he received information that the Axel D was in the Maldives and the DEA had a bug on it. For two hundred and fifty thousand dollars he would tell us where to find it. I smelled a rat. Jerry told him a few days earlier where the vessel was located. I said. "We aren't going to give those clowns a dime! I have a collection of transponders, I will fly down, take it off and put it on another ship."

Howard said, "Sorry, I already gave him the money."

"Well you damn-well better not have given him any of my money," I said hotly.

Jerry came to Howard's rescue and tried to smooth things over.

"Listen, nobody gives away over eighty thousand dollars of my money without asking me. It was not as if I was hard to reach. He could have come to the hotel and discussed it with us before handing it over if he did hand it over." I accused.

Howard was indignant. "How can you say such a thing?"

"When I've been screwed I get this unique feeling and I just got it."

Jerry escorted me out of the room and said, "Of course he ripped us off for the money, it's to be expected. Keep your eyes on the big picture. Twenty tons of good hashish will bring us seventy million dollars. Just let it go, please!"

We called the captain, he climbed the smokestack and found the bug glued inside where Howard's associates had placed it.

My instincts were firing again. It felt like a vampire bat had attached itself to my neck and was slowly draining my life force, but I hung around regardless. The promise of a profit rode over my intuition. I placated myself by taking in the beautiful countryside. Mallorca was covered in pink almond blossoms. Lambs skipped in a mosaic of paddocks enclosed in chest-high fences of fieldstones. Gnarled, old olive trees that existed before Christ confirmed the feeling of antiquity. Marrie fell in love with the island and said she would like to move there if we ever left France.

For some unknown reason I wanted one of those fastback Peugeots as a run-about car. They were considerably less expensive in Belgium than in France where they were made, so I caught a flight to Brussels and hired a taxi to take me to an address someone had given me of a dealer. The driver was a Turk who didn't speak English, I just handed him the address. He drove up to a business. However, it didn't look like a place to buy a car, I stepped out to ask. As soon as my feet touched the sidewalk, he peeled out with my briefcase, passports, twenty-five thousand in cash, and a suitcase full of expensive clothes.

Brussels had 3,500 full-time and part-time taxi drivers, I looked at photographs for two days and didn't see anything that resembled the creep. The taxi driver who drove me to the police station befriended me, took me to his home for dinner and supported me throughout the ordeal.

I reported the theft to the Brazilian Embassy since I was using my Brazilian passport. They said it would be two weeks before they would issue another as they had to give the Belgium police a chance to find the original. The Police gave me a paper stating that my passport had been stolen and granting permission to go and come from Belgium. To compound the problem I returned to France for the two weeks and then flew back to Brussels. Unfortunately, the embassy in Paris was bombed the day I arrived and the Belgium police were working overtime. Without a passport, they would not allow me back into the country.

I called my taxi driver friend who came to the airport detention center and visited me. We called the Brazilian Embassy and he spent all day working on the problem. During that long day I saw the police take hundreds of people and lay their hands on a black glass table. After a short delay all of their information lit up on the screen. I was quaking in my boots, afraid they would invite me to do the same. Late in the evening my friend returned with a new, ten-year Brazilian passport. We celebrated by going to dinner in a fine restaurant in Brussels and doing the town.

Ibiza had been on my mind ever since I was there in '76 and I wanted to show Marrie the island. We arrived at the ferry terminal in Barcelona and waited in the long line of cars, but the boat filled before we could embark. The agent was apologetic and gave me a ticket for one of the first places the next day. We went to a second-rate hotel where rooms rented for three-hundred dollars a night. The next morning we arrived rather early and saw a double line of cars a mile long. There was no way to get in. I took my priority paper to the workmen who only shrugged his shoulders. My only chance was to go to the back of the line and wait.

Only one car came in behind me. I was waiting at the counter watching the man give out tickets and it looked as though I would get the last one. The woman behind me was pushing with her large bosom and talking to the agent over my shoulder. We both saw there was only one more spot so she ran over to the glass at another window and began jabbering through the hole in Spanish. He left me, walked over and sold her the ticket.

This infuriated me and I told him that he knew I had a priority ticket and had been waiting a day. He didn't look up or acknowledge me. He was most arrogant as people are who are behind glass or protected in some way. In a few minutes he came out of his booth and started walking across the lobby. I met him and asked if he could put me on. He was a big man, weighing two hundred and fifty pounds and about thirty years old. He gave me a pissed off look, brushed his hands back and forth a few times and walked off. I hit him with a haymaker on the bottom of his listener and he went down like a sack of potatoes. On his way down I gave him a couple more and one connected with his mouth. A tooth stuck through the knuckle on my right hand, putting it out of commission. The family that received the ticket jumped in and two small men grabbed me by the arms. I didn't really struggle as I thought they were just stopping the fight and as far as I was concerned it was over. Then a third ran up and socked me in the mouth and I came undone. The floor was polished marble and slippery. Men were sliding all over. Someone started hitting me hard with something from behind. I looked around and Grandma was swinging her long strapped purse. It must have had a pistol in it or something with similar weight. Miriam ran up, gave her a gigantic shove and said in Spanish, "Leave my Papa in peace." I can still see her sliding across the floor, her dress up around her waist revealing pink knickers, her kicking out with spiked heels for traction reminded me of a turtle on its back.

The police rounded everyone up and took us to the station in the building. The sergeant looked us over and said that since we all had blood on us it looked rather even and he was not going to press charges. My guess is they enjoyed a little excitement now and then.

My hand hurt and as soon as we got out of there I went looking for a doctor. He disinfected the wound and gave me pain killers but the tooth had sunk deep into my knuckle. It throbbed with every heartbeat for a long time.

Ibiza and Mallorca were out, so we headed south to Grenada, Malaga and Seville. Although these places were lovely we didn't feel we wanted to settle. From Spain we drove back through France, Belgium, Holland, Germany and Denmark where we caught a ferry to Oslo, Norway. From Oslo we drove to Bergen where we arranged with a shipping agent to have our Jaguar swung onto the bow of a coastal freighter which we also boarded for a two-week journey to the top of Norway. The freighter carried mail and supplies to the remote colorful towns along the coast that have no other means of transportation.

Accommodation on the vessel was Spartan, but the food was good, yet different. For example, big platters of sardines and herring with boiled potatoes were on the table for breakfast. The Norwegians dug in like it was grits and eggs.

Located at various spots on the ship were primitive glass front slot machines where one could put a coin in the top, where it would then bounce off nails on the way down until it came to the bottom and either disappeared or several came back out. Miriam and Rhett loved it, and it must have given fair odds as they played for long periods without needing more money.

At Ovre Alta, on the northern tip of Norway, we disembarked. It is approximately two hundred miles north of the Arctic Circle in Lapland, the land of the midnight sun.' Reindeer were grazing alongside the road, some pulling sleds loaded with wood. Miriam's birthday was coming up and she wanted to fly to Amsterdam to see a special ballet performance, she and Marrie would wait for us there.

Rhett and I set out on the Ore Highway, an unpaved road that runs the length of Sweden. Rhett liked the Marty Robbins *Gunfighter Ballads* tape and asked me to play *Big Iron* over and over, he then would draw his little pistol and shoot. I noticed that he was gifted with perfect timing in music. If he wanted me to play a certain song, he would click out a rendition with his tongue.

Stockholm was a confusing place. Rain was slashing down. We kept going in circles, returning to a big hotel in the heart of town. I pulled in under the canapé, the porter opened the door, unloaded our bags and drove the car away. We walked in and found the place to be a luxurious hotel indeed. After freshening up in our room, which overlooked the harbor, we went downstairs for cocktails. I ordered a Roy Roger's for Rhett and a Chivas for myself and moved over to sit by a log fire while sipping our drinks. A classy looking casino was located across the foyer and people kept coming and going through the swinging doors giving us glimpses of sparkling chandeliers, gambling tables, and a lot of commotion.

Rhett asked, "Dad, can we go in there?

"No son, they won't let children in casinos."

"That little girl went in." I looked and sure enough, a little girl about five was playing while her parents were at a blackjack table.

We walked to the door and I asked the doorman if we could enter. He answered, "By all means, please come in gentlemen."

"Daddy, are you going to gamble?"

"Yes son, I'll try to win enough for supper at this blackjack table. Wish me luck." I slipped onto a vacant stool and exchanged a hundred dollars for some chips. The woman beside me left and Rhett asked, "Daddy, can I sit on the stool?"

The dealer was a dapper young man who missed nothing, he smiled and said, "Of course the young gentleman may join us."

I helped Rhett onto the high stool and when it was just a guess as to hit or stay, I would ask him and he usually said, "Hit," patted his hand on the table and frequently he was right.

"Dad, can I play?" The dealer answered in the affirmative for me and dealt Rhett a hand. I would tell him to either stay or draw. He was all-important as he held his hand flat out to the dealer and demanded, "Stay!" or "Hit!" Now the chips looked like real gold coins. After a while, his chips were stacked so high that he had trouble seeing over them, Patrons and tourists came over photographing this little blond, blue-eyed boy, holding his cards behind a pile of gold, calling out and making hand signals to either, "Hit!" or "Stay!"

I was broke, Rhett was rich and my stomach was calling me to dinner. It took some talking to get Rhett to join me but his stomach was on my side. I helped him off the stool and gathered up his gold in a bag to take to the cashier for exchange. "No way, Dad, that is my gold and I am going to take it home to Mom," he said. I explained that it was only fake gold and had no value except in this casino. I pleaded with him to allow us to exchange it so we could buy dinner. He went to crying as if I was robbing him. I let him keep his gold and we went to supper. Later that night while he was asleep, I went downstairs and cashed in the gold leaving him several pieces of each kind to take home to Mom.

When Marya finished her first year at the University of Paris, we sent her to Toronto where she met my sister Marijo. They rented two twenty-foot U-Haul trucks and had the furniture loaded, then set out along back roads to Quebec City. They were careful not to be followed and drove for miles along small roads before getting back on another highway. They were positive no one had followed them. The furniture was loaded into a 40-foot container in Quebec City and shipped to Jackie Chevalier in Marseille, France.

Jackie rented a truck and went to the agent in Marseille to receive the goods. The woman at the warehouse acted strangely and this alarmed him. He backed off and returned empty-handed. I called the storage facility in Canada and talked with the owner who told me that indeed there was something unusual concerning the shipment. He said the Royal Canadian Mounted Police had bugged the furniture and the two trucks that hauled it away. He was sorry and would have informed us had there been any way.

Two days later we were packed up, out of France and driving across Spain in a big 24-foot truck with Miriam sitting beside me while Marrie and Rhett followed close behind in the Jaguar. In Barcelona, we boarded the ferry to Mallorca.

We found an old stone house situated on a narrow peninsula on the west end of the island near the village of Andraitx. The house was built in the early nineteen hundreds by an English couple. The walls were made of fieldstones three-foot thick. It had a thick lead roof and few windows. As you entered, you felt a peaceful serene feeling; the feeling one has in a pleasant cave. The story was that the husband died and the widow lived alone in the house. She sold the property to an attorney in Palma, reserving the right to remain there for as long as she lived. The lawyer died and the option passed on to his children. They too all died. The old woman died at the age of a hundred and thirteen and I rented it from a grandchild, a notary in Palma, for five-thousand dollars a month.

Mallorca was lovely, particularly in February and I could never imagine growing tired of it; especially when the ewes lambed and the almond trees were covered in pink blossoms. The port of Andraitx was quaint with colorful fishing boats bobbing on the water below the striped canapés of the outdoor cafes. Marrie and I walked down to the port most every day for lunch and a bottle of wine. We enrolled in Spanish classes, took day trips in our new Jaguar, and saw many interesting places on the island. Some nights we drove to Palma, dined in a fine restaurant, and afterward went out on the town. A favorite place of ours was a former carriage house that had been converted into a bar and dessert spot. Here, classical music played softly, there were large displays of flowers and fruit that could be seen throughout the large room. Candlelight was everywhere casting shadows on the sandstone walls and floors. Rabbits roamed freely, doves cooed. At the stroke of midnight rose petals fell from the ceiling and floated down on the patrons at the sound of the Hallelujah chorus. It was all dreamy and romantic. We lived this wonderful storybook life for one full year.

Howard Marks and his wife Judy invited us for dinner a few times and I enjoyed talking with him. I always enjoyed Judy's company, she was a good woman. One night I mentioned that I was interested in finding a place on the sea, a location where I could safely grow a thousand acres of marijuana annually. If I could grow it with impunity, I would establish a cigarette factory and package a brand of "Roger's Reefers." They would be filtered and packaged like cigarettes in a white pack with a green marijuana leaf on both sides with the notice: "Warning, Roger has determined this product will knock you on your ass."

Of course, Howard knew just the man, one Anthony Moynihan, ex English Lord, a crony of Marcos in the Philippines, owner of the McArthur Hotel in Manila with big plantations of all sorts under his domain. Howard said that he had business in Hong Kong and that on his way home he would stopover in the Philippines and introduce me.

I flew from Rome to Thailand and met Philip Johnson and Kevin Bergstrom. Johnson knew Moynihan and warned me to stay clear of him. Phillip and Kevin looked and conducted themselves as winners. Against Johnson's strong warning I flew to Manila and met Marks at the McArthur Hotel, a rather seedy place. Howard introduced me to Lord Anthony Moynihan, a big-bellied pompous bag of wind and we did not get off to a good start. A limousine took us to a swank restaurant, we ordered drinks and Moynihan crossed his arms on his bulging belly, looked me straight in the eyes and said, "So Roger, you are wanted all over the world. The Philippines is the place for you. They can't touch you here."

"Glad to hear that Tony." Why on earth did Howard tell him about me?

"I have a virtual mansion on the outskirts of Baguio, the most beautiful city in the Philippines. I will rent it to you and your family for a pittance. Five maids and a chauffeur come with it."

"How much would this virtual mansion set me back in dollars?"

He leaned back, took a big drink and pretended to think. "Let's see, with the limo and all the help I suppose I could let it go for fifteen thou a month."

I didn't bat an eye. "When can we have a look?"

"First thing tomorrow. We will fly there in the Governor of Luzon's plane. What time would be convenient for you?"

"How about six o'clock?" I saw him flinch.

"Are you up that early?"

"Yeah, being raised on the farm has me accustomed to rising early and I never could break the habit."

I knew it irked him to get up early, but he needed to save face.

He tried to order everything on the menu, rejected several bottles of perfectly good wine, had the air conditioner turned down and in general made a complete ass of himself.

The conversation was steered into safer subjects. However, he soon disputed me as to the location of New Guinea. He said it was north of the equator and I knew it was south. He became loud and boisterous and said, "I will bet my hotel that New Guinea is north of the equator."

I didn't want his hotel, I had my eye on the bill, so I said, "I don't want your hotel, so I'll bet the price of dinner that New Guinea is ten degrees south of the equator."

On a bet, he would have to actually pay, he calmed somewhat, he had to accept after all the bragging. "All right, I accept the bet. We will look it up when we get back to the hotel."

"No way. We will settle this right now. Waiter!"

A waiter appeared and I handed him a twenty-dollar bill and asked him to find a map of the Pacific Ocean that had New Guinea on it and to hurry back and keep the change.

"Waiter! Another bottle of that fine wine." I was rubbing it in.

We drank the bottle, the waiter arrived with the map and of course, Moynihan lost.

The bill was four hundred and sixty-odd dollars.

He looked through his pockets, scrutinized his wallet and said, "Looks like I am a little short of cash tonight, may I borrow five-hundred until we get to the hotel?"

'Not I', said the fly. Howard didn't have the cash on him, so Moynihan sent for the manager who came over and signed a chit for the meal. That small win cost me thousands of times over.

Early the next morning we took off in the governor's twin-engine Piper in air so polluted we couldn't see the ground until we landed at Baguio. An old limousine was waiting on the tarmac and the driver took us directly to the house. It was big, with a spectacular view across a lush green valley but the house itself was cold and lonely and it felt as if evil spirits had resided there for many years.

While in Baguio, I went to see a famous 'faith healer.' Since I was fifteen years old I have had tinnitus in both ears. The ringing is loud and constant. There is no known cure and I was ready to try almost anything. I went to the 'healers' house and was kept waiting for fifteen minutes while he waited on imaginary customers. It reminded me of the story of the young lawyer who opened an office. A man came and asked for the lawyer and the secretary kept him waiting for the required length of time and then ushered him in. The lawyer continued to talk on the phone and after a while hung up, looked up at the man before him and asked what he could do for him. The man replied, "I'm from the telephone company, here to connect your telephone."

Anyway, the healer looks me up and down trying to figure how much I'll pay. I see right off he's a charlatan and a greasy one at that. I needed to pee and asked to use his bathroom. He was hesitant, but reluctantly agreed, explaining that the bathroom was broken but I could use it. He opened a door leading to another section of the house and it was filthy. The bathroom toilet overflowed with stale urine. I held my breath and backed out. He tried to sell me a little brown bottle of oil for three hundred dollars. "Put a few drops in your ears each day for a month and they will be healed." Yeh, sure. I passed and made my way back to the car.

From Baguio we flew to a plywood mill that Moynihan obviously had an interest in. Recently burned-out log trucks littered the grounds, calling-cards of the guerillas unhappy with the payoff. Many people were milling about but little work was going on.

Before noon we landed on one of the 'Three Sisters,' islands in the Luzon Straits. A relic left from W.W.II met us and I made the mistake of riding in the cab where the rust kept falling on me. The monstrous five-ton truck was special in that the front tires suddenly turned all the way to the left and we darted off the road. The driver stopped, backed up, straightened it out and proceeded on as though nothing happened. He let us out at a large grass-thatched building on the beach. The truck left and soon returned with a 600-pound red heifer shot in the head. They rolled it off the high body of the truck and it hit the ground with a thud. Knives were unsheathed and chunks of flesh were hacked off the animal before it was dressed.

Someone shot a chicken with an AK-47. A little overkill.

Explosions were echoing from the reef and I asked, "What is all the bombing about?"

Moynihan said, "Oh that's just the boys dynamiting fish for lunch."

While we were waiting for lunch they brought out an arsenal of AK-47s and we went target practicing on the beach. The automatic rifles were surprisingly accurate and I could hit coconuts repeatedly at long distances.

After lunch we loaded up in the giant truck and started across the island to scout out property for the plantation. Wild guava growing out of solid coral covered the island and there was no way I could farm in the stones. Howard asked me to take a soil sample just to please Moynihan, reluctantly I did. That would cost me.

On the return journey the driver stopped and picked up two men carrying a tightly woven bamboo litter hanging from a long pole. The litter was folded around a man which I learned was the men's father. The pole was placed across the side bodies of the truck and stuck out three or four feet on each side with the man in the litter swinging from the pole. I pointed out the danger and the pole was shifted, but not near enough. I ducked underneath and stood near the front of the truck. Sick looking body fluid ran out of the litter, perhaps he vomited… or died. The truck gathered speed and ran between two overhanging trees. The litter and all the people standing behind it were scraped off that truck like scum off a Louisiana swamp. Whether the fall killed the old man or not I don't know as they all preferred to walk thereafter.

We returned to Manila and had a serious meeting. Moynihan insisted on a million-dollar deposit on the island property with payments monthly for his tractors and workers. I told him that it was a little steep and his reply was that he had heard that a million dollars was just front pocket money to me. I threw the soil sample in the rubbish and Howard and I caught a plane to Bangkok.

Phil and Kevin came to the hotel, showed us a sample of some excellent pot and said there was an unlimited supply. I called Jerry with the news and he and Ron arrived in a few days.

Howard introduced me to his friend John Denby, a Mick Jagger look alike and a credit to Marks.

Howard said there was an American called 'Rummy' with an eighty-foot wooden sailboat trying to find a load and he wanted to introduce us. I turned the offer down as I didn't know this character or his people. Besides, we didn't need transportation as we had a 120-foot vessel standing by that could haul a hundred tons if we could afford it.

Jerry, Ron, Phil, Kevin, Howard and I got down to business. For a deposit of two million dollars and a percentage the Thai Navy would load us two-hundred miles offshore with twenty tons of superb marijuana. It was vacuum packed in nitrogen gas and consequently just as fresh when it was opened as the day it was packaged. This was the deal I had been looking for.

"Howard, will you transfer the deposit in Pakistan to this deal?"

"Sorry, it has already been given to the farmers in Pakistan.

I should have not expected otherwise.

Howard knew Bob Light from Washington State and John Ritter from British Colombia. They were professional unloaders who would do the favor for seven million US dollars. I knew that was gouging and figured Howard was in for at least half the amount so I offered to unload it for three million. Howard was hard against the idea and Jerry agreed with him saying we needed local knowledge. I said I could buy a heap of local knowledge with four million dollars. In any case, they did not want my expertise and the job went to strangers.

Two million dollars changed banks, the Axel D sailed into the South China Sea and the Thai Navy met it 200 miles offshore with the cargo. The pot was stored in the hold and she steamed for Canada. I returned to Mallorca.

Unbeknownst to the rest of us, Howard stayed in Bangkok for another week.

A month later Jerry called and reported that the Axel D had been unloaded and all was fine.

Howard sent John Denby to Vancouver to look after his interest which turned out not to have been ours. Scotland Yard called the Mounties and informed them that John Denby, a notorious criminal, was headed their way.

By sheer coincidence, Denby registered in the same hotel as Jerry and Ron. Spotters for the Mounties registered on all sides. Some were old women, others homosexuals dressed in bright colors, who Jerry and Ron remembered, but never dreamed they were spotters for the RCMP.

Rummy arrived on the old sailboat with seven tons of pot and a DEA agent.

Canadian Customs agents waited until all was unloaded into three trucks and then sprang the traps. Three men jumped into the icy water and one hid all day under the pier. They arrested eleven unloaders including John Denby. Agents busted into Jerry and Ron's rooms and found three million dollars, another couple of million in a rental car parked in the hotel basement. In Ron's pocket was the key to a storage locker with five million.

The Canadians knew that Ron and Jerry had nothing to do with the seven tons and had no idea where the ten million came from. All the off loaders were granted bail within twenty-four hours, but denied to Jerry, Ron, and Denby, as they were foreigners.

The off loaders were storing the marijuana and selling it for Ron and Jerry. Every few days they sent word that all was well and sales were going great.

I offered to come over and take care of things and was told to stay away, that everything was running smoothly.

After six months, all charges were dropped against Jerry and Ron they were released from jail and deported.

The off loaders said, "Get fucked, you brought this heat on us and we aren't going to give you a cent." Twenty-five million dollars ripped off, just like that!

Jerry hired a thug from the Mossad to collect the money. After a few days the man came back to Jerry, stuck a Glock pistol to his head and demanded two-hundred and fifty-thousand dollars for his efforts. Jerry gave it to him and felt lucky to escape with his life.

Howard had remained in Bangkok in order to load Rummy. If he could have afforded more pot why didn't he put it on our vessel? He knew us, but he had no idea who Rummy was. He then hooked Rummy and his DEA crew member up with the same unloaders. This fuck-up, coupled with him sending Denby to Vancouver, cost me ten million dollars.

29. IF AT FIRST YOU DON'T SUCCEED

Two Tons of Hash -- 'Nicely' Done Over -- It's All A Misunderstanding -- Lamb to the Slaughter

Jerry met me in Amsterdam to look at a ship. She was a five thousand ton, ice-class, Dutch-built, 'tween (double) deck freighter for sale at six-hundred thousand dollars. Jerry was impressed and I made a down payment of sixty thousand dollars to hold her for thirty days. I rode with the captain to the dry dock where the bottom was cleaned and painted and later the sides and superstructure. She was nice before, but with the new paint, she was dashing.

Once Jerry was arrested in Vancouver I was reluctant to invest so much in a vessel for which I had no immediate use. I asked for a thirty-day extension. They turned it down.

I flew to Amsterdam intending to go ahead and buy her. When I arrived at the dock I found she had been sold and was on her way to Norway. I called the owner in England, he told me he didn't think I was going to buy her so he sold her to someone else. I said that I understood, however, he must pay me back the deposit plus the cost of dry-docking and the paint job. He told me to go to hell, he was not going to pay me anything. As I was expecting something like this I replied that he did not know who I was and I knew who he was. I knew where he lived and if he did not pay me my money I would spend an additional ten thousand dollars to have his legs broken and when he got out of the hospital I would spend another ten. He had a sudden change of heart and said the money would be with the sales agent the next day.

Early the following morning I was standing by the door waiting anxiously for the agency to open. I was afraid he notified the police of my threat. The money was there and the agent gave me a check for 180,000 guilders that I took straight to his bank and cashed. The teller put the money in a plastic bank envelope and I put it in my inside coat pocket and walked to the train station where I caught a train up the coast to Den Helder.

The weather was bitter cold with a gale blowing off the North Sea. The canals were solid ribbons of ice. I inspected a similar size freighter and found it stripped clean of every spare part, wrench, cable, and rope. These items generally stay with the ship and cost a lot to replace. Other ships were waiting for inspection. On the return trip the train felt warm after the time spent on the cold ships and soon I was nodding off. Afraid that someone would notice the green bank envelope in my coat pocket I took it out and put it inside my undershirt and went to sleep. Upon arrival in Amsterdam, I awoke, stepped out and caught a tram to Leidseplein Square. As I walked into the Oyster Bar Restaurant, I handed my coat to the coat clerk. Suddenly I thought of the money. I felt in the coat pocket and remembered putting it in my underclothes, I went to feeling all around, patting myself and checking my coat two or three times before dashing out the door and catching a taxi back to the station. A thorough search of the area was in vain, as hundreds of people were milling about. I waited on the tram to return and searched in the aisles and under the seats. I knew the fat, bright green, ABN Bank envelope had been spotted straight away but I couldn't help going over the area, looking under benches and in trash cans. To lose over a hundred thousand dollars so stupidly will make a body sick. I went to the newspaper and asked about running an ad. The Dutchmen all laughed good-naturedly and told me I was in Amsterdam and not to waste good money chasing bad.

When that old hairy hand of luck changes, it changes all over.

My savings were melting away like a man running across a desert with a block of ice in an attempt to get to another oasis and a freezer before it's all gone. Howard told me of a ship in Holland that was seized by a bank for money owed and if I paid it out of hock he could haul a load of hashish out of Morocco. The debt was for fifty-thousand pounds, about a hundred- thousand dollars at the time. Howard said he would pay me double within three months for the loan and back it up with his house. This sounded like a sweet little deal to me and I flew off to Holland. Two London gangsters showed me the ship and introduced me to Horst Schultz, the German Captain and owner of the ship. I gave the fifty thousand pounds to the Englishmen and departed.

After a couple of weeks, I asked Howard about the ship, he replied that everything was fine as far as he knew. The next month I asked again and he said he wasn't sure what had happened with the ship, however, he heard there had been some problems. I flew back to Amsterdam and went to the docks. The ship was still chained to the same spot. A friendly guard invited me aboard and over a cup of coffee he told me the ship was up for auction in three days. A large bullfight size poster advertised the event.

I tried to telephone Captain Schultz but couldn't find his number through the international operator. I had his address in Ratzeburg, Germany, so I caught a flight to Hamburg and from there I obtained his number. I rang, he answered and was glad to hear from me and said he would be at the airport in one hour. He arrived promptly on time and drove back to his home in Ratzeburg where I rented a room in a lovely hotel.

Schultz and I hit it off like old friends and had many good laughs. He said the Bank of Hamburg would not accept the late payments on the ship and he gave the money back to the Englishmen the day after I left. Hmmm?

He told me he had an unlimited captain's license and was ready and willing to work in the hashish trade anywhere in the world. Just the man I was after.

Schultz knew of a ship for sale in Lubeck which didn't work out. We drove to Rotterdam to inspect another. It was fine, one-thousand six-hundred tons, I bought it for three-hundred and fifty-thousand dollars.

Back in Mallorca I told Howard that I bought a ship and had a captain ready to go. Howard called Jim, an Irishman who claimed to be connected with the IRA. Jim flew in and said he had two tons of hashish in Morocco that needed transportation to England. I told him I was ready and the price of shipping would be two million US dollars. Howard and Jim haggled and complained that they just could not pay that much. I said there was no way I would take less with me furnishing the ship and paying the crew. We were at an impasse, I went to the restroom. When I returned they were all smiles. They had decided to accept the deal. I got that special flush in the face that told me I had just been cheated, but didn't act on the warning.

Schultz delivered a load of steel to Italy and from there sailed to Malta. I flew down and bought a huge inflatable to unload the hashish and transport it to the beach. I also personally repaired a generator.

The load was waiting at Ceuta, an enclave in Africa, across from Gibraltar. Howard and I went to Algeciras, Spain to wait on the ship to arrive from Malta. While in Algeciras Howard and I went to Gibraltar and met two London gangsters driving a new Rolls Royce. They wanted us to haul two tons of hashish located several hundred miles south. A deal was struck--coordinates and light signals agreed upon for loading at sea and a time set.

When the ship arrived in Malaga we loaded it with fresh fruit and vegetables and I told Schultz about the additional merchandise, gave him the particulars and promised to increase his pay. He departed and anchored in the bay of Ceuta. Our loader went to the ship with his face wrapped and wearing an Arab robe. One and a half tons of hashish was hoisted aboard in big cargo nets, the anchor weighed and Schultz sailed south. Howard and I returned to Mallorca to wait.

In a few days Howard left Mallorca bound for England to oversee the unload while I waited in Puerto Andraitx for his phone call. The call was long overdue and I became worried that something had happened and the ship was lost or caught. My friend Justo Ajanares came to visit me and said hashish with red cellophane wrappers was all over London. I knew this to be the color of the wrapping of the load and wondered why Howard didn't call. After a few more days with no news I was ready to go to Morocco and see if the ship was perhaps there with the crew in jail but I deduced that if the ship had not reached England Howard would be on the horn.

I telephoned the home of Schultz in Ratzeburg, expecting to talk to his wife, but Schultz himself answered. I asked if everything was all right and he said he unloaded the cargo a week earlier and was wondering where I was.

Where the fuck was Howard?

A couple of days later Howard telephoned and in a sad, whiney voice, he said, "The merchandise is no good. We are having problems right now and there is a lot of heat. Nobody can move. "

"OK Howard, I will come to London tomorrow and take my share."

"Oh no, don't even think of doing that. Nobody can go near it right now. We will take care of things when everything cools down."

Two weeks later and still no word. I went to his house and told his wife Judy to tell him to call me that very day and to tell him I was pissed.

He called late that night and whined about it being the Easter season and nothing much was moving. I said I had to get enough money to pay the crew. He agreed and told me to go to Amsterdam the next day that he would have someone meet me at the American Hotel.

An obese young man with a lot of crack showing above his jeans arrived and handed me a satchel. I went to the room and counted two-hundred thousand dollars, only ten percent. Not even enough for the crew.

I called Schultz and told him to meet me at the American Hotel coffee shop, the best coffee shop in Amsterdam, as soon as he could. I then went to the ABN Bank, took two- hundred thousand out of my lockbox, and waited in the room for Schultz. Five hours later he arrived in a new BMW. It looked like he had counted on being paid. I paid him off and he left.

Howard returned to Mallorca with a new British passport that I had been waiting for. He said sales had picked up and the two million he owed me was ready. This was factoring in the hundred-thousand I had loaned him. He told me to go to Amsterdam the next day and the same man would meet me at the train station at four in the afternoon.

The only flight from Mallorca to Amsterdam was on KLM departing at eleven a.m. and arriving at one p.m. Marrie packed my bag. I took it and my new passport and like a sheep to the slaughter, I boarded the flight. After landing in

Amsterdam I had to choose one of several long lines of passengers from all over the world waiting to check through immigration. I stood in one of the queues, slowly making my way forward. I handed a tall young blond immigration officer my new passport, he took it, looked at the name, his head jerked up, he seemed surprised. "Is this your own passport sir?" He asked.

My heart beat hard against my ribcage as I answered, "Yes it is."

He reached above his head to the sign and reversed it to read *CLOSED* then walked around and took a firm grip on my upper arm in his big hand and said, "Come with me."

"Is something wrong with my passport sir?" He did not answer.

He conducted me into a room filled with turbaned men sitting against one wall and five immigration officers pouring over passports and arguing with the foreign men.

My officer said rather rudely, "Sit there," indicating a chair by the wall. I sat down and watched as he sat down and turned in a swivel chair, opened the passport and slipped it under a clip by the computer.

Before he had turned halfway around I slithered out the door and into the crowd. Whether or not he saw me leave I have no idea, but I assumed he did and I crouched down and ran through the crowd as fast as I possibly could without knocking people over. I opened an office door, entered a room and noticed that I was still carrying a package of books. I threw them on a table, crawled out a window and found I was still in the same situation, only another corridor, although this one did not have any people. I ran towards the end where the planes were parked. To the left of the boarding gate was a big stainless elevator door with the sign above, "Forbidden to enter." I pushed the button and the door opened. I stepped in, pushed the only button and went down to the ground level. The door opened onto an empty crew room. On a hangar was a KLM pilot's cap and a jacket with four gold stripes on the sleeves. I quickly put these on over my dark green suit. I noticed they were a tad too large as I looked myself over in a large mirror before walking out on the apron amongst the blue and white KLM 747s lined up like piglets to a sows tits.

I was in a dilemma. The recent photograph in the passport would soon be in the hands of every police officer and employee in the area. I had to do something fast. Several large garbage bins were an option and I considered hiding in one but figured they would be searched and decided against it. Just then, a KLM flight crew of fifteen or twenty came by headed for the gate. I fell in close behind. I noticed they each held up ID cards as they walked by a guard in a booth and I turned back. I was walking beside a twelve-foot tall chain-link fence with six strands of barbed wire in a Y on top. When I got to the corner of the terminal I bounded up the fence and balanced on the barbed wire before jumping down into the shrubbery below. The pain was electrifying! I could not believe it! I could not move. I had jumped into a barrier of tough needle-sharp spines two-inches long. I tore off the captain's jacket and pushed the shrubbery away from my legs then proceeded to stomp the jacket onto the next shrub. I was making slow progress when a blue van drove up on the other side of the fence. Two young police officers jumped out with pistols in hand, pointing at the sky. They yelled, "Halt, halt!" which only spurred me on. The barrier of spines was only about fifteen feet wide and I was soon through. There was a four-lane highway going into a tunnel just where I had to cross and cars and trucks were zipping in and out. I ran through the traffic. Standing on the curb on the farther side were four police officers, two men and two women. I walked past and I still remember the blonde, her hair in a bun, showing a goodly bit of cleavage with a gold cross hanging in the crevice.

I tried to walk casually as I entered the airport where at least five hundred people were waiting to meet arriving passengers. Wide, space age, moving sidewalks were transporting people to and from the trains. One said *NAAR DE TREINS* (to the trains), and I stepped on.

One floor down, I had the choice of two sleek new trains, one to Amsterdam, the other to Rotterdam. I chose the one bound for Rotterdam. I figured they knew I was on my way to Amsterdam. I walked through a couple of carriages, went into a toilet and closed the door. A lovely 'shhhh' sound corresponded perfectly with my feelings. I crammed the KLM uniform jacket and cap through the hole used for paper towels, washed the blood off my face and legs, combed my hair, and sat down on the toilet seat, ready to ride.

The train pulled out and I found a seat. After a few minutes, the train stopped. I got worried. The two young police officers on the other side of the fence had seen me go into the airport. No, they couldn't want me that bad I reckoned. We started up again and at the first stop I got off. This was out in a cow pasture and sitting across from the station was a three-carriage bus-train. Some people had already boarded and were waiting calmly. I boarded and took a seat on the back row because there was less glass windows in that area. While I was sitting there a muscle car raced up to the station. Two men jumped out and showed a paper to the agent who shook his head. I sunk down as low as I could as the car sped away.

The bus stopped in Alsmeer and I stepped off. Across the square was a haberdashery sign. I vaguely remembered it had something to do with ribbons and bows and I thought they might have needles and tweezers. It did. I purchased these items, found a park bench, and went to work on my hands first, then my legs, and I found that somehow my head was full of broken off thorns. I literally dug out hundreds of spines.

As I sat on the bench playing doctor and did some hard thinking. Did Howard turn me in? I remembered the night he and Jim capitulated so easily while I was in the bathroom. Did they agree to use me, split two million dollars and then turn me in? Was there something wrong with the passport? I thought not. The officer recognized the name before he examined it. Howard was found guilty by my court. Anyway, why not go to the train station and see what happened. I was still an hour early.

From the restaurant on the second floor of the station I looked at each person coming and going and no one vaguely resembling my contact showed up.

"Will you walk into my parlor?" Said a spider to a fly;
"T'is the prettiest little parlor that ever you did spy."

Fortunately I had another passport in the lockbox. I retrieved it and caught a train to Paris. A day or two later I took another one on to Madrid. From there I caught a domestic flight to the Canary Islands where I stayed for two months. While touring the archipelago I decided to move to the Soviet Bloc, perhaps Prague as it was well known as the Paris of the East.

I called Jerry Wills, he could not believe Howard had done such a dirty on me. He said that Howard had been in too many big deals and he had never heard of him doing anything so terrible. He called Howard several times and Howard vehemently denied turning me in and asked Jerry to have me return to Mallorca. He said he would convince me of his innocence and pay me.

No one would have recognized me in my disguise on the ferry back to Mallorca. I rented a hotel room in a village catering to Germans. Marrie visited me and we dined, danced and discussed the future. We were 45 years old that year and Marrie was at the zenith of her beauty. Her hair was turning silver and she looked tall and regal in a full, black, pleated, linen dress. It was cinched in at the waist with a wide belt and massive silver buckle amongst other fine accessories. Players from a German soccer team staying at the same hotel lined up to dance with her.

Marrie flatly refused my pleas to move to Prague and said the problem in Amsterdam was just a bad passport, everything could be worked out. God bless her she was in denial and refused to look at the danger we were in.

Marrie visited Howard at his house and he told her he wanted to pay me however we needed to talk. She made an appointment for the following morning in a breakfast café in Magaluff, a town popular with English tourists. I drove up in our fawn-colored Jaguar with license plates from 'The Kingdom of Andorra.' The long red plates with a king's crown attracted too much attention.

Howard arrived shortly after I did and we ate breakfast and he convinced me that he was all right. In the conversation he asked if I was still driving the Jag with the Andorra plates. I said I was and he told me to be careful because they were cracking down on tax-free plates. He gave a date and time for me to collect the two-million dollars and we parted.

"Take the keys out of the car door and put your hands on the roof." A gruff voice said in Spanish.

I whirled around and closing in were four older men in civilian clothes. The pistols in their hands left no doubt as to who they were. My right hand came up automatically and the heel caught the fittest looking one under the nose. He went down as I ran over him. One was too fat to be in the race, but the other two gave it all they had.

They ran through the tourists with their pistols in hand. I looked back, saw one of them stop and bend over but the thin one kept coming. I was gaining and by the third block I had a good lead. On my left was a hotel. I ran up the steps, slowed down and walked in, ran up the stairs and saw nowhere to hide. A window was open in the rear and I jumped out on to a roof and from there onto the ground. A stream with knee-deep grass on both sides ran behind the hotel. I jumped a fence, ran through the creek, bound over another fence and calmly walked into the kitchen of another large hotel. Chefs were busy making bread and pastries and I said "Buenos Dias" as I walked through. After several twists and turns I came to a big empty ballroom. I hid behind the stage curtain and sat down and caught my breath. After a few minutes I walked out front planning to find a taxi and leave. On the steps was a fat glassy-eyed man who looked vaguely familiar. He held out his hand offering to shake mine and it dawned on me that he was one of the four at the car. Back through the pastry chefs I ran causing a major wreck by knocking pans in all directions.

Knowing the fat cop had called on the radio and all my pursuers would be looking in the hotel, I ran down the creek and went around the far end of the first hotel. I walked calmly across the street and into a cabinet shop. A young man was working at a wood lathe and I noticed a three-wheeled truck in the shop. I said, "I need a ride to Palma and I will pay you fifty dollars," I handed him a fifty-dollar bill.

He dropped what he was doing and we got in the truck and took off. Police cars were coming from all directions with sirens blaring. The man looked around and said rather nonchalantly, "Wonder what's going down?"

"I have no idea," I said as we rode through them.

In Palma I gave him another fifty, forgetting I had already paid.

Seventeen million people visit Mallorca each year and there was no way the police could find me if I stayed in the crowd. I bought a pair of three-quarter length white trousers, a striped black and white pirate shirt and a cap with a plastic visor. I looked in a mirror and did not recognize myself. I then went to see my friend Justo and told him my woes. He had been a true friend even before we moved to Mallorca.

Justo was building an apartment building and he took me to one apartment that was not quite finished. The electricity was not on so we bought a hundred candles and I moved in. Marrie, Miriam and Marya brought me clothes and I begged Marrie to stay with me and let us leave Spain. No way. Every day she returned to the house in Puerto Andraitx, with excuses or some foolish reasons.

Howard went to visit Marrie, cried real tears and swore he had nothing to do with the trouble. "It's just those Andorra plates Marrie. They are tightening down all over Spain. I warned Roger. Hire a lawyer to find out."

Marrie did hire a lawyer. He went to the police and they laughed and asked why I ran, said it was only a matter of a fine and I could have taken the car out of the country. Marrie was very happy with this news. It was only a fine and now I could come home and the children could continue in the same school.

Had someone cast a spell on her? Had Howard given her some of his loco weed?

Jorge, the lawyer, had lived in Mallorca all of his life and was well connected. After talking with him for some time he almost had me believing it was the plates.

Paco, the taxi driver who drove the children to and from Palma had a brother on the police force. The brother said the problem was only the plates.

OK, perhaps it is the plates, but if so, why doesn't Howard just give Marrie the two million dollars? She went again and talked with him and Judy and returned totally convinced that I was paranoid.

"Marrie, I don't care what everyone says. Something bad is in the air. The passport in Holland. The police chase in Magaluf. Howard not calling for two weeks and now he will not give you the money. It does not add up."

"Roger you are making a mountain out of a molehill. It is the wanderlust in you. You would just love to take off, go to Russia today, and take us with you. Well I am not going! And you know that Rhett is in his first play this afternoon."

"Listen Sweetheart, I can't go to that school. It's crazy! I've been wearing disguises and hiding in this candlelit apartment for a week and now you want me to go to a public school play?"

"Oh, you infuriate me! You're so brave when it comes to doing what you want to do, like flying across the Rio Grande with your wheels in the sand but when it comes to your family it's 'oh no, I'm afraid'. What will Rhett think when he is on the stage and looks out and his father is not there?"

Marrie was a beautiful woman. I was in love. The sun was shining and Rhett was a handsome seven-year-old boy. Going against the feeling in my guts, I made the fateful choice… I would never go *home* again.

We had a long lunch with Howard on the terrace of a restaurant. The meal was excellent and the wine was good. I winced when Marrie told Howard we had to leave because Rhett was in his school play. We arrived at school, children and parents were all animated and festivities were in the air. Rhett ran to me, I picked him up and he pulled my face around so I had to look directly at him as was his custom. He was telling me something when I saw the car stop. The driver looked me directly in the eyes and quickly got out of the car with a plastic case in his left hand. He crouched as he hurried across the street towards me pulling out a machine gun.

I could have run but for some reason the energy just wasn't there. The first

Thought was that I had on slick leather wingtips and they would slip and slide. Then I saw all the children around me and Marrie and other women. Few fathers were present.

Other plain-clothes police officers were closing in. I pulled off my watch and handed it to Marrie along with my wallet as I knew what happens to property in police stations. I raised my hands but that made no difference. They knocked me in the head with guns, tackled me from all sides, handcuffed me and dragged me away.

Miriam and Rhett were expelled from the school. Parents would not allow their children to even speak to them. One was Rhett's best friend.

30. DESPERATION LEAP AND A SPANISH PRISON

The Man Who Prays -- Between the Sheets -- The Slow Grinding Wheels Of Justice

The prison was old and dingy, extremely hot during the day. The open barred cells were small with a narrow bunk. However, the food was good and each morning we went out into a small walled-in patio with a store where one could buy tobacco, coffee and pastries. We wiled away the days trying to keep in the shade of the high walls.

After some days I was taken to the court in Palma to be arraigned on extradition charges to Germany. Why Germany? I had never done anything in that country. The police officers kept laughing at how they had duped my lawyer. "We are the best policemen in the world," they bragged as they escorted me up several flights of stairs to the third floor. By American counting it's the third, by Spanish counting it's the second as they don't count the ground floor. I sat handcuffed in the witness box. Jorge Henri, the same lawyer who was duped about the plates sat beside me. Marrie and Rhett were in the audience, which was surprisingly large. The tops of palm trees were swaying in the breeze just below the windows. I kept wondering how tall they were and decided they must be thirty or forty feet.

We waited and then waited some more for the judge to arrive. Four police officers were guarding me and every few minutes two of them walked out for a smoke. The court recorder, who was very pregnant, sat behind a large desk facing the audience. She looked bored and kept filing her nails and trying to find something to look at.

I said to Henri, "I am going to kick that big window out and jump the next time two of those clowns go for a smoke."

"Don't be foolish, you will kill yourself." He whispered.

"How high are we?"

"I don't know, maybe fifteen meters. You will surely kill yourself if you jump," he said rather emphatically.

I didn't hesitate. I watched two of the police officers go out and I made a dash across the courtroom, jumped up on the court recorder's desk, jerked the big window further open, stepped onto the wide sill and looked down. I could hear a big sucking sound behind me and I am sure I heard Marrie's above the rest. It was a long way to the ground! I was looking down on the power lines and the tops of tall palm trees. A white car was parked close to the building leaving barely enough room for another car to pass in the narrow medieval stone street. Toward this target I leaped. On my way down a police car with the large number 78 on top came around the corner. As I hit the roof of the parked car glass flew up and it looked to me like snow going the wrong direction. The roof went all the way to the floorboards squashing the seats on the way down. I saw lots of stars, but jumped up and started running towards Paseo de Maritimo, a wide six-lane highway running along the waterfront. The patrol car reversed along beside me. A tall young police officer jumped out with a shotgun, ran up behind me and hit me between the shoulder blades---hard. I went down.

Marrie and Rhett were in front of the court when they brought me around. I could see great anguish on her face.

They took me into a holding cell below the court and started working me over. The four police guards were livid. I copped the beating for a little while and then one of the assholes got behind me and hit me hard on my ears with open hands. The pain blinded me and I came undone. It must have been energy similar to what a mother has to lift a car off her child. It came and there was no stopping me. I kicked and knocked policemen all over that cell and they could not get out quick enough.

Court was adjourned for the day. They took me back to the prison, threw me in a cell with a pile of broken bricks, a bunk with sagging wires to hold a non-existent mattress and that was it. A ring had cut my chin and the front of my shirt and T-shirt were covered in blood. A guard set a pitcher of water on the floor along with a washcloth, towel and blanket. I refused to clean up. The German Consul was coming to visit me and I wanted him to see me in this condition.

After several days the consul arrived and everyone, even the warden tried to get me to wash and change shirts. I had lived like an animal for the last four days and there was no way I was going to wash now. Finally, they allowed me to go into a room and see my visitor. He was aghast! Later in Germany I read his scathing report of the brutality in the Spanish prisons.

They transferred me to a corner cell on the top floor and at night guards came and took all my clothes. This was supposed to prevent me from escaping.

I was allowed a radio and one morning as I was listening to the news I heard that Dennis Howard Marks and his wife Judith Marks had been arrested in a worldwide sweep on narcotics traffickers. Arrests were made in the United

States, the U.K., Canada, Spain, Portugal, Pakistan, and the Philippines. More arrests were expected later in the day.

Howard was brought to the prison but they placed him in a different area. I sent him a package of necessities. The next day he showed up in the small yard and talked. He had been arrested on charges in Fort Lauderdale, Florida, where his brother-in-law, Patrick Stuart had made some transaction with fifty-thousand dollars. This somehow had been twisted around so as to make marijuana deals in Pakistan and Spain offenses in the US and they were asking for the extradition of twenty-two people from all around the world. My name was on the list.

"What on earth do they mean? What do they have against me?" I asked.

"Roger, Moynihan spilled his guts. They have you down as the agronomist for a worldwide marijuana trafficking organization. You are indicted in Florida with the rest of us. They are asking for your extradition to the United States on RICO charges," Howard said it with a bowed head.

"What did Moynihan say that I did?

"You have two overt acts listed in the indictment. The first is; you flew on an airplane from Rome to Manila with the intent to further the marijuana enterprise by growing a thousand acres of marijuana. The second is that you took a soil sample for the purpose of growing marijuana. The charge carries twenty years."

I could not believe it! Of all the things I had done in my life and to be indicted in the US for taking a soil sample in the Philippines - which I threw away? It was absurd!

Craig Fernando, a swaggering black-eyed Mexican-American DEA arrived, offered me a cigarette; just like they do in the movies, and gave me a rundown on how much trouble I was in. He said, "You are looking at ten to fifteen in Germany. There is the 25-year parole term and a RICO waiting in the US. It all adds up to around sixty years. If you are to ever see your family again in any place except a prison visiting room, I strongly suggest you join my team."

"What's your best offer, Fernando?"

"You tell us everything you know and testify against Howard and his cronies and I will guarantee that you will walk out after two years. I will have a United States Attorney here today to put it in writing."

"What about the German charges?"

"We will work through diplomatic channels and have them dropped."

"I'll think it over."

"The offer is on the table for twenty-four hours." He walked out of the room.

I went back to the patio and told Howard. He asked what I was going to do and I told him not to worry, I could not testify against Ron and Jerry.

"What have they arrested Judy for?" I had never known her to be involved.

"They have her down as the telephone operator for the Marks organization. Seems they had my phone tapped for some time and when anyone called, Judy told them where they could reach me."

"What about baby Patrick?"

"Since he is nursing they allow him to live in the prison with Judy."

"God, that's pathetic. It's unbelievable. Howard, I know something about the American judicial process. Have her agree to voluntary extradition and a magistrate will let her out the day she arrives on such chicken shit charges."

"My lawyer does not agree to that, says it will hurt my case when it comes up." He hung his head very low in shame as he said this.

"Howard, that will take two years, you can't let Judy and the baby sit in jail just because it 'might' affect your hearing. Listen Howard, Spain will do whatever the United States says. You can delay the inevitable, but you cannot stop it. You will be extradited and when you get there you will make a plea-bargain deal or spend the rest of your life in a penitentiary. Get Judy out now."

The selfish son-of-a-bitch wouldn't listen. Judy and Patrick were taken to the woman's prison in Madrid where her teeth and hair fell out. Caretakers mistreated Heather and Amber, their two beautiful little girls. Judy spent eighteen months in that hell with baby Patrick before they extradited her. The day she arrived in Florida the judge released her with a strong reprimand to the prosecutor and the DEA.

After several weeks in the Palma prison the Audencia National, (the national police), came, shackled me and Howard up, and transported us to the ferry. They escorted us down into the ship and locked us in a thickly padded cell. Several hours later we heard the engines start up and felt the ship quiver as she backed out of the docks. They gave us one jug of water and one empty jug for the twelve-hour sojourn. We were low in spirit. And no wonder--chained together in a padded cell deep in the bowels of a ship that was plowing through dark seas taking us away from our loved ones, perhaps never to return. I could see that Howard was distraught.

"Howard, would you like to pray with me?" He looked at me as if I had lost it. "I'm serious, I pray and the Lord often comforts and strengthens me. It can't hurt you. "No, you go ahead if you like."

I prayed for Howard and myself, for our loved ones whom we were leaving behind and asked for strength and guidance. Then I recited the twenty-third Psalm

"The Lord is my shepherd; I shall not want. He maketh me to lie down in green pastures: he leadeth me beside the still waters. He restoreth my soul: he leadeth me in the paths of righteousness for his name's sake. Yea, though I walk through the valley of the shadow of death, I will fear no evil; for thou art with me; thy rod and thy staff they comfort me. Thou preparest a table before me in the presence of mine enemies: thou anointest my head with oil; my cup runneth over. Surely goodness and mercy shall follow me all the days of my life and I will dwell in the house of the Lord forever. Amen"

Unbeknown to me I was called "The man who prays" as a police intelligence telephone code name. An appellation for which I am proud.

We were marched out of the ship into the bright sunshine of tomorrow and driven to a huge holding area. What purpose it was made for I can hardly guess. It was a big open building with row after row of cages for men. They put Howard in one and me in another, far away from each other. We had to yell to communicate.

The cages were twenty feet deep, eight feet wide with stiff wire for walls. Down the side was a narrow cement bench. We were left there for the next four days without a blanket or pillow. The bench was too narrow to sleep on while lying on my back so I lay on my side until my hips were raw. There was nothing at all in the cages and I was terribly bored. When a guard brought food I asked for a Bible. He returned with a very old and ragged one, for which I was very happy. I yelled to Howard bragging of my treasure and he yelled back for me to send part of it over. I ask which part he wanted and he said it didn't matter. I tore it down the middle and sent him the first half.

From Valencia, they took us to an old prison in Barcelona. The architecture was beautiful in a sick way. The main area had a high vaulted domed ceiling in mosaic tiles with classical Greek carvings on each pillar. The wings were wide with cells behind heavy oak and iron doors one would expect to see in a dungeon from the middle ages. The cells had thick iron bars high up near the ceiling and the place was filthy! I scrubbed ours and rinsed seventeen times before the water began to run clear. The next day they moved us to another wing and another putrid cell. This one needed rinsing twenty times. Every day it was a new wing and another cell to clean.

We met an angry young US DEA agent in one wing. He had flown to Barcelona with eight kilos of cocaine to make a sting, so his explanation went. He was arrested and got a sentence of ten years. The episode caused a scandal in diplomatic circles.

We spent a week in the crowded filthy Barcelona prison with no idea as to where we were going, or when. Guards banged on the heavy doors at four a.m. one morning, hand-cuffed us and loaded us into a truck with a half dozen other prisoners. Soon we began the long drive to Alcala de Henares, the modern prison near Madrid. This is the village where Miguel de Cervantes wrote Don Quixote after he escaped from prison. One of my favorite books.

After four or five hours we stopped at a gasoline station out in the country. Off to the right was a steep drop of fifty or a hundred feet down to a field of tall sugar cane. If I could only make it to the edge, I could escape. Two Guardia Civil Police took turns escorting us to the toilet while the third pumped gasoline. I watched Howard go and then another man. One of the guards seemed a decent enough chap, but the other was tall, lean, mean and just itching to use the machine gun in his hand. My turn came. I crawled out of the truck, keyed up and ready to make my move. Unfortunately I drew the bad guard and I knew he would kill me. From experience, I know that if you give a man a gun and badge he will shoot you in the back if you run and he has the chance. I think I can say this with some authority having been shot at hundreds of times.

The prison Alcala de Henares was a sprawling new two-story complex with ten separate modules. Each 'modulo' held fifty prisoners and one guard. The rooms were big with molded concrete bunks, tables and chairs. A six-inch green pipe sometimes had hot water supplying heat. The food was delicious. Each morning the guards came with an urn of coffee and a loaf of homemade bread. The recipe changed monthly. Hot chocolate was an option on weekends. I would dunk the hot fresh bread in the rich hot chocolate and pig out. The seafood paella was a weekly favorite. With a few pesos one could purchase a beer for lunch. On birthdays and special occasions fifteen or twenty of us each bought a beer and gave them to the lucky person who could get properly drunk.

The asphalt patio was about the size of a tennis court. In one corner was a small store run by a, Turk. He was a kick-fighting champion who had no problem with the Basque terrorists, gypsy throat slitters and the tame drug smugglers. He sold cigarettes, pastries and delicious coffee made from an espresso machine with steamed milk. The drug traffickers took turns buying all the pastries and leaving them on a table for everyone to enjoy.

The first week there an explosion jarred me out of bed. The next morning we learned that Basque terrorists had left a car loaded with high explosives parked beside the road near the prison. Two police officers had opened the door to check and only their shoes were found.

Howard hired the most expensive law firm in Madrid to fight his extradition and I asked him to let me tag along since he was paying with my two million dollars.

"My lawyer said it would be a conflict of interest," he lied.

Howard paid for his attorney, Ian Donaldson, to fly to Madrid and talk with him. Ian spent several hours with me, took his shoes off, propped his feet on the wire screen divider and asked the guard to bring Coca Colas and chips. I thought highly of Ian that I almost invited him to visit my daughter Marya who was studying at the Sorbonne at the time. I have often wondered what might have been. I heard he was an up and coming man in Canada, being groomed for Prime Minister.

At one end of the patio was a knee-high concrete wall and on top was an eight-foot chain-link fence. Beyond the fence was a space of dirt, ten or fifteen feet wide. Further on was a deep concrete moat with no water but containing electronic sensors instead. Beyond the moat was a twenty-foot concrete wall with a metal catwalk running along the top joining the guard towers. A most formidable barrier!

Each week prisoners were allowed to order three kilos of food from an outside grocery store. The wealthier prisoners gave the poorer men prison paper money to purchase three kilos and we received copious supplies of exotic cheeses, smoked salmon, ham, chicken, turkey, cantaloupes, watermelons, grapes, cucumbers, tomatoes, bell peppers and anything else a large grocery store sells. We set up a table in the patio and had a picnic every day.

Thousands of Styrofoam cups were knee-deep tangled in weeds beyond the fence. I sharpened a mop handle and began retrieving the cups one at a time. When all the cups were cleared I poured hundreds of five-gallon buckets of water on the soil. The spigot was a ways off, making it a big task. After the ground was thoroughly soaked I began pushing the mop handle into the earth about eight inches and slowly began breaking the ground.

This was hard work and my hands were soon blistered. The men ridiculed me for working so hard in the sun for nothing. My friend Fernando defended me.

We had fun playing backgammon and he spent an hour every day listening to me read Spanish novels and correcting my pronunciation.

After a few weeks the earth looked like a miniature field, plowed and harrowed, with rows laid off ready for planting. In the meantime I had been gathering seeds from different vegetables and placing them in jar lids filled with soil in my windowsill. When the plants were about three inches tall I placed them roots, soil and all, on the end of the mop handle and carefully guided them through the chain-link fence and eased them into holes already prepared. By carefully maneuvering the handle I could get them upright, rake soil all around the plant, pack it down and then pour a cup of water down a plastic tube which had been a covering for the mop handle. The plants grew profusely. I trimmed off all growth except for one vine or stem and wove this vertically in and out of the chain-link fence. Four months later watermelons, cantaloupes, cucumbers, tomatoes, bell peppers and eggplants, were weighing down the fence. I had to act mean to stop the men from overwatering. They all wanted a piece of this painting. So much beauty against such an ugly background was a paradox, so much so that a photographer from the 'El Spectador' came out and took pictures of the warden standing in front of it.

I received few packages. Only two that I can remember and they both came the same day. A guard knocked on my steel door. I stood at the back of the cell, head bowed, pockets turned out, hands open and facing forward. Only then would the two guards open the door. This time they had a package for me. I opened it and there was a lovely, leather-bound, Schofield Reference Bible. I was delighted. Marrie had sent it from Holland. As I opened the Bible to the first page I happened to notice the logo, a C with a line drawn through it and the words Claxton Publishing Co. Claxton, Georgia. I thought, 'isn't this strange', Marrie sending a Bible from Holland which was printed near my home in Georgia, to be sent to me in a prison in Spain?

Two hours later another knock, same procedure and I received another package. I opened it and there was a book, The Father Heart of God, sent by Jerry Pope, a man from Douglas, Georgia. I knew that he and his brother had prayed for their crippled father who was in a wheelchair and the father was healed and stood up and walked. As I opened this book I was surprised to see the same logo of Claxton Publishing Co. printed on the first page. What were the odds? A coincidence? I remembered the mosaic in front of a Synagogue in Miami that read, "A coincidence is just a small miracle where God chooses to remain anonymous." Yet if that was strange, what about this? There on the inside cover was a photograph of my friend, Floyd McClung, the missionary I met in Amsterdam!

I eagerly read his book and ordered others he had written. He told of how he and his wife had gone to Kabul, Afghanistan and began a mission for hippies who were searching for 'The old man on the mountain,' embracing other gods and becoming completely lost. He and his wife ministered to thousands in such a condition and helped many with tickets home.

After that era they went to Holland and started "Youth with a Mission." Each year this organization sends out over three thousand young people to all parts of the world to deliver The Gospel. In his book, he described Heatherveld, a retreat in Northern Holland where these young people are trained. I would find myself returning to that place in Holland many times.

Visits were limited to two hours a month. They could be either family or conjugal. The latter, called vis-à-vis in Spanish, was a sight to behold. Thirty men waited expectantly in one room. A door opened and we walked into a larger room where the women were lined up on the opposite wall. Some wearing bright red lipstick, spiked heels and miniskirts. Others wore long black dresses, black wool stockings and no makeup, but they all had two things in common, a set of sheets under their arm and an expression on their faces. They knew what they were there for and I could tell there had been some witty words spoken while waiting in the line.

A guard escorted each couple to a room, locked the door and said, "Dos horas."

In the room was a bed with a mattress encased in a thick plastic covering, a toilet, a lavatory, a big open shower, and absolutely nothing else. Having not seen one another for a month we didn't know just how to act. Should we rip off our clothes and jump in bed? No, we looked one another in the eyes to see if all was well and then hugged. We put the sheets on the bed and crawled in. During winter the room was freezing and the plastic covering was like ice. We got naked, jumped in bed, touched one another with icy hands, screamed and rubbed one another vigorously trying to warm up. After one hour and fifty-five minutes, the guard knocked on the door and said, "Cinco minutos (five minutes)." The visit was over for a month.

During the seventeen months I spent there, Marrie drifted away. One cannot leave his treasure unattended. Sometimes she missed our Vis-à-Vis and when she did come I knew something was wrong. It hurt. I felt like my guts had been kicked out. I understood suicide. I had no desire to know if there was someone else. I could not blame her for I could easily spend the rest of my life in prison. She returned from California and I watched the big blue and white jet fly over and lock onto the glideslope for Madrid International. I waited expectantly, my heart sank as the appointed hour passed. Should I get a divorce and tell her to go on with her own life while she was still young and beautiful? These thoughts were constant, particularly at night on my bunk. Dreams and reality floated, intertwined, married.

The Spanish Court ordered double extradition. First, I was to be extradited to Germany and once that sentence was over, I was to be extradited to the USA.

Walter, a handsome German hashish smuggler comforted me by telling me that I would only get seven or eight years in Germany for the hashish. Furthermore, they would credit me with three jail days for each day spent in Spain. Two years of jail time in Spain counted as six years in prison in Germany and one was paroled after two-thirds. So two years in Spain completed a nine-year sentence in Germany. This perked me up, but hard to believe.

Marrie flew to Lubeck, Germany, and asked for the best drug lawyer available. Frau Elke Blumberg came highly recommended. Marrie met and spoke with her and got on well. She and her husband, who was a judge, invited Marrie to dinner and Frau Blumberg confirmed Walter's story. She said that because of the severe conditions of the prisons in Spain, Germany did give three days jail time for time spent awaiting extradition. One served from one-third up to two-thirds of the head sentence and I could expect a sentence of ten years, or less if I pled guilty.

I discussed this with Howard and told him that since the hashish was his and Captain Schultz was testifying to that fact, it might be a good idea for me to say the same and get him extradited to Germany. Before the wheels could grind he would have been in jail in Spain for two years which covered a nine-year sentence. A German request for extradition took precedence over a US request since it was in the EC and he was looking at life in the US. Howard was skeptical, yet he was interested and asked me to investigate it further once I got there.

A guard came and told me I was on my way to Germany. It was during siesta and I didn't get a chance to tell my friends goodbye. The Guardia Civil chained me up and transported me to a holding cell at the Madrid Airport. It was nothing more than a concrete box sitting in the corner of a big room, a tiny thing, just big enough to walk into stooped over. The ceiling was dome-shaped reminding me of the above-ground graves in the cemeteries of New Orleans. They left me sitting in that tomb for seventeen hours without a drop of water or food.

Around seven o'clock the next morning they returned and told me I was to have a physical. As I stood by the tomb a man with wiry grey hair sticking straight out walked into the room, took one quick look at me, whirled around and strolled out. The physical examination was completed. The guards shackled my legs, handcuffed me, and left me in the cell.

Due to my ability to get handcuffs from behind me to the front, my hands were cuffed in a most unusual way. My left arm was pushed up between my shoulder blades, the right bent over my right shoulder and shackled to the left. This position is painful and burns after a short time.

The Guardia Civil drove up to a Hercules C-160 and motioned with their guns for me to get out. I stepped out onto the tarmac and looked around at twenty-five German soldiers surrounding the plane as if prepared for war. By that time the pain in my shoulders was excruciating. I hobbled out of the car bent over with my arms shackled over my shoulders and shuffled to the stairs loaded down with leg irons and chains.

The German police officers acted as if they were sorry for me and asked the Spaniards to remove all the hardware. Then a German police officer placed one pair of handcuffs on my wrists. I entered the plane escorted by the two young police officers who sat in the cargo area with me. They gave me coffee and breakfast. They were quite friendly and talkative and of course, I knew they wanted information so I kept the conversation light and jovial.

It was a clear day as I watched Paris drift by on our flight north. We continued on and landed at a military base near Munich. The two police officers handcuffed me to an armrest in the back seat of a Mercedes and drove north through picturesque landscape. In a couple of hours we stopped at a gasoline station where they took me to the restroom and brought me back to the car and attached me to the flimsy door rest. Then they went back in and took their time shopping and drinking a Pepsi. After some time they came out, got in the car, turned around and inspected my skinned red right wrist and burst out laughing. The door rest must have had a bar of steel installed underneath the innocent-looking leather and they knew it.

We arrived in Neumunster after dark where they dropped me off at a medium-security prison. The only problem was it was filled with informants. I was placed in a cell with informers on both sides. They kept me locked twenty-three hours a day and for my one hour of exercise I walked alone in a gated courtyard with a guard.

Fifty men all showered at the same time. We stripped off, got our towels, and marched to the showers. A guard yelled something, pulled a big lever, and hot water sprayed for five minutes. It stopped abruptly without warning. It was best if one was not still soaped up when it did. On the way back we were alone for a few minutes in the glass-roofed walkway. I looked up and saw an open skylight. In a flash I bounded up the braces, my naked body pink and steaming. As I neared the window a prisoner yelled, 'escape, escape, escape!' Guards came running. I climbed down and the next day I was transferred to the maximum-security prison in Lubeck.

31. ESCAPE FROM LUBECK, GERMANY

Work Will Set You Free -- Prison Doctor -- The Escape -- Honey I'm Home -- Border Crossing -- A Treasure in The Field

Lubeck is located in northern Germany on the Trave River near the Baltic Sea. A ring of canals separates the ancient inner city from the suburbs. This historic section has some of the finest medieval Gothic buildings in Europe. As I rode through in chains I admired the lovely old city with its church spires towering above the countryside.

My new abode was a cell in the basement away from Captain Schultzor and anyone else who might advise me. Each morning at five I was allowed one hour exercise in a tiny yard with two guards, one on each end, with another looking down from the guard tower. My wrists were manacled in cuffs with a solid stiff length of connecting steel, a most uncomfortable set of bracelets for an early icy morning stroll in the dark. The only good thing about solitary confinement was a large bathtub with claw feet in which I took a daily bath and luxuriated. This arrangement lasted for several months until I was sentenced.

I interviewed several boisterous and expensive lawyers and was beginning to despair of these crooks when Frau Elke Humbert showed up with Carol Hoptenor from Utah as interpreter. They were pretty, full of life and good vibes. I told Frau Humbert exactly what happened and she insisted I tell the court everything, nothing but the truth for her. I learned later that her husband was one of the judges in Lubeck. She said I would get a seven or eight-year sentence if I pled guilty and receive three days jail time credit for the seventeen months spent in Spain while fighting extradition. This meant I would get out immediately or after two years, depending on the sentence.

I asked her if Howard could get the same deal and she assured me he could. That clinched the deal and I told it roughly as it happened. Howard was indicted and the next day an extradition warrant was sent to Spain. This stopped his extradition to the US.

Within a week DEA agent, Craig Lavato and Assistant US Attorney Robert O'Neal showed up in Lubeck, went to the court and swore this was a plot contrived between Reaves and Marks. They explained that the hashish charge was mixed up with Marks' other charges and after a conviction in Germany it would be impossible to convict him in the US. Besides, if Marks' was extradited to Germany and received the maximum sentence he would be out within six months. They came to the prison and offered me another deal. If I testified, they would assist and I would walk out of prison. I turned them down and as punishment they wrote a nasty letter to the US Parole Commission.

The Germans dropped the charges against Howard and he was extradited to the US. I sent my sister Kay to Miami to visit Howard daily to see if he was going to testify against the rest of us. She had a conference call telephone system installed in her apartment so Howard could keep in touch. He got there too late to make a deal as too many others got there first. He did a plea bargain whereby for a guilty plea he got twenty-five years. He served eight years in the maximum-security federal prison in Terre Haute, Indiana.

I received an eight-year sentence with three to one for my time in Spain. I would have to serve one more year. There was no evidence and neither Schultz nor I ever saw the product. If I had had a good lawyer I could have said the Arabs had tricked us and it was not hashish. With this statement the maximum sentence would have been three years for conspiracy. It was, for this reason, I was kept incommunicado until after my confession.

After sentencing I was moved to a cell on the first floor. The only window looked out on a miniature artificial clay soccer field that was often covered in birds. They gave us bread in excess and the men threw pieces to the seagulls as they hovered almost upright waiting for the morsels. With the early morning sun shining through their white wings they were exquisite. Crows and ducks were regular visitors, although the gulls were boss.

One could earn up to a hundred dollars a week if he worked hard. My first job was in a dark room with BMW carburetor housings stacked to infinity. The prisoners' job was to take off all the burrs. I made two hundred dollars a month by working steadily. John, an African boy, made double by working as fast as anyone could possibly go. He was arrested on a train when his shoe broke, revealing several ounces of heroin. He could neither read, nor write, the guards pleaded for him to go to school but he refused. He said he was making ten times more in prison than he could make at home and he was saving for a bush-taxi when he returned.

X-ray envelopes were my next career. The cake pan paper was pre-cut and all one had to do was apply a thin strip of glue in just the right places, fold the paper to within a thousandth of an inch of perfection, run your fingers along while creasing the two sides and you were two cents richer. Two hours of that and your shoulder blades felt like they were on fire.

Enter McDonald's visors, millions upon millions of them. Our job was to tie a rubber band through a hole on each side of the visor. I tied a few million and quit. John took them to his cell and worked most of the night, adding another part to his taxi.

With time I moved up a flight of stairs every month or so until I caught up with Schultz and the *important* prisoners. Schultz ran the library and got me out of my cell often and we would laugh and talk. There was no such thing as protection, you were thrown in with your snitch and may the best man win.

My cell on the fourth floor was above the wall and I had a lovely view of the countryside.

The Germans were humane. They allowed us to have an electric coffee maker, stereo, metal fork, spoon, flat knife, a real paring knife, and a TV with remote. Once a week we could go to the basement where a family set up shop. There we bought most anything one could buy in a small market. Of special remembrance were the cakes. They had vanilla, chocolate, swirl, marzipan, lemon and nut, all vacuum packed in foil and they were divine. I even thought of exporting them.

Marya visited with her new husband Ashley and brought the whole family for support. It was so good to see my precious family together after all these long years. I remember vividly the image I had on entering the room. They were all standing there with such expectant expressions. Marya had on red lipstick and was obviously pregnant. Marrie was giving her motherly support. Ashley was waiting to see what was going to happen. Miriam's eyes were sparkling and Rhett was waiting for me to pick him up and hug him, even though he was getting a little big.

Marya's pick did not really surprise me. I just looked at my dear lovely daughter and then looked at Ashley and thought, 'no reason to say anything'. She knows. Some say that even God cannot change the past. I don't know about that, but I knew there was nothing I could do but love her and she was going to need lots of it. Did I wonder at the folly of such a beautiful gifted young woman with an apartment in Paris, attending the best university with a new BMW and giving it all up for this man in baggy jeans? I thought, 'Sweetheart, you are going to cry bitter tears over this decision'. I swallowed hard and congratulated them and hugged Marya many times. She returned with him to England where they lived in government housing. Her new husband drawing welfare while she sliced bologna in a deli.

Few prisoners spoke English and I had to learn German. I asked Frau Blumberg to bring me a German Berlitz course and I worked diligently on the lessons and kept the tape playing day and night until I had it memorized. The other prisoners were amused and often laughed at the unexpected words I came out with.

Carlos, a Colombian prisoner, was anxious to talk to someone in Spanish and he latched on to me every time we went to the exercise yard. At night he would scream out the window, disturbing everyone, a real no-no in Lubeck. One day he hit a man in the mouth and blood splattered. Guards came running. He passed a wicked-looking shiv' to me and I threw it over the wall. Carlos was not seen for days. When he returned he was a cured man. I asked, "What happened to you, Carlos?"

"Señor Roger, those sons of whores took me down to a dungeon, stripped me naked as the hour I was born, strapped me to a steel table with a hole for my ass to shit through. They strapped my arms sticking straight out, then they spread and strapped my legs. I couldn't move nothin' but my fucking head. On one side was a metal pipe from which I could suck sugar water and on the other side was the same with fresh water. Every day they hosed me off. On the fourth day they asked if I was ready to join society."

"What did you tell them Carlos?"

"I told them, fucking yea, I was ready!"

As far as I know, he never caused a moment's problem after that.

Trees were now the same color as when I arrived. I had watched them change in slow motion. It had been an interesting year.

Marrie was causing me anguish of the heart that was infinitely more painful than prison. This is very common with prisoners. I read somewhere that ninety-five percent of prisoner's wives are unfaithful within two years. Fidelity seems to be an unnatural state for the human race.

An old farmhouse with mossy sheds, haystacks, sheep, and a beautiful blond woman kept appearing in my dreams. I thought it was in Russia or the Ukraine and perhaps there was a new life waiting for me somewhere.

Soon, new problems emerged as the US put in a request for my extradition. I hired Thomas Eissing, a handsome young professor of law, a man I liked immediately. He was truthful about the extradition request. I would be extradited and our only hope was to eliminate the 25-year special parole term. A multi-million dollar gold coin laundering charge had been eliminated by the Spanish court.

Prisoners were taken to town for medical problems and I faked plenty. The rule was that one guard carried the Luger in a holster and the other carried the clip.

This way both had to agree to shoot. Sometimes the older guards would go on those trips. A very old wino worked on my floor and I was hoping to get him. No such luck, my escorts were always young soccer players. They escorted me from the van on a light chain wrapped around the handcuffs and attached to a metal T held in the guard's hand to prevent one from jerking free.

One day the wino was working on my floor and I complained of stomach problems. He stayed and two young guards escorted me to a lovely old home in the old section of Lubeck. As soon as we entered the office the doctor told me to drop my trousers and undershorts. A young woman was standing in the room and I looked at her. The doctor said, "Never mind her, she is used to this." I dropped my britches stood there naked from the waist down. He gave me a shot and told me to bend over the table. Before I could bend over my knees were buckling. He slapped a pad of grease on my butt and shoved a TV camera on a cable up my anus. As I was passing out I was groaning "Ohhhh, Uhhhh, Ohhhh, Uhhhh." When I came to the young woman was wiping my butt. The doctor said, "Your intestines are perfect, good day."

One of the better positions at the prison was cleaning the administration offices, my job was cleaning the three lawyer visiting rooms. All the employees left at four o'clock and three prisoners, accompanied by a guard, went in to clean. Each man went directly to his duty and in a few minutes all was clean and we went back to our wing.

Next it was heart problems. After a couple of complaints to the local GP he scheduled a visit with a specialist. The guard told me to get dressed and go downstairs for a trip to town. Marrie had smuggled in two one-hundred-dollar bills and I folded them tight and hid them in my sock. Of course, money was strictly forbidden. I had no idea why they were taking me downtown this time. I soon learned it was to the heart specialist. Without ceremony he had me lay on the table and pulled up my britches legs to attach the electrocardiogram leads for a 12 lead ECG'. Both guards couldn't help but notice the bulge of money under my tight sock. One guard just glared at it and then at me, but made no attempt to remove it. Perhaps he was not allowed to search me outside the prison, I don't know.

The doctor thoroughly examined me using a new machine to look at my heart on a monitor. It was beating clear as a bell. I could see it as good as if my chest was opened up and I was looking straight at it.

On the trip back the guard turned on the passenger seat of the van and glared at me. He never once batted an eye. There was a seat in front of me and I crossed my legs and removed the money from the sock, put my hand over my mouth and as I coughed the bills were in a new position. I bit down hard and made as much spit as I could to soften them and kept biting, but never could get them small enough to swallow. I stashed them between my gums and molars and hoped for the best. When we arrived at the prison I was taken to a cell in the basement and they searched me with a fine-toothed-comb. They made me open my mouth several times, stick my tongue out and turn it all about. Somehow they missed the contraband and I was free to go back to my cell.

The trip was on a Wednesday, it was raining hard and on the way back I saw my path to freedom. A medium-security prison surrounded with two fences abutted the maximum-security prison wall and a construction project was underway to expand the maximum-security portion. An excavator had dug a trench six feet deep and eight feet wide around the medium-security portion, leaving a row of white inverted cones of sand twenty feet tall. Concrete pillars were in place along the middle of the trench and large ten by thirty-foot slabs of pre-fabricated concrete panels were lying close by, ready to attach to the uprights. This would make a solid prison wall. Above the sally-port the contractor had removed a ten-foot-wide section of the tangled mass of razor wire in order to attach the new concrete slab to the existing wall.

A menacing guard tower arced out in a half-circle from the building above the sally-port. A guard sat with a high-powered rifle and a machine gun and there was no doubt he would kill you if you tried to escape.

The bars on the attorney visiting offices were rather light and made in the shape of flat music notes. A factory in the prison manufactured inflatable boats for the navy and their painters were made of strong rope. I traded a worker in the factory a ten-mark pack of stamps for a ten-foot section of rope. He wanted to know why? I said it was for skipping.

I called my new extradition lawyer and asked him to come at once.

My friend Lutz had a blue pullover with a snoopy on the front, a birthday gift from his daughter. I borrowed this and told him about my plans. He asked that I mail it to his home, which I promised to do.

The attorney had to come a long way and it would be Thursday morning before he could get there. He was dressed as usual in cords and a leather jacket with lots of character in the patina. After feeling him out a bit I said, "Thomas, I think I can get out of here. I will give you ten thousand dollars if you will pick me up several blocks away at such-and-such a cross street and give me a ride to the border with Holland."

"Don't be silly, you cannot escape just like that," and snapped his fingers. "This prison is fifty years old, and only one person has escaped in all those years."

"I know all that. Look, I will give you ten thousand dollars if I make it or not if you will only be there tomorrow at five o'clock."

He thought a bit and said, "That is something of a strong bet on your part. Do you understand that they will shoot to kill? The guards in the towers are picked especially for that job and are highly trained."

"I am well aware of all the facts. If I am killed, you are not paid. Otherwise, you will make ten thousand dollars at five o'clock tomorrow. Do you agree?"

"It's a deal. I will be there, but I do not think you will."

"Wonderful! What kind of car will you be driving?"

"A blue Volkswagen Combi."

"OK, make sure to take the license plates off the car or cover them with mud and be ready to get out of Lubeck."

Back in my cell I cut two heavy mop handles into four pieces and taped them together by pairs, attaching half the rope to each pair. I was ready.

All night I kept jerking awake as shiny brass machine gun bullets tore into my back.

The guard always stayed with the man cleaning the computer room and at 4:45 pm I walked into the lawyer's visiting room, closed the door and tore the curtains off the windows. Next I took out the mop handles and rope, wrapped it twice around two bars and tied a figure eight. Then I stuck the taped handles in and started twisting. When it would go no farther I stuck one end of the wood behind the bars and did a repeat on the adjoining two bars and watched as a space slowly grew wide enough for me to get through. As I tried to secure the last handles they slipped out of my hand and whirled in a blur, knocking the skin off my hands. When I could finally catch my breath I did a repeat of the first part and got them secured.

The window was chest high. I stacked three chairs, stepped up, climbed onto the windowsill and stuck my head through. My chest was too big and wouldn't go through. Off came Lutz' snoopy shirt and I hung it on the bars. I could get only half my chest through so I exhaled and kept exhaling, twisting and pushing my way through. My head and shoulders were hanging out in the pouring rain. Oxygen was running out fast. I tried to get back in and could not move either way. I pictured them finding me with my naked white top-half hanging out, my chest caved in between the bars and my face purple, and dead. In a few more seconds this was going to be the scene if I could not get on through. I had been wiggling from side to side and now I tried forward and backward. The skin got a grip on the bars and I inched through. The belt caught and I couldn't get my hips through with the belt and jeans on. I hung there, twisted around in the rain and undid my belt and jeans. They slid to my ankles as I fell six feet onto the ground below.

I was in the yard where the soccer equipment and gardening tools were kept. A fantail rake was nearby and I climbed up to the window trying to retrieve the snoopy shirt, but it kept falling off the rake. I had to give up the task. One guard tower looked over this area and I kept low behind a recess in the wall. That area of the prison had scaffolding installed all the way to the fourth floor as they were installing new windows and bars. I climbed to the top and onto the roof which was made of black tar and I knew my naked white body was shining against the background. Fortunately I was above the guard towers. I crawled to the end, jumped down to the second level roof and crossed over a narrow causeway to the administration building. There I had to climb up one floor. I managed to shimmy up a drainpipe and get a grip on the gutter. Normally I could have easily pulled up and over but I was out of air. My sneakers were pumping against the slick wet windows as I finally slid over. I was now on the roof directly above the sally-port gun tower. I lay there gasping for breath. My asthma was acting up and I had forgotten my inhaler. I lay there wheezing, waiting for more energy.

I watched a guard get out of the car with his wife and little boy. They walked to the door underneath a big double umbrella. While she was walking back to her car I made a dash for it. I jumped one floor down onto the tin roof of the gun tower. The guard yelled a deep HAAA! The mountain of sand was ten feet away and twenty feet below. I jumped and sank to my knees when I hit. Without slowing down I ran straight toward the woman and little boy and in a flash I was past them and taking some lengthy strides downhill. Sirens were blaring behind. The lawyer was waiting ahead. I ran as hard as I could.

I heard a crashing, slapping racket behind me, looked over my shoulder and saw parking meters hitting the ground like falling dominoes. The woman was driving down the sidewalk trying to kill me. A car was parked ahead and she tore a fender off as she swerved out. This was too perilous for me and anyway, I couldn't go to the lawyer with this maniac on my tail. I stopped and vaulted over a brick fence that just happened to have a supply of broken glass along the top to discourage such antics. My hands were cut and bleeding and so was my chest. I ran through vegetable gardens behind nice homes, sinking to my ankles in the wet plowed ground, and lost my shoes. Big maple trees and rhododendron shrubs were thick all along the embankment. I made my way through them, crouched on a tall retaining wall overlooking a street, and watched as an unmarked car took up his position at a corner. I backtracked to the opposite street and hid in some thick shrubbery. I was half-naked, bleeding, covered in goosebumps, and figured I would have to wait in this position until dark before moving. Then, right before my eyes was a blue VW easing down the street. The car was alone and the rain was pelting down. I yelled "Hey!"

Brake lights came on, I ran and jumped in. Thomas didn't say a word. He went to light a cigarette and I saw his handshake. I must have been a sight, for he took off his jacket and told me to put it on. I did, but nobody could see in as the windows were foggy and he was having trouble seeing the road. After a few turns we were on the autobahn bound for Hamburg. I was ecstatic.

At a telephone booth in a gasoline station I called Marrie in Spain. She answered, "Hello."

"Hi sweetheart" I said.

"How is it you are able to call this late?" she asked.

"Marrie, you have a husband again. I just escaped."

"Oh no! You haven't have you?"

"Yes Marrie, I'm on the autobahn now on my way to the farm."

"Oh my God, you have ruined our lives."

"Listen Sweetheart, don't get upset. I will be at the farm tomorrow. If you were to leave tonight on the ferry to Barcelona you could catch a train to Amsterdam tomorrow and we could be together tomorrow night and talk everything over."

"Are you crazy? What would I do with the children? I am not going to pack up and run just because you wanted to escape from prison. What about me? What about the children? Do you ever think about us?"

"Marrie I will be at Marulyne's tomorrow. Come if you want to, but please be careful. "Marulyne was Marrie's cousin's child and no one knew the name.

I got back in the car feeling like a sick dog that had just been kicked in the guts and it was best just to crawl in a ditch and die.

Thomas drove on to Hamburg, smoking one cigarette after another. He turned to me and said, "Did you see the old woman with the umbrella walking on the other side of the street?"

"No, I didn't see anyone."

"She saw you get in and I'm sure she reported it."

"Did you take the plates off the car?"

"No, I didn't think you would make it."

Once in Hamburg we twisted and turned down little streets in the pouring rain and stopped before a derelict ship. We ran up a sagging gangplank and knocked on a bulkhead door. An attractive redheaded Amazonian opened the door and invited us in. Two men were introduced. Both were out on bail for a murder charge and Thomas was defending them. He explained my situation and asked if they could drive me to the border of Holland. They readily agreed and he gave them a thousand marks for their trouble. My two hundred dollars were lost in action and so Thomas gave me two hundred marks for my journey.

"Do you happen to have a bottle of whiskey? I feel like celebrating my freedom."

"Whiskey you say?" shouted the redhead. "Do you want to get to Holland this year? If you do, you had better keep whiskey away from these characters!" She was boisterous and jovial.

"I need a drink bad! I have just escaped from prison, a crazy woman tried to run me over and my wife yelled at me and ordered me to go back. I think I deserve a bottle of Chivas Regal."

"By putting it that way my friend, I tend to agree with you. I will send my man for a bottle with the understanding that in no way you allow him to even smell it."

"You have my word of honor, kind lady."

"Those cuts look nasty, let me put something on them." She got a bottle of iodine and bathed my chest and hands.

One of the men returned with a half-pint bottle of Chivas Regal which made a statement all by itself. 'If we cannot drink, then I'll be dammed if you are going to drink very much either.'

The lady of the ship put on sausages for dinner. Cats came out of the rust. I went into a corroded head and showered while they scraped up some clothes. I remember the shoes having long pointed toes and the undershorts were covered in pink and blue clowns with red balls for noses. While we were waiting for the sausages to cook a big man came in and started talking to me, poking me in the chest to emphasize each point. The woman told me not to pay him any attention, that he was her father who had Alzheimer's disease. The sausages were done and she kindly gave one to her papa. The cats jumped all over him as he sat down to eat. He would take one bite and the cats took ten. I needed a coat and she took the one he was wearing and gave it to me. It was twice my size and later caused quite a fright.

It is not a crime in Germany to escape, but it is a six-month offense to steal their clothes. However, there is no charge if they are mailed back within forty-eight hours. All I got away with was a pair of jeans, socks, and underpants. The kind woman put them in a washer and promised to mail them the next day. She did.

The two men and I loaded ourselves up in an old car and started on the five-hour drive to the Dutch border. I chose a spot far away from any towns, northeast of Osnabruck. When we got near the frontier we turned north off the highway and followed a small logging road for a few miles. I got out and shook hands with my two assistants who wished me well and I began hoofin' it to Holland.

A bright silvery moon cast shadows on the trail as I walked underneath tall pines sighing in the breeze. The trail ended in a large flat cleared area. In the distance to the east was a line of trees that looked to be about a mile away. With a determined step, I set out, as I reckoned it to be the land of the Netherlands and freedom.

I came to a ditch that looked as though a monstrous tractor had pulled a turning plow with a six-foot blade which cut a furrow through the earth six-foot deep and turned it on a slick wet crest six-foot high. I guessed this was done several years previously because a few shrubs were growing out of the sides which I judged to be four or five years old. I waded down into the ditch. The water was cold and came up to my armpits and as I tried to climb out on the far side the mud caved in and I fell back into the water. After several attempts with the same results I thought of Paul Bunyan's, Christian, falling into the *Slough of Despond.*

I stood there neck deep in muddy water hoping 'Help' would come and show me the steps and a place to lay my burden down. That night 'Help' didn't come. I waded down to where an oak shrub was growing out of the bank. I climbed up, got a grip on the little tree, and managed to get out of the slough, but not for long. From the crest I saw another ditch fifty feet farther on and a little farther on was another. There were more beyond that. I began to despair.

This time I walked along the edge until I saw a shrub growing out of the far side and managed to cross this one with less difficulty than the last one, it was enough to drain my energy. As soon as I would crawl out of one there was always another. My bones ached. I was exhausted. I lay down on my back and rested. A full moon cast pink linings on puffy clouds as they drifted by and I wondered why I chose the brightest night of the year to sneak across the border.

As I sat up I heard a bell tinkle nearby. I looked around quickly but saw nothing. This got me moving and after a couple of hours I was across the sloughs.

I cannot ask anyone to believe this, but after the ditches there was a barrier of giant cement jackstones in a pile six feet high and extending for miles in both directions. I started to climb over and they turned under my feet and hands threatening to break my legs. When I got to the top I saw a railroad and another row of jackstones. I looked up and down the track and could see until the rails met in the distance. Beyond this line was another row of jackstones and another railroad and so on. I continued at a snail's pace, a crawl, no more. After the giant jackstones I came to a field with row upon row of smaller jackstones about four feet apart and three feet tall. I could jump this barrier, but had to stop and regroup for the next jump. Occasionally I would hear the little bell and be startled. I was afraid I was crossing a minefield on a strategic military installation and that I was about to be blown out of my pointed shoes.

Dark water blocked my way, but after what I had just come through I welcomed such a simple obstacle and waded in. Needle sharp spines on floating vines brought me up short. I backed out and took off the big coat, and as I did, the bell went off in my hands. The string that tightened the hood had metal tips and when they collided, I heard the little bell. I was somewhat relieved to have worked out where the sound was coming from and I pushed the coat in front of me as I slowly waded across the lake of neck-deep water.

On the far side I came upon trees and underneath the trees was a low farm fence that I stepped across and frightened a flock of sheep. Some of the sheep had bells around their necks. I smiled and exhaled deeply as they jingled away. I was out of the minefield and probably out of Germany and in Holland. After crossing the pasture I came to a paved road and saw a house with a car under the carport. Afraid of a bad or noisy dog, I crept slowly up the drive to the car, stooped down and read 'Nederland' on the license plate. I thought of kissing the ground, but refrained and blessed Holland in my heart.

Day had not yet broken and as I walked down the highway, where a man was waiting for a ride. He said he was on his way to work and I asked him if I could pay for a ride to town. He looked me over, figured I was a tramp and said he would ask the driver who would be along soon. When the car stopped, he stepped in and the car sped away.

It was thirty kilometers to the train station and I began to walk at a brisk pace that served to keep me warm. I arrived at around eight o'clock in the morning, totally exhausted. I bought a ticket to Zutphen with a one hundred mark note and the stationmaster gave me change in guilders without the slightest thought. I ate breakfast at the station and couldn't help but smile as people avoided me.

In Zutphen, I walked up to a taxi and asked him to take me to Dotherdijk, near Eefde. He demanded payment upfront. I remember it was twenty-five guilders. The driver stopped in the driveway of a lovely old farmhouse and I got out.

It was a bright sunny morning and all was incredibly quiet. I walked to the front door and knocked with some apprehension. No one answered. I knocked again and waited and still not a sound. Fresh car tracks led into the garage. As I was about to knock even harder the door slowly opened and a very pregnant blond woman opened the door. We stood there staring at one another.

"Roger?" She asked.

"Mita?" I asked in disbelief.

She looked me over and asked rather timidly, "What happened to you?"

I looked at her big protrusion and asked, "And what happened to you?"

We had a laugh. It had been ten years since I was last there and she had been a little girl playing with her goats.

"Come in. I will get Mom and Dad. They were out late last night and are still sleeping."

I waited in front of the fireplace and soon Mita came down, followed by Marÿa and Meint who looked at me in wonder. Marÿa was so surprised that she kept her hand over her mouth. Meint said, "Sit down and tell us all about it."

I told them of the escape and of some of the difficulties I had encountered on my journey to their door. I ended by saying that I needed a place to stay for a few days.

Mita said, "You can stay here for as long as you like," and turned scarlet.

Marÿa and Meint both echoed her invitation.

Two and a half years earlier, when I was first arrested in Spain, I had Marrie bury one hundred thousand dollars in the forest behind their house for just such a contingency. Meint and Marya were unaware of this but Marrie had told me the location in explicit detail. After coffee, Meint and I went treasure hunting. I had the directions down pat. I was to walk from the big Linden tree six steps toward the sheep shed, make a right turn toward the haystack and walk five steps. This was all very simple except there were a dozen big Linden trees. We found a thin steel rod and began sticking it in the ground and after an hour or two I hit pay dirt. Marrie had placed the money in a plastic keg and a special moisture absorbent material had kept it dry.

In the afternoon they took me to town and I bought new clothes. Mostly jeans, plaid shirts, and hiking boots. I made a couple of calls to start the process for a new passport and papers. I returned feeling like a new man.

They gave me a quaint little attic room with a sloping ceiling. There was room for only a single bed and a small closet but it was tailor-made for me. A window opened onto the sheep paddock and the lovely Dutch countryside.

Meint was a professor of tropical agriculture and had worked in Swaziland where his two oldest children, Merel and Meint Bass, were born. He then took a position with the World Bank in Iran where they adopted two children, Miguel and Marulyne.

As a child, Meint was a prisoner of war in Indonesia during the Japanese occupation and almost starved to death. His photograph is on the front of Time Magazine in 1945. He was so emaciated that he could only lie on his stomach because the bones would cut his skin in other positions. He was now working as an advisor for the Indonesian Government on a large coffee plantation project in Sumatra. Marÿa was active in Christian missionary work with the local women.

The story was that Mita got pregnant by a fifteen-year-old houseboy. The family, Marÿa in particular, was against abortion so they returned to Holland for the birth of the baby. In Holland you can choose your delivery date and they give you a shot to induce labor. Mita's scheduled date was within a few days.

Marÿa took her to the hospital and in the afternoon Rebecca was born. Marÿa mailed the following announcement: *Mita, Marÿa and Meint wish to inform you of the birth of their daughter, Rebecca.*

A couple of days later I rode a bicycle to the hospital with a bouquet. Mita was propped up in bed and as I handed her the flowers I leaned over to kiss her on the cheek and was surprised to receive a kiss on the lips. Marÿa walked in seconds later and my face was fiery red.

Every day I would ask Marÿa the same question, "Have you heard from Marrie?" and it was always the same sad shaking of her head in the negative. I decided she was not coming.

Mita came home from the hospital and soon we were all going to town and restaurants. I held the baby, Marÿa and Meint walked ahead and everyone thought we were two couples. People commented on how pretty the baby was, assuming I was the father. We had good laughs over it.

I bought a Toyota car and since I didn't have a driver's license Mita drove. I had an idea of using Holland as an offload sometime in the future and I set out with Mita driving to find the perfect spot. The Frisian Islands looked promising and we made several trips, going over on the ferry early in the morning and spending the day. These islands were quaint and enchanting and we looked in many hidden little places.

One afternoon Marÿa invited me to go to church. I said I would like to but since it was in Dutch I couldn't understand anything. She assured me it was in both English and Dutch so I agreed to go. Two cars loaded up and we set out. We drove for a long way and it was dark by the time we turned off the main highway. As we rode down a little lane and over a bridge I had the strangest feeling that I knew the place and I asked Marÿa if the place was called Heathervield. She said, "YES! How could you possibly know this?"

I told her how I met Floyd McClung in a barbershop in Amsterdam and three years thereafter I was in a maximum-security prison in Spain, fighting extradition to Germany and received the book, "The Father Heart of God" written by him and I asked, "Will he be here tonight?"

"No, he is working in Amsterdam. Do you know that he is a famous man in Holland? I just can't believe you know him."

Marÿa was sure this was some sign from the Holy Spirit and I knew it was too much to be a coincidence.

During the year in Germany I was all alone in a quiet cell and read the Bible right through several times. Each time I came to the Gospel of John, chapter three, where Jesus said to Nicodemus, "Verily, verily, I say unto thee, except a man be born again, he cannot see the kingdom of God." I would have great doubt and wonder if I was to die today, would I go to the kingdom of God? Am I born again? I prayed that devout men would someday lay hands on me and I would receive 'The Baptism of the Holy Spirit,' be changed and filled with 'joy unspeakable' as I had seen others receive.

The service was held in a large building and I guess there was over four hundred present. They started singing 'The Old Rugged Cross,' followed by other old hymns I knew. The words were projected onto a screen. Some songs were in English and others in Dutch. The congregation was rather too active for me as they were swaying back and forth and clapping their hands and raising them in praise.

I was still covered in cuts, scabs, and bruises.

The congregation got quiet and a lovely English woman sitting on the stage stood up and in an angelic voice said that it was now time for prophecy. For a space of five minutes there was silence, then, across the auditorium, a tall Dutch lady stood up with a Bible draped over her hand and she began to read. Even though she read in Dutch I understood every word. "Jesus said to Nicodemus, you must be born again!" My heart twisted in my chest and there was a hot burning within. The lady sat down and again it became very quiet. My chest felt like it had a chain around it with a binder squeezing. A space of three or four minutes passed as I sat there under conviction. Then directly behind me I heard a chair scrape the floor as someone stood up.

An old Dutchman with loose false teeth and in a very strong accent said in English, "There is a man here tonight who is in a deep black pit. The Holy Spirit has a message for you sir. He says for me to tell you that you are born again and farther along your walk with the Lord than you know. The spirit that lives in you is much stronger than the spirit that lives in the world. Will you please stand up so we can pray for you?"

I stood up.

It rained hard on our trip back to the house. Everyone was silent. We went in and sat around on the sofa and floor. Several devout young Christian men were present. Somehow I wanted to relieve the pressure and each time I made light of the experience verbally or in my thoughts, a bolt of lightning would strike nearby and the report almost broke the windows. It was as if God zapped me each time I denied.

After two months Marÿa received a call from Marrie. She was in Amsterdam with Rhett. I left at once. Mita was jealous. We met and found a suite of rooms in Vondel Park. Rhett was a precious little boy, nine years old and knew what was going on. Marrie was still the beautiful Marrie. I ached for her and our old life with the children but she was not prepared to leave Mallorca and go to Russia or South America where I would be safe.

"Marrie just tell me the truth. Do you still love me?"

"Yes, I love you Roger, but there are many rooms in my heart and you occupy one of them."

"And your friend Adrian, do you love him also?"

"Yes, I love Adrian. He also has a room in my heart. But it is not the kind of love I have for you."

"I understand you have several admirers and gentlemen friends. Do they all have a room in your many chambered heart?"

"There is no cause to be mean."

I cried so hard that I missed the tram stop and we had to catch one back to the hotel. Marrie and Rhett returned to Mallorca and I went back to the farm, Mita, and the family.

A nineteen-year-old goddess can be a soothing balm to a broken heart. Yet the heart stayed broken.

Our daughter Marya flew over with her baby, Maximillian, and stayed a few days on the farm with me. It was wonderful to have her. Marÿa a and Meint returned to Indonesia and I moved to a hotel.

What should I do? What could I do? Taking a chance of collecting all or part of the three million, three hundred and eighty-two thousand owed by Jorge Ochoa in Colombia won out. Mita drove me to Paris and returned to Holland the next day.

32. BACK TO COLOMBIA

Three Million Dollar Collection -- One Million Divorce Proposal -- Twenty Ton Load of Coke -- A King Needs His Queen -- 'The Rolling Stones' and a Large Crane -- Expensive Indiscretion

I caught a train south to Portugal. Sometime during the night I awoke when the train stopped at the Spanish border. The coaches were lifted off the French trucks and placed on the Spanish that has a wider gauge. This precaution is fine during a war, but a major inconvenience otherwise. The following evening I arrived in the old city of Porto. The only flight to Venezuela for the week had departed that afternoon so I spent a boring week eating excellent seafood and experiencing many delicious Port wines. There are several for any occasion and some are surprisingly delicious.

I was nervous at the airport because my picture was on the walls of every post office, immigration and customs office in Europe, but there was no problem as I boarded for the long flight across the Atlantic. In Caracas I changed planes for San Cristobal, a city near the border with Colombia. From there I took a taxi to Cucuta, Colombia, a hot, dirty, border town.

As I was buying a bus ticket to Barrancabermeja, the agent invited me into the back room and told me there had been many robberies on this particular road and the bus line was ensuring valuables and currency. He asked how much I was carrying in cash. I counted and there were over seven- hundred dollars. He made out an insurance policy, took the money and counted it on a table right in front of me, placed it in a thin clear plastic bag and told me to put it inside my sock, which I did. In Bucaramanga I checked into the Presidente Hotel and discovered I had been robbed of two hundred dollars. He had tricked me right before my eyes! Even though I was skeptical of him counting my money and watched him closely, he still managed to fool me. That made twice I had been bitten by that same dog, never again.

The President of Colombia stayed the night in the same hotel and soldiers were everywhere. I ate in my room and called the wife of Alfonso Carbajal, a banker I was in prison within Terminal Island back in 82. He received a sentence of 25 years without parole on the dreaded charge of Continual Criminal Enterprise. I told her I was on my way to Medellin; she warned me against going, saying it was extremely dangerous.

The following morning I caught an old school bus for Barrancabermeja, a village on the Cauca River. The bus broke down so I got out and flagged a truck that took me on to the river. It was a hot, dirty place, with sagging shacks along muddy potholed streets. I ate lunch in a restaurant and the proprietor took delight in preparing all kinds of creeping crawling animals into aphrodisiac dishes. Some were tasty, some were not, but all were blistering hot. I lived through lunch with the aid of plenty of cold beer and boarded a launch for the trip upriver to Puerto Barrio, a journey of about a hundred miles.

After an hour or so of skimming along the brown water the driver turned in towards a small settlement, ran the skiff up on the mud and we all got out with our belongings. A group of soldiers searched each person, hands-on. When he touched my ribs I jumped and laughed, pretending to be ticklish. This broke the serious façade. Everyone including the soldiers was laughing. We got back in the boat and proceeded upstream. The afternoon wore on and the man beside me went to sleep and laid his head on my shoulder. People smiled. I put my arm around him and pretended to stroke his shoulder and they broke up into fits of laughter.

We arrived in Puerto Barrio well after dark and it was a rush to obtain a seat in the tough-looking muddy Toyotas. Passage to Medellin was expensive and I shared a rugged, five-hour, bone-jarring ride with two other men. We arrived in the city at three in the morning through streets strewn with paper and garbage. I rented a room right in downtown Medellin and heard gunshots echoing through the streets until I fell asleep.

The next morning the hotel receptionist said he didn't' know what I was talking about when I asked about the gunshots during the night. When I walked out the streets were clean. It was as though the previous night had been a dream. I took a taxi to 'Envigado', a village south of Medellin and home of the Ochoa's. I found five-hundred-pound Papa Ochoa at the stables and received a warm welcome. I wanted to see Jorge and learned that he was in hiding, but he told me they could send him a message. I sat down and wrote a long letter explaining that I had not received the money and how Marcus had told me it was coming. He asked me to come back in two weeks and to come before daybreak so as to attract less attention. This I did several times. The bodyguards welcomed me graciously and invited me to go to the patio where the big man was waiting on his breakfast with his veterinarian. The cook brought out whole roast chickens with copious piles of baked potatoes, gravy, and a stack of tortillas. I had breakfast with him while we watched daybreak over Medellin. I never received a reply from Jorge.

While waiting around the stables a blond masseur for horses started up a conversation. He spoke rough broken English and was proud to be showing it off. I told him the name of the hotel I was staying at and he commented on how expensive it was and invited me to stay at his apartment nearby. I went with him to have a look and it was much more luxurious than I expected. It only had one problem, there was no furniture. A new mattress on the floor of each of the two bedrooms with clean white sheets and pillows were the only furnishings. There was absolutely nothing else in the place. He said that after Escobar and the Ochoas were arrested, the work of massaging horses had hit bottom so he had sold the furniture and went into a long story about all the antiques he once owned. We came to terms of five dollars a day for rent.

I moved in with my suitcase and paid by the day. He waited like a little child for me to pay him and immediately left to buy a big pizza or beer and he was broke within the hour. His redeeming feature was that he seemed to know everyone and everywhere we went people waved, called out and laughed with him. He was a perfect version of Mexican Joe. *Dancin', romancin*, always on the go, sun shining down on Mexican Joe.'

I met Ampara de la Cruz, a lady of distinction from one of the oldest families in Colombia. Presidents and governors sprinkled her lineage. The family farm was enclosed by the city of Medellin and she lived like a Spanish Doña in the middle of chaos. When we were introduced she stood there scrutinizing my every feature and later said that I was the very image of her dead husband.

Her story was a sad one. She was a virgin until the age of thirty when she married her husband. Within two years they had a daughter and a son. Her husband was a successful attorney in practice with his brother in Envigado. Ampara, nine months pregnant, was driving her husband home for lunch when a motorcycle pulled up beside them at the light in the village. The passenger on the motorcycle opened up with a machine gun, shooting her husband ten times and hitting Ampara three times. The husband leaned over, kissed the unborn baby goodbye and died. Ampara was rushed to the hospital and given a caesarian. A bullet had gone through the baby's head.

Ampara invited me to her home for Christmas dinner and I was impressed at how kind she was to her maids. As soon as the table was set she told them to leave and go to their families. Such kindness is rare in Latin America. Other evenings she came by and took me to restaurants overlooking Medellin and she made it clear that she was interested in marriage. I told her I was married but was having heartaches over my wife. I explained that I still loved my wife and I did not know if we could ever get together again. I told her about my escape from the German prison and the money Ochoa owed me. She was alarmed at my trying to collect the money and said she was sure that such money was the cause of her husband's death.

After much searching I got a lead on my friends, Marcus and Esmeralda, who had moved to Cali. I caught a bus to that city and began inquiring. After several days of searching, I found someone who gave me a phone number. I called and a surprised Marcus said he would meet me on the steps of the Cathedral downtown. I was somewhat afraid to meet him like that. If Ochoa had given him the money then maybe he would have someone shoot me on the cathedral steps. These thoughts occupied my mind as I stood close behind the great columns. Then I saw my old friend looking for me with his open honest face and I rejoiced. He and Esmeralda with their two children, Nicholas and Amileta, lived in a palatial apartment overlooking Cali and we all had a wonderful reunion.

I moved into a detached apartment across a large patio with big orange trees growing in planters. In the yard was a beautiful German shepherd, a parrot that talked and cried like a baby and a tortoise that came inside before earthquakes.

When I told them about the 'Lady of Medellin' they laughed at me. Then we received a call from Ampara who said she was flying down for the weekend with her sister as chaperon. Marcus and Esmeralda were even more dubious. However, when they met Ampara and her sister, both changed their opinions. They were impressed! The trip had a purpose, a wedding proposal. Ampara offered to pay Marrie one million dollars for a divorce if I would marry her and promise never to go near the business of drugs again. I thanked her and bowed out as graciously as I could.

Marcus hooked me up with the Rodriquez-Orejuela brothers who shipped more cocaine than Pablo Escobar, Jorge Ochoa, and the entire Medellin Cartel ever dreamed of. These brothers were shipping 20 tons at a time on a regular basis. They had Boeing 727's flying loads to the Federalés in Mexico who trans-shipped it in tractor-trailer trucks to Texas and California, crossing at borders where family members worked for US Customs.

They owned a fleet of fast banana boats that departed weekly for Belgium loaded with bananas and cocaine. General Manuel Noriega was in their pocket making untold millions by trans-shipping ether from Germany. Ether is the major ingredient used in manufacturing cocaine. Everyone was making money, big corporations too and they knew what they were doing. The brothers controlled the operation from the peasant farmers picking coca leaves in the mountains to sales and banking all over the world. These brothers were quiet and they were ruthless.

This level of trafficking is only possible with major US government employee involvement at the very highest levels. They say the DEA shipped more drugs than the CIA ever did. Some say the DEA was just a sub-branch of the CIA. But white boys in suits never go to jail.

Miguel, the elder of the brothers, took me out on the town and later to his home where the first thing that greeted us was a cougar. My thoughts were drawn uncomfortably back to Sonya and the eaten baby. I stayed with Miguel for three full days before he decided to do business with me. Once he accepted me, the doors were wide open.

Dan McKeon and his 'Playboy Centerfold' girlfriend Kim came over to Amsterdam after I escaped from the German prison. Dan offered me a wad of money which I refused but thanked him for the thought. He told me he had a 75-foot sailboat with a hidden compartment that could hold five tons of cocaine and he was ready to work. I called from Cali and told him I had a load to transport to California. We agreed on a price and he said he would be on his way within a week. My sister Kay went along as a crewmember on the trip south. They got as far as Acapulco and stopped. Dan said he needed some parts and flew back to the states and was gone for a month. The Arriella Brothers had the five tons waiting on the Pacific coast and were ready to deliver it out at sea. Dan kept procrastinating and finally he returned to the states and abandoned the deal. I later learned that he was testifying in a Federal Court in Rhode Island against his former fiancé and her husband who both received life sentences on a four-ton deal that Dan had organized for them. He also testified before a Federal Grand Jury about the five tons I negotiated with him.

After the deal with Dan fell through Miguel and I had a meeting. He asked, "Can you unload ships on the west coast of the United States?"

"Yes, I can. How much will be in each shipment?"

"Twenty tons."

"How much do you pay for this service?"

"Two thousand dollars a kilo for picking up the cocaine at sea and taking it to a safe storage place where my man can get to it."

Forty million dollars for a night's work was more than I expected.

"How far offshore will the ship drop the product?"

"The ship is a large container ship departing Peru en route to Korea. She will come as close to the coast as possible. I think it will be within twenty miles offshore perhaps only five. It depends on the location you choose."

"How will it be unloaded?"

"The crew will have it packed in a container on the very back of the ship. When they pass, they will throw a drag chute in the water and the cocaine will come out in 25-kilo waterproof bags attached to a line spaced two meters apart. The ship never slows down nor varies its course."

"When do you want to do the first load?"

"We are waiting on you, Señor."

Mother and my sister Nell met me in Nuevo Laredo, Mexico and we drove across the international bridge to Laredo Texas. Nell's husband David is the same height and age as I am so she brought his wallet and entire ID and gave it to me. They left their luggage in a motel room in Texas and drove down in a Ford Blazer. I left my luggage in my hotel room in Mexico and we drove back across with nothing to draw suspicion. The officer asked for our place of birth and the purpose of the trip. Nell was driving and she said we had never been to Mexico and had just gone down for the day. He waved us on. As soon as we got to their room, Nell returned to Mexico and retrieved my luggage.

One thousand dollars purchased me an authentic Georgia driver's license and after a few days of visiting and hiding I caught a flight to California. Cal Worthington, the celebrity car dealer gave me a deal of 10,000 blue chip stamps and a used car for my stack of hundreds.

Happy with the exchange I headed up the coast looking for 'The Spot'. In Morro Bay I rented a room with an artificial fireplace, a coffee pot, and a king-size bed. I arose early every morning and snooped around until dark. It's amazing what one can find in a month of serious looking.

Lonely can't begin to describe the feeling I had in that hotel room. I was empty inside, not the kind of feeling that's banished with bacon and beans. I wanted my family back.

On the strand in the village of Oceano, I rented a new four-bedroom house with luxurious white furniture and black granite floors in the kitchen and baths. A ten-mile white sand beach with porpoises frolicking in the surf was the front yard. Whales fed in the bay and I followed their progress as they surfaced and blew on their way down the coast.

Marrie seemed pleased I had found a place and flew over with Miriam and Rhett. I filled the house with flowers, bought cut glass vases and candle holders, and everything I could think of to brighten the place up. I was filled with excitement as they arrived. Marrie cried it was so beautiful but burst my bubble that night when she said she had not packed up when she left Spain and was returning in a few days.

"How long will it take you to pack?"

"At least a month, you can't expect me to just rush into these things at your whims."

"Marrie, you should be able to arrange packers from here and schedule them to be available when you get there and it couldn't possibly take more than three days to get everything done."

"Roger, you can't hurry me. Pam is coming over next month for a month then it will take a couple of weeks to pack."

"God, Marrie, I'm your husband! We haven't been together for three years and now you choose to be with Pam instead of me?"

"Roger, don't get angry. Pam and I have been planning this vacation for months."

"Is Adrian going to escort the two of you around Europe?"

"Don't be ugly!"

A few days later Marrie returned to Europe and it was many years before I saw her. Except in a prison visiting room.

Marya came over from England with baby Max and Miriam flew in from Spain the day after she graduated from high school. The three children and little grandbaby were some consolations. We bought a trampoline and put it up in the soft sand in front of the house and the place became the local hang out. Rhett and his new friends took over the big playroom with a pool table.

Ten miles south, on the way to Santa Maria, is a castle-looking-game park with miniature golf, go-carts, and all kinds of games. I took Rhett there often and he had many gunfights with Quick Draw McGraw. I bought rolls of quarters and we stayed as long as he wanted.

China Cove is a very small nook located behind a point about ten miles west of San Luis Obispo, California. It can boast of perhaps fifty feet of sandy beach surrounded by sheer walls of loose rock a hundred feet high. Two ruts run across a pasture and over the hill to this little inlet. A heavy wooden gate locked with a log chain nailed to a big post supposedly prevents the uninvited from entering. A brief inspection revealed that the chain was nailed to the post with regular nails. A simple claw hammer could easily remove the nails that could later be nailed back in the same holes and nobody would ever know that 20 tons of cocaine passed through.

Rhett and I headed for Los Angeles to look for used equipment. We found two heavy-duty ten wheeler dump trucks with gasoline engines for four thousand dollars each. They were old but in good shape. Commercial operators had changed to diesel and similar trucks with diesel engines cost ten times that amount. Next on the list was a used 20-ton road crane. As we were driving along Interstate 10, east of Los Angeles, I spotted one in a yard off to the right. I got off at the next interchange, went back and found the place. A small man wearing overalls walked up and in a heavy Arkansas drawl said, "Good afternoon, can I help you gentlemen?"

"And a good afternoon to you sir. We're looking for some equipment. What's the story on that old D8 over there with her tracks rusting off?" I wasn't interested in it, I was just making conversation until I got to the crane.

"She ain't for sale."

"What will you take for that old Caterpillar grader?"

"She ain't for sale either."

"Then I don't reckon you want to part with that old road crane over yonder?"

"No sir, I don't. You have just pointed out three of my bread and butter pieces."

"Looks like they have been sitting in the same tracks for a long time. What's the story on them?"

"Did you ever hear of that outfit from England called the Rolling Stones?"

"Yes sir, I think most everybody has heard of them from time to time."

"Well, they drove up here one morning in a big long limousine smoking marijuana cigarettes and bought that loader over yonder and the grader and crane you asked about. They then went and bought another two million dollars' worth of other equipment. They said they bought a ranch up on Mount Palomar and had it in mind to all work together and build the place up. They wrote me out a check and said they would be back soon. It's been 11 years and I ain't seen hide nor hair of 'em since. I read somewhere that the outfit broke up, but their office sends me a five hundred dollar check every month for storage."

The gentleman suggested a crane dealer down the road where I bought one in good condition for twenty-five thousand dollars.

Finding a warehouse where we could come and go at all hours of the night without prying eyes was somewhat difficult but eventually I found an ideal place in San Luis Obispo.

A vessel to drag the haul in from the sea to the cove was all that was lacking. Rhett rode with me from marina to marina as I searched for one. As we drove into Santa Barbara I asked him if he would like to stop and see his friend Paul. He smiled and said he would so we went to the home of Stan and Colleen Aristo who had been our neighbors and friends. Colleen was so surprised and happy to see us she just beamed. She was a pretty woman who had been the homecoming queen for Santa Barbara a few years back and she was still just as beautiful. She prepared lunch and cried as she told me that Stan left her for another woman. He told her he didn't love her anymore and wanted to go his way so now they were getting a divorce. He had been living with the other bimbo for a year; however, he came over once in a while and spent the night. She said Stan would be delighted to see us and she called and asked him to come over after work.

I told Colleen that I also had problems of the heart and told her about Marrie coming over and spending only a few days with me before returning to Spain. She could not understand how Marrie could possibly behave in such a manner and I thought Stan must have gone bonkers to leave Colleen and three young children for some young bimbo.

Stan came in a little after five and he had blown up out of all proportion by injecting steroids and pumping iron. I immediately saw the change in the man. I also knew that steroid abuse caused one's emotions to harden. Stan gave me a big bear hug, sat down at the table and accepted the offered wine. Colleen cried as he related his side of the story about how he was fed up with his business as a chiropractor with several men working and it took sixty thousand dollars a month to cover expenses. He said he did not love Colleen any longer and had finally moved out, but he felt responsible for them and he would be happy when Colleen met someone and married again.

After dinner he drove me to the marina in his hundred thousand dollar Mercedes sports car. We walked down the dock to his yacht, a sixty-foot, twin-engine, Chris Craft. It was in immaculate shape. We sat in the main salon and drank a goodly portion of a fifth of Chivas and he told me he was benching over five or six-hundred pounds, squatting six or seven-hundred and had been a winner at such-and-such meets. He was also the designated sports chiropractor for the American Olympic Team. The yacht was perfect for my purpose and I broached the subject.

"Stan, I have a job coming up and I'm in need of a yacht such as this. Would you consider renting it to me for a few days if the price was right?"

"Hell yeah old buddy. What's the deal?"

"I will pay you five hundred thousand dollars cash for the rent of your yacht for less than a week, if anything goes wrong I will run her on the rocks and burn her, you know you will never be implicated. You can report it stolen."

"You have got yourself a deal partner. Just let me know when you want to take her out." We shook rather too hard on the deal and returned to the house.

Colleen was waiting up and Rhett and Paul had already gone to sleep. I invited them both to bring Paul up on the weekend and said I would cook *Daddy's Chicken*, a favorite with all who had eaten it. Stan said they would be there at six o'clock Friday evening and stay the weekend. I was shown into the bedroom where Rhett was sleeping and Colleen was beaming as she and Stan departed for their quarters.

Friday evening the doorbell rang, I hurried to answer it in my new striped apron and there stood Colleen, alone. I looked around and asked, "Where's Stan?"

"I guess the son-of-a-bitch had a date." She said rather sad and bitterly.

"Well come on in, I have the wine open and waiting." Colleen, Rhett and I enjoyed a good supper and afterward she and I took a long walk on the beach. That night we sat on the patio and drank a couple of bottles of wine and feelings were charged. I said, "I feel uncomfortable knowing you and Stan all these years."

Colleen said, "I'll never kiss and tell." She spent the weekend with me and then the next. All I can say is, Stan is a damned fool. And I was one also because Colleen did tell Stan and he called the DEA and told them my address and about my request to rent the boat.

Miriam and Rhett were in the house. I was in my swimming trunks throwing clams into the ocean left by the early morning diggers. I knew I couldn't save but a fraction of them and was thinking of the old missionary in Africa. Someone told him that he couldn't save all the millions of souls and he replied, "No, but I can save this one and this one and this one."

Eight or ten 4-wheel drive vehicles surrounded me. Twenty or more men jumped out with as many muzzles pointed at me. They were yelling for me to lie down and I said, "Fuck off, where do you think I'm going?" They handcuffed me and put me in one of their new vehicles. The driver bitched as I smeared suntan lotion all over his new seats.

They drove me to the back of the house and left me in the car for a couple of hours while they searched and robbed the place. Thankfully, Rhett and I had buried the million-dollar coin a foot deep in the sand right next to a pillar in front of the house and made a mark above it. They took my Corum watch and listed it on the articles seized. Afterward, Miriam took it off the table and hid it in a flowerpot. They all screamed and took on accusing each other of being idiots for stealing it after it had been documented. Good girl, Miriam!

A United States Marshal chained me up with leg irons and cuffs then attached this hardware to a bolt in the floorboards of the back seat of the vehicle. On the way down to the Metropolitan Detention Center in downtown Los Angele he purposely drove forty miles out of the way to drive by the Penitentiary in Lompoc. As we passed, he said, "Reaves, take a good look at your new home. I expect you'll be there for many years to come."

33. LOMPOC, HELL FOR THE LIVING DEAD

An Un-reliable Cell Mate -- Lompoc -- Mikes Bin' Robbin' -- Pepe and the Rattlesnake -- The Quiet Man -- Doc Roger -- "Can You Help Me?" -- Chaotic Visions

We arrived at the Los Angeles, Metropolitan Detention Center and went through assigned security and prisoner induction routine. When the paperwork was done they threw me to the 'High Power' wing on the 22nd floor. This is where all high-risk prisoners are housed.

In the wee hours of the first morning I was just getting back in my bunk after taking a pee when the building started swaying. I looked out the four-inch-wide window and saw transformers exploding across the city. Each one had its own color, red, blue, yellow, and white. It looked like a scene from a W.W.II movie with the Japs bombing Los Angeles. The building felt like it was floating on waves of the ocean and swaying so hard I thought it had to come down. I yelled, "Rock and roll, early parole!" and hoped it came down with me on top of the heap. It didn't fall so I had to find some other way.

During my stay at MDC, one of the worst riots in US history erupted in south-central Los Angeles (April 1992) after the acquittal of four white police officers charged with the videotaped beating thirteen months earlier of a black suspect, Rodney King. Fifty-eight people died in the rioting. At night I would look down through my tiny window at the rubber-tired tanks patrolling the streets. Neither side of the window looked like the United States of America I thought I knew.

A prisoner who had worked on the construction of the building told me there was two feet between our wall and the outside wall and the entire structure was crisscrossed with hanging girders and beams. On the ground floor was supposedly a fire exit that had to remain unlocked. I began taking the guts out of the air conditioning vents as they were thin and made of extremely hard stainless steel. My roommate, Ron Throckmorton from Phoenix was all for it. One of us dug while the other watched. We could only work during the day while a lot of noise was going on as the rasping of metal against concrete echoed through the block and the floors above and below. It took two months of hard digging and our hands were ruined even though we wrapped the blades with cloth. The hole was made high up above my bunk where a calendar hid the evidence. When we pulled the plug out, I could see all the way to the ground floor, nine floors down.

Ron was hyperventilating with excitement when he came in. He had just left from a visit with his brother who was to pick us up after the four o'clock count and whisk us away in a fast car.

After the count the floor was closed down and everyone ordered out on the recreation patio. Guards began arriving with video cameras big enough to make a movie. They made a pretense of searching all the cells and taking a couple of men away and then they called my name and took me to the hole where I stayed for the next six months. Ron had lost his nerve or he was a snitch to begin with. In either case, he was awarded with a reduction of sentence and shipped to a prison farm.

The hole was a dirty dingy place with a thin plastic mattress, two short sheets, a thin foam pillow, and one blanket. The light stayed on 24 hours a day. We were issued 2200 calories, carefully measured out. They even counted the margarine pats and sugar for the one Styrofoam cup of lukewarm coffee. I was allowed one hour of exercise a day. The guards came at five a.m. and yelled," Recreation, be ready in five minutes." Most men didn't bother but I never missed one. It wasn't much, just a 15-foot square patio with a basketball hoop, however, three or four men would talk a little, which was something.

Harry Dwyer was the examiner for the parole board and he gave me 132 months for a parole violation. As far as I know that is the longest in US history. He said, "You must think you are like one of those Vietnam prisoners of war who can crawl out of those bamboo prisons at will. Well, I don't think of you in those terms. For the escape from the court in Spain, you will serve 24 months; for the escape from the German prison I am going to add another 24 months; for the attempted escape here in MDC, I am going to add another 24 months; and for the German conviction for transporting three and a half tons of hashish, I am going to add 60 months. That is a total of eleven years."

I stood up and said, "And I hope you burn in hell!"

The Santa Inez River flows gently through the idealistic Lompoc valley with thousands of acres of flowers in a mosaic of brilliant colors. On a bluff overlooking the river stands Lompoc Federal Penitentiary. An ugly, grey, monolithic structure of concrete and razor wire. A hell for the living dead. One thousand four hundred men are caught in its hideous maw and few there be that leave while still breathing. However, due to pressure from Washington, they try to keep the death in custody count down by getting the dying to the county hospital shortly before they expire.

Guards have 'The New Rock' stenciled across the backs of their jackets because Lompoc Penitentiary is where they moved the prisoners from the infamous Alcatraz when it was closed.

Upon my arrival at Lompoc I was put in "H" unit, better known as "The Hole," and what an appropriate name. This is the punishment unit, the official reason I was there was because I was not 'designated' which took three months. The true reason was to punish me further for the hole in the wall at MDC.

The place was full of angry Cubans. Ten years earlier they burned the prison in Atlanta and these miserable, forgotten men had been in the "hole" ever since. Most completed their sentences years before but were not eligible for release because they now had a record and no country would take them. Over ten thousand men were caught in this situation and over the years they became animals. Two men shared an existence in a cell five by eight feet. Two steel bunks with two-inch-thick mattresses, two small metal lockers, two metal hooks protruding from the concrete, a stainless steel basin, and toilet of the smallest size imaginable. A fluorescent light recessed in the ceiling covered with heavy wire constantly lit the cell. Many men saved their feces and urine to throw on the guards, sometimes the chaplains as well. Prisoners regularly set their mattresses on fire and pushed them between the bars. A guard stood at the end of the corridor and turned a fire hose on the smoldering cotton and there it lay, smoldering for hours.

Such a din of diabolical sounds no man ever heard. My next cell neighbor yelled so loud it vibrated my innards. Using toilet paper for fuel my cellmate boiled water, added a strong dose of cleanser, and threw it in the face of the neighbor, blinding him. New cellmate, new neighbor.

An old man taught me how to take the marks off used postage stamps by soaking them overnight in dental cream. This became my hobby. I collected stamps from the two hundred men, took the glue off an envelope, used this to glue a stamp on a fresh envelope and gave them away. It was fun for a while. I had Marrie coat a pretty daisy stamp with clear nail polish and we sent that stamp back and forth for years.

After three months in Dante's Inferno they moved me to "M" unit, the maximum-security unit, in the maximum-security prison where I existed for the next seven years and four months. Upon entering, everyone was suspicious of me. I had no tattoos, I did not look the part, and I was not accepted.

Some years prior to that existence I was a part-time beekeeper, gradually increasing my apiary to five hundred hives. Sometimes a new queen was needed and I would order one from a commercial apiarist. She arrived in a box with a screen on one side and a cube of hard sugar blocking the exit. If she was placed directly in the hive the bees killed her immediately. However, it took three or four days for them to eat the sugar, and by that time they were used to the intruder and accepted her. How similar are prisoners to bees.

My claim to jailhouse fame was my *Pink Card.* Only 45 federal prisoners in the United States were so honored. This was a hot pink plastic ID which I clipped onto a shoestring tied around my neck. Everywhere I went I had to give the card to the officer and he called control and said, "I've got Reaves in the library," yard, church, or wherever I went. When I left the unit a call was made declaring that Reaves was on his way to unit M, or wherever. Once a guard mistakenly took the card home with him when his shift ended and I was thrown in the hole overnight. The next day I was returned to my cell in the unit, but my little home was gone, it was a mess, everything had been stuffed in bags and placed in storage.

For two years I was down on the flats with a multitude of different cellmates. On the flats were three TVs, one for the blacks, one for the Mexicans, and one for the whites. The sound of each was broadcast on a particular radio frequency so one had to have a radio with earphones in order to watch TV. There were three tiers of cells, back to back, with a plumbing chase separating them and they faced outward across a void of twenty feet toward a window. The walls were made of eighteen inches of reinforced concrete. There was a basement with offices with an equal amount of cement and the same for the roof. I noticed that men didn't age as quickly here and I hypothesize to this day that it was because they were shielded from astral radiation more than most men.

After two years of being squeaky good I was awarded a single cell on the third tier. This move was like dying and going to heaven. No longer did I have to breathe other people's farts and cigarette smoke. Also, people are peculiar and it takes time to learn each new individual. These single cells are what the guards hold over the better-behaved men, one word of insolence and out you go. If a guard does not like you he can get you kicked out for any infraction, "the cell is cluttered," or "there are too many books causing a fire hazard." However, the men on the top tier knew this and were quiet, careful, and courteous. I had some wonderful neighbors and they became friends for life. I would like to introduce you to a few.

Phil Dimerza, good looking, solid muscle, karate expert, yoga, trained with the Ringling Brothers and Barnum Bailey Circus, heir to the throne of Iran. This caused the news to dub his trial "The Prince Defense," he is now serving fifty years without parole for large-scale marijuana sales.

James Marion, 'Big Jim,' six foot six, 400 pounds, kind, gentle, heart of gold, bookie for ball games, Christian, serving thirty years for marijuana sales, plus ten for giving a fool the telephone number of a helicopter pilot. 'Fool' was on the phone when his ride came and someone had to go tell him his taxi was here. He ran out, jumped onto one side of the machine causing it to cartwheel through three fences breaking the pilot's neck. Unfortunately, fool lived and had Jim's handwritten note in his pocket.

Vic, black, forty, muscular, could bench press over 400 pounds, quiet, easy-going, articulate, had a beautiful wife, serving thirteen life sentences for selling an agent one gram of cocaine on thirteen occasions.

Arthur and Victor Andonia, brothers, Lebanese, devout Catholics, quiet, kind, harmless, lovely families, serving 505 years for 101 sales of gold for cash in their gold business where they reported each transaction. Judge Ideman gave them, five years consecutive for each sale because he wanted the infamy of handing out the largest sentence in US history.

Jimmy Craft, gentleman, genius, marathon runner, from old aristocratic family, brother a banking billionaire, South Carolina Akin-Craft Highway named after his father, serving 80 years for cocaine possession. The government had three indictments in three different states at the same time. At sentencing, each conviction counted as a prior, thus compounding the sentence.

Yildren, 75 years old, East German spy, was to be exchanged two days after the Berlin wall fell. Now he doesn't have a country, as there is no East Germany. He could make keys to any door using dental plate putty or Pyrex dinner plates. He was once a diamond miner in Sierra Leon, great storyteller, harmless. Clinton refused to pardon him with the hundreds he pardoned as he was leaving office. Yildren missed out, as he had insufficient funds.

I ask you, just who are the evil ones here? Just who deserves to be locked up? Just who is lacking in moral and ethical fiber? The judge or the accused?

Chaplain John Burke was a saint! A more compassionate man I have never met. He was a retired tank commander and alcoholic who converted and became a born again, spirit-filled Catholic. He wore a raincoat and hat when he visited the men in the hole, he knew human waste would be thrown on him. He stopped and prayed with you while holding hands through the bars and would do anything he could for anyone who asked.

One night around midnight, my cell door opened with a loud clatter and a guard came and told me to get up and go to the chapel immediately. My heart froze in my chest and my mouth became so dry I could not swallow. My knees were so weak I had difficulty getting down the stairs. As I walked down the corridor

I prayed, 'Oh God, don't let it be Mother, or Marrie, or Marya, or Miriam, or Rhett, or Marijo, or Charlotte, or Nell, or Larry, or Kay, or Sharon, Oh God, let this cup pass from me'. Chaplain Burke was waiting in the doorway and I was thankful it was him. He said, "Roger, your son- in- law, John Cross, has been killed in a car accident in France and your daughter wants you to call her." He dialed the number direct and told me to talk as long as I wanted. Marya was beside herself with grief. She said, "Daddy, his head was lying on his chest and I just held him and talked to him until he became cold. Oh Daddy, what am I going to do? What am I going to do? I don't want to live. Oh Daddy if you could only come now!" I comforted her as best I could under the circumstances. I have never felt more grossly inadequate. My daughter needed me. But I was locked up and far away.

After I returned to my cell I got on my knees and prayed for Marya and the soul of John. I was very sad and troubled. Peace just wouldn't come and I asked God for help. I opened the Bible and read the very first page I opened to Matthew 22: 23-32:

"The same day came to him the Sadducees, which say that there is no resurrection and asked him, Saying, 'Master, Moses said if a man die having no children, his brother shall marry his wife and raise up seed unto his brother. Now there were with us seven brothers: and the first, when he had married a wife, deceased and having no issue, left his wife unto his brother: Likewise the second also and the third, unto the seventh. And last of all the woman died also. Therefore, in the resurrection whose wife shall she be of the seven? For they all had her.

Jesus answered and said unto them. 'Ye do err, not knowing the scriptures, nor the power of God. For in the resurrection they neither marry, nor are given in marriage, but are as the angels of God in heaven. But as touching the resurrection of the dead, have ye not read that which was spoken unto you by God, saying, 'I am the God of Abraham and the God of Isaac and the God of Jacob? God is not the God of the dead, but of the living.'"

At that moment I knew John was not dead and I was greatly comforted as I thought of him and other loved ones who had passed beyond the veil.

Days turned into weeks, weeks into months, months into years and the years mingled and ran together. My world was grey and colorless and only two things brought color and beauty to my dingy existence. Marrie came every Monday. She was always dressed up in pretty colors and her countenance was radiant and luminous. We spent three or four wonderful hours holding hands, talking about the children and making plans for our life once I was released. Lunch was cold sandwiches purchased from the vending machines, we didn't mind, we were together for a few hours and we were in love. The years and the hardships had only brought us closer together.

My other color came from dreams. Just before going to sleep I would pray to see Daddy, or Grandma, or an Uncle, or a friend from long ago in a dream and strange as it may seem, I sometimes had a dream of that person. Often the dream was back in the forties and the cars were older, from the thirties and on dirt roads. The clothes were of the same era. I remember one dream of Daddy and Uncle L.G. in a 1938 Chevrolet. They were dressed in suits and were wearing felt fedoras, cocked to one side exactly as they once wore them. Daddy has been dead over fifty years and I can recall his face better from that dream than from old memories. I dreamed in living color and woke to a grey and dingy world.

Mike was a tall, lean, soft-spoken colored man who kept his shoes spit-shined and his khaki clothes ironed to perfection. One afternoon as I was walking the track Mike passed me and I stretched my stride to equal his. We got to talking. I said, "Mike, how on earth did such a kind man as you end up in a place like this?"

He answered, "Rogers, (as he called me) I'm from down in South Carolina and times was hard. I was cropping' tobacco and pickin' cotton for five dollars a day when this little cousin of mine from New Jersey drives up in a brand new Pontiac and wearing designer clothes. I said, bro, what you doin?"

He said, "I been robbin'."

I said, "Man, what you mean you bin robbin'?"

"Like I say man, I been robbin'. Ain't nothin' to it."

He pulled out a little .22 revolver and said, "I goes in the stores about closing time, stick this little gun in the man's face and he empties his cash register. Like I said, ain't nothin' to it."

That evening we went behind Ma's house and shot up every mayonnaise and Clorox bottle in the garbage pile and before dark I was getting pretty good at it. I bought the little pistol off him and the next Saturday I went to town and did a couple of hold-ups but that little pistol didn't seem to scare 'em like I thought it would. So, I went and bought a twelve-gauge pump-action shotgun. I would go in those grocery stores on a Saturday night around nine o'clock when they was counting their money. Now all those stores have a rack of dried peas and butterbeans somewhere up around the checkout counter, I'd go through the door, jack a shell in the chamber and blast that rack with buckshot. When those butterbeans quit rollin' on that wooden floor, it got mighty quiet. I'd say, "This is an important day in your life. Don't make it your last. You knows what I'm after."

"Sometimes I got thirty or forty thousand dollars out of one of those little stores so I didn't have to do it but a time or two a year. I moved around from state to state and got away with it for twenty years. But then credit cards come out the take started getting less and less so I changed to banks. One afternoon I went into a bank over in Arkansas and made everyone lie down on the floor. There was a big fat man who gave me a bit of trouble and as he lay down his shirt came up and I saw a thirty- eight stub nose revolver in a holster on his belt. I was keeping my eye on him while the manager was emptying the safe and I saw this fool roll partly over and reach for his pistol. I pointed the shotgun at him and said, "Don't do it mister, don't do it." He pulled it on out and I cut him in two with buckshot. They caught me a few days later and I got life without parole, but I guess I was lucky it was a bank and the feds got me. If the state would a prosecuted, they would da' electrocuted me."

We continued walking around the track. There was a baseball game going on between the whites and blacks, we became aware of some tension. This must have been some playoff as there were only twenty or thirty whites who were mostly the players. Two or three-hundred black men were standing around and watching from the bleachers. Something must have sparked off, I saw the white pitcher and a black baseman tie into one another in a fiery fistfight. Faster than you can ever believe the three-hundred blacks in the bleachers poured onto the field and enveloped the white team as if a black canvas had covered the field. It took at least a half-hour for the guards to bring the riot under control and by that time some men had been badly hurt, black, and white. We were forced under gunpoint to lie down on the grass in exactly the place where the worst fighting took place. Guards came and bound our wrists behind our backs with plastic handcuffs. We lay in that position for hours. The moon came up, the stars came out and the dew fell heavily, yet we were not allowed to move off our bellies. Once all the casualties were removed they came with bright lights and inspected each person. If there was one drop of blood or one mark on one's hand he went one direction while the unmarked ones were returned to their unit. I got back to my unit after midnight and listened to the roar of the diesel buses as they took off for prisons all over the country loaded with men. The next morning over three hundred men had been transferred and I never saw Mike again. I know he didn't have a part in the riot, they had just made him lie down in the blood.

Pepe was just sixteen years old when he showed up on the Hi-Power floor at the Metropolitan Detention Center. He had been caught with a shotgun, guarding a ton of cocaine in a house. The judge gave him a life sentence without the benefit of ever being paroled. Pepe was a chubby happy lad. There was one hard man there who kept play wrestling and rubbing on him most shamefully. I befriended young Pepe and told him to stick with me and he would be all right. He stuck close and we became friends. He was transferred out, but I continued to think of him over the years and often wondered what happened with him.

One day I was sitting on a bench in the weight yard when a hard-looking, muscled up Mexican came over and said, "You don't remember me do you, Señor Roger?"

I looked at him closely and saw the deep-set eyes one often sees on men who have seen too much or those with no hope and I said, "No, I'm sorry, but I don't remember you."

"I'm Pepe."

I saw it then! Yes, it was the boy, he had grown up and filled out during the past seven hard years. I was truly happy to see him and I invited him to my cell. He sat down on the bunk. I asked him how he was doing and he said, "I'm not well Señor, I have lupus and I'm dying."

He pulled up his trouser leg and pressed the flesh. His finger went to the bone and the indent stayed there after he removed his finger. He had me push in on the muscle of his arm and it did likewise. After he told me about lupus I wanted to change the subject to something lighter so I asked him to tell me the story of the rattlesnake. He chuckled and said, "You remember that Señor Roger?"

"Yes Pepe, I remember it well, but please tell it again. Start from the beginning and don't leave anything out."

"OK, I was born on a little rancho in the mountains of Chihuahua, Mexico. My papa died when I was ten years old and left my mother and five little children. We were very poor and sometimes we didn't have enough to eat so I began catching rattlesnakes and my mother would cook them, and Señor, they are very good to eat. I caught so many that we made a pen to keep them in as you would chickens. We tended a little garden where we grew beans and corn and with this, we ate well.

Down the mountain, about five kilometers was a village. Every Saturday I could hear the music echoing up the canyon and I begged my mamma to let me go.

When I turned twelve, she surprised me one day by telling me I could go if I was back before dark. Oh, I was a happy boy as I set off down that mountain trail on my very first trip to the village alone. When I was about halfway down I came across a really big rattlesnake stretched across the road. Boy was I excited! I had never caught one that big before. I ran and cut a limb with a little fork, pressed it behind his head and picked him up partway. He was as big around as my leg and over two meters long with a long pod of rattlers. I got under him, pulled him over my shoulder, and set out for the village at a good clip. That snake was heavy and kept squirming and I kept going faster and faster. Finally, he squirmed and wrapped around my right arm several times with half of him dragging on the ground. I could not carry him like that and my grip began to weaken. I knew I could not hold him much longer and I could not turn him loose while he was wound around my arm. I was scared and didn't know what to do. I came around a bend and there hanging partway out over the road was a big boulder. I went up to it and began rubbing his nose back and forth, back and forth, until I rubbed his head off. And that Señor, is how I saved my life."

Artie lived in the cell directly behind mine. I lived in E17 and Artie lived in F17. We slept head to head, separated by three feet of concrete. I didn't know Artie very well, no one did. He was quiet and private. I heard he was a dangerous man, that he had been an assassin and had once had a school for this purpose. He was a handsome forty-five years old with pearly white teeth, a winning smile, and stood at a lean five feet ten inches tall. He worked-out often and was exceptionally limber. He graduated from university while in prison with straight A's. Artie had some kind of problem but he handled it his way. He was never in that long line of men waiting for their medication. Sometimes Artie went for months without speaking unless he absolutely had to and then for a while he became animated and the nicest fellow imaginable.

One night I had a horrible nightmare. I shot a policeman in the chest and then in the face with a large pistol. The blood flew, and the policeman fell backward dead. It was so vivid that I could see the brass buttons on his coat and the way his mustache drooped. I woke in a sweat. Never had I dreamed such a violent dream as I always run or hide in my dreams. This was so unlike anything I had ever thought or dreamed that I could not understand it. I thought, 'What has this place done to me?' I prayed to be delivered from whatever it was. Several times during the next day, I pondered over the strange dream.

After the four o'clock count Artie came to my cell and asked if I had any peanut butter. This was just his way of visiting and I was happy that Artie was back with us as he had been tuned out for a long time. I invited him in, he sat down on the bunk and I offered him a cup of coffee. We got to talking and I asked him how such a nice fellow as himself got into a place like this? Artie was ready to talk to someone and I heard quite a story. He once had a school where he trained assassins. He had been a hitman, could kill and have it look like a normal death. Once he was in the attic of a Senator's home for a week. He had a small hole drilled directly above her bed and he could lower a tiny tube to her face and pour a mixture of chemicals directly into her mouth causing a massive heart attack.

I asked how he got into the federal system and he told the following tale. He was in California's maximum-security Folsom Prison doing a life sentence for murder and he escaped. From there he made his way to Canada where he lived for some years. He bought a farm, married, and had a baby. When the baby was only two weeks old, he and his wife left the baby with relatives and started on a trip to the states. It was getting late in the day and instead of following the freeway he decided to take a side road through Idaho.

He said, "I pulled up to this podunk border crossing and stopped. Out of the hut swaggers a Mexican-American Customs agent and I knew there was going to be trouble. Well, he comes up to my side, I give him my passport and then he goes around to my wife's side. She didn't have a passport, which was not required, so she started to get out her driver's license and he saw two driver's licenses in her purse. He immediately left her and came over to my side with his hand on his pistol and told me to get out of the car. As soon as I got out he took a firm grip on my arm and escorted me into the office. I knew it was all over, so I drew my pistol from under my shirt, whirled around and shot him, first in the chest and then right between the eyes. An immigration officer was coming in the door. He turned and ran. I took a bead between his shoulder blades and fired. The screen door swung to at that moment and the bullet hit the jam and deflected. I started to shoot again but for some unknown reason I let him live. I ran to the car and we took off, but it was no use. The immigration officer followed us in his vehicle. We abandoned the car and set out through the woods. My wife was having medical problems after the baby and as we ran she started bleeding so badly we had to stop. Soon they were on our trail with dogs and I had to leave my wife. They arrested her that afternoon, but it took them two weeks to catch me in the woods. I thought they would kill me, but they didn't."

Artie got another life sentence in the federal system. His wife got twenty years as an accomplice.

I had dreamed Artie's dream.

Lompoc was a dangerous place by any standard, however, there were good times as well. The warden was a jolly fellow and allowed a lot of small stuff to pass. Once a month the inmates could cook a special meal. One month the Mexicans did their thing and the next the Asians had the day, no matter who cooked, at least once each month we ate like kings. The warden was also soft on Pruno, a wine made from orange juice and a few guards let it ride if it wasn't too obvious. On one birthday I drank about a gallon with my friends and got cross-eyed drunk. When the guard made his rounds we sprayed talcum powder and he just smiled. Songs were sung and wonderful tales told with much bravado. Phil named me "The Wino Warrior." I spent the remainder of the night embracing the toilet. I was cured of a repeat.

They nicknamed me Doc because I sewed men up who had been in knife fights, that is if the wounds were not life-threatening. Strangely, I enjoyed doing it. Often it was a friend and my work kept him from going to 'the hole' for six months and then being transferred. Sometimes both combatants came for stitches. I once put 40 stitches in a friend's hand, back and chest. My Dr.'s satchel contained alcohol, dental floss, a large bent sewing needle, and antiseptic cream. The men never flinched as I sewed them up. An average of one a month was stabbed to death.

'Stick'em' Steve was a colorful character, medium-sized, wiry, and about five feet nine inches tall. He came by his name from two different directions. One was that he sold heroin, and the other if you complained, he would stick 'em a blade through your liver.

He was a gifted artist who painted cards and had a lively business selling to other prisoners. He also did oil paintings of clowns, crying clowns behind bars, behind razor wire, or being hanged. I reckon these were some masterpieces and I considered buying one. However, after thinking about it, I didn't want anything in my house that would remind me of him for he was truly bad to the bone. He came into prison on a three-year sentence, killed a man, received a life sentence, killed another, and got another life sentence. In all, he was supposed to have killed thirteen men.

One afternoon, several of us were watching a movie in the TV room. This was a small glassed-in area with a television, a few folding chairs, and ten or twelve headsets with long leads. In walked Steve and turned the channel.

Someone said, "Hey man, we was watchin' the movie!"

Steve pulled up a chair and said, "Yawl all know I watch Bonanza every day at three o'clock."

Men started getting up and leaving one by one. Most of those men were not afraid of Steve. I wasn't. It just was not worth the outcome.

Steve's job was painting the buildings. One day as he was painting in the theater he got into a heated argument with his fat boss who was a young man without much experience. The boss threatened to send him to the chokie, or solitary confinement but relented.

At 6 a:m., the bars on the third floor shook the building as they were jerked out of their slots and the heavy chain dragged them to the open position. I got out of my bunk, dressed, picked up my coffee mug and walked down the catwalk towards the landing where we got hot water out of a spigot. Phil Dimerza, met me and said, "You don't want to go down there Roger."

"What's going on?" I asked

He just shook his head and said, "You don't wanna see."

Naturally this aroused my curiosity and I walked on down to the landing. Strange, there was nobody there. Usually a dozen men were waiting to get coffee water. Then I saw Steve and stopped. When he saw me he turned and I saw a metal shank sticking out of his chest at least two feet in front and several inches in back. When the doors opened someone had run into Steve's cell and plunged the pike through his chest and into the mattress. Steve walked right up to me and with the voice of a little boy said, "Can you help me?"

I replied, "No, Steve, I'm sorry, I can't help you."

He turned and asked, "Can anyone help me?"

He walked back over to the corner from where he came. Blood began trickling out of his mouth, he hung his head over the railing, and blood spattered onto the floor by the guard shack three floors below. The guard saw the blood and pushed his panic button. Within a half-minute fifteen or twenty guards burst through the door. The guard in our unit pointed up-stairs and the troop shook the building as they bound up the stairs with Steve's fat boss leading the pack. He ran right up to Steve but it took a few seconds for it to register, then he had a heart attack and fell dead at Steve's feet. Steve looked on with glassy eyes, crumpled down dead beside his boss.

The prisoners said that when Steve went to hell he reached in and took the other's soul with him.

Fourteen hundred men were locked down for two weeks and fed bread and water with an occasional slice of paper-thin pressed turkey.

The old warden was retiring and the guards warned us that big changes were in the makings. One day the new warden made his debut in the chow hall. Ugh! What a pretentious, pencil-necked, paper shuffling, bureaucrat. He was wearing a sharkskin suit and high gloss patent leather shoes. His hair was plastered smooth above a thin pale face that would make an undertaker cringe. Soon he made many cringe, even the suits in Washington that sent him.

The rules changed. Zero tolerance for drugs, alcohol, and food coming out of the chow hall. The special meal was abolished and the budget for food was cut. He vowed that no prisoner would ever eat a steak on his watch even if beef went to ten cents a pound, which it almost did. He made a punishment unit out of another block and there was an average of four to five hundred men in the hole at all times. He ordered a truckload of paint and wax, had the whole place painted and all the concrete floors polished till they sparkled.

Unicor was the prison factory where one thousand men worked fabricating cables for planes, missiles, and satellites. It was a profitable business and some of the profit went to an inmate trust fund. The new warden canceled it. If anyone asked about the trust fund or the proceeds of Unicor it was an automatic trip to the hole and a transfer. This money went directly into a retirement fund for high-ranking prison officials and a select few in Washington.

Warden Ridley had the concrete floor of the passageway from the units to Unicor waxed and polished. It was like polishing a busy street. He put a man on it full time and often this man had a helper. One day it started raining as I was coming in from the yard and the warden was headed to Unicor. The roof had a leak and the waxed floor had a small amount of water on it. Ridley's patent leather shoes slid out from under him and he was suspended in the air with arms wind-milling and feet kicking. His butt hit the concrete so hard he bounced a time or two. Oh, what a wonderful sight! I don't know if he broke anything but a bunch of us busted our guts laughing. Twenty men spent all night stripping the corridor.

The guards were given free rein. For the smallest infraction men were slammed into the wall, searched, handcuffed, and thrown in the hole. Children, no matter how small, were no longer allowed to sit on their father's lap in the visiting room. If a chair was moved or you spoke or nodded to another prisoner or his visitor your visit was terminated.

The prison had a staff of four hundred. Most were good people just making a living but there were six or eight sadistic killers that ran in packs. Stelliot and Fantana were an especially nasty pair who always had men up beside the wall searching them and whispering dreadful insults in their ears trying to make them 'go off.' They were real sickos and easily capable of killing a prisoner. Quite a few deaths occurred in 'the hole' and it was always blamed on an overdose. My jogging partner and friend Noah was thirty years old, in excellent health, and didn't use drugs, yet he died of an 'overdose.' I wonder which one killed him, why, and how?

A guard named Hurdel was bad, but there is an old saying that no matter how bad you are, there is always somebody 'badder'. Federal marshals brought in a prisoner from the state prison at San Quentin. This man had arms as big around as my thighs and was covered in tattoos all the way to his eyelids. The story was that the guards at San Quentin had introduced gladiator-style fighting at the prison. They would open a door on one side of an arena and allow a prisoner from a certain gang or ethnic group to enter. Then from the other side of the arena a prisoner from a rival gang or group would enter. The two men would be armed with whatever weapons they could get and fight until one killed the other while fifty or more guards stood on cat-walks above and made bets.

This big tattoo-covered man was a federal witness at the trial against the guards and they didn't want anything to happen to him so they put him in the hole of a federal penitentiary. Wasn't long before he was bored and tore the metal toilet out of the cement floor and continually slammed it into the bars. This caused a terrible racket that was above the usual din and it wasn't long before Hurdel shows up with his goon squad. They suited up and rushed the cell with Hurdel leading the pack. Ol' Tattoo grabbed Hurdel's shield, jerked it up and gave him an undercut that knocked him cold. Of course, the others beat him senseless. Two or three weeks later he was feeling better and tore the lavatory off the wall, slammed it into the bars, and was calling, "Come to daddy Hurdel. Come to daddy."

One night while sleeping I had a vision. Something different from any visions I had before. This one was surreal, black and white, in slow motion. In the vision I walked into 'M' unit and saw there had been a riot. Most of the glass had been blown out of the windows by concussion grenades. Smoke from the grenades floated in the air and the floor was covered in broken glass, blood, and water. A multitude of men was lying face down, handcuffed behind their backs with plastic handcuffs. I walked slowly through these men and I could tell what they were thinking or feeling, fear, pain, anger, dismay, and violation. I saw Chaplain Mike Crane with a knee in the back of a man putting on the cuffs and somehow I was not surprised. His face did not resemble a Christian chaplain's.

The following day I told the vision to Phil, Big Jim, Carlos Miralanda, Wayne, and Chaplain John Burke and all the men that I could remember whom I had seen on the floor. I told them something very bad was going to happen soon. When Marrie visited I told her in detail that we were going to have a riot. I wanted to warn everyone.

Officer Williams was a handsome, quiet, young man, about thirty years old, and was in charge of urine tests. During my visit I was called out and told I had to give a urine test. I replied that this was my visit and they could take a urine sample anytime. The guards told me to wait right there and that Officer Williams would come. I waited for two hours.

Officer Williams finally came through and said, "Hold on Reaves, I'll be right back." But he didn't come back and I knew Marrie was worried as I had been gone for two hours. Finally, I told the officer that he could do whatever he had to do, because I had to pee. I did and was allowed to go back in to my visit. Most likely, I cursed Williams.

At the door to the chow hall there was always six or eight and sometimes fifteen officers standing around, searching different ones as we came out. The chow hall was emptying as I was going out with my friend Jerry Wills when ahead of us all hell broke loose. Green, a tall, thin, stupid inmate from 'M' unit had gone out with a long, razor-sharp butcher knife taped to each hand. He stabbed Williams in the throat, killing him, then he stabbed Stelliot through the chest. Three other guards were seriously cut before they overcame him. Jerry and I ran to the right to get out of the melee. We ducked into the movie theatre, sat down near the front and watched "The Mosquito Coast." Sirens were blaring non-stop. The men heard what had happened and many started cheering when they heard Stelliot finally got what was coming to him. I thought, boys, you don't know what you are doing or thinking because we are all going to pay dearly for this.

The movie stopped partway through. A guard told us all to remain in our seats. After a couple of hours a black man started to the toilet and the guard told him to sit down. The inmate said he had to go to the toilet and he started in. The doors burst open, the goon squad stormed in dressed in black with masks and helmets. The light was coming in from the door behind them. I could see the silhouette of the truncheons raining down on him and see him being beaten and kicked to the floor and they still did not stop. They were screaming, "Down, down on the floor mother fuckers, with your hands behind your head!" Everyone did as instructed. Unfortunately I was sitting in a row of seats where the row in front had been removed. A huge masked black man came down that aisle and hit me behind the head so hard it cracked my skull and drove my nose into the concrete floor. My nose was split from the tip to my eyes. I lay there pouring blood. Someone handcuffed me behind my back so hard my wrists were cut and then picked me up by the handcuffs. They had a guard for each prisoner and we were put up beside the wall with our forehead resting on the wall with our feet wide apart. My right leg was shaking and jerking so that I couldn't control it. I belittled myself for shaking but later realized I had been traumatized and was in shock. We were marched to our unit and shoved into our cells. Late that night a very stupid guard named Clark, came up to my cell, pointed a rifle through the bars, and kept jabbing it at me.

I didn't receive any medical attention what-so-ever. We were locked down for a week with only dry bread and paper-thin pressed turkey.

After one week, we were marched to the chow hall. The corridors were lined with masked, angry guards holding shields and truncheons. We were not allowed to look up. Every privilege was taken away.

A boiler will only stand a certain amount of pressure.

Some weeks later a black singer had been scheduled for months to perform and the group was allowed in under heavy guard. The auditorium was packed with over six hundred angry, muscled up, black men. A pretty, sleek, black rap singer, with a slit in her skirt that reached to her hip got on the stage and began gyrating and rapping about black bondage. The house began to rock. A guard made the fatal mistake of hopping on stage, trying to force the entertainer off. He got a microphone sunk into his head. Other guards ran in and met a similar fate. Pure bedlam broke out. They called in for assistance from all over the prison. Marrie and I were in the visiting room, we noticed reinforcements moving back and forth. They would *suit-up* in front and run-in with ropes, shields, gas masks, and grenades. Some of the regular officers returned to the visiting room, hot and bloody with torn uniforms. It took three hours to get the auditorium under control and the men back to their units. Then it went off again in the units. One unit had a pool table and the prisoners threw the balls at the guards, injuring several badly. If they missed, the balls bounced off the concrete wall and they got another shot. In "M" unit, they filled thirty-gallon trashcans with boiling water and dropped them on the guards. One of the prisoners involved in the first World Trade Centre bombing caught a female guard, dragged her to his cell and ripped her clothes off. She was rescued without injury, and they said you could hear her screaming above the din. Marrie and I had the longest visit ever as she wasn't allowed to leave until after dark. Guards came, handcuffed me, and with a guard on each side escorted me back to my unit. As the door opened, right in front of me was the exact scene from my vision:

And it shall come to pass afterward, that I will pour out my spirit on all flesh; and your sons and daughters shall prophesy, your old men shall dream dreams, your young men shall see visions.
Joel 2:28

I have now been in prison for thirty-three years. I have come to realize why so many men end up here and it is simply that they were not loved and cared for as they should have been. They are from broken or dysfunctional homes, parents often poor and on welfare. They are unwanted, passed off to grandmothers or the state. The answer is simple. One must reach a certain criterion and get a permit to have a child. People need to be educated and money poured into bettering society, not starting endless wars. That shouldn't be so hard, one must have a permit to drive a motor scooter on our roads; how much more is the responsibility of bringing a child into the world?

34. BACK TO LUBECK

Double Crossed -- If You Want Something Done, Do It Yourself

Originally I received a 5-year sentence for moving the gold coins. The actual indictment read something like, "Reaves moved and sold gold coins that the United States Government would have seized had they known..." After some years of research in the law library I filed a writ of habeas corpus and won! I was transported back to the Metropolitan Detention Center in Los Angeles and went before Judge Ideman who reduced the sentence to three years.

While at MDC an extradition request arrived from Germany and the prosecutor offered me a deal whereby they would send me directly to Germany if I agreed to the extradition. As I had a year left to do on the parole violation it was a good deal for me. I figured I would do less than a year in Germany and have that charge out of the way. I also thought that by being extradited it would break the jurisdiction of the parole term. I accepted the deal and walked into the courtroom with my sassy public defender. Sitting on the bench was a nice-looking woman judge and behind the prosecutors bench was a chic young thing that smiled and gave me a secret little wave from her side. The judge ordered my extradition to Germany forthwith and I returned to my cell with expectations of going to Germany.

The case manager informed me that the German police would be there on Monday to fly me back to Germany.

Early Monday morning, marshals chained me and loaded me on the bus going back to Lompoc. I thought there had been some mistake, but the only mistake had been mine. Warden Ridley refused to release me from his prison because I had testified against him at the inquest over Officer William's death and told in detail about how I was treated. I asked him about the court order extraditing me to Germany forthwith and he said, "If you say one more word you will spend the rest of your time in the hole."

To take the case back to court would take more than a year and he knew it.

I spent twelve more months in that dismal dungeon before they chained me and drove me back to MDC where I spent a week in the 'hole' waiting on the German police. US Marshals arrived and presented me with my paperwork. Stamped in big red letters was *USE MAXIMUM RESTRAINTS*. I was chained with so much hardware that I jingled as I hobbled along. Three vehicles drove me to the airport, one in front and one in the rear. They *accidentally* parked a half-mile from the Lufthansa terminal. Two marshals walked in front with shotguns moving people out of the way, two more walked behind similarly armed, while another pair flanked me as I shuffled along taking 12-inch steps because the leg irons were so short. Everyone stopped to stare and I acted the part by nodding and calling out, "It's only an illusion ladies and gentlemen, only an illusion."

Two tall young German policemen stood by and watched as the US Marshals removed the hardware and handed me over. They escorted me into the plane without even a pair of handcuffs. My seat was reserved in the very back beside the wall. One sat beside me and the other sat across the aisle. A grumpy old flight attendant asked for our drink order and I said I would like a Chivas on ice. She didn't look at me. The young policeman repeated the order and she was all smiles. Despite the bitch that brought it, the airline dinner was delicious!

The guard at reception in Lubeck remembered me, smiled, patted my face and sang "Big Eight Wheel," gave a big laugh and brought out a big sealed box with 'Mr. Big' written in bold black letters. Everything was just as I had left it. The photographs were still on the boards, all my writing material and old letters were there to greet me. Even the tea was still good. Somehow, it was like coming home and I was pleased to be back. The change from Lompoc was drastic. The Germans had a memory for suffering and the conditions and authorities were humane.

Frau Elke Blumberg was on vacation for three weeks so she sent a young woman lawyer who didn't know doodle about my case. I was anxious to get started on the paperwork because I was sure the court would release me as soon as they learned that I had now spent over eleven years in prison for the hashish and the original sentence was eight years. When Frau Blumberg returned there was another delay for the Christmas holidays. After Christmas, she came and talked about money. Marrie sent her the money right away. Still she procrastinated. I very carefully explained how the US Parole Board punished me for the German offense and showed her the papers to prove it. February passed and still she didn't move.

Willie Honenburg, a fellow prisoner who had been there when I escaped, was a sharp young embezzler who conned a bank in Malaga Spain into delivering five million dollars in cash to a real estate establishment. Willie also knew the law and he began helping me write letters to the judge and prosecutor. Frau Blumberg was appalled.

The winter of 1998 was bitter cold and a deadly flu swept across Europe, killing many. I caught it and thought I really might die. I lost 30 pounds and scarcely had the strength to walk slowly up and down the stairs. Every day I called the prosecutor. At first he tried to make me angry, but I was too sick to take the bait. Finally he realized I had served far too much time and told me he would release me on Easter if I had a passport and a country that would accept me.

The representative for the U.S Counsel in Hamburg was a thoroughbred son of a bitch. He did everything in his power to prevent me from getting a passport. Every day I called his office and talked with his secretary and she would tell me that nothing had been done. My friend Willie was from Hamburg and connected with some tough people. He sent a gentleman to talk to this prick, and the next day my passport was ready.

I was too weak to carry my belongings down the stairs, but with great determination I somehow succeeded. Willie's friend was waiting on the curb. He loaded my things in his car and we sped off. Willie had been released a few days earlier and he was waiting in a Chinese restaurant nearby. We had a good reunion and a few drinks then his friend drove me to a post office where he helped me pack up the 200 Penguin classics and ship them home. Then he drove me to a good hotel near the airport in Hamburg.

35. HOME TO MARRIE

Brief Honeymoon

For months I had dreamed of going to France and visiting Marya and the grandchildren when I was released, but the Mayor of Lubeck prevented this by stamping my new passport with a great seal on the front page stating that I could never return to certain European countries under such-and-such convention.

That night I went to dinner and ordered a drink and a steak. The meal came and I sat there with tears rolling down my cheeks as I ate. The weakness from being sick and all the emotions of finally being free was overwhelming. Back in the room I called Marrie and told her I was arriving in Tijuana at 9 p.m. the following evening on Mexicana Airlines.

The 747 took off early. I sat on the left by a window and watched Holland go by, then the English Channel. Scotland was a deep green and it took a long time to traverse from south to north-west. I could make out the island of Skye and the new bridge connecting it to the mainland. White fluffy clouds covered the Atlantic all the way to Iceland and then it cleared for a good look from seven miles up. Greenland looked like a big frozen wilderness as we inched across. The day passed into night and we were an hour late and for once Mexico City was clear and lit up like day under a bright full moon. I hurried to the gate for my connecting flight to Tijuana and found the Mexicana flight had already departed so I booked a ticket on Aero Mexico and boarded just in time. I was so excited to be meeting Marrie after all the years. A big lump swelled in my throat and tears slid down my cheeks just imagining the moment. When I walked into the terminal she was not there. What happened? Did she have a wreck? Where was she? There was no one to call. I sat down on the curb with my suitcase and waited for hours. Around midnight the airport closed so I took a taxi to a cheap nearby hotel.

Six o'clock and I was back at the airport looking in every car that came by. At eight o'clock I called Miriam's apartment in San Diego, but the phone was busy for the next hour. At nine o'clock Marrie answered with, "Hello sweetheart, where are you?"

"Marrie I am at the Tijuana airport where I told you I would be. Why aren't you here?"

"Don't get angry. I was there and you were not on the flight and Mexicana said it was the last flight of the day, so I returned to San Diego."

"I have been trying to ring for the last hour, but the phone was engaged! Damn it Marrie, I have been in prison for eleven years and come home and you don't meet me, are you coming or not?"

"Roger, calm down, I will be there in two hours."

"Two hours? It's only a thirty-minute drive."

"I'll see you soon, Sweetheart."

I had several Bloody Marys and a big breakfast of huevos rancheros on the patio overlooking the runway and watched the planes landing and taking off. I went back downstairs and renewed my vigil of watching automobiles entering.

She pulled up to the curb. I threw my bag in the back seat and got in, pissed. Sick in body and heart. She was shocked at my appearance as I looked like death warmed over. We sped away and drove for hours through the wine country of Baja. After some time my anger abated and I asked her to find a doctor. Someone recommended one and we drove to the house. Walking in, we saw that everything was covered in dogs and dog hair and a short greasy fat man sitting pompously behind a desk. I immediately turned around and left without so much as a 'buenos dias'. We drove to a pharmacy where I asked for antibiotics. The pharmacist misunderstood and sold me expectorants. I became even sicker. I found a proper doctor who gave me a shot of penicillin and I began to improve.

We rented rooms at a small hotel on Rosarito Beach. Directly in front of our balcony was the area where they brought horses each morning to rent to tourists. Marrie was particularly fond of one mare with a tiny palomino colt. Rhett and his friend caught the train from Oceano to San Diego, stayed with Miriam a couple of days and she drove them down to Rosarito. Miriam would come down one evening each week and spent the weekends with us. We dined in the typical restaurants in Rosarito and Ensenada and bribed the bouncers to allow two seventeen-year-old boys into Husongs Bar and Grill. Back in San Diego Miriam's car had been stolen and stripped. Marrie and I drove from one *Jonkie (Junk Yard)* to another buying parts and having them bolted on until her vehicle looked new again. The honeymoon was over all too quickly with Marrie, Miriam and Rhett going north, and me going south.

36. FORTY MILLION DOLLAR PAYDAY

Not Invited -- Twenty Thousand Kilo's -- British Colombia -- Graduation -- Operation Millennium

Marcus and Esmeralda were delighted to see me and I stayed a month in their lovely home overlooking the Cauca valley. This area is a bird watchers paradise with over 400 permanent residents in addition to the hundreds of colorful species that fly through each year. Every day I took long walks along the streams while bird watching with binoculars.

Jorge Ochoa was around so I went to his house several times and started hanging around the stables trying to meet him, but he was avoiding me. One day his brother David invited me to ride with him. We got in the back seat with two pistoleros in front and drove around town doing errands. He then said he had to go to the funeral of a horse trainer who had been killed. We arrived at a big cathedral in downtown Medellin and waited as group after group followed a coffin out. Finally, our man was brought out on the shoulders of youths, some tall, some short, wearing shorts and T-shirts. They were followed by an awful marching band with girls in short shorts twirling batons. We followed the circus to the hearse and then returned to the car.

I wrote several long letters to Jorge asking for the three million, three hundred and eighty-two thousand dollars he owed, but never got a response. One evening I went to his house and the housekeeper invited me in. I talked to Jorge on the phone and he said he was in Bogotá and would not be back for a few days. Another time I was waiting across the street while a birthday party was going on behind the walls. The gate opened, the place was decorated with balloons, expensive Mercedes and Porsche cars were driving in, and I saw Jorge standing by the pool. I quickly entered with the cars. When he saw me he told his bodyguard to escort me to the street. My face was crimson red and I was disgusted with myself for spending eleven years in prison protecting someone who treated me like this. For several years agents of the DEA came to the prison in Lompoc and told me that I had the keys to the front door in my hand. All I had to do was testify against Jorge Ochoa and I could walk out a free man.

Marcus and I flew to Barranquilla, Colombia where we met a handsome young man driving a bulletproof car who wanted someone to unload a ship off the coast of British Colombia. We had a delicious meal in a Chinese restaurant and then went to this man's house, which was bulletproof. His gorgeous wife brought out the first lap top computer I ever saw. He brought up surprisingly good maps and I pointed out my old place off Pam Peninsula which he thought was perfect. The deal was the same as before, two thousand dollars per kilo for 20,000 kilos which had to be brought ashore and stored. Marcus said I should ask for a deposit, but I was so sure of the man that I didn't want to lose face or diminish myself in anyway.

I headed north.

Late 1990's. I had just been released from prison after 11 years.
Copyright - Marrie J. Reaves.

Miriam's eyes were sparkling when she met me in Tijuana. She gave the officer at the border a big smile and he waved us on without a second glance. We couldn't stop hugging and patting one another on the ride to San Diego. Marrie, Marya, Rhett, Maximillian, and baby Zillah were waiting anxiously at Miriam's apartment. Max was standing out front and when he saw us coming he ran around the building hailing our arrival. It was one tearful and joyous reunion!

Miriam graduated with honors from the University of California, San Diego in biochemistry and cell biology. We cheered loudly and were proud as she walked down the aisle to receive her degree. That afternoon we celebrated in a restaurant overlooking the Pacific and had a wonderful time. The next day she prepared a big picnic, with games, water balloons and other activities in a nearby park. Many friends and fellow students from school also attended and it was another memorable occasion.

At the picnic I told Rhett we were packing up and moving to British Columbia, Canada and he did the most unexpected, he sobbed. I had been selfish, only looking at life from my point of view and thought he would be delighted to go to British Columbia and fish and hunt with Dad. No way. He was born and raised on the coast of central California, his friends were there and at eighteen years old he wanted to be with them. I was torn emotionally over his sadness but thought he might really like the place if he would just go and have a look.

Marrie drove back to the house in Oceano with me lying low on the back seat for the last mile. Rhett opened the garage door and Marrie drove in. I stayed inside the house for a week, helping pack our belongings and eating Marrie's delicious cooking.

Rhett and his friends had planned a trip to the Colorado River and he was down in the dumps about missing it so I told him if he would just cheer up he could go to the river and catch us later in Canada. His smile and his big hug warmed my heart.

Marrie drove north along the coast highway stopping in Mendocino the first night. We woke up late, had a leisurely breakfast, walked around a bit and continued on. It took a week's traveling on winding country roads and staying in quaint B&B's before reaching the Canadian border.

Once across, I drove with my fake ID.

In Victoria we rented a suite in a high-rise hotel with an incredible view of the harbor and the San Juan Islands beyond. One evening as we were walking along the wharf a group of actors was performing. The Prince looked the crowd over and chose Marrie to be the Princess. The actor placed a crown on her head and had her repeat some lines after him and soon she was hamming it up and was every bit his equal. He had her lie on her back as though she was sleeping, my heart almost burst with love as I saw her lying there. If only I had a camera, everyone else did. For the remainder of our stay in Victoria people would pass and say, "Hello, there's the Princess."

My old lagoon was out. The timber had been cut and logging roads were everywhere. We began looking, driving every logging road from Port Hardy south to the middle of Vancouver Island. There were several choice spots to choose from and I narrowed it down to one after many visits to each. The woods abounded in bear, deer, grouse, and bald eagles. At one lagoon a doe so gentle she let us touch her.

In Nanaimo I purchased a 55-foot salmon trawler and a 16-foot hard-bottomed Zodiac with center console and radar. I wanted this vessel to run alongside the ship and attach it to the cargo in case of a miss in fog or bad weather. All warehouses in the area were full and the ones in Victoria were not appropriate so I decided to store the cocaine in the woods.

Traveling north up the main highway we came to a roadblock with a dozen law enforcement cars and motorcycles standing by. The northbound traffic was waved through but police were searching every southbound vehicle using dogs. I wondered what was going on. Two miles up the road Marrie and I switched positions and she drove back through. They were searching for illegal fish and bear gall bladders that were selling for five thousand dollars each. We found they only did this for a few weeks during the salmon run.

The ship was due to depart Lima within days and I was keeping in close touch with Marcus. One morning I called and a very nervous Marcus answered and told me to get out of there now. I asked what he meant and explained that I had just forked out a lot of money on two vessels. He repeated that I should leave as quickly as possible and for me to read the newspapers. I found a newspaper and the headlines read, 'Operation Millennium, 600 arrested worldwide in the largest sweep in the history of the war on drugs'. The American DEA had infiltrated the cocaine trafficking ring from the jungles of South America to the streets of Europe and America. Favio Ochoa's name was at the top of the list followed by my friend from Barranquilla.

37. LETS GO SAILING

Home -- Fake Driver's License -- A Boat Named 'No Name' -- A Man Named Margaret -- Home and Hospital Bills

The boats were soon sold back to the broker at a great loss and we were headed east along the Trans-Canadian Highway with Rhett driving the new Nissan Pathfinder we purchased the day before. The scenery was spectacular until we reached Banff. After the Rockies came the prairies which were interesting for a few hundred miles, then it became monotonous. We spent a day each in Medicine Hat, Regina, Winnipeg, and Sault Ste. Marrie, arriving in Cambridge, Ontario rather worn out.

Mom, Marrie's Mother, was delighted to see us. Dad had died a few years before but I could feel his presence everywhere and missed him deeply. Marrie showed Rhett where she went to school and the house where she grew up and all too soon it was time to leave.

The second Sunday in September is Homecoming at Sand Hill Methodist Church, and I was determined to be there. The US Customs agent at the border gave us a hard time about the car being purchased in Canada by a Canadian citizen living in the US holding a Green Card who was just going down to visit, blah, blah, blah. Finally, he got tired of his own bullshit and waved us through. The following day I was happy as we drove across the Georgia state line. It had been a long, long journey.

My sister Charlotte and her husband David own a large farm, a new house, and 180,000 chickens in the backwoods, end of the trail it was. Here is where I felt most comfortable. The ladies cooked and prepared food all day Saturday to take to Homecoming. Sunday morning we dressed up and set out for Sand Hill. What a joyous reunion it was! Folks had aged a lot in the seventeen years I had been away, however, the eyes and smiles were the same. There were a lot of hugs and hearty handshakes and I was happy to be home. The few hours were over all too soon and I wondered if I would ever get back.

Marrie had to do all the driving as I was afraid to drive with the fake California driver's license l was using for ID. We were planning a road trip back to Canada and I didn't want to fly using my real name and passport as that would prove to the US Parole Commission that I had been in the States. We drove to Tallahassee Florida where I rented a mailbox, then drove to the Department of

Motor Vehicles, walked calmly to the desk and told the pretty lady that I was from North Carolina, had recently moved to the area and had lost my license. She asked for ID and I gave her a Social Security card and birth certificate, plus several other items which she handed back. Within five minutes I was driving away with a real Florida driver's license in the name of David Gunn, my brother-in-law.

Since that was so easy we decided to get Marrie a license in the name of Nell Green, my sister. With the entire I.D. in hand we walked into the DMV office in Fort Lauderdale, went to the counter and met a hatchet-faced woman who gave Marrie a hard time and sent her to the Social Security office for further proof. We obtained the necessary papers and returned. She then brought up Nell's particulars on the computer and said, "I suppose you have been on a diet."

Marrie lied, "Yes, I have lost a lot of weight."

"And I suppose you dyed your hair from black to platinum." She smirked.

"When did you last renew your license?"

"I don't recall."

"Well, was it three months ago, or three years ago?"

"I don't recall."

She said, "Wait right there!" She gathered up the ID and walked through a door behind the counter and closed it.

We waited about two seconds, glanced at one another, and bolted through the front door, sprinted across the parking lot, and jumped into the Pathfinder. I turned the key, ran over the cement curbs in the parking lot, peeled off down the street, up an onramp, and into heavy freeway traffic. We both shook from the narrow escape, without a doubt the woman back at the D.M.V. was calling for backup.

Money was getting low and I had to do something. Larry was surfing the net one day and found three of our old bank accounts in the lost money section. The accounts had been turned over to the State of California twenty-five years back without notifying us. The state paid 5% interest compounded annually so the principle plus interest amounted to a nice sum. The accounts were verified but the bureaucrats needed all kinds of information before they would release the money. The Feds had a lien against me for a hundred million dollars and I knew that if they heard of this money they would seize it. After a lot of wrangling we finally received the funds.

Canada was a safer place to land contraband than the US, so Marrie and I flew to Halifax, Nova Scotia to look for an unloading spot for a boat or landing strip. We rented a car and visited every inlet from Cape Sable to Cape Breton Island. There were so many ideal places to choose from that I marked eight or ten of the best on the chart. We thoroughly enjoyed our month in Nova Scotia and even thought of buying a house with an orchard after the trip.

From experience I knew that if one had transportation someone would load you up with contraband, so I set out to find a sailboat I could afford and that was tough enough to do the job. Marrie and I looked at sailboats in every marina from Brunswick, Georgia to Key West, Florida, and finally settled on a 45-foot Sea Master in Fort Lauderdale. The vessel had been out of the water for ten years with the owners coming down every winter and camping in it. For some reason they had never named it and it was listed on the federal register as 'No Name.' The owners wouldn't allow a survey so I knew something was wrong. I waited until they were gone and had a marine surveyor do a survey on the hull, decks, and mast and he gave her a clean bill of health. A new six-cylinder diesel engine cost around six thousand dollars and I figured I would have to replace it. In addition, the sails were in poor condition, but another two thousand dollars purchased a used set that was like new. I offered fifty thousand and was surprised when they accepted. As soon as the money touched their hands they fled, making me wonder just what else was wrong with her.

The boatyard hoist lowered her into the water and I half expected her to sink but she sat there rather regally. With Marrie standing on the bow ready to drop the anchor in case of an emergency we went for a canal cruise and she behaved splendidly. Still, I was dubious.

The passport from the embassy in Germany was good for one year and I wanted to get to Nassau and have it extended for ten years before it ran out. I ordered sails, stocked her with food and wine and we set sail for Bimini in a gale. We sloshed around all night and just before dawn the propeller picked up a line that twisted around the shaft so tight it stopped the engine and it filled with saltwater. Bimini is a very small village and any work would have to be sent to Nassau or Miami. The wind was at forty knots right on our nose so I chose to return to Miami.

We were making 8 knots under a fully reefed headsail and by noon we passed under the bridge at Fort Lauderdale and were amongst multi-million-dollar yachts. Being in an unfamiliar vessel without an engine in such traffic was nerve-racking. I saw an empty fifty-foot space between two cream puffs tied to the dock of a swanky hotel, turned, ran forward, dropped the sail and docked it like parking a car. Marrie jumped off and took a hitch on a cleat. A dock boy dressed in whites came running over to us and said we couldn't tie up. I explained that we didn't have an engine and couldn't move. Of course, he didn't believe me and said he was calling a tug to tow us away. I asked him to allow us to stay. He looked a few minutes at his watch. Across the canal and down a ways I noticed a repair shop, so I stripped off my shirt, dove in and swam across. The owner was surprised to see me come in the shop, wet and dripping, not the usual appearance of his customers. He said he would do the repairs for me. He had never worked on sailboats. He took me back across in a motorboat and towed old 'No Name' to his shop.

We had wonderful service and they repaired the engine. When it was time to pay the bill it was less than the dock space would have cost where we originally tied up. Six-foot tarpons swam around the live bait dock, they were like pets. We ate in the local restaurants and drank in the bars for two weeks and all too soon it was time to leave our new friends and push on.

Bimini is only a spit of sand a few feet above sea level and difficult to see until you are very near. We entered the cut, cleared customs, and set off across the flats for Nassau. The flats are ten or twelve feet deep with coral heads scattered here and there and one has to be alert. As it was getting dark we dropped anchor in what looked like the middle of the ocean. A gale began to blow. The anchor chain jerked and rattled throughout the night. The GPS kept changing. I thought we were dragging anchor, yet after a few minutes it read the same. As a slate grey dawn broke over a choppy sea, two red-eyed exhausted sailors hoisted anchor and set sail.

By ten o'clock we were in deep water, sailing across the Tongue of the Ocean when a rusty craft loaded with tough-looking local men turned sharply and fell in close behind us. As I had no idea of their intentions it alarmed me. I thought they might be pirates. I turned a sharp left and they seemed surprised. Then they fell off several hundred yards to starboard and stayed there the remainder of the day. When the first tower of Nassau came into sight they changed course and sped away. Obviously they were lost and figured we were headed for Nassau.

We anchored in the same channel as the giant cruise ships with their loud discos at night making it unbearable to sleep. Their overweight, lily-white, whining clientele made me ashamed to call myself an American. To escape the noise and commotion we moved in front of an Ashram meditation center. They were kind gentle folks who invited us to use their washer, dryer, and water to fill our tanks.

The US Embassy was surrounded by sandbags and local Bahamian soldiers armed with machine guns. Several sliding bulletproof doors led to a receptionist. After waiting on a bench most of the afternoon the receptionist told us to return the next day which we did. I was sweating profusely from worry. I felt something was amiss and I couldn't shake off the feeling. However, after waiting for several more hours I got my passport with an extension for the full ten years.

Sunday morning we up-anchored and set sail south. The day was picture perfect with a gentle wind on our back and a big drifter pulling us along at 8 knots. Sometime after lunch the wind veered and was right on the nose rising to 40 knots. I took down the sails and cranked up the diesel and soon she went to pounding into the waves. Each time the bow fell off a fifteen-foot crest the boat would jar and Marrie was afraid. I laughed and told her there was nothing to worry about, this was what boats were made for. She went to screaming, yelling and pointing to the bow. I had no idea what she was going on about because my hearing is somewhat impaired. I ran forward, heard an awful ripping, tearing noise, and felt the vibration in the soles of my feet. My hair stood on end for a second or two as I thought the boat was ripping apart. Then it dawned on me that it was the 250-foot anchor chain paying out. I reached the bow in time to see the bitter end go over the roller and all was quiet. We had just lost a 55-pound anchor and all our chain. The hard pounding had caused the pin holding the anchor in place to come out and down it went.

The night was pitch dark. The wind was still forty knots, gusting to fifty as we rounded the west end of Marijuana Island, I called for help to enter the lagoon. The radio operator answered and said, "No one can move at night due to the dangerous coral heads." He then told me to turn left to gain sea room and I informed him that I was coming from the west and a left turn would put me on the reef. He insisted I turn left immediately. I disregarded this error on his part and continued on course. Marrie was afraid that he was right and I was wrong. I told her to watch the red light on the shore and that in three minutes exactly it would change from red to yellow and after four minutes it would turn green and we would hang a left and drop anchor after going in a little way. The lights changed colors as I knew they would and I motored slowly in until the bow was almost on the sand. I took the 30-pound stern anchor to the bow, attached a three quarter inch anchor rope 200 feet long, let it out all the way and she held.

Once the sun was up we wove our way for five miles through the coral heads to the marina and fuel dock. We stayed for a week and met the most interesting people of our entire journey.

When the wind eased up, we eased out and sailed to the Dominican Republic where I was hoping to have some teak work done, but was disappointed as they had nothing to work with. Nor anyone who knew how to do anything.

From the Dominican Republic we pushed straight through to the British Virgin Islands where we rested for a couple of days and visited 'The Caves' and a few other spots of interest. It only made us sad remembering our previous visit with the children on the beautiful *Jolly Swagman.*

In Saint Martin we worked and played hard for two weeks. A hurricane had ravished the island the previous summer leaving many wrecks in the lagoon. From one of the wrecks I purchased the keel and melted a ton of lead into 45-pound ingots to tape onto a stack of cocaine in order to sink it if I was boarded. Underneath the table, in the main salon I fiber-glassed in a 12-inch square sea chest through which I could drop stacks of kilo blocks that would sink directly to the bottom of the ocean. On a trial experiment I found that I could get rid of a hundred kilos in less than a minute.

Martinique was our next stop. We never did see immigration and customs even though we looked for them. The food was marvelous and surprisingly the French had changed their tune toward tourists. They were most friendly. From Martinique, we sailed non-stop to Grenada, and on into Prickly Pear lagoon, directly below the medical school.

We walked up to the university and waited for Miriam to finish her last exam. She knew we were on our way but didn't know when to expect us. When she walked out of the classroom with a group of friends she saw us and screamed, "Mamma, Daddy" and ran over, gave us big hugs and kisses and introduced us to her friends. We had a wonderful reunion with Miriam showing us all around the island. After a week both Miriam and Marrie bailed out on me and flew to the states.

Whilst in Grenada Marcus contacted me and let me know he had 250 kilos of coke ready to go. The 'blocks' were curved to fit in drums and were left over from a vessel that could not take the full load. The deal was sweet but they would only load in Venezuelan waters. I wanted to load in the Atlantic so we were at an impasse and I turned it down.

Hurricane season was upon us and *No Name* was one of the last boats still hanging around Grenada. I told Marcus that I had to get out of there and he said for me to head to Bermuda and he would get me loaded near there. I thought this was highly unlikely as Bermuda was two-thirds of the way north with a goodly portion of the danger passed. However, I had no choice but to go. I motor-sailed with the engine idling making an average of just over 150 nautical miles every 24 hours. The roller reefing on the headsail was acting up so I motored into Saint Martin, untangled and repaired the problem, fueled up, bought some fresh groceries, and was out of there in three hours.

Upon rounding the south end of the island I began hearing voices in the cabin. I listened intensely and it seemed it was in the Dutch language from bygone centuries. Men talked, sang songs, and then several men talked at once. I could never make out what they were saying but the voices were deep and masculine. It sounded ghostly and I searched in vain for the source and never did figure out what it was. But it was cause for several stiff ones.

A mighty hurricane paralleled my journey staying 200 miles to starboard all the way to Bermuda. In Georgetown I tied Zillah, the proper name we gave the yacht, to an old stone wharf in front of shops and restaurants.

Marrie flew in and we played and toured the island for a month. One night we invited Fernando, a Portuguese sailor from a nearby sailboat aboard for drinks. He was very interesting and told us he was a clairvoyant. Sometime after midnight he began talking randomly. Some of the things he said were rather right on and yet he didn't speak directly to Marrie or me, he just talked. He had explained beforehand that this was how the gift came to him.

He said, "You are going to meet trouble soon and Margaret will be the only one to get you out of the problem. Do you know anyone by the name of Margaret?" We both shook our heads and I had no idea what he was talking about.

Fernando left around two a.m., I placed the big window fan in the entrance to the main salon. Marrie made up the bed in the main cabin and I went into the forepeak cabin to sleep under the open hatch as it was very hot. Around 3 a.m., I heard Marrie say' "Ugh, ough, ugg," and then a loud slam. I was somewhat alarmed and asked, "Did you fall out of bed?"

Marrie screamed, "Roger, we have just been robbed, someone reached in and took my purse!"

I made a lunge for the dock, kicking the window fan out of the entrance and destroying it as I ran up in my skivvies. A man walking on the dock said, "He ran that way!" I took off in the direction he pointed, wondering if he was the thief. I could not have been over ten seconds behind, but I didn't see anyone. Back on the boat I tried to comfort Marrie as she told of waking up and seeing this face against the moonlight and a long muscular arm reaching in through a 14-inch square hatch above her bunk and taking her back-pack. I asked her what had been in the purse and found out how bad the robbery had been. Both our passports, two thousand US dollars, three thousand Canadian dollars, plus Marrie's jewelry and return airline ticket. Even the ring she inherited from her great Grandmother was in the bag. The thief got away with over fifty thousand dollars. We were downcast and sick at heart.

As dawn was breaking two police officers arrived and took the report, but I could tell they were not interested in a purse snatch.

When I first sailed in, I met two beachcombers who helped me with some rigging repairs. I cooked a few meals, served good beer and they continued to stop by. One of them arrived early at the boat as he had heard of the robbery. Marrie cooked breakfast and as we were eating he said, "I can help you recover the purse, there aren't many such people on the island and I know them all. The jewelry will start showing up tonight in the drug dens of St. George."

I replied, "I already put out an offer of five thousand dollars with the stipulation they can keep the money but must return all the jewelry, passports, and airline ticket."

"That should do the trick. By the way, in the underworld I am known as Margaret."

Before noon we knew the thief was called 'The Zipper Kid,' a fifty-year-old man who had a long history of stealing from the yachts and had recently been released from prison. I went to his parents' house looking for him. His father came out, was very kind, and said that he was sorry we had had such an encounter with his son. I told the old gentleman that my wife could identify his son and neither of us wanted to do that, we just wanted the purse back.

Two days later Margaret arrived with the purse. It was sandy from being buried on the beach. To our surprise the Canadian money was all there and one envelope containing a thousand US dollars was unopened. Gold chains and bracelets were the only things missing. I gave Margaret five hundred dollars and told him to tell the thief that the deal was that all the jewelry had to be returned. Margaret said the items missing had been sold and The Zipper Kid was happy we didn't want to prosecute. I didn't want to prosecute, I wanted his ass!

Marrie flew back to Georgia and I set sail for the states. With the wind and current against me I couldn't sail directly to Georgia so I went with the elements to North Carolina. Before leaving Bermuda I was unable to purchase charts. I only had an overlay of the east coast which was inadequate for navigation. After a week at sea I reached the coast fifteen miles south of Cape Hatteras, an area renowned as the 'Graveyard of the Atlantic.' I steered for the red and green light at the entrance to Okracoke, with a heavy sea breaking fifty yards on my left.

Then I found the lights were in line with the coast and it was confusing. I called the Coast Guard and gave my position and predicament. Some idiot told me I was off the coast of Virginia and for me to contact such and such a station in that state. I replied, "I know where I am. I am only asking for instructions for entering Okracoke."

Again he instructed me to contact the Virginia base, I told him I could not reach it with my VHF as it was out of radio range and I was speaking with him clearly.

I thought 'To heck with the idiots,' and I turned and headed back to sea, deciding on an overnight sail against the Gulf Stream down to Moorhead City which I knew had a deep, wide and well-lit entrance. When I was three or four miles out a voice with authority called on the radio and said they had been mistaken, that they were dispatching a vessel to guide me in and to expect to rendezvous at the entrance in one hour. I wondered what would take them so long but that was better than an all-night sail though and I was tired from the long passage.

I was headed south paralleling the coast and behind the breakers when a sudden squall with winds of over a hundred miles an hour hit knocking the vessel down so the masts were in the water and I was standing on the side of the cockpit. She righted and the sails were torn to shreds. The painter on the Zodiac broke and blew into the rigging where the flapping sails wrapped around it, it was pitch dark. I could barely open my eyes for the stinging water blowing in my face. The vessel was spinning like a top. I kept trying to look at the compass and every time it was in any direction slightly resembling east I applied full throttle and during other headings I reduced power. Fifteen minutes later the storm passed with the Coast Guard calling me non-stop. Their rescue vessel was aground and they were sending a cutter.

An hour later a small cutter came through the entrance all lit up and wanted to tow me in. I told them I had no need for a tow, I just wanted to enter the harbor. They kept asking if I was all right and I kept assuring them I was. I told them my sails were torn to shreds, doors were torn off lockers and there were busted glass and foodstuff strewn in the cabin, but I was alright. I followed close on their stern as they meandered through the backwoods of North Carolina and finally arrived at the docks. The fool in charge searched the boat and wrote me up for not having a bell. He said that if I did not get a bell, by noon the following day the vessel would be seized. This was a blue law from centuries past with no possible application today with radar and radios.

The next morning I went looking for a bell and of course, there were no bells for sale in Okracoke. I went to a seafood processing plant and asked a crabber to loan me his bell for a few minutes while I took a taxi to the station and showed the fool my bell. Where do they find these bureaucratic idiots?

After cleaning up the mess I headed across the shallow inland sea to Oriental, North Carolina, a lovely little town with a colorful shrimp fleet, good restaurants, and a complete chandlery. Marya was visiting from France and she drove down from New York with Max and baby Zillah. We drove and talked all night arriving in South Georgia early in the morning. I shall always remember that night with her driving and me holding little Zillah. To write the words makes my heart ache for something I'm missing.

My days were spent working on the farm. I crawled in drain pipes stuffed full of limbs by beavers and cleaned them out. David had an old Case front-end loader and I cleared land with it, helped in the chicken houses, and kept the roads scraped. After two months of hard farm work we moved to Mother's who wanted to use some of my stored up energy and I went to work around her house and really enjoyed it. Rhett and I jack-hammered out part of her driveway that was cracked by roots from the tall pines. We dug and cut the roots, then poured the drive and made some steps. A light in her living room had been flickering for years and two electricians had attempted to repair it and failed. A two-dollar rheostat and it was like new. I enjoyed these days working with Rhett, and Mother was delighted. When Mother couldn't think of anything else for us to do we went back out to Charlotte's house.

Miriam was in Medical School in Grenada and came home for the holidays. She took her Nissan Maxima out of storage and went cruising around Georgia. Rhett wanted a car, so David and I took him to the auction in Albany, Ga. and bought a Nissan 240 Z Fastback sports car. He was one happy young man as we followed him home and that night. Marya, Max, and little Zillah came home. We had a good time together over Christmas 2000. Rhett received a 12-gauge shotgun for a present and was having the time of his life going to dove shoots.

Marrie called me in from the yards where I was working and handed me the phone.

Clint was on the line and said, "Uncle Roger, Rhett, and Miriam had a bad wreck near Bo's trailer. Come quick, they're in bad shape."

The blood froze in my veins as I heard the news. I grabbed Marrie by the hand and we ran for the Pathfinder. In minutes we came to the wreck. The cars had hit head-on while coming around a curve on the dirt road going to the house. Miriam and Rhett were lying in the road with their arms around one another. Rhett was vomiting up copious amounts of blood and I saw that Miriam was in shock.

There was no way around the wreck. I tried to shove it aside with the 4-wheel drive but it wouldn't move. I backed up and with a running start jumped a deep ditch, knocked over young pines and jumped the ditch again, and backed up to where my babies lay dying in the road. I picked Rhett up and laid him in the back with Marrie cradling his head in her lap. Miriam got in the front seat with me. It was the longest forty miles I have ever driven. Log trucks were blocking the road and slow drivers on hills prevented me from passing. I was flashing lights and waving a white towel out the window and most people pulled over and let me pass. At the hospital they were all asleep or in first gear. After a yell or two they stepped into action. A nurse was almost fighting me as I lifted Rhett out of the car and carried him in. Her job was to apply a neck brace and get him on a backboard and then a stretcher. I said that his back was all right, he needed to get into the emergency room, NOW!

Miriam was more in danger of death than Rhett as one lung had collapsed and the other was going down. Within minutes they had her in surgery with a suction tube installed and she began feeling better. Later we found her seatbelt had broken.

Rhett's nose and eye socket were shattered and the blood he kept vomiting was from that injury. He was disorientated and his speech was slurred. They sent him to the trauma center at St Joseph Hospital in Savannah by ambulance

Marrie and I returned to Charlotte's where we took off our overalls and brogans, took a shower, threw some clothes in a bag, and headed for Savannah. As we were speeding through Fort Stewart Military Reservation an M.P. stopped us, and I explained to him that we were following an ambulance that passed through about an hour previously with our son who was in critical condition. He remembered the ambulance and escorted us for twenty miles across the reservation. The surgeon had to take his eyeball out and insert a Teflon plate to hold the eye, then place it back in. As soon as the operation was over and he came to, he felt much better, although the broken bones were pinching the nerves and tissue, causing him great pain.

Marrie and I were torn emotionally between wanting to be with Miriam and Rhett. For some reason we felt Rhett needed us more as he was delirious, broken and bleeding while Miriam was sitting up in bed, laughing and telling jokes. Rhett was released from hospital after five days and we drove directly to the hospital in Douglas and visited Miriam. While we were there Mike Harper's daughter Whitney and her friend Lee Ann came in and Rhett was stoked by the presence of two beautiful girls. Miriam walked around carrying her suction pump attached to a tube sticking between her ribs and I am sure that thing hurt, however, she never flinched or let on.

Hospital bills were enormous, our two cars were totaled, the last of our money was diminishing and I had to do something before going paralyzed broke.

38. ONE TON OF COCAINE TO AUSTRALIA

Fateful Journey -- Mid Ocean Transfer -- If You Want Something Done... -- Mexican Standoff -- Land Ho!

Gravel crunched as one of those monster trucks with balloon tires suitable for a 747 eased into the parking lot of the marina. Two Latin men, about thirty years old, wearing jeans and muscle shirts climbed down and Marcus followed. I thought, 'Oh God, I don't need this attention, I wish I had met them somewhere else.'

Marcus introduced them as David and Paco. My first thought was that they looked like the new generation of prisoners entering Lompoc doing life sentences. Then I decided it was such young men as these now doing the business. They looked the boat over and asked if I was willing to sail to Australia via the Cape of Good Hope with a ton of cocaine. I said it was a long and dangerous journey of 14,000 miles without being able to go into a port for repairs, but possible. After some haggling I settled on 20%. If the load sold for fifty thousand US dollars a kilo, as they expected, then my part would be ten million US dollars.

I explained that the vessel had to be re-rigged with heavier rigging, a set of heavy sails and a wind vane was a must. One of the young men asked me how much all this would cost and I estimated a price in the thirty-five-thousand-dollar range. He opened his valise and counted out the amount and asked how long before I could be ready to depart. I said it would take approximately six weeks.

Mechanics and riggers went to work and in a couple of weeks it was done. Everything was oversized and rigged. It looked like the boat could make the long and somewhat treacherous journey but I didn't know a soul who would go on such a trip with me.

Marcus returned and said the men had changed their minds and wanted to buy a more substantial vessel. That was fine with me as I could sell the sailboat and use theirs.

I recommended buying an oil supply vessel since they were mini tankers designed to carry fuel and water to the offshore rigs. Also, they had two engines with separate drives and propellers so if one failed you could get there on the other. He asked the price and I told him they cost from three hundred thousand to four hundred thousand and another hundred thousand to get one ready for the trip. Marcus told me to start looking and try to find one soon.

I listed the sailboat with a broker and headed for Louisiana, stopping in Mobile and several ports along the coast. Within three weeks I had narrowed it down to two vessels. The White Dove was for sale at four hundred and fifty thousand dollars, but recently the owner had come down to three hundred thousand and I thought this was the best deal. The vessel was 38 years old and in pristine condition. The owner, Jimmy Martin, had just spent five million dollars replacing it with a new vessel and he needed the dock space. He was also keen to receive as much cash as I could come up with. I could come up with it all in cash but was afraid he would just take it to the bank and declare it.

The particulars of the vessel were relayed to Colombia and I was told to go to New York, meet Paco, and pick up the money.

New York was fifteen hundred miles north, a hard two days drive. I stopped off in Georgia for Mother, who rode with me as far as North Carolina where we spent the night with my sister Nell and her family. I arrived in New York after dark and went to the Holiday Inn at La Guardia Airport and met Paco. We stayed there for a week. Rooms were two hundred dollars a night and Paco was out of money. I had about two thousand with me and it was going fast.

We moved to the New Yorker Hotel right downtown where we shared a room for a hundred and fifty dollars a night to cut down on expenses. Paco kept calling Colombia and a number in New York. Someone wanted to come by and get my vehicle and go for the money but I refused as I had no idea as to how hot this person was. Perhaps he was under surveillance? If so, the DEA would take photos of the license plates registered to Marrie and we would be targeted before we began.

After a week, a bad-looking fellow met Paco in the foyer and they walked off down the street. I followed at a distance, but ugly saw me, thought I was DEA and bolted. We waited several more days and Paco was getting hard to live with. He eventually made a call to Colombia and someone told him to go to a certain address and pick up the money. I was waiting in the lobby when he came back with a backpack and a duffle bag stuffed with a half-million dollars. We checked out, loaded up, and headed south.

Since I had a Florida driver's license I went to Tallahassee. A teller at Bank of America directed me to a young woman from Chile who took applications for new accounts. We chatted a bit in Spanish, she blushed and was a bit shy. When she typed in George Green and gave my previous bank account number in North Carolina the computer refused to accept the account and I knew what the problem was. The account in North Carolina had a George Green with a different driver's license number to accompany the Social Security number. The young woman blushed even deeper as she told me I could not open an account in the bank.

Two more banks turned me so I gave up the idea of opening an account in David's name. I would have to find another way. I took the money to Miami and met Paco and two other men and explained the problem I was having depositing the money in a bank. We took the money to their friend who would deposit it anywhere for a fee of 10%. In about fifteen minutes this delightful lady earned fifty thousand dollars. It was expensive, but it kept the deal alive.

Marrie was waiting at Mother's house so I drove up to Georgia. Several family members heard I was coming and there was a crowd waiting when I got there. We had a good supper, accompanied with storytelling and lots of laughter.

Joel Parrish was there and I had not seen him for a long time. He and my sister Kay had lived together for the past eight years, but I had been away. Everyone in three counties knew Joel as he was a baseball and football legend. There is, or was, a giant billboard on both ends of town with a painting of Joel charging with a football and underneath is the caption, "Welcome to Douglas Georgia – Home of Joel Parrish." Also, Joel's family had lived in Douglas for generations and his father was active in the Presbyterian Church for seventy years. When Joel was a boy he went to Sunday school for thirteen years without missing a Sunday. The citizens of Douglas love Joel, and that's a fact.

After supper, Joel and I took a walk around the nearby golf course and I explained my problem of trying to open a bank account to purchase a vessel. Joel was driving a truck seven days a week and ready to make some money and before we came to the far end of the golf course we had reached an agreement.

Joel and Kay drove to Saint Augustine, took the Zodiac, outboard motor, food, tools and most everything off the sailboat and brought it to Golden Meadows, Louisiana, where they met Marrie and me at the Motel. The next morning we met with the owner of the vessel, who told us he had an account in Hibernia Bank and it would be easier if we opened an account there. Joel did, with me sitting beside him answering questions the lady asked. She looked at us funny as she asked Joel questions and I answered.

The money was transferred to the account, the vessel changed hands and Joel was the proud owner of a 100-foot offshore supply vessel. We had no time to celebrate as we had work to do.

We hauled her out at Allied Marine where plumbers converted water tanks into fuel tanks and had her twelve water tanks, which held 40,000 gallons, hydro blasted and cleaned. We filled the freezer with choice cuts of meat and stuffed the larder with enough food to last a crew for a half year. Two hundred fuel and oil filters were loaded onboard along with spare parts for the five motors and a dozen pumps. Running out of water at sea has always been a fear of mine so I purchased a hundred one-gallon jugs of water and stored it in one of the rooms.

I carried one tone cocaine hidden in the bow of an oil rig re-supply vessel named 'The White Dove' - very similar to this vessel. It's giant fuel and water tanks allowed for a non stop journey Down Under.
Image courtesy Agnito Navicula 1999 - Ensco Ram - Wikipedia

For emergency electronics, I purchased a locating beacon, a handheld GPS, and a handheld VHF radio with a case of batteries to run them. These items were placed in a waterproof container and stored near the door in case we went down.

We needed a global satellite telephone to contact the shore party before landing. The Iridium system had been up and running the year before and then gone bankrupt. It was in service again, but there were no stores in which to purchase one. I called the number on the advertisement and they gave me a number in California. Someone at that number told me that he could send me one overnight if I had a credit card. I didn't, so I borrowed Joel's and ordered the phone which cost one thousand two hundred dollars and I gave Joel that amount in cash.

Once all was shipshape and ready to go Marcus said that I must go to Colombia for a meeting with the owners. I explained that I was afraid to go through customs and immigration. If they found out who I was, it was off to prison for parole violation and the end of the deal. We were at an impasse for several days and finally they agreed to meet me in San Jose, Costa Rica. I could go there and return on the dodgy driver's license.

I drove to New Orleans where I caught a flight via Miami that arrived on schedule. I went to the designated hotel and waited three days before Paco showed up. The next evening a driver picked us up and drove to a restaurant where I met three nice looking, slim men, about forty years old. We had dinner, drank a few beers and they were satisfied.

I returned to Louisiana without problems and went directly to the vessel. Joel, Marrie and I departed Golden Meadows southbound on the bayou for the 20-mile trip to the fuel docks on the Gulf of Mexico. This was interesting as I was unfamiliar with the vessel and the area. It was also hilariously funny with the errors I was making. As we were going through a lock, I saw a tug pushing a string of heavily loaded chemical barges our way. Over the radio, I heard, "Vessel, departing Golden Meadows locks southbound, this is the tug Taurus, give me two whistles please."

I shut down on the air horn with two long loud whistles and heard the chuckles echoing over the radio.

"Hello White Dove, in freshwater two whistles means pass me on the right."

I changed course without answering, happy with the knowledge that we were departing those parts.

As the lower rim of the sun touched the horizon we arrived at Port Fourchon on the Gulf of Mexico. The place was a hive of activity. Helicopters were taking off and landing in all directions, a seaplane was coming straight for me and oil supply vessels and fishing boats were as thick and active as ants in a freshly kicked bed. They were going forward, backward and sideways around the fuel dock that I was supposed to back into. It didn't take long to figure out this was not the place for me. I got out of there somehow without crashing.

A mile back up the canal we found a quieter fuel dock. The next problem was backing into the narrow slip with the current running one way and the wind blowing another. With Marrie motioning on one side and Joel on the other we got the Mammoth docked. It took five hours to pump 50,000 gallons of fuel through the hose holding the nozzle at all times as dock men are not allowed on vessels and there is a ten thousand dollar fine for any fuel spilled into the water.

At 2 a: m. the tanks were full and I was ordered to move immediately as several vessels were waiting and letting their impatience show. Oh boy, how am I going to do this? Just Marrie and me, alone in the middle of the night on an unfamiliar vessel with traffic on the water busier than ever! There was no choice, we had to leave. We untied the ship and pulled away. We steered up and down the water until we came to an unlit barge on the far side. I turned into the current and slowly approached. As we came alongside Marrie draped the eye of the heavy two-inch line over a stanchion and we were attached. I quickly ran down from the bridge and secured more lines. We locked up, got into the Zodiac, and began paddling across the bayou. As we reached the center we could see a ship bearing down towards us at twelve knots. I was scared. Marrie was terrified. We bent the paddles getting out of the way. The huge ship glided past our stern and we surfed to shore on its wake. We pulled the Zodiac out of the water, hid it amongst some rusty oil drilling pipes, and went for a taxi.

Back at the hotel we showered and went to bed. Our heads had just touched the pillow when the phone rang and the man from the fuel dock said we should get back as fast as possible because a tug had come for the barge and our abandoned vessel was illegally tied to it.

I threw my clothes in a suitcase and we peeled out. When we arrived a police boat was tied to the White Dove with both red and blue lights flashing.

I invited the police officer in for a cup of coffee and soon we were friends. *Soft words turneth away wrath.*

Joel showed up and we were ready to depart.

Both Marrie and I were heartbroken at the idea of being separated for the three-month journey. I was sick at heart as I kissed her goodbye knowing the chance I was taking with the vessel, the elements, and the years in a foreign prison if I was caught. Marrie stood on the dock waving and I, with an aching heart, watched and waved until I could no longer see her.

May 9, 2001. Our departure was on the day shrimp season opened. The entrance to the Gulf was jammed with small shrimpers with outriggers extended out thirty feet on both sides. A fishing boat dragging nets has the right of way and we were forced so far to one side that we hit bottom, hard. Eventually we inched our way out into the gulf amidst numerous oil wells. Night fell and we were in the thick of them. Rooster, a shrimper from the shipyard, warned us of unlit rigs and broken off wells and said we were in no way to traverse the area in the dark. We wove our way around one oil patch after another and at midnight we were running in the clear. The sea was moderately rough and soon both of us were losing our dinner over the railing. For the next two days the wind was coming directly from starboard causing her to roll constantly.

The steering was a new state-of-the-art GPS coupled to the autopilot. I had never seen anything like it and had a hard time with all the buttons. Joel had experience with computers and took on the task of reading the instructions, figuring it out, and later teaching me.

Extending forty miles out into our route was a string of reefs. I plotted waypoints in the autopilot with ample room to clear. I instructed Joel to keep her on course and went to bed. After a four-hour sleep I walked on the bridge and saw we were almost on the reef. I immediately changed course and asked Joel how we got into this position? He said he was looking at the chart and saw where we could save fifty miles by cutting the corner. He got a quick lesson in navigation, and map reading.

Sunday morning, May 12, 2001. Day 3. We ran out of freshwater. Both tanks were bone dry. One of the workers at the shipyard had left a toilet valve open and it had taken that long to drain the tanks. There was no choice. We had to go in. I decided on Key West and what a beautiful choice it was. I have never seen such shades of blue, sprinkled with every type water conveyances imaginable: tugs, dredges, flashy speedboats, and derelict old sailing yachts adding their flavor to the flotilla. We maneuvered our way through to the yacht fuel dock right downtown. Our ship was too big for the pier and the proprietor was afraid we would bash it in but I came in ever so gently and tied up. Two garden hoses were brought out to fill the empty water tanks and I decided to top off with diesel while we were there. Diesel was one dollar and sixty cents a gallon and I figured it should take 1,700 gallons yet it took 2,200 gallons. Jimmy had lied as to the amount it burned. Instead of burning the 550 gallons a day it was burning over 700. I would not have enough for the 12,000-mile trip from Cape Verde Islands to Melbourne Australia. What could I do? I decided to check it again when we reached Africa. We ordered two blackened grouper sandwiches to go and pulled out. Our sojourn in Key West lasted less than two hours.

The Gulf Stream was running a strong three knots and we stayed in the center of it. That night we passed Key Largo, Marathon, and Miami doing a screaming 12 knots. Upon reaching the 26th parallel we hung a right for our traverse down the Tongue of the Ocean and through the Bahamas. At daybreak we let out a 300-pound test line with a big dolphin lure. Joel pulled in a 12-pound king, then a thirty-pound bull dolphin. In the late afternoon I landed a 10-pound tuna and a four-pound bonito. We had plenty of fish and reeled in the line.

Tuesday morning, May 16, we were clear of the Bahamas and out in the blue Atlantic. A high-pressure area extended all the way across and it was smooth motoring. A school of frolicking dolphins joined us under the bow, darting off, then returning, leaping and rolling overlooking us straight in the eye. It was a delight to watch these enchanting animals play. They are truly happy creatures, although it saddened me to see so few. Thirty years before when Marrie, the children, and I sailed down the west coast of Central America we often encountered schools of three or four hundred frolicking dolphins over miles of oceans. They like to stay over schools of tuna. The giant tuna vessels send out helicopters to spot schools of dolphins to lead them to the tuna. Sadly, dolphins die in the tuna nets.

As soon as we crossed the tropic of Cancer we began seeing flying fish. Sometimes hundreds of these small silver fish with bulging eyes took to the wing like a covey of quail. They would all sail off in the same direction and it was fascinating to see them fly on such tiny wings. As is always the case, one would go much farther than the rest of the pack. Sometimes we found little ones on the instrument panel on the bridge, 15 feet above the water. Each morning there would be a dozen or more on deck ranging in size from two to fourteen inches. I picked up several of the bigger ones and fried them up for breakfast. They were good with grits.

Dead center of the Atlantic the starboard main engine quit. After some searching I found that fuel wasn't getting to it. Using the same reasoning as I did on the old Farmall tractors on the farm, I deducted that the line was stopped up somewhere. I figured the problem should be easy to remedy as there was an air compressor on board with a tank pumped up to 80 pounds per inch. I took the one-inch fuel line apart, stuck the air hose down, and using a rag for a stopper, let her rip. The engine room was suddenly pitch black and deathly quiet. Oh, shit! I had blown the fuel out of all the lines and back into the day tank. Groping on my hands and knees I found a flashlight that was pitifully inadequate in the darkness. I had to get a generator going for lights and to recharge the air pressure. After a few minutes I had a generator going and the problem lessened with bright lights shining on in. I got the port engine going so we were underway doing six knots. After taking out half the fuel lines I found a broken valve blocking the fuel to the starboard engine. I took the valve out and put the fuel line back together without a valve. In the process I took a bath in diesel and ran blindly for a shower. Later, I broke out in tiny blisters and a bad rash.

Nineteen days out of Key West we picked up the Cape Verde Islands on the radar screen. I was excited, but Joel more so, because he had never been outside the United States. I radioed Cape Verde Coast Control repeatedly and then this message came over the air, "Good morning, White Dove. This is American Warship so and so, may I help you?"

Did this ever surprise me and cause my heart rate to perk up a beat. I answered, "White Dove to Warship, I'm trying to reach Cape Verde Coast Control."

His response, "White Dove, Coast Control will not be open until eight o'clock, you can reach them on frequency 487942."

I shut down one engine and made my way slowly into the port, never contacting anyone on the radio. I ventured on in and tied up to a long filthy wharf.

Police, customs and immigration officers with long faces lined the wharf. I speak a little Portuguese so I greeted them with a cheery "Bom Dia." Angry stone faces glared back. They kept pointing to the flagpole and I realized they were pissed because I was not flying their courtesy flag. I needed a shipping agent, so I got on the Iridium phone and called Marya in France. She found the number of an agent in Praia and relayed it to me. I called and the man was there with a flag within minutes. I attached it to the flagpole and as it raised so did the frowns on the faces. They were all smiles after Joel invited them aboard and offered them our Budweiser. When we ran out of Budweiser and bought several cases of their green piss I realized why they liked our beer.

Since I could not show my passport and the vessel was in Joel's name, he was listed as Captain and I as Engineer. I gave them the David Gunn ID but they refused to allow me to get off the vessel. After two days they lifted the restriction so I could go to restaurants with the port captain and to town with the shipping agent to buy supplies.

It took 75,000 liters to fill the tanks and I figured it would take an additional 16,000 to reach Melbourne. The agent found sixteen one-thousand-liter plastic tanks on pallets enclosed in a steel cage. They were cleaned and delivered to the vessel, where we bolted them on deck and chained them down.

The dock by the vessel was filled with idle men and boys begging for our empty plastic jugs, lines, barrels, and anything else they saw. Several had to be driven off the deck with harsh words and gestures. Still, if we blinked, something went missing. One morning the din was louder than usual. I went out to see what was going on and there was Paco waiting to come aboard.

Joel, Paco, and I were working on deck securing the containers when two thieves slipped onto the bridge and stole Joel's CD player. Several people saw them and told us who they were. We put out a sizable reward but never got it back. Joel had two cases of CDs and one battery-operated player. As it turned out, this could have cost us our lives.

We planned to leave the next morning and the shipping agent asked for our passports to give to immigration. When he left, Paco said that he gave him his

Colombian passport. I came undone! "Why on earth did you give him your Colombian passport when you have a clean, new Spanish one in your pocket?"

All along, he and his bosses had insisted I stay far away from South America and anything to do with Colombia. They would not even allow me to go through the Caribbean and re-fuel in Trinidad where we could have saved twenty thousand dollars with the cheap fuel and cut 3000 miles off the trip. Paco bought a big bag of marijuana and had been sucking on joints regularly. His Colombian passport was compromised, as he had recently been released from prison in the Dutch Antilles for importing cocaine. Besides, I had already told the shipping agent I had a Spanish crew member.

I ran after the agent and found him in the customs and immigration building. I asked for Paco's passport, he gave it to me and I saw that his real name was Carlos Suarez. Then I handed him back the Spanish passport. He said the immigration officer had already seen the Colombian passport and it was better to continue with it. He also promised he would not tell about the Spanish one. The next morning as we were getting ready to depart a carload of long-faced officials arrived. The immigration officer said that Carlos Suarez (Paco) had two passports and they did a thorough search of the vessel. We departed with those officers lining the dock, looking as hostile as when we arrived. I had a great dread that they would notify the US authorities and we would be under the scrutiny of a satellite. I was ready to throw in the towel.

Carlos said the pick-up point had been changed from 50 miles southwest of the Cape Verde Islands to a location a thousand miles west. For a week I kept a western course, using one engine to conserve fuel. We reached the rendezvous point exactly on time and found an empty ocean. Carlos made a telephone call to Colombia and they told him to wait for eight hours. We steered south for four hours, then headed north for four hours, returning to nothing. This went on for forty-eight hours and I had a belly full of circling under a satellite. I told Carlos it was over and headed for Saint Martin. He also had enough circling under the satellite and was not against going in. En route, Carlos whistled into the mike every few minutes and a clear whistle responded. We had run across the loaders. They gave their position and soon we had them on the radar.

Dark heavy clouds hung low on the horizon ten miles to the south and I headed for them in order to conceal the exchange from the cameras of a satellite. We came together in rain and eight-foot seas. The Venezuelan vessel was an 80-foot steel derelict with a dozen half-naked brown bodies lining the rail. The captain circled and reversed into our stern where his men secured lines to heavy stanchions on both vessels. His vessel slammed into ours busting a hole in his just below the rail. Bales began sailing across and landing hard on our deck. One fell in the ocean between the two vessels and a young man dove in to retrieve it. The vessels were coming back together and he was most definitely going to be crushed. I engaged the gear and started towing the other vessel, keeping them apart and saving the fool's life. Towing worked better than standing still and slamming into one another, so I continued to tow. Bales kept flying over with Carlos trying to catch them to prevent them from tearing the corners on the rough deck. Joel was standing to one side looking at the circus. I wore a mask and watched through the rear window of the bridge.

I could see there was tremendous pressure on the lines each time we rode over a wave and I wanted to warn everyone but could not leave the wheel. The massive stanchion on the port side tore loose at its roots and a two-inch diameter line whipped across the deck with a fifty-pound steel Boland attached to the end, knocking Joel down. I abandoned the bridge and ran to attend to him. He was hurt badly and it looked like his arm was broken as it was swelling rapidly. The other vessel had turned around and their crew secured lines to our port side and were running parallel with us. They swarmed across on our vessel and Carlos was talking with some of them while the captain came on the bridge demanding food and fuel. I told him I could not part with one liter. We had already come a thousand miles out of our way and had waited on him for two days and now it would take several days to get back to our route. Then I explained that I had an injured crewmember I wanted to send ashore. He refused. I insisted. He was adamant. I offered money. There was no way he was going to allow Joel to know who he was or where he was going. He and I parted company on very unfriendly terms.

I had a complete medical chest on board and I gave Joel a shot of morphine that put him to sleep for several hours. When he awoke we decided his arm was not broken but it was twice its normal size. I told him he was going to have stretch marks. Nothing was funny to Joel.

On the trip from Cape Verde I removed three 14-inch wide oak timbers and cut a three-foot square hole in the metal deck in order to get the bales of cocaine into the rudder room. There was only one small manhole going to the room and I was sure the bales would not fit through it. As soon as we were on our way I removed the timbers and lowered the 40 bales through the hole and then went down and stacked them against the further side and secured them with chains and chain binders. On deck I placed six 55-gallon drums of oil along the rail and over the manhole cover, then chained and bound them in place.

About the only job Joel had, other than stand watch, was to remove the heavy drum of oil every day and check on the merchandise. I gave him the job because it was easy for him, seeing as he was so big. Every day I would say, "How is the rudder room Joel?" and he would reply, "Dry as a bone!"

The night after we loaded we crossed the shipping lane from South America to Europe and ships were coming at us all night. One showed up on radar doing forty knots. I woke Joel and we watched as he bore down on us and I thought it had to be an American warship. Whatever it was it steamed past a half-mile off our bow and disappeared over the horizon. Things like that are not good for one's heart.

We cruised along in beautiful weather until we crossed the equator and hit the SE trades at an angle and then things got rough. Green water was coming over the bow, the vessel rolled unceasingly and Señor Carlos was also green making many offerings to Neptune.

Early one morning after a particularly stormy night, Carlos woke me and said the boat was going in circles. I hurried to the bridge and sure enough, we were going in circles. I found the steering worked in either the full right or the full left positions, there was no in between and it had me at a loss as to what was wrong. I began taking hydraulic lines apart on the bridge. The fluid sprayed out under pressure so it was not the hydraulic pump. Then I went to work on the steering mechanism which took several hours to inspect.

Down in the engine room I noticed water running out a small pipe coming from the rear of the vessel. I tasted it. It was salt. Strange! Where was it coming from? Then it dawned on me and my blood ran cold. I ran up on the deck yelling for Joel. We ran to the rear and as we removed the drum of oil, I asked Joel how long it had been since he looked in the hole. He said he had never looked in, he just flipped the switch to the bilge pump for that room and nothing came out so he reported it, "Dry as a bone."

Before we got the manhole cover off I could hear tons of water sloshing back and forth. When the cover came off an empty plastic kilo bag popped out and I almost had a heart attack. I quickly removed the timbers and had a good look in the hole that was ¾ full of milky-white saltwater with bales of cocaine sloshing from one side to the other. I began grabbing them as they came by and was happy to see many were undamaged. However, empty kilo bags kept floating by. I tied a rope around my waist and with Joel holding one end I lowered myself into the cocaine swimming pool. With every roll of the vessel, water sloshed by violently in the 22-foot-wide compartment. On each 'slosh' I pulled out a 25-kilo bale. When all those were retrieved I started on the singles. I found 30 empty kilo packets and several more that were partially empty or damaged.

My teeth began grinding against one another and my vision was strange. It dawned on me, I was on a cocaine high! I got out of the violent sloshing cocaine bath and took a warm shower and drank some hot coffee as it was raining and I was freezing. After a few minutes I was back in the tank with a 5-gallon bucket dipping water. I dipped until my muscles seized up, then Joel took over. After three or four hours, we had dipped enough water out so I could dive down and unstop the drain pipe which was covered in a bucket-full of big flakes of paint.

Once the hole was empty I saw that a bale of floating cocaine had knocked the arm to the autopilot off and the bolts through the deck punctured the sloshing bales. I used haywire and jerry-rigged the autopilot so we could get underway.

After rescuing the cocaine, I placed it on the linoleum floor in the main salon to let the water run out of the bags. Some of the kilos were torn with white sticky water oozing out. The floor was slippery so I laid down burlap bags to walk on. Without realizing it, I was getting high by walking in the cocaine goo with bare feet. Later in the day I took it to a spare room downstairs and laid it out on the slats of empty bunk beds.

Carlos went into some type of shock. He was seasick and vomited. His limbs became rigid, he got very cold and I thought he was in danger of dying. I covered him in a pile of blankets, nursed him as best I could by mopping his brow, cleaning up his puke, talking gently to him, and making him chicken soup. When he recovered somewhat, he got out of bed, lay on the bench on the bridge, smoked marijuana and listened to the little CD player. I would sleep while he was supposed to be on watch and wake to the alarm going off on the bridge. However, he wasn't able to hear it because he was stoned and the volume of his music was loud. I worried when he was on watch because the radar alarm made a soft beep which he could never have heard in his condition.

Every day when I plotted our position it was several miles east of my estimate and it should have been a westerly drift with the wind and current. What was causing this I wondered? One night I walked on the bridge, we were headed ESE and I asked Carlos why the course change. He replied, "Which way is Australia? Tell me which direction is Australia from here?"

I answered, "Australia is 7000 miles due east of here."

He smiled and said, "Ok, I'm going east, what's your problem?"

"My problem is the 6,000-mile African continent with mountains 20,000 feet high between here and Australia and this boat can't fly." I tried to explain that the farther east we got the stronger the current and the waves against us. To mention the great circle route being shorter was futile. Australia was east and he was miserable.

Sometimes I had to turn the vessel into the waves in order to cook, but I wanted to get back on course as soon as possible. Each evening I cooked a good supper and put a lot of effort into doing so. Carlos covered whatever I cooked with catsup, honey, and sometimes condensed milk. If it happened to be a sirloin steak he took his good time chopping it up and stirring in all the aforementioned ingredients. By the time he had his plate to his liking everything was cold and Joel and I had finished eating. One night as soon as I finished eating I went on the bridge and turned to the correct heading and the boat started rolling. Carlos threw his plate full of mixture on the floor and stalked off to his cabin. He refused to speak to me all the next day. His face hung like a miserable hound and his personality matched his countenance. It was a mistake to say "Good morning."

One morning I walked on the bridge and perhaps I was not having such a good start and did say "Good morning," got the long face and pissed off expression. I yelled, "I know you are miserable, but you came along voluntarily and this is not a fucking morgue!"

His reply was, "I would rather be in prison than on this boat."

After a week the bags of cocaine were dry, so I went down and re-bagged all the loose kilos and took inventory. Thirty kilos were destroyed, twelve had dented places on the corners and a tiny bit of water damage, five were half-empty and seven were a quarter light. All added up, the loss was about thirty-five kilos. I wrote all this down on paper and put it in my pocket. Then I opened a forward fuel tank, lined it with lumber, and concealed the cocaine inside.

Joel and Carlos were on the bridge when I came up and gave Carlos the news along with the slip of paper. He stuck it in a diary he was keeping along with all other evidence he could find. I said, "Carlos, if you want to keep that as a souvenir then copy it off in your own hand."

He looked at me very hostile and said, "Tomorrow you can have your paper. You will pay for every kilo that was lost!"

"Carlos, I feel bad enough already. I will most certainly pay, but at the Colombian price, not the expected price in Australia."

"No, you will pay every peso at the Australian price!"

"Listen big shot, you are the supercargo on this vessel. It was your job to see that the cocaine was safe, but you have been too fucked up ever since you stepped on board to look after anything. Give me that bit of paperback NOW!"

"Tomorrow!"

Wham! A right hook came out all by itself knocking Señor Carlos into the bulkhead. The fight was on. Carlos dove in, grabbed me around the head and shoulder and wouldn't let go. The bridge was too small and we stayed locked like that until it got boring. I told Joel to pry him loose so we could go down and fight. Joel came over and separated us and we went down in the main salon. Carlos was thirty years younger and stronger but he didn't know anything about fighting. He also had trouble standing up on the pitching deck, which was a great advantage to me. I ducked his whopping swings and knocked him down, but it was just making him angrier. He would jump up and rush in again screaming and swinging. I would sidestep his savage wild blow and connect again. We fought our way through the cabin and onto the back deck and I was giving out. My anger had abated and it was senseless. I told Carlos to just stop, but he kept coming. He was angry because he had not hit me. I asked Joel to come between us and stop the fight. When Carlos got up, Joel put his big arms around him and said, "Here, here, take it easy fellow."

As I walked by Carlos kicked out at my groin and hit my leg near the jewels, while screaming, "I will *keel* you, I will *keel* you. We know where your mother lives!"

Señor Carlos was on very thin ice as I walked back to the bridge and considered what to do with him.

When Joel let him go Carlos ran into the kitchen, stuck a butcher knife in his belt and thus walked around the rest of the day. I also went in, got a bigger butcher knife and sat at the table sharpening it on a stone. I chuckled to think of Cookie Jack London's, 'The Sea Wolf'.

Later that night Carlos came in and said, "You want to *keel* me, come on, *keel* me, *keel* me!"

"I said, "Carlos, I don't want to kill you or anyone else. Don't you remember me holding your head and nursing you when you were sick? And how I have cooked every bite you ate and washed every dish. What is wrong with you that you are so miserable and angry?"

He answered, "You do have your good points and your bad points."

Don't we all?

We were three hundred miles south of the Cape of Good Hope in gigantic seas. I had no idea the earth's oceans could produce waves that big in the middle of deep water. They were like mountains with 20-foot curlers on top. We had to go with them, if we turned in either direction the vessel would have rolled. We were lifted up high, thrown forward and surfed down colossal walls of water. At the bottom of the trough the bow plunged deep under, then she would slowly rise up shedding the water as it poured waist deep over the deck. Then the bow pointed towards the sky when we started on the slow journey up the mountain. As we went over the crest, the propellers came out of the water and the engines screamed as they over-revved. The vessel was definitely not made for these violent seas, she was at home in the sub-tropical climate of the Gulf of Mexico. I was afraid she would break in half at any time.

Early one morning a full fifty-five-gallon drum of hydraulic oil got loose on deck and was floating and slamming into lifeboats and the other drums of oil. We had to secure it. We were using ten gallons of oil a day and if it busted other drums we would soon be 'dead' in the water. I yelled for all hands on deck. Joel came to the rear door, looked out, and said, "No fucking way!" and went back in. It was then I learned the true meaning of 'A loose cannon on deck.' Roping a bucking Brahma bull is tame compared to a bucking barrel of oil in three feet of swirling icy water.

We continued in an ESE direction until reaching the fiftieth parallel where we had the wind and current going with us. Giant albatross sailed by the bridge, their shadow scared me as it looked like an airplane. One old white one with feathers missing from one side of his head and some more missing from both wings stayed with us for days. His wingspan was a good 10 feet, probably close to 12. By soaring into the air currents only inches from the surface of the sea and using his head and tail as rudders, he would dive and glide all day without any perceptible wing motion. I watched him for days and never saw him land.

The Southern Ocean was chock full of Petrels and Shearwaters. Several were always circling the ship and one or two hanging like kites over the stern. When the propellers chopped up squid or other fish, they landed and had a feast. These little birds were a delight to watch and I know they are the best flyers in the world and the most graceful. They have a rapid, gliding flight, somewhat like the albatross. They have a wingspan of two to three feet and their plumage was a multitude of colors, black, grey, brown, white, and many with a white star in the center of their brown wings.

One morning before dawn, the radar picked up what looked like land. This was strange as there was no land for a thousand miles, but there it was. The sky began to turn pink in the east and I saw the light reflecting off the blue ice of a large iceberg several miles to the SE. Between the iceberg and us was a herd of whales blowing into the cold air. Their warm exhale spewed up like geysers, leaving puffs of white clouds that hung over the blue ocean with the iceberg as a backdrop.

It was in the dead of winter in the antipodes and we had no radio to receive the weather. The iceberg brought home the danger we were in should the weather turn nasty. With that thought in mind, I turned northeast. Ever since we reached the Southern Ocean, a low-pressure area had passed every fourth day, bringing cold rain and rough seas. I was ready for warmer climes.

I asked, "Carlos where are we going? I am headed northeast toward the southwest point of Australia and I need a destination, call now."

"No! I am supposed to call Wednesday and I will not call before."

Wednesday came and he telephoned. His mouth was all sugar and spice as he talked to David. When he hung up I asked for the position.

He said, "David has a position, but he is not going to tell us until it is necessary."

Before departing Louisiana, I received a fax with co-ordinates for unloading near Streaky Bay, South Australia. The charts showed this as an unbroken shore with reefs extending out over three miles with no shelter. Furthermore, it was 2000 miles farther than necessary and we did not need to cruise the Australian coast for ten days. I explained to Carlos that we had limited fuel because of going back towards Colombia a thousand miles. This wastage was compounded by the fooling around two extra days waiting to get loaded and then there was the fuel burned to get back to where we started and this had taken our reserve. I said that his man had to find a spot in South Western Australia, in the vicinity of Albany or Esperance.

Carlos called but did not mention South West Australia, he just said Western Australia. The next time he called they were north of Broome, double the distance of the original place. I heard Carlos repeating the following in loud, clear Spanish, "Longitude, one, one, seven, three, four, west, latitude." The first three numbers of the latitude were sufficient for me to know the position within a mile, as the longitude had to be on the coast.

Oh, God! They were broadcasting the unload spot for the world to hear. I had asked Carlos earlier if they had a code and he assured me they did. The only code they had was in plain Spanish. I would never go near any place as compromised as that spot. I would not even go near the north coast as I had read about the heavy surveillance in the north. There was no way I was going to follow the coast of Australia for a thousand miles to get into the hottest waters in the entire country. I called David, the offloader, while Carlos was asleep and told him to come south. When Carlos woke up I told him what I had done and he turned purple with rage.

With Carlos swearing that I would have to pay fifty thousand dollars for every missing kilo, coupled with the broadcasting of the position, I became very doubtful of ever getting paid. I had had enough experience with the last three loads for Ochoa; the load delivered to the off loaders in Canada and the Howard Marks debacle in Germany. I had been ripped off so many times and dealt with such incompetent, arrogant fools why should this one be any different? It was sure shaping up that way. With this in mind, I decided not to give them my share of the load. I knew I was honest, but I had no idea if the Colombians were. I pulled the card on the satellite phone, replaced it with one from a regular cell phone, and changed directions towards Shark Bay.

I planned to unload near the 26th parallel and hide the cocaine in the desert under rocks and sand. I would leave Carlos with it while I went back to the White Dove and motored north to Steep Point where I would open the seacock, start up the fire pump and point her out to sea on autopilot. Joel and I would get in the Zodiac and zip through the straights of the southern entrance to Shark Bay and on across to Denham, thirty-five miles away. There we would rent a 4-wheel drive vehicle and return for Carlos within four hours.

That night while sleeping on my bunk, I had a crystal clear vision in living color. Men in camouflage clothes with faces painted in camouflage paint were pointing rifles at me. I was lying on my stomach in the sand as they handcuffed me behind my back. I was saying repeatedly, "Poor, poor Marrie, poor, poor Marrie." I awoke from the vision, hot tears streaming down my face.

The next day Carlos came on the bridge and said he had had a terrible dream, but did not want to share it.

Two weeks later, at a little after midnight, on July 27, 2001 we motored into Dulverton Bay, mid-way up the coast of the vast and empty state of Western Australia. All lights had been extinguished hours earlier and it was dark, with only stars for light. A mile above us an aircraft was moving unusually slow and blinking a white light. Two vessels were creeping along the coast about five miles out and appeared to be trawling. After we passed, one of them followed us for a way and then turned back on his course. As we came into the bay, three cars raced over the sand dunes, their headlights waving up and down in the darkness. I asked Joel what he thought of the cars and he said, "Just some good ole boys going home from the pub."

We eased into the bay for about a mile before we saw a wave rising across the center. Steep shelving causes this and I had to reverse hard to get out of the danger. We still couldn't see a thing and I was afraid of going aground and the White Dove lying on its side in the tiny bay with daylight approaching. When we got back out about a mile, we lowered the two Zodiacs into the water and loaded them with the cocaine. I told Joel to return in one hour. Carlos and I got into the Zodiacs.

Carlos said, "No puedo, no puedo." (I can't, I can't)

"You can't what Carlos?"

"I can't drive."

"Shit! Why didn't you tell me before?" I tied the painter of his Zodiac to the one I was driving while he crawled over and got in with me and we started off. Carlos kept telling me he heard surf breaking, but I couldn't hear anything so I kept easing on in. Suddenly we were in a six-foot breaking surf and a long way from land. Unbeknown to me we were already through the danger, but I couldn't see anything so I turned around and went back through it with the bow pitching up at a 45-degree angle and then dragging the other inflatable behind.

I steered for the south side of the bay, spotted an area without much surf, gave it full power and rode a small wave in. We were carried up onto a slick sloping flat rock. I jumped out, secured the painter to a rock and took care of the rear inflatable which was still in the surf. Just as I got to it, a wave lifted it up and knocked me down, scuffing me up a bit. I got the painter secured and said, "Thank God!"

It was the end of a long and dangerous 14,000-mile voyage across three oceans, one being the roughest in the world. After 77 days cooped up with Joel and Carlos, I was truly thankful to be on dry land.

Carlos and I unloaded the inflatables onto dry rock, but the tide was coming in fast. The place was right out in the open so I took a flashlight and went looking for a place to hide the cocaine. The first thing I saw was fresh boot tracks in the sand. This was the area the cars left from and I hoped it was just a fisherman, but I was concerned. A hundred feet down the coast I found a perfect indentation in the rocks about eight feet above the water. I could not shake the feeling we were being watched.

We began moving the bales by walking on the sloping rock in knee-deep water. My sandal was torn off my right foot on the first trip and soon the skin was gone and it was bleeding and causing me a great deal of pain. This task was harder and took longer than I thought. Carlos took every step with a little flashlight in his mouth and after a few trips, he started complaining that he had cramps. He sat down on a dry rock, still holding the flashlight.

Joel returned, thinking Carlos's flashlight was a signal for him to come back. The bow was on top of me before I saw it and I went to yelling for Joel to go back. It was too dangerous for such a big vessel to be in so close. Joel came out on the bridge, heard me, and left.

After two or three hours of shouldering the heavy bales over the rough rocks and up the stone embankment I had all the cocaine in the hole, but my right foot was cut to ribbons and bleeding badly. The large inflatable with the new four-stroke motor had a busted tube on one side. The other Zodiac floated away with the rising tide and was 300 feet out in the bay, what a debacle!

I got out the waterproof bag with the GPS and two-way radio and tried to call Joel, but the batteries were dead. I took the batteries out of the GPS and put them in the radio and they were also dead. Carlos had used them in the little CD player and replaced them with dead ones. If we would have had to abandon ship, we would have died because of dead batteries in the emergency locating transponder and radio.

My teeth were chattering from the cold and exhaustion as I stood there watching the inflatable float away. I knew the water shelved a short distance to my right and such a place is an ideal spot for sharks to hang out waiting on seals to come ashore. It was with foreboding that I swam out into the black waters of Shark's Bay, kicking with a bloody foot. I kept my clothes on to conserve as much heat as I could, and soon they were waterlogged and pulling me down. I started doing slow breaststrokes, but the Zodiac seemed to be drifting away from me at almost the same speed I was swimming. I stopped to rest for a minute and off to my left, not twenty feet away, a big fin cut the water. I prayed, 'Oh God, don't let my life end this way.' Then it rose out of the water a foot high and cut the surface like a knife about ten feet to my right. I was petrified. I pulled my knees up to my chest and was afraid to move a muscle, but the wet clothes were pulling me under and I had to dog paddle to keep my head up. He surfaced directly in front of me and blew. The relief of discovering that it was a dolphin was so great it cannot be put into words. When I reached the Zodiac, I almost lunged over it as I shot out of the water with plenty of energy.

I wanted the new 4-stroke if we were going to Denham for a vehicle, so I paddled back in and changed the motors. The 15 horsepower Yamaha outboard had taken a beating in the surf and I was worried that it was full of water and wouldn't start, but on the first pull she was purring. I could have kissed it!

Before I left I asked Carlos to clean up the area and to let all the air out of the big Zodiac and sink it.

Joel was a couple of miles out and I climbed on board, took a warm shower, changed clothes and dressed my foot, which was in bad shape. Oh, how I wanted to head for Denham, but the beach was littered with a boat motor, Zodiac, fuel cans and other telltale signs that had to be looked after and I was doubtful Señor Carlos would do it.

The White Dove had to go to the bottom.

I went down to the engine room and unscrewed pipes that allowed seawater to flow in, threw switches that began filling all water and fuel tanks. Then I cranked up the big fire pump, opened the nozzles into the cabins, .and began filling them with seawater at a thousand gallons per minute. Then I went up on the bridge and put her on a westerly heading. Once the autopilot had locked on the new course, I ran down to the deck and jumped down into the Zodiac. The vessel was moving at ten knots. The painter was seized so tight that I could not pull the slipknot loose, so I cut it with my knife and watched the White Dove disappear into the night.

We came in through the surf and I jumped out to steady the Zodiac for Joel and got run over and completely submerged. Joel waded out in water above his waist and was soaked. I gave the inflatable a couple of swipes with a knife and it went to the bottom. Carlos was still sitting on the rock where I had left him holding the flashlight. He was wrapped in a blanket like an old Indian and complaining of cramps. The outboard and fuel cans were just as I had left them. I hurriedly put everything in the hole on top of the cocaine, covered it with camouflaged blankets, and then covered everything with rocks.

As it began to get daylight, I saw what looked like a buoy in the middle of the bay and as it got lighter, I saw it was both ends of the Zodiac sticking up about four feet high. Carlos had let part of the air out and pushed it off. What a fucking fiasco!

As we were ready to leave, we saw four fishermen on a high rocky outcrop about a hundred yards to the west. We watched as they brought in one big pink grouper after the other. They couldn't see us as long as we stayed in the hole, but if we moved out we were in plain view. Then Carlos said he would not stay with the cocaine, but insisted on going with us. It began to rain, so we got somewhat in the shelter of a rock overhang and watched the fishermen through binoculars. As the rain got heavier, three men left, only one remained and reeled in a 20-pound grouper. We thought, surely in this rain they will leave and we can get out of here.

“DOWN! DOWN! DOWN YOU SONS OF BITCHES OR WE’LL BLOW YOUR FUCKIN BRAINS OUT!”

I looked down the bore of a rifle and into the very face I had seen two weeks before in the vision. He wore a shaggy camouflage suit, smelled strongly of sage, and his face was painted green and yellow. I was looking him straight in the eye when he hit me with his rifle in the forehead above my right eye; knocking the skin and meat off a large area. I rolled over on my stomach and another goon grabbed me by the testicles, picking me partway off the sand while the first thug searched my pockets and body. He then handcuffed me so tight it cut off the blood supply to my hands. As I lay there all I could think of was, ‘Poor, poor, Marrie, poor, poor, Marrie. Would she die of grief when she found out?’ What was her life going to be like without me to help her? Never in my life had I been so sorry and would have done almost anything to turn back the hands of time for three months.

39. $400 MILLION DOLLAR DRUG BUST

Hakea Prison and "Mr. Suckie" -- Casuarina Prison and A Line of Lawyers -- Court Shenanigans, an Expose' On Blabber Mouths -- Bad Neighbors in the S.H.U -- S.H.U and the Pussy Cats

Two men picked me up by the handcuffs, sat me on a stone facing a cliff, and ordered me to keep my eyes closed. I could hear kilos of cocaine hitting the water and I knew what was up. The tide was running out and they hoped to retrieve the cocaine later on the beach or rocks. It was on the news three months later that kilo blocks of cocaine were still washing up on the beach to be found by members of the public. Only much later did I see the plain facts in my appeal paperwork: "700kg pure, 998kg. bulk." Over 250kg of cocaine had never made it to the furnace. The Colombian cartels do not ship 250kg of *cutting agents* with their loads halfway across the world. Perth and Sydney were awash in cocaine that year.

In a few minutes, someone came and asked if there were others on the vessel and I told him there was no one else. A large twin-engine Coast Guard plane circled once and then flew on out to sea in the direction of the White Dove. They loaded me in the back seat of a car with four men and we started down a long sandy road.

One man with a pockmarked face read me my rights, "Anything you say can and will be used against you in a court of law." He then brought out a tape recorder and wanted to interview me. I thought how absurd of him to think that even a fool would talk after the warning he just gave me. In another car, one did talk and kept talking.

The four still kept asking me questions and I continued to respond with the answer that I would not say anything until I talked with an attorney. Ole, pock face said he could get Andréa Horrigan on the phone in minutes, and that she was the best drug lawyer in Western Australia. I said, 'Yeah, I imagine she is, but I think I'll just wait and find my own, thank you."

They undoubtedly came from the town of Geraldton without stopping for fuel, because the gas tank was on empty. They drove twenty miles to a low stone house by a salt lagoon and purchased a tank of gasoline. For some reason they drove all around the desert in the area before heading south. Two men got out and Officer Scantleberry and a young police officer drove me to Geraldton. They were decent enough, stopped and bought me a meat pie and a drink at a roadhouse. Just before dark, they stopped to pee. The young policeman walked me to the edge of the bush and he was soon through and returned to the car and began to empty the trash into a container. I seriously thought of bolting, but I had on slick soled leather shoes that were untied and my foot was in bad shape. Besides, the young police officer was about thirty years old. However, I did have a chance and didn't take it, something I kicked myself over for a full year.

When we reached Geraldton, they drove to an apartment and allowed me to take a shower. They ordered me a juicy pepper steak with three airline size bottles of Chivas Regal. It was a fabulous meal and I thought of the men who ate their last supper before going to the electric chair and wondered if they enjoyed their meal as I was enjoying mine.

Several high-ranking Federal Police officers arrived and I spoke with them *off the record.* They wanted to do a video interview and they again insisted I talk to attorney Andréa Horrigan. I asked if they did plea bargains in Australia. They explained that their system was different, they write a sealed letter to the judge and he usually honored their recommendation. They said that if I gave them the name of the owner of the merchandise and cooperate with them, I could expect a sentence of approximately twelve years with a parole date of six or eight years and they would take me directly to the prison in Albany. I thanked them for the food, drinks and kind offer, but said I would wait a bit and find my own lawyer for professional advice.

I was taken to the jail in Geraldton and put in the cell with Joel. He seemed to be doing ok, although I could guess what he was thinking. I slept very little that night as I thought of the long lonely years ahead, spent in a prison as far from home as one could possibly get. Perth is the most isolated city in the world. I thought of my dear eighty-one-year-old mother who I would probably never see again, of the grandbaby just born, that I may never see. Would Marrie ever cook another meal and our family sit around the table together? Would I ever see the old church and cemetery and go to Homecoming? See the Old Place again, much less plant the orchard I had planned? Would I live long enough to go home, and if so who would be living? God only knew. The questions haunted me all night. To think that I had done this to myself and to the ones that loved me so dearly, just for money. Was I insane? The Bible verse kept echoing in my mind: "For the love of money is the root of all evil: which while some coveted after, they have erred from the faith and pierced themselves through with many sorrows."

The next day around noon they loaded Joel and I in the forward compartment of a completely closed van similar to a Brinks truck, then they brought in Carlos, Eduardo, and Fernando and locked them in the rear compartment. Eduardo and Fernando had been arrested in Geraldton at a caravan park and were accused of being the unloaders. We left on a bone-jarring, kidney busting, five-hour ride in the closed metal box before reaching Perth, the beautiful city by the sea I had dreamed of visiting.

The three Colombians climbed down out of the truck into a swarm of guards. Joel and I remained chained in the forward compartment. The rear door slammed to and locked, the truck started up and we pulled out. Sometime later, it stopped again, and then I could hear the beeping as it backed up. We were unloaded into a closed space with lots of guards. From there we hobbled along in our shackles and chains to a reception area where we were stripped and put through a prisoner induction. Sometime after midnight, we were taken to Unit 1 at Hakea Prison. Unit 1 is old, dark, and dingy. We were given sheets, a blanket, and pillow and ushered to adjoining cells. I said goodnight to Joel and quickly made up my thin stained mattress and was asleep by the time I got under the blanket.

Early next morning we stood beside our door for 'muster' and then went into a small eating area, where there were a toaster, jelly, and cereal. I got something to eat and found a table. When I finished I picked up a dishrag and wiped my hands and mouth. A very ugly man yelled, "Hey!" I had a strong urge to tie into him but decided it best to see which way the wind was blowing first. I should have beat the hell out of him then and there because we found out later he was a well-known snitch placed there to watch us.

During lunch a big bully beat up a small man and kicked him into a corner and soon thereafter we discovered we were in the unit for the troublemakers of the prison.

Behind Unit 1 was a small patio enclosed with a high wall. Several cement benches were placed around a goldfish pond and I choose this place to sit and eat. In the dirty pond were a few water plants and three goldfish with long lacy fins. 'Ol, Suckie' got his name by walking through the halls holding his dick, saying, "Suckie, suckle anyone want to suckie?" He came out and threw in a few slivers of bread and when the fish surfaced to eat, he hit the water with his flip-flop killing one of the little creatures. This inflamed me and in the twinkling of an eye a haymaker connected on the bottom of his listener and 'Ol, Suckie' was flat on his back in the pond. He went around screaming about how he was going to kill me, trying to raise support. However, Joel and I were a pair, and his 250 pound, six-foot-five football player physique was a natural deterrent.

Joel and I went walking around the basketball court and Joel stopped to light a cigarette with his lighter. We didn't know they were a special item in Hakea as they only sold matches in the commissary. A tough-looking man all covered in grim tattoos and hair down to his waist walked up and asked Joel for a light. Joel handed him his lighter and without a word the man lit up, handed Joel a packet of matches and walked off. Joel said, "Hey Buddy, give me my lighter."

Long Hair stopped, turned slowly and said, "You didn't give me a lighter, you gave me a packet of matches and I just gave them back to you."

With that, he walked off and met up with his mate. Both Joel and I saw him pass the lighter to his friend.

We walked up behind them and Joel said, "If this is some kind of joke it has gone far enough."

The pair walked on and sat down near a female guard on a long bench attached to the building. Joel walked up and kicked ol' long hair on his shinbone just where it connects to the knee bone and that kick raised ol' long hair and the bench several inches. Long hair's mate went to fumblin' in his pocket and out came the lighter. As he handed it over he said, "We was just joking."

News of the incident spread among the units and we had no further trouble.

FOUR-HUNDRED MILLION DOLLAR DRUG BUST
Largest in Australian history.
Captain Sinks Ship after Unloading One Ton of Cocaine.

These and similar headlines filled the papers and were repeated on television and radio for days. Joel and I were jailhouse stars. Many were very happy to meet us, however, the informants saw an opportunity and came crawling out of the sewers.

"Hey Captain, I got a brother that flies helicopters. If you got two million dollars he'll come and get you."

"Is that in Australian or American?"

He had to think a bit and then said, "That would be in American."

"Well, tell him to bring that baby on today, 'cause I'm ready to go to the house." Of course, I knew he couldn't pay for his next fix.

Joel and I were sitting down to supper when four guards entered and said, "Reaves, you and Parrish pack up! You have five minutes to get your shaving gear and anything else you want to take with you. Throw it in a pillowcase and get going, the truck is waiting."

"Where are we going," I asked.

"Never mind where, just get a move on if you want your things."

We were shackled, chained, and loaded in the back of the armored truck and transported through the night which we couldn't see from the inside of our coffin. They discharged us at Casuarina Prison and took us directly to the *chokie*. The cell was rather large with an 8ft. by 12ft. exercise area attached to the back. This was opened every day at 9 a:m. Two guards opened the cell door and I was ordered to sweep and mop. We got a ten-minute shower and upon returning to the cell there were clean clothes in a pile on the floor and the rear door open. This was repeated each day like clockwork. While out on a patio area, Joel and I could talk over the connecting wall through bars on the roof that were as thick as your leg. A lovely little eucalyptus grew just beyond the rear grill and honeyeaters swooped in every morning for the nectar. Their clear calls were beautiful.

Lawyers visited most every day. From all the publicity, they were keen to represent us. I had probably interviewed a dozen without finding one I trusted. Justine Fisher's name kept coming up, so I gave her secretary a call and asked for an interview. A few days later I walked in the lawyer's visiting room and a shapely blond dressed in a sharp business suit stood up and shook with a firm hand. Her blue eyes sparkled and the room was filled with good vibes. Within two minutes of listening and the sound of her voice, I knew she was the one to represent me.

As I had been caught red-handed sitting on a ton of cocaine, my only hope was to convince some tough judge that I wasn't Mr. Big, but a poor old man who had recently been released from prison after doing eleven years for a parole violation and was broke and lowly. The good thing was, it was largely true. Barrister Justine Fisher spoke eloquently and with her good looks, I figured that if anyone could get the job done, it was her. She signed me up as a client and went to work.

Within a week, she returned with startling news. The Australian Federal Police had been watching Fernando, the unloader, for a month. They had 1,600 pages of transcripts of him talking while in the motor home. His friend, Eduardo, was a snitch...

Carlos retained Andréa Horrigan for his attorney and had already pled guilty and told everything. Barrister Horrigan was going to ask for a life sentence.

Carlos began talking as soon as the car door shut at Shark Bay and when he arrived in Geraldton, the head of the Australian Federal Police, Australian Customs, and the prosecutor were waiting. Carlos talked into the cameras non-stop, from 6:23 p:m. until 11:17 p:m with a half-hour out for dinner. He was given three aspirin and three telephone calls to Colombia and told the police I was the captain of the vessel. His confession is called the four slap confession. They had to slap him once to get him started, and three times to shut him up

From the sentencing transcripts of his interview with the police it stated;

Supreme Court of Western Australia,
20 May 2002,
Versus the Queen and Carlos Arturo Suarez Meja.
Paragraph 27, "He immediately provided his full cooperation to the
Investigating authorities. He held nothing back"
Paragraph 54; "His cooperation extended beyond the initial interview".

I called Justine and told her of my find and the next day I was transferred to Hakea prison and the papers disappeared. I knew I was dead meat and the only thing I could do was try to save Joel. Justine got out her notepad and began taking notes as I told her the tale. After a few minutes, she stopped me and said that I was digging a hole for myself and hinted there was a possible defense of duress. I said, "That can only work for one and I have a record."

She stopped, looked me hard in the eyes, and said, "The penny just dropped."

I told of how Joel was a good man who had never been in trouble in his life and how I offered him ten- thousand dollars to put a ship in his name. I told him we would take it to Indonesia, sell it there and I would give him ten percent of the profit. We needed a satellite telephone and only Joel had a credit card with which to order one, I used it and gave Joel the money. In the middle of the Atlantic, when we met the load boat, Joel was terribly upset and wanted to get off. I tried to get the loaders to take him back to Colombia, but they were afraid he was a DEA agent and would not allow him aboard their vessel. Joel was a thousand miles from land, he couldn't swim to shore, and he had no other choice. I had told him that if he got on the radio and reported us, the Colombians would kill his family.

Justine said, "That sounds thin to me, let's just hope we can find twelve sane men and women who will buy it."

Marrie flew to Australia, the anguish on her face broke my heart. She suffered the indignities of the drug dog and searches ever day as she came to see me for the allowed one hour. The Australian dollar was forty-six US cents at the time and everything was inexpensive for us. We discussed buying a bed and breakfast in the wine region, her staying and visiting me throughout my sentence. She contacted realtors and had them looking.

Early one morning the Australian Federal Police kicked in the door and came crashing in with pistols drawn. While she stood there in her nightclothes, they searched and went through her wallet, finding eleven thousand dollars in US funds. They seized her money, jewelry, address book, and passport, then handcuffed her and took her downtown where she was fingerprinted and booked for entering the country with over five thousand dollars in Australian currency. They asked her where she got the money and she said that she brought it with her for her husband's legal fees. They claimed she had not declared it. She replied that the questionnaire very clearly asked if she was bringing over five-thousand Australian dollars into the country. Being that she didn't have one Australian dollar she checked the *no* box. The judge was just another lackey for the feds, did their bidding, and fined her one thousand dollars. The lawyer's fee was another grand. For several weeks she wrote and asked for the items they took from her, but never did get a response.

Marrie was frightened and traumatized by the experience and a few days thereafter, she told me she was leaving. When she kissed me goodbye and walked out of the visiting room door, it felt as though my heart was being torn from my chest. I can so vividly recall what she was wearing and the way she looked back over her shoulder and tried to smile as she walked around the corner. After all these years the tears still fall as I recall that day and wonder if I will ever see her face again.

We heard the police helicopter hovering overhead before they loaded us into the truck. Two Toyota Pathfinders with heavy bull bars drove side-by-side leading the procession. Next came a heavy-duty armored truck with Joel and I shackled inside. Two more armed vehicles brought up the rear. The helicopter hovered a few feet overhead with a mounted .50 caliber machine gun hanging out the door pointed at us. When we got out in the sally port of the courthouse, there were numerous reporters and cameramen. They usually just got the top of my head, but I stopped and flashed them a smile if I had the chance.

Men and women suited up in black bulletproof gear and helmets with double chinstraps were standing on the roof and all around the parking area holding automatic shotguns. Strapped to their chest were automatic pistols with extra ammunition, plus an assortment of other combat material as though they were at war. It was quite a sight.

I would hear, "Third floor clear, rear stairwell clear, second floor clear." Sometimes I tried to count all the police holding shotguns and once I counted thirty. I have no idea who they were trying to impress. My guess is they ask for a lot of money each year and this is just a way of putting on a parade, kind of like the military parades in the banana republics. At least they got to play with their toys for a while.

Once we were in the courthouse we were unchained in a large cell and the police seemed to leave, or at least they weren't visible. We were wearing our street clothes and guarding us was an older woman, another woman with a good build and a thin man. I asked permission to use the bathroom. The thin man opened the door and I went around the corner, used the facilities and returned. I told Joel this was a joke. We could leave anytime we wanted to. Then he went in and came to the same conclusion. We discussed it for a few minutes and then he said that if they opened the door he wouldn't leave because he was going to win his trial and go home. He was serious and needed my testimony to convince a jury, I chilled out, but I knew that I could have gone.

Several years later, eleven men saw the same weakness and took advantage. The news dubbed it "The Great Escape" and it became a political debacle. A new 150 million dollar courthouse was built; after the horses had bolted.

We spent two long boring months in the "chokie," then one day they transferred us to the Special Handling Unit, better known as the SHU. This is a maximum-security jail within a maximum-security prison, where the worst of the worse are housed. When we arrived, there were three others.

Dan Harvey, a quiet redheaded lad, had hidden an Allen wrench up his butt and a handcuff key in his penis. With the latter, he unlocked his handcuffs, then retrieved the Allen wrench and took the hinges off the rear door of the van. When it stopped for a traffic light, he got out, ran around the van, banged on the window, gave the guards the finger and loped away in the traffic. They got him eventually. They weren't happy. Hence the S.H.U.

Wayne was the only man ever to escape from maximum security Casuarina, built as the most secure prison in the southern hemisphere. He had been placed in a wooden box at the prison workshop and gone out the gates on the back of a truck. Wayne had been in the SHU for eleven years. Here, there was no escape.

John, who hated pedophiles, was doing life for a murder he didn't commit. There had been some strange prosecutorial conduct in his case. Earlier his friend was on trial for murder. The prosecutor summoned John to testify and gave him immunity. He testified that he killed the man and his friend went free. The prosecutor went ballistic and soon charged him with a murder he didn't commit. He was convicted and given a life sentence with a minimum of 25-years before becoming eligible for parole.

Three months after we were arrested Justine told me I must make up my mind about pleading, because if I put it off any longer I would not receive the third off for fast-tracking. She explained that I must make a taped video with the Federal Police asking me questions. The sentencing judge would carefully scrutinize this interview and it would play a big part in the number of years I received. She advised me to forget about the police and imagine I was talking directly to the judge.

With great apprehension, I took my seat in front of the camera and one of the two police officers began to ask me questions. It didn't take long for me to realize they knew the answers to the questions they were asking. If I was to get it just a little wrong, they continued to ask leading questions, such as, where was Joel standing when the bales of cocaine were being thrown over? Did he try to catch them? What was he wearing? Looking from the stern toward the bow, which side was he standing on? Did he talk to any of the loaders? Where were you when the cable broke? How many shots of morphine did you give Joel? Did he pass out? It was obvious they were concerned about their case against Joel and were trying to get me to slip up. It also became obvious that not one question was asked concerning Carlos.

For three hours, I sat on that hot box answering questions and relating the journey from my point of view. I told of how I did all the mechanical work, cooked, cleaned, washed dishes, navigated, loaded and unloaded the cocaine. I told how Joel was angry at being caught in such a precarious situation and how seasick Carlos was all the way down the South Atlantic and across the Southern Ocean with its hundred-foot waves. I said that Carlos was just a throwaway deckhand, who was only there to tell the Colombians what happened if something went wrong.

I wrote several letters to Carlos telling him that his lawyer was going to ask for a life sentence and begged him to change lawyers. I never got a response and wondered why? Soon he went before Judge Scott and the prosecutor asked for a life sentence. Andréa Horrigan stood up for his defense and said, "Your honor, the defense agrees with the prosecutor. In a crime of this magnitude, the only appropriate sentence is one of life." Her face was on the news all across Australia for two days as she said these words. The judge obliged both the prosecutor and the defense counsel and gave Carlos a life sentence with a minimum of twenty years before becoming eligible for parole. This was incredible.

This was the first case in Australian history where someone pled guilty, fast-tracked, and received a life sentence for drugs. The law states that one must receive a third off their sentence for a fast track plea of guilty and until that day, it was presumed one must have a determinate sentence, as you cannot receive a third off of a life sentence.

While sentencing Carlos, the judge said, "By your own admission, you were in charge of the load and responsible for the safe delivery of the cocaine. You instructed the captain as to where to go. You were the one organizing the liaison with the off loaders. Your remorse was complete. You came clean at the first opportunity and told everything, holding nothing back. You continued to work with the police subsequent to your initial interview. Except for these mitigating factors I would have given you a sentence of life, with 28 years to serve before becoming eligible for parole." There were five others to go to trial, and this set the stage for the prosecutor to ask for parity in the other cases.

Far too many lawyers in this large but sparsely populated state are in the pocket of the establishment. Defense lawyers more often than not do exactly what they are told and work with the prosecution to varying degrees. The most isolated city in the world produced a 'click' upper class. They all went to the same private schools, the same elite universities, screwed each other, and most likely used a good amount of my cocaine in both their professional and private time. Carlos was kind enough to also tell about the 45-foot sailboat in Florida and the Feds in America confiscated it. I appealed and they replied that I had conspired to transport a ton of cocaine from Colombia to Australia. However, it was determined that it was too small and another vessel was purchased. Yes, as the record states, Carlos continued to work with the police subsequent to going to prison.

Had Carlos kept his mouth shut and had his lawyer work with mine, then he would have gone down as a deckhand and received a sentence of 4 or 5 years, served a couple and been deported. His folly reminds me of a painting on the wall of the prisoner's law library at Lompoc Penitentiary with the caption: "More men are hung by the tongue than by the neck."

In order to prepare for my defense, we needed the complete transcripts of the co-defendant's proceedings. The prosecutor had accused me of lying during my police interview. Being there was only three of us on the boat and I knew that Joel said nothing, I wanted the transcripts of Carlos's confession.

Fernando a handsome 32-year-old Colombian walked into a business that rented Motor Homes and off-road vehicles. He inquired about renting such equipment and asked if he could pay with cash. Delilah, a Spanish speaking woman attended him and asked him to come back the next day.

She immediately called Australian Customs and made a very lucrative deal. Fernando returned the next day and that is when the discovery recordings began. Fernando rented a big motor home and a Toyota jeep with bull bars and sand tires. He and his A.F.P. snitch, Eduardo, drove north to Geraldton, where they rented a space at a caravan park on the ocean. Each day Eduardo would take a run and meet with his A.F.P. (Australian Federal Police) handler and give him the daily recordings, unknowing to the A.F.P... Australian Customs were dug in all around the caravan. A newspaper article said that the two did not know about each other and almost had a shoot-out, meaning two snitches.

Newspaper articles stated that Delilah was arrested along with us, which was a smokescreen.

When Marrie visited I entered the room with leg irons, hand-cuffed close to a waist chain, and escorted by two guards. While I was there I saw Delilah kiss Carlos and the next day Fernando. One morning after the visit Delilah followed Marrie out to the rose garden. She told her she had a helicopter coming and that if Joel and I could get to the dentist's office she would pick us up with Carlos and Fernando. Marrie whispered this to me the next day. I told her it was a trap, that if they had a helicopter coming they would not be waiting for Joel and I. Marrie said Delilah had two children and invited her to dinner at her house. I told her to be nice, however, decline, because I was sure she was working with the police.

A year later I was transferred from the SHU to general population. Phone calls cost $1.10 per min., so I asked Marrie to buy a phone only for me, and to not give the number to anyone, so that when I call she can say "Hello Sweetheart." I put this new unlisted number on the prison telephone system.

My then 85-year-old Mother was coming to visit. I was excited. At 2 am. the phone rang in California, perfect time to catch one unaware 'Police manual 101.' "Hello Marrie, Delilah here, how are you?" How did you get this number? "Don't worry Marrie I have ways." Marrie thought, I bet you do. "Listen Marrie, don't worry, remember what we talked about at Casuarina while we walked by the roses? Well, now I have two helicopters coming, one for Fernando at Hakea and another for Roger, Joel, and Carlos at Casuarina. Two helicopters will land exactly the same time. Here is my number, have Roger telephone me on a mobile and we can arrange the time."

My Mother and sisters flew over the next week and my mother was excited and whispered the number and told me the Colombians were going to get me out. I told her that this was a trap laid by the prosecutor, and that Joel was soon to go for his second trial and the prosecutor would love to indict us on conspiracy to escape as this would seal Joel's fate. I then went to Carlos and told him what Delilah said. He was adamant that she had not telephoned Marrie. I then had a friend call the number, and of course, Delilah answered, and soon hung up. Without any doubt in my mind, this was entrapment by the prosecutor. I went to the superintendent and asked him to please contact the prosecutor and the Federal police and tell them that Joel and I were not interested in a helicopter, and for them to leave my mother and wife at peace. Fernando's eyes are blind to the fact that Delilah is working with the Federal Police, and it is she who put him in the SHU and caused him years of pure misery. The woman knows that I see right through her wicked schemes, therefore she hates me, and tries to tarnish my good name.

KIDNEY FOR YEARS

OFFICE OF THE ATTORNEY GENERAL
RECEIVED
18 MAR 2002
DOJ
SOL GEN
DPP
WAEC
LEG AID
EOC
CSO
PC
PEFL DEV
SWDC
Draft Reply
Minister reply/letter
COS Reply
Direct reply
COS Reply/enc
Comment/Advice
Attention
Information
Action
Interim
Completed
MIN. NO: 9-12353 DATE DUE: 28/3/02

Mr. Jim McGinty
Attorney General
Level 12
Havelock Place
West Perth

Dear Mr.McGinty,

I am a fifty-nine-year-old American citizen awaiting sentencing on cocaine charges and expect a lengthy sentence. I have a fifteen-year sentence remaining in the U.S. of which I would have to do ten years should I be deported there. My remaining life expectancy is twelve years. There is little hope that I will ever get out of prison and see my home again, yet I remain hopeful.

Throughout history punishment against lawbreakers has been handed out by many different means and in all cases the offender gave up something which society deemed sufficient for his punishment. This usually was one's life, banishment from society, so many lashes of the whip, and in recent years, time in prison. This term can be reduced by 25% or 30% if one pleads guilty and 'fast tracks', another if one will tell the police all he knows of the case, and now I hear that prisoners who remain drug-free will be given special housing and additional time off. I wish to offer something much more valuable, a kidney.

Multitudes of suffering people from all walks of life go four times a week and spend the entire day on dialysis machines; over 150 in Perth alone. These people are waiting on a donor's kidney that most likely will never show up and they will get sicker and sicker until they die. I would like to save one of these person's lives.

I have written to The Kidney Foundation, and they informed me to talk with my doctor. The doctor here in the prison thought it an excellent proposal and suggested I write to you. As the doctor said, "everyone would win." If you, allowed this to happen other non-violent offenders would want to sign on, and possibly a great need could be fulfilled.

Your consideration will be greatly appreciated.

The response from the Attorney General was positive. He sent the request to the Executive Director of Prisons, who replied that he would evaluate the medical and financial implications...

I believe this was one of my better ideas and I wish I could have set precedent. Unfortunately, the spool of red tape was so long that it could not be accomplished before I went for sentencing.

Rain beat against the tin roof of the passageway leading from the holding cells to the courtroom. I hobbled along loaded down with shackles, chains, and dread. In a little anteroom, guards removed the chains, handcuffs and leg irons, then ushered me into a brilliantly lit courtroom. While standing in the doorway, I bowed to the judge attired in a black robe and white powdered wig. He resembled a kind neighbor who lived on a farm near our home when I was a boy. He nodded his head in acknowledgment to my bow and I proceeded to the prisoner's box. I noticed half a dozen policemen seated at the back in thousand-dollar suits and wondered how much they got per kilo for my cocaine? Reporters filled one side of the courtroom. I noticed one young woman of exceeding beauty, wearing a shiny wide wedding band. An artist, doing a sketch for a newspaper was the only person who looked at me. I acknowledged him and he gave a faint smile and nod. I looked around the court for a familiar face and saw no one that I knew. There was a lonely, hollow feeling inside and I remembered the words of the apostle Paul when he went before the court of Rome. "No man stood with me, but all men forsook me: I pray God that it may not be laid to their charge. Notwithstanding, the Lord stood with me and strengthened me."

"Court is now in session, Honorable Henry Wallwork presiding!" hailed the clerk.

"I acknowledge this letter from your daughter Marya, and I thank her for it. I also read your letter and viewed the video." He straightened up, adjusted his glasses, and read. "I sentence you to a prison term of twenty-five years, beginning on the 27th of July 2001. You will become eligible for parole after serving fourteen years, at which time you will be seventy-two years of age."

He looked up over his glasses, realized I was still seated, and yelled, "Stand Up!"

I stood.

The gavel fell.

Twenty heavily armed men from a special task force surrounded the area. They were decked out in their shiny new urban combat gear, all in a lovely shade of black. They probably didn't get to play in it much and I was reminded of the Waffen SS in Hitler's day.

I shuffled along in chains and leg irons and crawled on my knees up the steps into the armored truck. The truck pulled out preceded by two armed vehicles driving side-by-side with flashing lights. Two Toyota Land Cruisers with oversize bull bars followed close behind. The usual police helicopter with a mounted fifty-caliber machine gun protruding from the doorway hovered low overhead. The exhibition continued until I was back inside Casuarina Prison, supposedly the most secure prison in the southern hemisphere. The truck entered a sally port where the guards checked their weapons and then drove on to another enclosed building where a heavy metal door rose electronically and the truck reversed inside. I'd done this before.

I was unloaded and ushered into a holding cage at reception where the MSU (prison swat team) unchained me. One big man took a firm grip on the handcuff chain and told me to spread my legs and face him. Another unlocked the waist chain and then the locks on the chain going to the leg irons. Finally, the leg irons were removed and I was ordered to sit on a steel wire mesh bench, hold my hands apart and raise my thumbs. Only then, did he release the chain and unlock the cuffs.

Two burly prison guards ordered me to take off all my clothes. Then they searched every orifice and went over my entire body with a metal detector. Two other guards escorted me through a half dozen electronically operated doors. One pushed a button, looked into a camera and called out a number. I heard a click, the door opened. After a total of thirteen doors, we reached the SHU, my old home.

"Welcome to your new home Reaves," one guard mocked.

"Yeah, for the next twenty-five years," the other scoffed.

While I was at court, they had moved me from the cell I had been in for the past six months, knowing this added extra stress.

This particular cell was dingy and smelt of urine. A stained mattress was propped against the wall. Foul body odor permeated the air. The window was extra dirty, not allowing in much light. I was sick at heart and thought, "God, how will I ever get out of this mess?"

As I stood by the window, looking out at the yellow lights, I heard a big helicopter approaching. I could hear the blades flatten out as he hovered. It was so close that I squinted my eyes to keep out blowing sand. The noise filled my head, it filled the room. I heard it land and sit there idling for ten seconds or so and then it revved up and took off. I pressed my face to the bars for a better view, but saw nothing. Only then did I realize it was a supernatural vision.

Back in the SHU, things were changing. The 12 cells filled with some most unsavory characters. One young prisoner was especially difficult to live with. He had been stabbing people and threatening staff; hence his arrival in the SHU. We all shared a washing machine and every day he threw his stinking, dirty clothes on top of the machine and left them there. If we wanted to wash, we had to move his clothes first. I emptied a quart of tomato ketchup on them, but he stole someone else's clothes, it made no difference to him. He left his dishes unwashed on the counter, we either had to wash them or put up with the flies. Some days he turned his stereo up and blasted us all out. As he was a good fighter, the men ignored him. It's a wonder he lived through his time in the SHU, as there were definitely some there who could and would have snuffed out his life as easily as they would pinch out a candle flame.

One day in walked a big man who was obviously on medication for mental problems. He whispered when he talked and told some doubtful tales of his exploits. Several of the men hated him.

About one o'clock in the afternoon, I was lying on my bunk about to go to sleep when my door was rudely opened and a man who I was having trouble with came in and told me that Joel wanted me out on the patio.

"Get the hell out of here. If Joel wants me he knows where to find me."

'No man, he wants you on the patio now."

"Fuck off!"

The door closed and I lay there angry and wondering what that was all about. Then I heard what sounded like a scuffle going on in the adjoining cell and I knew a fracas of some sort was taking place. I listened for a bit and then all was quiet except for what sounded like a head being kicked into the wall repeatedly. All of a sudden, it dawned on me that this might be Joel's head and I jumped up and ran next door clad in my skivvies. Just as I got there, outran my enemy with a shank. Doubled over and inside the cell lay 'Whisperer' with two men kicking his head into the wall every time it bounced off. Blood was everywhere.

I yelled, "Stop it! Stop it! You're killing him!"

They stopped and looked at me and then one of them yelled. "Get him out of here, the son-of-a-bitch is bleeding all over my house."

I grabbed Whisperer under his arms and dragged him to the common area where I put him in a chair in front of control where I thought they would see him at any moment. I wanted to get as far away as possible, I ran for the shower to get the blood off. As I went back by the cell, I heard one of the kickers yell at the other "Get a bucket of water and mop quick, the fuckin' blood's running out the door."

Some weeks later, Whisperer looked me up and thanked me. He said they had lured him into the cell and had him sit down to read something. While he was bent over reading, one of them stabbed him in the ribs with the shank, which fortunately hit a rib and bent. They tried several more times and ol' Whisperer was just plain lucky. He showed me his ribs, which looked like a woodpecker had landed there and gone to work.

Another bad fight, which I can't say anything about, left one of the combatants blind in one eye.

Feral cats lived in the no-man's land between the razor wire fences and the SHU. One of the ferals had a litter of kittens and we began feeding her through the hole where three concrete blocks were turned on the side to give us ventilation and a small view from the exercise yard. After a few weeks, only two kittens were left and they began to ease in with mom for the sardines and milk we left out. To begin with, they would flee whenever they saw someone, but gradually they got braver and braver.

John in particular wanted a kitten, so he set a trap using a bowl of milk placed under a cardboard box, propped up with a ruler tied to a long piece of dental floss. Just before dark, the kittens came in and started drinking, he jerked the dental floss, the box fell and we had two little yellow kittens trapped underneath. Now those things were wild and I knew they would claw and bite, I ran for gloves, and Hobbit and Harvey cut a hole in the top of the box and each caught a kitten. You can't imagine what a big deal that was. Every man there wanted to hold the kittens. Some stood back and scoffed, but it wasn't long before their true colors came out and they were holding and petting the kittens.

The men wove little collars, strings were attached and the kittens secreted in waste paper baskets in the cells to hide them from the guards. Once they got somewhat gentler, we tied a long piece of dental floss to the collar and let them go outside to visit with mom. John named his Megs and Wayne and Harvey shared the other and named him Boris. Those hard men pampered the kittens like they were babies, giving them baths in shampoo and brushing their hair. Boris was bigger than Megs and Harvey belittled John for not feeding his kitten. When they were about half-grown Boris got the sniffles and stopped eating for several days. Harvey was beside himself as the kitten wheezed and lost weight. When he recovered, Megs was bigger and the shoe was on the other foot.

As they got older, they spent more and more time outside with their former family. One big old tom would sniff these pampered young toms and straddle them trying to mate. I figured he was just confused with the shampoo and perfume smell emanating from another tomcat, but John was beside himself when he saw this and said, "That's a fool pedophile tomcat. Look, he don't do it when we're looking!"

A box trap was set and within a couple of days old yellow was trapped underneath. John put on heavy kitchen mittens, cut a hole in the cardboard box, and caught a hurricane, barely managing to hang on to the writhing mini tiger. As the fur flew, he ran inside, filled the kitchen sink with water and shoved old tom under. The awful meowing and bubbling spoiled our supper and we were all dirty on John. This didn't faze him, his eyes just sparkled as he threw the wet carcass in the trash can.

40. HYPOCRITES

Out And About -- How Many Children Killed Via Cocaine? -- Who Runs The Drug Trade?

When one is placed in the SHU, one has no idea as to how long he will be there. The shortest time I heard of was six months and the longest was eleven years, with an average of two or three years. It's a dismal place and I hated it. Every day was the same and everything and everybody was grey and gloomy. Cameras recorded our every move and a half dozen guards monitored us from behind a heavy one-way mirror. It is somewhat like the situation depicted in the movie, 'The Silence of the Lambs.' I had been there over a year, was sick of the sameness and wondered aloud as to how long Joel and I would be there.

One afternoon I awoke from my siesta and walked out into the aisle. Joel was putting his things on a cart and I saw another loaded with his TV and other belongings standing beside the door. I asked, "Where are you going?"

"To general population," came the reply.

I went up to the one-way mirror, leaned my head over to talk through the narrow slot, and said in a loud clear voice, "What about me?"

The whole bunch busted out laughing and kept mocking, "What about me. What about me!" They had gone to all that trouble just to watch my response and I had not disappointed them.

Fifteen months from the day we arrived the speaker crackled, "Reaves and Parrish, pack up, you are out of here." Oh, what wonderful words. I could have cried for joy.

We had no idea as to where we were going, but we were packed up and stood by the door in short order. One guard, not the normal three, escorted us out into the bright sunshine. The flowers were so wonderfully colorful and the grass seemed to exude a living green essence. My first impulse was to lie down and roll in it and I thought of the mules Daddy shut up in the lot for half the year while the crops were growing. Once the crops were in, they were turned loose and they tore out running, kicking, and farting. Once they ran for a while, they lay down in the dirt and rolled over and over. I had that exact feeling, I think it is unhealthy for a human to never touch the earth and get grounded. They sent us to unit 3 and gave us cells side by side.

The first day I was out, I got a pass to the library, asked for a job, and was hired. Previously in the SHU, about once a month, a guard wheeled a cart loaded with about a hundred books. We were allowed to borrow three. As many of the men didn't use this service I checked out books in their name and over the time I read a great many.

One morning I was working in the library when a new woman came in and was asking about a book. As I was helping her, she leaned over close to me and asked in a soft kind voice, "Are you in for sex offenses?"

I understood why she asked the question. Usually older men who enter this place are often sex offenders, so I took no offense and answered, "No ma'am, I'm in for cocaine charges."

"Oh, just how much cocaine did you have?"

"Only one ton."

Her eyes immediately lost their sparkle and filmed over. The smiling conspiratorial face changed to one of hate. Her soft sweet voice changed instantly to one of disgust and I believe her fingernails grew into claws. She hissed, "How could a man like you have anything to do with such poison for our children?"

"Well ma'am, I did it for the money."

"Do you realize how many children are killed every year in Australia by cocaine?"

"No Ma'am, I don't know exactly, but I will bet the farm that the number is zero. However, I do know that a large number of your Aboriginal children are dying or becoming brain dead every year from sniffing gasoline fumes and nothing is done about that. Could it be that taxes are paid on gasoline or is it that those children are less valuable than the rich kids in town?"

The woman became white-hot with rage. Mr. Nesbit, the librarian, came from the back room and got into the fray, pulled the tigress off me and with a parting shot he said, "You may be right, but we're going home tonight."

Now, had I been a pedophile and raped a little boy, she would have invited me to her office for a cup of tea and we would have talked about my childhood.

I suppose this twisted view, which is shared by so many psychologists, judges, and prosecutors is that they themselves have a fixation on sex and understand these perverted sexual offenders. Whereas, one who traffics in drugs and makes tons of money leaves them feeling jealous.

The media is also responsible as they put their spin on whatever comes up and want sensation. "Ship loaded to gunnels with cocaine as machine gun-toting smugglers enter our waters," sells better than, "Man has sex with child."

A disgraced, but well known high profile Australian lawyer named Andrew Fraser came out publicly one day on the news here in Western Australia in early 2011. He said that he had seen a judge lock away a man for ten years on a cocaine charge; then, he had done lines of cocaine with that very same judge that very same day in his chambers! Such is the utter and total hypocrisy of the drug laws and the people who apply them! I recommend you read his book, *'Snouts in the Trough'*, and his many other books exposing police and judicial corruption.

Another judge with forty years' experience in the legal and judicial profession retired in this state, and for the first time in their long careers, stated publicly, that the drug laws were a waste of time. They went on to explain that drug use needed to be treated as a medical and psychological problem, not a criminal problem. Most of the crime associated with drugs is about getting money to get the drug. As a drug addict told me once, "I don't have a drug problem, I have a money problem."

Here in Western Australia the police commissioner came out publicly and answered questions by the media about how cocaine was not a high priority for him as it did not cause the same social problems methamphetamine brought on. He went on to publicly warn certain "high profile media personalities" that they might want to cease their well-known partying with certain "high profile sports stars". These were extraordinarily frank comments.

Then there were the comments of Supreme Court judges in this state regarding my guilt in transporting such a 'dangerous drug' into the country. They charged that the drug caused "untold damage to the community". These comments were laughable. I'd like to see them quote some statistics.

If I sound like I'm whining, I am, not because I was caught, but because I can't stand the self-evident hypocrisy of the entire prohibition issue. I took the risk, I knew the rewards and I knew the punishment. But to have to be 'ministered to' by self-serving hypocrites is too much. "Remove the beam in thine own eye," as Jesus so eloquently put it.

Jorge Ochoa, former Colombian Cartel kingpin and once a personal friend of mine, said recently in an interview, that the drug problem was: "everyone's problem". From the *one gram on the weekend* hobbyist, to the Wall Street bankers who happily process billions of dollars in drug money annually; knowing exactly where it has come from. This liquid cash flow props up the stock market and their own cocaine habits.

My friend Barry Seal was involved with Iran/Contra, Colonel Oliver North and Papa Bush, CIA Director and soon to be US president. They were major drug traffickers, swapping illegal arms shipments for drugs in the 1980s. They utilized drug profits made from cocaine to finance "black ops" all around the world. Congress would not approve such funding so the "killing squads" and pay off's to businessmen and government officials were financed by the drug trade. This got rid of unwanted populist politicians who were refusing to bow down to US corporate-driven foreign policy in Central and South America. They were politicians who wanted to look after their own people and not the profit sheet of some fat and lazy Wall Street corporation.

They made a documentary called "Kill the Messenger" (2006) where an FBI whistleblower (Sibel Edmonds) exposed American, Turkish and Israeli top government officials involved in the drug, drug money laundering and illegal weapons trade.

They say the drug trade is worth $600 billion a year and is central to the world's economy, impossible to let go. No massive drug profits would result in a bad balance sheet for the banking world. However, the jails would empty, police, lawyers, and judges, as well as prison guards, would be out of a job and your kids would most likely walk the streets safely at night. People in power have become rich because of the drug war. Others drunk with power, for instance, federal judge, Gilbert, said that he is going to give out one million years to drug offenders before he retires.

While bankers, politicians, and sections of the armed forces have a field day with the drug trade, propping up your 401K; *lil' old Roger* sits in jail at the cost of $90,000 a year

As one Italian gangster once famously quipped, "Organized crime exists because of the greed of the average man on the street." Enough said.

Mother, my two sisters, Marijo and Charlotte flew to Australia, and we had wonderful visits every day. They would visit me for an hour and then Joel would get his turn. All too soon, they had to depart. Tears flowed freely as I saw my old mother walk out the door. I knew I would never see her face again.

Six months after we were released from the SHU we transferred to the self-care unit. It was like dying and going to heaven. Forty-eight men are in self-care and divided into four units of twelve men each. Weekly loads of fresh meats and vegetables are brought in, the men cook for themselves and I mean some of these men can cook! We are not fenced in like the other units and the flowerbeds could compete with many in botanical gardens. The guards are housed in a compound in the center of the four units and don't bother us. Everything is relaxed and easy. I suppose this is the best place in the whole world to be in prison.

Some might complain that prisoners should not get such conditions in a maximum-security prison, but a reward system is vital for the good order and management of hundreds of men in such cramped conditions. Give a man nothing to lose, leave him with no hope and nothing to look forward to; then he becomes a danger to himself and others. The prison environment becomes very dangerous for both prisoners and staff alike without this type of reward system.

Nothing is ever perfect and self-care was no exception. Joel and I moved into 'C' wing and the first person we met was Hal or 'Mother Hal,' as he was often referred to. Hal welcomed us and seemed to bend over backward to help. He typed up a new list with our work areas explicitly laid out. He cooked pies and cakes and was always in the kitchen wearing a tight singlet, short shorts, and sweating into the food. It was obvious from the start that he wasn't liked by the men and attached himself to us just to have a friend.

Hal's was a rather amusing case. He was or is a crossdresser, or transvestite, but a transvestite in that he likes to wear women's clothes. He dressed up in his Batman suit, played cat burglar, and broke into some of the richest homes in Perth. Once he got in through the vents, he spent hours dressing in the ladies' clothes and shoes. He would video his antics, despite the home owner's presence in the house, including them in the video while they were asleep. When he was tired of this, he would go into the bathroom, take their toothbrushes, brushed his anus and stuck them up his ass, afterward hanging them back in their slots. Whether these tales are true or not, it was talk among the men. The policeman who finally caught him, after fifteen or so similar episodes, said he had a hard time running him down, even though Hal was wearing a long white gown and high heel shoes.

Wasn't long before the new wore off and Hal was under our skin also. If you cooked an egg and sat down to eat it, he started bitching about the dirty frying pan left on the counter. He noticed every little thing and was vocal about it. Several times I yelled at him in a threatening manner and told him that he wasn't running a damned thing as far as I was concerned. One night I prayed, "Lord, please move that aggravating man from my life."

The next morning I came out of my cell to go for a cup of coffee and Hal was packing up. I didn't say anything and soon he was gone. I asked and was told that he went to crisis care. I stopped and said, "Thank you Lord."

41. JOEL AND A RIGGED COURT

Under Duress -- May 2003, Third Trial -- Walking On Air

Early on, when we were interviewing lawyers, we met one dapper young Italian attorney who said, "One of you can beat this case. Do you realize they don't know jack-shit, they only know what you tell them and then they try and put the pieces together?" The following week, this attorney was indicted on drug charges and put in prison. However, the seed was planted and we decided Joel should take it to trial.

We knew Joel was in for an uphill battle because he was caught sitting on a ton of cocaine, the ship was registered in his name, the Iridium phone was purchased using his credit card and the bank account used to purchase the vessel was also in his name. When we entered Africa, he was listed as Captain and paid for the fuel and supplies, of which Señor Carlos kept meticulous records.

During my taped interview with the Federal Police, I was emphatic in my statement that I duped him into buying the vessel and that he knew nothing about the cocaine until we met the other vessel in the middle of the Atlantic. I said that Joel couldn't just jump in and swim to land, as it was a thousand miles away. Furthermore, the vessel that loaded us refused to allow Joel to travel back with them. The cocaine was packed in burlap bags that got wet and Joel's fingerprints were not on them. I swore that I let Joel know that if he got on the radio and told, the Colombians would kill his family. This was grounds for a defense of duress.

Joel went to trial and his lawyer made mincemeat out of the prosecutor. One Juror even went so far as to give Joel secret little 'thumbs up'. The prosecutor knew he had lost the case and the following dirty theatrical production was played out with the judge and prosecutor as key actors. What I am about to describe happens more often than you think. Rigging juries is a routine affair when the state wants a conviction at all costs.

The trial had been going on for a week and on the last day, a juror stood up and said, "Your honor, I found all this information on the internet last night, so I copied it and gave a copy to each of my fellow jurors this morning. I hope you have no objections, but I just thought you should know."

The judge asked the bailiff to fetch the papers and read what had been written about Joel and the trial. The judge acted as if he was angry and declared a mistrial. Joel's lawyer cried foul, objected, and pleaded to have the one juror replaced with one of the substitutes, not so, the actors must stick to the script.

Seven months later a new trial was held and this time the prosecutor was ready, as they knew what Joel's defense was going to be. Joel's lawyer summoned Carlos to the stand and asked him if it wasn't true that Joel wanted to get off the vessel in the middle of the Atlantic and the Colombian boat would not allow him to board. Carlos crossed his arms and said, "I say nothing."

Had he verified my statement Joel would have walked free that day, but he had already talked for hours, told everything, and somehow made an agreement whereby he would not testify in open court.

The jury was out for two days and finally returned with a verdict of "Hung Jury."

The third trial was set for May 2003, almost two years after we were arrested. I knew Joel needed more help and it came to me that if we could get two Supreme Court Judges from Georgia to testify to Joel's good character, it just might tip the balance in our favor. I kept after Joel to telephone Judge Jerome Adams and Judge Earl McRae, in the US. After considerable brow beating, he put their names on his telephone list and called. Both were happy to hear from Joel and they knew he would never have been in this mess if it had not been for me. They readily agreed to testify on Joel's behalf.

The courts here all have video hookup, but it was unknown in South Georgia. Yet I knew it was available, I had visited a doctor of agriculture at the experiment station in Tifton, Georgia when he got a call from an agent in the field with detailed pictures of squash, infected with a wilt disease. The doctor identified the disease and gave instructions as to what to spray. All this took less than five minutes and I was impressed.

I continued calling family in Georgia, insisting the system was available, however, I kept getting a negative response. Finally, Charlotte, my sister called the University of Georgia and discovered they had video hookups in one of their auditoriums right there in Douglas. Of course, all of our calls are monitored and recorded and I expect the prosecution and Federal Police had no problem obtaining copies.

"Reaves, pack up, you are leaving for Hakea in fifteen minutes."

Mrs. Longshore, a very nice lady and also the assistant superintendent was walking by and I asked, "Why are they transferring me to Hakea?"

She replied, "It is something near you, but you are not involved."

I asked, "May I be allowed a five-minute visit with Joel before I go."

"No, you cannot talk with him."

With that, I knew they were transferring me so I couldn't help Joel during his trial.

They shackled and chained me, loaded me in the back of the vault and away I bounced. In Hakea, I was housed in unit 7, the oldest most dismal unit there. After one week in that shit hole I was transferred to unit 8, which was wonderful compared to where I had been. I got a job in the library and enjoyed my time there with the young prisoners awaiting trial.

On trial number three Joel was found not guilty. When I heard this news, I could have walked on air. No mention was made of this loss by the prosecutor on the television. The newspaper ran a tiny article giving all the credit of him winning the trial to the two Supreme Court Judges testifying to the good character of Joel. The reporters said this was the deciding factor in the trial.

Joel never went back to Casuarina. They took him directly to the immigration holding facility at the Perth airport and deported him back to the United States

After all we went through, I received one letter from Joel.

When Joel returned he found his mother in poor condition after a car accident, he cooked and looked after her for a year until she died. As he was recovering from that shock, his eighteen-year-old daughter was killed in a motorcycle accident. During a storm, a tree fell on his house causing severe damage inside. He was diagnosed with cirrhosis of the liver and as of the time of writing, Mother said he was in the hospital in need of a transplant.

February 2004. The state of Western Australia was upset I had got Joel home and now they were going to get their pound of flesh with interest! The Crown wanted more time and they appealed my sentence which they considered far too lenient.

Shackles and chains were removed and I was escorted into a strange courtroom. I bowed to the three judges on the bench and neither looked up or recognized me. I could feel their vibes and evil intent filling the room. Somehow this didn't affect me as I already knew I would not get relief here and whether I did fourteen years or one-hundred and forty years made no difference to me, as I wasn't going home for a very long time, if ever.

This was a very different court to that of the court of Justice Henry Wallwork. Justice Wallwork was a former defense attorney, whereas these three were ex prosecutors. I think that prosecutors should never be elevated to judges as they have a persecuting spirit. They are natural accusers who can never hurt or give out enough years to fill the emptiness within their own souls. They follow their master, the prince of this earth who is the accuser of all men. They are as Isabella said four hundred years ago.

"But man, proud man
Dressed in a little brief authority
Most ignorant of what he's most assured.
His glassy essence, like an angry ape
Plays such fantastic tricks before the high heavens
As would make the angels weep." *William Shakespeare, Measure for Measure*

The prosecutor, a Mr. Bimbo, stood up and began ejaculating in a loud voice. There were three judges, a big-headed pompous sort sat in the center; a self-righteous small woman was on his right; and an arrogant proud man was spread out over his chair on the left. Was the judge *spread all over his chair* an example to follow? His demeanor was disgusting and not worthy of a court of law. I couldn't help but picture such a man in a compromising position - other than his chair.

As the prosecutor spoke, I saw three heads nodding in unison and I thought, 'This shit has been rehearsed. All they need to do is shout *Amen* every once in a while to make the charade complete.' The prosecutor ended his rant with, "The crown asks for nothing less than a life sentence with a minimum time of imprisonment of 30 years before becoming eligible for parole."

Justine Fisher stood up when the prosecutor finished and began to tell of the twenty-three years parole I had in the states. Chief Justice Malcolm said, "Ms. Fisher, we are not going to listen to that argument, because the defendant will probably not live long enough to finish the sentence we are going to give him. So we won't worry about a sentence elsewhere."

Justine then started on her second point, which was that the law states that the court must give one third off any sentence for a plea of guilty and fast-tracking and that one could not take a third off life. Malcolm said, "Ms. Fisher we are not going to sit here and listen to that argument. Are you saying that if one mass murderer kills a thousand children and gets life, then another mass murderer kills seven hundred children and gets life, and then your mass murderer comes before the court and is not as bad because he only killed five hundred children? Are you going to stand there and argue that he should not get a life sentence because he was not as bad as the first two? No, we are not going to listen to that argument."

To Justine's credit, she tried a few more points, but it was of no use. Malcolm sat there looking throughout the courtroom with glassy eyes, trimming his nails, and at every opportunity he cut her off. His behavior was despicable and not something the general public would approve of.

Malcolm handed down a life sentence with 18 years to serve before becoming eligible for parole.

I thought, "You poor misguided fools. You have no idea of the injustice you are guilty of. You're proud and arrogant spirits in such a position of power, makes you far worse than many of the prisoners who come before you."

I understood why Jesus prayed thus for the ones who nailed Him to the cross, "Father forgive them, for they know not what they do."

It was not in me to forgive at that time and I cursed him saying, "Lord curse him as you did Nebuchadnezzar. May they drive you from men and thy dwelling shall be with the beast of the field and they shall make thee to eat grass as oxen and they shall wet thee with the dew of heaven."

Afterward, Malcolm was confused in court and his speech was without reason. A major murder case was thrown out because of his foolish remarks, they removed him from his exalted position and put another in his place. It was said that he was suffering from a mental illness. That may well be true.

The Spirit that lives in me is truly stronger than the spirit that lives in the world.

42. A NICE LETTER FROM "MR. NICE"

Lil' Snitches Revenge -- Solitary Man

'Bad Bill' McCreed dug up information about me and was spreading a rumor as fact, that I was a "dog", the absolute worst thing to be called in a jail. He was repeating, badly, the plot between myself and Howard Marks to keep Howard from being extradited to the US by me saying the hashish load was his. He knew the truth as the book, "Hunting Marco Polo" explains the whole incident and clearly states that it was a conspiracy between Reaves and Marks to keep Marks from being extradited from Spain to the United States. That didn't matter to Bad Bill and Carlos as they set out to ruin my reputation. They thought they could get me run off the compound and into the protection unit.

Both wanted me out of the way for their own reasons. Carlos knew that I had the paperwork on him and he and McCreed were very close. McCreed had served a long sentence some years back for the rape and murder of a Native Australian girl. After the rape, he dragged her behind his pickup until she came apart. He completed that sentence and was released, committed another rape, and was back, serving seven years on the new charge.

I heard something about this plot against me before I returned and I was ready. When I would walk up to a group of men they would fall silent, there were none of the smiles and handshakes I had expected. I explained to a few of the men, but the stigma just wouldn't go away, so it was time to act. I got a pass to the library and walked up to Bill. He spoke before I could say anything. He said, "Don't speak to me. You're a dog and I don't talk to dogs." Now a dog in Australia is a snitch or informant and this is the worse insult one can sling.

I looked him in the eye and said, "OK baby rapist, or do you prefer *boss boy*? Come on down and the undertaker will wipe your fat ass before this day is over."

I walked down to self-care and prepared myself for the worst, he didn't show.

The next day I wrote to Howard explaining the situation and to his credit, he replied with a nice three-page letter stating that I had never testified against him or done him any harm. I made several copies, passed some around, and pinned others on the bulletin board. Soon everything was sweet and I was back in the fold.

Two months passed as one and then another came up and shook my hand, but Carlos and his cronies were not about to give up so easy.

The speaker blared, "Reaves come to control." I walked over and the officer handed me a blue pass and told me to go to reception. I wondered what this could mean, when I got there, I found out soon enough. I walked through the door, the first person I saw was head of security. Four rough hands grabbed me, slammed me against a wall, handcuffed me, and then pushed me down into a chair before the desk of the head of security. He read, or said, that he was placing me in solitary confinement and applying to the Director of Prisons for my placement in the SHU. I asked for what reason he was doing this and he said it was for violation of section 32, which is "For the good order and management of the prison." That catchall could mean anything. I knew I had done nothing wrong and I knew where it was coming from.

They put me back in the same cell where I had spent two months, but this time they had a couple of pure fiends working the area. The next morning at nine o'clock the cell door opened and standing there were two guards, a broom and a mop bucket. I walked out in the hall, reached for the broom and said, "Good morning."

The tall thin guard named Young stomped up, got in my face and yelled, "Shut your fuckin mouth and clean your god-dammed cell. We ain't here for conversation!"

It is a terrible thing for a man to have to suffer such an insult.

During my two months in that situation, I often heard this guard yelling, "Shut your fuckin' mouth you black cunt!" or, "You fuckin' nigger."

The bad ones associate later apologized for being there and said this coward was just riding a white pony. As I didn't understand the meaning, I asked and he explained that this man only abused helpless people to make himself feel bigger.

Mr. Robert Jennings, the superintendent, is a real gentleman and I know if he saw or knew of such goading and disrespect, he would fire the man. However, these cowards are shrewd. They guard one another's back and it's difficult for those in authority to see them in action. Should Mr. Jennings show up they would smile, bow and lick his boots, he has no idea as to who they really are.

The second morning, I returned the few steps from the shower and found my cell stripped. Mattress, pillow, sheets, blankets, towel, soap and every other little thing I had was in a pile in the hallway. Beside the pile was a sheet torn into thin one-inch wide strips and each strip tied together. The men use this type of string and tie something heavy onto one end, throw it down the hall where their friend gets hold of it somehow, they can pass tobacco or whatever else back and forth. I had never seen the string and I knew right off that fat Stevenson, the guard had planted it on me. For the next two months, my cell was stripped every morning. I had nothing at all except the walls and the springs to the bed all day.

I am lactose intolerant and also have celiac disease, whereby I can't eat wheat, rye, or oats. The guards knew this and they made sure I received Weetabix and milk for breakfast. Lunch was often macaroni and cheese or sandwiches and I could eat very little of this food. Soon I lost 25 pounds and had sores in my hair and on my face.

Carlos was head honcho in the commissary and each week I was allowed to purchase a few things. I remember ordering a black pen to write letters and he sent a red one. I ordered old-fashioned potato chips and he sent chicken flavored. I ordered Coca Colas and he sent vanilla cola. I returned these things and nothing ever came back, even though I was charged.

Mr. Hyde, a gem of a man and assistant superintendent, came by every morning. I'm sure it was he who influenced the Director of Prisons to have me released. Michelle, a caring psychologist accompanied Mr. Hyde and I could see the concern on her face when they came in. One morning the door opened and a new guard told me to gather up my things, that I was going back to self-care. I could not believe it as most everyone who goes to solitary with a request for transfer to the SHU, goes to the SHU. As Officer O'Keefe, a quiet guard escorted me out he said, "Reaves, I want you to know I did not approve of the way you were treated." Such comments are rare and most appreciated.

When I got out of the chokie, I had lost my cell, my job, my clothes, and most everything I owned. To replace the cell and clothes was aggravating and time-consuming, the job was another matter. I work full time for seven dollars a day which is not bad compared with the United States penal system. With this, I pay for telephone calls to loved ones, buy a new pair of jogging shoes each year and a few canteen items. But now, I would have to start from scratch. One thing you learn when incarcerated; get ready to start all over again at a moment's notice.

43. THE FINAL WORD

Moral Dilemma -- Spiritual Reflections -- Daddy's Poem

Today is my 73rd birthday. I remember back over ten years ago when my daughter Marya and grandson Maximillian visited from France and showered me in hugs and kisses. There is no family visit this last decade.

While I lay in my bunk I note all of Australia is taking a holiday and are barbecuing and celebrating, being that January 26 is Australia Day, something like Thanksgiving in the United States. Native Australian's call it "Invasion Day."

Three years and six months from today I am scheduled to go before a parole review board at which time I have a chance of being released. I will be seventy-six years and six months old at that time.

I wonder what I will say at the parole hearing. "Sorry?" On that particular subject I find myself torn. Have you ever seen a hospital E.R on a Friday night? Now count the marijuana and cocaine cases on those stretchers? Yeh, that's right, you won't require any fingers to count the cases - you won't see any. But the alcohol and tobacco-related admissions to E.R. will require both hands, all your toes and a good many friends to form a conga line of *ample digits*. But why let facts and statistics get in the way of a government crusade? Just say no?

When I was a tobacco farmer I was a gentleman. How do you reconcile that to the half-million people that die from tobacco-related diseases each year in the United States? Tobacco executives dine with Presidents.

We all saw what happened when they banned alcohol in the first quarter of the 20th century. It made a lot of very rich American and Canadian families respectable; for example, the Kennedy family and Canada's Bronfman's. We all know the Kennedy's. The Bronfman's own most of Canada and half of the United States. Granddaddy was a bootlegger! Just don't tell the grandkids.

When I made whiskey back in Georgia and the still blew up, everyone knew. Marrie was ashamed to go to church or the grocery store. Then we moved to California and the next year we visited friends up in the Napa Valley. This young couple had a lovely little stone house, a twenty-acre vineyard, and made their own wine. It was a charming little farm and Marrie asked, "Roger, could we ever have a place like that?"

A wry grin came across my face and I replied, "Sweetheart, I remember just last year you were ashamed of such a business?"

She replied, "Yes. But it was illegal in Georgia. Here it's legal!"

I remember men spending twelve years in Alcatraz for alcohol 'crimes'. When they were released they walked across the street and bought whiskey at the bar, whiskey having been legal for twelve years.

The trail of dead bodies and the gangster personalities that were conjured during that nasty prohibition period still sells books today. It seems we still haven't learned or, are there signs that governments have finally realized you can't "lock up the problem"? Well, actually, you can, but it's going to cost you billions to do so and rip apart the very fabric of society. You will also scare people into accepting a police state where the police don't come to get your 'kitty cat' out of the tree with a smile anymore, they bring a tank. And they do love those all-black uniforms with an optional ski mask.

Maybe there are simply way too many people in *suits* making way too much money to see an end to the war on drugs?

Soon it will be the fifteenth day of February 2016; our wedding anniversary. Marrie and I will have been married for fifty-two years. My greatest regret in life is that I have been in prison and separated from her for over half those years. For the first twenty-one years of my life I was searching for Marrie, then, after finding her and winning her hand, we lived in bliss and were inseparable for eighteen years. Then, it was as if some evil malignant force ripped us apart. It was so awful it was as if we could scarcely breathe. I struggled terribly until I made it back to her. Oh what joy, to be together again! We fled to South America and then onto Europe only to be caught and torn apart yet again. The last thirty years of my life have been longing for and striving to get back to Marrie. I pray we will have some years together still. When I leave this prison, we will go to the tropics together.

I have spent thirty years of my life in some of the worst prisons in the world. Several years of that time were spent in solitary confinement. I know there are spiritual dimensions, both good and bad, that strongly influence our lives. Over the years, I have slowed down and little by little, I have turned towards God, influenced greatly by my wife's example. I clearly remember the vision I had that night in the SHU and I know it is coming, I just don't know when.

Then there is the colorful vision of the Heavenly Host, which I will someday see and I have no idea as to whether I am in the flesh or in the spirit when this occurs, but that does not matter because I am there.

Long ago, I had a vision of the moment I leave this body and pass through the veil. I can vividly recall the scene and remember the peace that engulfed me. I am a very old man on a veranda, sitting in a chair with wide wooden arms. I am wearing khaki trousers and a white shirt. Across my lap is a folded blanket in the style and color of the Indians of Central America. I was in the spirit as I got out of the chair and came to a lacy white veil, as delicate as mist. I watch as I walk into the white mist and I know that I am immediately going to meet many loved ones, many that I did not recognize while in the flesh.

There is always hope. Always. I agree with the evangelist who ended his program with, "Rejoice and be of good cheer, for something good is going to happen to you today!" Yes and it often comes from the most unexpected direction.

Miriam, Marrie, Marya
Copyright - Marrie J. Reaves

Daddy's Poem
Written by Miriam, my daughter.

A year ago I became a poet, when I wrote your birthday prose.
And here I am today, ready to give it another go.
First, I would like to wish you, a very Happy Birthday to be.
And to thank you very much, for without you, I would not be me.
Secondly, I want to say, that your support has been immense;
It has been true, honest, and loving, and free from all pretense.
Thirdly, it goes without saying, your love has surpassed all my wrongs,
And you always made me smile, with one of your country songs.

I can remember on Cuervo, Daddy, with you holding me in your arms,
As you sang Jim Reeves to me, and talked about the farm.
I can see you walking through the door, from one of your travels far and wide.
And the thought of you coming home, Daddy, kept a twinkle in our eye.
I can smell you as I did, when I used to climb into your bed.
And you would talk to me again, about one of the adventures that you led.
I can see me and Marya asleep, in one of your airplanes extraordinaire,
And remembering wondering to myself, why there wasn't an available chair!

I remember having to meet you, and worrying that you wouldn't be there.
But you would pop from behind some corner, and give us all a happy scare.
You gave us presents in Key Biscayne, and hotel pleasures galore,
And three dozen roses you gave to us, as we came through an airport door.
When I saw your face in Amsterdam, at the luggage carousel,
You looked like a boy with a secret, that you were really dying to tell.
You taught me mathematics, in the sands of a faraway place,
And taught me how to sail, when we left without a trace.

We climbed glaciers in Argentina, and saw the blues of their beautiful caves,
And witnessed the majestic beauty, of such a jagged crystalline maze.
I learned how to change gears, on the dirt roads through Brazil,
And we ate hotdogs in Paraguay, a memory we smile over still.
We talked about lions, elephants and bears, on a hacienda in Uruguay,
But decided it was better, if to Europe we did fly!
Oh the old world and all its luxury! What a good time it was!
From South America to the Krasnapolsky-- I think we fell in love!

The European jaunt? Well, it is to be considered a book in and of itself.
But it is a story about beauty and knowledge, suspense and worldly wealth.
We went from Holland to Sweden and we went from France to Spain,
And I promise you that I have no regrets--I would definitely do it again!!!
I would see the world with you anytime, sir! There is not a doubt in my mind.
Because being by your side Daddy, always ensures a wild good time!
So our path took a little turn, and we are back in the US of A.
But life here isn't so bad, and I'm plum content to stay.

I am happy to be near you, although I'm not as close as I was before,
But because of your love and encouragement, I've been able to open new doors.
I am grateful to be in school, and I am genuinely happy where I am,

And I even like when you call to tell, to study hard for my next exam!
What a life you have given me, Daddy! It is a tremendous and magical gift.
We already have so many stories to tell. There are far too many to list.
But I want to thank you again this day, with a very BIG Happy Birthday to You!
And to tell you just a few more things, that I know in my heart to be true.

That I love you Daddy, with all your wrongs and your rights.
That you are the head of our family, and have kept us all bound tight.
That you have an honest love in your heart, for God and all mankind,
And you truly do believe in yourself, when you say it will all be fine.
I know you will be there to catch me, if I waver and start to slip,
And I would know that I'd want you as my captain…on any sinking ship!
I also know a new chapter is written. It's almost time to move on,
It's time to sail another sea, and witness a brand new dawn.

It will be good to see you at the helm again, as you point out our destination.
And to laugh and dance on the upper deck, while the boat glides through with patience.
It will be good to see you on the go, as I know you like to be,
And to know you can open any door, without requiring a key!
But while we revel in our days together, we will know better than to hurry,
Because as you have told me many times before…**Life is an Incredible Journey!**

EPILOGUE

The manuscript that has now been turned into the book you are reading was first begun in early 2001. For reasons I cannot entirely explain, it has taken over fifteen years to get this memoir to you. But here it is, rough and ready. Take it or leave it. This is my life – or at least a large part of it.

Hollywood star, Tom Cruise is playing the character of my friend and colleague Barry Seal in a movie called "Mena". Due out in early 2017. A chronicle of the life and death of a complicated and mysterious man linked in with Colonel Oliver North, Iran/Contra, Bill Clinton and George Bush Sr. – to name a few.

A lot of people in a lot of high places are going to be worried about what dirt gets re-hashed about that very, very, very ugly period in US history. Hillary is running for president - it could get nasty. She and husband Bill are heavily implicated in "Mena" and drug trafficking. There's already been a plane crash with two dead on the set while filming in Colombia. Some say the line of dead bodies surrounding the Clintons and their rise to power is very, very long. I'll leave it for others to probe into, many already have. So many so, that the word "homicide" was changed to "Arkanside". Why the producers decided they simply "must" film in Colombia is anyone's guess. The company that operates the aircraft is said to have intelligence connections. Not long after the plane crash on set, Jorge Ochoa's brother died of a heart attack in a Bogota hospital. Maybe he got a copy of the script?

I remember so clearly the distinct periods of time in Colombia where landing strips were busier than JFK Airport. There were times where I feared a mid-air collision there were so many big CIA planes flying with their lights out after dusk. People seem to accept government direct involvement in the drug trade as almost normal now - expected.

Now, with Hollywood producing several new high budget movies exposing government involvement in the drug trade, it is high time we all look at ending drug prohibition once and for all. Right now, over two million men and women sit incarcerated in prisons at great cost to the American taxpayer as it is for similar countries all over the world. For most, violence played no part in their 'crime' and if it did, it was rooted not in the drug they chose to consume, but in the drug prohibition and high cost.

Prohibition is, and always has been, a failure that has ripped societies apart - not protect them. The *war on drugs* is not a war on drugs. It is a *war on people* – your sons, daughters, mothers and fathers, brothers and sisters, next-door neighbors.

While alcohol, tobacco, poorly tested pharmaceuticals, McDonald's and candy manufacturers decimate the population with their direct and indirect costs to health and community well-being - cocaine and marijuana do not even feature as a blip in the statistics.

Now marijuana is legal in several states in the US but I have spent 33 years in prison because of the law at the time.

It seems we are *particular* and *discerning* about what substances raise our ire and demands for retributive justice even if we will shove indiscriminately, any old bit of overly processed garbage food down our gullets for our hearts, livers and bowels to pay for later – not to mention the taxpayer. One man's poison is another man's pleasure. One day legal, then, with the stroke of a pen, it is illegal and worthy of public hatred and derision. All the while, large numbers of the public from all corners of life drive the demand, the price, and the accompanying violence. They are not 'conscious consumers', they are 'victims' - according to the law. Maybe they just know what they like? I like Chivas Regal on the rocks. I hope they don't make that illegal. Apparently, I'm safe – for now. Though there is no 'bar' in the prison it's the thought that counts and I would hate to think I will die without one last taste of *my* favorite indolent pleasure.

We are fast approaching the end of an era. Drug prohibition is moving from a criminal matter to a medical and educational one. The experiment in Portugal has been a huge success. Three grams of any "drug" is now treated with an on the spot fine. The prisons have emptied; crime rates have plummeted; police and prison officers, lawyers, and judges look for other employment. So why hasn't this self-evident success story been followed by others? Is it just blind adherence to ideology? It would seem there is much more to the issue than that. The advanced industrial societies cannot admit (openly), that not only is a vast swathe of their respective populations addicted too, and happily consuming drugs – their economies and in particular their banking and financial sectors are completely addicted to the vast rivers of liquid drug money that flow into their coffers. No bankers are in jail, but I am, and so are tens of thousands of others. I hope you're happy. I'll wear a suit next time and get an MBA and handle the cash – perhaps equally profitable with far less chance of punishment.

To move the drug trade to where it should be – manufactured and distributed by approved government agencies (as they are now doing with marijuana in certain US states) - would see a vast change in certain segments of the economy. Hotels, luxury car manufacturers, construction, and real estate would take a hit as it often did in Miami when drug interdiction efforts pushed smuggling routes elsewhere for a spell. They say Sydney Australia in its modern form was built on the heroin trade of the 1970s and early eighties from just the activities of one large mafia don (Abe Saffron) and the myriad of respectable suits that supported him in the background; usually bankers and financial advisers. Not to mention the police and state politicians he had in his pocket. It's the same all over the world. All the while policing agencies stand mute, unable to stem the tide or as some would say, perhaps unwilling? Their jobs depend on the trade and the vast profits ensure corruption is rife amongst nearly all policing and intelligence agencies throughout the world. Without police and intelligence agency co-operation, the drug trade simply cannot flourish. But you keep telling yourself law enforcement will solve the problem with more laws that take away more of your basic civil rights. You just keep telling yourself that. We will be in tyranny before we know it. Perhaps we already are.

The time has come. End the war. Take it from someone who knows – you are destroying society with this *war on drugs* madness. As long as vast profits are possible, with government agencies taking part in the drug trade and human greed prevailing; no amount of new laws and "tough on drugs" public relations stunts will save your community and your public institutions.

I take full responsibility for my actions. Actions that have cost me and my family dearly. It's time for society as a whole to take responsibility for *their* actions and *their* addictions that drive demand. No more "whipping boys". Enough said.

I hope you enjoyed this book. It's an account of my life - in part. My journey is not yet over, there is much more to come. I hope you were entertained. I've seen many wonderful things, flown over countless lush landscapes and sailed the vast oceans with my beautiful wife and children, and met many wonderful people, living a life few can imagine. But also reflect and rejoice on the opportunity to end this mad war that makes retired generals and police chiefs rich, pays for lawyers and judges' new Mercedes, and keep prisons full of your sons and daughters.

Sincerely,
William Roger Reaves

FUTHER INFORMATION

BOOKS

"Chasing the Scream", Johann Hari – "A must Read" ***excellent!***
"Barry And The Boys", Daniel Hopsicker
"The Kings Of Cocaine" - Guy Gugliotta & Jeff Leen
"Hunting Marco Polo - Pursuit And Capture Of Howard Marks" - Paul Eddy & Sarah Walden
"The Politics Of Heroin: CIA Complicity In The Global Drug Trade" - Alfred W. McCoy
"The Big White Lie: The Deep Cover Operation That Exposed the CIA Sabotage of the Drug War" - Michael Levine
"The Clintons War On Women" - Roger Stone & Robert Morrow

VIDEO'S - MOST AVAILABLE ONLINE/YOUTUBE

"The Mena Connection" - Documentary, Terry Reed (High-level government drug dealing involving Barry Seal, Bill Clinton, and George Bush Snr)
"The Clinton Chronicles" - Documentary detailing the incredible rise to power of Bill and Hillary Clinton.
"The Truth & Lies Of 9-11" - Live Audience presentation, Michael Ruppert (Drug money laundering, Wall Street)

"Kill The Messenger" - Documentary, 2006 (Details the unholy alliance between Israel, Turkey and the United States in drug dealing, drug money laundering, illegal weapons trade, and illegal nuclear weapons parts proliferation through the eyes of FBI whistleblower Sibel Edmonds)
"Cocaine Cowboys" - Documentary, Directed by Billy Corben (Details the drug trade and personalities out of Miami)
"Double Crossed" - Movie, Starring Dennis Hopper (1991 film about Barry Seal)

MOVIES

"Kill The Messenger" - Jeremy Renner (Details the life and death of real-life reporter Gary Webb who first broke the story of CIA complicity in the crack cocaine epidemic that hit the streets of L.A in the eighties)
"Training Day" - Denzel Washington, Ethan Hawke (Police corruption and drug dealing)
"The Departed" - Jack Nicholson, Leonardo DiCaprio, Matt Damon (Police corruption, drug dealing and high level organized crime infiltration of police)
"Layer Cake" - Daniel Craig (Details the drug trade in London and how it reaches to the top levels of the establishment)

My heartfelt thanks to my dear friend Brendon with whom I shared many hours walking and talking at Her Majesties pleasure. Without his encouragement, regular prison visits, over the phone discussions and word processing skills, this manuscript might well still be languishin.

Printed in Great Britain
by Amazon

78039473R00305